Gerald P. Mulderig

DePaul University

The Heath Handbook

Thirteenth Edition

Instructor's Annotated Edition

D. C. Heath and Company

Lexington, Massachusetts   *Toronto*

Address editorial correspondence to:

D. C. Heath and Company
125 Spring Street
Lexington, MA 02173

Acquisitions Editor: Paul A. Smith
Developmental Editor: Linda M. Bieze
Production Editor: Martha Wetherill
Designer: Alwyn Velásquez
Production Coordinator: Charles Dutton
Permissions Editor: Margaret Roll
Cover design: Alwyn Velásquez

Acknowledgments: Seven paragraphs (on pp. 235–37) from "The New Generation Gap" by Neil Howe and William Strauss in *The Atlantic Monthly*, December 1992, pp. 67–69. Reprinted by permission of *The Atlantic Monthly*. Poetry by Wallace Stevens (on p. 328) from "Thirteen Ways of Looking at a Blackbird" by Wallace Stevens from *Collected Poems* by Wallace Stevens. Copyright 1923 and renewed 1951 by Wallace Stevens. Reprinted by permission of Alfred A. Knopf, Inc. Poetry by Emily Dickinson (on pp. 334 and 355) reprinted by permission of the publishers and the Trustees of Amherst College from *The Poems of Emily Dickinson*, Thomas H. Johnson, ed., Cambridge, Mass.: The Belknap Press of Harvard University Press. Copyright © 1951, 1955, 1979, 1983 by the President and Fellows of Harvard College.

International Standard Book Number: 0-669-34131-2 (Student Edition)
0-669-34133-9 (Instructor's Annotated Edition)

Library of Congress Catalog Number: 94-76932

10 9 8 7 6 5 4 3 2 1

Preface

With his publication of the first edition of *The Heath Handbook* in 1907, Edwin C. Woolley established a new standard for composition textbooks in the twentieth century. Though Woolley's tone was dogmatic and his approach to correctness uncompromising, the unprecedented comprehensiveness of his book and the clarity of its organization—350 numbered rules, beginning with a definition of good usage and ending with the proper placement of a postage stamp on an envelope—made it an immediate success.

Our understanding of the writing process, and of the way writing should be taught and learned, has changed dramatically in the nearly nine decades since Woolley's handbook first appeared. But comprehensive coverage and clear organization remain as desirable in a handbook at the end of the twentieth century as they were for Woolley and his contemporaries. Accordingly, I have sought to make this thirteenth edition of *The Heath Handbook* the most complete, most accessible version ever published. It preserves all of the features that users of the past edition have commended, including the following:

- Attention to the recursive and idiosyncratic nature of the writing process, with thirteen chapters devoted to planning, drafting, and revising an essay and a unique guide to classroom collaboration and peer editing.

- Discussions of grammar, style, punctuation, and mechanics that are clear, well illustrated, and accompanied by engaging connected-discourse exercises on topics ranging from astronomy to surgery, from Gertrude Stein to Thomas Edison, from the Harlem Renaissance to the Chicago Fire, from traveling by train to writing with a word processor.

- Well-chosen examples of strong prose by student and professional writers.
- A complete guide to the research process, including practical directions for using the latest versions of MLA, APA, and endnote documentation and two fully annotated student research papers.
- An engaging tone, clear explanations, and an accessible organization.

But the many changes in this new edition of *The Heath Handbook* illustrate the opportunities that the revising process always lays before us. More than half of the book's forty-three chapters have undergone significant rewriting, all of its sentence-level exercises have been redesigned, forty new exercises have been added, and both the glossary of usage and the glossary of grammatical and stylistic terms have been expanded and extensively revised. Users of past editions of *The Heath Handbook* will notice the following major enhancements in this edition:

1. Increased attention to the drafting process.

Chapter **5**, "Organizing an Essay," has been greatly enlarged to include advice about developing a rhetorical plan for an essay, selecting an appropriate pattern of organization, and beginning the process of drafting. New examples have been added to the discussion of writing introductions and conclusions, and new exercises throughout the chapter focus attention on various aspects of the drafting process.

2. Expanded discussion of revising.

Chapter **10**, "Revising the Essay," has been expanded and reorganized to present a case study of the revising process; the chapter now follows a student paper from its first version to its final draft, illustrating the writer's use of peer critique and her instructor's comments as she develops a final draft. Chapter **11**, "Revising Paragraphs," has been extensively revised to provide clearer discussion of specific details in paragraph development and to offer new examples of strategies for achieving coherence within and between paragraphs. Throughout Chapter **12**, "Revising Sentences," the text has been revised and reorganized for added clarity; moreover, all of the chapter's exercises have been revised, and a new section on faulty predication has been added to the discussion of mixed constructions in section **12f**. Chapter **13**, "Revising Diction," has also been extensively rewritten and completely reorganized for easier accessibility; additions to this chapter include three new exercises on using inclusive language in section **13e**.

3. Expanded, up-to-date treatment of the research process in an electronic milieu.

Chapter **18**, "The Library," addresses the needs of students working in an electronic library by including up-to-date discussion of on-line library catalogs (**18a**), on-line data bases (**18e**), and CD-ROM data bases (**18e**). Helpful illustrations and well-annotated bibliographies of major data bases accompany the text, which also offers extensive coverage of traditional sources of information, including standard reference works, periodical indexes, and government documents. Chapter **20**, "Composing the Research Paper," not only presents clear guidelines for avoiding plagiarism and citing sources but also includes a new section on strategies for incorporating quotations into one's own writing (**20c**). Like the twelfth edition, this book offers comprehensive instructions for documenting research in MLA, APA, and endnote styles. Model MLA works cited citations, APA reference list citations, and endnote citations are provided for every type of source that a student is likely to encounter, and two fully annotated student research papers illustrate MLA and APA methods of citation in practice.

4. A complete guide to the newly revised APA documentation style.

The thirteenth edition features all the major revisions in APA documentation style as presented in the new *Publication Manual of the American Psychological Association*, fourth edition (1994). Instructions in Chapter **22**, "Using APA Documentation," for composing reference list citations and for formatting the research paper, as well as the sample paper in Chapter **23**, follow the APA's latest directives.

5. Revised and expanded treatment of punctuation.

For greater clarity and easier access, the twelfth edition's single chapter on punctuation has been divided into six new chapters that offer expanded coverage of the fourteen major marks of punctuation in English (Chapters **31** to **36**). The emphasis throughout these six chapters has been on clear explanations, carefully chosen examples, helpful exercises, and an organization that enables the reader to locate information quickly and easily.

6. A new chapter for ESL writers.

New to this edition, Chapter **43**, "Writing English as a Second Language," addresses the particular concerns of ESL students with clear discussions of definite and indefinite articles; subjects, verbs, and expletives in sentences; phrasal verbs and progressive verb forms; the use of gerunds and infinitives after verbs; the ordering of cumulative adjectives; and the placement of adverbs.

7. A revised design that includes more than seventy quick-reference boxes.

Streamlined for greater readability, the book's design also includes more than seventy reference boxes enabling readers to locate key information quickly and easily. Each chapter opens with a quick-reference box that summarizes the chapter's contents, provides definitions of key terms, or illustrates major principles or rules. Within chapters, other boxes highlight important points or provide handy checklists—for example, a guide to patterns of organization (**5c**), a list of wordy connectives to avoid (**8c**), a table of useful transitional words and phrases (**11b**). A convenient index of the information in all of these boxes is located inside the back cover.

Supplements

The new *Instructor's Annotated Edition* of *The Heath Handbook* is a large-format edition featuring on-page teaching tips and answers to exercise items, as well as suggestions for further professional reading. It helps instructors prepare for and lead classroom use of the handbook and facilitates checking student answers to exercise items.

Several resources can help students using *The Heath Handbook*. For additional practice in planning, writing, and revising, students can benefit from *The Heath Workbook for the Heath Handbook* by Dusky Loebel. A separate *Answer Key for the Heath Workbook* is also available. *Heath Grammar Review Software,* for Macintosh and IBM-compatible computers, provides three diagnostic tests and 300 multiple-choice exercise items to help students improve sentence-level grammar skills. As another resource for improving their writing, students can receive, at a nominal cost, either *The Bantam Roget's Thesaurus,* a completely up-to-date reference of synonyms and antonyms in a dictionary format, or the Dell *American Heritage Dictionary.*

Students using *The Heath Handbook* have available the option of a ten-week subscription to *Newsweek* magazine at a nominal price. With fresh, new ideas for a composition course, *Newsweek* introduces students to important contemporary issues and the writing that best conveys them. Instructors who choose this option for their students can also receive a complimentary subscription to *Newsweek* for the academic year. *Using* Newsweek *with Your D. C. Heath Handbook,* by Albert C. d'Amato, provides sample syllabi and assignments for developing students' reading, writing, and revising skills using *Newsweek* and *The Heath Handbook* in tandem.

Acknowledgments

I enjoyed the support and assistance of many colleagues and friends as I prepared this edition of *The Heath Handbook.* Special thanks are due to Robert Acker of the DePaul University Libraries, who shared his expertise in on-line information systems; to Demarie Jackson of the American Psychological Association; and to Eileen Seifert, whose contributions to the exercises and reference boxes were invaluable. Chris Rutigliano, the copy editor for this project, read the manuscript with care and insight, making innumerable wise suggestions and catching many errors before they could find their way to the printed page.

Teachers and reviewers of *The Heath Handbook* offered me a host of valuable comments that helped to shape this thirteenth edition. I am grateful to Richard R. Bollenbacher, Edison State Community College; Betty L. Dixon, Rancho Santiago College; Connie W. Douglas, Tulane University; David Fuller, Northern State College; Joanna Gibson, Texas A&M University; Owen W. Gilman, St. Joseph's University; David E. Hartman, St. Petersburg Junior College; Douglas Hunt, University of Missouri, Columbia; Karen J. Jones, St. Charles County Community College; David M. Kvernes, Southern Illinois University, Carbondale; Janet Madden-Simpson, El Camino Community College; Margaret McCampbell, Catonsville Community College; Barbara Merkel, Cazenovia College; Patricia Y. Murray, California State University, Northridge; Susan B. Norton, Trident Technical College; Linda

Marianne Taylor, Tri-County Technical College; Jeff Watkins, Mt. Hood Community College; and Martha A. Whitt, University of Tennessee, Martin.

My wise and patient editors at D. C. Heath and Company once again deserve the highest praise and my deepest thanks. Paul Smith's enthusiasm for this project and his personal support have, as always, been constantly reassuring. Linda Bieze's thoughtfulness and good sense played a major role in shaping the text, and her unfailing encouragement surpassed even her anxiety over my inability to write faster. And Martha Wetherill's concern for detail and eye for good design have made a difference on every page of the book. I feel fortunate indeed to have been associated with an editorial team of such talent and good cheer.

Gerald P. Mulderig
Chicago, Illinois

Contents

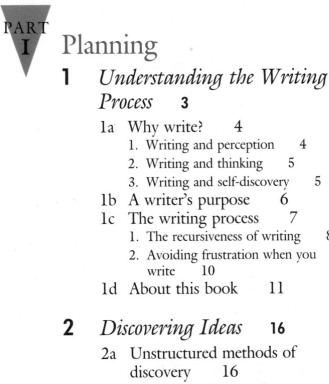

Writing

PART III

Revising

PART IV   Critical Reading and Thinking

PART
V

The Research Paper

17 *The Research Process*   **359**

PART VI   Grammatical Usage

PART VII Punctuation, Spelling, Mechanics

31 *End Punctuation: Period, Question Mark, Exclamation Point*   **653**

PART VIII Special Writing Situations

PART I

Planning

I ▼ *Under-standing the Writing Process*

As you begin this book on writing, it may surprise you to know that no less a person than Plato had serious doubts about the value of learning to write. More than 2,300 years ago, the Greek philosopher argued in one of his works on rhetoric that a person's education is better served by oral discussion and debate than by writing. Unlike a speaker or teacher, he pointed out, a printed book cannot answer its readers' questions, nor can it in turn pose questions to make sure that readers have correctly understood what they have read. According to Plato, those who become dependent on the written word will gradually lose their powers of memory and the ability to think on their own. Believing their knowledge greater than it actually is, they will become conceited and complacent, a burden rather than an asset to their society.

No matter what we think of Plato's doubts about the value of writing, we shouldn't overlook the important fact that he used writing to express those doubts. If he had not, his ideas would probably be unknown today. Plato's written attack on writing suggests in a paradoxical way the inevitability of written communication in the exchange and transmission of ideas. During the centuries since he lived, technological advances ranging from the development of inexpensive paper to the invention of the desktop laser printer have continued to underscore the central role of writing in our civilization. Indeed, our lives would be unimaginable without the written word. Try to picture a world with no books or newspapers, no greeting cards or instruction manuals, no bills,

This book begins with an issue that should be fundamental in any consideration of the writing process: the intrinsic value of writing, introduced by the allusion to Plato's *Phaedrus*. Most students are used to thinking about writing primarily as an activity directed at others; unless they have adopted the practice of keeping a personal journal, they may not have become very sensitive to the changes that can occur within themselves through the act of writing. But writing is a valuable activity not only because it can affect the way readers think and act, but also because it helps writers develop into fuller human beings, more conscious of the surrounding world, more aware of their intellectual processes, and more deeply committed to the ideas they consider important. Writing is a way of seeing the world, of coming to understand one's ideas more fully, of arriving at a fuller conception of who one is and what one believes. In short, as Janet Emig has pointed out in her frequently cited essay, writing is a mode of learning.

Not many first-year college students have been taught to think of writing in these terms—a point that can be illustrated by asking students

1a

> QUICK REFERENCE: *The Writing Process*
>
> *Communication triangle*   The configuration of elements present in virtually every writing situation: a writer, a reader, and a subject, linked by a written text.
>
> *Purpose*   A writer's awareness of the ways in which the components of the communication triangle affect the content, style, tone, and form of his or her writing.
>
> *Recursiveness*   A term used to describe the typically cyclical nature of the writing process, whose three phases—planning, drafting, and revising—may be repeated many times during the composition of a single text.

recipes, advertisements, or love letters, and you will realize that we write, quite simply, because we must.

1a   Why write?

For a moment, though, let us suppose that writing was not essential to communication in our culture but was instead an activity that we could choose to engage in or not, as we wished. What value could we assign to writing under such circumstances? What benefits does it offer the writer as an activity pursued for its own sake?

1.   Writing and perception

In the first place, writing heightens our awareness of the way in which language shapes reality. Writing brings us into contact with language in an especially direct way, demanding that we make deliberate choices from among many alternative ways of identifying, and hence

beginning a college writing course what they have learned about writing in high school. For many, writing as they have learned it in high school is primarily a matter of content and form. They have been taught that they must have something interesting to say, that they must follow certain conventions of organization, that they must be clear and logical. All of these guidelines have a certain virtue, of course, but they may be insufficient for the kinds of writing required in college and in life.

perceiving, the features of our world. Consider, for example, the different implications of the following similar statements:

Deborah is a *loyal* supporter of the president.
Deborah is a *devoted* supporter of the president.
Deborah is a *zealous* supporter of the president.
Deborah is a *fanatical* supporter of the president.

At what point does loyalty shade into devotion? Devotion into zeal? Zeal into fanaticism? Writing forces us to take positions on such questions, to decide how we will describe, and therefore understand, the world we inhabit. Whenever we choose one label (*zealot*) and reject another (*fanatic*), we further define for ourselves the nature of that world. No wonder that respect for the power of language has been the cornerstone of Western education for 2,500 years. We participate in that intellectual tradition, increasing our consciousness of the links between language and perception, each time we write.

2. Writing and thinking

By forcing us to give our ideas concrete form, writing also leads us to understand those ideas more fully. Unlike an impromptu debate with friends over a late-night pizza, a written argument makes us attend to the quality and reasonableness of our ideas; the logical leaps that may pass unnoticed in conversation show up in writing as glaring fallacies. When we write, we enter naturally into a kind of internal dialogue with ourselves as we search for the words and sentences that will best capture our elusive thoughts. Because it requires such precision, the act of writing is a uniquely powerful means of discovering and refining our ideas about any subject.

3. Writing and self-discovery

Writing not only leads us to the discovery of new ideas but also offers opportunities for discovery of the self. When we commit ourselves in writing to an idea, a perspective, a belief, or an argument, we also come to understand ourselves better. Bound up with the intellectual growth that accompanies writing is the personal growth that

1b

results from taking a firm position on an issue, from deciding to see the world in one way rather than another. The commitment that is part of every important writing act forces us to come to terms with what we really believe, with who we really are.

1b   A writer's purpose

When we use writing not only to explore our ideas but also to communicate those ideas to others, we place ourselves in a configuration of elements often referred to as the *communication triangle*.

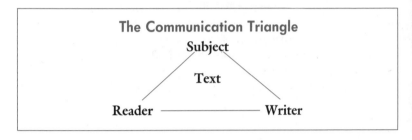

The Communication Triangle
Subject
Text
Reader ——————— Writer

It would be difficult to imagine an act of writing that did not include these four components. Writing obviously presumes a subject, a specific selection from the writer's fund of experiences. Virtually all writing, moreover, is addressed to a reader of some sort. (Even a private journal has at least a single reader: what writer of a journal does not go back and review entries written weeks, months, or years before?) And linking writer, reader, and subject is the written text itself, whether in the form of a letter, an essay, a memo, a novel, or a poem.

These elements, which surround us whenever we attempt to communicate through writing, vary endlessly and thus demand great adaptability from us as writers. When our audience of readers changes, so must the style and content of our writing. No one would use the same language to address a child, an intimate friend, and a senior business colleague. Our approach to writing also changes when our subject or our closeness to the subject changes. The personal tone of an autobiographical essay differs from the more formal tone of a research paper partly because of a writer's different relationship with the material in each case. Finally, our writing changes as the form in which we write

As an introduction to the more sophisticated writing that students may be doing in college, section **1b** presents the writing process in *rhetorical* terms—as the creation of a text shaped by a writer's relationship to a subject, a reader, and an occasion (or purpose) for writing. As the diagram on page 7 makes clear, the discussion of the components of the communication triangle in **1b** not only makes an important point about the writing process but also serves as an outline of the first portion of the book. Chapter **2** concentrates on the subject to be written about and presents several ways of probing a topic for interesting angles to develop in writing. Chapter **3** will take up the question of the reader at greater length, offering a rationale for understanding one's audience and a systematic method of analyzing readers before one begins to write. In Chapter **4**, the focus shifts to the writer—in particular, to the tone of his or her writing. Chapters **5**, **6**, and **7** examine the form of the text itself by turning to the organization and development of essays and paragraphs.

1c

changes. Business letters, for example, require that we follow conventions different from those that govern the writing of term papers or of sonnets.

When we speak of a *purpose* in writing, we mean an awareness of the complex ways in which the components of each new communication triangle affect the content, style, tone, and form of what we write. As you will see, this broad concept of a writer's purpose informs much of what is said about writing in this book. The next six chapters, for example, will develop the notion of purpose in writing by considering the questions that the communication triangle suggests.

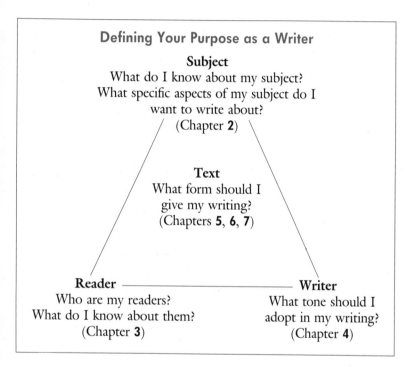

Defining Your Purpose as a Writer

Subject
What do I know about my subject?
What specific aspects of my subject do I
want to write about?
(Chapter **2**)

Text
What form should I
give my writing?
(Chapters **5, 6, 7**)

Reader
Who are my readers?
What do I know about them?
(Chapter **3**)

Writer
What tone should I
adopt in my writing?
(Chapter **4**)

1c The writing process

Rarely do any of us begin a writing task prepared with complete answers to these questions about our purpose. The act of writing

The unavoidably sequential arrangement of topics in this book may suggest to some students that the writing process itself is similarly linear, a series of steps that, once mastered, will invariably lead to the production of successful papers. Section **1c** attempts to dispel this notion by stressing the cyclical, or recursive, nature of the composing process, as well as the plain messiness of writing, illustrated by a page of the original handwritten manuscript for this chapter. Among the most important things that a student can acquire in a composition class are a respect for the unpredictability of the writing act and a self-conscious awareness of the idiosyncratic features of his or her own composing process. True, there are rules that govern many aspects of the form that writing takes—spelling and punctuation rules, for example—but this handbook tries to give equal weight to the many options for composing that are available to each person who picks up a pen or sits down at a computer keyboard.

1c

is partly deliberate, but partly intuitive as well; intention and inspiration mingle when we write. We clarify and define our purpose as we participate in the scratch-it-out, stop-and-go process that writing always entails.

Some people try to avoid writing, or at least to postpone it, because they find this process frustrating and discouraging. They make the mistake of believing that writing should be a clean and smooth act, word following word until all of their thoughts have been translated neatly onto the page before them. But writing isn't a matter of simply translating ideas into words on a page. Instead, as suggested above, it involves the far more complex process of discovering the meaning and implications of one's ideas. No matter how clearly you may think you have formulated your thoughts in your mind, putting them down on paper has a way of revealing new angles for you to consider, new questions for you to answer. It's by searching for ways to secure our free-floating thoughts in writing that we find out what we really understand and believe. If this process is often a slow and uncertain one, we shouldn't be surprised.

1. The recursiveness of writing

For most of us, writing involves frequent stops and starts, the outward signs of our minds at work. The fact that you don't effortlessly fill page after page with your writing doesn't mean that you're not getting anywhere; most writers stop to revise and rethink what they have written well before they get to the end. That's what has happened in the handwritten draft reproduced on the following page—the original draft of the paragraph you just read. As you can see, the revising began immediately, with the adding and deleting of words, phrases, and whole sentences. And if you compare this draft with the final version of the paragraph above, you'll see that even more changes followed.

Some writers work more neatly and methodically than this, others much less so. Most writers, though, move forward only by repeatedly going back to an earlier point and rethinking what they have written. For that reason, writing is sometimes described as a *recursive* process, one in which thinking, writing, and revising are not sequential steps but rather stages in a cycle that a writer repeats many times. Each portion

~~Many~~ Some people try to avoid, or at least to postpone, writing because they find it frustrating & discouraging. They mistakenly persist in believing that the art of writing should be ~~neat &~~ clean & direct, word inevitably following word until all of their thoughts have been translated neatly onto the page before them. But writing ~~is not~~ isn't the <u>translation</u> of ideas into words on a page; it's the <u>discovery</u> of the meanings and the implications of these ideas. ~~By finding~~ ways to fix ~~our ideas~~ your thoughts into written words, ~~we discover what they mean to us and to others. When we write,~~ you also ~~we~~ find out what ~~we~~ you really ~~mean~~ intend. We shouldn't be surprised to discover that ~~it is~~ writing is often a slow, uncertain, unpredictable task.

as are not you and I

to say

No matter how clearly ~~you~~ we may think ~~that we~~ ~~you~~ have formulated ~~your~~ our ideas in ~~your~~ our mind, the art of writing them down on paper has a way of ~~raising new questions,~~ revealing new perspectives & raising new questions.

1c

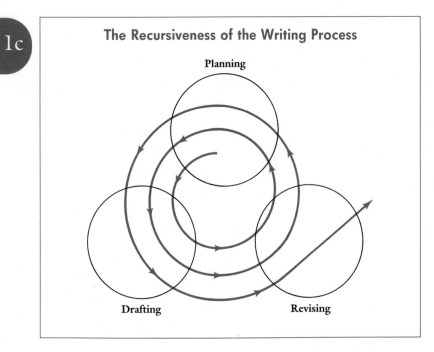

The Recursiveness of the Writing Process

Planning

Drafting

Revising

of a draft may reveal possibilities for revision, each revision prompting the writer to consider anew his or her subject and purpose, each reconsideration of the subject leading to a new tentative draft.

2. Avoiding frustration when you write

The difficulty of expressing ideas in writing is frustrating to all of us at one time or another. But you can minimize that frustration if you anticipate—and then, perhaps, even enjoy—the recursiveness of the writing process. Before you begin, prepare for the fact that you may eventually delete and discard much of what you write, replacing it with ideas that you don't yet have, ideas that will come to you only after you have immersed yourself in your writing. Take pleasure in observing how your ideas change and evolve as you commit them to writing, and pay attention to your own distinctive behavior as a writer. For example, how do you cope with being stuck? Do you reread what you have just written in an attempt to recapture some of the momentum that got you as far as you are? Do you try to refocus your thoughts on your subject? Get up and walk around for a while? Or just daydream until inspiration strikes again? Becoming a writer is partly a matter of identifying the habits that make you most productive and sticking to them whenever possible. Still, that won't necessarily make writing easy. Even experienced writers prepare to spend more time wandering through deserts of mental blankness than luxuriating in pools of creative energy.

1d   About this book

This book is about many elements of the writing process. As this chapter has already suggested, that process varies greatly from person to person. Indeed, though convention governs some aspects of writing, like punctuation and grammatical usage, many others are so idiosyncratic that it's impossible to prescribe the best procedures for you to follow. If you have not done so already, you'll have to decide for yourself where and when you are most productive as a writer, which writing materials you're most comfortable with, and what strategies of composition are most fruitful for you.

What this book offers is advice that you may find helpful to incorporate into your own writing process. The remainder of this first section presents some methods of exploring a subject before you begin to write, examines the concept of audience and its relation to the writing process, and discusses the nature and varieties of a writer's voice. Later chapters on the form that writing takes will consider topics that range from composing effective sentences to organizing research papers. Also included are strategies for revising prose, principles of critical reading and thinking, and a survey of the conventions of grammar, usage, and mechanics. Remember, though, that the form of this book imposes on these subjects a linear order that is not true to the actual process of writing. Subject, audience, form, and purpose are interrelated, inseparable elements. Planning, writing, and revising are components of the process that overlap and blur.

1d

EXERCISE 1

Make a list of the materials and circumstances that you find most conducive to writing. Consider, for example, the following questions:

1. Where do you write most easily (at a desk, in a comfortable chair, in bed)?
2. When are you most productive as a writer (early morning, midday, late at night)?
3. What kind of paper do you prefer to use (legal paper, unlined typing paper, notebook paper)?
4. What instrument do you usually write with (pencil, ballpoint pen, keyboard)?
5. What surroundings do you prefer (silence, conversation, music)?

Compare your list with the lists of others in your class. What do the results reveal about the idiosyncratic nature of writing?

EXERCISE 2

Read the following professional writers' descriptions of the way in which they go about writing. What aspects of their writing processes are also part of your writing process? What differences do you find between their methods of writing and yours?

1. I write when I feel like it and wherever I feel like it, and I feel like it most of the time: day, night, and during twilight. I write in a restaurant, on a plane, between skiing and horseback riding, when I take my night walks in Manhattan, Paris, or in any other town. I wake up in the middle of the night or the afternoon to make notes and never know when I'll sit down at the typewriter.

   —Jerzy Kosinski

2. I like [writing] at home [best] because . . . it's the only place where you can really promise yourself time and keep out interruptions. My ideal way to write a short story is to write the whole first draft through in one sitting, then work as long as it takes on revisions, and then write the final version all in one, so that in the end the whole thing amounts to one long sustained effort. . . . I can correct better if I see [my work] in typescript. After that, I revise with scissors and pins. Pasting is too slow, and you can't undo it, but with pins you can

Exercise 1

This exercise is the first of four that are intended to focus the student's attention on the specific features of his or her own writing process. It can be used as the basis of a class discussion and as a means of generating raw material for the essay called for in Exercise 3 below.

Exercise 2

To reinforce the point that each writer's approach is unique and that there is no single, "correct" method of writing to be learned, this exercise deliberately juxtaposes contradictory descriptions of the composing process. Kosinski, for example, talks about writing wherever he goes, on airplanes and during walks through cities, whereas Welty states her preference for composing in the uninterrupted silence of her home. Vidal asserts that he never revises until the first draft is finished, while Heller describes revising every three or four pages for hours. Steinbeck recommends writing as quickly as possible, but Gass complains that he has to write with excruci-

1d

move things from anywhere to anywhere, and that's what I really love doing—putting things in their best and proper place.

—Eudora Welty

3. Now everything [I write] finds its initial expression in longhand and the typewriter has become a rather alien thing—a thing of formality and impersonality. My first novels were all written on a typewriter: first draft straight through, then revisions, then final draft. But I can't do that any longer. . . . I haven't any formal schedule, but I love to write in the morning, before breakfast. Sometimes the writing goes so smoothly that I don't take a break for many hours—and consequently have breakfast at two or three in the afternoon on good days.

—Joyce Carol Oates

4. Whenever I get up in the morning, I write for about three hours. I write novels in longhand on yellow legal pads. . . . For some reason I write plays and essays on the typewriter. The first draft usually comes rather fast. One oddity: I never reread a text until I have finished the first draft. Otherwise it's too discouraging. Also, when you have the whole thing in front of you for the first time, you've forgotten most of it and see it fresh.

—Gore Vidal

5. I ordinarily write three or four handwritten pages and then rework them for two hours. I can work for four hours, or forty-five minutes. It's not a matter of time. I set a realistic objective: How can I inch along to the next paragraph? Inching is what it is.

—Joseph Heller

6. When I am between books, as I am now, I sit in an armchair and think and make notes. Before I start a book I've usually got four hundred pages of notes. Most of them are almost incoherent. But there's always a moment when you feel you've got a novel started. You can more or less see how it's going to work out. After that it's just a question of detail.

—P. G. Wodehouse

7. The following are some of the things I have had to do to keep from going nuts. . . . Abandon the idea that you are ever going to finish. Lose track of the 400 pages and write just one page for each day, it helps [sic]. Then when it gets finished, you are always sur-

ating slowness. Most students will probably identify with specific points from several different authors' descriptions of their work.

1d

prised. . . . Write freely and as rapidly as possible and throw the whole thing on paper. Never correct or rewrite until the whole thing is down. Rewrite in process is usually found to be an excuse for not going on. It also interferes with flow and rhythm which can only come from a kind of unconscious association with the material.

—John Steinbeck

8. I write slowly because I write badly. I have to rewrite everything many, many times just to achieve mediocrity. Time can give you a good critical perspective, and I often have to go slow so that I can look back on what sort of botch of things I made three months ago. Much of the stuff which I will finally publish, with all its flaws, as if it had been dashed off with a felt pen, will have [been] begun eight or more years earlier, and worried and slowly chewed on and left for dead many times in the interim.

—William Gass

9. The most important [of my writing rituals] is that I need an hour alone before dinner, with a drink, to go over what I've done that day. I can't do it late in the afternoon because I'm too close to it. Also, the drink helps. It removes me from the pages. So I spend this hour taking things out and putting other things in. Then I start the next day by redoing all of what I did the day before, following these evening notes. When I'm really working I don't like to go out or have anybody to dinner, because then I lose the hour. If I don't have the hour, and start the next day with just some bad pages and nowhere to go, I'm in low spirits.

—Joan Didion

10. If I'm stuck, I try to get myself unstuck before I sit down again [to write] because moving through the day surrounded by people and music and air it is easier to make major motions in your mind than it is sitting at the typewriter in a slightly claustrophobic room. It's hard to hold a manuscript in your mind, of course. You get down to the desk and discover that the solution you had arrived at while having insomnia doesn't really fit.

—John Updike

EXERCISE 3

Use your answers to Exercises 1 and 2 to write a short essay on your writing process. Be as specific as you can about the strategies you ordi-

---

Exercise 3

Assign the essay described in this exercise early in the course, ideally during the first week. In the context provided by Exercises 1 and 2 above, it will give students an opportunity to reflect on themselves as writers, and it should offer you insights into what they hope to obtain from your course. Consider making copies of the papers to redistribute at the end of the term so that students can write a final essay on the ways in which the course has confirmed or altered their conceptions of their own writing processes.

Exercise 4 (page 15)

This final exercise shifts the focus to the different composing styles that we employ in different rhetorical situations. Thus it looks ahead to the discussions of audience and voice in Chapters **3** and **4**.

narily follow to plan, draft, and revise a piece of writing. What aspects of your writing process are you particularly comfortable with? Are there others that you would like to change or improve? If so, why?

1d

EXERCISE 4

Write an essay in which you compare the strategies you use to compose two different types of writing, such as a letter to a friend and a paper for a class. What elements of your writing process are common to both? How do you account for whatever differences you find?

For Further Reading

Britton, James. "Writing to Learn and Learning to Write." *Prospect and Retrospect: Selected Essays of James Britton.* Ed. Gordon M. Pradl. Montclair: Boynton/ Cook, 1982. 94–111.

Chorny, Merron. "A Context for Writing." *Reinventing the Rhetorical Tradition.* Ed. Aviva Freedman and Ian Pringle. Ottawa: Canadian Council of Teachers of English, 1980. 1–8.

Emig, Janet. "Writing as a Mode of Learning." *College Composition and Communication* 28 (1977): 122–28.

Perl, Sondra. "Understanding Composing." *College Composition and Communication* 31 (1980): 363–69.

Young, Richard, and Patricia Sullivan. "Why Write? A Reconsideration." *Essays on Classical Rhetoric and Modern Discourse.* Ed. Robert J. Connors, Lisa S. Ede, and Andrea A. Lunsford. Carbondale: Southern Illinois UP, 1984. 215–25.

2 Discovering Ideas

$\mathbf{W}$hy is one writer able to create a substantial, convincing essay, while another, working with a similar subject, produces writing that is thin and stale? Good subjects don't alone guarantee good essays; the successful writer also knows how to probe a subject for interesting and important angles to develop in writing. This chapter describes several such strategies for making your thinking more productive and creative.

You can use these methods of discovery no matter what kind of paper you are working on. If your assignment is an autobiographical paper or a personal experience essay, these techniques should help you recall aspects of your life that you can use as the basis for your paper. If you are writing in an academic discipline such as art or political science or psychology, you may expect these procedures to raise issues that you will want to explore with additional reading or research. In either case, you will have discovered ideas to build on as you write.

You don't need to master every one of these strategies. In fact, because writing is such an idiosyncratic activity, they won't all be equally useful to every writer. Experiment with several of these approaches, and then concentrate on using the ones that seem to work best for you.

2a Unstructured methods of discovery

An *unstructured approach* to discovering ideas for writing may be defined as one in which you let your mind go in whatever direction it chooses. The important thing, however, is that you pay attention to

One of the hallmarks of contemporary composition teaching is the renewed emphasis on rhetorical invention—the process of exploring ideas for writing. Invention was the cornerstone of classical rhetorical practice (Aristotle placed it squarely in his definition of rhetoric as "the art of *discovering* in any given situation all the available means of persuasion" [italics added]), but when the influence of classical rhetoric waned, so did the popularity of rhetorical invention. From the second half of the nineteenth century until the 1950s, departments of English virtually abandoned classical rhetoric, and invention consequently disappeared from writing instruction in America. Although many teachers of English have once again become interested in classical rhetoric during the last twenty or thirty years, invention remains a subject frequently overlooked in high-school and even in college writing courses.

Chapter **2** deliberately avoids the rather intimidating term *rhetorical invention* and discusses alternative approaches to invention under the headings of "Unstructured Methods of Discovery" and "Structured Methods of Discovery." It also avoids presenting more different methods of discovery

> **QUICK REFERENCE: *Methods of Discovery***
>
> | | |
> |---|---|
> | *Unstructured approaches to discovery* | Methods of exploring ideas that rely on the mind's natural creativity and powers of association rather than on predetermined procedures or steps. Brainstorming, free writing, and journal writing are examples. |
> | *Structured approaches to discovery* | Methods of exploring ideas that systematically employ external aids to thinking, such as a fixed set of questions to answer or a checklist of topics to consider. |
> | *Brainstorming* | The free, intense exploration of an idea guided simply by the mind's natural powers of association. |
> | *Free writing* | A discovery technique that generates ideas through concentrated periods of undirected, continuous writing. |
> | *Writer's journal* | An ongoing, written record of one's reflective, probing, and speculative responses to the world. |

2a

your mind's activity and make note of all the ideas it turns up. Only at the end of the discovery process, as you begin to shape your paper, should you go over your notes to decide which ideas you will use and which you will discard. (For suggestions about organizing your raw material, see **5a**, **5b**, **5c**, and **5d**.)

1. Brainstorming

Brainstorming is the free and uncontrolled play of the mind with any idea. When we engage in brainstorming, we let our mind's natural powers of association direct the discovery process. The difference

than any student could realistically be expected to master, and instead explains a few useful alternative methods thoroughly.

Strictly speaking, rhetorical invention involves the *systematic* exploration of a subject, usually by examining it in relation to a set of questions or categories. Aristotle's "topics"—definition, comparison, cause and effect, for example—are the classical model for this approach to invention. Section **2a** discusses three less formal, but currently more popular and often equally useful, methods of discovering ideas for writing: brainstorming, free writing, and journal writing.

Two points about all of these methods of invention cannot be stressed enough. First, they must always be performed with pen or pencil in hand; otherwise, they will yield no written record of the material they generate and will be of little more use to the writer than random daydreaming. Second, the ideas generated by these methods should never be "edited" until the entire list has been produced; ideas that initially seemed trivial or useless may turn out to be surprisingly valuable as one's paper begins to take shape.

2a

between brainstorming and mere random thought is that in a brainstorming session we *write down* all the ideas that come to us so that we finish with a concrete record of our thoughts. The very act of noting each idea, moreover, often prompts the mind to generate still more related ideas.

You may jot down the ideas that occur to you through brainstorming in a simple list like the one below. In this case, a student began to consider writing about some aspect of the subject "gymnastics."

Nick's brainstorming

```
Gymnastics
--many people think gymnastics is boring
--they're right
--practice boring, especially stretching,
    warm-up exercises
--setting up and breaking down equipment mo-
    notonous
--leg lifts are very boring
--very painful
--how you do them
--flat on your back
--if you do them wrong you get extras
--leg lifts for punishment as well as exer-
    cise
--gymnastics is good for you, though
--getting a high score is worth the effort
--one of the top sports
```

```
--becoming increasingly popular thanks to the
    Olympics
--more people beginning training . . .
```

When you brainstorm, you should not "edit" your thoughts in order to produce a neat, orderly list of ideas. Brainstorming, as its name suggests, is a wild, intense activity; its initial results are supposed to be chaotic and disorganized. The time to edit, to look over the ideas you have generated and select those that seem most promising, will come later, as you plan the structure and development of your paper.

Some writers like to use a mapping diagram like that on page 20, rather than a straight list, in the brainstorming process. At the center they place the main idea that they wish to explore. Then, as new ideas come to mind, they write them down on connecting lines drawn out from the center of the page, grouping related ideas together and extending the subgroups as far as possible. One advantage of mapping is that it connects related ideas. Like a straight list, though, the mapping diagram is also tentative and exploratory, and like any method of discovery, it should be expected to generate much more material than you can use in a single well-focused essay. Only when you have extended your ideas as far as possible should you go back to decide which ones might work in your paper.

The illustrations above both involve a subject drawn from the writer's personal experience, but you can also use brainstorming techniques when you are writing a paper based on your reading. In this case, your brainstorming notes will probably fall into two categories: ideas *from* the readings that strike you as important, and ideas *about* the readings that occur to you as you read. In such notes you may be able to discover the focus and basic content for your paper.

Consider this assignment from an introductory sociology course.

Compare the structure and the functions of the family and the values surrounding children and community in modern China and the Israeli kibbutz. Refer to assigned readings by Melford E. Spiro ("Is the Family Universal?") and Bruce Dollar ("Child Care in China"). Length: 2–4 pages, typed.

2a

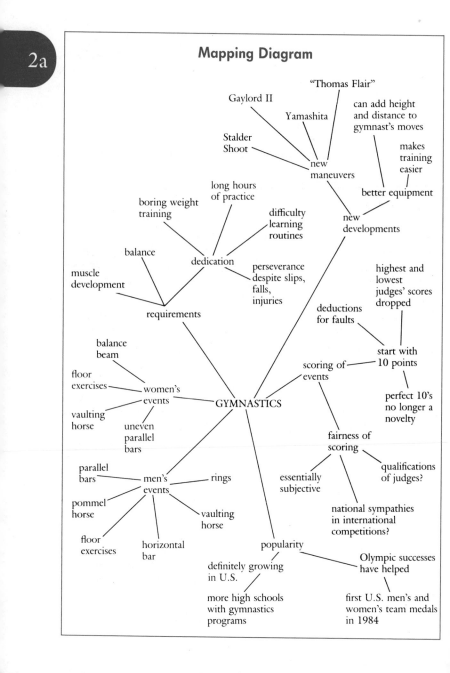

Mapping Diagram

"Thomas Flair"

Gaylord II

Yamashita — can add height and distance to gymnast's moves

Stalder Shoot

makes training easier

new maneuvers

long hours of practice

boring weight training

difficulty learning routines

better equipment

balance

dedication

new developments

muscle development

perseverance despite slips, falls, injuries

highest and lowest judges' scores dropped

requirements

deductions for faults

balance beam

floor exercises

women's events

scoring of events

start with 10 points

vaulting horse

GYMNASTICS

perfect 10's no longer a novelty

uneven parallel bars

fairness of scoring

parallel bars

men's events

rings

essentially subjective

qualifications of judges?

pommel horse

vaulting horse

national sympathies in international competitions?

floor exercises

horizontal bar

popularity

Olympic successes have helped

definitely growing in U.S.

more high schools with gymnastics programs

first U.S. men's and women's team medals in 1984

After reading the two articles, one student jotted down these preliminary notes.

Ellen's brainstorming

```
"Is the Family Universal?"
    Murdock: four functions of nuclear family
        1. sexual
        2. economic
        3. reproductive
        4. educational
    Kibbutz one such group
        --an agricultural collective in Israel:
        communal living, collective ownership
        of all property, communal rearing of
        children
    Education & socialization function of
        "nurses" and teachers, not parents
    Parents are important to psychological de-
        velopment of child

"Child Care in China"
    Several major ideas about child rearing
        --subordination of personal to social
        needs, respect for productive labor,
        altruism, cooperation, integration of
        physical w/intellectual labor--tend to
```

```
        develop kind of citizen China wants--
        values
    Importance placed on group activities
    Toys too heavy for one child
    "Multiple mothering" of Chinese tradition
```

Reflecting on these notes, she then sketched out the following more organized thoughts about the two articles.

Ellen's organized notes

```
  Likenesses
        both value children
        both emphasize group rather than individual
        both separate economic and educational
          function from others
        cooperation preferred over individual ac-
          tion
        both provide psychological security for the
          child
        family life strong
        both altruistic

  Why important?
        family is institution that guarantees fu-
          ture of society
        I see this now better than before--all val-
          ues are focused on children
```

```
society's way of life and values are im-
    pressed in the way children are treated--
    socialization isn't just education; it's
    the whole atmosphere of the society in
    its attitude toward children
```

The notes Ellen had made about her readings led her to a perspective on the material and to a possible focus for her paper—the similar ways in which cultural values are impressed on children in Israel and China. Formal research, of course, would require much more thoroughness in note taking and documentation (see Part V, *The Research Paper*). But for this shorter, more informal paper, brainstorming offered a valuable first step.

2. Free writing

When you brainstorm, you jot down bits and pieces, fragments of ideas that occur to you as you let your mind roam freely. Another way of capturing your thoughts in flight is *free writing*. Free writing differs from brainstorming in that you attempt to catch the flow of your thoughts by writing them not as a list of fragmentary ideas, but as a continuous thread of sentences.

Free writing often begins with an idea or question that sparks your thought. Your opening question may be as vague as "What can I say that's worth reading?" or as specific as "What were the principles of the Chicago school of architecture?" Once you have written your question down, follow it by quickly writing or typing whatever comes to mind as you think about your reply to it. Remember that your question is merely a starting point. Don't attempt to answer it fully, or even to focus your writing around it; let your thoughts take you in whatever direction they will. Try not to pause at all as you write, particularly not to consider such matters as correct punctuation or spelling. If you think you have run out of things to write or are not able to think of words for what you want to say, try rewriting your last five words again and again until something new comes to mind. Your object is to fill your pages with writing, not to compose a coherent essay on the spot.

2a

Some writers actually time themselves when they engage in free writing, trying to get as many words as possible on the page in ten- or fifteen-minute intervals. The idea behind free writing is that our minds will come up with many good ideas if we simply give our thought processes free rein. As in brainstorming, though, it is important that you write down all your ideas as they come to you. It's the written record of your thoughts that distinguishes free writing from daydreaming and that provides concrete material for writing later on.

Here is a brief sample of one student's free writing on the topic of Eastern religions.

Kathleen's free writing

```
     I've been thinking about a bunch of the "ism's"
we talked about in history yesterday. Most are
confusing to me—-how to achieve the desired ef-
fect? For example, Confucianism stresses that
the believer must achieve inner harmony. What
exactly does that mean? You are at peace with
yourself and others, I assume, but how do you
go about it? This brings me to the next "ism"—-
Taoism. This one has a more definite approach—-
become one with Tao, the force which permeates
the universe, by withdrawing from society and
doing nothing. But without more instruction, I
am lost just as with the first. Both seem to
concentrate on inner peace, but seem rather im-
practical. These ideas are just too abstract
for my taste. I think I prefer the third reli-
gion we talked about, Buddhism. One Buddhist
```

sect relied on the compassion of the Buddha in
order to gain salvation. This faith in Buddha
seems similar to that of Western religions. Another sect practiced meditation in order to
achieve enlightenment. Somehow these sects of
Buddhism seem more comprehensible to me--
something I can relate to and understand better. But I guess I need to learn more about all
three religions before I draw conclusions about
them.

In this free-writing sample, Kathleen has correctly been more concerned with getting her ideas down on the page than with structuring
her sentences precisely. By the end of the piece, she has not only explored her initial reactions to Confucianism, Taoism, and Buddhism,
but has also defined a direction for further research—research that
could lead to a more sophisticated comparison of the three religions. As
in this example, free writing will often point you in interesting directions if you give it the opportunity.

Like brainstorming, free writing also works with writing based on
reading assignments. In this case, you may find it useful to begin with
rough notes that you have already taken on your sources. With your
notes before you, simply let your mind and your pen or keyboard take
over. Below, for example, is some of the free writing that Ellen did after
jotting her notes on child rearing in China and on the Israeli kibbutz.

Ellen's free writing

Emphasizes group rather than individual. What
does this mean? The community values of the society are focused on communal success not on
the individual. Best illustrated by the way
children are brought up--most activities occur

2a

in groups not in individuals—examples of the
building blocks that are too heavy for children
to pick up. This forces (Chinese teachers said)
group cooperation. More than one child was
needed to pick up blocks—whole Chinese society
is focused on group effort. Thus we see that
children are taught values they will live by
for the rest of their lives, thus maintaining
the society's values (maybe this should be part
of the introduction). Well, it's not really
teaching—the blocks are designed to force students to learn to cooperate. It's the whole atmosphere that is intended to reinforce the
values.

How is this related to the family? Family
is the institution that guarantees the future
of a society. In China the family has three of
the four functions that Murdock mentions: economic, sexual, reproductive, not education—
also one that Spiro mentions, affection. This
means that the family is not fully part of educational system because the family would tend
to individualize—in a society that emphasizes
group identity you would have to take children
away from the family, but even the substitute

```
family is very loving. Do not punish, only cor-
rect.
```

Neither of these two "paragraphs" is perfectly coherent, nor should we expect them to be. More important in free writing is maintaining the rapid flow of thought. What Ellen has sketched out here are ideas that she can develop further in other, more deliberately planned paragraphs. After some additional free writing, she will begin to reflect on the best way of organizing her ideas. She may underline sentences in her free writing that seem especially important; she may copy key sentences onto another sheet of paper; she may even group ideas together in a rough sort of outline. With pages of written notes before her, she is in a good position to think about the content and structure of the essay she is going to write.

3. Keeping a journal

Scientists record their observations and ideas in journals—and so do poets. The fact that journal writing has proven a useful tool to people across the intellectual spectrum should lead writers of every type to consider the value of keeping an ongoing record of their responses to the world they live in.

This kind of journal is not one that simply records the events of your daily routine—whom you saw, what classes you went to, what tests you studied for, whom you ate dinner with, what magazine you browsed through, what time you went to bed. Instead, it's a journal of ideas—your thoughts and questions about the people, issues, and events in your world. Such a journal is probing and speculative rather than simply factual. And it is also personal, not because its contents are private (they don't necessarily have to be), but because it reflects your unique outlook on the world. The journals of two different people will be as different as the people themselves.

Journal writing differs from free writing in several ways. Whereas free writing is a rapid, almost unconscious activity, writing in a journal is a more leisurely, more reflective, more thoughtful activity, conscious rather than automatic. And while free writing is a technique that writers

2a

use sporadically to generate material on specific subjects, journal writing is a sustained, ongoing activity. A journal presumes a kind of continuity; you collect entries together, whether in a notebook or on a computer disk, so that you can go back to reread and reconsider what you have written earlier. Such rereadings may in turn spark new journal entries.

Journals offer opportunities for freedom and experimentation, but they also call for a degree of discipline. Nothing about a journal can ever be labeled "right" or "wrong"; its format and contents are whatever you want them to be. Consequently, you should use a journal to play with ideas, to ask questions that you can't fully answer, to be serious and silly, outraged and outrageous. Experiment with different styles of writing; use your journal to explore not only different aspects of your world, but different sides of yourself. One of the benefits of such a journal should be increasing your feeling of ease when you write—both physical ease (the act of putting words on a page) and intellectual ease (the process of grappling with ideas). But you will achieve such benefits only if you have the discipline to make writing in your journal a regular habit. Plan at the outset to write at least a paragraph or two in your journal several times a week, and provide a record of your journal's development by dating each entry.

In the following journal entry, notice how the student writer has gone beyond a mere listing of events to include commentary on Henry James as a novelist, reflections on himself as a reader, and even some fun with terminology learned in his psychology class.

Brad's journal entry

September 23

Last week I picked up The Portrait of a Lady, by Henry James. I remembered that I enjoyed The American, and I thought that The Portrait of a Lady might also be good, considering it was written by the same author. I sat down to read it, and thought that I didn't mind it

being slow because I had only started. Something was bound to happen soon. I was reading
about forty pages a day, and each time I sat
down I expected at least one slightly enter-
taining thing to occur. Four days later I was
trying to tell myself that this was not an idi-
otically boring story. "Something will surely
interest me soon." "This is how British women
were in those days." "She's not really disgust-
ingly snobbish."

But eventually I got really mad and began
to attack Henry James: "I'm surprised anyone
could stand to read this stuff." Then I fought
with myself: "Well, The American was pretty
enjoyable. I must be missing something good
here." I had been fighting like this all the
time I was reading. At least I knew I was trying to keep an open mind. But finally my id got
a choke hold on my superego and started dragging him around by his hair. When my superego
gave in, my ego suggested that I drop the book,
go to the library, and check out a good Follett
spy novel.

Of course this isn't literary analysis, and it isn't supposed to be; it's a
record of an immediate personal response. What makes this passage a
good journal entry—besides the genuineness of Brad's voice as a writer

2a

and his obvious sense of humor—are the provocative questions it suggests. Why exactly does he react so negatively to Isabel Archer, the title character in *The Portrait of a Lady*? Why does this novel appeal to him so much less than *The American* did? What's different about James's handling of the two books? All of these are good topics for Brad to consider when he writes in his journal again. Journal entries that raise such interesting questions not only inspire additional journal entries, but may also be the genesis of a more formal piece of writing.

EXERCISE 1

Using either listing or mapping, explore one of the general subjects below, or another subject of your choice. Generate as many ideas as you can in one sitting. Wait at least a few hours and then come back to the same subject. Can you add some new ideas to those you wrote down earlier? Repeat this procedure several times, and then review all the ideas you have jotted down. Which ideas interest you? Which do you think you could make interesting to someone else?

1. Fitness
2. Learning to drive
3. Children
4. Jealousy
5. Music

6. Television commercials
7. Solitude
8. The environment
9. City life
10. Rural life

EXERCISE 2

Select a chapter from one of your textbooks, and use the brainstorming method described on pages 17–23 to explore its contents. What key ideas in the chapter did you identify? What ideas of your own were you able to generate in response to the chapter you read?

EXERCISE 3

Write steadily for ten minutes on one of the topics below or on another subject of your choice. At the end of ten minutes, select what you consider to be the most important idea in your free writing, copy it onto the top of a clean page, and write again for ten minutes without stopping. When you have finished, underline the best ideas from your two sessions of free writing and try to rewrite them into a single coherent paragraph.

1. My greatest accomplishment so far in life has been _____.
2. The most important person in my life is _____.

Exercise 1

Once students have used brainstorming to generate ideas about a subject, they will need to be able to sort through these ideas, selecting out those that are appropriate to their purpose and audience. Hence, the final two questions in this exercise ("Which ideas interest you? Which do you think you could make interesting to someone else?") are particularly important because they ask students to reflect on their material in terms of their own interests and those of their readers.

Exercise 2

Ideally, this exercise should generate not only ideas *in* the chapter but original ideas *about* the chapter.

Exercise 3

Like Exercise 1, this exercise is intended to make students sort through their ideas, selecting those that can be linked together in a coherent piece of writing.

3. My life would be much better if _____.
4. I always feel good when _____.
5. The most important decision that I will have to make this year is _____.

2b Structured methods of discovery

We called the previous approaches to discovery "unstructured" because they follow no predetermined pattern. The results of brainstorming, free writing, and journal writing depend solely on the unpredictable way in which ideas surface in your mind. In contrast, *structured approaches* to discovery follow an orderly plan, usually a fixed set of questions to answer or a checklist of topics to consider. Like the methods of discovery described above, structured methods demand mental alertness and concentration. For some writers, though, the direction provided by structured methods of discovery makes them more productive than brainstorming, free writing, or journal writing.

One of the simplest—and most effective—structured approaches to discovery is the set of questions learned by every novice journalist:

Who?

What?

When?

Where?

Why?

How?

Armed with these questions, a journalist is expected to be able to assemble the essential information about any subject that he or she is investigating. By expanding this formula with additional questions under each of these main headings, we can create a useful structured approach for examining any subject for writing.

Before we do that, however, a few words are in order about the most effective way of using such a set of questions. Many students trying such a discovery procedure for the first time mistakenly believe that their task is to come up with a single answer for each of the questions involved. Two things are wrong with that conception of structured discovery procedures. First, if this approach is to be

Many first-year college students have not been trained to regard the process of exploring ideas for writing as a separate stage in the writing process, and they will need practice in the methods described in this chapter if they are to learn to use them effectively. Have the entire class explore a subject with the discovery questions in **2b**, covering the chalkboard with the information that the students produce. Once students have seen how much material these approaches can generate, let them repeat the procedure with a new subject in small groups, again with one student in the group writing down on paper everything that the others are able to contribute. Before students try out these approaches on their own, then, they will have had the chance to observe their potential usefulness.

2b

successful, your goal must be to produce *as many responses as possible* to each question. You should not treat these questions like examination questions for which there is only one correct answer; instead, reflect on each one carefully, using it to squeeze from your mind as much information about your subject as you can. Second, you must recognize that not every question will be relevant to every topic. Don't feel that this approach is not working if you don't have an answer for every question.

Remember, too, that the answers you get from asking these questions are not themselves topics for a variety of different papers, but raw material that you will eventually refine into a single essay. As with brainstorming and free writing, your initial objective is to collect as much diverse information about your subject as possible. Later, as you begin to organize your paper (see Chapter **5**), you will be able to pull out the best ideas from your notes and consider how they can be most effectively organized, and whether they can be further developed. Like brainstorming and free writing, therefore, structured methods of discovery are useful only if you work through them with pen in hand, jotting down all the ideas that occur to you and assembling pages of working notes on your subject.

Now let's look at an expanded version of the journalist's set of questions. In the questions below, *X* represents the subject you are thinking of writing about.

A Writer's Discovery Questions

Who?

   Who created X?

   Who cares about X?

   Who benefits from X?

   Who suffers because of X?

What?

   How is X defined?

   How would you describe X?

What is X similar to?

What parts make up X? How are they related to one another?

When?

When did X occur?

How long did X last?

What events preceded X?

What events followed X?

Where?

In what setting did X occur? What were the physical surroundings?

What other circumstances made X possible?

How might X have been different if the circumstances had been different?

Why?

What are the causes of X?

What are the consequences or effects of X?

Why is X important?

How?

How did X come to be?

How does X work?

To see the versatility of these questions, consider the way in which one student used them to generate ideas about her hobby, photography. Reflecting on the questions above yielded several pages of notes, among which she was gradually able to find a controlling idea for an essay on the subject. Here is just a portion of Julie's notes, those that she made in response to the second set of questions, under the heading "What?"

Excerpt from Julie's discovery questions

2b

What?

How is photography defined?

```
A chemical process involving light, an im-
age, and a light-sensitive material.
```

How would you describe photography?

```
As a knack or gift.
As a hobby--but photography requires more
equipment than most hobbies--can be expensive
(film, developing)--takes time for photographer
to become really skilled.
As a talent.
As a profession.
As an art form--photography is more highly
technical than most art forms--also, the artist
is restricted by many conditions beyond her
control.
As a form of personal expression.
```

What is photography similar to?

```
Painting--but the photographer's imagina-
tion is limited by lighting, setting, subjects,
equipment.
Writing--photographs can tell a
story--either a single picture, or a series
```

```
of photographs--images and setting establish
mood--subjects' faces can convey emotion.
```

What parts make up photography? How are they related to one
another?

```
     Photographer herself.
     Equipment: camera (more than one?), lenses
(normal, telephoto, zoom, wide-angle--necessary
for maximum creativity); filters (UV, skylight,
polarizing, star-effect, colored--for effective
color reproduction and special effects); tri-
pod; flash; camera case and equipment bag.
     Subjects: human (posed, candid), land-
scapes, animals (hard to control).
     Experts for developing, printing, enlarging
(without first-rate processing, all the photog-
rapher's efforts are futile).
     Purchasers of photographs: magazines, news-
papers, friends.
```

This small portion of Julie's notes suggests the potential value of structured inquiry. Working through these and the other questions, Julie
recognized for the first time the conflict that existed between her attraction to photography as a medium of creative expression and the
many elements of photography that she could not control—equipment
limitations, unpredictable conditions for work, unreliable processing,
and the like. In the opposition that she discovered between her natural
abilities and the inescapable restrictions imposed on those abilities, she
was able to find a central idea for a paper: balancing the rewards of
photography against its intrinsic frustrations.

Exercises 4 and 5 (page 36)

By offering students the opportunity to decide for themselves which type
of discovery procedure seems to be more productive, these exercises make
the point that neither approach is inherently superior. Like the writing
process itself, the appeal of various methods of discovering ideas should be
expected to vary from writer to writer.

For Further Reading

Aristotle. *On Rhetoric: A Theory of Civic Discourse.* Trans. George A.
    Kennedy. New York: Oxford UP, 1991.

2b

Exploring a subject in this systematic way takes concentration, persistence, and imagination. But by enabling you to think carefully about many sides of your topic, such a procedure can help make you a writer with something worth saying.

EXERCISE 4

In Exercise 1 (page 30) you used brainstorming to explore a possible subject for writing. Now examine the same subject using the Writer's Discovery Questions on pages 32–33 above. Are you able to generate new information?

EXERCISE 5

Choose another subject and explore it first with free writing (follow the directions in Exercise 3, page 30) and, a day later, with the Writer's Discovery Questions presented in this section. Which approach to discovery—unstructured or structured—seems to work better for you?

Corbett, Edward P. J. *Classical Rhetoric for the Modern Student*. 3rd ed. New York: Oxford UP, 1990.

———. "What Is Being Revived." *College Composition and Communication* 18 (1967): 166–72.

Fulwiler, Toby, ed. *The Journal Book*. Portsmouth: Boynton/Cook-Heinemann, 1987.

Harrington, David W., et al. "A Critical Survey of Resources for Teaching Rhetorical Invention: A Review-Essay." *College English* 40 (1979): 641–61.

Lauer, Janice M. "Issues in Rhetorical Invention." *Essays on Classical Rhetoric and Modern Discourse*. Ed. Robert J. Connors, Lisa S. Ede, and Andrea A. Lunsford. Carbondale: Southern Illinois UP, 1984. 127–39.

Young, Richard. "Recent Developments in Rhetorical Invention." *Teaching Composition: Twelve Bibliographical Essays*. Ed. Gary Tate. Fort Worth: Texas Christian UP, 1987. 1–38.

3 *Considering Your Audience*

The term *rhetoric* has long been associated with the concept of persuasion. The politician seeking the votes of her constituents is practicing rhetoric, as is the courtroom attorney arguing for his client's innocence. But *rhetoric* may also refer more broadly to the use of language in order to produce any effect—sympathy, anger, euphoria, contempt—in an audience of hearers or readers. If we think of rhetoric in this larger sense, we can see that virtually every act of human communication contains a rhetorical element. We may not spend our days asking for votes or pleading for the lives of clients, but at the very least we usually want the people around us to believe that we are worth listening to. Inspiring that belief in our friends and associates is itself a rhetorical act, no matter what the subject under discussion may be.

3a The rhetorical situation

The relationship between you and your audience—whether in conversation or in writing—is called the *rhetorical situation*. In spoken dialogue, you can easily see whether or not other people understand what you are saying, and their expressions and comments will let you know immediately that they approve or object. The case is much different when you write. Alone with your thoughts and your keyboard, you can only imagine how readers will react to what you write. Whenever you pause to think about the best arguments to use or to consider how a sentence will sound to your readers, you are demonstrating your sensitivity to the rhetorical situation in which you find yourself.

Good writers are able to alter their writing to suit widely different audiences and rhetorical situations. All of us, in fact, make similar

Is there any kind of writing that does not have a rhetorical goal of some kind? Students confronted with this question may claim that "objective" or "factual" writing—such as that found in a newspaper, an encyclopedia, or a textbook—is not intended to affect readers but simply to inform them. But how seriously would we regard a newspaper account written in slang, or an encyclopedia whose articles had the sophistication of comic books? Even writers of informative prose have at least one rhetorical goal in view—to convince the reader of their authority as sources of information.

Chapter **3** presents rhetoric in this broad sense, as the use of language to affect an audience in some—in any —way. Most students in an initial college composition course are willing to accept this definition in the abstract; the difficulty arises when they are asked to apply it in their writing, to adjust their writing for different audiences. One of the hardest myths to overcome in any writing class is the myth of the general reader, the belief—held by students who have been trained to concentrate on content rather than on audience—that most writing is addressed to a vague general

3b

QUICK REFERENCE: *Rhetoric and Audience*	
Rhetoric	In its broadest sense, the use of language to produce any effect in an audience of listeners or readers.
Rhetorical situation	The relationship between you and your audience, whether in conversation or in writing.

adjustments of tone and style every day. If you are explaining a suspension bridge to a small child, you don't use the vocabulary of a civil engineer. If you are showing a campus visitor through your college library, you don't use the familiar tone that is suitable with close friends or family members. If you are embroiled in a heated debate, you don't use arguments that you know will only further antagonize your opponent. The person who is sincerely trying to communicate makes every effort to find language appropriate to his or her audience.

In a writing course, students are sometimes directed to consider others in the class as their audience. In most business and professional writing, however, your readers may not be as familiar to you as your fellow students are. To cope with writing tasks in the real world—with business letters and technical reports, for example—you will need to be able to adapt your writing to the specific rhetorical situations at hand. And such adaptation will require that you know how to analyze and understand your audiences.

3b Analyzing audiences

Many beginning writers like to think that they are writing for the "general reader." In fact, such a person doesn't exist. Few subjects, after all, can realistically be said to interest all people, or even most people. If you think carefully about any paper you have written in the past, you will realize that no matter how broad its appeal, you can imagine readers for whom it would be inappropriate or simply uninteresting. Even the members of your composition class—the audience you may consider most like yourself—come from different geographical areas, ethnic and

audience whose specific characteristics cannot be ascertained and are not likely to be directly relevant to a writer's work anyway.

Many composition textbooks—even many so-called "rhetorics"—comment on the importance of understanding one's audience but fail to explain how students are supposed to acquire this important knowledge. Section **3b** offers a specific method of audience analysis, followed in **3c** by a sample of the way in which such analysis can lead to awareness both of one's audience and of one's purpose and true subject. This is material that is unfamiliar to—and difficult for—most students; instructors should realize that most classes will need substantial practice in such analysis. Chapter **3** and the exercises that follow it provide sufficient material for at least three class sessions.

religious backgrounds, and family situations, and those differences may profoundly affect their reactions to what you write.

Once you recognize that your audience is never people in general, but always a particular selection from humanity, you must consider ways of identifying and understanding that audience, for only if you understand the disposition of your readers can you write effectively for them. Every complex argument has several sides, and no single approach will satisfy all possible audiences. Do your readers already understand your subject, or must you provide background information? Do they already share your beliefs, or must you persuade them to see your subject as you do? The answers to such basic questions will necessarily affect the content and tone of your writing.

Some writers try to visualize an individual member of the audience they are addressing. But this strategy will not be of much value if you lack specific knowledge about your audience. Instead, you might try posing a series of specific questions about your readers. Such questions, like those below, take some of the guesswork out of understanding your audience.

Questions for Analyzing Audiences

Audience's background

What do I know about my audience's
1. age?
2. social status?
3. level of education?
4. political positions?
5. moral beliefs?

Audience's relation to subject and writer

1. What does my audience already know about this subject?
2. What else do I want my audience to know?
3. What do I want this audience to think of me as a person?
4. What evidence or arguments will be convincing to this audience?

3c

Of course, not all of these questions will be relevant in every case. But for most writing tasks this checklist will provide a helpful way of reflecting systematically on your audience and rhetorical situation.

3c Using audience analysis to shape your writing

As you respond to these questions, you must consider how your answers will affect the writing you are about to do. For example, if you are writing in a technical field such as architectural engineering, you will freely use the specialized vocabulary of the field if your readers share your expertise, but not if they are laypeople. Neglecting to consider your audience would be disastrous in either case: you'd be incomprehensible to nonspecialists if you used technical language, but if you failed to do so with an audience of engineers, you'd look like a rank amateur rather than a professional. Similarly, if your subject is politics, the strategies you use to mobilize readers who already share your beliefs will be utterly different from the approach you would take to convert opponents to your position.

In the following audience analysis, note how one student's use of the questions above leads him to a fuller understanding of his audience and hence to a clearer conception of his purpose in writing. In this case, the student had decided to write a letter to be published in his campus newspaper about damage to furnishings in the university library. Should such a letter be directed to the students responsible for the damage, or should it be directed to the rest of the students on campus, the indirect victims of the vandalism? The writer's analysis of these two groups of readers helps him decide which audience to address and what approach to take in his letter.

Marc's analysis of his audience

Audience's background

1. Age

   —all students on campus approximately my age
   —vandals act younger than they are
   —socially immature?

If students are to appreciate the important role of audience in the writing process, they must have practice not only in analyzing audiences but in actually writing for different audiences. Ideally, all of the essay assignments in a first-year composition course should involve writing for specific audiences. Students might be asked near the beginning of the course to try writing two papers on the same subject, each addressed to a different audience (this assignment is likely to work best if the instructor first discusses with the class some sample subjects and audiences). Or they might be asked, after doing Exercise 1 on page 43, to write on subjects that would interest readers of a local newspaper and to mail the final versions of their essays, recast in letter form, to the newspaper for possible publication. Even when audience is not the specific focus of the assignment, its importance can be reinforced if students are required to include with each paper they write a statement of the audience that they are addressing and a brief explanation of the way in which they have adapted what they wrote to that audience.

2. Social status

    —most students from middle-class backgrounds
    —about a third have part-time jobs
    —some paying entire university tuition without help from parents

3. Level of education

    —academically speaking, same as mine
    —but what about social education, i.e., respecting other people's property and rights?

4. Political positions

    —not relevant

5. Moral beliefs

    —wrecking furniture a kind of stealing: steals from university, which must pay to replace damaged items; steals from other students, who are deprived of good study conditions
    —do vandals see matter this way, as a moral issue?
    —probably not
    —if they do, then little apparent sense of guilt

Audience's relation to subject and writer

1. What does my audience already know about this subject?

    —students who use the library to study know about extent of damage to chairs, couches, and study carrels
    —other students may not know about issue at all
    —vandals know what has been done *and* who's responsible

2. What else do I want my audience to know?

    —if my audience is student body at large, I want them to know the seriousness of the problem, and to know that there are students like me who are angry, who feel that something should be done to stop vandalism
    —if audience is vandals, I want them to know that there are students who condemn their actions

Exercise 1 (page 43)

This exercise gives students the opportunity to examine how well other writers have adjusted their prose to their intended audiences, but instructors who intend to use it should first offer their class practice in the skills that the exercise requires before turning students loose to try it on their own. A good idea is to duplicate one or two actual letters to the editor—preferably polemical ones—and to distribute them to the entire class for discussion and analysis. Of course, the "Letters" section of the average American newspaper will supply both excellent and awful examples of popular rhetoric; distinguishing between the two is one of the points of this exercise.

—which approach is more effective in stopping vandalism?
—which audience should I address?

3. What do I want this audience to think of me as a person?

—reasonable —or outraged?
—is it possible to be sympathetic to vandals?—I don't see how
—so should I appear angry?
—is any approach going to matter if my audience is the vandals themselves?
—do they care what I think?—probably not

4. What evidence or arguments will be convincing to this audience?

—if audience is vandals, could try to appeal to their respect for others' rights—but do they have any such respect?
—can I realistically expect to change such people's actions with a single letter?
—better possibility: try to persuade other students that vandalism can be stopped if students mobilize against it
—examples from other campuses available?
—also, present vandalism as an attack on their rights
—their tuition pays for damage
—vandals are stealing from them
—no one is more directly concerned than students themselves
—their responsibility to take action

By systematically examining two possible audiences—the vandals and their victims—Marc was able to define both his audience and his purpose more clearly. The vandals, he gradually realized, represented an audience whose actions he could not possibly hope to affect with a single letter to the college newspaper. On the other hand, such a letter might be able to mobilize the majority of the student body against the few who were guilty of the destruction.

As this example suggests, analyzing your audience must be an early step in the writing process, since an understanding of your audience's background and needs will inevitably shape the content of your writing. The more complete the notes you can make about your audience, the better prepared you will be to make decisions about the content, organization, and tone of your writing.

Exercise 2 (page 43)

Students will probably need to practice this exercise more than once before they develop a solid grasp of the method. You may want to begin by devoting part of a class period to an analysis of a single audience by the whole class, with everyone's comments and suggestions recorded on the chalkboard. Once all the information about the audience in question has been listed on the board, the class can consider which are the most important points and how they would affect what a writer wrote. As a second exercise in audience analysis, the class might be broken into small groups, with one student reading through his or her audience analysis point by point as others in the group add suggestions to the information that the writer has listed. The point here is that students beginning to experiment with audience analysis should share the results of their analyses; by hearing and considering the supplementary comments of others, they will be better prepared to analyze audiences later by themselves.

3c

Examine the role that awareness of audience has played in shaping a letter to the editor or an opinion column published in a recent edition of your local newspaper. Consider the following issues about writer and audience that we have discussed in this chapter:

1. How does the writer's choice of subject define the audience for whom he or she is writing? What readers would be *outside* that audience?
2. How does the writer demonstrate his or her understanding of the audience's background? What can you conclude about the age, social status, level of education, political positions, or moral beliefs of the reader whom this writer seems to be addressing?
3. How much knowledge about the subject does the writer presume? What background information does he or she supply for the reader?
4. How does the writer wish to be regarded by the reader? What kind of person does he or she seem to be? Rational? Emotional? Serious? Witty?
5. What evidence or arguments does the writer use to support his or her position? Can you imagine a reader for whom this evidence would *not* be convincing?

EXERCISE **2**

Using the Questions for Analyzing Audiences on page 39, write out an analysis of the next audience for whom you intend to write. Underline what you consider to be the most important points in your analysis. How will these points influence what you write?

For Further Reading

Booth, Wayne C. "The Rhetorical Stance." *College Composition and Communication* 14 (1963): 139–45.

Ede, Lisa. "Audience: An Introduction to Research." *College Composition and Communication* 35 (1984): 139–54.

Ede, Lisa, and Andrea Lunsford. "Audience Addressed/Audience Invoked: The Role of Audience in Composition Theory and Pedagogy." *College Composition and Communication* 35 (1984): 155–71.

Elbow, Peter. "Closing My Eyes As I Speak: An Argument for Ignoring Audience." *College English* 49 (1987): 50–69.

Kroll, Barry M. "Writing for Readers: Three Perspectives on Audience." *College Composition and Communication* 35 (1984): 172–85.

Porter, James E. *Audience and Rhetoric: An Archaeological Composition of the Discourse Community.* Englewood Cliffs: Prentice, 1992.

Thomas, Gordon P. "Mutual Knowledge: A Theoretical Basis for Analyzing Audience." *College English* 48 (1986): 580–94.

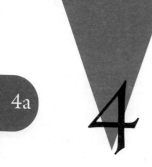

4 *Choosing a Voice*

Writing begins as dialogue; it is one person speaking to another about something important to both. One of the pleasures of writing is discovering that we do not as writers have to give up the sense of self that enlivens conversation, for we can create in our writing the many different voices we use in speaking.

4a A writer's voice

In spoken dialogue, your facial expression, gestures, and tone of voice determine to a great extent the way your audience responds to what you say. The pitch, volume, and pace of your speech tell your listeners whether you are serious or mocking, decisive or doubtful—in short, how you feel about your subject matter. In writing, you must translate these physical and auditory signals into visual symbols so that the eyes of your readers will "hear" the tone of your voice. The more proficient you become as a stylist, the more voices you will have at your disposal. Your written voice—like your speaking voice—can vary in tone from ironic to passionate, from annoyed to outraged, from humorous to grim.

Of course, developing a personal voice in writing is complicated by the fact that our language comes from a public stock. We cannot each invent a new language; no one would understand us. Yet the linguistic symbols that limit us also enable us to be who we are. We assert our identity by choosing from the language we find around us the words and styles that best suit our personalities and our purposes.

The first step in developing your writer's voice, therefore, is recognizing that you can make choices. If you carefully examine the voice

Like sensitivity to audience, awareness of one's voice as a writer is a subject that receives little attention when students are taught to concentrate primarily on content and organization in their writing. Many beginning college students have already learned the "right" voice to use in their academic work—impersonal, formal, perhaps somewhat stilted—and they may be shocked to be told at this point in their academic careers that there are some occasions when contractions and first- and second-person pronouns are not only acceptable but necessary.

Chapter **4** may encourage students to explore the range of possible voices available to them as writers. It deliberately avoids vague directives like "Write with an authentic voice"—good advice, to be sure, but not very useful to many beginning writers. Instead, by presenting voice as the combination of the writer's attitudes toward subject and audience, this chapter tries to offer students a specific way of understanding where a writer's voice comes from and how it can be modulated.

> QUICK REFERENCE: *A Writer's Voice*
>
> *Voice*   In writing, the sum of the stylistic qualities that suggest a writer's attitude toward his or her subject and reader. Sometimes referred to as the *tone* of one's writing.

in your past writing, you may be surprised by how often you have surrendered your power of choice and unconsciously borrowed the phrasing and tone of people around you. The language of parents and friends, of the media and the bureaucratic world, inevitably creeps into the writing that most of us do. In some situations, though, you have no doubt found yourself writing with genuine feeling and power. The composition of a letter to someone you care for or the assertion of a value you believe in can move you to choose your words carefully, to rewrite sentences again and again until you feel certain that what you have written will move your reader. In such a creative act you can almost hear your voice in the words on your page and see the look of recognition on the face of the person you are addressing. Making this experience a part of every writing act is the goal of all serious writers.

To a large extent, the voice in our writing—what we might also call the *tone* of our writing—depends on two relationships: our attitude toward our subject, and our attitude toward our reader. We will consider both of these relationships in the sections that follow.

4b Voice and subject

Before you can write with any distinguishable voice, you must first decide for yourself how you feel about your subject. In the broadest terms, writers might be said to regard their subjects either positively or negatively. But the range of possible attitudes within each of these large categories is enormous, limited only by each writer's range of emotional responses. The city council's plan to reduce funding for public transportation may *concern* one citizen, *disturb* another, *anger* a third, *outrage* a fourth. An act of kindness between acquaintances may inspire

This chapter includes writing samples that clearly illustrate the variations in voice that the chapter describes. Consider using them not only as topics for discussion in class but also as models for practice. After discussing attitudes toward subject in **4b**, for example, you might ask students to bring to the next class a short piece of their own writing in which they have tried to create a clear attitude toward the subject. Have several students read their papers to the class, and see if the class as a whole can identify what the writer's attitude is.

4b

appreciation, affection, admiration, or devotion, depending on the people involved.

To convey our attitude toward our subject in writing, we must rely on carefully chosen words and details. In the passage below, for example, the writer does not explicitly state his attitude toward nurses, but his admiration and respect are nonetheless clear because the details he includes emphasize efficiency, sensitivity, and personal concern.

Details convey attitude toward subject

The nurses, the good ones anyway (and all the ones on my floor were good), make it their business to know everything that is going on. They spot errors before errors can be launched. They know everything written on the chart. Most important of all, they know their patients as unique human beings, and they soon get to know the close relatives and friends. Because of this knowledge, they are quick to sense apprehensions and act on them. The average sick person in a large hospital feels at risk of getting lost, with no identity left beyond a name and a string of numbers on a plastic wristband, in danger always of being whisked off on a litter to the wrong place to have the wrong procedure done, or worse still, *not* being whisked off at the right time. The attending physician or the house officer, on rounds and usually in a hurry, can murmur a few reassuring words on his way out the door, but it takes a confident, competent, and cheerful nurse, there all day long and in and out of the room on one chore or another through the night, to bolster one's confidence that the situation is indeed manageable and not about to get out of hand.

—Lewis Thomas, *The Youngest Science: Notes of a Medicine Watcher*

In the same way, May Sarton helps us to understand her feelings about the life she lives by presenting details from her daily routine.

Details convey attitude toward subject

For me the most interesting thing about a solitary life, and mine has been that for the last twenty years, is that it becomes increasingly rewarding. When I can wake up and watch the sun rise over the ocean, as I do most days, and know that I have an entire day ahead, uninterrupted, in which to write a few pages, take a walk with my dog, lie down in the afternoon for a long think (why does one think better in a horizontal position?), read and listen to music, I am flooded with happiness.

—May Sarton, "The Rewards of Living a Solitary Life," *New York Times*

Sarton's paragraph might perhaps be reduced to the assertion "My solitary life is satisfying." But without the details with which she has described her day, we would not fully understand her sense of satisfaction. As writers, we must remember that merely asserting our attitude toward our subject is insufficient. If we want our readers to understand our feelings, and perhaps even to share them, we must rely on carefully chosen diction and details that will show our readers why we feel as we do.

All of this is not to suggest that every writer's attitude toward his or her subject can be precisely labeled, or even that every piece of writing will always reveal its writer's attitude. Many writing situations call for the objective reporting of information, such as we find in the following passage.

Objective reporting

If low-income and working-class nonvoters suddenly appeared at the polls, would they change American politics? According to careful studies of the question, the answer is no. Pollsters find that the political views of nonvoters—at least on matters that appear on the ballot—are not terribly different from those held by voters. Careful analysis by political scientists suggests that if nonvoters were to vote, they would shift the electorate slightly to the left on economic issues, such as jobs, government spending, public works, and the like, but slightly to the right on social issues, such as busing, abortion, and other life-style questions.

—David Osborne, "Getting Out the Vote," *Atlantic*

Of course, we should remember that apparent objectivity in writing is also the result of a writer's choice—the decision *not* to reveal one's attitude toward the subject.

4c   Voice and audience

If we have clearly defined our attitude toward our subject, we have laid the groundwork for writing with an honest voice. But equally important to a writer's tone is the relationship that the writer seeks to establish with his or her readers. Just as we easily shift our spoken language to suit the many different people whom we address throughout the day, from family members to strangers, we must be ready to

After discussion of **4c**, have students write two paragraphs on the same subject, one establishing a very close reader/writer relationship, one with greater distance between writer and reader. Let the class as a whole decide which paragraph seems more appropriate. Such a discussion should ideally lead students to understand the interrelatedness of subject, audience, voice, and purpose.

Exercise 1 (page 52)

1. *Subject:* Didion's immediate subject is her baby, but the paragraph gradually broadens to comment on modern life.

   Attitude toward subject: A variety of details suggest Didion's closeness to her baby: the act of kneeling beside the sleeping child to press their faces together; the description of the child as "open and trusting"; the author's stated wish that she could give the child more than she has been able to offer her. This last point introduces Didion's attitude toward the life that she leads. The passage suggests that Didion finds

4c

adapt our written language to each rhetorical situation that we confront as writers.

Some writing situations naturally require that we use language that suggests a personal relationship with our readers. In letters to close friends, for example, we tend to use the simplified sentence structure of conversation, the diction of colloquial speech (including contractions and slang), and the first-person and second-person pronouns *I*, *we*, and *you*. If we did not, our writing would seem stilted and artificial. For other writing tasks, however, such as the writing of a research paper, distance between writer and reader is more suitable than intimacy. In such writing, we strive to create polished sentences that will suggest our careful thinking; we adopt a more formal diction (including, perhaps, specialized words appropriate to the discipline in which we are writing); and we tend to avoid the first-person and second-person pronouns.

It is important to realize, however, that no absolute rules will help us in determining how to approach our readers when we write. "Never use *I*" might be an acceptable guideline for formal academic writing, but in other writing situations it would be as absurd as a rule like "Always use slang." Instead, we must think carefully about the kind of relationship with our audience that is appropriate to our rhetorical situation, and about the means available to us for creating this relationship in our writing.

The examples of a letter to a friend and a formal research paper are just two points on a vast continuum of potential writer/reader relationships. Along the continuum are an infinite number of degrees of closeness between writer and reader, ranging from the greatest distance to the greatest intimacy. At one end, for example, is the writing found in many professional journals, which uses distance between writer and reader as one means of suggesting the writer's authority.

Great distance between writer and reader

This paper has shown that a direct generalization of assumptions that Davis and Hinich have shown to be sufficient for multidimensional median voter results in *deterministic* voting models is sufficient for multidimensional median outcomes in *probabilistic* voting models. Among other things, this is an indication of just how strong the assumptions that they originally studied are. The generalization that was studied here is similar in

her life lacking, but that she has come to terms—reluctantly—with the inadequacies of her existence. Missing from her own life and her daughter's is a sense of family and home; for her daughter there are to be no cousins, no heirlooms from her great-grandmother, no family picnics. In their place, Didion can offer only material goods—"a xylophone and a sundress from Madeira."

Attitude toward reader: Both the details and the personal pronouns in this passage help to draw the reader into Didion's life, causing us to sympathize with her resignation.

2. *Subject:* Kendall's subject is the sudden popularity of English at the beginning of the fifteenth century.

Attitude toward subject: Though Kendall is essentially reporting a historical fact, several words and phrases in his paragraph suggest his delight and excitement over this fact: "amazing suddenness," "the

spirit to the original assumptions of Davis and Hinich—both in its explicit use of pseudo-norms and scaling functions and in its retention of symmetry for the distribution of the voters' ideal points in the society. As a consequence, it should be recognized that this generalization itself is also highly restrictive—and could easily fail to hold in a specific economy that is of interest.

—Peter J. Coughlin, "Davis-Hinich Conditions and Median Outcomes in Probabilistic Voting Models," *Journal of Economic Theory*

The distance between writer and reader in this passage results partly from the writer's highly technical vocabulary—"multidimensional median voter results," "probabilistic voting models," "pseudo-norms and scaling functions"—which places the passage outside the realm of ordinary conversation between two individuals. The long, densely structured sentences reinforce this distance, as does the writer's deliberate avoidance of personal pronouns. In the first sentence, for example, he has chosen to write "This paper has shown . . ." rather than "I have shown. . . ." Similarly, he later uses the passive voice to remove both himself and his reader from the text:

"The generalization that was studied here . . ."
[rather than "The generalization that *I studied* here . . ."]

"As a consequence, it should be recognized that . . ."
[rather than "As a consequence, *you should recognize* that . . ."]

In this case, as in much writing intended primarily to report or inform, the writer's main interest is his subject rather than his reader. The formal voice of a scholar is more appropriate to such a writing situation than the familiar voice of a friend.

Informative writing need not be impersonal, however, even when the subject is a grand one. In the following passage, for example, Kenneth Clark compares two major artists of the Middle Ages, the painter Giotto and the poet Dante, yet his tone borders on the informal.

Moderate distance between writer and reader

Although I think that Giotto was one of the greatest of painters, he has equals. But in almost the same year that he was born, and in the same

---

Englishness of England," "to enjoy with keener awareness the flavor of living." Students might be asked to consider what phrasing Kendall might have used if he had considered the rise of English a *bad* thing.

Attitude toward reader: Kendall's diction and syntax give the passage a slightly formal tone: "French well nigh disappeared," "cast in the vernacular," "there developed the impulse," "not only to enjoy with keener awareness . . . but also to record . . ."

3. *Subject:* This passage is taken from an essay in which Buckley describes passengers on a train—including himself—who endured an overheated car rather than complain. As the paragraph evolves, it becomes clear that Buckley's subject is life in an age of increasing technological development.

Attitude toward subject: Buckley looks at modern life with clear regret. In the past, he writes, Americans were assertive; when they "were too

part of Italy, was born a man who is unequalled—the greatest philosophic poet that has ever lived, Dante. Since they were contemporaries and compatriots, one feels that it should be possible to illustrate Dante by Giotto. They seem to have known each other and Giotto may have painted Dante's portrait. But in fact their imaginations moved on very different planes. Giotto was, above all, interested in humanity: he sympathised with human beings and his figures, by their very solidity, remain on earth. Of course there is humanity in Dante—there's everything in Dante. But he also had certain qualities that Giotto lacked: philosophic power, a grasp of abstract ideas, moral indignation, that heroic contempt for baseness that was to come again in Michelangelo; and, above all, a sense of the *un*earthly, a vision of heavenly radiance.

—Kenneth Clark, *Civilisation: A Personal View*

On the whole, Clark's diction here is as lofty as his subject. Phrases like *philosophic power* and *heroic contempt for baseness* are not part of most people's everyday conversation. But Clark pulls the tone of this passage toward the informal by interjecting himself in its first sentence ("I think"), by using a contraction ("there's everything in Dante"), by tending to write sentences of only moderate length, and by starting several sentences with the conjunction *but,* often regarded as a somewhat colloquial sentence opener.

These features are among the characteristics that we usually expect to dominate less formal writing. In the paragraph below, for example, written as an introduction to a personal essay, the writer combines liberal use of the personal pronouns *I* and *you* with generally informal diction to draw the reader into the world of his experience.

Moderate intimacy between writer and reader

The solid vibration that goes through your arms and body when you perfectly connect a wooden bat with a leather-covered baseball is a feeling of pure exhilaration. My love affair with hitting baseballs began with stickball games on my street, continued through Little League, junior high, and high school, and persists even now when I go to the Revere batting cages, where occasionally some Boston Red Sox players hit. I've consistently been a good hitter through the years, with the exception of a period of steady decline from the end of my sophomore year in high school through half of my junior year. During this batting slump, I wondered whether I had completely lost the ability to hit a baseball well. What was

hot, or too cold, [they] got up and did something about it." Now, in contrast, we have "[withdrawn] into helplessness," unwilling to assert responsibility for anything in our environment.

Attitude toward reader: Because he is presenting an argument that he wants the reader to accept, Buckley uses the first-person pronouns *I* and *we* to draw the reader into the situation that he describes. Still, the rather sophisticated diction of the passage keeps it from becoming informal: "observable reluctance," "centralized political and economic power," "technification of life," "conditioned to adopt a position of helplessness."

4. *Subject:* Genealogical research.

Attitude toward subject: Williams's passage projects strong enthusiasm for her subject: "an interesting and fascinating adventure," "heartily recommend that you inaugurate a search."

I doing wrong? Was I striding too soon? Were my hands coming around too fast? Was I rotating my hips improperly? I consulted every book on hitting to check the mechanics of my swing. I changed my stance a hundred times. But still my batting slump hung on.

—David A. Miller, student writer

In the language of advertising and popular journalism we often see an attempt to establish an even closer bond between writer and reader. Notice the especially direct appeal to the reader in the following magazine announcement, soliciting suggestions for new articles. Here the writer creates an extremely informal tone by generously using personal pronouns, contractions, colloquial diction, and slang.

Great intimacy between writer and reader

Our Eyes and Ears

"Frontlines" needs you, the legions of *MJ* faithful and faithless, the fifth column in the war for irreverence and investigation. Send us your troubling and bubbling items, yearning to breathe free.

Although we can't acknowledge every item sent in, we do acknowledge those we use. What's more, if we use something you tip us off to, we'll rush you $15 and a *Mother Jones* T-shirt.

—*Mother Jones*

We can summarize a few of the stylistic features that characterize the continuum of relationships between writers and readers in a table like the one below.

Determining Distance Between Writer and Reader

Greater Distance ⟵——————⟶ *Greater Intimacy*

Formal or Technical ⟵— *Diction* —⟶ Informal or Colloquial

Longer ⟵———— *Sentence Length* ————⟶ Shorter

Fewer ⟵———— *Personal Pronouns* ————⟶ More

Attitude toward reader: It would be difficult to imagine a passage that established a closer relationship between writer and reader. The personal pronouns, the imperative in the first paragraph ("Start right in your own home. . . ."), and the generally colloquial diction all work to spark in the reader the enthusiasm that the writer feels for her subject.

5. *Subject:* Bassett's subject is the series of calamities that struck the Northern Plains.

Attitude toward subject: The details and diction of this passage suggest that Bassett feels sympathy for the plains in the face of the devastation she describes: "plagued by disasters," "hailstorms battered to the ground," "fire rose like an angry dragon," "[c]oyotes scampered on singed feet."

4c

The tone of all writing results from choice. Effective writers are so conscious of their writing voice that they bring a distinctive touch even to routine writing situations. If you resolve to be personally committed to any act of writing, to care about what you say and how you say it, such involvement will compel you to write vigorous prose. Writing becomes a mechanical task only when we fail to listen to our voice and to the imagined response of our reader.

EXERCISE 1

Analyze the writer's voice in each of the passages below. What is the writer's subject? In which cases do details or diction reveal the writer's attitude toward that subject? Does the writer's relationship with the reader tend toward distance or intimacy? How does the writer create this relationship?

1.   It is time for the baby's birthday: a white cake, strawberry-marsh-mallow ice cream, a bottle of champagne saved from another party. In the evening, after she has gone to sleep, I kneel beside the crib and touch her face, where it is pressed against the slats, with mine. She is an open and trusting child, unprepared for and unaccustomed to the ambushes of family life, and perhaps it is just as well that I can offer her little of that life. I would like to give her more. I would like to promise her that she will grow up with a sense of her cousins and of rivers and of her great-grandmother's teacups, would like to pledge her a picnic on a river with fried chicken and her hair uncombed, would like to give her *home* for her birthday, but we live differently now and I can promise her nothing like that. I give her a xylophone and a sundress from Madeira, and promise to tell her a funny story.

　　—Joan Didion, "On Going Home," *Slouching towards Bethlehem*

2.   In England, until the end of the fourteenth century, the government, the business community, the courts, the towns, kept their records in French or Latin; lords and knights conducted their correspondence in French, when they corresponded at all. Then with amazing suddenness, in a span of less than fifty years during the first decades of the fifteenth century, French well nigh disappeared and Latin faded. The rolls of Parliament, chronicles, letters, town records, were cast in the vernacular. The Englishness of England had arrived. At this same time there developed the impulse not only to enjoy with

Attitude toward reader: Bassett is close to her subject but maintains moderate distance from her reader. The diction and syntax of the passage are not overly formal, but there are no personal pronouns to form a close bond between the writer and reader here.

6. *Subject:* The introduction to a magazine article about the villages and scenery in a remote, mountainous region of Greece, this paragraph focuses on the hike that Ron Hall has just concluded.

Attitude toward subject: Despite the discomforts of his trip—aching feet, a difficult "slog" up the mountain, perspiration and blinding mist—Hall has clearly relished the adventure. In the camp he has reached, the warm stove and the "comforting aroma of drying socks and steaming soup" seem to cancel out the hardships of the journey. In the final line, as he turns to "feast on the extraordinary panorama" around him, his diction leaves no doubt about the delight he feels.

keener awareness the flavor of living, the drama of character, but also to record these manifestations.

—Paul Murray Kendall, *The Art of Biography*

3.   I think the observable reluctance of the majority of Americans to assert themselves in minor matters is related to our increased sense of helplessness in an age of technology and centralized political and economic power. For generations, Americans who were too hot, or too cold, got up and did something about it. Now we call the plumber, or the electrician, or the furnace man. The habit of looking after our own needs obviously had something to do with the assertiveness that characterized the American family familiar to readers of American literature. With the technification of life goes our direct responsibility for our material environment, and we are conditioned to adopt a position of helplessness not only as regards the broken air conditioner, but as regards the overheated train. It takes an expert to fix the former, but not the latter; yet these distinctions, as we withdraw into helplessness, tend to fade away.

—William F. Buckley, Jr., "Why Don't We Complain?" *Esquire*

4.   If you have never attempted to trace your lineage, and would enjoy an interesting and fascinating adventure that may well develop into a family project, and lead to a lifetime avocation, I heartily recommend that you inaugurate a search for your very own family tree which is located somewhere in the great forest of humanity. I can almost hear you ask: "Where do I start?" Start right in your own home, where you will find evidences of family history all about you.

There is no magic formula to follow in tracing family history because each search presents different problems, and the solution of one problem usually leads to several new and unsolved ones. You simply take a logical approach, as in any other field of research, and work from the known facts to the unknown. *Time* and *place* are the basic factors in the solution of all genealogical problems.

—Ethel W. Williams, *Know Your Ancestors: A Guide to Genealogical Research*

5.   For the Northern Plains, it was a year plagued by disasters. First came the drought, the result of sparse rainfall in the spring and summer. Then came the grasshoppers, great brown clouds that descended on crops of wheat, barley, oats, and finally the grasslands. What the

Attitude toward reader: "Here I am," Hall announces in his first sentence, the personal pronoun and the present tense functioning together to draw the reader into the scene. The first-person pronouns are also put to humorous use in the lines that follow, where Hall invites the reader's laughter by readily depicting himself as an out-of-shape hiker in newly purchased designer boots. Although Hall's sentence structure is hardly conversational, colloquial phrases like "three-hour slog" and "sweat on my brow" help to maintain his casual informality with the reader.

7. *Subject:* Falling asleep.

Attitude toward subject: Although the almost clinical detail in this passage gives the impression of objective reporting, the adjective *curious* in the first line suggests Farb's mild fascination with his subject.

Attitude toward reader: Farb's style is direct and engaging, but he nonetheless maintains moderate distance from his reader. To see how much more directly he could have involved the reader, we need only

4c

grasshoppers left behind, the hailstorms battered to the ground. In August, lightning from a dry thunderstorm struck randomly across the state, igniting rotten logs, brush, and needles in Montana's forests. As strong winds fanned the tiny flames, the fire rose like an angry dragon, sucking in air, heating it, and blasting it through the trees at speeds of up to sixty miles an hour. Herds of elk and deer raced ahead of the wall of fire. Coyotes scampered on singed feet into nearby canyons. For days, the flames crowned the tops of Ponderosa pine and Douglas fir, leaping from ridge to ridge in a brilliant nighttime spectacle of soaring embers that could be seen thirty miles away.

—Carol Ann Bassett, "After the Big Fire in Next-Year Country," *American West*

6.   Here I am in the Astrakas mountain refuge, six thousand feet up in the high Pindus Range of northwestern Greece, savoring that comforting aroma of drying socks and steaming soup, at once remembered from childhood camps of long ago. My feet have been eased, aching but unblistered, from my Italian-designer walking boots, bought just a few days earlier at a tough-looking adventure emporium in London's Covent Garden. (They had been polite enough not to laugh when I said I was planning to heave my unathletic frame around these rugged mountains.) The mule and goat tracks up to the refuge were a hard three-hour slog, which was not made easier by wisping cloud that combined with the sweat on my brow to mist up my spectacles, so that I had to walk most of the last mile blind. But now, after a few moments by the heat of the stove, normal vision has been resumed, and I can feast on the extraordinary panorama around me.

—Ron Hall, "Greece on the Precipice," *Condé Nast Traveler*

7.   A number of curious experiences occur at the onset of sleep. A person just about to go to sleep may experience an electric shock, a flash of light, or a crash of thunder—but the most common sensation is that of floating or falling, which is why "falling asleep" is a scientifically valid description. A nearly universal occurrence at the beginning of sleep (although not everyone recalls it) is a sudden, uncoordinated jerk of the head, the limbs, or even the entire body. Most people tend to think of going to sleep as a slow slippage into oblivion, but the onset of sleep is not gradual at all. It happens in an instant. One moment the individual is awake, the next moment not.

—Peter Farb, *Humankind*

insert personal pronouns into a few of his sentences: "You may think of going to sleep as a slow slippage into oblivion, but the onset of sleep is not gradual at all. . . . One moment you are awake, the next moment not."

8. *Subject:* This passage, the introduction to the income-tax form used by most taxpayers in the United States, encompasses a number of themes all related to taxes: the importance of tax revenue, the respect due to taxpayers, and the ongoing attempts of the Internal Revenue Service to simplify the taxpaying process.

Attitude toward subject: Peterson's relentlessly upbeat prose puts everything related to taxation in the most positive light. The description of what taxes do is vague but comforting ("provide essential social services," "fund scientific and health care research"). The process of paying taxes, we are assured, is getting easier, and new electronic returns provide a "faster refund." The IRS itself, certainly not one of people's

8. Dear Taxpayer:

As the Commissioner of Internal Revenue, I want to thank you on behalf of the government of the United States and every American citizen. Without your taxes, we could not provide essential social services; we could not defend ourselves; we could not fund scientific and health care research. Thank you for paying your taxes.

You are among the millions of Americans who comply with the tax law voluntarily. As a taxpayer and as a customer of the Internal Revenue Service, you deserve excellence in the services we provide; you deserve to be treated fairly, courteously and with respect; and you deserve to know that the IRS will ensure that others pay their fair share. . . .

We realize that the tax law is complex and sometimes frustrating. We want to do what we can to make tax time easier for you. To that end, we are simplifying our forms and procedures to reduce the burden on taxpayers. This year, we revised the tax table so that more taxpayers can simply look up the tax they owe instead of doing the arithmetic. Also, if you have a small business, check to see whether you can file new Schedule C-EZ, where taxable profit is computed in only three lines.

Don't forget the option to file your tax return electronically. Electronic returns are more accurate and you can get a faster refund.

Our goal is to transform the tax system by the end of this decade. To achieve the excellence in service that you deserve, we are literally "reinventing" the Internal Revenue Service, making our internal organization more efficient and less bureaucratic. As we improve our organizational structure, we also will do a better job of serving our customers, the taxpayers. We believe in accountability. Please let us know if you have any suggestions for ways to improve our service to you.

Thank you again for your dedication to our country.

—Shirley D. Peterson, "A Note from the Commissioner," *1040 Forms and Instructions*

favorite government agencies, is described as becoming "more efficient and less bureaucratic," and taxpayers are cast as "customers" who will receive better "service."

Attitude toward reader: Peterson's prose is carefully crafted to put a human face on government and to break down the stereotypical view of bureaucratic language as jargon-ridden, impenetrable, and impersonal. The liberal use of personal pronouns in this passage, the short, simple sentences, and the frequent direct addresses to the reader ("[C]heck to see . . . Don't forget . . . Please let us know . . .") all attempt to make us feel as close to this unpopular and often mysterious government agency as possible.

For Further Reading

Gibson, Walker. *Persona*. New York: Random House, 1969.
———. *Tough, Sweet and Stuffy: An Essay on Modern American Prose Styles*. Bloomington: Indiana UP, 1966.

PART II

Writing

5 *Organizing an Essay*

Our preceding discussion of the initial planning that you should do as a writer focused on the three points of the communication triangle—discovering ideas about your *subject,* drawing conclusions about your *reader,* and making decisions about your own voice as a *writer.* Part II of this book considers the choices you must make as you draft an essay, and thus it focuses on the fourth element of the communication triangle—the written *text* that links writer, reader, and subject. We begin with the overall structure of an essay. Chapters **6**, **7**, **8**, and **9** will then examine in greater detail its component parts—unified and well-developed paragraphs, effective sentences, and precisely chosen words.

5a Limiting your subject

Effective writing often depends on the writer's ability to limit the scope of a subject appropriately. We are never able to write everything that could be said about a topic, simply because all writing tasks have length limits of some kind. In the case of college writing, this limit is usually imposed by the instructor to whom the paper is submitted. Your instructor is probably not going to count the number of words in your paper, but he or she may not be pleased by a paper that is several pages longer than what was assigned. When you write an essay exam in class, the limits are even more absolute. Once class time is up, you will be expected to have isolated the important points in the questions you answered and to have discussed them adequately.

One of the purposes of college writing in all disciplines is to provide you with such practice in deciding what is really important about

The guidelines for limiting a subject presented on pages 60–62 continue the themes of the first part of the book by following the communication triangle discussed in Chapter **1**: the first point focuses on the writer, the second on the reader, the third on the material related to the subject itself. As guides to inquiry, like the questions for exploring a subject and for examining one's audience in Chapters **2** and **3**, these questions should not be expected to produce a perfectly limited subject each time they are used. But considered thoughtfully in the initial stage of planning a paper, they can help a writer to make some productive early decisions about the direction a paper might take and to rule out unmanageable possibilities.

5a

your subject. You practice limiting a subject in college writing because the writing situations you will confront in the world after graduation impose similar strict limits. Business reports, advertising copy, magazine articles, dissertations, books—all of these force writers to limit their subjects according to the time and interests of their readers.

As these examples suggest, the act of focusing one's writing is principally a response to fundamental questions of purpose and audience, the inevitable constraints in every writing situation. Consequently, there are no easy procedures for limiting a subject that will work in all situations. But recognizing the role of purpose and audience in this process makes it possible for us to construct some useful questions to pose as we approach any writing task.

Guides to Limiting Your Subject

What interests you as a *writer*?

What might interest your potential *readers*?

What information is available about your *subject*?

Suppose, for example, that you have been concerned about the importance of conserving the world's natural resources. When you begin to consider this large subject, you may be tempted to despair over the number of important topics that you could write about: the threats to natural wilderness areas; the diminishing amount of agricultural land available to grow food for the world's population; the limited supplies of oil and natural gas; the use of other sources of energy (solar, geothermal, nuclear) and their potential advantages and hazards; the pollution of the air by exhaust gases from factories and cars; the pollution of rivers and lakes by industrial wastes, sewage, and acid rain; the production of pure drinking water in urban areas; the necessity of controlling population growth. All of these are certainly important subjects, yet they could not all be treated adequately even in a book-length study.

5a

How do you start? You might use the following guides, based on the three points of the communication triangle, to help you narrow your topic.

1.   Consider what you know about yourself

What aspect of your subject is most interesting or important to you? Why? If you have lived in America's farming belt, then you are probably concerned about such issues as the increasing urbanization of rural land, the erosion of topsoil, and the potential dangers of long-term pesticide use. If you live in a large urban area, then you have no doubt experienced the effects of smog and read about sewage treatment and waste disposal. You may have grown up near one of the nation's massive nuclear power plants; in that case, you have certainly formed opinions, favorable or unfavorable, about the use of nuclear reactions to produce electricity. If you enjoy outdoor activities like boating or backpacking, then you have probably been grateful for the existence of clean lakes and unspoiled mountain trails. There's a simple point here: choose an angle on your subject that genuinely interests you. All successful writers care about their subjects; they use their backgrounds and natural inclinations to steer them toward the kinds of subjects that they will be able to write about with genuine interest and concern. You should too.

5a

2. Consider what you know about your readers

If you could tell your readers only one thing about your subject, what would it be? Why? As noted in Chapter **3**, a thorough consideration of your audience can lead you to a clearer sense of your purpose in writing. A clear sense of purpose, in turn, helps you limit your subject. Suppose, for example, that your essay is to be duplicated and distributed for comments to the members of your writing class. What can you say about your subject that is new to them? What aspect of your subject might they identify with? What might they consider important about your subject? You can narrow a paper on any topic by regarding it as an essay with a specific point that you want your readers to carry away with them.

3. Consider what you know about your subject

What aspect of your subject could you develop best with the material you have at hand? Behind this question is the simple fact that you can't write effectively without something to say; thus, you should not limit your subject to an area in which you have only scanty knowledge. For some topics, you will be able to use the discovery methods discussed in Chapter **2** to generate information from your own personal experience; on other occasions, you will think of potentially interesting approaches to your subject that can be researched in a library. But don't try to take on a narrow subject without adequate information about it; doing so will invariably make the writing process exasperating and will result in a finished essay that is thin and unconvincing. Always select from among the many possible aspects of your subject the ones about which you have substantial and important knowledge.

EXERCISE 1

The suggestions for narrowing a subject (pages 59–62) will work best *after* you have explored a subject and considered your intended audience (see Chapters **2** and **3**). But to test their effectiveness, try using them to limit one or more of the following broad subjects, or another equally

Exercise 1

Since it is usually not possible to restrict a subject effectively before one has generated ideas about it, this exercise should ideally be done with a subject that students have already explored using one of the approaches in Chapter **2**. The sample subjects listed here might be used as a classroom exercise to demonstrate the potential usefulness of the restricting questions in **5a**.

general subject of your choice. Which of the suggestions seem to be most helpful?

1. Family relationships	6. Religion
2. Music	7. Transportation
3. Science	8. Animals
4. Your hometown	9. Space exploration
5. International relations	10. Peace

5b Formulating a thesis statement

Like all stages of the writing process, the process of limiting a subject cannot be described by rigid rules or formulas. Sometimes, the suggestions above may immediately lead you to see how your subject should be focused; at other times, you may fully understand what you want to say only after you have begun to draft a paper. Regardless of your method, as your understanding of your precise subject evolves, you should try to formulate your controlling idea in a single sentence or two known as a *thesis* or *thesis statement*.

1. Components of a thesis statement

A thesis statement may begin as a tentative expression of your paper's main point, subject to change as your ideas work themselves out on your page. In its final form, however, the thesis must be specific and unambiguous, for it establishes a kind of contract between writer and reader, a promise about the content of the paper that is to follow. Typically, a thesis contains two elements: the precise subject of the essay and a word or phrase that even further limits this subject. The importance of that restricting word or phrase is illustrated in the example at the top of page 64, which shows how a single subject may be limited in different ways.

A clear thesis often implies a method of development. Though the subject in each of the thesis statements on page 64 is the same, the different ways in which it is restricted will produce three quite different essays. The first thesis will lead to a paper that explores the threat that underground water pollution poses to human life, examining its effect on the health and livelihood of Americans in western states. The paper that develops from the second thesis statement will be much more

The questions posed in **5a** are designed to yield a narrowly focused subject. Section **5b** continues this discussion of the focusing process by explaining how such a precise subject may be further restricted to generate a thesis statement.

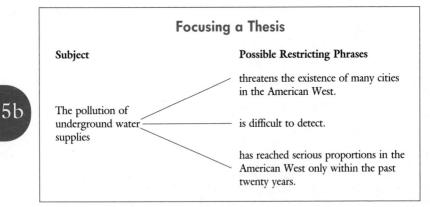

technical in nature; we might expect it to deal with such matters as the engineering difficulties involved in reaching underground water supplies and the scientific process of testing them for pollution. In the third case, we might anticipate a paper that takes a historical perspective, examining the causes of underground water pollution and explaining why this phenomenon is a relatively recent one.

2.   Precision in a thesis statement

Much of a thesis statement's potential usefulness is lost if either its subject or its focus is vaguely stated. Sometimes a writer may believe that he or she has composed a thesis with a clear subject, when in fact the thesis contains only a generalized topic, not the actual subject that the writer intends to develop.

Vague subject   *Many experiences* help a person develop a respect for the rights of others.

This general statement may perhaps provide a kind of background for a paper, but notice that it does not contain a specific subject. What experiences does the writer intend to describe? Compare the thesis statement above with this one, which substitutes the writer's specific subject.

Precise subject   *Sharing a college dorm suite with five other students* helps a person develop a respect for the rights of others.

Sometimes the problem with a thesis is not that its stated subject is too vague but that the thesis does not limit the subject adequately. In each of these thesis statements, for example, the writer begins with a sufficiently specific subject but fails to restrict it in a way that makes the paper's point clear.

Vague restriction Climbing Long's Peak as a teenager *was a very important experience* for me.

Vague restriction The Vietnam War years *had a great impact* on this country.

5b

In what ways was climbing Long's Peak important? What effects of the war in Vietnam have endured in America today? Without such information, these thesis statements merely announce a subject; they do not commit the writers to anything specific, nor do they help the reader to anticipate what will follow. In contrast, the thesis statements below add to the same subjects a more precise restriction.

Precise restriction Climbing Long's Peak as a teenager *restored my faith in my ability to set and accomplish goals.*

Precise restriction The Vietnam War years *created divisions in American society that have lasted into the 1990s.*

In both of these thesis statements, the subject is focused in a way that provides the writer with direction and that arouses expectations in the reader about the paper's development.

A writer who uses a thesis statement merely to announce what he or she plans to do in a paper often neglects to include any restriction of the subject at all.

Announcement of subject with no restriction In the following paper, I will discuss my decision to spend my senior year in high school as an exchange student in Ireland.

Avoid thesis statements that rely on this and similar formulas, such as "I will use my essay to consider. . ." and "This paper will examine. . ." In the case above, the writer's subject—his decision to attend school abroad—is clear, but his dependence on a formulaic announcement of this subject has obliterated any trace of the way he intends to develop his paper. Revised by the addition of a precise restriction, the thesis statement reveals the writer's plan to the reader.

| **Precise subject and restriction** | I decided to spend my senior year in high school as an exchange student in Ireland *because I wanted to learn about my family's roots.* |

3.   Placement of the thesis statement

Typically, a thesis statement is placed near the beginning of an essay, often in the opening paragraph. In that position, it serves both the reader and the writer in several important ways. For the reader, it provides a way of focusing attention that will make the task of reading easier. Some beginning writers mistakenly feel that a precise thesis near the beginning of a paper gives away too much of the paper's point and may therefore cause readers to lose interest in an essay from the very start. What such writers forget is that readers need to know where a paper is leading if they are to follow its development and evaluate its arguments. Your readers, after all, do not have the same familiarity with your subject that you do. They do not begin to read with an understanding of the connections between points that you have worked out for yourself, nor will they necessarily grasp the logic of your organization immediately. A clear, specific thesis gives the reader a head start in comprehending the ideas that follow.

A well-formulated thesis is of as much value to the writer as to the reader. For the writer, it serves as a constant reminder of the direction that the paper should be taking. Every new argument, each specific detail, should in some way advance the focus of the thesis statement. Once a draft of the paper is complete, you can check its development against the idea stated in the thesis. Does the paper stick to the subject and focus that you established in the thesis? Does it develop these ideas completely and specifically? A good thesis provides an important standard for evaluating a paper's development and logic.

Theoretically, a thesis may be placed anywhere in an essay, as long as it is prominent enough to be recognized as the thesis by the reader. In an inductive argument, for example, the thesis—the main idea being argued—is often held until the end, after all the relevant evidence has been presented. A thesis placed in the concluding paragraph may also provide a dramatic turn to an essay and give the reader a sense of discovery. But no matter where the thesis occurs, it should offer your readers a clear and precise statement of your paper's focus.

EXERCISE 2

Complete each of the following thesis statements in two *different* ways by adding two different restricting phrases. Make a list of the main points you might use to develop a paper for each of the thesis statements you produce.

Example

The campus radio station . . .

Thesis #1: The campus radio station gives students firsthand experience with sophisticated broadcasting equipment.

Thesis #2: The campus radio station plays a blend of music that fails to attract either students on campus or the public at large.

1. The study of history [or another field] . . .
2. Volunteer work in one's community . . .
3. Reading science fiction [or some other type of literature] . . .
4. Growing up in the country [or a city or a small town] . . .
5. Living away from one's family . . .

5c   Developing a plan for your essay

As we have seen, the starting point for a well-focused essay is a thesis with a precise subject and restriction. A writer who has been able to formulate such a thesis probably already has some sense of the direction that the essay will take. But many writers pause early in the composing process to organize their thoughts and construct a conscious, if tentative, plan for their writing.

1.   Remember your reader

As you begin thinking about how to present your ideas in the body of your paper, you might consider how much space you will need to allot for developing each of the various sections of your essay. A clear conception of your reader and your purpose can help you make such decisions.

What does your reader need to know?

What does your projected reader already know about your subject, and what will he or she need to know? This key distinction will inform not only the content but also the proportions of your paper.

Exercise 2

This exercise might be used to generate class discussion of the alternative ways of restricting a thesis, and of the ways in which the choice of one thesis over another affects a writer's thinking about the development of a paper. Have students suggest several different alternatives for each thesis, write each one on a separate section of the chalkboard, and then let the class as a whole list possible details for the development of each proposed thesis. Compare the results.

This expanded discussion of planning the organization and development of an essay encourages students to remember the rhetorical nature of the work they are undertaking. Essays are written to be read, and so the writer's first considerations must be the knowledge and stance of his or her readers.

Background with which your reader is likely to be familiar can be sketched concisely, but when you discuss information that is likely to be unfamiliar to your reader or difficult for your reader to understand, you will need to rely on much more thorough treatment. You cannot omit details or explanations that your reader needs to understand the point you are trying to make.

5c

Does your reader agree or disagree?

Similar guidelines apply in papers that take argumentative stands on controversial issues. When you know that your reader is likely to agree with what you say or when you are presenting factual information as background, your writing can be brisk and economical. But when you cannot assume your reader's agreement or when you take a position that you know your reader is likely to disagree with, you will need to develop every step of your argument with thoroughness and care.

If your essay hinges on logical argument, you will want to consult Chapters **14** and **15** for information about the components of a written argument. Chapter **14** focuses on the structure of an argument and provides useful definitions and illustrations of a number of key concepts—premise, inference, fact, judgment, and assumption. Chapter **15** explains and illustrates errors in reasoning that can weaken an argument in the eyes of a critical reader—hasty generalizations, mistaken causal relationships, reasoning by analogy, avoiding the question, false alternatives, and non sequiturs.

2.   Find a pattern of organization

Just as important as the quality of the ideas in your essay is the order in which you present your ideas. If your reader can't follow the overall design of your paper, your ideas or examples, no matter how telling, will be wasted. To write a coherent essay, you will need a plan for arranging the facts, details, or arguments that form the substance of your essay.

A checklist of several standard patterns of organization is located on pages 70 and 71 along with the typical purpose for which each pattern is used. You can find further information about most of these patterns in Chapter **7**. Although they are discussed there in the context of developing paragraphs, keep in mind that these patterns are equally effective for organizing the content of larger texts, like essays or research papers.

3.   Use an informal outline

As you plan the shape of your essay, you will also need to consider which ideas are the main points that you wish to make and which are subordinate points that will function primarily as background or support. In making these distinctions, many writers rely on an informal or a formal outline, a written sketch of an essay's contents that displays its main and subordinate points.

Unlike formal outlines, which are discussed in **5d**, *informal outlines* may be as casual and idiosyncratic in design as you wish. Their purpose is merely to give you a preliminary plan, one that may well change several times as you begin the actual process of writing an essay. An informal outline provides a way of assembling and organizing the information and ideas that you have acquired either from research or from the methods of discovery discussed in Chapter **2**. Sketched out on paper, it enables you to identify possible opportunities for adding, deleting, or rearranging material.

A writer who wishes to argue the thesis "Grades are an obstacle to education," for example, might first draft a rough outline that simply lists the points to be incorporated into the paper.

```
Effects of grades
    --become an end in themselves
    --may lead some students to select easy
        courses
    --may create distance between students and
        instructors
    --may provoke cheating or plagiarizing
```

5c

Checklist of Patterns of Organization

Pattern	Typical Purpose
Lesser to greater	To organize examples clearly and effectively. To enhance the strength of one's argument.
Spatial or geographical order	To organize the details of a physical description.
Chronological order	To explain a past incident. To describe a process.
Definition	To explain a term or concept.
Classification	To analyze a subject made up of various smaller elements.
Comparison or contrast	To point out similarities or differences between two subjects.
Cause and effect	To explain the connection between a result and events or actions that preceded it.

```
--limit students' attention to materials for

    tests

--change instructor's role from teacher to judge
```

Later, as the writer's plan begins to gel, the same outline might evolve into something like the following, an outline that now rearranges this

---

This checklist of patterns of organization provides a handy summary of the functions that various organizational patterns serve and also gives brief directions for employing the patterns. For examples, refer students to corresponding sample paragraphs in Chapter **7**.

Method

Move from weakest to strongest or least valuable to most valuable point or argument. Move from the less controversial to the more controversial issue, from the less complicated to the more complicated point, from the least convincing to the most convincing evidence, etc.

Arrange details in the order in which they would normally be perceived—from front to back, left to right, east to west, etc.

Present a series of events in the order in which they occurred. Present a sequence of steps in the order in which they are performed. See **7b**.

Place the subject in a larger category of related elements and explain how it differs from the other elements in that category. See **7d**.

Identify and describe the various groups of elements into which the subject can be divided. See **7e**.

Organize the essay with a point-by-point comparison of similarities or differences (alternating comparison). Organize the essay by dealing fully with the first subject before considering the second (divided comparison). See **7f**.

Begin with the result and trace its various causes. Begin with a cause and examine its various effects. See **7h**.

5c

material into two categories and that differentiates between the paper's main and subordinate points.

```
Students' attitude toward teacher
    --see teacher primarily as judge rather than
        instructor
```

5c

```
    --develop reluctance to consult teacher out-
         side class

  Students' attitude toward course
    --avoid challenging courses to protect aver-
        age
    --concentrate only on what is required for
        tests
    --ultimately develop narrow intellectual
        range
```

But remember that even at this stage, outlines are temporary and can be changed as an essay begins to take shape. Don't follow your tentative headings so rigidly that they become a straitjacket instead of a support. Be prepared to add new material that occurs to you as you write, to delete points that you are unable to develop satisfactorily, and to rearrange points for clarity and emphasis.

EXERCISE 3

On which of the subjects below do you already have a reasonably firm position? For each such case, formulate a thesis statement that would be the foundation for an essay of between five hundred and seven hundred words. Then select one thesis statement and consider how you might develop your essay. Construct an informal outline of the essay's possible contents.

  1. Violence in television
  2. The appeal of science fiction
  3. Sex education in schools
  4. The role of the SAT in the college admissions process
  5. The death penalty
  6. Defense spending
  7. The study of foreign languages

Exercise 3

Less directed than Exercise 2, this exercise would work well as a homework assignment that students would either submit to the instructor or discuss in small groups in class.

8. The eating habits of American young adults
9. Prayer in public schools
10. Drunk driving

5d Constructing formal outlines

Like informal outlines, *formal outlines* may change during the writing process as a writer discovers new ideas or new ways of organizing ideas already at hand. But even in their initial stages, formal outlines look very different from informal ones, and that difference in design offers writers both a challenge and an opportunity.

1. Uses of formal outlines

Because they follow a strictly prescribed logic and pattern, formal outlines make greater demands on a writer than do informal outlines. But their strict logic also gives formal outlines several valuable uses.

As an aid to drafting

Some writers find that the rigor involved in constructing a formal outline forces them to consider each main and subordinate point that they formulate with special care. Because formal outlines not only divide main points into subordinate points but also indicate a virtually infinite range of smaller subdivisions, they provide writers with a way of exactly visualizing an essay's contents and analyzing its structure.

As an aid to revising

Formal outlines can also assist in the revision of a rough draft or an unsatisfactory final version. When a paper seems to lack coherence, balance, or tight logical structure, constructing a formal outline of the paper's contents can help you diagnose its problems. An outline enables you to translate the vague feeling that something is wrong with a paper into specific knowledge about where you may have strayed from your thesis, which points need further development, and where stronger transitions would improve coherence.

Even writers who consider some type of informal outlining an essential part of their composing process may find that formal outlining, with its strict logic and pattern, is a hindrance rather than an aid. Remembering that writing is an idiosyncratic process, you might present formal outlining to your students as a resource to consider rather than as a requirement to fulfill each time they compose and submit a paper.

As an aid to critical reading

Finally, a formal outline can often provide a fruitful way of examining another writer's plan and structure. Suppose, for example, that you have read three essays on Lincoln's use of power during the Civil War and are to write on the authors' differing assumptions about the presidency. By constructing three accurate outlines and thereby highlighting in visual form the crucial differences among the essays, you can save yourself from skimming over and over the same paragraphs and snatching at random phrases or details. Formal outlining is also useful when you are asked to refute another writer's argument. By outlining his or her essay, you can isolate the key issues and examine the evidence and logic that support them. Outlining your reading, in short, enables you to discover someone else's views as you clarify your own.

2. Types of formal outlines

There are two main types of formal outlines: the topic outline and the sentence outline. Each has its particular uses and limitations.

Topic outlines

The *topic outline* begins with the entire thesis statement, the main idea being developed in the paper. After the thesis, though, its entries are words or brief phrases, numbered and lettered to show the relative importance of the paper's supporting ideas. (For notes on the scheme of numbers and letters used in constructing outlines, see the next section, "Conventions of formal outlines.")

Effective topic outline

The Complexity of Laughter

Thesis: Although there are several theories of laughter, no single one accounts for the quite distinct emotions that cause it.

    I. Single explanation theories of laughter
       A. Social punishment
           1. Mocks differences
           2. Shows feeling of superiority
       B. Defense against social taboos
           1. Relies on dirty jokes
           2. Is relief of tension

    C. Sudden surprise
       1. Stimulated by the unexpected act
       2. Is delight in being startled
  II. Complex experience of laughter
    A. Descriptions of feelings
       1. "To have the last laugh"
       2. "To laugh at"
       3. "To laugh off "
    B. Descriptions of vocal expressions
       1. "To chuckle"
       2. "To giggle and titter"
       3. "To snicker"
       4. "To guffaw"
 III. Inadequacies of theories of laughter to experience of laughter
    A. Failure to account for description of feelings
       1. No sudden pleasurable surprise in social punishment theory
       2. No sense of superiority in social taboo theory
       3. No self-embarrassment in pleasurable surprise theory
    B. Failure to account for sheer joy
       1. No explanation of lovers' spontaneity by any theory
       2. No explanation of delight in success by any theory

5d

For short papers or reports, a topic outline may well offer sufficient detail, but it is only as useful as the headings that it contains. A topic outline built on vague headings and subheadings like "Introduction," "Body," "First point," or "Conclusion" does little to help a writer visualize the structure of an essay. Consider the following example:

Vague topic outline

The Change from High School to College

  I. Introduction
    A. High-school ideas
    B. Reasons for these ideas
  II. What my first impressions were
    A. Two examples
    B. Results
 III. Conclusions
    A. Why I have changed my mind
    B. Advice to high-school seniors

The vague entries here largely undercut the potential value of outlining. Though they suggest the paper's general direction, they fail to help the writer organize ideas or consider supporting evidence.

Sentence outlines

5d

For long papers, a *sentence outline* may be more valuable than a topic outline. Because each entry in a sentence outline is a complete sentence, the form of the outline makes possible a thorough consideration of a paper's contents. In the example below, the effective topic outline on pages 74–75 has been expanded into an even more specific sentence outline.

Effective sentence outline

The Complexity of Laughter

Thesis: Although there are several theories of laughter, no single one accounts for the quite distinct emotions that cause it.

I. The theories tend to explain laughter by a single emotion or cause.
   A. Laughter is social punishment inflicted by the majority.
      1. It mocks differences in dress, behavior, and belief.
      2. It is a feeling of superiority and satiric awareness.
   B. Laughter is a defense against social taboos.
      1. It is stimulated by the dirty joke and obscene remark.
      2. It is a safety-valve response relieving tension.
   C. Laughter is the expression of pleasure in the sudden surprise.
      1. It is stimulated by the unexpected physical or verbal act.
         a. The physical is often the sudden fall or thump.
         b. The verbal is usually a witty remark.
      2. It is delight in being startled.
II. The experience of laughter is not a simple one.
   A. Our feelings while laughing vary.
      1. Vindictively we "have the last laugh."
      2. In amusement we "laugh at" something.
      3. In embarrassment we "laugh it off."
   B. The vocal expressions of laughter vary.
      1. We "chuckle" in a low tone when inwardly satisfied.
      2. We "giggle and titter" in rapid, high-pitched sounds when silly.

   3. We "snicker" in sly, half-suppressed tones at another's plight.
   4. We "guffaw" in loud tones when heartily enjoying ourselves.
III. The theories are inadequate to the experience of laughter.
   A. No theory accounts for the ways we describe our feelings.
      1. The theory of laughter as social punishment neglects the laugh of sudden pleasurable surprise.
      2. The theory of laughter as a defense against social taboos minimizes the laugh of punishment and mockery.
      3. The theory of laughter as pleasurable surprise slights the laugh of self-embarrassment.
   B. All theories omit the laughter of sheer joy of being and doing.
      1. They do not account for the spontaneous laughter of children, lovers, and parents.
      2. They do not account for the triumphant, delighted laugh of the successful artist or athlete.

Notice that the sentence outline contains far more information and reveals a more detailed analysis than the topic outline. The sentence outline has the advantage of compelling you to formulate more explicitly the structure, details, and arguments that you plan to use in your essay.

3.   Conventions of formal outlines

The following system of alternating numbers and letters is nearly universal in outlines:

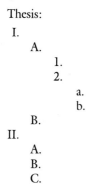

Thesis:
   I.
      A.
         1.
         2.
            a.
            b.
      B.
   II.
      A.
      B.
      C.

An outline begins with the thesis statement, the main idea to be developed in the paper. Roman numerals indicate the major subdivisions of the idea stated in the thesis. Capital letters, arabic numbers, and small letters mark further and further subdivisions. In topic outlines, capitalize the first letter of the word beginning each heading, but do not use end punctuation, because the entry is not a sentence. In sentence outlines, start with a capital letter and end with a period or other appropriate punctuation.

5d

The key to the logic of every outline is coordination and subordination. Coordinate points—those of equal importance—are indented the same distance from the left margin; under them, farther from the left margin, come subordinate, or supporting, points. In the outline above, for example, I and II are main points of equal importance, A and B are points of equal importance supporting I, and 1 and 2 are points of equal importance supporting A.

If an outline is to function as a tool for analysis, these conventions must be taken seriously. A writer who divides material like this negates the whole reason for outlining.

Illogical and confusing

    I. Advantages of outboard motors
        A. Relatively inexpensive
        B. Attachable to any small boat
    II. Easily transportable

"Easily transportable" is logically a subtopic under I, "Advantages of outboard motors." It should be made parallel with A and B.

Revised to clarify coordination and subordination

    I. Advantages of outboard motors
        A. Relatively inexpensive
        B. Attachable to any small boat
        C. Easily transportable
    II. Disadvantages of outboard motors
        A. Troublesome to repair on the water
        B. Limited fuel capacity

When one subheading includes material covered in other parallel headings, the subdivisions are said to overlap. Overlapping subdivisions suggest that the writer has not analyzed the material fully.

Poorly analyzed—overlapping

I. Organized welfare groups
    A. Early relief organizations
    B. Red Cross
    C. United Way
    D. Relief organizations today

Logically, "Relief organizations today" *includes* the Red Cross and United Way. If the pattern of development is to be chronological, the writer should stick to it consistently and make Red Cross and United Way subdivisions under modern welfare agencies.

Clearly subdivided

I. Organized welfare groups
    A. History of early relief organizations
    B. Relief organizations today
        1. Red Cross
        2. United Way

One last word about subdivisions: convention demands that each subdivided topic must have at least two headings. The argument runs that dividing something must produce at least two parts. Occasionally, however, a lone subhead is a useful means of *reminding yourself* of an example, illustration, or reference to be included when you are writing.

Examples noted

I. Extension of Mohammedan power under the early caliphs
    A. Eastward and northward
        1. For example, Persian and Greek lands
    B. Westward
        1. For example, Syria, Egypt, and northern Africa

Though they may be useful in working outlines, such lone headings should be eliminated from the final version of an outline.

5d

For practice in mastering the pattern of a formal outline, construct a topic outline of the student paper that appears at the end of this chapter, on pages 90–96. What strengths in the organization and development of this paper does your outline reveal?

5e Writing a first draft

Recent television commercials for a popular brand of athletic footwear and apparel depict well-known sports celebrities pushing themselves through rigorous athletic training and competition. And then three words appear on the screen: "Just do it." Getting the first draft of an essay down on paper requires a similar kind of commitment and exertion. But because a draft is a preliminary version of your paper, you needn't be overly concerned with the logic of its organization or the tightness of its coherence, much less with fine points of spelling and mechanics. Your goal should be simply to flesh out your thesis, to produce a written version of the ideas in your head, however tentative and incomplete this composition may be. If you take the process of revision seriously, you will discover that every draft that follows this first one will be more complete, more satisfying, and closer to what you really want to say.

1. Rely on your best writing habits

Chapter **1** stressed the idiosyncratic nature of the writing process and asked you to consider the physical circumstances that you find most conducive to writing. Having inventoried those circumstances for yourself, you should make every effort to exploit them. If you work best in the early morning, don't wait until late at night to begin your draft. If you're most comfortable composing at a computer, don't start your draft with a pen and a blank sheet of paper. If you need quiet to write, don't try to work within earshot of televisions, radios, or others' conversations. Of course, when a new idea occurs to you or an elegant sentence suddenly takes shape in your head, write it down wherever you are. Don't risk losing such a thought by waiting for just the right circumstances for writing.

Section **5e** is intended above all to keep beginning writers from panicking or freezing as they start a first draft. It stresses the tentative nature of a draft and offers advice on making the drafting process manageable and on overcoming writer's block. Its final section prepares students for the discussion of revision that follows in Chapters **10** to **13**.

2.   Segment your work

Whether composing a magazine article, a business report, a novel, or a poem, most writers reduce their work to a manageable size by considering it as a series of separate, smaller writing tasks. You, too, may find it helpful to think of your essay as a whole made up of several parts and to divide your writing into separate segments.

One convenient way to segment your writing is to work paragraph by paragraph. If you have written an informal or formal outline of your paper, you may already have a rough idea of the correspondence between sections of your outline and paragraphs in the essay you are planning. The building blocks of an essay, paragraphs are units of written discourse that have their own characteristic shape. Somewhat like essays in miniature, they are typically organized around a main idea, which is sometimes stated in a single sentence or two known as a paragraph's "topic sentence." To become more comfortable with the structure and development of paragraphs, see Chapters **6** and **7**, which present and analyze sample paragraphs of various types.

3.   Be prepared for getting stuck

Because even the most determined writers can get stuck in the middle of a draft, unable to pin down the words or thoughts they need to continue, you should prepare yourself with strategies for coping with writer's block. Leave blanks in your text whenever you can't think of the words you need to express a thought or finish a sentence; the words will come to you later. Don't feel that you have to write the sections of your paper in sequence; skip any section that gives you trouble and go on to the next. Try talking with someone else about your idea for the essay; verbalizing what you want to write can often help you regain momentum. Be ready to depart from your outline or plan when it doesn't seem to be working; a session or two of free writing (see **2a**) might help you discover a new direction. For your first draft, remember that your goal is a limited one: not to do it right (there will be time for polishing later), but just to do it.

4.   Be willing to revise

No matter how clearly you conceive your essay as you start to write, its content and form will change as you begin to connect words, sentences, and paragraphs. And if you are like most writers, you will finish your first draft both with a sense of accomplishment and with a feeling that many sections of your essay could be—indeed, must be—changed, either shortened, lengthened, clarified, moved to a new position, or deleted altogether.

As suggested in Chapter **1**, such feelings are entirely normal; they indicate your sensitivity to the role of revision in the writing process. For help as you consider how to revise your essay, you might begin by reading the discussion of revision in Chapter **10**, which differentiates between large-scale and small-scale revision and illustrates both varieties by analyzing the early and final drafts of a student essay. Chapters **11**, **12**, and **13** then suggest revision strategies for all the components of an essay—its paragraphs, sentences, and diction.

EXERCISE 5

Before beginning to write the first draft of your next paper, compose an informal or formal outline and divide this plan for your essay into a set of smaller writing tasks.

EXERCISE 6

Save the first draft of the next essay you write (remember to save a hard copy if you work on a computer) and compare it with the final draft that you eventually produce. How substantial were the changes that you made? Looking at the final draft today, can you think of additional changes that you could still make?

5f   Writing introductions

Few rules of writing are binding, but it is ordinarily desirable that an essay's introduction (1) attract and hold the reader's attention, (2) indicate the subject matter of the paper, and (3) reveal in some way the writer's attitude toward the subject. As these guidelines suggest, you can usually write an effective introduction only *after* you have formulated your thesis statement. In fact, since the success of an introduction depends on a writer's understanding of the complete essay, many writers work on their introductions only after they have written everything else for a paper.

Exercise 6

This exercise prepares students for the discussion of revision in Part III by asking them to consider their current revising habits and by suggesting that even finished texts may eventually become candidates for further revision.

Although it avoids dogmatic pronouncements about the form that an introduction must take, **5f** offers specific strategies for shaping an introduction around a thesis statement.

How long is an introduction? Again, there are no fixed rules, but introductions are usually proportionate in length to the texts that follow them. For an essay of two or three pages, a one-paragraph introduction might be sufficient. A longer magazine article may begin with an introduction of two or three paragraphs. And a book may require an introduction that is an entire chapter in length.

Among the many techniques for writing introductions are the three illustrated in the following sections.

5f

1. Beginning with the thesis statement

If you remember that any beginning can be changed, or even discarded, you should not be hesitant about drafting an introduction. One way of getting started, especially for short papers, is to begin with your thesis statement.

> *The pedestrian malls that appeared in the downtown shopping districts of many American cities twenty years ago were a mistake that threatened the very cities they were intended to revitalize.* Believing that they could win shoppers back from the new suburban shopping malls, city planners around the country tried to replicate the feeling of a mall in the city center. They banned automobiles from certain downtown streets, filled in the former traffic lanes with landscaping, benches, and meandering concrete paths, and waited—in vain, it turns out—for shoppers to forsake their suburban malls and come back to downtown department stores. What these planners failed to realize is that people shop at malls because they can drive to them easily and park close to the stores they want to patronize. With downtown stores in many cities now struggling for financial viability, city planners of the 1990s are rushing to demolish the urban malls that discouraged people from driving downtown to shop.

The thesis statement that opens this paragraph leaves no doubt about the writer's subject ("pedestrian malls") and restriction ("mistake"). The sentences that follow it provide the reader with useful background, but the paragraph doesn't stray from its initial focus. The last sentence reiterates the failure of city-center pedestrian malls and suggests that the essay will go on to discuss specific cases of cities that are demolishing them.

2. Beginning with a quotation

If your subject is a published work, you might try opening with a key quotation from the text you are going to discuss, as the student writer of the following example did.

> It is the "quick, compact imagery of a single statement that forms the basis of Navajo poetry," says Oliver LaFarge. *This remark can well be illustrated in LaFarge's own story of Navajo life,* Laughing Boy, *a novel in which things are perceived and identified through "quick, compact imagery."* The first image of the novel ties the protagonist, Laughing Boy, to his environment: "His new red headband was a bright color among the embers of the sun-struck desert, undulating like a moving graph of the pony's lope"—a simple statement, but a "compact image" of the movement of a man on his horse over flat ground.

In this paragraph, the writer has used a quotation from LaFarge to provide the focusing phrase for the thesis statement: "*Laughing Boy* is a novel in which things are perceived and identified through 'quick, compact imagery.' "

3. Building up to the thesis statement

Perhaps the most sophisticated introduction is one that gradually builds up to the thesis statement. Placing the thesis at the end of an introduction enables you to begin with background information that establishes a context for your main point. Moreover, a thesis in this position leads smoothly into the first paragraph of the body of the paper. In the following introductory paragraph, for example, notice how the student writer uses a brief historical survey to frame her thesis.

> Beginning in the 1960s, the United States saw a growing militancy among Native Americans. During this time, these people began to put aside their intertribal difficulties and feuds, and to unite and support each other's causes. The American Indian Movement (AIM), with its militancy and activism, soon drew national attention to the oppression and discrimination of Indian peoples. AIM, however, worked outside the established system, battling for Indian rights on the streets. *Now Native Americans have gone beyond this strategy and are waging battle from a new front—the courtroom.*

Without the perspective provided by the opening sentences of this introduction, we would not understand the significance of the writer's thesis, which focuses on the new legal action being taken by Native Americans.

In the next example, another student writer has used the same strategy to establish a context for his analysis of a short story.

5f

> It's often difficult for us to pause and analyze our relationships with other people. Instead, we find it easier to live each day as it comes without forming personal commitments or attachments. Sooner or later, though, everyone realizes that it is impossible to live with a person and not really care whether he or she will be there tomorrow. *The two characters in Dan Jacobson's short story "Led Astray" come to this realization and discover that no relationship can exist without feeling.*

To appreciate the effectiveness of this approach, notice that the thesis statement and the introductory sentences in this paragraph could not simply be flipped around in the reverse order. The thesis is not merely attached to the introductory sentences; rather, it appears to develop out of them.

In the following student paragraph, the writer uses his opening sentences for a different purpose—to create an informal tone and to establish himself as an authority on his subject.

> The Hawaiian Islands are anchored in a position where they receive sea swells the year round. The contour of the ocean floor and the structure of the reefs turn these swells into beautiful breaking waves, which make Hawaii a surfer's paradise. I have been surfing in this paradise every day for the last seven years, and I can tell you that there is probably no more purely natural act than surfing. You are at one with nature's most basic element— the living sea. *But as changing times bring "progress" to the islands, surfing in Hawaii will also be forced to change.*

The opening sentences of this introduction concisely tell us that the writer speaks from experience and hence prepare us to accept his thesis with its clearly stated subject ("surfing in Hawaii") and restriction ("will . . . be forced to change").

A writer who requires more room to establish a context for his or her thesis may need to expand an introduction to several paragraphs. In the following two-paragraph introduction to a five-thousand-word magazine article, for example, notice how the person described in the first paragraph and the authority cited in the second paragraph together form the foundation for a thesis about homelessness that the writer positions at the end of this two-paragraph block.

5f

> Several years ago in New Orleans, I met a young African-American woman, Virginia, who at the age of twenty-one was on her own in the world with two small children. She had just gotten out of a shelter after being homeless for a year, and over the coming twelve months she and her boys would become homeless several times again. Even when they had somewhere to stay, Virginia was so close to the edge, so precariously situated, that it took only the slightest mishap or misstep to send her back onto the street.
>
> Michael Harrington once wrote that we should not talk about "poverty," but about poverties. He meant that there are so many ways of being poor that no single description or analysis can apply to them all. Virginia's situation shows that the same thing is true of homelessness. *There are in actuality a variety of homelessnesses, each one different from the others in terms of causes, particulars, and solutions. Furthermore, the kind Virginia endures—a recurrent homelessness so much a part of the cycle of poverty that it becomes a predictable part of people's lives—gets much less attention than it deserves.*
>
> —Peter Marin, "Virginia's Trap,"
> *Mother Jones*

Again, the writer's clear statement of his subject ("recurrent homelessness") and restriction ("gets much less attention than it deserves") focuses the reader's attention on the direction the article is going to take.

No matter what form of introduction you use, remember that confidence, authority, and solid content characterize the most successful opening paragraphs. Stay clear of any beginnings that sound trite and obvious: "Our modern world is an ever-changing one." "It is obvious to everyone that today's children watch too much television." Such beginnings discourage even the most determined reader.

EXERCISE 7

Write two *different* introductions for a paper that would develop *one* of the thesis statements that you produced in Exercise 2 on page 67 or Exercise 3 on pages 72–73. Which introduction do you like better? Why? Would the essays that followed these introductions be likely to differ? If so, how?

Exercise 7

Have each student read his or her two introductions either to the class as a whole or to a few other students in small groups, and let the rest of the students discuss their reasons for preferring one over the other.

5g Writing conclusions

Just as an introduction may be written last, after a writer has finally arrived at a full understanding of what it is that he or she wishes to say, a conclusion may be drafted at any time in the writing process. Some writers hear a resounding final line echoing in their heads even before they have sketched out the body of an essay. Others begin writing with no idea about the way a paper will conclude. In drafting conclusions, as in all other aspects of writing, you should try to remain flexible and adaptable, ready to capitalize on inspiration whenever it may strike.

5g

Of course, not every paper requires a conclusion. A particularly short essay, for example, may not need the added sense of completeness that a conclusion provides. When a conclusion is called for, however, it should be more than a sentence or paragraph attached to the end of an essay with a mechanical transition like "Therefore . . ." or "In conclusion . . ."

1. Ending with a sense of finality

Rather than merely summarizing what has gone before, the best conclusions mark the arrival of the essay at the destination announced in its introductory paragraph. An essay should end with the ease and authority of a musical composition that brings its themes to a unified, harmonious resolution, giving the reader a sure sense of finality. For example, consider this ending to a student's seven-hundred-word essay on Chekhov's play *The Seagull.*

> When the curtain falls on *The Seagull,* one has the feeling that the story is not at all ended, that the action continues behind the curtain. Reflecting on this, one may find that the secret of Chekhov's effect lies in avoiding the overly dramatic, the play in which everything builds to one climax centered in one character. Chekhov has allowed the themes of love and death, of dreams and reality, to unfold in the random, senseless way that they occur in our lives.

2. Ending by bringing ideas together

A writer may also conclude strongly by making connections between ideas explored earlier in the paper. In the following student example, an analysis of Robert Pirsig's *Zen and the Art of Motorcycle*

Maintenance and Ralph Ellison's *Invisible Man,* note how the writer links Phaedrus and the Invisible Man, the protagonists of the two novels.

5g

> Participation in life and the celebration of its possibilities are what both Phaedrus and the Invisible Man finally affirm. They are able to do so as a result of their personal quests. Yet they both set out in ignorance, not knowing the direction they are actually headed in. At the end, when the Invisible Man says, "Who knows but that, on the lower frequencies, I speak for you?" it is a warning that most of us are still back at the very beginning simply because we think we're not or, worse yet, because we don't even think about it.

3.   Ending by echoing the introduction

Often the feeling of completeness that a well-written conclusion conveys can be created by recalling a word or phrase from the introduction. The student surfer whose introduction was quoted above went on to argue that the increasing number of surfers in Hawaii would either have to discipline themselves to share the waves or have to expect state regulation of the sport, and he concluded by emphasizing the concept of the living sea and the inevitability of change—two key ideas from his opening paragraph.

> Unless we treat the sea with the consideration that it deserves as a source of wonder, pleasure, and life, sacrificing our own selfish desire to catch the big wave regardless of who or what is in the way, we can look forward to the regulation of surfing. Police patrolling the beaches, floodlights stuck into the sand for day and night surfing, licenses, permits, tickets—these are not pleasant prospects. But neither are the fights, the racial name-calling, the indifference to another surfer's safety that one encounters all too often in Hawaiian waters. To live in a world of change, we must learn to change ourselves.

Similarly, the writer on homelessness, who began his article by recounting his first meeting with Virginia, the homeless young mother, recalled that introductory paragraph by concluding with a description of his last contact with her.

> During the busy season [at her new hotel job], Virginia could clear $175 a week for rent, food, clothing, toys, etc.—enough to get by and

perhaps save a bit. But during the off-season, her take-home pay would be lower than her expenses. She could get some food stamps, as long as she reapplied for them every time her income dipped. But what about other expenses? She'd no doubt fall behind, just as before; then the phone would be cut off, the lights would go, there would be a monthly struggle to come up with the rent—and, sooner or later, she'd be homeless again.

    I can't help worrying that that's exactly what has happened to Virginia. When I talked to her several months ago, work had slowed and she was having terrible problems. And recently, I tried to track her down but failed. The phone at her apartment had been disconnected. At the hotel, they told me that Virginia didn't work there anymore, and they didn't know where she'd gone.

5h

First and last encounters with Virginia frame this article—and dramatize her desperate plight.

    No competent writer dashes off a conclusion at the last moment. When we finish reading an essay we should feel that it had to end as it did. Writing that creates this sense of completion is the result of careful thought and painstaking revision, but its effectiveness justifies the effort.

EXERCISE 8

Examine an article in a magazine such as *Scientific American, Atlantic Monthly,* or *Natural History,* and consider the following points about its organization and development:

1. Does the article have a clear thesis? Where is it stated?
2. What are the main points with which the author develops the thesis?
3. What kind of evidence or support does the author present for each of these main points?
4. Is the conclusion of the article related to its introduction? How?

5h   A sample student essay

    This chapter closes with a student paper illustrating the elements of a successful essay discussed above—an appropriately limited subject, a precise thesis statement, a smooth introduction, well-balanced development, and an effective and substantial conclusion. This paper was inspired by E. B. White's frequently reprinted essay "Once More to the Lake," in which he describes a week-long vacation with his

Exercise 8

Students may have difficulty locating the thesis in a magazine article, for the piece may not contain the kind of thesis presented in this chapter. Nonetheless, a connection of some kind between the introduction and the conclusion should be evident, as should the author's main points of development. If you are using an anthology of essays in your course, you can reinforce the issues raised in this chapter by examining some of those essays with these questions.

son at a lake in Maine where his own family had spent the month of August each year when he was a boy. For White, the experience vividly brought back childhood memories that kept him eerily suspended between youth and adulthood. "I began to sustain the illusion that my son was I, and therefore, by simple transposition, that I was my father," he writes. "I would be in the middle of some simple act, I would be picking up a bait box or laying down a table fork, or I would be saying something, and suddenly it would not be I but my father who was saying the words or making the gesture. It gave me a creepy sensation." Watch how student writer Janet Lively analyzes a similar experience in her own life.

5h

Janet Lively

Professor J. Wallace

English 100

December 2, 1994

                    Breaking the Chain

Janet's opening sentences establish a clear context for the essay by succinctly but vividly describing her baby-sitting duties. We learn who was involved, and when and where the events that she describes occurred. By including the phrase *best summer job*, Janet also prepares us to share her favorable attitude toward her subject.

        Jenny was six, Marcia was eight,
and I was sixteen when we spent the
summer together. Although the pay was
terrible, baby-sitting for those
brown-eyed, skinny little girls was by
far the best summer job I ever had.
They lived just down the block and
therefore played on the same playground, explored the same forbidden
creek bottom, and rode bicycles over
the same bumpy paths that I had known
intimately as a child. Simultaneously

supervising and sharing in their activities, I felt emotions similar to those
that E. B. White expresses in his essay
"Once More to the Lake." "[I]t would
not be I but my father who was saying
the words or making the gesture,"
writes White of his memory-filled vacation with his son. Like White, I startled myself more than once that summer
by echoing my mother's words and
phrases to Marcia and Jenny. White's
experiences gave him a "creepy sensation"; mine made me wonder for the
first time what kind of parent I would
be.

A key quotation from White's essay leads Janet to her thesis statement, which presents a precise subject (her baby-sitting experience) and a clear restricting phrase ("made me wonder . . . what kind of parent I would be").

5h

    At sixteen, I was still under the
authority of my parents, who in my es-
timation were unreasonably protective.
Each time I left the house, I would
have to detail to my mother exactly
where I was going, who I was going
with, when I would be back. Walking out
the door, I was invariably told to wear
my seat belt, check for fire escapes,
cross only at stoplights, stay clear of

Janet organizes her second paragraph around what she felt was her mother's unreasonable protectiveness—background that we need to understand the point she wants to make about her own behavior as a baby-sitter.

5h

Notice the well-
chosen, specific
details with which
she makes her
point.

public rest rooms, and leave a phone
number that I could be reached at. Even
at Marcia and Jenny's age I had thought
my mother's perpetual admonishments ridiculous, but as a teenager I deeply
resented them. Specifically outlining
my every plan to my parents was particularly irritating, and I had vowed repeatedly to myself that I would never
place such demands on my own children.

In this paragraph,
Janet begins to
develop the idea
raised in her
thesis: what did
the restrictions
that she imposed
on Marcia and
Jenny—so much
like the protective-
ness of her mother
—predict about
her own future as
a parent?

Again, specific
details make the
situation
convincingly real.

Nonetheless, my tiny, energetic
wards never left the house that summer
until I had found out where they were
going and when they would return, and
had extracted a promise from them that
they would not ride their bicycles
around the block. Marcia and Jenny argued as fervently against the restrictions I placed on them as I had pro-
tested against my mother's rules. Why
couldn't they walk half a mile alone to
visit a friend? Why should they stay
out of Colleen's pool just because her
mother wasn't home? To my surprise, I
usually responded with the precise

phrases I had so often heard my mother use with me. That frightened me. My mother's words were filled with genuine concern, never harshness, but they were her words, and I scared myself by spewing them out so automatically. Even though I felt that my mother worried needlessly and restricted me unnecessarily, I found myself worrying about and limiting my girls to the same degree. I was "raising" Marcia and Jenny in the same manner that my parents had raised me, which was most likely similar to the way they had been raised. Was I destined to raise my own children in the same way? It seemed to me suddenly that I was trapped in an unbreakable chain of parental behavior from which I would never be able to escape.

But at the same time that I felt and acted like my mother out of concern for Marcia and Jenny's safety, I also closely identified with the freedom they wanted and understood the resentment they felt at the rules I laid

5h

Here's the sentence that gave Janet the idea for her title ("Breaking the Chain").

Against the sternness of her parental role, developed in the preceding paragraph, Janet now balances an effective description of the way in which

5h

Marcia and Jenny's games reminded her of her own childhood.

Specific details and diction (scamper, high-pitched giggles) bring the scene to life.

down. Thus, like White, I experienced the startling sensation of living a dual existence. Down deep, I knew how difficult it was for the two of them to pinpoint their play areas, because summer days weren't meant to be planned. They lived their vacation as spontaneously as my friends and I had, waking each morning with the wonderful knowledge that they had the whole day before them with nothing, but everything, to do. A typical day might begin by playing "Barbies" in a friend's cool basement, followed by a game of jump rope in someone else's front yard; after lunch, they'd reassemble, perhaps to construct a fort behind still another friend's garage. Sitting on the porch, watching them scamper from yard to yard and listening to their high-pitched giggles, I became one of their group and reexperienced the carefree feeling that had come with summer before camps and jobs occupied my summer days. I couldn't let them play kickball in the

street or walk unaccompanied to the
Dairy Spot, but I hated to put any kind
of limits on their glorious freedom.

   Despite my worries about those
little girls that summer, and about my
future as a parent, I truly enjoyed
those three months. Spending time with
Marcia and Jenny allowed me to relive
the pleasures and freedom of my early
summers on Maplewood Street, just as
White's vacation with his son enabled
him to relive his childhood summers at
the lake. The experience of acting out
the dual roles of parent and child was
unsettling to me that summer, much as
it had been for White, but I've since
been able to resolve the conflict it
created within me. Now that I've been
away from my parents' authority, I realize that the "chain" of parental behavior is not as unbreakable as I had
thought. As I grow older, I realize
that I am different from my mother after all. I <u>can</u> raise my children with
fewer restrictions--if I'm able to

5h

Janet effectively links her conclusion to her introduction by again mentioning E. B. White's essay, her starting point.

She then connects the major ideas of the paper by explaining how she has resolved the conflict that she described above.

The rhythm of Janet's last sentence creates a satisfying sense of finality.

Exercise 9 (page 96)

This exercise offers guided practice in some of the principles of focusing and organizing that are discussed in this chapter. A general subject ("inci-dent in your life") and focus ("forced you to reconsider your assumptions about yourself or your world") are provided; the student must identify a precise incident in his or her life that will become the subject of the paper and must use the introduction and thesis to state what precise assumptions this event challenged. A loose, tripartite pattern of organization for the

```
recall, as I did that summer, how it

feels to be a child.
```

The marginal notes on Janet's essay not only highlight the principles of essay organization discussed in this chapter but also point out the clear organization of its paragraphs and the specificity of its details and diction. Those are subjects to be examined further in the chapters that follow.

5h

EXERCISE **9**

Using Janet Lively's essay above as a model, write an essay of 500 to 700 words on an incident in your life that forced you to reconsider your assumptions about yourself or your world. To organize your essay, begin by composing a precise thesis statement and an informal or formal outline of your paper's contents. Try to include the three segments that make up Janet's essay: appropriate background about yourself, description of the important incident in your life, and analysis of the incident's effect on you.

---

paper is also suggested; students should be urged to treat it as a way of thinking about their subjects rather than as a mold into which the contents of their papers must be fitted.

For Further Reading

Arrington, Phillip, and Shirley K. Rose. "Prologues to What Is Possible: Introductions as Metadiscourse." *College Composition and Communication* 38 (1987): 306–18.

Coe, Richard M. "If Not to Narrow, Then How to Focus: Two Techniques for Focusing." *College Composition and Communication* 32 (1981): 272–77.

Haswell, Richard. "The Organization of Impromptu Essays." *College Composition and Communication* 37 (1986): 402–15.

Larson, Richard L. "Structure and Form in Non-Narrative Prose." *Teaching Composition: Twelve Bibliographical Essays*. Ed. Gary Tate. Fort Worth: Texas Christian UP, 1987. 39–82.

6 *Constructing Paragraphs*

The concept of a paragraph is no doubt familiar to you. Just about everything we read—from novels to newspapers, from textbooks to cookbooks—is printed with indentations that mark new paragraphs. And in most of your writing, you also probably adopt the tradition of using paragraphs to divide what you write into separate chunks. At the same time, you no doubt recognize that such divisions are not arbitrary, that paragraphs have a certain logic behind them. But how can we define more precisely what paragraphs are? And can we determine some principles for writing good paragraphs? These are among the questions to be explored in this chapter. Later chapters will consider two other aspects of paragraphing: methods of developing paragraphs (Chapter 7) and points to keep in mind as you revise paragraphs (Chapter 11).

6a Recognizing paragraphs

Try to imagine, for a moment, a world with no paragraph indentations. Every book, every newspaper, every magazine would present a solid page of type, with no white spaces inviting you to pause and rest, even momentarily. Reading under these circumstances would be tedious and tiring. But would paragraphs exist, even if the indentations that signaled them did not? To find out, try reading the following short magazine article, printed without its original paragraph indentations. In particular, consider this question: without the indentations, has this text now become a single long paragraph, or are the original separate paragraphs still here, and still perceptible, with a little extra work on your part?

This discussion of paragraph structure is organized around topic sentences because they offer many beginning writers help in controlling paragraphs. But balancing this traditional approach is an introductory section that presents paragraphs as *rhetorical* constructions, that is, as units whose design exists primarily for the reader's benefit. And the chapter avoids dogmatic pronouncements about the placement of topic sentences within paragraphs or about the necessity of a topic sentence in every paragraph. For instructors who wish to present their students with still other approaches to paragraph construction, the readings listed at the end of the chapter offer a number of possibilities.

6a

In the course of almost four decades of research, Dr. Paul MacLean of the National Institute of Mental Health has determined that there is a zoo in the human brain. More precisely, there are in the human brain evolutionary holdovers from our animal origins, he says, that influence our behavior and thinking. In its evolution, the human forebrain has expanded in size while retaining three basic formations that reflect our ancestral relationship to reptiles, early mammals, and recent mammals. Radically different in size as well as chemistry, and in an evolutionary sense countless generations apart, the three formations constitute a hierarchy of three brains in one—a triune brain. The reptilian core, or "biological brain," which MacLean calls the R-complex, is involved in basic social behavior and preservation of the self and of the species. It contains built-in formats for the instinctual behavior of dominance and territoriality. As an example of human behavior that reflects that protoreptilian impulse, MacLean offers the "place preference" of lizards, which is no different, he says, from Archie Bunker's territorial attitude about his favorite chair. The limbic system, or "emotional brain," is a holdover from early mammals. Its integration of internal and external experiences accounts for the ineffable affective feelings required for self-preservation and for perpetuation of the species. Without the limbic system (a term that MacLean coined) there wouldn't be the kinds of behavior that distinguish mammals from reptiles—namely, nursing in conjunction with maternal care, vocalization for the purpose of maintaining contact, and play. The neomammalian formation, or "intellectual brain," is found only in the higher mammals. It makes language and rational thought possible for man and fosters cultural life. According to MacLean, the triune brain obliges us to view ourselves from three perspectives. As a further complication, there is evidence that the two older formations lack the necessary neural machinery for verbal communication. Despite [this] built-in incompatibility of the three brains, Mac-Lean is not without hope for man. The continuing influence of our animal origins, millions of years strong, will not be easily transcended, but it can be, MacLean says in his forthcoming book, *The Triune Brain.*

—John White, "On the Brain," *Esquire*

6a

Despite the way in which this passage is printed, you probably approached it by mentally dividing the text into separate chunks, in order to follow it more easily. When the author tells us in the introductory sentences that the human brain retains traces of three earlier formations, we expect him to discuss these three brains in the rest of the article. And that is indeed what he does in three middle paragraphs, each devoted to a different brain formation. After describing the three, he concludes with a paragraph commenting on the necessary conflict among them.

Here, then, is how the article above originally appeared.

In the course of almost four decades of research, Dr. Paul MacLean of the National Institute of Mental Health has determined that there is a zoo in the human brain. More precisely, there are in the human brain evolutionary holdovers from our animal origins, he says, that influence our behavior and thinking. In its evolution, the human forebrain has expanded in size while retaining three basic formations that reflect our ancestral relationship to reptiles, early mammals, and recent mammals. Radically different in size as well as chemistry, and in an evolutionary sense countless generations apart, the three formations constitute a hierarchy of three brains in one—a triune brain.

The reptilian core, or "biological brain," which MacLean calls the R-complex, is involved in basic social behavior and preservation of the self and of the species. It contains built-in formats for the instinctual behavior of dominance and territoriality. As an example of human behavior that reflects that protoreptilian impulse, MacLean offers the "place preference" of lizards, which is no different, he says, from Archie Bunker's territorial attitude about his favorite chair.

The limbic system, or "emotional brain," is a holdover from early mammals. Its integration of internal and external experiences accounts for the ineffable affective feelings required for self-preservation and for perpetuation of the species. Without the limbic system (a term that MacLean coined) there wouldn't be the kinds of behavior that distinguish mammals from reptiles—namely, nursing in conjunction with maternal care, vocalization for the purpose of maintaining contact, and play.

6a

The neomammalian formation, or "intellectual brain," is found only in the higher mammals. It makes language and rational thought possible for man and fosters cultural life.

According to MacLean, the triune brain obliges us to view ourselves from three perspectives. As a further complication, there is evidence that the two older formations lack the necessary neural machinery for verbal communication. Despite [this] built-in incompatibility of the three brains, MacLean is not without hope for man. The continuing influence of our animal origins, millions of years strong, will not be easily transcended, but it can be, MacLean says in his forthcoming book, *The Triune Brain*.

Whenever we read, we look for such divisions because, in order to read with understanding, we need to be able to identify the main ideas in the text before us and to perceive their relationship to one another. If we lived in a world where paragraphs were never marked, we would have to find them on our own as we read. To put it another way, if paragraphs were unknown in our world, we would simply have to invent them.

We might say that paragraphs have a primarily *rhetorical* function. That is, they are intended by a writer to affect a reader in some way—in this case, to help a reader identify and follow the writer's principal ideas. Underlying this concept of a paragraph are two principles. First, a paragraph should ordinarily be unified around a single thought. If the function of paragraphing is to help point out a writer's main ideas, then it follows logically that separate ideas should be developed in separate paragraphs. Second, if the reader is to make sense of the text, all the paragraphs in a given piece of writing must be related to one another in some clear way.

Rhetorical Guidelines for Paragraphing

1. Paragraph breaks help a reader identify the writer's main points; therefore, *each paragraph in a text should be unified around a single idea.*
2. Paragraphs help a reader follow the writer's chain of ideas; therefore, *paragraphs in a text should be related to one another in some clear way.*

Sometimes, of course, we create paragraphs almost unconsciously. When we are writing well, we find ourselves deeply involved in our subject and able to discover new ideas and connections as we go along. On such lucky occasions, we usually paragraph by the instinctive feeling that one section is complete and that we are ready to begin a new one. At other times, we may become aware of the proper places for paragraph breaks only gradually, as we make slow progress through the cycle of writing and revising discussed in Chapter 1. As a writer, you should be prepared to discover paragraphs in your writing where you had not previously seen them. Look for opportunities to combine short paragraphs, be ready to divide longer ones, and don't hesitate to move a sentence from one paragraph to another. Paragraphs are molded out of clay, not carved in stone; experienced writers expect to reshape them as they work toward a final draft.

6a

EXERCISE 1

Each of the following passages has been formed by printing two consecutive paragraphs without indentation. Separate each passage into two paragraphs again, and explain your reason for dividing them where you did. What is the main idea in each of the paragraphs you identified? Is the relationship between those ideas clear?

1.   Whoever said that people who do the least complain the most must have known my boss, Miss Eleanor. By hiding behind paperwork that takes the other store managers only a fraction of the time to finish, she is able to push the jobs she should be doing on whoever else is within earshot. Across the entire store one can hear her yelling for a clerk to bring her a file folder or a cash register tape lying only a few feet away. Her voice, fierce and commanding, together with her stony face and dark eyes, freezes everyone around her in fear. Eleanor is as vain as she is fearsome. In front of her desk she has a three-foot square mirror in which we see her constantly making faces, admiring herself, and talking to herself. In her nearby "private" cabinet she has two cans of hair spray, a box of bobby pins, several combs and brushes, a set of electric curlers, enough makeup to make Frankenstein look acceptable, and half a dozen issues of *Vogue* magazine. It's no wonder Miss Eleanor is always so busy.

—Cathy Kwolik, student writer

Exercise 1

Note that students are not yet asked to identify topic sentences in this exercise (although these paragraphs do have rather clear topic sentences) but simply to separate the passages into paragraphs according to the two main ideas developed in each selection.

1. The second paragraph begins with "Eleanor is as vain as she is fearsome." The main idea in the first paragraph is Miss Eleanor's laziness; in the second, it is her vanity. The comparison established in the second topic sentence ("as vain as she is fearsome") links that paragraph neatly with the final sentence of the first paragraph.
2. The second paragraph begins with "The misnomer is understandable. . . ." Whereas the first paragraph focuses on the manufacture of Panama hats, the second traces the history of their name, picking up the idea in the first paragraph's opening sentence.
3. The second paragraph begins with "By about the beginning of the sixteenth century . . ." The main idea in the first paragraph is the

6a

2.   The first thing you have to know, if you are going to be serious about Panama hats, is that genuine Panamas are not made in Panama at all and never have been. They are made in Ecuador—that is, the raw body of the hat is made in Ecuador, handwoven out of very thin strips of jipijapa palm leaves. Nor are they woven underwater, as many people seem to think; the leaves are simply woven while moist. The hat body is then sent off to hat makers around the world to be sized, blocked, and trimmed. But the important part, the weaving, has already happened in Ecuador. The misnomer is understandable: Sailors and traders first encountered the hat when they went ashore in Panama more than 150 years ago. Naturally, they called it a Panama hat, and the name they gave it stuck. All the more so when Teddy Roosevelt was photographed wearing a Panama hat at the construction site of the Panama canal. In the ensuing rush to buy Panama hats, no one took the trouble to straighten out the name, not even the Ecuadorians who had made Roosevelt's hat.

—John Berendt, "The Panama Hat," *Esquire*

3.   Medieval courtiers saw their table manners as distinguishing them from crude peasants; but by modern standards, the manners were not exactly refined. Feudal lords used their unwashed hands to scoop food from a common bowl and they passed around a single goblet from which all drank. A finger or two would be extended while eating, so as to be kept free of grease and thus available for the next course, or for dipping into spices or condiments—possibly accounting for today's "polite" custom of extending the finger while holding a spoon or small fork. Soups and sauces were commonly drunk by lifting the bowl to the mouth; several diners frequently ate from the same bread trencher. Even lords and nobles would toss gnawed bones back into the common dish, wolf down their food, spit onto the table (preferred conduct called for spitting under it), and blow their noses into the tablecloth. By about the beginning of the sixteenth century, table manners began to move in the direction of today's standards. The importance attached to them is indicated by the phenomenal success of a treatise, *On Civility in Children,* by the philosopher Erasmus, which appeared in 1530; reprinted more than thirty times in the next six years, it also appeared in numerous translations. Erasmus' idea of good table manners was far from modern, but it did represent an advance. He believed, for example, that an upper-class diner was distinguished by putting only three fingers of one hand into the bowl,

crudeness of medieval table manners; in the second, the subject is their gradual refinement. The two paragraphs balance each other nicely.

4. The second paragraph begins with "To do away with the inevitable confusion . . ." The first paragraph explains the multiple correct answers that one might have received to the question "What time is it?" The second paragraph focuses on the convention called to eliminate this confusion.

5. The second paragraph begins with "But the definition is also true . . ." Offering a somewhat humorous explanation of the comment that entrepreneurs don't "know any better," the first paragraph suggests that they are often inexperienced, out of touch with reality, and lacking in essential business skills. By focusing on the idealistic dedication of entrepreneurs to their business enterprises, the second paragraph presents a more positive interpretation of the same comment.

instead of the entire hand in the manner of the lower class. Wait a few moments after being seated before you dip into it, he advises. Do not poke around in your dish, but take the first piece you touch. Do not put chewed food from your mouth back on your plate; instead, throw it under the table or behind your chair.

—Peter Farb and George Armelagos, *Consuming Passions*

4. Until 1883 a Chicagoan asked to tell what time it was could give more than one answer and still be correct. There was local time, determined by the position of the sun at high noon at a centrally located spot in town, usually City Hall. There was also railroad time, which put Columbus, Ohio, six minutes faster than Cincinnati and 19 minutes faster than Chicago. Scattered across the country were 100 different local time zones, and the railroads had some 53 zones of their own. Typically, a traveler journeying from one end of the U.S. to another would have to change his watch at least 20 times. To do away with the inevitable confusion, the railroads took the matter into their own hands, holding a General Time Convention in the fall of 1883 at the Grand Pacific Hotel at LaSalle Street and Jackson Boulevard, the site of the present Continental Bank Building [in Chicago]. Its purpose: to develop a better and more uniform system of railroad scheduling. The convention secretary, William F. Allen, editor of the *Official Railway Guide* in New York, proposed that four equal time zones be established across the country. Five were actually adopted—Intercolonial (now Atlantic, including Nova Scotia and New Brunswick in Canada), Eastern, Central, Mountain and Pacific.

—June Sawyers, "The End to Falling Back and Forth in 100 Time Zones," *Chicago Tribune*

5. I once heard an after-dinner speaker define *entrepreneur* as "a person who doesn't know any better." We all recognized ourselves and laughed. Entrepreneurs seldom do know what they're getting into when they start. They are people so fired up with a vision that they go blind to everyday realities—which is a good thing, since otherwise they would never even attempt to do the impossible things they so often succeed in doing. Moreover, entrepreneurs often lack a basic grasp of business skills. I certainly did. But the definition is also true in another, more literal sense: entrepreneurs know nothing better than their own enterprises. They have the noblest missions and the finest products in the world. It doesn't matter if they make duct tape

or artificial hearts; they believe they have what it takes to alter history. And they are right, at least for themselves and their own companies— and sometimes for history too.

—Kye Anderson, "The Purpose at the Heart of Management," *Harvard Business Review*

6b Using topic sentences

Writers separate their ideas into paragraphs so that readers will be able to follow those ideas more easily. Sometimes a writer also succinctly states the main idea of a paragraph in a sentence or two known as a *topic sentence*. Just as a thesis statement directs the reader's attention to the central idea in an essay, a topic sentence, when it exists, aids the reader in more readily grasping a paragraph's point. Like a thesis, it usually introduces both a subject and a specific aspect of that subject, or focus. Like a thesis, too, a topic sentence is in some sense an arguable statement, one that leads to, or even demands, specific support or proof in the rest of the paragraph.

1. Formulating a topic sentence

Which of the following two sentences meets the criteria for a topic sentence described above?

a. Abraham Lincoln was born in what is now Larue County, Kentucky.

b. A food processor, as more and more good cooks are discovering, is an indispensable kitchen tool.

Because it does not raise an idea that requires further comment, but instead simply states a fact, the first sentence could not be a strong topic sentence. This sentence presents a clear subject—Lincoln's birth-place—but it does not contain a focusing idea about that subject that could be developed further. In contrast, the second sentence has both a clear subject, *food processor,* and a controlling focus, *indispensable*. When we read this sentence, we naturally expect it to be followed by discussions that will explain why a food processor is in fact indispensable in one's kitchen. What tasks does it do well? Does it save time? Or eliminate waste? Such a topic sentence, with a clearly stated subject and focus, prepares the reader for the direction the paragraph is going to take.

A well-formulated topic sentence offers benefits to the writer as well, by providing a kind of blueprint that directs the development of the rest of the paragraph. Organizing paragraphs around topic sentences in your first draft can help you generate content for each paragraph by focusing your attention on the specific point that you must develop. And keeping your topic sentences in mind as you revise an essay is a way of checking that all the sentences in a paragraph really belong there.

6b

EXERCISE 2

Which of the following could make good topic sentences? Identify the subject and the specific focus of each. How might you develop those sentences into paragraphs?

1. Sunspots, magnetic storms on the sun's surface, are responsible for a number of important phenomena on earth.
2. Acquiring an inexpensive metal detector can be the start of a profitable hobby.
3. In most of the United States, the average annual rainfall is between fifteen and forty-five inches.
4. The second-largest French-speaking city in the world, Montreal is also the largest city in Canada.
5. The most important requirement for a successful long-distance runner is not endurance but concentration.
6. Last July two friends and I went backpacking in the Smoky Mountains.
7. A person suffering from heatstroke must receive correct treatment swiftly.
8. The plays of Hrotswitha von Gandersheim, a tenth-century German nun, often suggest that she had a lively sense of humor.
9. Airmail service in the United States began in 1918.
10. *The Grapes of Wrath* is John Steinbeck's novel about dispossessed Oklahoma farmers.

2. Positioning a topic sentence

Topic sentences are often found near the beginnings of paragraphs. In this position, a topic sentence arouses expectations in the

---

Exercise 2

1. Good topic sentence. Subject: sunspots. Focus: important phenomena.
2. Good topic sentence. Subject: acquiring a metal detector. Focus: profitable.
3. Poor topic sentence: merely states a fact.
4. Poor topic sentence: merely states a fact.
5. Good topic sentence. Subject: requirement for long-distance runner. Focus: concentration.
6. Poor topic sentence: merely states a fact.
7. Good topic sentence. Subject: heatstroke victim. Focus: correct treatment.
8. Good topic sentence. Subject: Hrotswitha von Gandersheim's plays. Focus: indication of her lively sense of humor.
9. Poor topic sentence: merely states a fact.
10. Weak topic sentence. The phrase "dispossessed Oklahoma farmers" does not do enough to focus the paragraph's development.

reader about the paragraph's development. A good paragraph satisfies those expectations with relevant, specific, convincing information.

The following paragraph, from the student essay at the end of Chapter **5**, illustrates the way in which a topic sentence placed at the beginning of a paragraph predicts the paragraph's development.

6b **Topic sentence first**

> *At sixteen, I was still under the authority of my parents, who in my estimation were unreasonably protective.* Every time I left the house, I would have to detail to my mother exactly where I was going, who I was going with, when I would be back. Walking out the door, I was invariably told to wear my seat belt, check for fire escapes, cross only at stoplights, stay clear of public rest rooms, and leave a phone number that I could be reached at. Even at Marcia and Jenny's age I had thought my mother's perpetual admonishments ridiculous, but as a teenager I deeply resented them. Specifically outlining my every plan to my parents was particularly irritating, and I had vowed repeatedly to myself that I would never place such demands on my own children.

The focusing phrase here is *unreasonably protective,* and the writer goes on to develop that idea by clustering specific details from her experience around three main points.

> *Topic sentence:* Parents were unreasonably protective
> - Information she had to provide before leaving house
> - Warnings her parents gave her as she left
> - Her growing resentment as a teenager

Although the beginning of a paragraph is a natural place for focusing our thoughts, there is nothing sacred about starting a paragraph with a topic sentence. A topic sentence may be placed anywhere—after a transitional sentence, in the middle of a paragraph, or at the end as a kind of conclusion. When a topic sentence comes in the middle of a paragraph, it usually links the sentences that precede it with the material that follows it, as in this example.

Topic sentence in middle

> In the Western world, the person is synonymous with an individual inside a skin. And in northern Europe generally, the skin and even the

clothes may be inviolate. You need permission to touch either if you are a stranger. This rule applies in some parts of France, where the mere touching of another person during an argument used to be legally defined as assault. *For the Arab the location of the person in relation to the body is quite different.* The person exists somewhere down inside the body. The ego is not completely hidden, however, because it can be reached very easily with an insult. It is protected from touch but not from words. The dissociation of the body and the ego may explain why the public amputation of a thief's hand is tolerated as standard punishment in Saudi Arabia.

—Edward T. Hall, *The Hidden Dimension*

6b

This paragraph's opening sentences on Western ideas about personhood provide the context for the writer's subsequent explanation of the Arab conception of the person. The topic sentence—the fifth sentence—introduces the writer's main idea, the contrast between Western and Arab attitudes, with the focusing phrase *quite different*. We might outline the development of this paragraph in the following way.

- Western world views "person" and "body" as the same
- Even superficial physical contact may be considered a violation of the person

Topic sentence: Arab conception of "person" is different

- Person is deep inside the body
- Punishment of the body does not threaten the person within

When the topic sentence concludes a paragraph, it usually pulls together sentences that have led up to it. In these cases, the subject and focus of the paragraph are left implied until the reader reaches the topic sentence, as in the following paragraph.

Topic sentence last

Seen from an aeroplane high in the air, even the most gigantic skyscraper is only a tall stone block, a mere sculptural form, not a real building in which people can live. But as the plane descends from the great heights there will be one moment when the buildings change character completely. Suddenly they take on human scale, become houses for human beings like ourselves, not the tiny dolls observed from the heights. This strange transformation takes place at the instant when the contours of the buildings begin to rise above the horizon so that we get a side view of them instead of looking down on them. The buildings pass into a new stage of existence, become architecture in place of neat toys—for *architecture means shapes formed around [people], formed to be lived in, not merely to be seen from the outside.*

—Steen Eiler Rasmussen, *Experiencing Architecture*

This topic sentence could have been placed at the beginning of the paragraph, but by reserving it until the end the writer creates an effective sense of climax. We might outline the paragraph's structure as follows.

- Buildings are merely sculptural forms when viewed from far above
- Buildings become architecture when viewed in human scale, from the side

Topic sentence: Architecture means shapes formed to be lived in by human beings

The practice of constructing a paragraph around a focusing sentence is a useful one, but it's possible for a paragraph to be well unified even though it does not contain an explicit topic sentence. The important thing, though, is that its main idea must be evident to the reader. The following student paragraph, for instance, has no stated topic sentence, but its central idea is still clear.

Implied topic sentence

Classes at the medieval University of Paris began at 5 A.M. First on the agenda were the ordinary lectures, which were the regular and more important lectures. After several ordinary lectures and a short, begrudged lunch hour, students attended extraordinary lectures given in the afternoon. These were supplementary to the ordinary lectures and usually given by a less important teacher, who may not have been more than fourteen or fifteen years old. A student would spend ten or twelve hours a day with his teachers, and then following classes in the late afternoon, he had sports events. But after sports, the day was not over. There was homework, which consisted of copying, recopying, and memorizing notes while the light permitted. Nor was there much of a break. Christmas vacation was about three weeks, and summer vacation was only a month.

If we were to formulate a topic sentence for this paragraph, it might be something like "The long school day at the medieval University of Paris made heavy demands on students." That's the idea clearly implied by the paragraph's development.

> *Implied topic sentence:* Medieval school day made heavy demands
> - Ordinary lectures from 5 A.M. till lunch
> - Extraordinary lectures after lunch
> - Sporting events in late afternoon
> - Tedious homework until darkness fell

6b

As you can see, an implied topic sentence works only when the development of your paragraph leaves no room for doubt about its point. Most of the time, you should probably make an effort to include a topic sentence somewhere in your paragraph, rather than risk leaving your reader uncertain about your main idea.

EXERCISE 3

Identify the topic sentence in each of the following paragraphs. What subject and specific focus does it introduce? How do the rest of the sentences in the paragraph develop that idea?

1.   Violence as a way of achieving racial justice is both impractical and immoral. It is impractical because it is a descending spiral ending in destruction for all. The old law of an eye for an eye leaves everybody blind. It is immoral because it seeks to humiliate the opponent rather than win his understanding; it seeks to annihilate rather than to convert. Violence is immoral because it thrives on hatred rather than love. It destroys community and makes brotherhood impossible. It leaves society in monologue rather than dialogue. Violence ends by defeating itself. It creates bitterness in the survivors and brutality in the destroyers.

   —Martin Luther King, Jr., *Stride toward Freedom*

2.   Commercial interruption is most damaging during that 10 per cent of programming (a charitable estimate) most important to the mind and spirit of a people: news and public affairs, and drama. To many (and among these are network news producers), commercials have no place or business during the vital process of informing the public. There is something obscene about a newscaster pausing to introduce a deodorant or shampoo commercial between the airplane crash and a body count. It is more than an interruption; it tends to

---

Exercise 3

1. The topic sentence is the first sentence. Subject: violence. Focus: impractical and immoral.
2. The topic sentence is the first sentence. Subject: commercial interruption. Focus: most damaging during news and public affairs programming.
3. The topic sentence is a combination of the first two sentences. Subject: Missouri caves and cave dwellers. Focus: not well/many serious problems.
4. The topic sentence is the first sentence. Subject: surgery and writing. Focus: what they have in common. (Selzer uses the topic sentence to state his disagreement with the observation that they have *little* in common.)
5. The topic sentence is the first sentence. Subject: children's attitudes about food. Focus: transformation into a question of self-determination.

reduce news to a form of running entertainment, to smudge the edges of reality by treating death or disaster or diplomacy on the same level as household appliances or a new gasoline.

—Marya Mannes, "The Splitting Image," *Saturday Review*

3.   All is not well for caves or cave dwellers in Missouri. Many serious problems now exist in the effort to preserve caves in their original condition. Casual visitors often turn into vandals, breaking formations and chasing off the easily scared bat populations. In addition, holes and pits on the surface caused by natural cave collapses are being used as dumps, resulting in contamination of water systems in the caves. Another increasingly serious problem is the growing contamination of caves by septic tank drainage. The contamination of Devil's Icebox Cave by septic tanks, for example, has caused national groups such as the Sierra Club to organize a cave preservation program. Finally, the Army Corps of Engineers has been responsible for flooding hundreds of caves with its river-damming projects in the state.

—Scott Stayton, student writer

4.   At first glance, it would appear that surgery and writing have little in common, but I think that is not so. For one thing, they are both sub-celestial arts; as far as I know, the angels disdain to perform either one. In each of them you hold a slender instrument that leaves a trail wherever it is applied. In one, there is the shedding of blood; in the other it is ink that is spilled upon a page. In one, the scalpel is restrained; in the other, the pen is given rein. The surgeon sutures together the tissues of the body to make whole what is sick or injured; the writer sews words into sentences to fashion a new version of human experience. A surgical operation is rather like a short story. You make the incision, rummage around inside for a bit, then stitch up. It has a beginning, a middle and an end. If I were to choose a medical specialist to write a novel, it would be a psychiatrist. They tend to go on and on. And on.

—Richard Selzer, "The Pen and the Scalpel," *New York Times*

5.   Children often transform what should be a matter of nutrition into a question of self-determination. For some youngsters the benevolence of their parents' assertions that carrots are good for you, that they help you see in the dark, is lost in the suspicion that they are

being tricked into tasting something nasty. Distrust flavors the carrots, they *do* taste unpleasant, and the child is even more adamantly opposed to eating them. The parents insist, the child resists, and battle lines are drawn. The issue is no longer whether vegetables are indeed good for you, but whose willpower is to prevail. The ability to sustain her refusal becomes a matter of survival for the child. I recall that the longer I held out, the more I feared that giving in would topple my tower of autonomy. Those who would suggest that my parents simply were not authoritative enough underestimate the depth of my young conviction.

— Susan Young, student writer

6c Adjusting paragraph length

Just as the structure of a paragraph is designed for the reader's benefit, so also the length of a paragraph is determined by its helpfulness to the reader. Indeed, we might say that the appropriate length of a paragraph is directly related to its structure. The key question is always this: *How much evidence do you need to develop the idea in your topic sentence?* Pages consistently cluttered by short, underdeveloped paragraphs scatter the reader's attention and give the impression of a writer unable to think an idea through completely. On the other hand, if too many sentences are combined without paragraph indentations, the reader will have a difficult time isolating the writer's main ideas. Paragraphs that run consistently to more than a page are little better than no paragraphing at all, since they force the reader to do work that is the writer's responsibility.

Ordinarily, then, we might say that a paragraph should be longer than one sentence but shorter than a page. But note that the length of paragraphs varies considerably in different kinds of writing. In formal, scientific, or scholarly writing, paragraphs may be four hundred words or longer. In magazine articles, the average length is below two hundred words. In newspapers, paragraph breaks occur even more frequently—every fifty words or so—in order to maximize white space in the narrow columns of text. If you're in doubt about the length of a paragraph you're working on, ask yourself the following questions about your paragraph's purpose and rhetorical design.

Checklist for Determining Appropriate Paragraph Length

1. What is the main idea in this paragraph?
2. Have I provided enough evidence, detail, or discussion to develop it to my reader's satisfaction?
3. Have I included irrelevant material that should be moved to another paragraph or discarded?

6c

1.   Using a short paragraph for emphasis

Occasionally, you may want to use a very short paragraph to call attention to an important shift in the line of thought or to emphasize a crucial point. Such paragraphs are effective but should be used carefully and sparingly. Notice in the following example that the student might have joined his short paragraph to either of the others. He chose instead to make the two sentences into a separate transitional paragraph and thus to stress the importance of his early training and the shock he was to receive.

Brief transitional paragraph for emphasis

. . . I know from personal experience the truth of Erich Fromm's criticism that the American male is forced to repress his feelings. Our society does tend to suspect emotional outbursts in a man as signs of "abnormality." From childhood onward, I was taught to "control" my emotions. I was told constantly that good little boys don't cry; they act like big strong men. The little boy who fell off his tricycle and got up with a smile was admired and recommended as a model to be emulated by the rest of the tricycle set. Nor were feelings of pain the only emotion I was encouraged to suppress. Anger, hostility, envy, and melancholy were all taboo, and this training was almost impossible to resist.

By the age of thirteen, I was a true believer in this Spartan code. It was at this age that I was first startled into doubting it.

My uncle had been ill but had kept this fact secret from . . .

2.   Paragraphing dialogue

In a narrative, any direct quotation, together with the rest of a sentence of which it is a part, is paragraphed separately. The reason for this convention is to make immediately clear to the reader the change of speaker.

Speakers paragraphed separately

> "But 'glory' doesn't mean 'a nice knock-down argument,'" Alice objected.
> "When *I* use a word," Humpty Dumpty said, in a rather scornful tone, "it means what I choose it to mean—neither more nor less."
> "The question is," said Alice, "whether you *can* make words mean so many different things."
> "The question is," said Humpty Dumpty, "which is to be master—that's all."
>
> —Lewis Carroll, *Through the Looking-Glass*

6c

The same convention is usually observed in cases where the speaker is not named each time.

Unidentified speakers paragraphed separately

> "Would you like to go to South America, Jake?" he asked.
> "No."
> "Why not?"
> "I don't know. I never wanted to go. Too expensive. You can see all the South Americans you want in Paris anyway."
> "They're not the real South Americans."
> "They look awfully real to me."
>
> —Ernest Hemingway, *The Sun Also Rises*

However, brief dialogue that is closely related to the narration may be included within a paragraph.

Short dialogue included in paragraph

> Now and then Mr. Bixby called my attention to certain things. Said he, "This is Six-Mile Point." I assented. It was pleasant enough information but I could not see the bearing of it. I was not conscious that it was a matter of any interest to me. Another time he said, "This is Nine-Mile Point." Later he said, "This is Twelve-Mile Point." They were all about level with the water's edge; they all looked alike to me; they were monotonously unpicturesque. I hoped Mr. Bixby would change the subject.
>
> —Mark Twain, "Old Times on the Mississippi"

6d Controlling paragraphs within an essay

Rarely are we called on to write a single, isolated paragraph. More often, we have to be able to develop and control individual paragraphs in the context of a longer composition. In the following essay, the student writer demonstrates just such a firm sense of paragraph unity and appropriate paragraph length. Considered separately, each paragraph here makes a clear point, developed with specific details that interest and satisfy us. But the paragraphs of this essay also fit together neatly, leading us as readers through the writer's experiences and his reflections on them. The result is an effective piece of writing, well organized and complete. (The paragraphs in this essay have been numbered for easy reference in Exercise 4.)

I Surrendered

1.   Social order, it is said, can only be maintained through the restriction and prohibition of our often whimsical impulses (taking off from school or work, swimming nude, indulging in casual sex). Thus we find ourselves inhibited by a civilization that was supposed to ensure our well-being. Parents, public opinion, and the law condition us to keep the lid tightly clamped on our drives for free and outward expression of inner needs: we are made to stop and evaluate our actions and thoughts and to feel guilty when they are not acceptable. And because this guilt often makes us tense and ill at ease, we give up and submit. This guilt is what I understand Freud to be describing in *Civilization and Its Discontents,* and it is what I learned to be a melancholy truth when I went hitchhiking up the West Coast with my sleeping bag and thoughts of being free to do what I wanted.

2.   My hitchhiking trip with a white friend from Long Beach to Canada was plagued by social pressure even before it began. Two weeks before we started, reports over the news about hitchhikers being axed in their sleeping bags, as well as drivers being robbed, beaten, or killed, did not make our trip sound like a good idea to my family. My family was also concerned that reports like these make drivers hesitant to stop for anyone unless they have a gun under the seat. That was just the beginning, though. I could have handled the fears others had for me, but the guilt I was made to feel was harder to cope with.

Exercise 4 (page 116)

Note that this exercise links the material on essay organization in Chapter **5** with the information about paragraphs in this chapter.

1. The last two sentences of the introductory paragraph constitute Reece's thesis; the subject is hitchhiking up the West Coast, and the restricting idea is experiencing guilt that makes us "give up and submit."
2. Paragraph 3 develops the idea of guilt, mentioned in the last sentence of paragraph 2. Note the other transitional markers between paragraphs in the essay: *also* at the start of paragraph 4; the phrase *that episode* at the start of paragraph 6.
3. Though both paragraphs involve Reece's feelings of guilt after talking with his brother-in-law, the first deals with dangers to hitchhikers in general, whereas the second focuses on the problems that Reece might face because he is black.

3.   My brother-in-law and I had a long discussion about the dangers of hitchhiking. The list was a frightening one that included the possibility I might be hassled and jailed by the police or be robbed and stranded. I felt quite guilty about running off and frolicking around while everyone worried about me, and this guilt took some of the pleasure—the thrill, day-to-day suspense, and excitement—out of the trip. Instead, it made me wary and insecure.

6d

4.   My brother-in-law and I also discussed the fact that very few blacks hitchhike in the live-on-the-road manner I was about to, which means sleeping in forests, communes, or freeway shrubbery, or going into strange towns and meeting all kinds of people. He suggested that if tension in any given situation forced a serious racial confrontation, my friend would surely turn to the safe side and against me. This kept me wondering all through the trip, and to my dismay, kept me looking for hints of racism in him. My new suspicions cast a shadow over the trip and added to the guilt I was already feeling.

5.   Hitchhiking is illegal in California, but the law is not usually enforced if the hitchhikers stay on the curb. We carefully heeded this policy and had no problems at all until just south of San Luis Obispo, where we were searched for weapons. There we were insulted by a pair of California Highway Patrol officers while they went over us. Among the many insults was the one directed at me, asking me who I was going to rape next. But, knowing how public opinion would side with the police if we retaliated, we kept our mouths closed. We knew that if the police reported subduing a couple of wandering, violent deadbeats, the stereotype of the shiftless young bum begging for food would justify the police in the public's view and set people's minds at ease. So we checked our natural impulse to fight back, but we were angry with ourselves for having to do so. We felt guilty for not standing up for our rights.

6.   Even with that episode behind us, the rest of the trip didn't bring me the sense of freedom I'd hoped for. The possible presence of dope in the cars of the young people who picked us up made me uneasy. But not my friend. He indulged heavily in marijuana all the way up the coast whenever he could get some. I knew that if we were arrested for dope it would go on my record, damage my chances in the future, and hurt my family badly. One morning, near Eureka, California, my friend and another hiker who joined up with us smoked as much

---

4. Paragraph 5: "We . . . had no problems at all until just south of San Luis Obispo, where we were searched for weapons." Paragraph 6: "The rest of the trip didn't bring me the sense of freedom I'd hoped for."
5. The idea of surrender, introduced in Reece's thesis statement, also closes the essay.

marijuana as they could hold. I was fearful that a band of night-roaming vigilantes would swarm on us and take us away. Later, in Canada, I felt guilty the very first time I got in line for a feed-in. I was self-conscious because the food was paid for by Canadian taxpayers and was meant for needy people. We had enough money to buy food.

7.   It now seems that everything we did, beginning with the very thought of hitchhiking, was meant to prove we weren't as trapped as the people we left behind. But when it came to the wild, free expression of inner drives, I couldn't throw off the wet blanket of society. I couldn't even go skinny-dipping in the Russian River because there were people around and I was afraid of what they might think if I stripped. We loved Canada and its forests, but we came back. Even though the air and water were like nectar in comparison to those of Los Angeles, we returned to the smog and noise and people. We discarded the forests, rivers, and meadows for the benefits and security of our social surroundings. I surrendered.

—Samuel Reece, student writer

For further information about maintaining coherence between paragraphs, see **11b**.

EXERCISE 4

Reread Samuel Reece's essay "I Surrendered" (above) and consider the following questions.

1. What is Reece's thesis statement?
2. How do the final sentences of paragraph 2 provide a transition to paragraph 3?
3. Why has Reece separated paragraphs 3 and 4, both of which involve his brother-in-law's advice?
4. What is the topic sentence in paragraph 5? In paragraph 6? How does Reece develop each of these topic sentences?
5. How does Reece link his concluding paragraph with his introduction?

For Further Reading

Becker, A. L. "A Tagmemic Approach to Paragraph Analysis." *College Composition and Communication* 16 (1965): 237–42.

Braddock, Richard. "The Frequency and Placement of Topic Sentences in Expository Prose." *Research in the Teaching of English* 8 (1974): 287–302.

Christensen, Francis. "A Generative Rhetoric of the Paragraph." *College Composition and Communication* 16 (1965): 144–56.

Eden, Rick, and Ruth Mitchell. "Paragraphing for the Reader." *College Composition and Communication* 37 (1986): 416–30.

Popken, Randall L. "A Study of Topic Sentence Use in Academic Writing." *Written Communication* 4 (1987): 208–28.

Rogers, Paul, Jr. "A Discourse-Centered Rhetoric of the Paragraph." *College Composition and Communication* 17 (1966): 2–11.

7 *Developing Paragraphs*

What happens in a paragraph—the form that its contents assume—is often determined by the subject itself. If you are writing out a description of an automobile accident for your insurance company, you will probably let chronological order dictate the structure of your material (signaled left turn, waited for traffic light to change, started across intersection, suddenly saw other car coming through red light). On the other hand, if you are discussing two political candidates in your school newspaper, you might find your paragraphs taking shape around comparisons of the candidates' positions on several key issues. In short, in words that the great American architect Louis Sullivan wrote a century ago, "Form follows function."

Sometimes, however, the subject you are writing about may not arrange itself on your page with inevitable clarity and logic. For these occasions, it's useful to be acquainted with a number of basic patterns of paragraph development. Readers unconsciously expect to be able to discern such patterns and may be confused by a paragraph whose sentences seem to be pointed in no clear direction. Controlling patterns of paragraph development, therefore, is another way of making your writing more effective by satisfying your readers' expectations.

Before we consider some widely used methods of paragraph development, though, a caution and a hint. The important caution to keep in mind about these strategies is that, in actual practice, they are rarely used independently of one another. Instead, they naturally and inevitably overlap; development by examples, for instance, also implies development by detail. Thus, you should probably regard these patterns less as a set of alternatives than as a master list of techniques to select from and combine freely.

117

As the introduction to this chapter suggests, paragraph development, like paragraph structure, is essentially a rhetorical concern: we organize the material in paragraphs so that our readers will find their way from one key idea to the next. Ultimately, that clear progression of ideas is more important to the success of a paragraph than adherence to any one of the methods of paragraph development described in this chapter—a point emphasized by the schematic outline that accompanies each sample paragraph in this chapter.

Indeed, students should be reminded that paragraphs developed by a single method of development are the exception rather than the rule. More often, as this chapter points out, paragraphs illustrate a combination of methods. Still, knowledge of and practice with these various methods is a first step toward writing paragraphs that are at once more complex and more typical of modern prose.

> QUICK REFERENCE: *Methods of Paragraph Development*
>
> Because in actual practice the methods of paragraph development often overlap, consider these patterns not as alternatives but as a repertoire of techniques to select from and combine freely.
>
> • Specific details
> • Narration (chronological order)
> • Examples
> • Definition
> • Classification
> • Comparison or contrast
> • Analogy
> • Cause and effect

The hint: you should consider these approaches not simply as ways of *arranging* the contents of a paragraph, but also as ways of *generating* content both for paragraphs and for entire essays. In this sense, these strategies resemble the methods of discovering ideas that we discussed in Chapter **2** (indeed, you'll probably recognize occasional overlap with the structured methods of discovery in **2b**). Phrased as questions, they can help you reveal new and potentially interesting angles of your subject to write about.

7a Development by specific details

A paragraph lacking specific details may strike a reader as dull and uninspired, even though its central idea is clear. Part of every writer's obligation is to supply the details necessary to support a paragraph's main idea. As a writer, you need to be able to distinguish between paragraphs that make effective use of details and paragraphs that only seem to be developed specifically, but in reality offer little precise information that would move a reader to accept your argument or share your perspective.

> ## Using the Methods of Paragraph Development as Methods of Discovering Ideas
>
> - With what specific details can I describe X?
> - In what order did the events surrounding X occur?
> - What examples of X do I have?
> - How can I define X?
> - How can I classify types of X?
> - What components or examples of X can I compare?
> - What is X analogous to?
> - What are the causes and consequences of X?

7a

Writing with specific details begins with recalling as precisely as possible the event to be described and then re-creating the taste, touch, sound, and sight with carefully chosen words. In the following paragraph, for example, the writer effectively uses striking visual and auditory details to support the assertion in his topic sentence—that nature programs on television offer "a clean and well-lighted simultaneity . . . of the things you'd never see in a thousand walks in the wild."

There's a driving rainstorm tonight, the city is completely obscured from view, and I'm watching a show about the rain forest. My TV screen is a brilliant canvas of bright red beads set into a field of multicolored triangles: a close-up of red mites on the back of a harlequin beetle. Now, over surreal horizons of harlequin thorax, come tiny scorpions preying upon the mites. Paper wasps, meanwhile, are spitting rainwater off of their nest and cooling their brood with wing pulsations. A poison-arrow frog is dumping its tadpoles into a droplet of water at the base of a bromeliad. Golden toads are courting in misty pools atop the one mountain in this world where they can be found. There's a sudden wide shot of a night sky with a white-gold moon that gives way now to the luminous orb of a leaf toad's eye, and then a shocking, screen-size, green triangle: the head of a katydid. I can hear its chewing, and then the soft paddings across dead leaves of an approaching tarantula. The tarantula pounces. I listen to its pincers piercing the waxen abdomen of the katydid. "We soon get through with Nature," Thoreau once noted in his journals. "She excites an expectation which she cannot satisfy." Thus, the modern TV nature show: a clean and well-lighted simultaneity of the unseen; of the things you'd never see in a thousand walks in the wild.

— Charles Siebert, "The Artifice of the Natural," *Harper's*

- Red mites on the back of a harlequin beetle
- Paper wasps spitting rainwater off of their nest
- Poison-arrow frog at the base of a bromeliad
- Golden toads courting in misty pools
- Luminous orb of a leaf toad's eye
- Shocking green triangular head of a katydid
- Soft paddings of an approaching tarantula

Topic sentence: The TV nature show offers a clean and well-lighted simultaneity of the unseen

Of course, specific details in a paragraph must be relevant to the writer's purpose. The objective is not to provide an exhaustive inventory of all possible details but to select the most vivid and most representative ones. The details in the following paragraph, for example, are probably only a few of those that the writer could have included to describe the campus building that he taught in, but because they are so specific and so well chosen, they effectively convey the excitement he sensed there.

The thing that most struck me during my first months in Campbell Hall was the level and variety of activity, the vibrancy of the place. The walls were covered with posters, flyers, and articles clipped from the newspaper: a multicolored collage of announcements from the Ethnic Studies Centers, the EOP staff, and politically active students and faculty. There were notices about American Indian dancers and Japanese watercolors and forums on labor history—one poster with a photograph of Filipino cannery workers, another with black women bent before machines in a textile mill. There were calls for legal defense funds and vigils for justice. There was news about military atrocities in Chile, CIA murders in Africa, the uprooting of the American Indian. A slow walk down the hall provided an education in culture and politics disconnected from the lives of most Americans, a reminder of culture denied, of the brazenness of power.

— Mike Rose, *Lives on the Boundary*

Topic sentence: The most striking aspect of Campbell Hall was the level and variety of activity

- Walls covered with posters, flyers, and newspaper articles
  - Notices about American Indian dancers, Japanese watercolors, forums on labor history
  - Calls for legal defense funds and vigils for justice
  - News about military atrocities, CIA murders, uprooting of the American Indian

7b

EXERCISE 1

Write two different paragraphs on one of the topics below. In the first, make the diction as vague and general as you can. In your second paragraph on the subject, substitute specific details to make your description vivid and interesting.

1. A public swimming pool on a hot day
2. A fair or carnival
3. A college dining room at noon
4. The street or road you grew up on
5. A subway or bus late at night

EXERCISE 2

Using Mike Rose's description of Campbell Hall as a model, write a paragraph that describes a place you know well. Make sure that all the details in your paragraph contribute to creating a single, dominant impression.

7b Development by narration

Narrating events—reporting what happened, and in what sequence—is part of our daily interaction with other people. Effective written narration depends on the exact selection of details, arranged in such a way that a reader can easily follow the order of the events in question.

Sometimes a paragraph of narration includes a topic sentence that focuses its development around a specific idea. In the following paragraph, for example, the focusing word is *grandiose*.

In fourth grade I embarked upon a grandiose reading program. "Give me the names of important books," I would say to startled teachers. They

Exercises 1–9

As they do the first nine exercises, students should be aware that they are practicing methods that they will normally use in conjunction with one another.

soon found out that I had in mind "adult books." I ignored their suggestion of anything I suspected was written for children. (Not until I was in college, as a result, did I read *Huckleberry Finn* or *Alice's Adventures in Wonderland*.) Instead, I read *The Scarlet Letter* and Franklin's *Autobiography*. And whatever I read I read for extra credit. Each time I finished a book, I reported the achievement to a teacher and basked in the praise my effort earned. Despite my best efforts, however, there seemed to be more and more books I needed to read. At the library I would literally tremble as I came upon whole shelves of books I hadn't read.

—Richard Rodriguez, *Hunger of Memory*

Topic sentence: I embarked upon a grandiose reading program
- Startled teachers by requesting important books
- Refused to read anything written for children
- Reported achievements and basked in praise
- Trembled at shelves of books remaining to be read

But a paragraph developed by narration doesn't always need a thematic focus, or even a topic sentence, to hold it together. Chronology alone may be sufficient. The paragraph below, describing the Battle of Hastings between King Harold of England and William of Normandy in 1066, has no topic sentence; its unity and coherence arise from the precise time markers that the writer has inserted to orient us to the sequence of events.

Bringing his troops south again with all possible speed, Harold arrived in London on October 6. Five days later, having collected all the reinforcements he could muster under his banner, he marched south for the Sussex Downs, where he hoped to take William by surprise and to cut him off from his ships, which lay at anchor at Hastings. As it happened, it was Harold who was caught by surprise. Riding out of Hastings early on the morning of October 14, William and his knights came in sight of Harold's infantry near Telham Hill at nine o'clock. The Normans advanced on the attack immediately, before the small English army was even drawn up in battle array. It was a hard-fought battle, in which the Normans had to throw in one mounted attack after another against the English front, but at the end of the day Harold was killed, and his remaining followers fled from the field.

—Christopher Hibbert, *Tower of London*

[No topic sentence]

- October 6: Harold arrived in London
- Five days later: marched south toward Sussex Downs
- October 14, nine o'clock: surprised by William and his knights near Telham Hill
- At end of day: killed after hard-fought battle

EXERCISE 3

Write a paragraph developed by narration on one of the subjects below, or another subject of your choice. Begin by listing points you might include and, if possible, formulating a topic sentence.

1. The process by which you selected your college or university
2. The way you usually go about writing a paper
3. The stages in which your friendship with another person developed
4. The last time you found yourself in an embarrassing situation
5. The last time you were pleased with what you had accomplished

7c   Development by examples

An example is a member of a larger class or category, chosen to illustrate the class to which it belongs. Typically, the topic sentence of a paragraph developed by examples introduces the class that the writer wishes to develop. In this paragraph, for example, the class to be illustrated is "sources of contaminants."

Many contaminants contribute to air pollution inside offices, and they have a variety of sources. The worst offender, for smokers and nonsmokers alike, is ambient cigarette smoke, which contains benzene, formaldehyde and other carcinogens. Wet-process copiers give off odorless hydrocarbons, causing fatigue and skin irritations. Dry-process copiers leak ozone, an irritant to the eyes and respiratory tract. Computer screens exude low levels of radiation.

— Susan Gilbert, "Hazards of the Toxic Office," *Science Digest*

Topic sentence: Contaminants in office air have a variety of sources

- Cigarette smoke contains benzene, formaldehyde, and other carcinogens
- Wet-process copiers give off odorless hydrocarbons

- Dry-process copiers leak ozone
- Computer screens exude radiation

The four sources of office air pollution mentioned here are not all that could be cited. Rather, they are typical members of the class, presumably selected in this case because of their prevalence and importance.

Often examples are introduced in a paragraph with the transitions *for example* or *for instance*. But even without these transitional markers, the structure of a paragraph developed by examples should be evident to a reader if the category that the examples illustrate is clearly stated at the outset. In the following paragraph, the illustrated category is "remedies [that] meet the test of modern scientific medicine."

> Undoubtedly many of the witch-healers' remedies were purely magical, such as the use of amulets and charms, but others meet the test of modern scientific medicine. They had effective painkillers, digestive aids, and anti-inflammatory agents. They used ergot for the pain of labor at a time when the Church held that pain in labor was the Lord's just punishment for Eve's original sin. Ergot derivatives are still used today to hasten labor and aid in the recovery from childbirth. Belladonna—still used today as an antispasmodic—was used by the witch-healers to inhibit uterine contractions when miscarriage threatened. Digitalis, still an important drug in treating heart ailments, is said to have been discovered by an English witch.
>
> —Barbara Ehrenreich and Deirdre English, *For Her Own Good: 150 Years of the Experts' Advice to Women*

Topic sentence: Some witch-healers' remedies meet the test of modern scientific medicine

- Ergot used for the pain of labor
- Belladonna used to prevent miscarriage
- Digitalis discovered by an English witch

EXERCISE 4

Write a paragraph developed by examples on one of the subjects below, or another subject of your choice. Begin by listing points you might include and formulating a topic sentence.

1. The sameness of fast-food restaurants
2. A new trend in popular music

3. Lack of understanding among people
4. A problem in our society
5. Creativity

7d   Development by definition

In informal logic, definition involves referring a term to a general class of related elements (its genus) and then distinguishing it from others in that class. Before examining definition as a method of paragraph development, we should perhaps consider this basic use of the term.

1. Simple definition

To take a simple example, we would begin defining a pen by classifying it as a "writing instrument." However, since the class "writing instrument" also includes a number of other elements—pencils, felt markers, typewriters, to name just a few—we would have to go one step further and differentiate it from these and other members of the class. A pen, we might therefore continue, is "a writing instrument that makes use of a hard point and a colored fluid."

Term	Class	Differentiation
pen	writing instrument	makes use of a hard point and colored fluid
pencil	writing instrument	with a core of solid-state material like graphite inside a wooden or plastic case

A description of an object can include all kinds of specific details—the pencil has a chewed end and is coated with yellow paint embossed with the motto "Quinn's Lumber Yard"—but these details are irrelevant to the definition of the term. Similarly, examples do not by themselves constitute a definition, although they may help to clarify one. To say that a Dixon Ticonderoga No. 2 Soft is an example of a pencil is not the same as specifying what the meaning of the term *pencil* is.

You may be able to define an unfamiliar term in a sentence by *apposition,* that is, by following the term with a word or phrase that clarifies its meaning.

Simple definition by apposition

7d

The x-ray showed a crack in the *tibia,* or *shinbone.*

Please analyze the importance of the *denouement —the final unraveling or outcome of the plot—* in *Lord Jim.*

Tonight the moon will be in *apogee,* that is, *at the point in its orbit farthest from the earth.*

2. Extended definition

When you are dealing with complex terms or terms used in a special sense, you may have to devote a paragraph or more to definition. The following student paragraph illustrates such an *extended definition.* The writer first classifies Sarah Woodruff and Clarissa Dalloway as belonging to the class of people whom she labels "heroic." Then, to differentiate her subjects' heroism from that of others in the class, she rejects one set of meanings for the term (control and domination) and presents another (sensitivity, endurance, independence). She closes the paragraph with examples that show how each of her subjects meets this definition of "heroic."

The central characters in John Fowles's *The French Lieutenant's Woman* and Virginia Woolf's *Mrs. Dalloway* are women who embody certain heroic qualities that set them apart from what one character calls "the great niminypiminy flock of women in general." These two women, Sarah Woodruff and Clarissa Dalloway, are not heroic in the traditional masculine, aggressive sense of the word. They do not seek to control or to dominate but to cultivate a sensitivity, to endure, and to remain free of masculine narrow-mindedness. They possess a power that allows them to remain open to the compelling vitality of life. Their heroism is their ability to be responsive to reality, to feel even if it entails suffering and uncertainty; and this heroism spurs others on to live in the presence of life, with all its beauty and terror. Sarah is a free woman, and through her sensitivity, forbearance, and courage, she liberates Charles, a man caught in the petrifying forces of Victorian society, preoccupied with duty and piety.

Clarissa Dalloway's radiant, vital presence at her party, a ritual of community, helps to liberate her guests from their shells of individual solitude and memory. It is in this sense and these ways that they are heroic.

Topic sentence: Sarah Woodruff and Clarissa Dalloway embody heroic qualities

- Not in the masculine, aggressive sense of the word
- But in their sensitivity and openness to the compelling vitality of life
  - Sarah Woodruff liberates Charles from duty and piety
  - Clarissa Dalloway liberates party guests from shells of solitude and memory

7d

3. Guidelines for definitions

A few rules apply to the writing of all definitions, simple and extended. First, avoid circular definitions, that is, the use of the term being defined in the definition itself. "Democracy is the democratic process" and "An astronomer is one who studies astronomy" are both circular definitions. When words are defined in terms of themselves, no one's understanding is improved.

Second, avoid definitions composed of long lists of synonyms. When a paragraph begins, "By education, I mean to give knowledge, develop character, improve taste, draw out, train, lead," the readers know they are in for the shotgun treatment. The writer has indiscriminately blasted a load of abstract items at them, hoping one will hit. Precision and thoughtfulness are more important to a good definition than sheer volume.

Third, avoid loaded definitions, definitions that rely on evocative or inflammatory language. Their purpose is usually emotional impact rather than clarity. The negative phrasing of a definition like "Euthanasia is the outright murder of a helpless human being" makes the writer's bias unmistakable. Conversely, "By euthanasia I mean merciful intervention in another human being's suffering" is a definition heavy with positive suggestions. Such judgments—for that is what they are—are sometimes used for powerful effect in persuasion but they do not lead toward clarification if offered as definitions.

EXERCISE **5**

Write a paragraph developed by definition on one of the subjects below, or another subject of your choice. Begin by listing points you might include and formulating a topic sentence.

7e

1. Satisfaction
2. Commitment
3. Masculinity
4. Femininity
5. Concern for others

6. Propaganda
7. Caution
8. Neatness
9. Challenge
10. Anxiety

7e Development by classification

A writer using classification to develop a paragraph enumerates and describes the main divisions of a subject, either for clarification or as an introduction to further discussion. Underlying classification is the notion that the elements of any large group—classic cars, college students, home computers—can be divided into a number of subgroups ("There are three basic types of X"), and that the classification will better help us understand the category as a whole. In the following paragraph, for example, the noted anthropologist Margaret Mead uses classification to lead us to a new perspective on the concept of "culture."

> The distinctions I am making among three different kinds of culture—*postfigurative,* in which children learn primarily from their forebears, *cofigurative,* in which both children and adults learn from their peers, and *prefigurative,* in which adults learn also from their children—are a reflection of the period in which we live. Primitive societies and small religious and ideological enclaves are primarily postfigurative, deriving authority from the past. Great civilizations, which necessarily have developed techniques for incorporating change, characteristically make use of some form of cofigurative learning from peers, playmates, fellow students, and fellow apprentices. We are now entering a period, new in history, in which the young are taking on new authority in their prefigurative apprehension of the still unknown future.
>
> —Margaret Mead, *Culture and Commitment*

Topic sentence: Cultures may be divided into three types
  • In postfigurative cultures, authority derives from the past
  • In cofigurative cultures, learning is exchanged among peers

- In prefigurative cultures, the young apprehend a still unknown future

Mead's paragraph illustrates a number of the principles of classification. First, a classification makes sense only if the things being classified are grouped according to some clearly understood principle or feature. For ease in record keeping, a college typically classifies its students according to a number of different principles: year of study, major, place of residence (dormitory, fraternity/sorority house, off-campus apartment, parents' home, etc.), to name just a few. Such classifications provide a useful means of organizing data, but a classification is usually worth writing about at length only if it also helps us understand something more fully or more clearly. Margaret Mead classifies cultures according to the sources of their members' education, and by doing so she gives us an important new perspective on some differences between our own culture and others that have preceded us.

The second feature of a successful classification is that it is exhaustive; that is, all the members of the larger group must fit into one or another of the categories of the classification. A college's students could not be classified sensibly as history majors, psychology majors, and music majors unless the college offered only these three fields of study. The three categories in Mead's paragraph illustrate the exhaustiveness necessary to a successful classification: societies are either postfigurative, cofigurative, or prefigurative; there are no other possibilities.

You routinely use classification every time you sort your laundry, plan a shopping trip, or organize the papers on your desk. Classification also becomes an important pattern of organization for writing when it helps you lead your readers to a new understanding of a complex subject.

7e

EXERCISE **6**

Write a paragraph developed by classification on one of the subjects below, or another of your choice. Begin by listing points you might include and formulating a topic sentence.

1. Relatives
2. Summer jobs
3. Extracurricular activities

4. Desires
5. Decisions

7f Development by comparison or contrast

When we wish to point out the similarities or differences between two subjects, comparison or contrast is the logical method of development. The writer of an effective comparison/contrast paragraph indicates at the start the two subjects that will be treated and organizes the details related to each in a way that is easy for the reader to follow.

1. Alternating comparison

Comparisons are usually structured in one of two basic ways. In the first, known as an *alternating comparison,* the writer switches back and forth between two subjects throughout the paragraph, creating for the reader a point-by-point comparison based on specific aspects of the two subjects. The writer of the following paragraph, for instance, uses an alternating structure to compare books and films.

> There are other ways in which our freedom of choice is more limited with respect to film. While reading a book, we can imagine things quite freely even within the limits set by the description of the writer. Before *Gone with the Wind* was adapted to film, readers could picture Rhett Butler however they wished, although presumably basing that picture on the descriptions provided by Margaret Mitchell. But from the release of that movie on, Rhett Butler will always look like Clark Gable; indeed, that will be hardly less so even for readers who have never seen the film, so famous has that portrayal become. When we read Mary Shelley's novel *Frankenstein,* we may or may not be able to overcome the visual image imposed by all the movie *Frankenstein* monsters. But when we see the film *Frankenstein,* it is impossible for us to overcome the visual image; that is all there is, it is right in front of us, and we cannot make it any different. Moreover, a film can only show us what can be shown; the eye can only see what can be seen by the eye, a limitation not shared by the mind's eye.
>
> —Morris Beja, *Film and Literature: An Introduction*

Topic sentence: Film limits our imagination more than books do

- Book version of *Gone with the Wind* allowed readers to picture Rhett Butler however they wished

- Film version of *Gone with the Wind* has forever linked Rhett Butler and Clark Gable
- Book version of *Frankenstein* may enable us to create our own visual image of the monster
- Film version of *Frankenstein* limits our imagination to the image on the screen

The first two sentences in this paragraph indicate that a comparison between films and books is to follow, and the words *more limited* and *imagine* specify the basis of the comparison. Beja alternates between books and films in developing the rest of the paragraph because his point—that films impose limitations on the imagination that books do not—can best be illustrated by juxtaposing specific books and their film adaptations.

7f

2. Divided comparison

In the second type of comparison, called *divided comparison,* a writer deals fully with the first subject before turning to the second, thereby dividing the paragraph approximately in half. This approach works well when the subjects cannot be compared on a point-by-point basis and the writer is more interested in describing each at length. In the following divided comparison, the beginning of a longer paragraph, E. B. White reflects on one of the changes that have occurred at his favorite lake since he visited the place as a boy.

> Peace and goodness and jollity. The only thing that was wrong now, really, was the sound of the place, an unfamiliar nervous sound of the outboard motors. This was the note that jarred, the one thing that would sometimes break the illusion and set the years moving. In those other summertimes all motors were inboard; and when they were at a little distance, the noise they made was a sedative, an ingredient of summer sleep. They were one-cylinder and two-cylinder engines, and some were make-and-break and some were jump-spark, but they all made a sleepy sound across the lake. The one-lungers throbbed and fluttered, and the twin-cylinder ones purred and purred, and that was a quiet sound, too. But now the campers all had outboards. In the daytime, in the hot mornings, these motors made a petulant, irritable sound; at night, in the still evening when the afterglow lit the water, they whined about one's ears like mosquitoes. . . .
>
> —E. B. White, "Once More to the Lake," *Collected Essays*

[Implied topic sentence: The new outboard motors were less agreeable than the earlier inboard ones]

- Inboard motors
  - Made a sleepy sound
  - Throbbed, fluttered, purred
- Outboard motors
  - Made a petulant, irritable sound
  - Whined like mosquitoes

7g

Although this paragraph lacks an explicit topic sentence, White's opening sentences introduce the subject of the paragraph, outboard motors, and clearly suggest the comparison that is to follow ("only thing that was wrong now," "unfamiliar nervous sound"). Structurally, the paragraph hinges on the transition *but* at the beginning of the seventh sentence, which divides it into two parts, the first describing the agreeable sounds of the old inboard motors, the second expressing White's mild annoyance with the newer and noisier outboards.

EXERCISE 7

Write a paragraph developed by comparison or contrast on one of the subjects below, or another of your choice. Begin by listing points you might include and formulating a topic sentence.

1. Discussing and arguing
2. Two close friends
3. Photography and painting
4. High-school and college computer courses
5. Yourself and your brother or sister

7g Development by analogy

One special type of comparison is analogy, a comparison between two essentially unlike things, one familiar to the reader, the other unfamiliar. As a method of illustration, a clever analogy can sometimes make a difficult concept easier to understand. In the following student paragraph, for example, the writer was faced with the problem of showing how the characters in William Faulkner's short story "Spotted Horses" could continue to admire and tolerate a man who continually fleeced them. To solve this problem, the student used the apt analogy of a game of pool with Willie Hoppe, for many years the world champion.

"That Flem Snopes," says the narrator. "I be dog if he ain't a case now." The townspeople had respect for a good horse trader and Flem Snopes was that. Since money was of grotesque importance to these people who had to dig for every penny, they admired a man who could come by it easily and cleverly. Ironically, when Flem skinned someone of his last nickel and kept the fact to himself, the people would interpret Flem's silence as sheer modesty, while the victim laughed off as hopeless any thought of retribution. Their admiration for and toleration of Flem is not hard to understand. It was like a game of pool in which you lose so decisively to Willie Hoppe that you feel no bitterness—merely a sense of pride and awe at having played the master at all. After Willie has beaten you and quietly taken off the stakes, you admit sheepishly to others you were licked before you started and put the cue back on the rack instead of taking it into some dark alley to wait for Willie. Most people didn't even try to beat the time-honored master, Flem Snopes, at his game of swindling.

- Townspeople admired Flem's ability to acquire money so easily
- His victims laughed off any thought of retribution

Topic sentence: The people's admiration for and toleration of Flem was like the attitude of someone who had lost a game of pool to Willie Hoppe

- You feel pride and awe at having played the master at all
- You admit sheepishly that you were licked before you started

Professional writers often use analogy to make difficult technical or abstract ideas accessible to the average reader, and they take care, while developing their paragraphs, to be sure that the readers regard the analogies as illustrations, not proofs. In developing the following paragraph on theories of gravitation, for example, Lincoln Barnett refers to his analogy as "this little fable."

The distinction between Newton's and Einstein's ideas about gravitation has sometimes been illustrated by picturing a little boy playing marbles in a city lot. The ground is very uneven. An observer in an office ten stories above the street would not be able to see these irregularities in the ground. Noticing that the marbles appear to avoid some sections of the

7h

ground and move toward other sections, he might assume that a [semi-magnetic] "force" was operating which repelled the marbles from certain spots and attracted them toward others. But another observer on the ground would instantly perceive that the path of the marbles was simply governed by the curvature of the field. In this little fable Newton is the upstairs observer who imagines that a "force" is at work, and Einstein is the observer on the ground, who has no reason to make such an assumption. Einstein's gravitational laws, therefore, merely describe the field properties of the space-time continuum. . . .

—Lincoln Barnett, *The Universe and Dr. Einstein*

[Implied topic sentence: The difference between Newton's and Einstein's ideas about gravity is like the difference between two perspectives on a game of marbles]

- Newton's perspective: from ten stories up
  - Attributes movement of marbles to unseen forces repelling and attracting them
- Einstein's perspective: at ground level
  - Recognizes that path of marbles is governed by curvature of playing surface

EXERCISE 8

Select a technical concept from a field that you know well (for example, art, auto mechanics, carpentry, chemistry, photography) and explain it in a paragraph that develops an analogy between this technical concept and a concept that would be familiar to a lay audience.

7h Development by cause and effect

In a paragraph developed by cause and effect, a writer stresses the connections between a result or results and the preceding events. Some cause-and-effect paragraphs are primarily persuasive. Their purpose is to make the reader feel the forcefulness of the writer's conclusions, or at least see the grounds for those conclusions. Other cause-and-effect paragraphs are essentially explanatory. They are intended to help a reader understand a necessary relationship between causes and effects.

A cause-and-effect paragraph may begin by stating an effect and then explaining its causes, or it may open with a cause and go on to explore its various effects.

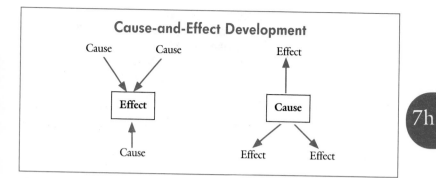

More often, however, causes and effects are intermingled in a subtler way, as in the following paragraph about television's influence on politics.

> While the public and politicians are often blamed for being more concerned with images than with issues, the image bias may be inherent in the way we now get political information. Through television, we come to feel we "know" politicians personally, and our response to them has become similar to our response to friends and lovers. Just as we would not marry someone on the basis of a résumé or a writing sample, so are we now unwilling to choose Presidents merely on the basis of their stands on the issues. We want, instead, to know what they are "really like." However, the current drive toward intimacy with our leaders involves a fundamental paradox. In pursuing our desire to be close to great people or to confirm their greatness through increased exposure, we destroy the distance that enabled them to appear great in the first place.
>
> —Joshua Meyrowitz, "Politics in the Video Eye: Where Have All the Heroes Gone?" *Psychology Today*

Topic sentence: The emphasis on image is inherent in the way we get political information

- Television has made us feel that we "know" politicians personally
  - We want to know more than their stands on issues
  - We want to know what they are "really like"
- This intimacy has replaced the distance that enabled our leaders to appear great

Two pairs of causes and effects are explored in this paragraph. The first sentence states an effect (the emphasis on political "image") whose cause (television's ability to make us feel close to politicians) is explained in the three sentences that follow. The last two sentences introduce a related issue: our desire for intimate knowledge of our leaders, Meyrowitz points out, is a cause whose ultimate effect is the collapse of their appearance of greatness. Such sophisticated analysis demands careful thinking as well as precise control of a paragraph's structure and organization.

EXERCISE 9

Write a paragraph developed by cause-and-effect analysis on one of the subjects below, or another subject of your choice. Begin by listing points you might include and formulating a topic sentence.

1. Why I am frustrated by _____.
2. Why I prefer _____ to _____.
3. Why I usually refuse to _____.
4. Why I am always willing to _____.
5. Why I don't believe _____.

7i A more typical case: combined methods of development

As the start of this chapter indicated, most writers find themselves using a combination of the methods of development. To illustrate this point, the following long paragraph has been separated into segments developed in turn by definition, contrast, and example.

Topic

I never have much confidence in people who talk a great deal about "their image" or "so-and-so's image"; they make me wonder if they even care about what the real thing is.

Definition

By image, I don't mean an accurate copy or truthful likeness. I mean, rather, the same thing that PR types, bureaucrats, and political managers too often mean: a counterfeit, a phony projection, a manipulated picture intended to give the illusion of actuality.

Contrast

In daily situations where actual performances can be judged and experienced firsthand, rather ordinary ones like house painting or plumbing, no one spends much time worrying about the image of the performer. These performers are very different from the rigged ones on TV: either the walls are smoothly rolled and the faucets are fixed, or they aren't; the painter or plumber is competent or not so competent. But in some parts of our society, we are not even supposed to think about the reality as long as the image is "good."

Example

Recently, while watching a talk show, I was struck by one guest, a candidate for office, who kept harping on our need for "the image of strong leadership." The more he dwelled on his opponent's failure to project such an image, the more I wondered what policies the speaker stood for, what he would do if elected. And when he defended his expensive media blitz as part of "getting my image across" to the voters . . .

A good paragraph is a "bounding line" that encloses its own distinct material. The phrase belongs to the artist and poet William Blake: "The great and golden rule of art, as well as of life, is this: That the more distinct, sharp, and wirey the bounding line, the more perfect the work of art. . . . How do we distinguish the oak from the beech . . . one face or countenance from another, but by the bounding line and its infinite inflexions and movements? . . . Leave out this line, and you leave out life itself: all is chaos again."

EXERCISE 10

Choose one of the subjects that you wrote about in the exercises above and write a paragraph on the same subject developed by a different method. For example, if you defined "commitment" (Exercise 5), now try *contrasting* it with a slightly different concept such as "fanaticism." If you classified summer jobs (Exercise 6), now try *describing* a particularly satisfying or distasteful summer job that you have had. If you analyzed the cause of one of your frustrations (Exercise 9), now try *classifying* all the things that

---

Exercise 10

This exercise is much less directed than the first nine; its purpose is to emphasize the important way in which the choice of a method of development can shape the writer's thinking about a subject. Thus, as noted on pages 118–19, the methods of paragraph development presented in this chapter can serve like the questions in **2b** as ways of thinking about one's subject before writing. Readers of Aristotle's *Rhetoric* will of course recognize the traditional methods of paragraph development as an adaptation of the Aristotelian topics.

Exercise 11 (page 138)

Students will probably discover that the overwhelming number of paragraphs they examine combine methods of development or follow no readily discernible method. They should come to see, therefore, that the clarity of

frustrate you. Pay attention to the way in which the choice of a method of development may determine how you think about a subject.

EXERCISE 11

Closely examine the paragraphs of several articles in a magazine such as *The New Yorker, Psychology Today, Rolling Stone,* or *Scientific American*. What methods of paragraph development can you identify? How often do the paragraphs seem to be developed by a combination of methods? Based on your findings, write a paragraph about paragraph development in published writing.

a paragraph depends less on a consistent method of development than, as stated above, on clear connections between the writer's main ideas in the paragraph. For more on paragraph coherence, see **11b.**

For Further Reading

D'Angelo, Frank J. "Topoi and Form in Composition." *The Territory of Language: Linguistics, Stylistics, and the Teaching of Composition*. Ed. Donald A. McQuade. Carbondale: Southern Illinois UP, 1986. 114–22.

Meade, Richard A., and W. Geiger Ellis. "Paragraph Development in the Modern Age of Rhetoric." *English Journal* 59 (1970): 219–26.

Winterowd, W. Ross. "The Grammar of Coherence." *College English* 31 (1970): 828–35.

8 Writing Effective Sentences

W hat characteristics make one sentence "strong," another "weak"? Answering that question brings us to the subject of style in writing. Although the precise sources of a writer's style may be as difficult to isolate as the components of a professional basketball player's style or the elements that characterize the style of service at a fine restaurant, the study of writing style does repay our effort. Through it a writer is able not only to appreciate more fully the mastery of other writers but also to enlarge his or her own repertoire of stylistic skills.

The specific focus of this chapter is sentence style. We begin with three qualities that are always virtues in a sentence—unity, emphasis, and conciseness. From there we will move on to consider strategies that can enhance the rhythm and variety of your sentences.

If concentrating on your sentence style is a new experience for you, you may at first find it difficult to break old habits and to experiment with new patterns. But you cannot increase your stylistic fluency if you are not willing to take a few risks. Like proficiency in all skills, stylistic skill comes with practice and experience. Seek out opportunities to use the following strategies in your prose and you may be surprised by the new confidence and sophistication of your writing.

8a Writing unified sentences

A unified sentence makes its point clearly and unambiguously. This is not to suggest that a unified sentence must be a short one; it may in fact include many details if their relationship to one another and to the sentence's main idea is clear. But a sentence is not a container designed

139

This chapter explains and illustrates some key features of effective sentences—unity, conciseness, variety, and effective coordination and subordination. It also describes the virtues of parallel constructions and the different effects created by cumulative and periodic constructions. Students should be encouraged to view the topics of this chapter as a set of relatively easy stylistic strategies that can give their prose sophistication and self-assurance.

For a separate discussion of grammatical problems at the sentence level—unclear pronoun reference, dangling and misplaced modifiers, split constructions, shifts, and mixed and incomplete constructions—see Chapter **12**, "Revising Sentences."

8a

QUICK REFERENCE: *Strategies for Writing Effective Sentences*

Write unified sentences (8a).	Divide rambling sentences by identifying separate ideas and grouping them into separate sentences. Eliminate less important information. Combine strategies if necessary.
Use coordination and subordination for emphasis (8b).	Identify relationships between sentence elements as equal or unequal. Use coordinating conjunctions to connect equal elements. Use subordinating words to show unequal relationships.
Write concise sentences (8c).	Omit redundant words, phrases, and clauses. Replace nominalizations with more direct verbs. Eliminate wordy connectives and unnecessary repetition. Use the active voice rather than the passive. Avoid unnecessary expletives as sentence openers.
Use parallelism (8d).	Arrange parallel sentence elements—words, phrases, clauses—in parallel grammatical constructions.
Experiment with cumulative and periodic constructions (8e).	A cumulative sentence places the main idea first and elaborates with details and modifiers. A periodic sentence places the main idea at the end for emphatic effect.
Vary sentence length (8f).	Prevent monotony by using a mixture of sentence lengths and structures.
Vary sentence openers (8g).	Try beginning sentences with single modifiers, prepositional phrases, inverted word order, appositives, verbal phrases, absolute phrases, and dependent clauses.

to hold all the available information on a subject. To create unity in a sentence that rambles on from point to point, first isolate the various ideas that the sentence includes and then look for ways to divide the sentence into two sentences or to eliminate less important information.

1. Divide rambling sentences

8a

The simplest way to achieve unity with a rambling sentence is to divide it into two or more separate sentences. The following sentence is a candidate for such revision. As it stands, it tries to cover too much ground, from the first cries for woman's suffrage to the passing of the Nineteenth Amendment.

Ununified sentence Many people objected when the cry for woman's suffrage was first heard, and the opposition continued for decades, until finally men began to realize that women were entitled to the vote, and in 1920 the Nineteenth Amendment was ratified.

Revise this sentence by identifying the separate ideas it contains and grouping them in different sentences.

Sentence 1 Many people objected when the cry for woman's suffrage was first heard.

Sentence 1 The opposition continued for decades.

Sentence 2 Finally men began to realize that women were entitled to the vote.

Sentence 2 In 1920 the Nineteenth Amendment was ratified.

Revised as two sentences Many people objected when the cry for woman's suffrage was first heard, and the opposition continued for decades. Finally, however, men began to realize that women were entitled to the vote, and in 1920 the Nineteenth Amendment was ratified.

In this revised version, the first sentence is now unified around the idea of opposition to woman's suffrage, the second around the granting of suffrage to women.

2.   Eliminate less important information

Sometimes an ununified sentence can be revised simply by eliminating unimportant ideas that intruded when the sentence was first drafted. That's what has happened in the following case.

8a

> **Ununified sentence**   Inexpensive word processors, which first became available to the public in the late 1970s and which, like other technological innovations such as computer chips and digital recording, are part of what sociologists call the postindustrial revolution, have made a significant dent in the electric typewriter market, which includes secretaries, students, and teachers, among others.

Again, revise by listing the distinct ideas in this sentence and considering their importance to its main point.

> **Keep**   Inexpensive word processors first became available to the public in the late 1970s.
>
> **Eliminate**   Inexpensive word processors, like computer chips and digital recording, are part of what sociologists call the postindustrial revolution.
>
> **Keep**   Inexpensive word processors have made a significant dent in the electric typewriter market.
>
> **Eliminate**   The electric typewriter market includes secretaries, students, and teachers, among others.

The information about computer chips, digital recording, sociologists, and the postindustrial revolution is only tangentially relevant to the point that word processors are cutting into the sale of electric typewriters. And most readers would probably not need to have the members of that market listed for them.

> **Revised with less important information eliminated**   Inexpensive word processors have made a significant dent in the electric typewriter market since they first became available to the public in the late 1970s.

3.   Combine strategies

Neither of the strategies above may alone be sufficient to unify some disorganized sentences. In these cases, you may need both to divide the sentence and to scrutinize its contents for extraneous ideas to delete.

Ununified sentence	The earliest known examples of sculpture date from the Paleolithic period, which ended about twenty thousand years ago and is sometimes called the Old Stone Age, making sculpture one of the oldest arts, many pieces of sculpture having been found in caves or old burial grounds in various parts of the world.

8a

The point here seems to be the great antiquity of sculpture, but it is obscured by the sentence's rambling structure and excessive detail.

Sentence 2	The earliest known examples of sculpture date from the Paleolithic period.
Sentence 2	The Paleolithic period ended about twenty thousand years ago.
Eliminate	The Paleolithic period is sometimes called the Old Stone Age.
Sentence 1	Sculpture is one of the oldest arts.
Eliminate	Many pieces of sculpture have been found in caves or old burial grounds in many parts of the world.
Revised as two sentences with less important information eliminated	Sculpture is one of the oldest arts. The earliest known examples of sculpture date from the Paleolithic period, which ended about twenty thousand years ago.

In this revised form, the first sentence succinctly makes the main point, and the second sentence supports it with specific detail.

EXERCISE 1

Improve the unity of the following sentences by dividing them into separate sentences and/or by eliminating unnecessary information.

Example

Ununified	Ever since the introduction of personal computers, one of their most popular applications has been word processing, which is a method of writing on an electronic screen, and for both novices and

Exercise 1

Answers will vary.

1. A computer might at first seem intimidating to someone who has no background in electronic technology. However, anyone who writes can learn how to use a word processor. [divide sentence, eliminate unnecessary information]
2. Although using a word processor requires little more skill than typing does, composing on a word processor is much more efficient than writing on a typewriter. [eliminate unnecessary information]
3. You do not have to know how to program computers or even understand how they work. Once you learn a few simple operations, you can begin composing. [divide sentence]
4. You will need to learn the procedure for beginning a file, which varies depending on the word-processing program being used, and the procedure for moving text around on the screen. [eliminate unnecessary information]

professionals, word processing has revolutionized the act of writing.

Revised   Ever since the introduction of personal computers, one of their most popular applications has been word processing. For both novices and professionals, word processing has revolutionized the act of writing.

8a

1. A computer might at first seem intimidating to someone who has no background in electronic technology, which has reshaped so much of modern life, but anyone who writes can learn how to use a word processor.
2. Although using a word processor requires little more skill than typing does, composing on a word processor is much more efficient than writing on a typewriter, which is a machine that is rapidly becoming obsolete.
3. You do not have to know how to program computers or even understand how they work, but once you learn a few simple operations, you can begin composing.
4. You will need to learn the procedure for beginning a file, which varies depending on the word-processing program being used, such as WordStar, WordPerfect, MultiMate, or Word, and the procedure for moving the text around on the screen.
5. Knowing how to insert and delete text is helpful because most writers use these operations frequently, and both commands can be performed with a few keystrokes or clicks of the computer "mouse."
6. But a beginner should not worry about reading every page of the instruction manual, which may be very densely written and full of unfamiliar terminology, before creating a document because mastery of most computer commands comes with practice rather than study.
7. Many writers find that they can compose more efficiently with a word processor because they can easily revise as they write, and efficiency is a valuable benefit of technology.
8. Changes that a writer might be reluctant to make during typing because such changes are so complicated, particularly if one's typewriter does not have a correction feature, can be accomplished on the computer screen in seconds.
9. To produce a copy of the finished text, you will also need a printer, which converts electronic impulses to typescript, and like computers, printers are becoming more sophisticated and less costly.

5. Knowing how to insert and delete text is helpful because most writers use these operations frequently. Both commands can be performed with a few keystrokes or clicks of the computer "mouse." [divide sentence]
6. But a beginner should not worry about reading every page of the instruction manual before creating a document because mastery of most computer commands comes with practice rather than study. [eliminate unnecessary information]
7. Many writers find that they can compose more efficiently with a word processor because they can easily revise as they write. [eliminate unnecessary information]
8. Changes that a writer might be reluctant to make during typing can be accomplished on the computer screen in seconds. [eliminate unnecessary information]
9. To produce a copy of the finished text, you will also need a printer. Like computers, printers are becoming more sophisticated and less costly. [divide sentence, eliminate unnecessary information]

10. Early dot-matrix printers produced rather crude characters, but new laser printers can create professional-looking documents, because they offer a wide variety of fonts and graphic design elements, even though they are surprisingly inexpensive.

8b Creating emphasis with coordination and subordination

8b

Coordination and **subordination** are terms used to describe the either equal or unequal relationship between elements in a sentence. The Latin roots of these words indicate their difference in meaning:

ordinare, "to arrange in order" ⟶ *co,* "with"

sub, "under"

As their name suggests, *co*ordinate constructions rank sentence elements *with* each other. That is, they connect elements that are logically and grammatically equal, giving the same emphasis to both and hence leading a reader to regard them as equally important. Coordinate constructions are usually formed by connecting a pair or series of words, phrases, or clauses with any of the seven **coordinating conjunctions.** (For information about using coordinating conjunctions in parallel constructions, see **8d.**)

The Seven Coordinating Conjunctions

and	nor
but	or
for	so
yet	

---

10. Early dot-matrix printers produced rather crude characters, but new laser printers can create professional-looking documents. Even though they are surprisingly inexpensive, they offer a wide variety of fonts and graphic design elements. [divide sentence]

A *subordinate construction*, on the other hand, ranks one element *under* another in a sentence. It presents elements as unequal in importance, shifting the reader's attention to one element at the expense of another. Subordinate constructions often begin either with **subordinating conjunctions** or with **relative pronouns.**

8b

Subordinating Words

Subordinating conjunctions

after	before	than	where
although	even though	though	whereas
as	how	unless	wherever
as if	if	until	whether
as though	since	when	while
because	so that	whenever	

Relative pronouns

that	which	whoever	whomever
what	whichever	whom	whose
whatever	who		

---

1. Using coordinate and subordinate constructions

Sometimes you can use either a coordinate or a subordinate construction to combine separate ideas into a single unified sentence. The choice will depend on the relative importance of the ideas. Do you wish the reader to perceive them as equal or unequal in importance?

Ideas to be combined into one sentence   Matthew checked the spelling in the report. Theresa checked the calculations.

Coordinate construction balances Matthew's work and Theresa's	Matthew checked the spelling in the report, and Theresa checked the calculations.

In this sentence, the coordinating conjunction *and* directs the reader to regard Matthew's work and Theresa's as equally important. The two clauses in the sentence receive equal emphasis and are called **coordinate clauses.** But if you connect these ideas by placing a subordinating conjunction before either clause, you shift the focus of the sentence and the reader's attention to the opposite one.

8b

Subordinate construction shifts emphasis to Theresa	While Matthew checked the spelling in the report, *Theresa checked the calculations.*
Subordinate construction shifts emphasis to Matthew	While Theresa checked the calculations in the report, *Matthew checked the spelling.*

The clause that follows the subordinating conjunction is called the **subordinate** (or **dependent**) **clause;** the other clause, on which the sentence's emphasis falls, is the **main** (or **independent**) **clause.** (For additional information about independent clauses and dependent clauses, see **25g.**)

Note that subordinating conjunctions not only control emphasis in a sentence but also indicate different kinds of relationships between clauses—for instance, time (*after, before, since, until, when, while*), cause and effect (*because, since*), condition (*if, unless*), contrast (*although, even though, though*). As the following examples indicate, selecting different subordinating conjunctions to connect the clauses above would create sentences that are very different in meaning.

Acts in sequence	*After* Matthew checked the spelling in the report, Theresa checked the calculations.
Acts in reverse sequence	*Before* Matthew checked the spelling in the report, Theresa checked the calculations.
Repeated or habitual acts	*Whenever* Matthew checked the spelling in the report, Theresa checked the calculations.

2. Avoiding weak coordination

Because the sentences involving Matthew and Theresa are closely related in content, they make sense whether connected with a coordinating conjunction (*and*) or with a variety of subordinating conjunctions (*while, after, before, whenever*). But not all sentences can be handled so flexibly. When ideas that are not related or not logically equal in importance are mistakenly connected with a coordinating conjunction, more than emphasis is lost. Such a sentence may seem confusing and incomplete.

Faulty coordination produces confusion	Elizabeth Michaels chaired yesterday's meeting and is the company's newest computer whiz.

Using the coordinating conjunction *and* to link the two ideas in this sentence—that Michaels chaired the meeting and that she is the company's newest computer genius—makes them seem somehow comparable. But these ideas are not related, at least not in any sense that the sentence makes clear, and their dissimilarity produces an unfocused, puzzling sentence. A subordinate construction, such as a relative clause, would enable the writer to focus the sentence on either of these ideas by subordinating the other.

Subordinate construction places emphasis on the meeting	*Elizabeth Michaels,* who is the company's newest computer whiz, *chaired yesterday's meeting.*
Subordinate construction places emphasis on computer skill	*Elizabeth Michaels,* who chaired yesterday's meeting, *is the company's newest computer whiz.*

3. Recognizing faulty ("upside-down") subordination

As we have seen, when one idea in a sentence is placed in a subordinate construction, the emphasis in the sentence automatically shifts to the *other* idea. A writer who forgets this principle may accidentally place the sentence's main idea in a subordinate construction. This error, sometimes called *upside-down subordination,* creates confusion in a sentence by erroneously directing the reader's attention to the less important idea.

Upside-down subordination	As Mr. Boardman drove off the road, *he tried to kill a bee inside the car.*
Correct subordination	As Mr. Boardman tried to kill a bee inside the car, *he drove off the road.*

8b

The main idea here is clearly driving off the road, not killing the bee, but the pattern of emphasis is reversed in the first sentence, where the writer has mistakenly placed the main idea in a subordinate clause introduced by the subordinating word *as.*

EXERCISE **2**

Improve the emphasis of the following sentences either by substituting subordination for coordination or by correcting upside-down subordination. For the first five sentences, revision suggestions are provided in brackets.

Example

Weak coordination	Black Kettle was a chief of the Cheyenne, and they lived primarily in eastern Colorado in the 1860s. [*who*]
Revised	Black Kettle was a chief of the Cheyenne, who lived primarily in eastern Colorado in the 1860s.

1. Black Kettle believed that fighting the white settlers was futile, and he repeatedly attempted to make peace. [*who* or *because*]
2. Major E. W. Wyncoup assured Black Kettle that his tribe would be safe at Sand Creek, and he commanded the troops at Fort Lyon. [*who*]
3. On the basis of this assurance, the Cheyenne settled at Sand Creek, and they awaited a decision from the white leaders about Black Kettle's peace offer. [*where* or *while*]
4. Wyncoup's actions, which led to his being recalled from his post in November of 1864, did not suit his superiors. [upside-down subordination]

Exercise 2

Answers will vary.

1. Because Black Kettle believed that fighting the white settlers was futile, he repeatedly attempted to make peace.
2. Major E. W. Wyncoup, who commanded the troops at Fort Lyon, assured Black Kettle that his tribe would be safe at Sand Creek.
3. On the basis of this assurance, the Cheyenne settled at Sand Creek, where they awaited a decision from the white leaders about Black Kettle's peace offer.
4. Wyncoup's actions, which did not suit his superiors, led to his being recalled from his post in November of 1864. [upside-down subordination]
5. Major Scott Anthony, who was his replacement, agreed to the promise that Wyncoup had made to the Cheyenne. [upside-down subordination]
6. Meanwhile, a band of Arapaho under Chief Left Hand had joined the

8c

5. His replacement, who was Major Scott Anthony, agreed to the promise that Wyncoup had made to the Cheyenne. [upside-down subordination]
6. Meanwhile, a band of Arapaho under Chief Left Hand had joined the Sand Creek settlement, and it now numbered about seven hundred, including five hundred women, children, and elderly people.
7. Near the end of November, a former minister, who was Colonel Chivington, arrived at Fort Lyon with a cavalry troop.
8. Anthony sent Chivington and a hundred soldiers to Sand Creek, and they attacked the settlement at dawn on November 29, 1864.
9. Black Kettle raised a white flag over his tent, and the soldiers ignored it.
10. They killed between four and five hundred Native Americans, and most of the dead were women and children.
11. The soldiers took a hundred scalps, and these were later displayed in a Denver theater.
12. Left Hand was killed at Sand Creek, and Black Kettle escaped the massacre.
13. Black Kettle still hoped for peace, and in the years after the Sand Creek massacre he signed two additional treaties with the government.
14. The Cheyenne chief negotiated in good faith, and the government soon violated the terms of both treaties.
15. General George Armstrong Custer's cavalry attacked the Cheyenne without warning on November 27, 1868, and Black Kettle and hundreds of his people were killed.

8c Writing concise sentences

Superfluous words weaken a sentence. But there is a difference between brevity in writing, which is sometimes a virtue, and conciseness, which always is. Any sentence can be made brief by paring words and details; the difficulty is knowing what to strike out and what to retain. Concise writing manages to include all the essential information without wasting words.

Too wordy By the time trading ended on Wall Street yesterday, the stock market had fallen down forty points, which was significant because it was the sharpest decline since a similar drop seven months ago.

Too brief The market plummeted yesterday.

Sand Creek settlement, which now numbered about seven hundred, including five hundred women, children, and elderly people.
7. Near the end of November, Colonel Chivington, who was a former minister, arrived at Fort Lyon with a cavalry troop. [upside-down subordination]
8. Anthony sent Chivington and a hundred soldiers to Sand Creek, where they attacked the settlement at dawn on November 29, 1864.
9. Although Black Kettle raised a white flag over his tent, the soldiers ignored it.
10. They killed between four and five hundred Native Americans, most of whom were women and children.
11. The soldiers took a hundred scalps, which were later displayed in a Denver theater.
12. Although Left Hand was killed at Sand Creek, Black Kettle escaped the massacre.
13. Since Black Kettle still hoped for peace, in the years after the Sand Creek massacre he signed two additional treaties with the government.

| **Appropriately concise** | The stock market fell forty points yesterday, the sharpest decline in seven months. |

Answering a young man's question about how to become a good stylist, the English writer Sydney Smith once said, "You should cross out every other word. You have no idea what vigor it will give your style." Though exaggerated, Smith's advice makes an important point. Notice how the deadwood in the following passage blocks the reader's way.

8c

> Because *of the fact that* I wanted to major in *the field of* business, I *proceeded to* take several courses in *the area of* accounting in *the period of* my sophomore year. *During the time* when I was a junior, I *was* still *of the belief* that business was my best choice for *the purpose of* making a living.

When we eliminate the words that contribute nothing to this passage, the sentences make their simple point more directly.

> Because I wanted to major in business, I took several courses in accounting in my sophomore year. As a junior, I still believed that business was my best choice for making a living.

As you look for opportunities to eliminate wordiness in your own writing, keep in mind the six main types of wordy constructions discussed below.

1. Redundant words, phrases, and clauses

The word *redundancy* comes to us from the Latin word meaning "to overflow." In writing, redundancy is a flood of words that repeat the same ideas. Redundancy does not clarify; it merely bores.

| **Redundant** | When the poet writes *in his poem* that the character was never "odd in his views," he means that the man was a conformist, *accepting the standards of his society in all respects.* |
| **Concise** | When the poet writes that the character was never "odd in his views," he means that the man was a conformist. |

Redundant phrasing often results from needlessly spelling out the meaning of a word that can stand alone. Poets, as we know, write

---

14. Though the Cheyenne chief negotiated in good faith, the government soon violated the terms of both treaties.
15. When General George Armstrong Custer's cavalry attacked the Cheyenne without warning on November 27, 1868, Black Kettle and hundreds of his people were killed.

poems; we do not need to be reminded of that fact in the sentence above. Nor do we need a definition of the word *conformist*. Notice similar duplication in the following sentences.

8c

> **Redundant** Over the years, she began to suspect that she was being exploited by her relatives, *that they wanted to take advantage of her and use her.*
>
> **Redundant** The criticisms I want to make are major ones *that you ought to consider carefully because of their importance.*
>
> **Redundant** We like to be appreciated for our talents *that we possess,* and we hope to be praised for our achievements *that we have attained as individuals.*

In these sentences, the italicized words provide superfluous definitions of the simple concepts "exploitation," "major," and — in the last example — "our." Below are some common redundant phrases to be on the watch for.

Redundant Phrases

attractive *in appearance*	complete *entirely*
cooperate *together*	perplexing *in nature*
red *in color*	refer *back* to
repeat *again*	round *in shape*
several *in number*	small *in size*
tall *in height*	young *in age*

---

2. Nominalizations

The noun form of a verb is called a **nominalization.** We need nominalizations in our language—words like *argument, explanation,* and *life*—in order to talk about abstract concepts. Nominalizations weaken a writer's style, though, when they are pressed into service in place of more direct verbs. When a writer uses a verb phrase containing a nominalization instead of a verb, the result is almost always a wordy sentence.

Wordy nominalizations	*It is the* city council's *intention* to *make a decision about* the future of the Maple Street park at tomorrow's meeting.
Concise	The city council *intends* to *decide* the future of the Maple Street Park at tomorrow's meeting.

8c

As the sentences above illustrate, nominalizations not only generate useless, extra words; they also mask the action being described and deprive a sentence of the punch that only a strong verb can deliver.

Nominalizations are one of the hallmarks of what is occasionally called the bureaucratic style, the style of some writers in business and government who mistakenly persist in believing that more words are better than fewer, that indirectness is better than directness. We encounter this style so often that it is sometimes difficult to recognize, let alone resist. Below is a list of common nominalizations to watch out for, together with their more direct equivalents.

Eliminating Nominalization

Nominalization	More concise verb
I am of the belief that . . .	I believe . . .
She reached the conclusion that . . .	She concluded . . .
He will make a determination of . . .	He will determine . . .
We held a discussion of . . .	We discussed . . .
She provided an explanation of . . .	She explained . . .
He has the intention of . . .	He intends to . . .
We are in need of . . .	We need . . .
They made a recommendation that . . .	They recommended . . .
I will conduct a study of . . .	I will study . . .

The key to improving a sentence containing a nominalization is recognizing the nominalization and identifying the action that it conceals. Once you state that action as a verb and the actor as its subject, the other elements in the sentence will usually fall into place. Your new sentence will always be more direct, more economical, and more forceful than the original.

3.   Wordy connectives

8c

Join elements in your sentences as directly and economically as possible.

Wordy connective	The most prolonged cold spell of the century occurred *during the time in which* Jerry was living in Iowa.
Concise	The most prolonged cold spell of the century occurred *while* Jerry was living in Iowa.
Wordy connective	Sarah continued to study German *because of the fact that* she hoped to become an interpreter.
Concise	Sarah continued to study German *because* she hoped to become an interpreter.

Below are some examples of wordy connectives and their more concise equivalents.

Eliminating Wordy Connectives

Wordy connective	Concise
at this point in time	now
because of the fact that	because
due to the fact that	because
during the period when	when, while
for the purpose of providing	to provide
in order to prove	to prove
in the event that	if
in a great many cases	often
the majority of	most
on the occasion when	when
the way in which to	how to

4. Unnecessary repetition

Repetition is not always a flaw in writing. In fact, as you will see in the discussion of parallel structure in **8d**, the artful repetition of syntactic structures can please the ear and enhance the meaning of a sentence. But repetition that creates awkwardness rather than emphasis should be eliminated.

8c

Repetitious	The *problem* of the homeless is a formidable *problem*.
Concise	The problem of the homeless is formidable.
Repetitious	If *you* read the *story* carefully, *you* will find a pattern of imagery in the *story* that makes the *story* mean more than *you* first thought the *story* did.
Concise	If you read the story carefully, you will find a pattern of imagery that enlarges its meaning.

The best way to isolate cases of unnecessary repetition is to read your writing out loud, trusting your ear to detect the jarring sound of a word or phrase that occurs too frequently.

5. Overuse of the passive voice

A verb is said to be in the **active voice** when the grammatical subject of a sentence does the action presented in its predicate.

Active verb	She *wrote* the book.
Active verb	He *read* the book.
Active verb	The critics *praised* it.

Who wrote the book? *She* did. Who read it? *He* did. The subjects of these sentences do the actions that their verbs describe.

Occasionally, though, the person or thing *acted upon* in a sentence is more important than the one who acts; in this case, the sentence can be written with the object or recipient of the action placed in the subject position. The verb in such a sentence is said to be in the **passive voice.**

Passive verb	Her book *was nominated* for the Pulitzer Prize.
Passive verb	Only exceptional books *are selected* for this award.

The actions here—nominating and selecting—were performed by people not important to the sentences, hence not identified in them. If we wanted to insist on using only active verbs, we could write *A jury nominated her book for the Pulitzer Prize,* but doing so would radically shift the emphasis of the sentence, mistakenly directing the reader's attention to an anonymous group of people and away from the real point of the sentence—the book and the honor it received.

A passive verb is not only appropriate but necessary when the doer of the action in the sentence is unknown.

> **Passive verb**   My car *was* apparently *stolen* during the night.

The conventions of scientific and technical writing dictate the frequent use of the passive voice as well, since it is the experiment and not the experimenter that is important.

> **Passive verbs**   A cubic centimeter of water *was added* to the solution, and the test tube *was heated.* No reaction *was observed.*

Problems with passive verbs

Even in these cases where passive verbs are legitimate and necessary, they present one disadvantage over active verbs: because they are always formed by combining a past participle with some form of the verb *be,* passive verbs are always less concise than active verbs. Add to that the fact that in most writing the doer of an action is more important than the recipient of the action, and you have two reasons to avoid using passive verbs unnecessarily.

> **Unnecessary passive**   After my first draft *has been completed* and the paper *has been set* aside for a day or two, revising *is begun* by me.
>
> **Unnecessary passive**   Classics like Charles Dickens's novels *will* always *be appreciated* by readers.
>
> **Unnecessary passive**   "Who ever reads an American book?" *was asked* by an English critic in the nineteenth century.

Rewritten in the active voice, these sentences become more concise and forceful. Not only can the active verbs be expressed in fewer words, but the prepositional phrases needed to identify the actors here—*by me, by readers, by an English critic*—can be dropped when those actors are placed in the subject position.

More concise active	After I *have completed* my first draft and *have set* the paper aside for a day or two, I *begin* revising.
More concise active	Readers *will* always *appreciate* classics like Charles Dickens's novels.
More concise active	"Who ever reads an American book?" an English critic *asked* in the nineteenth century.

Passive constructions often obscure the true actor in a sentence, making it confusing as well as wordy.

Confusing passive	The changes that *had been made* in the conservation bill by the committee *were accepted* by the Senate, which voted to pass the bill.

One can hardly tell what happened here. Who did what? The actors are the committee and the Senate; active verbs make their roles easier to perceive.

Clearer active	The Senate *passed* the conservation bill that the committee *had amended.*

The point is to be able to distinguish between active and passive verbs and to use passives only when they are necessary and appropriate. Be especially sensitive to those wordy passive constructions that, like the nominalizations discussed above, often surface in bureaucratic prose, sometimes as a deliberate means of concealing the actor or actors in a sentence.

Passive conceals actor	It *has been determined* that a tax increase, however unpopular, offers the only solution to the budget deficit. [Who has determined this?]
Passive conceals actor	It *was thought* that the world's natural resources were inexhaustible. [Who thought this?]

Writing in the active voice demands more careful thinking and more exact phrasing.

8c

| **More exact active** | Only a handful of the people who seriously considered the question thought that the world's natural resources were inexhaustible. |

6.   Unnecessary expletives

There is/are . . . and *It is* . . . are common constructions known as *expletives*. Placed at the beginning of a sentence, an expletive delays—and hence often emphasizes—the sentence's actual subject.

| **Emphatic** | There is no reason to doubt Mayor Smith's integrity. |

To see how the expletive *there is* works, read the previous sentence aloud and note that your voice naturally rises after the expletive and stresses the words *no reason*. Similarly, in the sentences below, observe how the expletive *it was* adds special emphasis to the words that immediately follow it.

| **Emphatic** | It was Mayor Smith [not someone else] who established a new standard of integrity in municipal government. |
| **Emphatic** | It was her new standard of integrity [not some other virtue] that set Mayor Smith apart from previous mayors. |

Carelessly used, however, expletives may merely add words that do nothing to make a sentence clearer or stronger.

| **Wordy** | There are many citizens who believe that Mayor Smith's administration restored the public's confidence in local government. |
| **Wordy** | It is now necessary for us to demand a similar level of integrity in all city officials. |

In these cases, the sentences become both more concise and more emphatic if we delete the expletives and begin with the true subjects.

| **Concise** | Many citizens believe that Mayor Smith's administration restored the public's confidence in local government. |
| **Concise** | We must now demand a similar level of integrity in all city officials. |

Exercise 3 (page 159)

Answers will vary.

1. In the nineteenth century, technology was beginning to develop, and early science fiction was in large part a response to this change. [eliminate *there were* construction, repetition]
2. Many people believe that Mary Shelley's book, *Frankenstein; or, The Modern Prometheus,* published in 1818, is the first science-fiction novel. [eliminate *there are* construction, nominalization, unnecessary repetition]
3. An important early influence on SF was H. G. Wells, whose many novels included *The Invisible Man* and *The War of the Worlds,* both published in the late 1800s. [eliminate redundancy, wordy connective]
4. The nineteenth century also saw the beginnings of what was to become a major SF publishing market, magazines. [eliminate redundancy]

EXERCISE 3

Revise the sentences below to make them more concise. Be prepared to explain which of the following types of wordiness you have eliminated: redundancies, nominalizations, wordy connectives, unnecessary repetition, overuse of the passive voice, and unnecessary expletives.

Example

8c

Wordy   Today most people in our modern world are familiar with science fiction, but it may not be known by them that a long history has been had by science fiction.

Revised   Today most people are familiar with science fiction, but they may not know of its long history. [The revision eliminates redundancy ("Today . . . our modern world"), unnecessary repetition ("science fiction . . . science fiction"), and passive verbs ("may not be known," "has been had").]

1. In the nineteenth century, there were great technological developments that were beginning to develop, and early science fiction was in large part a response to these changes.
2. There are many people who are of the belief that Mary Shelley's book *Frankenstein; or, The Modern Prometheus,* a novel published in 1818, is the first science-fiction novel.
3. An important early influence on SF was H. G. Wells, whose novels were many in number, including *The Invisible Man* and *The War of the Worlds,* both published in the period of the late 1800s.
4. The nineteenth century also saw the first beginnings of what was to become a major SF publishing market, magazines.
5. Although often these magazines frequently contained stories inferior in quality from a literary standpoint, it is a fact that many articles by many well-known writers were published in them, including the writer Edgar Rice Burroughs, the originator and creator of Tarzan.
6. The term *science fiction*—abbreviated SF, never "sci-fi"—didn't come into general, widespread use until the 1930s.
7. Due to the fact that science fiction includes many different and various types of literature, it is difficult to define.
8. Writers of SF are characterized by an insistence that the events they portray are possible.
9. Over the years, science fiction has continued to grow and develop.
10. Among the recent trends in SF are more radical political themes and the trend toward more work by women writers.

---

5. Although these magazines frequently contained stories inferior from a literary standpoint, they also contained articles by many well-known writers, including Edgar Rice Burroughs, the creator of Tarzan. [eliminate redundancy, *it is* construction, unnecessary repetition, passive verb]
6. The term *science fiction*—abbreviated SF, never "sci-fi"—didn't come into widespread use until the 1930s. [eliminate redundancy]
7. Because science fiction includes many different types of literature, it is difficult to define. [eliminate wordy connective, redundancy]
8. Writers of SF insist that the events they portray are possible. [eliminate nominalization]
9. Over the years, science fiction has continued to develop. [eliminate redundancy]
10. Among the recent trends in SF are more radical political themes and more work by women writers. [eliminate unnecessary repetition]

8d

Revise the sentences below to make them more concise. Be prepared to explain which of the following types of wordiness you have eliminated: redundancies, nominalizations, wordy connectives, unnecessary repetition, overuse of the passive voice, and unnecessary expletives.

Example

Wordy   In some way, shape, or fashion, everyone laughs.

Revised   Everyone laughs in some way.   [The revision eliminates redundancy ("way, shape, or fashion").]

1. But as individuals, we each laugh at those things that we each individually find amusing.
2. In intellectual humor, people use their minds; in order for a person to laugh at a pun, for example, there must first be a realization by a person that a single word may have two different and distinct meanings.
3. In contrast, slapstick humor, on the other hand, is visually humorous.
4. In other words, what that means is that something that is seen by a person appears to be funny, like a man slipping on a banana peel and slipping and falling.
5. Unfortunately, it is true that one person's humor may be another person's pain.
6. There are in-jokes, which belong to a certain group or clique, and which reinforce a listener's feeling of inclusion and belonging only in the event that he or she is a member of the group.
7. But if a joke refers to something that is not understood by the listener, such a joke can be a way and means of making the person feel excluded.
8. Ethnic jokes, too, can also be painful on the occasion when it is one's own ethnic origin that is the target of the humor.
9. Despite these problems, humor is still needed by each and every one of us.
10. It is an enjoyable and pleasurable release from the everyday tension of our daily lives.

8d   Creating parallelism

The human eye and the human ear favor balance and harmony. We like matchings and pairs, equity, pattern, order. Once a major chord is struck in a piece of music, we expect to hear it again, just as we

Exercise 4

Answers will vary.

1. But as individuals, we laugh at those things that we each find amusing. [eliminate unnecessary repetition]
2. In intellectual humor, people use their minds; in order for a person to laugh at a pun, for example, he or she must first realize that a single word may have two different meanings. [eliminate nominalization, unnecessary repetition, redundancy]
3. In contrast, slapstick humor is visually humorous. [eliminate redundancy]
4. In other words, something that a person sees appears to be funny, like a man slipping on a banana peel and falling. [eliminate redundancy, passive verb, unnecessary repetition]
5. Unfortunately, one person's humor may be another person's pain. [eliminate *it is* construction]

appreciate looking at surfaces where planes and colors complement one another. In writing, this ordering of like element with like element is called **parallelism,** or **parallel structure.** Parallel structure balances word with word, phrase with phrase, clause with clause. It is one of the most basic of stylistic devices, one that is appropriate in many writing situations.

8d

Parallel words and phrases

The middle-class values by which we were raised—
    the work ethic,
    the importance of education,
    the value   of property ownership,
          of respectability,
          of "getting ahead,"
          of stable family life,
          of initiative,
          of self-reliance—
are, in themselves, raceless
   and even assimilationist.

         —Shelby Steele, "On Being Black
         and Middle Class," *Commentary*

Parallel clauses and sentences

A schedule defends from chaos and whim.
  It is a net for catching days.
  It is a scaffolding on which a worker can stand and labor with both
     hands at sections of time.
A schedule is a mock-up of reason and order—willed, faked, and so
brought into being;
  it is a peace and a haven set into the wreck of time;
  it is a lifeboat on which you find yourself, decades later, still living.
        —Annie Dillard, "Schedules," *The Writing Life*

1. The rhetoric of parallel structure

   Although the following sentences are a rather extreme example of parallel structure, they offer a good illustration of the effects that can

6. In-jokes, which belong to a clique, reinforce a listener's feeling of belonging only if he or she is a member of the group. [eliminate *there are* construction, redundancy, wordy connective, unnecessary repetition]
7. But if a joke refers to something that the listener does not understand, it can be a way of making him or her feel excluded. [eliminate passive verb, unnecessary repetition, redundancy]
8. Ethnic jokes, too, can be painful when one's own origin is the target of the humor. [eliminate redundancy, wordy connective, *it is* construction, unnecessary repetition]
9. Despite these problems, each of us still needs humor. [eliminate passive verb, redundancy]
10. It is an enjoyable release from the tension of our daily lives. [eliminate redundancy]

8d

be created with parallelism. To appreciate the way in which parallel structure works in this passage, try reading it slowly out loud.

> The cunning and attractive slave women disguise their strength as womanly weakness, their audacity as womanly timidity, their unscrupulousness as womanly innocence, their impurities as womanly defencelessness; simple men are duped by them, and subtle ones disarmed and intimidated. It is only the proud, straightforward women who wish, not to govern, but to be free.
>
> —Bernard Shaw

The first independent clause of Shaw's compound sentence states its subject and predicate simply. The phrases functioning as the direct objects of the verb (*what* do these slave women disguise?) have exactly the same construction because they are grammatical equals in the sentence. We might illustrate their parallel relationship by diagramming them like this.

their strength as womanly weakness

their audacity as womanly timidity

disguise

their unscrupulousness as womanly innocence

their impurities as womanly defencelessness

The parallelism of Shaw's sentence does not end there. In the independent clause following the semicolon, *simple men* are balanced against *subtle ones,* and *disarmed* and *intimidated* form parallel elements in the predicate of the second clause.

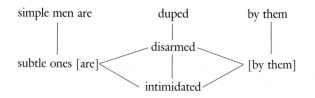

The sections of the sentence on either side of the semicolon are themselves contrasted in parallel fashion. The active voice of the verb in the first clause (*disguise*) is balanced against the passive voice of the verbs in the second (*are duped . . . disarmed and intimidated*); aggression is balanced against passivity.

The brisk second sentence introduces parallel objects of the verb *wish* with the correlatives *not . . . but*.

the . . . women who wish
— not to govern
— but to be free

8d

The initial pair of adjectives (*cunning* and *attractive*) defining the subject of the first clause (*slave women*) is here paralleled by a new pair of adjectives that describe the different women in this second sentence (*proud, straightforward*). Shaw ingeniously suggests the inequality between the two types of women by replacing the *and* that connects the adjectives in the first sentence with a comma in the second. A new rhythm is established.

This analysis of just two sentences suggests the concentration of ideas and the range of effects that a writer can create using parallel structure. Parallelism compares and contrasts, affirms (*both . . . and*) and negates (*neither . . . nor*) by putting like or different elements in similar constructions. Perhaps the fact that we have two eyes, two legs, two sides of the brain, two hands (*on the one hand . . . on the other hand*) accounts for our pleasure when elements in a sentence are balanced, and our dissatisfaction when they are askew.

Whatever the reason for our attraction to equality and balance, parallelism is indispensable for good writing. The guidelines that follow will help you use parallel structure effectively in your own prose.

2.   Coordinate pairs

Sentence elements joined by coordinating conjunctions—particularly by *and, but,* and *or*—should be similar in grammatical structure. Balance nouns with nouns, phrases with phrases, clauses with clauses.

Faulty   He likes reading all the books he can lay his hands on and to write whenever the mood strikes him.

He likes
— reading . . .
— to write . . .

The reader is jarred by the faulty parallelism of the gerund *reading* with the infinitive *to write*. To create parallel structure, rewrite the sentence with two infinitives or two gerunds.

8d

Parallel   He likes *to read* all the books he can lay his hands on and *to write* whenever the mood strikes him.

He likes
  to read . . .
  to write . . .

Parallel   He likes *reading* all the books he can lay his hands on and *writing* whenever the mood strikes him.

He likes
  reading . . .
  writing . . .

In the first sentence below, the conjunction *and* connects an infinitive phrase and a subordinate clause beginning with *that*—two structures that are not parallel. The second sentence presents one way of revising for parallelism.

Faulty   Students in composition classes learn to read with attention and that coherent essays must be written.

Students . . . learn
  to read with attention
  that coherent essays must be written

Parallel   Students in composition classes learn *to read* with attention and *to write* coherent essays.

Students . . . learn
  to read with attention
  to write coherent essays

The sentence could be rephrased to emphasize the parallelism even more.

Parallel   Students in composition classes learn *to read attentively* and *to write coherently*.

Students . . . learn $\left\{\begin{array}{l}\text{to read attentively}\\[1em]\text{to write coherently}\end{array}\right.$

3. Elements in a series

Like coordinate pairs, three or more elements in a series must be grammatically parallel to one another.

> **Faulty**   I concluded that she was intelligent, witty, and liked to make people feel at home.

The first two elements after the verb *was* are adjectives; the third is another verb. The lack of parallelism is clearly revealed if we construct a diagram of the sentence.

she was $\left\{\begin{array}{l}\text{intelligent}\\\text{witty}\\\text{liked to make people feel at home}\end{array}\right.$

The faulty parallelism can be corrected by making all three elements adjectives.

> **Parallel**   I concluded that she was *intelligent, witty,* and *hospitable.*

she was $\left\{\begin{array}{l}\text{intelligent}\\\text{witty}\\\text{hospitable}\end{array}\right.$

The sentence might also be rewritten by inserting another *and* to create two parallel noun clauses.

> **Parallel**   I concluded *that she was* intelligent and witty and *that she liked* to make people feel at home.

I concluded $\left\{\begin{array}{l}\text{that she was} \left\{\begin{array}{l}\text{intelligent}\\\text{witty}\end{array}\right.\\\text{that she liked to make people feel at home}\end{array}\right.$

4. Repetition of words

Sometimes it is necessary to repeat a conjunction, preposition, or other preceding word to make a parallel construction clear.

Unclear   My adviser told me that I spent far too much time worrying about what was expected of me and I needed more confidence in myself.

Clearer   My adviser told me that I spent far too much time worrying about what was expected of me and *that* I needed more confidence in myself.

$$\text{My adviser told me} \begin{cases} \text{that I spent . . .} \\ \text{that I needed . . .} \end{cases}$$

Unclear   Because she had been teaching for twenty years and she could remember being a student herself, I listened to her advice.

Clearer   Because she had been teaching for twenty years and *because* she could remember being a student herself, I listened to her advice.

$$\begin{rcases} \text{Because she had been teaching . . .} \\ \text{because she could remember . . .} \end{rcases} \text{I listened to her advice}$$

Occasionally, the absence of such a preceding word can significantly distort the meaning of a sentence.

Unclear   The vineyard is often visited by tourists who sample grapes and connoisseurs of wine.

$$\text{tourists who sample} \begin{cases} \text{grapes} \\ \text{connoisseurs of wine} \end{cases}$$

Clearer   The vineyard is often visited by tourists who sample grapes and *by* connoisseurs of wine.

The vineyard is often visited
- by tourists who sample grapes
- by connoisseurs of wine

5. Correlatives

Conjunctions that occur in pairs are called **correlatives:** *either . . . or, neither . . . nor, not only . . . but also, both . . . and.* The rule to follow when you use correlatives is that the parts of speech immediately following each conjunction must be identical.

Faulty   William Blake is not only famous for his poetry but also for his illustrations.

William Blake is
- not only famous for . . .
- but also   for . . .

Not only in this sentence is followed by the adjective *famous; but also,* however, is followed by a prepositional phrase beginning with *for.* In this case, the faulty parallelism can be corrected simply by rearranging the words in the sentence:

Parallel   William Blake is famous *not only for* his poetry *but also for* his illustrations.

William Blake is famous
- not only for . . .
- but also for . . .

Consider the following similar case.

Faulty   He either is a liar or a remarkably naive person.

He
- either   is   a liar
- or   a remarkably naive person

This sentence can be revised in three different ways to create parallelism around the correlatives *either . . . or.*

8d

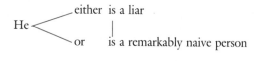

He ⟨
  either is a liar
  or   is a remarkably naive person

He is ⟨
  either a liar
  or   a remarkably naive person

Either he is a liar,
or   he is a remarkably naive person

In the final example below, the faulty parallelism could be corrected by inverting *both* and *to*, but doing so would produce the awkward split construction *to both raise*. A better solution is to add another *to* after *and*.

Faulty   The legislature hoped both to raise taxes and stimulate business.

The legislature hoped ⟨
  both to raise taxes
  and stimulate business

Parallel   The legislature hoped *both to* raise taxes *and to* stimulate business.

The legislature hoped ⟨
  both to raise taxes
  and to stimulate business

6. Dependent clauses

A dependent clause is never parallel to an independent clause in a sentence, and it should not be connected to the independent clause by *and* or *but*.

Faulty   She is a woman of strong convictions and who always says what she thinks.

The clauses can be put into proper relationship to one another by omitting the coordinating conjunction.

Correct She is a woman of strong convictions who always says what she thinks.

An alternative is to rewrite the sentence with two parallel dependent clauses.

8d

Parallel She is a woman *who has* strong convictions and *who* always *says* what she thinks.

$$\text{She is a woman} \begin{cases} \text{who has strong convictions} \\ \text{who always says what she thinks} \end{cases}$$

Faulty parallel constructions like those in the following sentences are corrected in a similar way.

Faulty In the middle of the sleepy village is a statue dating from 1870 and that depicts General Lee on horseback.

Parallel In the middle of the sleepy village is a statue *that* dates from 1870 *and that* depicts General Lee on horseback.

Faulty He appeared before the committee with a long written statement, but which he was not allowed to read.

Parallel *He* appeared before the committee with a long written statement, *but he* was not allowed to read it.

7. Logical sequence of ideas

Elements that are parallel in grammatical structure should also be parallel in sense. Used carelessly, a parallel construction can lead to an illogical series or an awkward sequence of ideas, as in the following sentence.

Illogical Her many friends, her recent marriage, and her slumping business could not offer Amy the happiness she had known while in college.

The items in this series are not parallel in meaning. A person might reasonably be expected to find happiness in friends and marriage, but not in a slumping business. Only the first two of these ideas can be expressed in a parallel construction.

> **Correct**   Neither her many friends nor her recent marriage could offer Amy the happiness she had known while in college.

8d

A similar juxtaposition of positive and negative ideas in the following sentence creates a puzzling effect.

> **Illogical**   During his last year in law school, David rose to the top of his class, worked on the law review, and decided not to enter law practice.

> **Correct**   During his last year in law school, David rose to the top of his class and worked on the law review. However, he decided not to enter law practice.

Sometimes the part of a sentence that should be parallel to another part is so far away that the writer may lose track of the sentence's sense.

> **Illogical**   I try to stay awake in chemistry class, fortifying myself with coffee, pinching myself at intervals, hanging by my fingernails on the professor's every word, but falling asleep nonetheless.

Falling is not logically parallel to the three other participles in this sentence, which describe the writer's strategies for staying awake. The parallel pair of ideas is *trying to stay awake* and *falling asleep*. The sentence should be rewritten with parallel independent clauses.

> **Parallel**   *I try* to stay awake in chemistry class, fortifying myself with coffee, pinching myself at intervals, hanging by my fingernails on the professor's every word, but *I fall asleep* nonetheless.

I try to stay awake ⟨ fortifying myself . . .
                      pinching myself . . .
                      hanging by my fingernails . . .

but

I fall asleep nonetheless

Exercise 5 (page 171)

Since faulty parallelism can almost always be corrected in several different ways, answers to this exercise will vary.

1. Stonehenge, the ancient circle of stone monuments in southern England, was apparently used for religious, practical, and astronomical purposes.
2. Hipparchus, who lived around 150 B.C., was the first astronomer to attempt classifying stars and mapping their paths.
3. Hipparchus not only developed trigonometry but also invented the astrolabe, a device for measuring the altitude of heavenly bodies.
4. His successor, Ptolemy, is credited with having cataloged more than a thousand stars and with having firmly established the theory that the universe revolves around the earth.
5. The Ptolemaic system not only influenced the ancient world but also dominated thinking about the cosmos until the sixteenth century.

EXERCISE 5

Revise the following sentences to correct faulty parallelism.

Example

Faulty   The earliest astronomers used the stars to make calendars and also in order that they could mark the time of religious rites.

Parallel   The earliest astronomers used the stars *to make* calendars and *to mark* the time of religious rites.

8d

1. Stonehenge, the ancient circle of stone monuments in southern England, was apparently used for religious, practical, and for astronomical purposes.
2. Hipparchus, who lived around 150 B.C., was the first astronomer to attempt classifying stars and to map their paths.
3. Hipparchus not only developed trigonometry but also he was the inventor of the astrolabe, a device for measuring the altitude of heavenly bodies.
4. His successor, Ptolemy, is credited with having cataloged more than a thousand stars and with the fact that he firmly established the theory that the universe revolves around the earth.
5. The Ptolemaic system not only influenced the ancient world but also it dominated thinking about the cosmos until the sixteenth century.
6. Until quite recently, astronomy, religion, and the subject of philosophy were connected in people's minds.
7. For centuries, people clung to the Ptolemaic theory and as they resisted the idea that the earth might not be the center of the universe.
8. A hundred years after Copernicus proposed this theory in the sixteenth century, the idea was still considered heretical and to be dangerous.
9. More recently, Edmund Halley, famous for the comet he discovered and that he tracked, helped to dispel some of the myths surrounding the solar system and its workings.
10. Today, the occasional confusion of astronomy and astrology remains as a sign of the blending of the rational and mysterious ideas—a mixture some people are unwilling to give up.

EXERCISE 6

Create at least one parallel construction in each of the following sentences by adding appropriate words, phrases, or clauses. Change the original sentence slightly if necessary.

---

6. Until quite recently, astronomy, religion, and philosophy were connected in people's minds.
7. For centuries, people clung to the Ptolemaic theory and resisted the idea that the earth might not be the center of the universe.
8. A hundred years after Copernicus proposed this theory in the sixteenth century, the idea was still considered heretical and dangerous.
9. More recently, Edmund Halley, famous for the comet he discovered and tracked, helped to dispel some of the myths surrounding the solar system and its workings.
10. Today, the occasional confusion of astronomy and astrology remains as a sign of the blending of the rational and the mysterious—a mixture some people are unwilling to give up.

Exercise 6

Answers to this exercise will vary. Several students might be asked to put their versions of the same sentence on the chalkboard for discussion by the

8e

Example

The afternoon sunlight filtered through the trees.

Parallel words added: The afternoon sunlight filtered through the *leaves and branches* of the trees.

Parallel phrases added: The afternoon sunlight filtered through the trees, *casting shadows* on the blanket *and making reading* difficult.

Parallel clause added: The afternoon sunlight filtered through the trees, *and a light wind brushed across the grass.*

1. Vince's pictures of the Bradley Warehouse fire were the start of his career as a professional photographer.
2. The fire occurred after all the employees had left for the day.
3. Vince had just started working as a night security guard at the warehouse.
4. Of course, no matter where he was, Vince kept his camera handy.
5. When he smelled smoke, he immediately called the fire department.
6. While he waited for the fire trucks to arrive, he took pictures of the blaze.
7. Once he was nearly injured when a burning beam fell close to him.
8. At that point, Vince decided that he had enough pictures.
9. The newspaper offered to buy the best of his shots.
10. Vince's pictures were good enough to get him a job at the newspaper.

8e Writing cumulative and periodic sentences

Sentences are sometimes characterized as cumulative or periodic, depending on where their main ideas occur.

1. Cumulative sentences

A *cumulative sentence* states its main idea first and then follows it with modifying words, phrases, or clauses.

I began to keep a journal when I discovered that my life was interesting, my dreams colorful, and my thoughts rather remarkably profound.

---

class. The best revisions of the original sentences in the exercise will add substantial new information without creating an unnatural or awkward rhythm. Below are some possibilities.

1. Vince's pictures of the Bradley Warehouse fire were the start of his career as a professional photographer and the end of his life in Scranton, Pennsylvania. [parallel phrases]
2. The fire occurred after all the employees had left for the day and the building had been locked up. [parallel clauses]
3. Vince had just started working as a janitor and night security guard at the warehouse. [parallel words]
4. Of course, no matter where he was, Vince kept his camera and film handy. [parallel words]
5. When he smelled smoke and realized the danger, he immediately called the fire department. [parallel phrases]
6. While he waited for the fire trucks to arrive, he located the center of the fire and took pictures of the blaze. [parallel phrases]

My brother stared at the unopened letter, trembling, pale, oblivious to the students who crowded past him in the stairwell.

Both of these cumulative sentences open with the main idea, to which are added phrases and clauses that provide supplementary information. Cumulative sentences offer a writer two advantages. First, they are clear, direct, and relatively easy to control. We generally speak in cumulative sentences, making a statement and then elaborating on it with details or qualifications. Every writer who can identify the main idea of a sentence has the beginning of a possible cumulative sentence. Second, such sentences are wonderfully flexible. Once the main idea of a sentence is on the page, a writer can freely arrange modifiers after it, varying its length and rhythm.

2. Periodic sentences

Periodic sentences are opposite in structure from cumulative sentences. In a periodic sentence, the main idea is held until the end—until the period—and the sentence begins instead with all the subordinate details. A periodic sentence can very effectively engage the attention of the reader, who is made to continue reading until the point of the sentence is revealed.

When I discovered that my life was interesting, my dreams colorful, and my thoughts rather remarkably profound, *I began to keep a journal.*

Trembling, pale, oblivious to the students who crowded past him in the stairwell, *my brother stared at the unopened letter.*

Periodic sentences are suspenseful and conclusive, since the weight of their statement falls on the long-awaited predication. And because they are artful and deliberate, such sentences give the reader an impression of thoughtful arrangement. Placed strategically after a series of cumulative sentences, the periodic sentence, surprising the reader by reversing the expected pattern, has an emphatic effect.

But periodic sentences also present a writer with certain hazards. For one thing, since they are less characteristic of contemporary prose than cumulative sentences are, periodic sentences used excessively give writing a slightly old-fashioned ring. Moreover, a periodic sentence

7. Once he was nearly injured when a burning beam fell close to him and showered him with embers. [parallel phrases]
8. At that point, Vince decided that he had enough pictures and that he should get out of the burning building. [parallel clauses]
9. The newspaper offered to buy the best of his shots and to run them in the next morning's edition. [parallel phrases]
10. Vince's pictures were good enough to get him not only a byline in the next edition but a permanent job at the newspaper. [parallel phrases]

whose main idea is not important enough for the emphasis that it inevitably receives may sound anticlimactic or even ridiculous.

> As the rainy night grew darker and the mysterious banging and howling in the attic stairway increased, I decided to make a peanut-butter sandwich.

8e

No one can prescribe when to use a cumulative sentence, when a periodic one. Such a choice must grow out of your subject, the surrounding sentences in your prose, and your instinctive sense of appropriateness. But only when you have mastered both forms will you be able to choose between them consciously and deliberately.

EXERCISE 7

By adding different sets of appropriate modifiers, rewrite each of the following sentences first as a cumulative sentence and then as a periodic sentence. Do you prefer one version of your sentence over the other?

Example

> No one seemed to be living in the house.
>
> Cumulative version: No one seemed to be living in the house, which loomed darkly against the stormy sky, its broken windowpanes and rotten siding suggesting years of neglect.
>
> Periodic version: Although the grounds were neatly cared for and lights burned within the curtained windows on the second floor, no one seemed to be living in the house.

1. The college faced a serious financial crisis.
2. Most of its residence halls needed renovation.
3. Another top priority was expansion of the library.
4. The last fund-raising campaign had fallen millions of dollars short of its goal.
5. The president reached a decision.
6. Some academic programs would have to be eliminated.
7. Students and faculty were outraged.
8. Many felt that cutbacks should be made in other areas.
9. A faculty committee began to look into the matter.
10. The committee's role was only advisory.

Exercise 7

Like Exercise 6, this exercise offers students the opportunity to choose between different stylistic strategies. Several students might be asked to put both versions of each of these sentences on the board, and the class as a whole can consider the effects of cumulative and periodic constructions.

8f   Varying sentence length

When the sentences in a passage are all approximately the same in length and structure, as in this opening passage from a published article, the result can be tedious reading.

Monotonous sentence length

> Nonsense bears the stamp of paradox. The two terms of the paradox are order and disorder. Order is generally created by language, disorder by reference. But the essential factor is their peculiar interplay. Elizabeth Sewell, in a penetrating analysis of nonsense, stresses the idea of dialectic. Yet her analysis deals almost exclusively with the formal structure of order. . . .

No reader can be expected to maintain interest in such prose for very long. Most of us, after all, read for pleasure as well as for information, and we expect writers to appeal to our desire for prose that satisfies and delights. The kind of monotonous prose in the example above can be revised effectively simply by varying the length and structure of the sentences.

Varied sentence length

> Nonsense bears the stamp of paradox, whose two terms are order and disorder. Although order is generally created by language and disorder by reference, the essential factor is their peculiar interplay. Elizabeth Sewell stresses the idea of dialectic in a penetrating analysis of nonsense, yet her analysis deals almost exclusively with the formal structure of order. . . .

The six sentences of the original, each approximately ten words long, have here been combined into three sentences of thirteen, eighteen, and twenty-five words. Related ideas are joined more clearly, and the second sentence's opening adverbial clause (*Although order* . . .) eliminates the monotony caused by a series of sentences that all begin with their subjects. Moreover, the progressively increasing length of these three sentences leads the reader more smoothly into the rest of the article.

Becoming familiar with the English sentence structures described in Chapter **25** is the first step toward developing variety in your writing.

Experiment with prepositional and verbal phrases; look for opportunities to use subordinate clauses; try to mix simple, compound, complex, and compound-complex sentences in your prose. At the same time, vary the length of your sentences. Remember that a string of long sentences is just as tiring to a reader as a series of short ones. It's the mixing of sentences of different lengths that keeps most readers engaged in a text.

8g Varying sentence openers

One important way of giving your prose new sophistication is by varying the first elements in your sentences. Many of us think of the main idea first and are therefore inclined to place it first in a sentence. But when every sentence in a piece of writing begins with its subject, as in the first passage quoted above, the effect is wearying dullness. Try experimenting with some of the alternative ways of opening sentences described below.

1. Single modifiers

When a single **modifier** (see **25c**) is placed at the start of a sentence, rather than buried somewhere else, it inevitably draws attention. The result is an emphatic sentence opening.

> Fay checked through the reports carefully, despite distracting noises coming from the office next door.

> *Carefully,* Fay checked through the reports, despite distracting noises coming from the office next door.

> The exhausted street musician began to pack up his collection of instruments.

> *Exhausted,* the street musician began to pack up his collection of instruments.

2. Prepositional phrases

Like single modifiers, **prepositional phrases** (see **25f**) can often be pulled from a later position in a sentence and placed at its beginning for variety and greater emphasis.

The weather in this city is completely unpredictable.
In this city, the weather is completely unpredictable.

U.S. auto manufacturers have begun to reestablish their credibility with American consumers during the past five years.
During the past five years, U.S. auto manufacturers have begun to reestablish their credibility with American consumers.

8g

3. Inversions

An *inversion* reverses the normal word order of a sentence by placing the **predicate adjective** (see **25e**) or **direct object** (see **25d**) before the verb. Use this effective construction sparingly.

Judy's red hair was barely visible behind the piles of paper on her desk.

Barely visible behind the piles of paper on her desk *was* Judy's red hair. [positions of subject and predicate adjective reversed]

I consider international peace the most important issue of our time.

International peace I consider the most important issue of our time. [direct object placed before subject and verb]

4. Appositives

Though usually placed after the nouns they refer to, **appositives** (see **25f**) can precede them and may be used to begin a sentence.

Those stained-glass windows, a gift of the college's first graduate, are irreplaceable.

A gift of the college's first graduate, those stained-glass windows are irreplaceable.

David, an unwilling partner in the scheme, feared that he would lose more money than he would make.

An unwilling partner in the scheme, David feared that he would lose more money than he would make.

Some readers would say that both of these sentences have been improved by beginning with the appositive, which in each of the original versions interrupts the flow of the sentence in its position between the subject and predicate.

5. Verbal phrases

8g

Look for opportunities to convert verbs in a sentence into **participial phrases** or **gerund phrases** (see **25f**) as beginning elements.

> Alina was worried about the legal implications of the document and refused to sign it.

> *Worried about the legal implications of the document,* Alina refused to sign it. [participial phrase]

> I considered many ways of using my medical training and finally decided to work in the field of public health.

> *After considering many ways of using my medical training,* I finally decided to work in the field of public health. [preposition with gerund phrase]

6. Absolute phrases

An **absolute phrase**—usually made up of a noun plus an adjective or participle (see **25f**)—is a distinctive sentence opener. Use it for emphasis and economy.

> Mark tried to attract Julie's attention by waving his arms wildly.
> *His arms waving wildly,* Mark tried to attract Julie's attention.

> Jill's patience was exhausted, and she began to raise her voice.
> *Her patience exhausted,* Jill began to raise her voice.

7. Dependent clauses

Moving a **dependent clause** (see **25g**) from the end of a sentence to its beginning shifts emphasis, and changes a cumulative sentence into a periodic one.

> The mayor refused to sign the proclamation because most of the city council members advised against it.

> *Because most of the city council members advised against it,* the mayor refused to sign the proclamation.

Sometimes an independent clause can be reduced to a dependent clause and used as a sentence opener.

Exercise 8 (page 179)

Answers will vary.

1. Arriving in Chicago in 1887, Wright found work as a draftsperson for the architect Joseph Lyman Silsbee. [verbal phrase]
2. After less than a year, Wright was hired as assistant to Louis Sullivan, the most famous architect of his day. [prepositional phrase]
3. In 1889 Wright married Catherine Tobin and built his now-famous house in the Chicago suburb of Oak Park. [prepositional phrase]
4. Soon afterward, Wright and Sullivan argued because of Wright's violation of an agreement not to accept independent commissions, and they parted company. [single modifier]
5. As Wright's family grew, the Oak Park house was enlarged and extensively remodeled. [dependent clause]
6. After adding a studio and office to the house in 1895, Wright made

Service at the oldest restaurant in town has been declining, but the prices have steadily risen.

Although service at the oldest restaurant in town has been declining, the prices have steadily risen.

Ultimately, you must decide which of these strategies best suit your writing. Read your prose aloud, experiment with new stylistic techniques, and work toward developing a style that reflects your own personality.

8g

EXERCISE 8

The following sentences all begin with the subject. Rewrite each so that some other element functions as the sentence opener.

Example

Original   Frank Lloyd Wright, perhaps the greatest of American architects, studied engineering briefly at the University of Wisconsin, but he never completed his degree.

Revised   Perhaps the greatest of American architects, Frank Lloyd Wright studied engineering briefly at the University of Wisconsin, but he never completed his degree. [An appositive is used as the sentence opener.]

1. Wright arrived in Chicago in 1887 and found work as a draftsperson for the architect Joseph Lyman Silsbee.
2. Wright was hired after less than a year as assistant to Louis Sullivan, the most famous architect of his day.
3. Wright married Catherine Tobin in 1889 and built his now-famous house in the Chicago suburb of Oak Park.
4. Wright and Sullivan argued soon afterward because of Wright's violation of an agreement not to accept independent commissions, and they parted company.
5. The Oak Park house was enlarged and extensively remodeled as Wright's family grew.
6. Wright added a studio and office to the house in 1895, and from this point until about 1910, Oak Park was the hub of his professional career.

Oak Park the hub of his professional career from this point until about 1910. [verbal phrase]
7. Among the first of his so-called prairie houses were the strikingly innovative houses that Wright designed for his neighbors—houses that startled the conservative community of Oak Park. [inversion]
8. Borrowing industrial materials such as reinforced concrete, Wright created a new domestic architecture. [verbal phrase]
9. By raising the main living area of his houses to the second floor, Wright increased the sense of privacy, but he maintained the horizontal appearance of his design by eliminating the attic. [verbal phrase]
10. Dramatically open, the interiors of Wright's houses always permit one to see at least a portion of the adjacent rooms. [single modifer]

Exercise 9 (page 180)

Various student revisions of this paragraph might be discussed in small groups, or the members of each group might be directed to work together in preparing a joint revision.

7. The strikingly innovative houses that Wright designed for his neighbors were among the first of his so-called prairie houses, and they startled the conservative community of Oak Park.
8. Wright borrowed industrial materials such as reinforced concrete to create a new domestic architecture.
9. Wright raised the main living area of his houses to the second floor to increase the sense of privacy, but he eliminated the attic to maintain the horizontal appearance of his design.
10. The interiors of Wright's houses are dramatically open, because one can always see at least a portion of the adjacent rooms.

EXERCISE 9

Most of the sentences in the paragraph below are of about the same length, and all begin with the subject. Rewrite the paragraph to increase variety in sentence structure and sentence length. Add new material as necessary.

Selecting an apartment in a strange city is a task full of unknowns. The first step is finding the apartments you want to inspect. You will probably need a recent city map to guide you. A city map, however, doesn't give you all the information you need. It doesn't tell you that there's a noisy factory across the street from the apartment you saw advertised. You have to arrive at the apartment to discover that. The reliability of your new landlord is another very important question. Your landlord may seem friendly when you first meet. He or she must be available when your pipes begin to leak. Acquiring information about your new neighbors may also be difficult. An apartment complex may be quiet when you visit it during the day. You may not meet your neighbors until after you have moved in. They may have a state-of-the-art stereo system that keeps you awake nights. It may even rattle the dishes in your cupboard. Your signature on a lease may condemn you to a year of frustration.

For Further Reading

Corbett, Edward P. J. "Approaches to the Study of Style." *Teaching Composition: Twelve Bibliographical Essays*. Ed. Gary Tate. Fort Worth: Texas Christian UP, 1987. 83–130.

Graves, Richard L. "Symmetrical Form and the Rhetoric of the Sentence." *Essays on Classical Rhetoric and Modern Discourse*. Ed. Robert J. Connors, Lisa S. Ede, and Andrea A. Lunsford. Carbondale: Southern Illinois UP, 1984. 170–78.

Lanham, Richard A. *Style: An Anti-Textbook*. New Haven: Yale UP, 1974.

Miles, Robert, Marc Bertonasco, and William Karns. *Prose Style: A Contemporary Guide*. 2nd ed. Englewood Cliffs: Prentice, 1991.

Williams, Joseph M. *Style: Ten Lessons in Clarity and Grace*. 2nd ed. Glenview: Scott, Foresman, 1985.

9 *Choosing Words*

Like all languages, English is constantly changing. New words are added as names are required for new inventions, discoveries, and ideas: *laser, transistor, fax, meson, tagmeme.* Old words acquire new meanings as they are used in new ways: *half-life* (physics), *snow* (television), *hardware* (computers), *digital* (audio recording). And some words disappear as the need for them vanishes; such is the case, for example, with a whole vocabulary dealing with horse-drawn vehicles. Words gain or lose prestige: *strenuous* and *mob,* once considered slang, are now in standard usage. As all of these examples suggest, an important part of being a writer is developing a genuine curiosity about words.

9a Using the dictionary

A dictionary is an attempt to record the current uses and meanings of words. Although many people believe that a dictionary tells them what a word *ought* to mean or how it *should* be used, a modern dictionary tries to be an accurate and objective record of what is actually being said and written. It discriminates among the current meanings of a word and tries to indicate the ways in which each is used. Since words and constructions differ in prestige value, a conscientious lexicographer will also try to record the current status of words, usually by usage labels such as *Dialectal* or *Regional, Obsolete* or *Archaic, Informal, Colloquial, Nonstandard,* or *Slang.*

1. Unabridged dictionaries

Unabridged dictionaries seek to be comprehensive guides to the language. Containing hundreds of thousands of entries, they

181

Every professional writer knows the value of a dictionary, but many beginning writers may not have had the opportunity to become familiar with all of the features of a standard desk dictionary. This chapter opens with an introduction to those features and a series of exercises that will lead students to new discoveries about the contents and usefulness of their dictionaries. From there, the chapter goes on to consider the more complicated issue of levels of usage. The material in this chapter might be introduced profitably at any point in a writing course.

For a discussion of diction problems, see Chapter **13**, "Revising Diction."

9a

QUICK REFERENCE: *Types of Dictionaries*

Unabridged Dictionaries	Comprehensive, multivolume dictionaries with extensive entries on the origins of each word and the history of its usage. Example: *The Oxford English Dictionary*.
Abridged Dictionaries	Condensed, one-volume versions of unabridged dictionaries, thorough enough for almost all writing tasks. Example: *The American Heritage College Dictionary*.
Pocket Dictionaries	Small paperbacks helpful for checking spelling, but otherwise inadequate for serious writers.

---

typically trace not only the origins of each word but also the history of its usage. Large, often multivolume works, unabridged dictionaries are invaluable sources of information about the development and present status of the language. They are found in a library's collection of reference works.

The Oxford English Dictionary. 2nd ed. 20 vols. Oxford: Clarendon, 1989.
[Commonly known by its initials, the *OED* is the standard historical dictionary of the language, tracing and illustrating the development of each word from its earliest recorded appearance to the present. The latest edition of the *OED* supersedes the earlier thirteen-volume edition of 1933 and its four supplements.]

The Random House Unabridged Dictionary. 2nd ed. New York: Random House, 1993.
[The most recently revised of the major unabridged dictionaries, the *Random House* is also available in a CD-ROM version.]

Webster's Third New International Dictionary of the English Language.
    Springfield: Merriam-Webster, 1986.
[Controversial when it first appeared in 1961 because of its
minimal inclusion of labels to designate nonstandard and
disputed usage, *Webster's Third* is second only to the *OED* in
comprehensiveness.]

9a

2. Abridged dictionaries

Abridged, or condensed, dictionaries provide a selection of the
data contained in their unabridged counterparts. Often called *desk* or
college dictionaries, they combine convenience, reasonable cost, and
thoroughness adequate for almost all writing tasks. The following
abridged dictionaries, frequently updated, are all reliable reference
tools:

> *The American Heritage College Dictionary*
> *Merriam-Webster's Collegiate Dictionary*
> *The Random House Webster's College Dictionary*
> *Webster's New World Dictionary*

Note that these abridged dictionaries are not the same as so-called
pocket dictionaries. Those smaller, paperbound volumes may be useful
for checking spelling and pronunciation, but their information about
what words mean and how they are used is insufficient for serious
writers.

3. Dictionary abbreviations and symbols

To use a dictionary effectively, you must understand the abbreviations and symbols it uses. You will find them explained in its
introductory section. Below are entries from four college dictionaries,
followed by notes on the information they provide.

Spelling and syllabication

When more than one spelling is given, the one printed first is
usually preferred. Division of the word into syllables follows the conventions accepted by printers.

spelling & syllabication   etymology
↓   ↓

¹**im·ply** (im plī′) *vt.* **-plied′, -ply′ing** ⟦ ME *implien* < OFr *emplier* < L *implicare,* to involve, entangle < *in-,* in + *plicare,* to fold: see PLY¹ ⟧ **1** to have as a necessary part, condition, or effect; contain, include, or involve naturally or necessarily [*drama implies* conflict] **2** to indicate indirectly or by allusion; hint; suggest; intimate [an attitude *implying* boredom] **3** [Obs.] to enfold; entangle—*SYN.* SUGGEST

reference to discussion of synonyms   usage label
↑   ↑

²**im·ply** \im-'plī\ *vt* **im·plied; im·ply·ing** [ME *emplien,* fr. MF *emplier,* fr. L *implicare*] (14c) **1** *obs:* ENFOLD, ENTWINE **2:** to involve or indicate by inference, association, or necessary consequence rather than by direct statement < rights ~ obliga­tions > **3:** to contain potentially **4:** to express indirectly < his silence *implied* consent > *syn* see SUGGEST *usage* see INFER

illustrations of use
↑

Pronunciation

A key to the symbols used to indicate pronunciation of words is usually printed on the front or back inside cover of the dictionary. Some dictionaries also run an abbreviated key to pronunciation at the bottom of each page or every other page. Word accent is shown by the symbol (′) after the stressed syllable or by (') before it.

Parts of speech

Abbreviations (explained in the introductory section of the dictionary) are used to indicate the various grammatical uses of a word; for example, *imply, v.t.* means that *imply* is a transitive verb.

---

¹With permission. From *Webster's New World Dictionary.* Third College Edition. Copyright © 1988 by Simon & Schuster, Inc.

²By permission. From *Merriam-Webster's Collegiate Dictionary.* Tenth Edition. © 1993 by Merriam-Webster, Inc., Publishers of the Merriam-Webster® Dictionaries.

pronunciation   part of speech   meanings
↓   ↓   ↓

³**im·ply** (im·plī) *v.t.* **·plied, ·ply·ing 1.** To involve necessarily as a circumstance, condition, effect, etc.: *An action* implies *an agent.* **2.** To indicate or suggest without stating; hint at; intimate. **3.** To have the meaning of; signify. **4.** *Obs.* To entangle; infold.—**Syn.** See INFER. [< OF *emplier* < L *implicare* to involve < *in-* in + *plicare* to fold. Doublet of *EMPLOY.*]

    —**Syn. 1.** *Imply* and *involve* mean to have some necessary connection. *Imply* states that the connection is causal or inherent, while *involve* is vaguer, and does not define the connection. **2.** *Imply, hint, intimate, insinuate* mean to convey a meaning indirectly or covertly. *Imply* is the general term for signifying something beyond what the words obviously say; *his advice* implied *confidence in the stock market.* *Hint* suggests indirection in speech or action: *our host's repeated glances at his watch* hinted *that it was time to go.* *Intimate* suggests a process more elaborate and veiled than hint: *she* intimated *that his attentions were unwelcome.* *Insinuate* suggests slyness and a derogatory import: *in his remarks, he* insinuated *that the Senator was a fool.* ↑

full discussion of synonyms

9a

Inflected forms

Forms of the past tense and past and present participles of verbs, the comparative or superlative degree of adjectives, and the plurals of nouns are given whenever there might be uncertainty about the correct form or spelling.

Etymology

The history of each word is indicated by the forms in use in Middle or Old English, or in the language from which the word was borrowed. Earlier meanings are often given.

Exercises 1 and 2 (page 187)

Answers will vary. The class may be broken into small groups to compare their sentences in Exercise 1.

---

inflected forms
↓

⁴**im·ply** (ĭm-plī′) *tr.v.* **-plied, -ply·ing, -plies. 1.** To involve by logical necessity; entail. **2.** To express or indicate indirectly: *His tone implied disapproval.* See Syns at **suggest.** See Usage Note at ←
infer. 3. *Obsolete.* To entangle. [ME *implien* < OFr. *emplier,* to enfold < Lat. *implicāre.* See IMPLICATE.]

reference to ⎯
discussion of
usage

Meanings

Different meanings of a word are numbered and defined, sometimes with illustrative examples. Some dictionaries give the oldest meanings first; others list the common meanings of the word first.

Usage labels

Descriptive labels, often abbreviated, indicate the level of usage: *Archaic, Obsolete, Colloquial, Slang, Dialectal, Regional, Substandard, Nonstandard,* and so on. Sometimes usage labels indicate a special field rather than a level of usage—for example, *Poetic, Irish, Chemistry.* If a word has no usage label, it may be assumed that, in the opinion of the editors, the word is in common use on all levels; that is, it is *Standard English.* Usage labels are often defined and illustrated in the explanatory notes in the front of a dictionary.

Synonyms

Many words have closely related or nearly identical meanings and require careful discrimination. A full account of the distinctions in

---

⁴© 1993 by Houghton Mifflin Company. Reprinted by permission from *The American Heritage Dictionary of the English Language,* Third Edition.

Exercise 3 (page 187)

1. *alibi:* a plea of having been elsewhere. From L *alius,* "other," and *ibi,* "there." The notion of "another place" is thus encapsulated in the word's etymology, as are the two *i*'s and one *l* of the spelling.
2. *capitol:* when uncapitalized, the building in which a state legislature meets; when capitalized, either the building in which the U.S. Congress meets or the temple of Jupiter on the Capitoline hill in Rome. From L *Capitolium,* "chief temple," from L *caput,* "head."
3. *cohort:* a group, especially of soldiers (in the Roman army, one-tenth of a legion); informally, an associate or colleague. From L *cohors,* "an enclosed yard, a crowd."
4. *concave:* hollow and curved. From L *concavus,* from *con* and *cavus,* "hollow." The association with cave and cavity helps to keep this word separate from its opposite, *convex.*
5. *denouement:* the final unraveling of a plot or the complications thereof. From F *desnouement,* from *des-* ("dis") and *nouer,* "to tie," from L *nodare,* "to knot." Hence, to unknot, untie.

meaning among synonyms (for example, *suggest, imply, hint, intimate,* and *insinuate*) may be given at the end of the entry for each word, or cross-references to its synonyms may be provided.

EXERCISE 1

In looking up the meanings of words, try to discover within what limits of meaning the word may be used. Read the definition as a whole; do not pick out a single synonym and suppose that this and the word defined are interchangeable. After looking up the following words in your dictionary, write a sentence for each one that will unmistakably illustrate its meaning.

anachronism	innocuous	precocious
eminent	materiel	sinecure
fetish	misanthropy	sophistication
hedonist	nepotism	taboo
imminent	philanthropy	travesty

9a

EXERCISE 2

Look up each of the following words in the *Oxford English Dictionary,* in another unabridged dictionary, and in an abridged one, and write a one-page report illustrating how the larger dictionaries explain the use of each word more carefully and clearly than the smaller one. Give the title, the publisher, and the date of each dictionary.

Bible	color	idealism
catholic	court	liberal
chariot	evolution	nose

EXERCISE 3

How may the etymologies given by the dictionary help one to remember the meaning or the spelling of the following words? Look up their origins in an abridged dictionary, or for more information, in a dictionary of etymology like *The Barnhart Dictionary of Etymology,* ed. Robert K. Barnhart (N.p.: Wilson, 1988). (Note that when a series of words has the same etymology, the etymology is usually given only with the basic word of the series.)

alibi	insidious	privilege
capitol	isosceles	sacrilegious

6. *insidious:* sly, wily, treacherous. From L *insidiosus,* from *insidiae,* "a trick or ambush"; related to *insidere,* "to lie in wait for, to sit in or on," from *in* and *sedere,* "to sit."

7. *isosceles:* having two equal sides (of a triangle). From Gr *isoskeles,* from *iso-,* "equal," and *skelos,* "leg." The notion of "equal legs" clarifies the current meaning.

8. *magnanimous:* noble, generous, unselfish. From L *magnus,* "great," and *animus,* "soul."

9. *malapropism:* a ridiculous mistaking of one word for another. From Mrs. Malaprop, a character in Richard Brinsley Sheridan's play *The Rivals* (1775). Her name, in turn, comes from F *mal à propos,* "not to the purpose."

10. *peer:* a person of equal standing with another. From L *par,* "equal."

11. *privilege:* a special or particular right. From L *privus,* "single, private," and *lex, leg-,* "law."

12. *sacrilegious:* injurious or disrespectful to sacred things. From L *sacer,*

cohort	magnanimous	sarcasm
concave	malapropism	subterfuge
denouement	peer (noun)	thrifty

9a

EXERCISE 4

Most dictionaries put abbreviations in the main alphabetical arrangement. Locate the following abbreviations and their meanings.

at. wt.	Ens.	LL.D.
CAB	ff.	OAS
colloq.	KB	PDT
e.g.	l.c.	Q.E.D.

EXERCISE 5

Consult the dictionary for the distinction in meaning between the members of each of the following pairs of words:

neglect—negligence	instinct—intuition
ingenuous—ingenious	nauseous—nauseated
fewer—less	eminent—famous
admit—confess	criticize—censure
infer—imply	increment—addition

EXERCISE 6

In each sentence, choose the more appropriate of the two italicized words. Be able to justify your choice.

1. Many in the class were *disinterested, uninterested* and went to sleep.
2. David's charming innocence is *childlike, childish*.
3. People often *complemented, complimented* Carolyn and Tom on their children's good manners.
4. Ellen is *continuously, continually* in trouble with the police.
5. I am quite *jealous, envious* of your opportunity to study in Europe.
6. Linda is so *decided, decisive* in her manner that people always give in to her.
7. If we give your class all of these privileges, we may establish *precedents, precedence* that are unwise.
8. Mark always makes his health an *alibi, excuse* for his failures.
9. Scott was *anxious, eager* to collect the prize money he had won.
10. The audience at the city council meeting was entirely *composed, comprised* of citizens outraged over rising taxes.

"sacred," and *legere*, "to take"; after the phrase *sacra legere*, "to purloin sacred things." Knowledge of this word's etymology may help one remember the correct placement of its *i*'s and *e*, in contrast to the spelling of *religious*, especially since that word has affected the pronunciation of *sacrilegious*.

13. *sarcasm:* a biting or cutting remark. From F *sarcasme*, from Gr *sarkazein*, "to tear flesh," a derivation that explains the quality of language denoted by the current word.
14. *subterfuge:* a device or action used to escape something unpleasant. From L *subterfugere*, "to escape secretly," from *subter*, "secretly," and *fugere*, "to flee, escape."
15. *thrifty:* frugal, industrious, thriving. From ON *thrifask*, "to thrive."

Exercise 4

at. wt.	atomic weight
CAB	Civil Aeronautics Board

EXERCISE 7

Find the precise meaning of each word in the following groups, and write sentences to illustrate the differences in meaning among the words in each group.

1. abandon, desert, forsake
2. ludicrous, droll, comic
3. silent, reserved, taciturn
4. meager, scanty, sparse
5. knack, talent, genius

9b

9b Levels of usage

Every good dictionary tells you the contexts in which the use of a word is appropriate, its customary usage. *Standard English* includes the great majority of words and constructions that native speakers would recognize as acceptable in any situation or context, whether spoken or written. All words in a dictionary that are not otherwise labeled are, in the judgment of the editors, Standard English and acceptable for general use. Other words and constructions, which for various reasons have a more limited use, are labeled to indicate their narrower range of acceptability. For example, words commonly used in only one part of the country (such as *frappé* for "milk shake") are accompanied by a regional designation (in this case, *New England*). Other labels—like *colloquial, informal,* and *slang*—indicate words that are appropriately used only in informal contexts. And still other labels—*Archaic, Obsolete,* and *Rare*—identify words that are no longer in common use at all.

1. Edited English

Edited English, the usual written form of the language, is relatively formal Standard English. It is the language of books from reputable publishers, good magazines, and most newspapers. Edited English is defined not merely by choice of words, but by widely accepted conventions of spelling, punctuation, grammatical usage, and sentence structure. The general subject of this book is Edited English, the normal means of official communication in the professions and in business and industry.

It may sometimes be difficult to determine whether a usage is acceptable in Edited English because authorities on language often

colloq.	colloquial, colloquialism, colloquially
e.g.	for example (L *exempli gratia*)
Ens.	ensign
ff.	folios; following; fortissimo (music)
KB	kilobyte
l.c.	left center (of a stage); lower case (typography)
LL.D.	Doctor of Laws (L *Legum Doctor*)
OAS	Organization of American States
PDT	Pacific daylight time
Q.E.D.	which was to be demonstrated or proved (L *quod erat demonstrandum*)

Exercise 5 (page 188)

1. The word *neglect* can be a noun or a verb; *negligence* can only be a noun. As a noun, *neglect* indicates a lack of care or attention, *negligence* a habitual neglect or a legally culpable level of carelessness.

9b

Levels of Usage

Standard English	The great majority of words and constructions that native speakers recognize as acceptable in any context.
Formal English	Language that appears in scholarly or scientific articles, formal speeches, and official documents. Includes words and phrases that rarely appear in conversation or casual writing.
Colloquial English	Conversational language appropriate for casual communication with friends but possibly out of place in writing.
Nonstandard English	Language whose usage is not accepted by most educated readers.
Slang	Words with a humorous or exaggerated meaning used in extremely informal contexts.

differ among themselves, particularly in cases where the language seems to be changing. For example, many speakers deplore the use of the word *impact* as a verb meaning "to affect" or "to have an impact on." But the most recent editions of three leading dictionaries differ widely on this point: one accepts the usage with no label; another accepts it but labels it *colloquial;* and the third marks it with the warning *usage problem.*

Faced with such disagreement, what should you do? If you use *impact* to mean "affect" and someone challenges you, you can certainly defend yourself by citing *Merriam-Webster's Collegiate Dictionary,* which makes no objection to it. But being challenged is a nuisance, and controversial usages may in any case distract your readers from the point you wish to make. If the main purpose of your writing is to get something said, be wary of usages that need lengthy defense.

2. These words might almost be said to be antonyms, *ingenuous* meaning "simple, artless, candid," and *ingenious* meaning "clever, original, inventive."
3. *Fewer* is used with things that can be counted ("fewer coins"), *less* with amounts that cannot be counted as individual items ("less money").
4. To *admit* is simply to concede, grant, or acknowledge; to *confess* carries the connotation of admitting wrongdoing.
5. To *infer* and to *imply* are opposite ends of the same process. You *imply* something by suggesting or hinting it; you *infer* something when you draw an inference from what someone else has said.
6. *Intuition* is an instantaneous apprehension, immediate and irrational, but characteristic only of people. *Instinct,* on the other hand, is a native, inborn, unlearned response occurring in animals as well as human beings.
7. That which is *nauseous* causes nausea; one who is *nauseated* is suffering from nausea, perhaps from having come into contact with something nauseous.

2. Formal English

Formal English appears in scholarly or scientific articles, formal speeches, official documents, and any context calling for scrupulous propriety. It makes use of words and phrases, such as *scrupulous propriety,* that rarely occur in conversation and that would seldom appear in casual writing. As another example, consider the verb *endeavor.* This is a perfectly good word that everyone knows, but its use is limited almost entirely to formal, written English, and even there it is not common. It is likely to give a bookish flavor to casual writing, and it is almost never used in speech. (Try to imagine yourself handing a friend a piece of writing with the request, "Endeavor to read this.") Formal English also includes technical language—the specialized vocabularies (sometimes called *jargon*) used in such professions as law, medicine, and the sciences. Technical language can be very precise and economical, but it is unintelligible to the ordinary reader and out of place in most Edited English, except in such special circumstances as legal documents, medical reports, and scientific papers.

9b

The basic principle of good usage is to fit the level of your language to the situation and to the expected reader. The most formal English is for the most formal occasions, such as a commencement or a funeral, or for official personages, such as college presidents in their public speeches and writing. In the most formal English, one might *endeavor to assuage one's consternation;* less formally the writer might simply say *attempt to calm your fears.*

3. Colloquial English

Colloquial English means, literally, conversational English. Everyone's language is more casual and relaxed among friends than in public speech or writing. Examples are adjectives such as *pricey* for "expensive," verbs like *get away with* something, and adverbs such as *sure* in the sense of "certainly" (*I sure would like . . .*). When words and constructions are labeled *Colloquial* (some dictionaries use *Informal* for the same purpose), you should consider whether they may be jarringly out of place in the context of your writing. If in doubt, look for more formal synonyms.

8. An *eminent* person is one who is outstanding or distinguished; the term is always complimentary. A *famous* person, on the other hand, is merely someone who is widely known; the term may be complimentary, but it is not necessarily so.
9. The word *censure* is the stronger in this pair, carrying connotations of blame and implying graver faults than *criticize.*
10. The word *addition* is the more general term here. An *increment* is a measurable amount of increase, and the term is used particularly when the increase is one of a series.

Exercise 6 (page 188)

1. *uninterested* [*Disinterested* means "having no personal interest in." *Uninterested,* which means "lacking interest in," is called for in this sentence.]
2. *childlike* [*Childish* usually carries a pejorative connotation; in this sentence, it would be at odds with the word *charming.*]

4. Regional English

Regional English refers to language that is common only to speakers in a limited geographical area. These words are often standard in speech and informal writing in the regions where they are found, and sometimes they are useful additions to the local vocabulary. But for general public writing, including most college writing, they should be avoided when equivalent words in national currency are available. Some examples of regional words and expressions are *gumband* for *rubber band*, *banquette* for *sidewalk*, and *stand on line* for *stand in line*.

5. Dialect and nonstandard English

A *dialect* is a variety of a language spoken in a particular region of the country or by a socially identifiable group of persons. Speakers of a dialect may use not only special vocabulary but also distinct grammatical structures that differ from those of Standard English. Speech forms that are restricted to a particular social dialect are often labeled *Nonstandard* (sometimes *Substandard*) in dictionaries. The use of *learn* for *teach* or *she don't* for *she doesn't* is Nonstandard in this sense.

To the modern linguist, all the dialects spoken by different groups in American society are equally expressive varieties of English, even though many of their features are not appropriate in Edited English. However, the social prestige and broad acceptability associated with Standard English make it important for educated persons to be able to distinguish this form of English from other types. Since a regional or social dialect's grammatical rules may differ from the rules of Standard English, students who are bidialectal have two sets of grammatical rules to keep in mind. They must be aware of those areas where their spoken English and written English conflict, and they may have to proofread their written work with special care to make certain that it follows the conventions of Edited English.

The labels *Nonstandard* and *Substandard* are also used to indicate a wide variety of usages not accepted by most educated readers but not necessarily associated with dialects at all: misspellings, unconventional punctuation, idiosyncratic grammatical constructions, and certain widespread usages that educated people have qualms about writing. Examples are words such as *irregardless* for *regardless, imply* for *infer,* and *flaunt* for *flout,* and grammatical errors such as *between you*

---

3. *complimented* [To *complement* is to complete or bring to perfection (e.g., furniture and carpeting that complement each other). The word meaning "to express praise or admiration" is spelled with an *i.*]
4. *continually* [This word, meaning "intermittently" or "repeatedly," indicates that Ellen frequently gets into trouble. In contrast, *continuously* ("without interruption") would mean that she never gets out of it.]
5. *envious* [This word means "discontent over another's possessions," usually with the desire to have them for oneself; *jealousy* adds the elements of resentfulness and rivalry.]
6. *decisive* [Both words denote a manner that is firm and unhesitating, but *decisive* also implies making decisions or settling disputes.]
7. *precedents* [*Precedence* is the right to precede, or go before someone else, and would be meaningless here.]
8. *excuse* [*Alibi,* though often used informally in the sense of "excuse," more properly denotes a physical "being elsewhere," which does not fit the sense of this sentence.]

and I (where *me* is correct). Many other common problems of this nature are listed in the Glossary of Usage at the end of this book. Expressions labeled *Nonstandard* have no place in Edited English, unless in direct quotation.

6. Slang

Slang is the label given to words with a forced, exaggerated, or humorous meaning used in extremely informal or colloquial contexts. To call a person whose ideas and behavior are unpredictable and unconventional *a kook* or to describe his or her ideas as *for the birds* satisfies some obscure human urge toward irreverent, novel, and vehement expression. Some slang terms remain in fairly wide use because they are vivid ways of expressing an idea that has no exact standard equivalent: *stooge, lame duck, shot* of whiskey, card *shark.* Such words are becoming accepted as Standard English. *Mob, banter, sham,* and *lynch* were all once slang terms. It is quite likely that, eventually, such useful slang words as *honky-tonk* and *snitch* will also be accepted as Standard.

A good deal of slang, however, reflects nothing more than the user's desire to be colorful, outrageous, or part of a particular in-group, and such slang has little chance of gaining complete respectability. Sports commentators and disc jockeys, for example, often use a flamboyant jargon intended to show off their ingenuity and cleverness and to establish their credentials as members of a select group or inner circle who keep up with the times. For centuries criminals have used a special, semisecret language, and many modern slang terms originated in the argot of the underworld: *gat, scram, squeal* or *sing* (confess), *push* (peddle).

Slang should be used with discretion in writing, since most slang terms fit only uncomfortably into Edited English. Furthermore, much slang goes out of fashion very quickly, and dated slang sounds more quaint and old-fashioned than Formal English. In the 1950s, to call someone a *square* identified the speaker as a youthful, up-to-date person; today, a person who uses this term seems stuck in a bygone era.

The chief objection to the use of slang is that it so quickly loses any precise meaning. Calling a person a *nerd,* a *twerp,* or a *dweeb* conveys little more than your feeling of dislike. *Cool* and *bummed out* are the vaguest kind of terms, lumping all experience into two crude divisions,

9. *eager* [This word means "exhibiting enthusiastic interest or desire"; while *anxious* also indicates anticipation, it includes a sense of uneasiness or apprehension. But *anxious* is gradually gaining acceptability as a synonym for *eager.* Whereas 72 percent of the Usage Panel of the *American Heritage Dictionary* rejected such a usage in 1969, only 52 percent of the 1993 Usage Panel found it unacceptable.]
10. *composed* [To *compose* is to make up or constitute; in contrast, to *comprise* is to include or to be composed of. Here is one way to remember the correct usage of these words: *compose* can be followed by *of* in a sentence ("the audience was composed/made up of citizens"), but *comprise* can't be.]

Exercise 7 (page 189)

Answers will vary. A good discussion of the differences in meanings here might be started by having several students read their sentences for each word.

pleasing and unpleasing. Try to get several people to agree on the precise meaning of *nerd* and you will realize how vague and inexact a term it is. The remedy is to analyze your meaning and specify it. What exactly are the qualities that lead you to classify a person as a *twerp* or a *nerd?*

If, despite these warnings, you must use slang in serious writing, do it deliberately and accept the responsibility for it. Do not attempt to excuse yourself by putting the slang term in quotation marks. If you must apologize for a slang term, do not use it.

9b

EXERCISE 8

With the aid of a dictionary and your own linguistic judgment (that is, your ear for appropriateness), classify the following English words as *Formal, Informal, Colloquial,* or *Slang.*

1. crank, eccentric, [a] character
2. hide, sequester, sneak
3. irascible, cranky, grouchy
4. increase, boost, jack [up the price]
5. decline, avoid, pass [up]
6. pass [out], faint, swoon
7. necessity, [a] must, requirement
8. inexpensive, [a] steal, cheap
9. snooty, pretentious, affected
10. crib, steal, plagiarize, pilfer

EXERCISE 9

For each of the following Standard English words, supply one or more slang terms and, to the best of your ability, judge which are so widespread that they have already begun to creep into highly informal writing (for example, letters to friends, college newspaper columns) or seem likely to do so in the near future.

Example

to *sleep* [to *crash,* to *catch some z's,* slang]

1. money
2. to relax
3. a skilled performer
4. to be going steady or to be in love
5. failure

Exercise 8

In decreasing order of formality:

1. eccentric (F, I); [a] character (I); crank (C)
2. sequester (F); hide (F, I); sneak (C)
3. irascible (F); grouchy (C); cranky (C)
4. increase (F, I); boost (I, C); jack [up the price] (C)
5. decline (F); avoid (F, I); pass [up] (I, C)
6. swoon (F [archaic or literary]); faint (F, I); pass [out] (C)
7. necessity (F, I); requirement (F, I); [a] must (I, C)
8. inexpensive (F, I); cheap (I, C); [a] steal (S)
9. pretentious (F); affected (F, I); snooty (I)
10. pilfer (F); plagiarize (F, I); steal (F, I); crib (C)

6. to tell off
7. pleasant or enjoyable
8. to vomit
9. liquor
10. to ignore or disregard
11. complaint
12. a dull person
13. an unconventional person
14. to be unfairly treated
15. puzzling

9b

EXERCISE 10

Pick five or six slang terms widely used around campus and ask at least five people to define the meaning of each term in Standard English. How much agreement do you find? Now look up the same words in the *New Dictionary of American Slang,* ed. Robert L. Chapman (New York: Harper, 1986). How accurate are this dictionary's definitions of those words? What new information about their origins does the dictionary provide?

Exercises 9 and 10

Answers will vary. These exercises should open an interesting discussion of current English.

For Further Reading

Simpson, Mary Scott. "Teaching Writing: Beginning with the Word." *College English* 39 (1978): 934–39.
Stotsky, Sandra. "The Vocabulary of Essay Writing: Can It Be Taught?" *College Composition and Communication* 32 (1981): 317–26.

PART III

Revising

10 Revising the Essay

From childhood on, we learn to ask others what they think and to pay attention to the opinions they express. Serving on committees in school or in our community, exchanging views on a recent film, sorting out tangled relationships with friends, relatives, or lovers—in these and dozens of other situations we depend on the opinions of others to deepen our understanding or guide our actions. We count on others to help us test and focus our ideas, to make us notice what we might otherwise have overlooked. At our best, when our egos do not intrude, when we don't feel threatened, we realize how vital the insights of other people can be, how much we can gain by collaborating. Such moments are possible in writing, too, particularly in the stages of revision.

10a Understanding revision

Revision, as the Latin roots of the word suggest, is "seeing again"—the chance to rethink an argument, reconsider evidence, rearrange ideas, rephrase sentences. As we observed in Chapter 1, many writers revise as they compose. But most writers also take time after completing a draft to review their work. Because revision at this stage of the writing process is just as idiosyncratic as every other aspect of composing, no one can prescribe rules for revising that will always work for you. What follows, instead, are some general principles for you to keep in mind as you look for ways to revise a draft of an essay.

As Chapter 1 noted, no description of the composing process can adequately represent its recursiveness or its variations among different writers. Although the first three sections of this book place "revising" after "planning" and "writing," we know that most writers revise as they compose and may make discoveries about their intended meaning throughout the composing process. And revising itself is a complex process that cannot realistically be segmented as it is in these four chapters of Part III. The goal of these chapters is not to represent the process of revision, but to shift perspectives on it, helping students to see more readily the different possible targets for revision in what they have written.

Above all, students should finish this section of the book with a clear understanding of the difference between macro revision (the focus of this and the following chapter) and micro revision (the subject of Chapters 12 and 13). Macro revision is stressed first because beginning writers tend to be less comfortable with large-scale rethinking of the organization and development of an essay than they are with sentence-level changes. For an

10a

> QUICK REFERENCE: *Types of Revision*
>
> Revision is the process of rethinking the content and the form of an essay (from Latin roots meaning "to see again"). It occurs on the following two levels:
>
> *Macro revision*   Revision that focuses on the larger elements that make an essay successful, including the sharpness of its focus, the clarity of its organization, and the appropriateness and specificity of its supporting evidence.
>
> *Micro revision*   Revision that deals with smaller changes, such as improving the clarity and conciseness of sentences, refining parallel constructions, and making diction more specific.

1. Recognize the two types of revision

Some students become so preoccupied with making sentence-level changes in their writing (substituting words and correcting punctuation, for example) that they overlook larger matters. Experienced writers, in contrast, recognize that effective revision occurs on two different levels. *Macro revision* involves the larger elements that make an essay successful: the sharpness of its focus, the clarity of its organization, the appropriateness and specificity of its supporting evidence. *Micro revision,* on the other hand, deals with smaller changes, like those ensuring that sentences are clear and concise, diction is specific, and punctuation is correct.

This chapter and the next will deal with macro revision—revision that focuses on the design of the essay as a whole and the strength of its paragraphs. In Chapters **12** and **13** we will turn to micro revision—revising sentences and diction. Separating the levels of revision in this way makes them easier to discuss and, more important, reminds you to focus on large as well as small matters when you revise. Don't conclude, however, that you should revise on only one level at a time. In reality, most writers constantly move back and forth between larger and smaller elements as they revise their work.

illuminating discussion of this point, see the article by Nancy Sommers cited at the end of this chapter.

2. Leave time after finishing a draft before you revise

This is perhaps the most frequently given—and most frequently ignored—piece of advice about revising. All of us occasionally find ourselves writing against the pressure of a deadline, and in such circumstances we compress writing and revising into a single, continuous process. When possible, though, it's a good idea to allow some time—at least a few hours, ideally a few days—to elapse between drafting an essay and revising it. You need such time to detach yourself from your work, to put some distance between yourself and your enthusiastic first efforts. Returning to an essay after such a break, you bring a degree of objectivity that will help you spot weaknesses in your writing and a fresh perspective that will help you find better ways of communicating what you want to say.

10a

3. Analyze your draft systematically

Sometimes we are prompted to revise by the instinctive feeling that a passage doesn't sound right, or that it doesn't say what we wanted it to. Intuition is a valuable guide; a passage that sounds wrong to you after you've written it probably won't sound any better to your readers. Still, we can't always depend on intuition alone to identify opportunities for revision. It's also a good idea to examine a draft systematically, considering its main elements one at a time.

4. Be open to possible changes in your draft

No revision will succeed, though, if you are so committed to the words on your page that you resist considering significant changes in what you have written. One of the hardest tasks that any writer faces is deleting lines, perhaps even paragraphs, that took hours to put down on paper and starting afresh to find a better way to get the point across. And yet, unless we are prepared to make such changes, there is little point in reviewing a draft at all.

Genuine revision demands your willingness to reconsider not just the phrasing of your essay, but its purpose and design. It requires that you be ready to let go of passages that may have seemed acceptable when you originally composed them and to search for stronger

Consider the following questions as a springboard for a class discussion about the idiosyncratic nature of the revising process.

1. How many students in the class actually do leave substantial time between drafting and revising? Why don't the others do so?
2. How many follow their intuition and make changes in an essay when they feel they are necessary? How many resist the impulse to revise? Why do they do so?
3. How often have students been willing to discard a large portion of an early draft?
4. How satisfied are students with their past revising strategies?

evidence and more effective patterns of organization. No wonder that professional writers usually expect to spend as much time revising a paper as they did writing it in the first place. They know that the small changes they make in a draft have a way of leading them to larger ones, and they approach revision prepared to discover new ways of shaping the composition as a whole.

10b Using your peers' suggestions in revision

10b

Professional writers almost always ask their colleagues to comment on the writing that they do before completing a final draft. If you have a friend or roommate who is willing to read your drafts with a critical eye, you should consider enlisting that person's advice for your revising too. Make it clear that you are not simply looking for compliments on what you've written; instead, you want to know about parts of your paper that the reader considers unclear, weakly developed, hard to follow, or just dull. Ask your reader to make brief comments in the margins of your draft, and then talk over his or her reactions to it. You may find that discussing your paper with someone who has read it will help you not only to understand its problems but also to think of ways to correct them.

1. Participating in a peer editing group

Your instructor may assign you to a group of four or five students who read and comment on early drafts of one another's papers throughout the academic term. If you haven't been in such a group before, you may not be sure what kind of advice to give to the other writers in your group. In fact, you may not feel that your advice is very valuable at all. But it is. You don't have to be an accomplished writer to offer useful advice on someone else's paper; you simply have to be a careful, sympathetic, honest reader. Here are some guidelines to consider as you look for appropriate comments to make.

Be considerate

Most of us feel that we have invested some part of ourselves in what we write, particularly if the paper deals with a subject from our

Students not only benefit from but usually enjoy the opportunity to discuss drafts of one another's papers. The guidelines for participating in a peer editing group and the model Peer Editing Worksheet presented in this section may be helpful to instructors who have felt the need for a way to structure the work that their students do in small groups or who have been reluctant to use small-group work in their classes.

experience or an issue that we care strongly about. To avoid hurting another writer's feelings, therefore, you should avoid making sweeping negative judgments about an essay, such as "This paper bored me," or "I don't know why you'd want to write about *this* subject." Such comments can wound the writer without helping him or her to see how the paper might be improved.

Be honest

On the other hand, a host of purely positive comments won't be of much value to another writer either. If everyone in the group says, "I thought your paper was great—I wish mine were that good," the writer may briefly feel gratified, but later, when he or she sits down alone to try to revise the essay, such compliments won't be very helpful. The best advice here is also the simplest: say what you really feel after reading the paper, touching on both its strengths and its weaknesses. Always begin with something that you think the writer has done well, but then go on to discuss elements of the paper that could perhaps be handled better.

10b

Be specific

Although most writers will be interested in your general reactions to their papers, the only really useful suggestions for revision are specific ones. Use your comments, whether oral or written, to point to the precise parts of the paper that you think the writer should reconsider. Don't say, "I think some of the evidence in this paper is weak"; instead, identify the places where the evidence doesn't convince you: "The examples that you give in paragraph 3 don't seem to support your thesis." Don't say, "Sometimes your paragraphs are hard to follow"; instead, specify the places where you have difficulty: "I get lost after the third sentence in paragraph 2."

Be prepared with comments on both the macro and the micro levels

We have noted that revision proceeds on two levels, a macro level that focuses on large issues like purpose, organization, and evidence, and a micro level concerned with sentence-level matters. The revision suggestions made by a peer editing group should also address both kinds of issues. Observations about word choice and comma usage can be useful, but they alone won't help a writer make a badly organized paper coherent, or an unfocused paper clear. Everyone in a peer editing group should also be prepared to make comments on the macro level—for example, comments about the clarity of the paper's focus and organization, about the appropriateness of the writer's tone, or about the strength of the evidence that the writer has cited to support the paper's main points.

2. Using a peer editing worksheet

10b

If you are still unsure about the specific kinds of comments that may assist another student who is about to revise a paper, you and the other members of your group might find it helpful to begin by filling out a Peer Editing Worksheet like the one on pages 205–06.

Don't think of the Peer Editing Worksheet as a scorecard; rather, use it as a way of opening up a discussion of the paper under consideration. Using the worksheet, members of the group individually evaluate the paper. Then, with the help of the paper's author, they compare and discuss their written responses.

Both agreement and disagreement among the group's members can be useful to the writer of the paper. Strong agreement—for example, about the effectiveness of a certain paragraph or the awkwardness of a specific sentence—provides either reassuring evidence of the paper's strengths or convincing proof of its weaknesses. Disagreements can be equally valuable. For example, when several readers formulate a paper's thesis statement in sharply different ways, the writer has probably failed to make clear the focus of the paper. The group members' next step in such a case should be to determine why they were unable to agree on the writer's main point. Perhaps the thesis statement should be reworded so that its subject or restriction is more precise. Or perhaps it needs to be moved to a more prominent position in the paper. By highlighting areas where at least some readers failed to grasp the writer's intentions, disagreements among group members should provoke a

Feel free to adapt the generic Peer Editing Worksheet to suit the demands of specific assignments. Try to include two types of questions: (1) questions that ask the readers to locate features that you expect the paper to include (in this case, for example, a thesis supported by specific evidence) and (2) questions that ask readers to evaluate the strength of certain key features of the paper (for example, its introduction, its conclusion, its organization and development).

Keep peer editing groups small—four or five students at most — and leave plenty of time—probably an entire class period — for students to read and think about the papers in their group, to fill out Peer Editing Worksheets for each paper, and most important, to discuss among themselves their evaluations of the group's papers. Remember that both agreement and disagreement among the members of a peer editing group are valuable. Agreement generally points either to strengths in the paper or to weaknesses that the writer will need to consider when revising. Disagreement opens up opportunities for discussion among members of the group.

Peer Editing Worksheet

Writer's name_____   Evaluator's name_____

1. What does this paper's introduction accomplish? Does it introduce the writer's subject? Does it arouse your interest in the paper? _____

   _____

   _____

   _____

2. What is the thesis statement in this paper? _____

   _____

10b

3. Briefly state the paper's main points, and then comment on how effectively each of these points supports the paper's thesis.

Main Point	*Effective Support for Thesis?*
(a) _____	(a) _____
_____	_____
(b) _____	(b) _____
_____	_____
(c) _____	(c) _____
_____	_____
(d) _____	(d) _____
_____	_____

4. If you were writing this paper, what other points might you use to support its thesis? _____

   _____

   _____

   _____

5. Identify the most successful and the least successful paragraphs of the paper, and explain why you selected them. Consider such matters as the following: Is the paragraph's main idea clearly indicated? Is the paragraph's development effective? Is the paragraph's organization easy to follow?

Most successful paragraph: _____
Reason: _____
_____

Least successful paragraph: _____
Reason: _____
_____

10b

6. Identify two or three of the strongest sentences in the paper, and explain why you selected each (for example: vivid diction, effective use of parallel structure, good sense of the writer's voice).

Strongest Sentences (give paragraph number and sentence number)	Reasons
(a) _____	_____
(b) _____	_____
(c) _____	_____

7. Identify two or three of the weakest sentences in the paper, and explain why you selected each (for example: confusing syntax, vague diction, awkward phrasing).

Weakest Sentences (give paragraph number and sentence number)	Reasons
(a) _____	_____
(b) _____	_____
(c) _____	_____

8. What does the paper's conclusion accomplish? Does it bring the paper to a strong close? _____
_____
_____
_____
_____

discussion of the paper that will help the writer to identify opportunities for effective revising.

The completed Peer Editing Worksheets are valuable not only as starting points for the discussion of a writer's paper, but also as aids to the writer when he or she begins to revise the paper. At the close of the discussion, all the members of the group should give their completed worksheets to the writer, so that he or she may draw on their comments and advice while revising the essay. The written observations that peer editors have made about the effectiveness of the paper's introduction and conclusion, about the strength of its supporting evidence, about its most successful and least successful paragraphs, and about its strongest and weakest sentences can help to guide the writer's reshaping of the essay long after the group has finished talking about it.

If you haven't engaged in such collaborative efforts before, or if you don't know the other members of your group very well, you may at first feel a bit uncomfortable with small-group work. Be patient. As the group begins to jell, you'll find it easier to join into discussions of other writers' papers and of your own. Such experience, you'll discover, will sharpen not only your powers of careful reading, but your writing skills as well.

10c

EXERCISE 1

Ask two friends to read a draft of your next essay and to record their reactions on a Peer Editing Worksheet like the one on pages 205–06. How much correlation do you find between their responses? If possible, bring both friends together to discuss their reactions to your paper.

10c Using your instructor's suggestions in revision

The written comments that an instructor makes on a draft of your essay are your most obvious source of assistance as you consider how to revise. Your instructor may make several different kinds of marks on your paper: short correction symbols like those printed inside the back cover of this book; numerical references to specific sections of this book (5a, 12d, and the like); brief notes or questions in the margins of the paper; and a slightly longer final comment on the paper's strengths and weaknesses. All such marks will be helpful, but you shouldn't necessarily expect them to provide a step-by-step plan for revising your paper. Revision, after all, is not simply a matter of following someone else's directions; rather, it's a creative process, a process through which you make your own discoveries about what you have written. Thus you should plan to use your instructor's comments not as a blueprint for revision but as a guide to reflecting on what you have accomplished in your paper and thinking about improvements that you might make.

0d

EXERCISE 2

Look over several papers that your instructor has marked and returned to you. Do the instructor's comments point mainly to the need for micro revision, or to opportunities for macro revision? Do similar problems, at either level, turn up in more than one paper? Use your instructor's marks to make a personal checklist of things to keep in mind when you revise your next essay.

10d From early draft to final paper: a revision in progress

To show you how the comments of peers and the suggestions of an instructor can help a writer discover a new plan for organizing and developing an essay, this section presents a student paper as it develops from a promising but unfocused draft into a coherent essay with a clear organization and point.

1. Preliminary draft

The following paper is Rhonda Allen's first *finished* draft—not a *rough* draft, but a draft of the essay that is as polished as she could make it before seeking the advice of her peers and instructor. As you read it, think about the questions in the Peer Editing Worksheet on pages 205–06. How would you assess the strengths and weaknesses of this paper?

Section **10d** illustrates some major steps in the process of revision, showing how comments from a student's peers and instructor play a role in shaping the final draft of a paper. Although sentence-level problems in the student paper are noted, the focus of this section is on the larger issues of organization and development.

Rhonda Allen

Professor D. Jacobs

English 105

February 8, 1995

Social Insecurity

Young people today hold high hopes for their futures, and why not? We live in America—the land of opportunity. If one speaks with a factory worker or with a yuppie though, it quickly becomes apparent that a major concern in everyone's mind is what will happen when they reach retirement age. It certainly is in mine. Politicians would respond with Social Security as the promise of retirement. But the majority of us are not politicians, and do not believe Social Security will be there once we reach our golden years. Nothing I heard in the last presidential campaign concerning this issue served to reassure me otherwise.

There is little doubt that Franklin Roosevelt was one of our greatest Presidents. When he conceived Social

10d

Security in the New Deal era of the 1930s, he had a breakthrough idea. Until then, working- and middle-class retirement security was virtually nonexistent.

A vexing problem in Washington these days is, however, that Social Security in the 1990s "ain't what it used to be." Designed to provide reasonable "security" for the elderly, the current amount received monthly does not come close to meeting the basic costs of the recipients. Barely being able to keep gas turned on and food on the table does not foster a sense of security for most Americans.

Social Security was begun in order to provide for America's working-class retired persons. The scope of the program has grown considerably since the 1930s to where it now includes retarded persons, disabled persons, some single parents, and other selected individuals singled out for inclusion. These people do indeed need governmental support,

but the Social Security machine and its
in-place infrastructure has seemed to
be the vehicle of choice, rather than
creating new, more specialized programs.

Another problem with Social Security is that it lags behind the changes
in America's economy. Inflation has
consistently outpaced the cost-of-
living adjustments made to the Social
Security program.

Social Security is an agreement in
kind between a person and the government. I pay into the program all my
working years and help to take care of
today's elderly. Then when I reach retirement age, the workers of tomorrow
will be paying into the program and
supporting me. This all-for-one-and-
one-for-all attitude seems logical and
simple enough. But with the problems
cited and many others not touched on,
the program is quickly heading for an
all-for-one-and-none-for-all conclusion. Social Security is nothing more

10c

0d

than a governmental program in need of a major facelift.

Perhaps I am being presumptuous in assuming a program I started paying into before I even understood what it was for should support me in my later years. What right do I have to the thousands of dollars I will have paid into it?

Conscientious adults must look at the reality of the situation. We cannot count on Social Security being there. At its present rate the program will never survive. Through individual retirement accounts, certificates of deposit, and the like, we must plan on our own for supporting ourselves in our golden years.

We all need to realize the truth of the matter; Social Security has not always been in such a dismal state. When it was created it worked beautifully, because the birthrate was high and contributors far outnumbered recipients. Since 1964 and the end of the

so-called baby boom, America's population has begun to age rapidly. Today
there are almost three contributors for
every recipient. Projections into the
twenty-first century estimate a time
when recipients will nearly equal contributors and eventually outnumber them
if present trends continue. The mathematics here is not difficult, and yet
our leaders in Washington continue to
ignore it. Why they do is not the purpose of this essay. The fact is they
do, and we as concerned citizens must
realize the gravity of the situation
and prepare ourselves accordingly.

10d

EXERCISE 3

Use the Peer Editing Worksheet on pages 205–06 to analyze Rhonda
Allen's paper. Write out your responses to the worksheet questions as if
you were commenting on the paper as a member of her peer editing group.

2. Peer comments

The following worksheet is one of the Peer Editing Worksheets from Rhonda Allen's peer editing group. Remember that other
students may have responded differently to many of these questions.
Even if they offer conflicting advice, the responses on a set of Peer
Editing Worksheets provide a valuable starting point for rethinking
one's paper.

Exercise 3

This exercise gives students practice in working with a Peer Editing Worksheet. After students have completed a worksheet, their written results
could serve as the starting point for a class discussion of Rhonda Allen's
paper. Or students may compare their responses with those on the worksheet in the next section (see Exercise 4).

10d

Peer Editing Worksheet

Writer's name *Rhonda A.*   Evaluator's name *Tony M.*

1. What does this paper's introduction accomplish? Does it introduce the writer's subject? Does it arouse your interest in the paper? *Intro raised questions about Social Security in the future. Does arouse interest — after all, I'll be retired someday too.*

2. What is the thesis statement in this paper? *Not sure — seems to be about problems with Social Security (?)*

3. Briefly state the paper's main points, and then comment on how effectively each of these points supports the paper's thesis.

Main Point	*Effective Support for Thesis?*
(a) *Roosevelt conceived Soc Sec in 1930s*	(a) *No — not related to current problems*
(b) *Soc Sec doesn't meet needs of recipients*	(b) *Yes — current problem that will get worse*
(c) *Scope of Soc Sec has grown*	(c) *Good point but not really explained*
(d) *Inflation has outpaced Soc Sec*	(d) *Good — clear problem*

4. If you were writing this paper, what other points might you use to support its thesis? *Is your point that we should do something to solve the problems with Soc Sec? Then be more specific.*

5. Identify the most successful and the least successful paragraphs of the paper, and explain why you selected them. Consider such matters as the following: Is the paragraph's main idea clearly indicated? Is the paragraph's development effective? Is the paragraph's organization easy to follow?

Remember to stress to students that this is a *representative* worksheet, not an example of all the "right" answers. Their own responses to Rhonda Allen's paper may coincide with some of these or differ from them. The primary function of the worksheet is simply to structure the discussion of a student's paper.

Most successful paragraph: ___¶ 6___

Reason: ___Made me think about how Social Security is supposed to work.___

Least successful paragraph: ___¶ 2___

Reason: ___Doesn't say much. I expected to find out more about the problems with Soc Sec here.___

6. Identify two or three of the strongest sentences in the paper, and explain why you selected each (for example: vivid diction, effective use of parallel structure, good sense of the writer's voice).

10d

Strongest Sentences (give paragraph number and sentence number)	Reasons
(a) ¶ 8, first sent.	Good urgent tone
(b)	
(c)	

7. Identify two or three of the weakest sentences in the paper, and explain why you selected each (for example: confusing syntax, vague diction, awkward phrasing).

Weakest Sentences (give paragraph number and sentence number)	Reasons
(a) ¶ 3, first sent.	Slang
(b) ¶ 4, last sent.	Don't understand
(c) ¶ 9, last sent.	Too vague

8. What does the paper's conclusion accomplish? Does it bring the paper to a strong close? ___I was disappointed. I expected to find out how to change Soc Sec or prepare for retirement, but you don't actually explain what we can do.___

EXERCISE 4

Compare your comments from Exercise 3 with the student comments on the Peer Editing Worksheet above. Where did you agree with those comments? Where did you disagree?

3. Instructor's comments

The following paper is again the first finished draft of Rhonda's paper but with marginal comments from her instructor and a final suggestion for reorganizing the essay. Notice how the instructor's comments focus the writer's attention on problems and suggest (but don't prescribe) ways of solving them. The instructor has used some of his marginal comments to point out problems that call for micro revision—for example, the agreement errors in paragraphs 1 and 4, the vagueness and jargon in paragraph 4, the inexact diction in paragraph 6. But as his final comment indicates, this paper's most serious weaknesses demand revision at the macro level. To revise the paper effectively, Rhonda will have to be willing to reorganize its contents, pulling together related ideas that are scattered throughout this draft of the essay, deleting material that confuses the paper's structure, and discovering a focus for her analysis.

Rhonda Allen

Professor D. Jacobs

English 105

February 8, 1995

Social Insecurity

Young people today hold high hopes

for their futures, and why not? We live

in America—the land of opportunity. If

one speaks with a factory worker or

with a yuppie, though, it quickly be-

comes apparent that a major concern in
(everyone's) mind is what will happen   *agr*
when (they) reach retirement age. It certainly is in mine. Politicians would   *awk*
respond with Social Security as the   *sent*
promise of retirement. But the majority
of us are not politicians, and do not
believe Social Security will be there
once we reach (our golden years.) Nothing *cliché*
I heard in the last presidential campaign concerning this issue served to
(reassure) me otherwise.   *ww*
                                          trans?
    There is little doubt that Fran-
klin Roosevelt was one of our greatest
Presidents. When he conceived Social
Security in the New Deal era of the   *thin ¶ - how is*
1930s, he had a breakthrough idea. Un-   *it related to*
til then, working- and middle-class re-   *your introduction?*
tirement security was virtually nonex-
istent.

    A vexing problem in Washington
these days is, however, that Social Security in the 1990s ("ain't what it used *avoid slang*
to be." (Designed) to provide reasonable
"security" for the elderly, the current   *dm*

10d

amount received monthly does not come close to meeting the basic costs of the recipients. Barely being able to keep gas turned on and food on the table does not foster a sense of security for most Americans.

awk
sent

Social Security was begun in order to provide for America's working-class retired persons. The scope of the program has grown considerably since the 1930s to where it now includes retarded persons, disabled persons, some single parents, and other selected individuals singled out for inclusion. These people do indeed need governmental support, but the Social Security machine and its in-place infrastructure has seemed to be the vehicle of choice, rather than creating new, more specialized programs.

10d *again, no clear*
connection with
previous ¶

vague — explain
or delete

jargon/agr

Another problem with Social Security is that it lags behind the changes in America's economy. Inflation has consistently outpaced the cost-of-living adjustments made to the Social Security program.

very thin
¶ — expand,
or combine
with another?

Social Security is an agreement (in
kind) between a person and the govern-   ?
ment. I pay into the program all my
working years and help to take care of
today's elderly. Then when I reach retirement age, the workers of tomorrow
will be paying into the program and
supporting me. This all-for-one-and-   **10d**
one-for-all attitude seems logical and
simple enough. But with the problems   *doesn't add*
cited and (many others not touched on,)   *much —*
                                            explain or
the program is quickly heading for an   *delete*
(all-for-one-and-none-for-all conclu-) ← *Could be*
sion.) Social Security is nothing more   *clearer*
than a governmental program in need of
a major (facelift.)   *ww—overhaul?*
    Perhaps I am being presumptuous in
assuming a program I started paying   *another under*
into before I even understood what it   *developed ¶*
was for should support me in my later
years. What right do I have to the
thousands of dollars I will have paid
into it?
    Conscientious adults must look at
the reality of the situation. (We cannot)   *unclear—*
count on Social Security being there.)   *when?*

At its present rate the program will never survive. Through individual retirement accounts, certificates of deposit, and the like, we must plan on our own for supporting ourselves in (our golden years)

same cliché as ¶1

10d

shouldn't this historical back-ground come earlier? Combine with ¶ 2?

We all need to realize the truth of the matter; Social Security has not always been in such a dismal state. When it was created it worked beautifully, because the birthrate was high and contributors far outnumbered recipients. Since 1964 and the end of the so-called baby boom, America's population has begun to age rapidly. Today there are almost three contributors for every recipient. Projections into the twenty-first century estimate a time when recipients will nearly equal contributors and eventually outnumber them if present trends continue. The mathematics here is not difficult, and yet our leaders in Washington continue to ignore it. (Why they do is not the purpose of this essay.) The fact is they

Combine this material with earlier ¶s on SSA's problems?

what is its purpose? Not clear.

do, and we as concerned citizens must
realize the gravity of the situation
and prepare ourselves accordingly.

Disappointingly vague. What exactly do you want readers to do?

Your subject is an important one, and you seem to have given it considerable thought. But as I suggest above, the focus and organization of this paper are not very clear. When you revise, I think you should (1) decide what point you want to make and state it explicitly, and (2) improve the coherence of your analysis by combining some of the short paragraphs that deal with the SSA's history and current problems.

10d

EXERCISE 5

Look over the marginal notes made by Rhonda's instructor. Which ones call for macro revision—that is, changes that will involve reorganizing the paper's contents and rethinking its development?

4. Final draft

In the revised paper that follows, notice above all the clearer structure that Rhonda has imposed on her material. Following the suggestions made by her peer editing group and her instructor, she has combined short paragraphs, eliminated extraneous information, and given her analysis a clearer point. In its final form, Rhonda's essay presents a more coherent analysis of the problems with Social Security, and it ends more conclusively with her opinion about the changes that are needed.

Exercise 5

The instructor's comments that point to the need for macro revision include the following:

Paragraph 2: Thin paragraph; connection to introduction unclear.
Paragraph 4: No clear connection with previous paragraph.
Paragraphs 5, 7: Thin development.
Paragraph 9: Information in this paragraph should be combined
    with earlier points. Vague conclusion.

10d

Rhonda Allen

Professor D. Jacobs

English 105

February 15, 1995

Social Insecurity

Young people today hold high hopes for their futures, and why not? We live in America, the land of opportunity. Yet looming in the back of most of our minds is worry about what will happen to us when we reach age sixty-five. To this concern, politicians respond that Social Security is the promise of retirement. But those of us who are not politicians are unconvinced that Social Security will be there when we need it. Regrettably, nothing I heard in the last presidential election persuaded me otherwise.

The problems facing Social Security today have not always existed. Conceived during the New Deal era of the 1930s, Social Security worked well at its onset. At that time, the birth-rate was high and contributors far out-

This revised paragraph, focusing on the origins of the Social Security Administration, draws on material from the second and ninth paragraphs of the original draft.

numbered recipients. Social Security provided a guaranteed income for millions of working- and middle-class retired persons where none had existed before.

In recent years, however, problems have arisen in the Social Security Administration. In the first place, the scope of the program has grown considerably since the 1930s. Now those receiving benefits from the retirement account include retarded persons, disabled persons, and some single parents. Moreover, with the end of the so-called baby boom, America's population has begun to age rapidly, while the number of working contributors to the Social Security program declines. As a result, today there are only about three contributors for every recipient, and projections into the next century point ominously to a time when the number of recipients will equal and then exceed the number of contributors. A final problem with Social Security is that it

This paragraph, on the Social Security Administration's growing problems, unites material from paragraphs 4, 5, and 9 in the earlier draft. Transitional phrases make the main points clear: *In the first place, Moreover, A final problem . . .*

10d

lags behind changes in America's economy. Inflation has consistently outpaced the cost-of-living adjustments made to the Social Security program, and consequently the amount that most people receive each month does not come close to meeting their basic expenses.

10d

This transitional paragraph, a shortened and clarified version of the original paragraph 6, leads Rhonda to the recommendations that she wants to make in her final paragraph.

Social Security was supposed to be an agreement between each citizen and the government. I pay into the program all my working years to help take care of today's elderly. Then when I reach retirement age, the workers of tomorrow will be paying into the program and supporting me. In theory this plan seems simple enough, but the realities of the 1990s indicate that it cannot continue to function in this way for long.

The closing paragraph of the revised essay is much more specific than the conclusion of the earlier version. Here Rhonda makes two precise recommendations:

If the Social Security Administration is to survive into the twenty-first century, we need to replace elected officials who refuse to acknowledge the program's precarious condition with others who realize that decisive action to correct its ills is needed now. And we must be willing to reconsider the program's goals. I believe that we must return Social Security to its original purpose, retirement security for the elderly. For others who have been receiving Social Security benefits, we will need to initiate new programs, along with new methods to fund them. Unless we are prepared to undertake such reform, more and more elderly Americans in the years ahead will find that "Social Security" is just a broken promise.

that we elect officials who are prepared to deal with the problems facing Social Security, and that we consider restructuring the program.

10d

In contrast to the inconclusive ending of the first draft, the final line of this essay powerfully suggests the urgency of the problem.

EXERCISE 6

Many writers fail to revise effectively because they feel too closely tied to the structure and language of their first draft. If you sometimes hesitate to tamper with the early draft of an essay, try the following procedure. After completing a draft of your paper, put it aside for a day or more, and then write a new version of the essay without looking at the original draft. Compare the two versions. Do you find that the changes you made in the second version were more substantial than the changes you ordinarily make when you revise?

For Further Reading

Butturff, Douglas R., and Nancy I. Sommers. "Placing Revision in a Reinvented Rhetorical Tradition." *Reinventing the Rhetorical Tradition.* Ed. Aviva Freedman and Ian Pringle. Ottawa: Canadian Council of Teachers of English, 1980. 99–104.

Faigley, Lester, and Stephen Witte. "Analyzing Revision." *College Composition and Communication* 32 (1981): 400–14.

Flower, Linda, et al. "Detection, Diagnosis, and the Strategies of Revision." *College Composition and Communication* 37 (1986): 16–55.

Lanham, Richard A. *Revising Prose.* 2nd ed. New York: Macmillan, 1987.

Sommers, Nancy. "Revision Strategies of Student Writers and Experienced Adult Writers." *College Composition and Communication* 31 (1980): 378–88.

Sudol, Ronald A., ed. *Revising: New Essays for Teachers of Writing.* Urbana: NCTE, 1982.

Revising Paragraphs

Paragraphs are the timber writers use to construct papers. Depending on the writer's blueprint, they can be cut into various sizes and shapes and planed down or nailed together, and they can serve as doors, joists, or flooring. Problems occur, however, when a beam is too thin to support the weight it must bear, or when it is cracked and knotty, or when the tongue and groove do not match. To put it another way, effective paragraphs have the thickness of evidence needed to sustain their ideas, they are unsplintered and intact, and they are firmly joined together. This chapter will discuss two of the most common weaknesses in paragraphs—lack of development and lack of coherence—and some means of repair. (To be sure that you understand the main characteristics of effective paragraphs, you may wish to read or review Chapters **6** and **7**.)

11a Inadequate development

Although its central idea may be clear, an underdeveloped paragraph is too brief, general, thin, or dull. Developing a paragraph does not mean padding out a simple statement or repeating the same idea in different words. It means taking the time to be clear, accurate, and specific.

1. Recognizing vagueness and generalities

As you read the following account of a group of first-year students meeting their adviser and having dinner together, pay particular attention to what you *don't* find out about the event:

Chapters **6** and **7** dealt with principles of effective paragraph construction and development. In this chapter the focus shifts to *deficiencies* in paragraphs, problems whose elimination falls in a general way under the rubric of "revision."

As in Chapter **10**, the emphasis here is on macro revision—revising that involves changes above the sentence level.

11a

> **QUICK REFERENCE:** *Revising Paragraphs*
>
> | | |
> |---|---|
> | *Improve paragraph development* (**11a**). | Identify vagueness and generalities; substitute appropriate specific details. |
> | *Improve paragraph coherence* (**11b**). | Use transitional words and phrases to indicate relationships between sentences. Link sentences by repeating pronouns. Repeat key words that are related to your central idea. Use parallel structure to highlight parallel ideas. Establish clear connections between paragraphs. |

Mr. Miller was not what I had expected of a faculty member. He was not over fifty years old. He was not wearing thick glasses. He was, in contrast, about twenty-six, rather athletic looking, and a very interesting conversationalist, not only in his own field, but in every subject we discussed.

My classmates, most of whom I had not met before, were also a surprise. There were no socially backward introverts, interested only in the physical sciences, as I had feared. I found instead some very interesting people with whom I immediately wanted to become friends. Some were interested in sports, some in music, some in politics. Each individual had something to offer me.

The Millers did a marvelous job of preparing the dinner. We did a marvelous job of eating it. However, the real purpose of the dinner was to become acquainted with at least one of our faculty members and about ten of our fellow students. In this endeavor we were also quite successful, for the discussions begun during the meal lasted for a long time after and as a matter of fact, some of them were continued the next day.

This year's adviser dinner was very rewarding, and I believe it should remain a tradition. The students really get to know each other, and a few of the faculty are pleasantly surprised.

A reader might well wonder why the dinner should be continued as a tradition. Nothing the writer says carries real conviction because nothing is developed concretely. These paragraphs raise more questions than they answer: (1) Why should the writer have expected his adviser to be an ancient, nearsighted bore? (2) What was Mr. Miller's "field" and what did he talk about? (3) What exactly did his classmates' various interests "offer" him? (4) If the meal was so memorable, what was it and how many servings did he have? (5) What was talked about so enthusiastically and "for a long time after" the meal?

What has gone wrong here? In place of specific information, the writer has relied on unoriginal, formulaic phrases *(very interesting conversationalist, socially backward introverts)*, vague generalities *(some were interested in sports, some in music, some in politics)*, and unexplained events (the dinner conversation). The paragraphs are not developed; they merely repeat the same idea unconvincingly — that the adviser's dinner was a good chance to discover that faculty and students were in some vague way interesting.

11a

2. Using specific details

Specific details cut out fuzziness and give a paper sharpness and depth. Consider these sentences from the essay above: *The Millers did a marvelous job of preparing the dinner. We did a marvelous job of eating it.* Do they mean that the Millers barbecued two dozen hamburgers and tossed a spicy bean salad for a delicious buffet meal on paper plates? Or do they mean that the Millers gave a sit-down dinner, complete with white linen, silver setting, and candlelight, and served roast turkey, hot rolls, and two vegetables? Either of these alternatives is better than the empty generality of the original. A buffet dinner for thirteen people implies relaxed hosts, students going for several helpings, and comfortable informality. A sit-down dinner for thirteen people implies busy hosts, reserved guests, hushed requests for the gravy, and long, earnest discussion as the coffee lingers in cups and the candles melt. Whatever the case was, specific wording would help readers see the event and prepare them for the point that the writer wants to make about it.

Often a paragraph can be dramatically improved by the simple substitution of specific details for generalities, without further revision. For example, in the two versions of the paragraph below, taken from the first and the final drafts of a student essay about a senior class trip to Florida, notice how the writer has increased the effectiveness of his writing without adding significantly to its length, just by substituting

For further discussion of specific language, see **13b**, **13c**, and **13d**.

specific details and concrete diction. The italicized passages indicate the places where he made changes.

Vague original

> When we left our high-school parking lot that Saturday morning, no one was prepared for the discomforts of the trip ahead. We did a variety of things to pass the time, but monotony soon crept in. Also, I became cramped from sitting for long periods of time. When night finally came, we slept sitting up in our seats. Some slept on the aisle floors, where food and drinks had been spilled.

Revised with specific details

> When *the Greyhound bus roared out* of our high-school parking lot *at 6:30* that Saturday morning, no one was prepared for the discomforts of the trip ahead. For a while we *sang songs and played cards* to pass the time, but monotony soon crept in. Also, after *seven or eight hours of sitting in the same seat,* I became stiff and cramped. When night finally came, most of us *dozed restlessly* sitting up in our seats, while others *huddled* on the *narrow* aisle floors where *potato chips* and *Coke* had been spilled.

11a

It's the choice of words, not the number of words, that makes the difference. In the second version, all the discomforts of the trip—the hours of sitting in the same seat, the restless dozing in uncomfortable seats, the desperate attempts to sleep by huddling on the sticky bus floor—have become concrete and tangible.

3. Revising an underdeveloped paragraph

If your instructor or peers comment that your paragraphs are inadequately developed, try using either of the following strategies as you revise.

Identify generalities

Examine the paragraph carefully for vague generalities, needlessly abstract words, and clichés, and underline them. For instance:

```
When they are young, children are free and

can be themselves. They are protected from na-
```

ture's hardships by our <u>modern-day society</u> and
by our <u>complex technology</u>. They only have to
<u>keep out of trouble</u>. Mostly they are <u>free to do</u>
<u>whatever they want</u>. But as they <u>get older</u>, they
have more and more <u>duties and responsibilities</u>
put upon them. They begin to <u>lose their freedom</u>
<u>and become conformists</u>.

11a What does the imprecise phrase *When they are young* really mean? Substitute a more exact phrase—perhaps, *Before they begin elementary school.* Instead of writing vaguely that young children are *free* and able to *be themselves,* why not describe them more specifically as *playful, spontaneous, and imaginative*? Which of *nature's hardships* is the writer thinking of? Hunger? Disease? Exposure to cruel weather?

Underlining may also reveal that certain generalities, if they mean anything at all, are untrue or need extensive qualification: Do children who bike to school, who roam where they wish afterward, and who spend time in the evenings with their friends really *lose their freedom and become conformists*? Or, to take a very different view, is it true that our *modern-day society* and our *complex technology* protect a poor child from crime, sickness, and dilapidated housing?

Construct lists of supplementary details

Make a list of all the possible details or examples you could add to the paragraph. You won't be able to use all of these, of course, without drowning your reader in specifics, but a written list of details offers you a starting place for making judicious and effective additions to your paragraph.

In the following example, notice how the student has identified places where he might insert additional details and has made a preliminary list of the kinds of items that he could include:

Working as a door-to-door salesperson in
and around St. Louis last summer gave me more

than just extra spending money. It gave me a chance to meet types of people* I might otherwise never have known, and some practical experience* I am glad I had.

* Construction workers living in trailers — retired jazz musicians living in boarding houses — young couples renovating inner-city duplexes — retirees in suburban condos

* Sizing up a person's interests and tastes — keeping my temper when insulted — making friends with hostile dogs — thinking on my feet

From such a list of specific details, a writer is able to choose those that best support the point he or she wishes to make.

EXERCISE 1

Take a notebook to one of the following locations and make a long list of all of the specific details (including what you see, what you hear, what you smell) that you might use to describe it. Use some of these details to write a one-paragraph description of the place you visited. Give your paragraph unity by selecting details that work together to create a single dominant impression.

A neighborhood hardware store

An airport terminal, a bus depot, or a train station

A restaurant or a cafeteria

A main street in a town or a large public plaza in a city

A sports arena

Exercise 1

This exercise might also be used as the basis of a longer writing assignment. In either case, its purpose is to give students practice not only in accumulating but in *selecting* specific details.

Plan a tentative outline for an upcoming paper and list as many specific examples or details as you can for each major idea or stage in the analysis. Write a first draft using all of your evidence. Then study your draft with the following questions in mind: Do all the examples and details warrant inclusion? If some are more effective than others, why are they? Do some of the examples or details bring others to mind that you had not included? If so, is any of the new material more effective than your original evidence?

11b Lack of coherence

Within every paragraph, the sentences should be arranged and linked in such a manner that readers can easily follow the thought. It isn't enough for readers to know what each sentence means; they must also see how each sentence is related to the one that precedes it and how it leads into the one that comes next. Without transitional devices to indicate such relationships, even a reasonably well-unified paragraph can be difficult to follow.

Most writers rely on four primary devices for achieving coherence: transitional words, linking pronouns, the repetition of key words, and parallel structure.

1. Transitional words

Transitional words and phrases help to indicate relationships between sentences. Notice how carefully used transitional words help us follow the writer's argument in the following passage.

Transitional words provide coherence

Past and future are two time regions which we commonly separate by a third which we call the present. *But* [contrast] strictly speaking the present does not exist, or is at best no more than an infinitesimal point in time, gone before we can note it as present. *Nevertheless* [contrast] we must have a present; *and so* [cause and effect] we get one by robbing the past, by holding on to the most recent events and pretending that they all belong to our immediate perceptions. If, *for example* [example], I raise my arm, the total event is a series of occurrences of which the first are past

Transitional Words and Phrases

Cause or effect	Contrast	Addition
as a result	but	also
because	however	besides
consequently	in contrast	furthermore
hence	nonetheless	in addition
since	on the contrary	moreover
so	on the other hand	next
therefore	still	too
thus	yet	

Example	Comparison	Conclusion
for example	in the same way	in conclusion
for instance	likewise	in short
specifically	similarly	to conclude
		to sum up

before the last two have taken place; *yet* [contrast] I perceive it as a single movement executed in one instant of time.

—Carl Becker, *The Heavenly City of the Eighteenth-Century Philosophers*

2. Linking pronouns

Sentences may also be linked by pronouns that have clear antecedents. Notice in the following example how Henry James achieves coherence by repeating the pronoun *it,* which refers first to *symbolism,* then to *suggestion.*

Linking pronouns provide coherence

In *The Scarlet Letter* there is a great deal of symbolism; there is, I think, too much. *It* is overdone at times, and becomes mechanical; *it* ceases to be impressive, and grazes triviality. The idea of the mystic *A* which the young minister finds imprinted upon his breast and eating into his flesh, in sympathy with the embroidered badge that Hester is condemned to wear, appears to me to be a case in point. This suggestion should, I think, have just been made and dropped; to insist upon *it,* and return to *it,* is to exaggerate the weak side of the subject. Hawthorne returns to *it* constantly, plays with *it,* and seems charmed by *it;* until at last the reader feels tempted to declare that his enjoyment of *it* is puerile.

—Henry James, *Hawthorne*

3.   Repetition of key words

Paragraph coherence may also be maintained by the repetition of key words that are related to a central idea. In the following passage, pay special attention to the key words *darkness, deep sea,* and *blackness* and the words related to them by contrast, such as *sunlight, red rays,* and *surface.*

Repeated key words provide coherence

Immense pressure, then, is one of the governing conditions of life in the *deep sea; darkness* is another. The unrelieved *darkness* of the *deep waters* has produced weird and incredible modifications of the *abyssal* fauna. It is a *blackness* so divorced from the world of the *sunlight* that probably only the few men who have seen it with their own eyes can visualize it. We know that *light fades out rapidly with descent below the surface.* The *red rays* are gone at the end of the first 200 or 300 feet, and with them all the *orange and yellow warmth of the sun.* Then the *greens* fade out, and at 1,000 feet only a *deep, dark, brilliant blue* is left. In *very clear waters* the *violet rays* of the spectrum may penetrate another thousand feet. Beyond this is only the *blackness* of the *deep sea.*

—Rachel Carson, *The Sea Around Us*

4.   Parallel structure

Continuity is also created and sustained when several sentences within a paragraph all begin with the same grammatical structure. Such grammatical parallelism shows the reader which ideas in the paragraph are parallel in importance as well. In the following paragraph, for example, Shelby Steele uses parallel sentence beginnings—*It became* . . .

It spawned . . . It was redefined . . . It was imbued . . . —to highlight the main points that he wishes to make about his subject, racial identification.

Parallel structure provides coherence

For blacks, the decade between 1960 and 1969 saw racial identification undergo the same sort of transformation that national identity undergoes in times of war. *It became* more self-conscious, more narrowly focused, more prescribed, less tolerant of opposition. *It spawned* an implicit party line, which tended to disallow competing forms of identity. Race-as-identity was lifted from the relative slumber it knew in the fifties and pressed into service in a social and political war against oppression. *It was redefined* along sharp adversarial lines and directed toward the goal of mobilizing the great mass of black Americans in this warlike effort. *It was imbued* with a strong moral authority, useful for denouncing those who opposed it and for celebrating those who honored it as a positive achievement rather than as a mere birthright.

—Shelby Steele, "On Being Black and Middle Class," *Commentary*

5. Maintaining coherence between paragraphs

The main devices for maintaining coherence between paragraphs are the same as those for providing coherence within a paragraph—transitional words, linking pronouns, repeated key words, and parallel structure. Equally important is the *arrangement* of the material so that a paragraph begins with some reference to the idea that has come before, or ends with some reference to the idea that is to be taken up next. In the following paragraphs, notice how often the writers begin a paragraph by overtly referring to an idea developed in the previous paragraph. Such a strategy helps the reader move easily from paragraph to paragraph, never losing the thread of the argument.

Two world views, reflecting fundamentally different visions of society and self, are moving into conflict in the America of the 1990s. A new generation gap is emerging. In the late 1960s the fight was mainly between twenty-year-olds and the fifty-plus crowd. Today it's mainly between young people and the thirty- to forty-year-olds.

In these gaps, the old 1960s one and the emerging 1990s facsimile, there have been two constants: Each time, the same conspicuous

Note the parallel structure used to achieve coherence within the second paragraph of this essay *(Each time . . . Each time . . .).*

generation has been involved. Each time, that generation has claimed the moral and cultural high ground, casting itself as the apex of civilization and its age-bracket adversaries as soul-dead, progress-blocking philistines. The first time around, the members of that generation attacked their elders; now they're targeting their juniors.

We're talking about Baby Boomers. Born from 1943 to 1960, today's 69 million Boomers range in age from thirty-two to forty-nine. Defined by its personality type, this generation is somewhat different from the group defined simply by the well-known demographic fertility bulge (1946–1964). At the front end, the grown-up "victory babies" of 1943—peers of Janis Joplin and Bobby Fischer, Joni Mitchell and Geraldo Rivera, Oliver North and Rap Brown, R. Crumb and Angela Davis, Newt Gingrich and Bill Bradley—include the first Dr. Spock toddlers; the fiery college class of 1965; the oldest Vietnam-era draft-card burners; the eldest among "Americans Under 25," whom *Time* magazine named its "1967 Man of the Year"; and the last twenty-nine-year-olds (in 1972) to hear the phrase "under-thirty generation" before its sudden disappearance. At the back end, the grown-up Eisenhower babies of 1960 are the last-born of today's Americans to feel any affinity with the hippie-cum-yuppie baggage that accompanies the Boomer label.

The younger antagonists are less well known: America's thirteenth generation, born from 1961 to 1981, ranging in age from eleven to thirty-one. Demographers call them Baby Busters, a name that deserves a prompt and final burial. [. . .] The novelist Doug Coupland, himself a 1961 baby, dubs his age-mates "Generation X" or "Xers," a name first used by and about British Boomer-punkers. Shann Nix, a journalist at the *San Francisco Chronicle,* suggests "posties" (as in "post-yuppies"), another name that, like Coupland's, leaves the generation in the shadow of the great Boom.

We give these young people a nonlabel label that has nothing to do with Boomers. If we count back to the peers of Benjamin Franklin, "Thirteeners" are, in point of fact, the thirteenth generation to know the U.S. flag and the Constitution. More than a name, the number thirteen is a gauntlet, an obstacle to be overcome. Maybe it's the floor where elevators don't stop, or the doughnut that bakers don't count. Then again, maybe it's a suit's thirteenth card—the ace—that wins, face-down, in a game of high-stakes blackjack. It's an understated number for an underestimated generation. [. . .]

What separates the collective personalities of Boomers and Thirteeners? First, look at today's mainline media, a hotbed of forty-year-old thinking. Notice how, in Boomers' hands, 1990s America is becoming a somber land obsessed with values, back-to-basics movements, ethical rectitude,

Again, parallel structure sustains coherence within the fifth paragraph (*Maybe it's . . . Then again, maybe it's . . . It's . . .*).

political correctness, harsh punishments, and a yearning for the simple life. Life's smallest acts exalt (or diminish) one's personal virtue. A generation weaned on great expectations and gifted in deciphering principle is now determined to reinfuse the entire society with meaning.

Now look again—and notice a countermood popping up in college towns, in big cities, on Fox and cable TV, and in various ethnic side currents. It's a tone of physical frenzy and spiritual numbness, a revelry of pop, a pursuit of high-tech, guiltless fun. It's a carnival culture featuring the tangible bottom lines of life—money, bodies, and brains—and the wordless deals with which one can be traded for another. A generation weaned on minimal expectations and gifted in the game of life is now avoiding meaning in a cumbersome society that, as they see it, offers them little.

11b

For evidence of this emerging generation gap, take a look at a *Fortune* magazine survey earlier this year asking employed twentysomethings if they would ever "like to be like" Baby Boomers. Four out of five say no. Peruse recent surveys asking college students what they think of various Boomer-sanctioned moral crusades—everything from "family values" to the "New Age movement." By overwhelming margins, they either disapprove or are remarkably indifferent. Recall the furious Thirteener-penned responses that appeared just after the media's celebration of the twentieth anniversary of Woodstock, or after the recent turn away from yuppie-style consumption ("Let the self-satisfied, self-appointed, self-righteous baby-boomers be the first to practice the new austerity they have been preaching of late," Mark Featherman announced in a *New York Times* essay titled "The 80's Party Is Over"). Notice the pointed anti-Boom references in such Thirteener films as *Running on Empty, Pump Up the Volume, Heathers, True Colors,* and *Little Man Tate,* or in the generation-defining prose of such emerging young writers as Coupland, Nix, Brett Easton Ellis, Nancy Smith, Steven Gibb, Eric Liu, Gael Fashingbauer, David Bernstein, Robert Lukefahr, and Ian Williams.

—Neil Howe and William Strauss, "The New Generation Gap,"
The Atlantic

EXERCISE 3

Analyze the individual paragraphs of a paper you wrote recently to determine which of the following devices you used to create coherence within paragraphs.

Transitional words

Linking pronouns

Note the parallel structure—in this case, repeated imperatives—within the eighth paragraph as well (*[T]ake a look . . . Peruse . . . Recall . . . Notice . . .*).

Repetition of key words

Parallel structure

Which of these strategies did you use most frequently? Where could you have also employed some of the others?

EXERCISE 4

Analyze the connections *between* paragraphs in one of your recent papers. How often did you use the beginning of a paragraph to refer specifically to a point made in the previous paragraph? Where else might you have employed this strategy?

11b

12 *Revising Sentences*

If paragraphs are the timber for building papers, then by analogy sentences are the kinds of wood chosen for the paragraph. Each kind of wood has its own texture, color, and strength; some are harder to work with than others; some are more likely to warp than others. Pine is soft, serviceable, and easy to come by, rather like an ordinary sentence with a colorless verb such as *have* or *be*. Maple is hard and close-grained, like a complex sentence with careful subordination and perhaps a parallel construction. Oak is heavy and strong, like a long, formal periodic sentence. Each wood—like each sentence—has distinctive qualities and functions. But when one uses unseasoned wood or oversized nails, the boards may buckle or splinter. So, too, with sentences: handled wrongly, they can warp or fracture.

During the preliminary stages of writing, our sentences may be only roughly hewn. Trying to maintain the creative flow of ideas, we may quickly put down words as they come. Fragments and fused sentences, mixed constructions and faulty parallelism—these may be the raw materials that confront us when we begin revising. And because revising entails rethinking, the work that remains may be challenging. Rethinking demands that we carefully inspect the structure, clarity, and smoothness of each sentence that we have written. If we are serious about revising, few sentences will survive such scrutiny intact.

Revising sentences entails more than repairing their coherence and clarity, however. Because different words—like different woods—have their particular textures, colorings, and associations, experienced writers also pay attention to their diction as they reshape their sentences. For convenience, these two aspects of revision are discussed in separate chapters. The first chapter, this one, stresses ways of revising structures that are awkward, confusing, or misleading. Chapter **13**, "Revising

Chapter 12 takes up revision at the sentence level, focusing on a variety of syntactic and stylistic problems. For discussion of unity, conciseness, and variety in sentences, see Chapter **8**. For discussion of sentence fragments, comma splices, and fused sentences, see Chapter **30**.

Answers to the exercises in this chapter may be expected to vary widely. In most cases, the answer provided is the one that requires the fewest changes in the original sentence.

Quick Reference: *Revising Sentences*

Avoid ambiguous, remote, and broad pronoun reference (**12a**)

Unclear	The beginning of this book is more interesting than the conclusion, *which* is unfortunate.
Revised	Unfortunately, the beginning of this book is more interesting than the conclusion.

Eliminate dangling modifiers (**12b**).

Dangling	*Supported by most voters, smoking* will be banned in restaurants by the new ordinance.
Revised	*Supported by most voters, the new ordinance* will ban smoking in restaurants.

Move misplaced modifiers (**12c**).

Misplaced	She wrote the full story of her recovery from drug addiction *in only a month*.
Revised	*In only a month,* she wrote the full story of her recovery from drug addiction.

Avoid split constructions (**12d**).

Split	Stunned by the accident, we found it difficult *to* accurately *describe* the other car.
Revised	Stunned by the accident, we found it difficult *to describe* the other car accurately.

Eliminate confusing shifts in voice, person, number, mood, and tense (**12e**).

Shift	When *one* tries hard enough, *you* can accomplish almost anything.
Revised	When *you* try hard enough, *you* can accomplish almost anything.

Avoid mixed constructions (**12f**).

Mixed	*The reason* their fuel bills were lower *is because* they installed solar heating last year.
Revised	*The reason* their fuel bills were lower *is that* they installed solar heating last year.

12

Finish incomplete constructions (**12g**).

Incomplete	Modern languages *have* and always *will be* an important element in our curriculum.
Revised	Modern languages *have been* and always *will be* an important element in our curriculum.

Diction," stresses ways of choosing the most appropriate and effective words. But remember that this division is for convenience only: both elements are part of a rigorous strategy for sentence revision.

12a

12a Unclear pronoun reference

A pronoun is a substitute for a noun. The noun it stands for is called the **antecedent** because it usually goes (Latin: *cedere*) before (*ante*) the pronoun.

antecedent   pronoun
Rita Martinez lives in Boulder, but *she* often visits relatives in San Diego.

antecedent   pronoun
When her *plane* left the airport, *it* was already behind schedule.

Note, though, that the antecedent—despite its literal meaning—may *follow* the pronoun in some constructions.

pronoun   antecedent
Although *it* was behind schedule, the *plane* finally took off.

As you read over your sentences with an eye to revising them, examine every pronoun to make sure its antecedent is clear.

1.   Ambiguous reference

When persons of the same sex are mentioned in a sentence, confusion may occur about which person a pronoun refers to.

Unclear	The novelist Virginia Woolf frequently told her sister Vanessa, who was a painter, that *she* was a great artist. [Whom did Woolf regard as a great artist—her sister or herself?]
Revised	The novelist Virginia Woolf considered her sister Vanessa a great painter and frequently told her so.

Do not use a pronoun in such a way that it might refer to either of two antecedents. If there is any possibility of doubt, revise the sentence to remove the ambiguity.

12a

Unclear	In *Nostromo*, Conrad's style is ironic and his setting is highly symbolic, so that *it* sometimes confuses the reader. [Does *it* refer to the novel *Nostromo*, Conrad's style, his setting, or a combination of these? Clarify the sentence by eliminating the pronoun.]
Revised	Conrad's ironic style and highly symbolic setting in *Nostromo* sometimes confuse the reader.
Revised	In *Nostromo*, Conrad's style is ironic, and his highly symbolic setting sometimes confuses the reader.

Both of these sentences are now clear, but note that each says something different.

2. Remote reference

A pronoun too far away from its antecedent may cause misreading. Either repeat the antecedent or recast the sentence.

Unclear	By 1890, architects in Chicago had perfected the floating raft foundation, a thick mat of concrete with embedded steel rails that would evenly distribute the weight of a heavy structure. *It* could support a building of sixteen or more stories—an unheard-of height. [The pronoun *It* is too far removed from its antecedent, *foundation*, and seems instead to refer to the noun *structure*.]
Revised	By 1890, architects in Chicago had perfected the floating raft foundation, a thick mat of concrete with embedded steel rails that would evenly distribute the weight of a heavy

structure. *Such a foundation* could support a building of
sixteen or more stories—an unheard-of height.
[The antecedent has been substituted for the pronoun in
the second sentence.]

Revised   By 1890, architects in Chicago had perfected the floating
raft foundation. This thick mat of concrete with embedded
steel rails could support a building of sixteen or more
stories—an unheard-of height.
[The sentences have been recast to eliminate the
pronoun.]

3.   Broad pronoun reference: *this, that, which*   12a

In speech we often use the pronouns *this, that,* and *which* to
refer broadly to the idea expressed in a preceding clause or sentence. In
writing, however, such loose pronoun reference can be misleading or
confusing. If the preceding clause contains a noun that might also be
mistaken for the antecedent, the reference may be ambiguous as well. In
such cases, revise the sentence to eliminate the pronoun or to give it a
definite antecedent.

Unclear   The beginning of the book is more interesting than the
conclusion, *which* is unfortunate.
[On first reading, the pronoun *which* seems to refer to
conclusion. The writer wants *which* to refer to the whole
idea of the main clause, but the noun at the end gets in
the way.]

Revised   Unfortunately, the beginning of the book is more interesting
than the conclusion.
[The pronoun has been eliminated and the sentence is
crisper.]

In the following sentence, *which* is being made to stand for more than
it can clearly express.

Unclear   In the eighteenth century, more and more land was
converted into pasture, *which* had been going on to some
extent for several centuries.
[*Which* is intended to refer to the process of conversion,
but no such antecedent is present in this sentence.]

Revised   In the eighteenth century, more and more land was
converted into pasture, *a process that* had been going on to
some extent for several centuries.
[The vague pronoun reference has been cleared up by
adding *process*, a noun that summarizes the idea of the
main clause and gives the pronoun *that* an antecedent.]

Because its intended antecedent in a preceding sentence may not be
clear, the pronoun *this* should not stand alone as the beginning word in
a sentence.

12a

Unclear   The Japanese fugu, or puffer, is one of the most lethal fishes
in the world, its poison 275 times deadlier than cyanide, yet
it is considered a choice dish in Tokyo, Kyoto, and other
cities, where it sells for more than $200 a plate. *This* means
that its preparation must be controlled and supervised.
["This *what?*" the reader may well ask, since the idea
serving as the antecedent of *This* is unclear. The revision
will depend on what the writer means.]

Revised   This *toxicity* means that its preparation must be controlled
and supervised.

Revised   This *costliness* means that its preparation must be controlled
and supervised.

4.   Indefinite use of *it, they, you*

English contains a number of idiomatic expressions using the
impersonal pronoun *it: It is hot. It rained all day. It is snowing.* The
pronoun *it* is also used clearly in sentences like "It seems best to go
home at once," in which *it* anticipates the real subject, *to go home at once.*
Avoid, however, the *it* that needs a clear antecedent and has none.

Unclear   The Tzotzil Indians are only nominal Catholics, using *its*
symbols and adapting them to the traditional Mayan
religion.
[The intended antecedent of *its* has to be inferred from
the noun *Catholics*, but that word means people who
belong to a church rather than the institution itself.]

Revised   The Tzotzil Indians are only nominal Catholics, using the
symbols and the names *of the Church* and adapting them to
the traditional Mayan religion.

Unclear   Lewis Thomas, author of *The Lives of a Cell,* was a physician and writer who spent his spare hours practicing *it.*
[The sentence lacks an activity that could be the antecedent of *it.*]

Revised   Lewis Thomas, author of *The Lives of a Cell,* was a physician who spent his spare hours practicing writing.

Be equally careful to avoid using the pronoun *they* in a sentence where its antecedent is only implied rather than actually stated.

Unclear   If intercollegiate sports were banned, *they* would have to develop an elaborate intramural program.
[Who, the writer should rigorously ask, are *they?* The answer appears in the revised sentence.]

12a

Revised   If intercollegiate sports were banned, *each college* would have to develop an elaborate intramural program.

Unclear   At registration *they* made us line up on the outside of the gymnasium and wait until *they* called the first letter of our last names. *They* made some of us stand in the rain for hours.
[Revise the sentence to identify participants in the event more exactly.]

Revised   At registration *college officials* made us line up on the outside of the gymnasium and wait until *a monitor* called the first letter of our last names. Some of us had to stand in the rain for hours.

The indefinite use of the pronoun *you* to refer to people in general is widespread in conversation and frequent in informal writing: *Around here, you never know what the neighbors will say.* Edited English, however, still restricts *you* to mean *you, the reader,* as in *You can use these review questions to enhance your understanding of the poems,* and requires the substitution of the pronoun *one* or of a noun.

Informal   Small classes give *you* a chance to take part in discussions.

Revised   Small classes give *one* a chance to take part in discussions.

Revised   Small classes give *the student* a chance to take part in discussions.

While the impersonal or general use of *you* is both natural and appropriate in certain informal contexts, it is clearly inappropriate in other contexts.

> **Inappropriate**   During the American Revolution *you* were forced to choose sides.
> [The pronoun *you* cannot possibly mean *you, the reader,* in this context.]
>
> **Revised**   During the American Revolution *colonists* were forced to choose sides.

If the pronoun *one* seems stilted, try recasting the sentence.

12a

> **Awkward**   In proofreading, *one* should catch all of *one's* careless errors.
>
> **Better**   In proofreading, *writers* should catch all of *their* careless errors.

EXERCISE 1

Revise the following sentences to correct unclear pronoun reference.

Example

> **Unclear**   The amount of cholesterol in an egg is admittedly high, but it is an excellent source of protein.
>
> **Revised**   The amount of cholesterol in an egg is admittedly high, but eggs are an excellent source of protein. [ambiguous reference corrected]

1. Many people like to cook eggs because you can prepare them so easily.
2. Fried or scrambled eggs can be ready in minutes; this means that they are a perfect quick meal.
3. With only a little practice, one can also prepare fancier dishes, which makes eggs a versatile food.
4. Before cooks beat egg whites for meringues, they should be at room temperature; this makes them fluff.
5. A cook should put the egg-white mixture into a bowl, turn the mixer on high, and slowly add sugar to it.
6. Baking a meringue successfully requires low humidity, which explains why meringues don't always come out right.
7. A soufflé is even trickier to prepare; one has to fold the yolks gently into fluffy egg whites without causing them to deflate.

Exercise 1

Answers will vary.

1. Many people like to cook eggs because they are so easy to prepare. [indefinite *you*]
2. Because fried or scrambled eggs can be ready in minutes, they are a perfect quick meal. [broad reference]
3. Eggs are also a versatile food; with only a little practice, one can also prepare fancier dishes. [broad reference]
4. Before a cook beats egg whites for a meringue, they should be at room temperature, so that they will fluff. [ambiguous reference, broad reference]
5. A cook should put the egg-white mixture into a bowl, turn the mixer on high, and slowly add sugar. [remote reference]
6. Baking a meringue successfully requires low humidity—a condition that explains why meringues don't always come out right. [broad reference]

8. If possible, bake the mixture in a soufflé dish rather than a standard oven-proof bowl because it distributes the heat more evenly.
9. This ensures that the soufflé will rise.
10. One cook told her apprentice that she had to learn to be patient.

EXERCISE 2

Revise the following sentences to correct unclear pronoun reference.

Example

> **Unclear**   Socrates, the self-appointed critic of ancient Athens, made many enemies, which resulted in his being brought to trial in 399 B.C.
>
> **Revised**   Socrates, the self-appointed critic of ancient Athens, made many enemies; as a result, he was brought to trial in 399 B.C. [broad reference corrected]

1. The charges against him were behaving impiously and corrupting the young people of Athens, but they were ridiculous.
2. Contemporary political intrigue apparently played a role in the trial of Socrates, but it remains unclear today.
3. Socrates might not have received the death penalty from the court had he not mocked it openly.
4. They sentenced him to imprisonment until he poisoned himself by drinking hemlock.
5. Socrates accepted the cup of poison calmly, which was the way he had lived his life.

12b Dangling modifiers

A **modifier** is a word or phrase that functions in a sentence to limit or describe another word or group of words. If there is no word or group of words in the sentence for the modifier to describe or limit, the modifier is said to *dangle,* as in the following sentence.

> **Dangling**   *Having eaten our lunch and waited an hour to digest our food,* the lake felt cool and pungent on that first hot afternoon of summer.

The literal syntax of this sentence states that the lake, well fed and well rested, felt cool on a summer afternoon. Of course, that is not what the writer meant, but it is the only meaning possible, because the writer has

7. A soufflé is even trickier to prepare; one has to fold the yolks gently into fluffy egg whites without causing the whites to deflate. [ambiguous reference]
8. If possible, bake the mixture in a soufflé dish rather than a standard oven-proof bowl because a soufflé dish distributes the heat more evenly. [remote reference]
9. Even heating ensures that the soufflé will rise. [broad reference]
10. One cook told her apprentice that new cooks have to learn to be patient. [ambiguous reference]

Exercise 2

Answers will vary.

1. The ridiculous charges against him were behaving impiously and corrupting the young people of Athens. [remote reference]
2. Contemporary political intrigue that remains unclear today apparently played a role in the trial of Socrates. [ambiguous reference]

failed to include the subject that the modifying phrase is actually intended to describe.

Almost all dangling modifiers occur at the beginning of the sentence, and almost all result from oversight. Once detected, they can be mended in either of two ways.

1. Supply the noun or pronoun that the phrase logically modifies.

modifier

Revised   *Having eaten our lunch and waited an hour to digest our food,*

word modified

we plunged into the lake, which was cool and pungent on that first hot afternoon of summer.

2. Change a dangling phrase into a complete clause.

clause replaces modifying phrase

Revised   *After we had eaten our lunch and waited an hour to digest our food,* swimming in the cool and pungent lake on that first hot afternoon of summer was a delight.

1.   Dangling participial phrases

Participial phrases are verbal modifiers that function in the sentence as adjectives do. When a participial phrase begins a sentence, it must be followed by the word it modifies, that is, by the person or thing doing the action expressed by the participle or being described by it.

Dangling   *Analyzing Joan Didion's style, her essay* seemed to me to be cool, detached, and uncommitted to purpose or point of view.
[This sentence says, erroneously, that the essay is doing the analyzing, not the reader.]

Revised   *Analyzing Joan Didion's style, I* discovered that the writing, especially in this essay, was cool, detached, and uncommitted to purpose or point of view.

Dangling   *Supported by a wide majority of voters, smoking* will be banned in public buildings by the new ordinance.
[Contrary to what this sentence seems to say, it is not smoking, but the ordinance banning smoking, that has wide public support.]

3. Socrates might not have received the death penalty had he not mocked the court openly. [ambiguous reference]
4. The court sentenced him to imprisonment until he poisoned himself by drinking hemlock. [indefinite *they*]
5. Socrates accepted the cup of poison as he had lived his life—calmly. [broad reference]

Revised   *Supported by a wide majority of voters, the new ordinance* will ban smoking in public buildings.

Dangling participles at the end of a sentence are less frequent than those at the beginning, but they are equally confusing and awkward.

Dangling   The mountains were snow-covered and cloudless, *flying over the Rockies.*

Revised   *Flying over the Rockies, we* saw snow-covered, cloudless mountains.

Revised   *When I flew over the Rockies,* the mountains were snow-covered and cloudless.

12b

A dangling participle should not be confused with an **absolute phrase,** which is an acceptable construction. Such a phrase consists of a participle *and* a subject; it is grammatically unconnected to the rest of the sentence.

His mind preoccupied with his marital problems, William forgot his lunch date with the chancellor.

The dinner for the new athletic director started late, *the guest of honor having been caught in the five-o'clock traffic.*

For more on absolute phrases, see **8g** and **25f.**

2. Dangling gerunds

A **gerund** is a verb form ending in *-ing* that is used as a noun. A gerund phrase dangles when the subject of the gerund—the doer of the action—is not apparent to the reader.

Dangling   *After explaining my errand to the guard,* an automatic gate swung open to let me in.
[Obviously, a gate cannot explain an errand to a guard, or to anyone else, but the sentence fails to say who the true actor is.]

Revised   *After explaining my errand to the guard,* I drove through the automatic gate, which had opened to let me in.

Revised   *After I had explained my errand to the guard,* an automatic gate swung open to let me in.

Dangling	*In doing research,* notes should be entered on separate index cards. [Because the sentence does not say *who* is doing research, the gerund phrase dangles.]
Revised	*In doing research, a writer* should enter notes on separate index cards.
Revised	*When you do research,* you should enter notes on separate index cards.

3.   Dangling infinitives

12b

An **infinitive,** a verb preceded by the word *to,* is said to dangle when the subject of its action is not expressed. Always look carefully at an infinitive phrase to make certain that *who* is doing the action is clearly expressed.

Dangling	*To develop a lively writing style,* a variety of sentence structures should be used. [*Sentence structures* cannot develop a lively writing style; only people can.]
Revised	*To develop a lively writing style, one* should use a variety of sentence structures.
Revised	*If you want to develop a lively writing style,* you should use a variety of sentence structures.
Dangling	*To be considered for law school, the LSAT* must be taken. [Who is being considered? That person, the subject of the infinitive *to be considered,* must appear in the sentence.]
Revised	*To be considered for law school, an applicant* must take the LSAT.
Revised	*If a person wishes to be considered for law school,* he or she must take the LSAT.

4.   Dangling elliptical clauses

Sometimes we omit the subject and full verb from a dependent clause and write *while going* instead of *while I was going,* or *when a child* instead of *when he was a child.* Such shorthand phrasing results in an **elliptical clause,** which is perfectly acceptable as long as its subject is made clear in the rest of the sentence. If the subject of an elliptical clause is not clear, the construction dangles.

Dangling   *When six years old,* my grandmother died.
[The omission of the subject *I* here results in a confusing—even ludicrous—sentence.]

Revised   *When I was six years old,* my grandmother died.

Dangling   Do not add the beans *until thoroughly soaked.*
[Who or what is about to get wet? Clarify the sentence by expanding the elliptical clause.]

Revised   Do not add the beans *until they have been thoroughly soaked.*

5. Permissible dangling constructions

Some idiomatic verbal phrases, such as *to begin with, judging from past experience, considering the situation, granted the results,* or *to sum up,* have become well established and need not be attached to any particular noun.

Judging from past experience, he is not to be trusted.

Granted the results, what do they prove?

To sum up, all evidence suggests that the decision was a fair one.

12c Misplaced modifiers

A modifier is **misplaced** if it is not near enough to the word it is intended to modify. In English, word order is crucial to meaning. Adjectives, adverbs, and phrases or clauses that function as modifiers must be placed close to the words they are intended to limit or define. The difference that the placement of a modifier makes in a sentence becomes clear if we observe what happens in the following sentence when the adverb *only* is moved about.

The notice said *only* [said *merely*] that clients were invited to see the exhibit on the third floor.

The notice said that *only* clients [clients *alone*] were invited to see the exhibit on the third floor.

The notice said that clients were invited *only* [invited for the one purpose] to see the exhibit on the third floor.

The notice said that clients were invited to see the exhibit on the third floor *only* [the third floor *alone*].

Some modifying phrases and clauses can be moved around to various positions in the sentence. An introductory clause, for example, can often be shifted from the beginning of a sentence to the middle or the end.

> *Whatever the public may think,* I am sure that Picasso will be remembered as one of the greatest artists of our times.
>
> I am sure, *whatever the public may think,* that Picasso will be remembered as one of the greatest artists of our times.
>
> I am sure that Picasso will be remembered as one of the greatest artists of our times, *whatever the public may think.*

12c

This freedom, however, has its dangers. Movable modifiers may accidentally be placed so as to produce misreadings or real ambiguities. Unlike the dangling modifier, which cannot logically modify any word in the sentence, the misplaced modifier may seem to modify the wrong word or phrase in the sentence.

Misplaced	She wrote the full story of her recovery from drug addiction *in only a month.* [This sentence says that the recovery took only a month. Compare the revised version, which says what the writer actually intended.]
Revised	*In only a month,* she wrote the full story of her recovery from drug addiction.

Be especially careful to place adverbs exactly where they belong in the sentence.

Misplaced	He scolded the student for cheating *severely.*
Revised	He *severely* scolded the student for cheating.

Misplaced	I have followed the advice *carefully* given by the manual.
Revised	I have *carefully* followed the advice given by the manual.

Modifiers are said to *squint,* or to look two ways at once, when they are placed so that they might refer to either a preceding word or a following word in the sentence.

Squinting	The tailback who injured his knee *recently* returned to practice. [Is the injury recent, or the player's return to practice? The modifier must be moved to eliminate ambiguity.]
Revised	The tailback who *recently* injured his knee returned to practice.
Revised	The tailback who injured his knee returned to practice *recently*.

12d Split constructions

12d

Avoid splitting the parts of a verb phrase with a long modifying phrase or clause.

| Split | I *have,* more than the rest of the class, *been* in a panic since the term paper was assigned. |
| Revised | More than the rest of the class, I *have been* in a panic since the term paper was assigned. |

Split infinitives—that is, infinitives with a modifier between the *to* and the verb—are also usually considered awkward and should be avoided.

| Split | Stunned by the accident, we found it difficult *to* accurately *describe* the other car. |
| Revised | Stunned by the accident, we found it difficult *to describe* the other car accurately. |

However, if eliminating a split infinitive would result in even clumsier phrasing, let it stand.

| Acceptable split | To avoid insolvency, the city's transit system will have *to* nearly *double* ridership during the coming year. |

Most readers would find the only alternative—*have nearly to double*—more objectionable than the split infinitive in this sentence.

EXERCISE 3

Revise the following sentences to eliminate dangling and misplaced modifiers and split constructions.

Exercise 3

Answers will vary.

1. Produced by eruptions on the floor of the Pacific Ocean, the Hawaiian Islands contain some of the world's largest volcanoes. [dangling participle]
2. Some volcanoes continue to be associated with myth and ritual. For example, Hawaii's Kilauea Volcano is said by many villagers to be the home of Pele, the goddess of volcanoes. [split construction]
3. To appease Pele and bring good luck, villagers sometimes offer flowers and gin to the volcano. [dangling infinitive]
4. Scientists have paid a great deal of attention to Kilauea, which erupts frequently. [dangling participle]
5. The eruptions there are usually mild ones, though; spurting lava and steam, the volcano sometimes gives tourists quite a show. [misplaced modifier, dangling participle]
6. Unfortunately, not all volcanoes are so benign. [misplaced modifier]

12d

Example

Dangling Derived from Vulcan, the Roman fire god, glowing rivers of molten lava are suggested by the word *volcano*.

Revised Derived from Vulcan, the Roman fire god, the word *volcano* suggests glowing rivers of molten lava. [dangling participle corrected]

1. Produced by eruptions on the floor of the Pacific Ocean, some of the world's largest volcanoes are found in the Hawaiian Islands.
2. Some volcanoes continue to be associated with myth and ritual. For example, Hawaii's Kilauea Volcano is, by many villagers, said to be the home of Pele, the goddess of volcanoes.
3. To appease Pele and bring good luck, flowers and gin are sometimes offered to the volcano.
4. Erupting frequently, scientists have paid a great deal of attention to Kilauea.
5. The eruptions usually there are mild ones, though; spurting lava and steam, tourists sometimes get quite a show.
6. Not all volcanoes are, unfortunately, so benign.
7. Burying people under almost fifty feet of ash, A.D. 79 saw the deadly eruption of Mount Vesuvius, which wiped out Pompeii.
8. Producing deadly gas as well as giant tidal waves, tens of thousands of lives were lost in 1883 when Krakatoa erupted.
9. Destroying acres of forestland, few people were fortunately killed by the more recent eruption of Mt. St. Helens in Washington state.
10. Described as dormant, active, or extinct, geologists continue to be fascinated and awed by volcanoes.

EXERCISE 4

Revise the following sentences to eliminate dangling and misplaced modifiers and split constructions.

Example

Dangling Begun in 776 B.C., the Greek god Zeus was honored by the original Olympic games.

Revised Begun in 776 B.C., the original Olympic games honored the Greek god Zeus. [dangling participle corrected]

7. Burying people under almost fifty feet of ash, the deadly eruption of Mount Vesuvius wiped out Pompeii in A.D. 79. [dangling participle]
8. Producing deadly gas as well as giant tidal waves, Krakatoa took tens of thousands of lives when it erupted in 1883. [dangling participle]
9. Fortunately, the more recent eruption of Mt. St. Helens in Washington state killed few people, although it destroyed acres of forestland. [dangling participle, misplaced modifier]
10. Described as dormant, active, or extinct, volcanoes continue to fascinate and awe geologists. [dangling participle]

Exercise 4

Answers will vary.

1. At first consisting only of footraces, the games gradually included new events like boxing and chariot racing. [dangling participle]

1. At first consisting only of footraces, new events like boxing and chariot racing were gradually added to the games.
2. Occurring every four years, the popularity of the Olympics steadily increased, and they eventually became the greatest of Greek festivals.
3. To qualify for competition, ten months of training had to be completed.
4. Athletes who won Olympic contests heroically returned to their home city-states.
5. The games were held continuously until they were abolished in A.D. 394, considered too pagan by the Christian emperor of Rome.
6. The Olympic games were, in 1896, revived in Athens.
7. For merely attending the games in ancient times, death was the punishment for women.
8. In 1912, however, fifty-seven women were present to fully participate in the Olympics.
9. By shattering world records in the two-hundred-meter race and the broad jump, Hitler's attempts to make the 1936 Berlin games a tribute to Aryan superiority were thwarted by Jessie Owens, the black American track star.
10. The Olympics were struck by tragedy in 1972 when Arab terrorists in Munich took Israeli athletes hostage, ending in seventeen deaths.

12e Confusing shifts

Shifts in sentence structure often lead to confusion. If the first clause of a sentence is in the active voice, the second clause should not be in the passive voice unless there is a good reason for the change. Similarly, a sentence that begins in the present tense should not switch to the past tense halfway through, and one that starts with the first-person *I* point of view should not shift to the second-person *you*. Revise sentences to ensure consistency in voice, person, number, mood, and tense.

1. Confusing shifts of voice

A shift from the active to the passive **voice** almost always involves a confusing change in the subject as well, and thus makes a sentence doubly awkward.

2. Occurring every four years, the Olympics steadily increased in popularity and eventually became the greatest of Greek festivals. [dangling participle]
3. To qualify for competition, athletes had to complete ten months of training. [dangling infinitive]
4. Athletes who won Olympic contests returned heroically to their home city-states. [misplaced modifier]
5. The games were held continuously until they were abolished in A.D. 394, because the Christian emperor of Rome considered them too pagan. [dangling participle]
6. In 1896 the Olympic games were revived in Athens. [split construction]
7. For merely attending the games in ancient times, women could be punished by death. [dangling gerund]
8. In 1912, however, fifty-seven women were present to participate fully in the Olympics. [split construction]
9. By shattering world records in the two-hundred-meter race and the

Shift   After *I* finally *discovered* an unsoldered wire, the *dismantling* of the motor *was begun.*
[The subject of this sentence shifts from the *I* of the dependent clause to the *dismantling* of the independent one; the voice shifts from active in the first clause to passive in the second. The sentence would be logically consistent if both verbs were in the passive voice: *After an unsoldered wire was found, the motor was dismantled.* But the passive voice is not required by the sense of the sentence. Repeating *I* as the subject of the independent clause produces subject and voice consistency.]

12e

Revised   After *I* finally *discovered* an unsoldered wire, *I dismantled* the motor.

Confusing shifts from the active to the passive voice can also lead to questions about agency.

Shift   He *left* the examination after his answer *had been proofread.*
[The passive verb in the second clause leaves us wondering who proofread the answer. The repeated subject and active voice of the revised sentence clarify the meaning.]

Revised   He *left* the examination after he *had proofread* his answer.

2.   Confusing shifts of person or number

A writer who fails to concentrate on the pronouns in a sentence may create a shift in **person**—for example, from the third person *(he, she, one)* to the second person *(you)*. The result is almost always a fuzzy, unfocused sentence.

Shift   When *one* tries hard enough, *you* can do almost anything.

Revised   When *you* try hard enough, *you* can do almost anything.

Revised   When *a person* tries hard enough, *he or she* can do almost anything.

Revised   When *we* try hard enough, *we* can do almost anything.

Revised   When *people* try hard enough, *they* can do almost anything.

A shift in **number** from singular to plural confuses the reader and results in faulty pronoun agreement.

broad jump, Jessie Owens, the black American track star, thwarted Hitler's attempts to make the 1936 Berlin games a tribute to Aryan superiority. [dangling gerund]
10. The Olympics were struck by tragedy in 1972 when Arab terrorists in Munich took Israeli athletes hostage; the incident ended in seventeen deaths. [dangling participle]

Shift   If a *customer* is ignored or kept waiting, *they* should complain to the management.

Revised   If a *customer* is ignored or kept waiting, *he or she* should complain to the management.

Revised   If *customers* are ignored or kept waiting, *they* should complain to the management.

3.   Confusing shifts of mood or tense

A sentence should end in the same **mood** with which it begins. If the opening mood is an order or a command, the sentence is an imperative and should not shift without good reason to the indicative mood.

12e

Shift   First, *locate* the library on the campus map; then *you should find* the card catalog and the reference section.
[The first clause is an order, a command addressed in the imperative mood to an understood *you*. The second clause, which is a statement giving advice, is in the indicative mood. The revision puts both clauses in the imperative mood.]

Revised   First, *locate* the library on the campus map; then *find* the card catalog and the reference section.

Different verb **tenses** may, and often do, occur within a single English sentence, but illogical shifts in tense should be avoided.

Shift   I *stood* on the starting block and *looked* tensely at the water below; for the first time in my life I *am* about to swim the fifty-yard freestyle in competition.
[The sentence describes events that all occur at the same time, yet the verbs shift illogically from past tense to present tense. The revisions put all verbs in one tense or the other.]

Revised   I *stood* on the starting block and *looked* tensely at the water below; for the first time in my life I *was* about to swim the fifty-yard freestyle in competition.

Revised   I *stand* on the starting block and *look* tensely at the water below; for the first time in my life I *am* about to swim the fifty-yard freestyle in competition.

Remember that it is a convention to use the historical present in writing about literature: *Hamlet stabs Laertes. Isak Dinesen writes about South Africa.* Be careful in this case not to lapse by habit into the past tense.

> **Shift** At the beginning of the *Divine Comedy,* Dante *finds* that he has strayed from the True Way into the Dark Wood of Error. As soon as he *realized* this, Dante *lifted* his eyes in hope to the rising sun.
>
> **Revised** At the beginning of the *Divine Comedy,* Dante *finds* that he has strayed from the True Way into the Dark Wood of Error. As soon as he *realizes* this, Dante *lifts* his eyes in hope to the rising sun.

12e

For further information about the tense and mood of verbs, see Chapter **29**.

EXERCISE **5**

Revise the following sentences to correct shifts in voice, person, number, and tense.

Example

> **Shift** If a visitor went to Harlem in the 1920s, you would find a thriving cultural center.
>
> **Revised** If a visitor went to Harlem in the 1920s, he or she would find a thriving cultural center. [shift in person corrected]

1. Because this section of New York City was home to one of the largest black communities in the country, it becomes a magnet for black artists, writers, and intellectuals.
2. A black artist could come to Harlem from another part of the country and find an audience for their work.
3. The movement that came to be called the Harlem Renaissance produces such important writers as Claude McKay and Jean Toomer.
4. Langston Hughes was perhaps the best-known writer of the Harlem Renaissance; poetry, plays, novels, and children's books were published by him.
5. What most white people knew about Harlem, though, was limited to the jazz clubs you found there, places like the famous Cotton Club.
6. Nightclubs lined Lenox Avenue, which in those days is widely regarded as the center of Harlem's entertainment industry.

Exercise 5

Answers will vary.

1. Because this section of New York City was home to one of the largest black communities in the country, it became a magnet for black artists, writers, and intellectuals. [shift in tense]
2. A black artist could come to Harlem from another part of the country and find an audience for his or her work. [shift in number]
3. The movement that came to be called the Harlem Renaissance produced such important writers as Claude McKay and Jean Toomer. [shift in tense]
4. Langston Hughes was perhaps the best-known writer of the Harlem Renaissance; he published poetry, plays, novels, and children's books. [shift in voice]
5. What most white people knew about Harlem, though, was limited to the jazz clubs they found there, places like the famous Cotton Club. [shift in person]

7. When a white person talked about these places, they used terms like *exotic* and *sensual*.
8. Such labels reflected the narrow view of black culture that is prevalent in white society despite the richness of the Harlem Renaissance.
9. Unfortunately, the plays and books about blacks that reached a large white audience tended to be those that perpetuate prevailing stereotypes.
10. The Great Depression settled over the country in the 1930s, and Harlem's period of intellectual and artistic activity was ended by it.

12f Mixed constructions

A sentence that begins with one grammatical structure and then shifts to another is called a **mixed construction.**

1. Prepositional phrase misused as subject

A **prepositional phrase** is a modifier, and it therefore cannot function as the grammatical subject of a sentence. When a prepositional phrase begins a sentence, a reader expects a noun or pronoun to follow; if it doesn't, as in the case below, a garbled sentence results.

Mixed	*By requiring* drivers to have their cars periodically inspected *is one way* to cut down on accidents.
Revised	By requiring drivers to have their cars periodically inspected, *we can cut down* on accidents.
Revised	*Requiring* drivers to have their cars periodically inspected *is one way* to cut down on accidents.

[In the first revision, the pronoun *we* now follows the prepositional phrase and serves as the subject of the sentence. In the second revision, the preposition *by* has been dropped, and the resulting gerund phrase (see **25f**) becomes the subject of the sentence.]

2. Adverb clause misused as subject

An **adverb clause** is also a modifier and therefore cannot be the grammatical subject of a sentence. Using such a clause as a subject produces a badly mixed construction.

---

6. Nightclubs lined Lenox Avenue, which in those days was widely regarded as the center of Harlem's entertainment industry. [shift in tense]
7. When white people talked about those places, they used terms like *exotic* and *sensual*. [shift in number]
8. Such labels reflected the narrow view of black culture that was prevalent in white society despite the richness of the Harlem Renaissance. [shift in tense]
9. Unfortunately, the plays and books about blacks that reached a large white audience tended to be those that perpetuated prevailing stereotypes. [shift in tense]
10. The Great Depression settled over the country in the 1930s and ended Harlem's period of intellectual and artistic activity. [shift in voice]

Mixed	*Just because* you're angry *doesn't justify* your rudeness.
Revised	*The fact that* you're angry *doesn't justify* your rudeness.
Revised	*Your anger doesn't justify* your rudeness.

[In the first revision, the adverb clause has been replaced by the noun *fact* followed by a noun clause in apposition (see **25g**); together they make up the sentence's subject. In the second revision, the subject is the noun *anger*.]

3.   Adverb clause misused as complement

12f   A common mixed construction involves the ungrammatical use of an adverb clause beginning with *because, when,* or *where* as a **predicate noun**.

Mixed	*The reason* their fuel bills were lower *is because* they installed solar heating when they remodeled their house.
Revised	*The reason* their fuel bills were lower *is that* they installed solar heating when they remodeled their house.
Revised	Their fuel bills were lower because they installed solar heating when they remodeled their house.

[In the first revision, a noun clause (see **25g**) replaces the adverb clause as the predicate noun. In the second revision, the sentence has been recast without a predicate noun; the clause beginning with *because* now correctly functions as an adverb.]

Mixed	One *thing* that keeps me from driving to the city *is when* I think of the traffic jams.
Revised	One *thing* that keeps me from driving to the city *is the thought* of the traffic jams.
Revised	I won't drive to the city because of the traffic jams.

[In the first revision, the noun *thought* replaces the adverb clause as the predicate noun. In the second revision, the sentence has been recast without a predicate noun.]

Mixed	*Symbiosis is where* dissimilar organisms live together in a mutually advantageous partnership.
Revised	*Symbiosis is a state where* dissimilar organisms live together in a mutually advantageous partnership.

Revised *Symbiosis is the* mutually advantageous *partnership* of
dissimilar organisms living together.
[In the first revision, the noun *state* replaces the adverb
clause as the predicate noun; the clause beginning
with *where* is now an adjective clause modifying *state*.
In the second revision, the predicate noun is *partnership*.]

4. Faulty predication

Faulty predication, a fourth type of mixed construction, occurs
when a writer loses track of the grammatical subject of a sentence and
inadvertently links a subject and predicate that don't make logical sense
together.

12g

Mixed *Increases* in state appropriations for new highway
construction *are expected to rise* next year.
[The *appropriations,* not the *increases,* will rise. The
sentence may be made more logical by revising either
the subject or the predicate.]

Revised *State appropriations* for new highway construction *are expected
to rise* next year.

Revised *Increases* in state appropriations for new highway construction *are expected* next year.

Mixed A *decision* about the source of funding *will be determined* next
month by the legislature.
[The legislature will *determine* the source of funding, but
it will *make* a decision. Again, revise by adjusting either
the subject or the predicate.]

Revised The *source* of funding *will be determined* next month by the
legislature.

Revised A *decision* about the source of funding *will be made* next
month by the legislature.

12g Incomplete constructions

Do not omit words necessary for grammatical completeness,
particularly in compound constructions.

1. Incomplete verb forms

When both verbs in a compound construction are in the same tense, an auxiliary verb need not be repeated.

Information will be sent to all students who *have signed* up for the Education Abroad program and [have] *paid* the fee.

However, when the verbs in a compound construction are in different tenses, the grammatical sense of the sentence usually requires that they both be written out in full.

12g

Incomplete	Modern languages *have* and always *will be* an important element in the college curriculum. [One could not say that languages *have be an important element*. The verb form *been* is needed to complete the sentence.]
Revised	Modern languages *have been* and always *will be* an important element in the college curriculum.

2. Omitted prepositions

English idiom requires that certain prepositions be used with certain adjectives and verbs. We say, for example, *interested in, aware of, devoted to*. We expect others to *agree with*, or to *object to*, or even to *protest against* our plans. When the verbs or adjectives in a compound construction take different prepositions, both prepositions must be included. If you are in doubt about the right preposition to use, a standard college dictionary will guide you. (See also **13f**.)

Incomplete	He was *oblivious* and *undisturbed by* the noise around him. [The preposition *by* can be used with *undisturbed* but not with *oblivious*. A second preposition must be inserted.]
Revised	He was *oblivious to* and *undisturbed by* the noise around him.
Incomplete	No one could have been more *interested* or *devoted to* her constituents than Senator Chong. [One can be *devoted to* constituents, but not *interested to* them. A second preposition is needed.]

Revised No one could have been more *interested in* or *devoted to* her constituents than Senator Chong.

3. Incomplete comparisons

In comparisons, do not omit words necessary to make a complete idiomatic statement.

Incomplete She is as witty, if not wittier, than her brother.
[If we delete *if not wittier* from this sentence, the statement says *She is as witty than her brother,* which makes no sense.]

Revised She is as witty *as,* if not wittier *than,* her brother.

Revised She is as witty as her brother, if not wittier.

Incomplete Leonardo da Vinci had one of the greatest, if not the greatest, minds of all time.
[No one, not even Leonardo, can have the greatest *minds.*]

Revised Leonardo da Vinci had one of the greatest minds, if not the greatest *mind,* of all time.

Incomplete Robert's expectations were more modest than his brother.
[This sentence erroneously compares Robert's expectations and Robert's brother. Each of the revised versions correctly expresses a comparison between the two men's *expectations.*]

Revised Robert's expectations were more modest than *those of* his brother.

Revised Robert's expectations were more modest than *his brother's.*

Incomplete The food here costs no more than any other restaurant in town.
[This sentence mistakenly compares the cost of food and the cost of restaurants. Adding the preposition *at* to the sentence clarifies its meaning.]

Revised The food here costs no more than [it does] *at* any other restaurant in town.

12g

Exercise 6 (page 264)

Answers will vary.

1. In reality, our facial movements may also have physiological functions. [faulty predication]
2. Israel Waynbaum, the French physician who investigated this topic many years ago, claimed that smiling actually creates happiness. [adverb clause misused as subject]
3. Crying, on the other hand, may be as good as, if not better than, tranquilizers, because it numbs the brain. [incomplete comparison]
4. The fact that we are not conscious of our facial movements does not mean that there is no reason for them. [adverb clause misused as subject]
5. When we wince in pain, for example, we may be unaware of and oblivious to the way our faces contort. [omitted preposition]
6. But making such an expression controls the flow of blood to the brain. [prepositional phrase misused as subject]

Avoid the illogical use of *any* and *than*.

Incomplete	For many years the Empire State Building was taller than any building in New York. [*Any building in New York* includes the Empire State Building, and a building cannot be taller than itself.]
Revised	For many years the Empire State Building was taller than any *other* building in New York.

Make sure the reader can tell what is being compared with what.

12g

Incomplete	Claremont is farther from Los Angeles than Pomona.
Revised	Claremont is farther from Los Angeles than Pomona *is*.
Revised	Claremont is farther from Los Angeles than *it is* from Pomona. [In the two revisions, both terms of the comparison are completely filled in, and there is no ambiguity about what is being compared.]

Many commercials and advertisements make claims that rest on incomplete comparisons. Both the student of language and the consumer should challenge such ungrammatical and empty statements.

Incomplete	Philsoc Gas gives more and better mileage for the dollar. [We should ask, more and better *than what?* Than a team of mules? Than another kind of gasoline? If so, which one?]
Incomplete	Buy Flakies, the crunchier, crisper, better-tasting breakfast cereal. [Again: than what?]

Note that the words *so, such,* and *too* when used as comparatives are completed by a phrase or clause indicating the standard of comparison.

I am *so* tired *that I could drop.* I had *such* a small breakfast *that I was starving by noon,* and when we stopped for lunch, I was *too* tired *to eat.*

EXERCISE 6

Revise the following sentences to eliminate mixed and incomplete constructions.

7. Contracting our facial muscles actually diverts blood from the face. [prepositional phrase misused as subject]
8. Similarily, the reason we touch our faces may be that we need to stimulate our minds. [adverb clause misused as complement]
9. So it makes sense that rubbing our foreheads has been and always will be a sign of thought. [incomplete verb form]
10. Being conscious of and alert to our expressions may have an effect on others and on ourselves. [omitted preposition]

Example

Mixed   Because our facial expressions show emotion makes us think that their only purpose is to communicate with others.

Revised   Because our facial expressions show emotion, we may think that their only purpose is to communicate with others. [misused adverb clause corrected]

1. In reality, the purposes of our facial movements may also have physiological functions.
2. Israel Waynbaum, the French physician who investigated this topic many years ago, claimed that when we smile actually creates happiness.
3. Crying, on the other hand, may be as good if not better than tranquilizers, because it actually numbs the brain.
4. Just because we are not conscious of our facial movements does not mean that there is no reason for them.
5. When we wince in pain, for example, we may be unaware and oblivious to the way our faces contort.
6. But by making such an expression controls the flow of blood to the brain.
7. In contracting our facial muscles actually diverts blood from the face.
8. Similarly, the reason we touch our faces may be because we need to stimulate our minds.
9. So it makes sense that rubbing our foreheads has and always will be a sign of thought.
10. Being conscious and alert to our expressions may have an effect on others and on ourselves.

12g

EXERCISE 7

Revise the following sentences to eliminate mixed and incomplete constructions.

Example

Mixed   The development of the Motion Picture Production Code in 1930 was when the film industry began to be censored.

Revised   The development of the Motion Picture Production Code in 1930 marked the beginning of censorship in the film industry. [misused adverb clause corrected]

Exercise 7

Answers will vary.

1. Sound films, invented in the 1920s, presented a broad range of new subjects to moviegoers. [faulty predication]
2. Censoring movies reduced their sexual content. [prepositional phrase misused as subject]
3. A movie could include adulterers if they were essential to its plot, but they had to end up less happy than any other characters in the film. [incomplete comparison]
4. The demand for and popularity of gangster movies made violence an issue. [omitted preposition, adverb clause misused as complement]
5. When James Cagney became a star as big as, if not bigger than, Mae West, the censors began to worry about violence in movies. [incomplete comparison]
6. One reason the censors looked at gangster movies was that they wanted to make Americans aware of and committed to the saying

12g

1. The invention of sound films in the 1920s presented a broad range of new subjects to moviegoers.
2. By censoring movies reduced their sexual content.
3. A movie could include adulterers if they were essential to its plot, but they had to end up less happy than any characters in the film.
4. The demand and popularity of gangster movies is where violence became an issue.
5. When James Cagney became as big if not a bigger star than Mae West, the censors began to worry about violence in movies.
6. One reason the censors looked at gangster movies was because they wanted to make Americans aware and committed to the saying "Crime does not pay."
7. Revealing the method of committing a crime was a violation as serious, if not more serious, than depicting violence, for the censors felt that people might imitate crimes they saw in the movies.
8. Because censors were worried about the authority of police meant that all law-enforcement officers had to be portrayed as honest.
9. The reason censorship exists in a society is because some people believe it can control the society's ills.
10. Different things will be censored in different generations, but censorship has and always will be a controversial issue.

"Crime does not pay." [adverb clause misused as complement, omitted preposition]
7. Revealing the method of committing a crime was a violation as serious as, if not more serious than, depicting violence, for the censors felt that people might imitate crimes they saw in the movies. [incomplete comparison]
8. Because censors were worried about the authority of police, all law-enforcement officers had to be portrayed as honest. [adverb clause misused as subject]
9. Censorship exists in a society because some people believe it can control the society's ills. [adverb clause misused as complement]
10. Different things will be censored in different generations, but censorship has been and always will be a controversial issue. [incomplete verb form]

13

Revising Diction

Every word in our language has a long history behind it, a fascinating ancestry of origins, of slowly changing meanings, of curious and forgotten uses as well as current, living ones—in short, an *etymology*. For instance, the word **diction,** meaning word choice, is derived from the Latin *dicere,* "to say," and ultimately from the Indo-European root *deik,* "to show or to point out," as its kinship with the Latin word for finger, *digitus,* and the English *digit* reveals. To know the root or roots of a word is to know something valuable about the source of its power to name.

The more fully we understand the ways in which words "name" the features of our world, the more precise and effective our diction can be. Granted, no word can ever duplicate the reality of the thorn that pierces our thumb, the sunset that moves us to silent joy, or the turbulence of first infatuation. Recognizing this limitation of language, however, writers who are attentive to diction achieve precision and depth by selecting words that most nearly approximate their thoughts and feelings.

13a Understanding denotation and connotation

The first of the complex ways by which words name is through their denotations and connotations. Their **denotations** are their most literal meanings. For instance, to take a stark example, *body, corpse,* and *cadaver* can all have the same denotation—a dead human being. **Connotations,** on the other hand, are a word's overtones, echoes, emotional colorings, and associations. Thus we would hardly speak of going

Chapter **9** introduced such basic issues about words as etymology and levels of usage. This chapter goes beyond the groundwork laid in the earlier chapter and focuses on judgments that students should be prepared to make about the words they use in their writing. Which connotation is appropriate to this context? At what level of abstraction should this idea be presented? Are these verbs as strong as they could be? Is this language free of sexist bias? Is this idiom correct? By concentrating on such issues, Chapter **13** introduces students to the kind of critical examination of their diction that should be an important part of the revision process.

13a

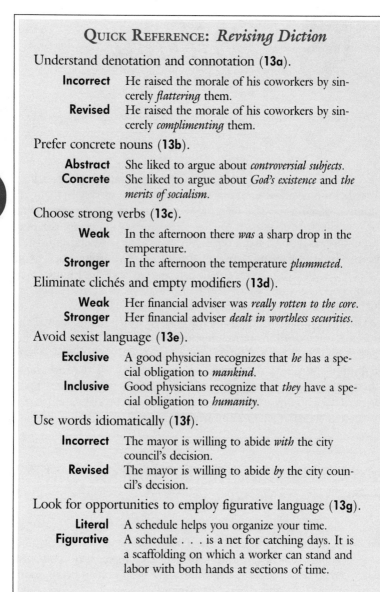

QUICK REFERENCE: *Revising Diction*

Understand denotation and connotation (**13a**).

Incorrect	He raised the morale of his coworkers by sincerely *flattering* them.
Revised	He raised the morale of his coworkers by sincerely *complimenting* them.

Prefer concrete nouns (**13b**).

Abstract	She liked to argue about *controversial subjects*.
Concrete	She liked to argue about *God's existence* and *the merits of socialism*.

Choose strong verbs (**13c**).

Weak	In the afternoon there *was* a sharp drop in the temperature.
Stronger	In the afternoon the temperature *plummeted*.

Eliminate clichés and empty modifiers (**13d**).

Weak	Her financial adviser was *really rotten to the core*.
Stronger	Her financial adviser *dealt in worthless securities*.

Avoid sexist language (**13e**).

Exclusive	A good physician recognizes that *he* has a special obligation to *mankind*.
Inclusive	Good physicians recognize that *they* have a special obligation to *humanity*.

Use words idiomatically (**13f**).

Incorrect	The mayor is willing to abide *with* the city council's decision.
Revised	The mayor is willing to abide *by* the city council's decision.

Look for opportunities to employ figurative language (**13g**).

Literal	A schedule helps you organize your time.
Figurative	A schedule . . . is a net for catching days. It is a scaffolding on which a worker can stand and labor with both hands at sections of time.

Eliminate jargon (**13h**).

Jargon	Let's *interface* at lunch to *finalize* this draft.
Revised	Let's *meet* at lunch to *finish* this draft.

to a funeral home to view the *corpse* of a friend, let alone the *cadaver*. *Body* is the most intimate in its connotations, expressing the sad acknowledgment that someone we care for is no longer there and that those familiar features will soon be gone forever; the word, in this context, connotes a commonly shared grief over an irrevocable reality. By contrast, *corpse* and *cadaver* connote the coldly impersonal, the anonymous, the institutional, as when police officially speak of finding an unknown corpse in a field or when medical students speak of dissecting a cadaver.

13a

1. The importance of context

The connotation of each word must be appropriate to the context. For instance, *to compliment* and *to flatter* may denote the same action—giving praise to another person—but consider the difference in their connotations. Usually, *to compliment* (or *compliments*) is used in the context of generous, justified praise given publicly or freely: "I'd like to compliment you on your performance." In contrast, *to flatter* (or *flattery*) connotes excess, even deception. Sometimes it may be harmless enough, as when we speak of "a photographer who flatters his subjects." More often, though, it connotes gratifying vanity, favor seeking, blandishments. Still, if forced to choose between being called a *flatterer* and an *apple-polisher,* most of us would probably elect the former. The context in which *apple-polishing* is used is unmistakable: blatant insincerity and favor seeking that are obvious to everyone, except perhaps the recipient.

Some connotations stem from our deep, often unconscious associations. When, for example, Phyllis Thompson concludes a poem "When I die, I will turn to bone / Like these. And dust of bone. And then, like God, / To stone," she draws on these associations in rhyming *bone* and *stone:* hardness, dryness, gray-whiteness, inertness. Drawing on equally deep but different associations, the poet Andrew Marvell three centuries ago praised "a green thought in a green shade." He knew very well that readers of English after his lifetime would bring to the phrase the positive associations of grass, trees, growth, life, and tranquillity.

2. The value of a dictionary

In short, context—the relevant environment of speaker, audience, and subject—is critical. But the context in which a given word is appropriate may not always be as evident as in the examples we have seen above. It's easy to decide whether you want to describe your best friend as *slender, slim,* or *skinny.* However, deciding how to choose from among such similar terms as *reparation, redress, restitution,* and *indemnity* may give almost any writer pause. For cases like these, you will need to rely on a good desk dictionary, such as those discussed in Chapter **9.** Many of these dictionaries not only provide the precise meaning of a word, but also discuss the subtle differences in connotation among terms that have similar denotations. You can't become a truly confident writer without such a book at your side.

EXERCISE 1

Pick four or five words that interest you (nouns, verbs, adjectives, or adverbs) and look them up in the *Oxford English Dictionary* in your library. The *OED* (its familiar title) is the indispensable reference for anyone curious about our language: it gives a word's first known appearance in print, its changing uses (with historical examples), and the fullest record we have of its connotations and denotations. Write a paragraph in which you (1) note each word's primary shifts in meaning, and (2) indicate what you take to be its primary connotations and denotations now.

EXERCISE 2

Choose three words that have similar denotations: for example, *to please, to gratify, to delight; concerned, involved, committed; fame, celebrity, stardom.* Then write a paragraph on the differing connotations of each word, and compose a sentence or two to show how the word is used in context. Consult a standard desk dictionary if you're unsure about the exact meaning of any word.

Exercise 1

Answers will vary.

Exercise 2

Answers will vary. Students might be asked to put their three sentences on the board for discussion by the entire class. What other similar words might be added to each set? How do their connotations differ?

13b Preferring concrete nouns

The second of the complex ways by which words name is through their abstractness and their concreteness. Words that name specific, tangible things are **concrete;** words that designate general qualities, categories, or relationships are **abstract.** An abstract term like *food* is a name for a whole group of concrete things: tomato soup, fried chicken legs, alfalfa sprouts, sliced apples, and cheesecake.

1.   The abstraction ladder

Note, though, that *abstract* and *concrete* are relative, not absolute, terms. In his influential book *Language in Thought and Action,* the linguist S. I. Hayakawa used what he termed an "abstraction ladder" to show how a concrete object can be perceived at greater and greater levels of abstraction. To understand Hayakawa's point, consider the example on page 272, which offers increasingly abstract perspectives on a specific ancient oak tree known as "Charter Oak."

The point is that we need general words as well as specific ones. For certain subjects or in certain contexts, we have to generalize, abstract, deal in whole categories. And at its own level of generality such prose can have great precision. The English philosopher John Stuart Mill, writing on *The Subjection of Women* in the late 1860s, is as intelligible to us now as he was to his contemporaries because of such precision.

Effective abstract diction

For, what is the peculiar character of the modern world—the difference which chiefly distinguishes modern institutions, modern social ideas, modern life itself, from those of times long past? It is, that human beings are no longer born to their place in life, and chained down by an inexorable bond to the place they are born to, but are free to employ their faculties, and such favorable chances as offer, to achieve the lot which may appear to them most desirable. Human society of old was constituted on a very different principle. All were born to a fixed social position, and were mostly kept in it by law, or interdicted from any means by which they could emerge from it.

Because he is arguing general principles rather than specific cases, Mill necessarily relies on abstract nouns—modern *institutions* and *social ideas,* human *faculties* and *chances.* But as every writer knows, abstract

13b

The Abstraction Ladder

The tree *Charter Oak* that exists at the atomic and sub-atomic level, incredibly complex and constantly changing.

The physical tree *Charter Oak* that we experience; the limited number of features that our nervous system selects from the complex reality.

The word *Charter Oak* itself, which is the name we give the particular perceived object but which is not the object itself.

The word *oak,* which stands for what *Charter Oak*$_1$, and oak$_2$, oak$_3$, and so on share in common—in short, thousands of oaks of different ages, sizes, and conditions.

The word *tree,* which stands for the traits we have abstracted that oaks, palms, pines, and so on share in common.

The word *plant,* which includes any living organism that cannot move voluntarily and usually makes its own food by photosynthesis—trees, flowers, bushes, and so on.

The word *organism,* which includes any living thing.

(left margin: more concrete) (right margin: more abstract)

13b

terms must at some point be given the substance of concreteness. In the following contrasting excerpt, for example, Jonathan Swift uses concrete diction to make his contemporaries—and us, two hundred years later—see and hear and feel the physical reality of war in the eighteenth century.

Effective concrete diction

And being no stranger to the art of war, I gave him a description of cannons, culverins, muskets, carabines, pistols, bullets, powder, swords, bayonets, battles, sieges, retreats, attacks, undermines, countermines, bombardments, sea-fights; ships sunk with a thousand men, twenty thousand killed on each side; dying groans, limbs flying in the air, smoke, noise, confusion, trampling to death under horses' feet; flight, pursuit, victory; fields strewed with carcasses left for food to dogs, and wolves, and birds of prey; plundering, stripping, ravishing, burning and destroying. I assured him that I had seen them blow up a hundred enemies at once in a siege, and as many in a ship, and beheld the dead bodies drop down in pieces from the clouds, to the great diversion of all the spectators.

Here Swift translates *war* into the concrete realities that the abstract term too often obscures—"dying groans, limbs flying in the air, . . . fields strewed with carcasses left for food to dogs . . . dead bodies [dropping] down in pieces from the clouds . . ."

2.   The value of concrete nouns

13b

This passage from Swift should suggest why teachers of writing urge their students to be specific, to be concrete. Concrete language compels our attention by its immediate appeal to the world of our experience. While the best writing shifts gracefully between abstract and concrete, overdependence on colorless abstractions makes for tediously dull reading. Consider the following examples.

Abstract	For dinner we had some really good food.
Concrete	For dinner we had barbecued steaks and sweet corn.
Abstract	She liked to argue about controversial subjects.
Concrete	She liked to argue about religion and politics.
More concrete	She liked to argue about God's existence and the merits of socialism.

In paragraphs, or entire papers, that settle for "really good food" and "controversial subjects," no real thought is taking place; like an unfocused camera, the writer is not registering anything in particular.

When you examine the diction of your sentences, remember that a specific statement often requires no more space than a vague one, yet it can communicate much more information.

Vague	One member of my family has recently begun her professional career.
Concrete	Last week my sister Lynn joined the law firm of Bailey, Harney, and Johnson.

Exercise 3 (page 274)

Students should note that the point of this exercise is not simply to trace the etymology of the words given (cf. Chapter **9**, Exercise 3, page 187), but to observe the evolution of meaning in each case.

1. *cereal*   Originates with Ceres, the Roman goddess of agriculture. Originally an adjective, the word pertained to the goddess, then to grain (which, as an all-important crop, might well be expected to have her special attention); later a noun, it denoted any grain grown for food (a sense still current in British usage). Finally, it has become a noun denoting a prepared breakfast food made from grain (an American usage originally).

2. *chapter*   From the Latin *capitulum,* "little head." The word was first used to refer to a main subdivision or section of a book, particularly of the Bible. Then, from the practice of reading a chapter of Scripture at a meeting of a monastic or religious order, the word came to denote the meeting itself, and then the group that met. Finally, this last

You will achieve only as much reality in your papers as your words actually name; you may find that the effort to think concretely takes time and imagination, but it's the only way you have of discovering and sharing your meaning.

13c

EXERCISE 3

With the help of a dictionary (and perhaps a dictionary of Roman and Greek mythology) discover the concrete particular in which each of these words originated. Write a brief explanation of why and how you think some of these words came to mean what they mean today.

cereal	cupidity	hackneyed	panic
chapter	erotic	infant	paradise
comma	genius	language	surgery

EXERCISE 4

Choose three concrete nouns and take them up three or four rungs on the abstraction ladder, beginning above the atomic and subatomic rung.

EXERCISE 5

Choose three abstract nouns (for example, *wealth, humanity, art*) and take them down four or five rungs on the abstraction ladder.

13c Choosing strong verbs

Anemic writing almost always results when, rather than using a vigorous verb, we connect subject and complement with the verb *be*. So-called **linking** or *copulative* **verbs** also include *become, seem, appear,* and *remain.* Of course, we cannot entirely avoid linking verbs because we need them to indicate logical equivalents.

> The commission's downtown development plan *was* disappointingly vague.

> Most physicians in Russia *are* women.

In cases such as these, the linking verb functions like an equal sign, equating the subject and complement in a sentence. But used excessively, linking verbs make for bland and monotonous prose.

---

meaning was further generalized to denote a group of members of any organization (as in "the local chapter of the sorority").

3. *comma*   From the Greek *komma,* from *koptein,* "to cut off." From meaning "a phrase or group of words," this term came to refer to the punctuation mark that separates phrases or groups of words within sentences.

4. *cupidity*   From the Latin *cupidus,* "eagerly desirous"; from the god Cupid, son of Venus and Mars and the personification of desire. The word originally meant "ardent desire or lust" but has come to refer more specifically to the lust for wealth.

5. *erotic*   From Eros, in Greek mythology the god of love, son of Aphrodite, identified by the Romans with Cupid. Hence, the adjective means "of or pertaining to the passion of sexual love" and is particularly used to describe the literature of sexual desire.

6. *genius*   From the Latin *genere,* "to beget." Originally the word referred to the classical pagan belief in the tutelary god or attendant spirit (the genius) assigned to every person at birth to govern the person's

Weak verbs

William LeBaron Jenney *was* the nineteenth-century Chicago architect who *was* the inventor of the skeletal-frame skyscraper. Jenney's Home Insurance Building of 1884 *was* apparently the first tall building in which an iron-and-steel frame *was* the main support, rather than load-bearing exterior walls of brick or stone. But though Jenney *was* a technical innovator, he *was* not a man with a clear aesthetic vision. His early buildings *are* often collections of discordant elements and eclectic ornamentation. Jenney's Manhattan Building of 1891, for example, *seems* to be a number of separate buildings set on top of one another. There *is* a lack of unity in its design that *is* immediately evident.

13c

Linking verbs like those in the passage above are not the only verbs that create dull prose. *Occur, take place, prevail, exist, happen,* and other verbs expressing a state of affairs also make for needlessly colorless writing.

Weak	In the afternoon a sharp drop in the temperature *occurred*.
Stronger	The temperature *dropped* sharply in the afternoon.
Weak	Throughout the meeting an atmosphere of increasing tension *existed*.
Stronger	As the meeting progressed, the tension *increased*.

Make your verbs work. Good writers enliven their observations by selecting sharp verbs and by using verbals as modifiers. Consider these sentences from an essay by the naturalist Edward Hoagland.

Strong verbs

Mountain lions spirit themselves away in saw-toothed canyons and on escarpments, and when conversing with their mates, they coo like pigeons, sob like women, emit a flat slight shriek, a popping bubbling growl, or mew, or yowl. They growl and suddenly caterwaul into falsetto—the famous scarifying scream functioning as a kind of hunting cry close up, to terrorize the game. They ramble as much as twenty-five miles in a night, maintaining a large loop of territory which they cover every week or two.

The verbs that assert—*spirit away, coo, sob, emit, growl, caterwaul,* and *ramble* — and the infinitive *to terrorize* are reinforced by the action of the

fortunes and determine his or her character. Later, it came to denote one's bent or turn of mind (the spirit being internalized to the possessor, as it were). Finally, the term has come to signify, in its most common meaning, a native intellectual power of the most exalted type, especially an instinctive and extraordinary capacity for imaginative creation, original thought, and discovery. It can be applied either to that power ("she has a genius for mathematics") or to the person possessing it ("she is a mathematical genius").

7. *hackneyed* From Old French *hacquenee,* "an ambling horse." Since such an easy-to-ride horse was particularly suitable for hiring out, a hackney soon was a horse for hire, and later a carriage. *Hackneyed,* therefore, began by meaning "for hire" and later came to mean "overused."

8. *infant* From Latin *infans,* from a participle meaning "unable to speak." This one attribute has given its name to the entire state of being a baby ("infancy").

9. *language* From Latin *lingua,* "tongue, language." The part of the

verbals, *conversing, popping, bubbling, scarifying, functioning, hunting,* and *maintaining.* Even the nouns *shriek, growl, mew, yowl, scream,* and *loop* contribute to the energy of the passage, since in other contexts they function as verbs and carry these active connotations with them. Action verbs and verbals make us feel, see, hear, smell; they appeal to our senses and body knowledge, our primary ways of knowing and understanding.

For some further advice on using verbs effectively, see **8c**.

EXERCISE 6

Revise the passage on page 275 that illustrates weak verbs, eliminating as many linking verbs as possible. A possible revision of the passage's first sentence is provided as an example.

Example

> **Weak verbs**   William LeBaron Jenney was the nineteenth-century Chicago architect who was the inventor of the skeletal-frame skyscraper.
>
> **Revised**   William LeBaron Jenney was the nineteenth-century Chicago architect who invented the skeletal-frame skyscraper. [one linking verb eliminated]

13d Eliminating clichés and empty modifiers

In his classic essay "Politics and the English Language," George Orwell criticized modern writing by describing it as the process of merely "gumming together long strips of words which have already been set in order by someone else, and making the results presentable by sheer humbug." Often these "long strips of words" are stock phrases known as clichés—trite, familiar expressions that involve no thought on the writer's part and evoke no feeling from the reader. Thus we may read about members of an *all-American family* who are *pleased as punch* to live in the *land of opportunity,* where they *work like the devil* to *make their dreams come true.* This string of clichés is admittedly exaggerated, but even a single cliché in a sentence suggests that the writer does not

body most obviously used in speech gives its name to the system of speech.

10. *panic*   From Pan, Greek god of forests, pastures, flocks, and shepherds, who was supposedly capable of inspiring people (or sheep) with a sudden, irrational fear—hence the modern meaning of a quickly spreading, unreasonable fear.

11. *paradise*   From Greek *paradeisos,* "garden." Originally *paradise* was used to denote the Garden of Eden; later the term was generalized to mean "heaven," "a place of great beauty," or "the condition of great happiness."

12. *surgery*   From Latin *chirugia;* from Greek *cheirougia,* "handicraft" (from *cheir, cheiros,* "the hand," and *ergein,* "to work"). The word has specialized to refer to a certain sort of skilled work with the hands— the treatment of disease by manual operations, such as the removal of the diseased part by cutting.

Common Clichés to Avoid

acid test	left out in the cold
all boils down to	more than meets the eye
as luck would have it	other side of the coin
beat a hasty retreat	proud possessor of
bitter end	quick as a flash
breathless silence	rotten to the core
deep, dark secret	slow but sure
depths of despair	straight from the shoulder
few and far between	trials and tribulations
green with envy	uphill battle
growing by leaps and bounds	walking on air
heave a sigh of relief	water under the bridge
hit the nail on the head	work hand in hand
in this day and age	worth its weight in gold
jumping on the bandwagon	young in spirit

13d

care enough to seek out an original way of presenting his or her thoughts. The box above lists some examples of the ready-made phrases that careful writers try to avoid.

Remember that enclosing a cliché in quotation marks does not make its use acceptable in writing, any more than deliberately tripping an alarm system would exculpate a burglar from his or her crime. If you rely on the language's ready-made phrases, you can't escape the charge of unoriginal thinking.

Like clichés, empty modifiers such as *really, very, much,* and *so* give the impression of a writer who is unwilling to take the time to find a more precise, emphatic, and original way of expressing his or her ideas.

Weak   The mayor was *really* angry over the city council's refusal to approve her proposed budget for the new fiscal year.

Weak   I was *so* happy to hear about David's new job.

Exercises 4 and 5 (page 274)

Answers will vary.

Exercise 6 (page 276)

Answers will vary. The revision that follows eliminates six of the original passage's ten linking verbs.

William LeBaron Jenney was the nineteenth-century Chicago architect who *invented* the skeletal-frame skyscraper. Jenney's Home Insurance Building of 1884 was apparently the first tall building in which an iron-and-steel frame *provided* the main support, rather than load-bearing exterior walls of brick or stone. But though Jenney was a technical innovator, he *lacked* a clear aesthetic vision. His early buildings *rose* as collections of discordant elements and eclectic ornamentation. Jenney's Manhattan Building of 1891, for example, *resembles* a number of separate buildings set on top of one another. The lack of unity in its design is immediately evident.

> **Weak**   Marcelle believes that proponents of medical
> experimentation on live animals are *very* bad people.

Why settle for such weak phrasing when the language offers a range of
more emphatic possibilities?

> **Stronger**   The mayor was *enraged* by the city council's refusal to
> approve her proposed budget for the new fiscal year.
> **Stronger**   I was *thrilled* to hear about David's new job.
> **Stronger**   Marcelle believes that proponents of medical experi-
> mentation on live animals are *detestable* people.

13d   Every time you are tempted to place a *very* before a word, look that
word up in a good college dictionary and try to discover a stronger
equivalent that will convey the meaning you want in all its intensity. Or
else just leave out the modifier. In most cases, your sentence will be
stronger without it:

> **Weak modifier**   The evidence points to only one conclusion—the
> company was engaging in *very* deliberate fraud.
>
> **Stronger**   The evidence points to only one conclusion—the
> company was engaging in deliberate fraud.

EXERCISE 7

Identify clichés and empty modifiers in the following sentences. Can you
suggest an alternative wording that is more emphatic?

Example

> **Original**   I always feel really calm when I am around my friend
> Henry because his perspective on life is as steady as a
> rock.
>
> **Revised**   I always feel tranquil when I am around my friend
> Henry because of his balanced perspective on
> life. [empty modifier and cliché revised]

1. Henry's love for others shines like the sun.
2. Even when people walk all over him, he remains as cool as a cucum-
ber.
3. When my coworkers treat me very badly, I have to make a conscious
effort to keep the lines of communication open with them.

Exercise 7

The weakness of clichés should be evident to students who attempt to
revise these sentences, for one can only guess at the precise meaning intended here. Answers will of course vary widely.

1. Henry's love for others is evident to everyone who knows him. [cliché
eliminated]
2. Even when people take advantage of his shyness, he remains unper-
turbed. [clichés eliminated]
3. When my coworkers treat me insolently, I have to struggle to keep
working productively with them. [empty modifier eliminated, clichés
eliminated]
4. In contrast, Henry easily overlooks wrongs done to him. [clichés elim-
inated]
5. Henry has taught me critical lessons about dealing with other people,
lessons that will stay with me until old age. [empty modifier eliminated, cliché eliminated]

4. In contrast, it is as easy as pie for Henry to forgive and forget.
5. Henry has taught me very important lessons about dealing with other people, lessons that will stay with me even if I live to a ripe old age.

13e Avoiding sexist language

One of the most important changes to occur recently in English is an increased sensitivity to sexist language—usages that treat men and women unequally or that betray stereotypes about what it means to be female or male. Unfortunately, inequality and stereotyping persist in our culture; the point is that language should not be used in a manner that serves to perpetuate this condition. To put it another way, language that refers to women and men should be *inclusive* rather than *exclusive*.

Publishers, professional organizations, broadcasters, and the general public have become steadily more concerned with avoiding language that fosters notions of inequality between women and men. As a result, writers who are not alert to the kinds of sexism described below increasingly run the risk of alienating their readers.

1. Avoid using *man* in a generic sense

Writers and speakers who attempt to defend the traditional use of the word *man* to mean "all human beings" argue that its connotation is generic, that it does not suggest individual men but people in general. In phrases such as *the average man* or *every man for himself,* they say, *man* simply means "person."

In reality, this notion that *man* has a generic connotation rather than a sex-specific one is easy to disprove. We need only consider a sentence like the following one.

> On this campus, unfortunately, any man who wants an active social life has to be a member of a fraternity or a sorority.

Why does this sentence jar? The ending startles us precisely because we do not read the word *man* in the beginning of the sentence in a generic sense, but instead attach to it a male connotation that subsequently clashes with the word *sorority* at the sentence's end. A number of alternative wordings, each with a different meaning, are possible.

Acceptable	On this campus, unfortunately, any man who wants an active social life has to be a member of a fraternity. [*Man* is not used here as a generic noun; the sentence is now *about* men only.]
Acceptable	On this campus, unfortunately, any woman who wants an active social life has to be a member of a sorority. [The sentence is now about women only.]
Acceptable	On this campus, unfortunately, any student who wants an active social life has to be a member of a fraternity or a sorority. [The language is now sex neutral; it includes both women and men.]

3e

Avoiding the allegedly generic *man* is easy. For *man*, substitute *person* or *human being* or whatever other noun fits the context (like *student* in the example above). For *mankind*, use *humanity* or *human beings*.

Exclusive	We are committed to hiring the best man for the job.
Inclusive	We are committed to hiring the best *person* for the job.
Exclusive	Since the beginning of history, man has been an inventor and an innovator.
Inclusive	Since the beginning of history, *human beings* have been inventors and innovators.
Exclusive	AIDS is the most recent example of mankind's struggle against the mystery of disease.
Inclusive	AIDS is the most recent example of *humanity's* struggle against the mystery of disease.

The same principle applies to compounds with the word *man*. A reasonable sex-neutral substitute is always available: for *manmade*, use *synthetic*; for *manpower*, use *workforce*. Finally, also avoid using the word *man* as a verb.

Exclusive	Representatives of the senior class will man the information booth during orientation for new students.
Inclusive	Representatives of the senior class will *staff* the information booth during orientation for new students.

2. Avoid using the pronoun *he* in a generic sense

Like *man,* the pronoun *he* (together with *his, him,* and *himself*) has often been used in a generic sense to refer to people in general when its antecedent is indefinite. But also like the noun *man, he* is demonstrably not a sex-neutral pronoun. If it were, the following sentence would make sense.

> Everyone who attended this year's meeting of the National Organization for Women increased his understanding of the organization's agenda for the rest of the decade.

13e

When the context clearly implies women as well as men, the pronoun *he* immediately seems out of place. Why? Because, despite traditionalists' claims to the contrary, *he, his,* and *him* are inevitably sex-specific terms. And if *his* excludes women in the sentence above, it does the same in each of the sentences below as well. Indeed, the personal pronouns in these sentences *define* their contexts as exclusively male.

Exclusive   Each participant in the race should take his place at the starting line by nine o'clock.

Exclusive   A good writer often does his best work in solitude.

Exclusive   Every attorney in the firm understood himself and his colleagues better after the meeting.

Avoiding the sexist use of the pronoun *he* is simply a matter of substituting *he or she.* When that alternative seems awkward, recast the sentence using plural nouns and pronouns.

Inclusive   Each participant in the race should take *his or her* place at the starting line by nine o'clock.

Inclusive   A good writer often does *his or her* best work in solitude.

Inclusive   *All the attorneys* in the firm understood *themselves* and *their* colleagues better after the meeting.

3. Use sex-neutral language to identify people's roles

With few exceptions, all roles in our society are occupied by women and men. The language used to refer to people in their roles should therefore be free of references to gender like the suffix *-man*.

Using Nonsexist Terms for Occupations

Sex specific	Sex neutral
businessman	businessperson
chairman	chair, chairperson
congressman	representative, member of Congress
fireman	firefighter
housewife	homemaker
mailman	mail carrier
male nurse	nurse
policeman	police officer
salesman	salesperson
woman judge	judge
workman	worker

The same rule applies in the case of words that were formerly given the feminine endings *-ess* or *-trix*, which suggest that women are occupying roles defined by men and that they should be distinguished from their male counterparts.

Avoiding Terms with Feminine Endings

Sex specific	Sex neutral
actress	actor
authoress	author
aviatrix	aviator
poetess	poet
sculptress	sculptor
stewardess	flight attendant

13e

4. Use parallel language to discuss men and women in parallel contexts

Perhaps the most insidious variety of sexist language involves the unequal treatment of men and women in the same context. When women and men are discussed in parallel contexts, the terminology that designates them should also be parallel. Consider the following examples.

Nonparallel	Two male students and a coed were accosted at knifepoint while walking across the campus last night.
Parallel	Two *male students* and a *female student* were accosted at knifepoint while walking across the campus last night.
Nonparallel	That company has a history of hiring more men than girls.
Parallel	That company has a history of hiring more *men* than *women*.
Nonparallel	The ladies' basketball team has a better record than the men's team.
Parallel	The *women's* basketball team has a better record than the *men's* team.
Nonparallel	I now pronounce you man and wife.
Parallel	I now pronounce you *husband* and *wife*.
Nonparallel	The only guests who have not yet arrived are Hank Evans and his wife.
Parallel	The only guests who have not yet arrived are *Hank* and *Patricia* Evans.

13e

EXERCISE 8

Suggest sex-neutral alternatives for the following terms.

1. caveman
2. clergyman
3. craftsman
4. deliveryman
5. draftsman
6. layman
7. television anchorman
8. repairman
9. sportsman
10. weatherman

Exercise 8

1. cave dweller
2. cleric, member of the clergy
3. craftsperson, artisan
4. delivery person
5. draftsperson, drafter
6. layperson
7. television anchor
8. repairer
9. sports enthusiast
10. weather forecaster, meteorologist

13e

Identify examples of sexist language in the following passage, originally published in 1965. Revise the passage using more inclusive language.

> Biography must always be a flawed achievement and the biographer, a man who fails before he begins. There is no Othello with whom to compare Shakespeare's Othello. There is no Trojan war with which to compare the *Iliad*. You cannot visit Satan in hell in order to learn how well Milton has taken him off. No one can accuse Thackeray of failing to tell all about Becky Sharp. But a biography is always publicly haunted by the life which it has attempted to recapture, and a biographer is always privately mocked by the evidences which that life has left behind. Unlike other writers, he must create a world out of materials which exist independently of what he does with them and of which he has had no part in the fashioning. No character that the novelist or the dramatist creates can be more intelligent, more complex, more sensitive, than his maker; whereas it is the lot of the biographer to pursue a man who is very likely to have been more ambitious, more subtle, more daring, and sharper of wits than he. In the race of art, a biographer must hoist himself by his bootstraps in order to run at all.
>
> —Paul Murray Kendall, *The Art of Biography*

Identify examples of sexist language in the following passage, originally published in 1983. Revise the passage using more inclusive language.

> Bridges typify progress more than any other structures built by man. They span obstructions in his path and open new routes of communication. As need increases, they are thrown across wider rivers and deeper valleys. Considered from the beginning, the growth of bridge building seems almost biological, sometimes accelerated by fertile civilization and sometimes blighted by barbarism. The bridge engineer acts as agent in this evolution of the bridge. He is directed by economic conditions over which he has no control, and he is himself a product of these conditions. In the early days, he was an architect unhampered by the complexity into which building operations have since fallen. He built structures so that they appeared correct to his eye. If they fell, he rebuilt them with sturdier proportions. The results were more pleasing in appearance than many of the coldly scientific modern bridges. In this way were built the marvelous Roman aque-

Exercise 9

Answers will vary. One possible revision follows.

> Biography must always be a flawed achievement and the biographer, a writer who fails before beginning. . . . Unlike other writers, biographers must create a world out of materials which exist independently of what they do with them and of which they have had no part in the fashioning. No characters that the novelist or the dramatist creates can be more intelligent, more complex, more sensitive, than their maker; whereas it is the lot of biographers to pursue subjects who are very likely to have been more ambitious, more subtle, more daring, and sharper of wits than those who write about their lives. In the race of art, biographers must hoist themselves by their bootstraps in order to run at all.

ducts and bridges, the picturesque medieval spans and the beautiful masterpieces of the Renaissance.

——Charles S. Whitney, *Bridges: Their Art, Science and Evolution*

13f Observing idiom

An **idiom** is an expression peculiar to itself in a language, one whose meaning cannot be explained by the ordinary meaning of its individual words. Idioms, in short, are arbitrary, as when we say *make out* (succeed), *make up* (reconcile), and *make do* (be satisfied with). They are as fixed as the Spanish *Hace frio* ("It's cold"), which literally and unaccountably to one learning the language translates as "It makes cold."

13f

In English, we often rely on prepositions to indicate subtle but essential relationships. To take a stand *on* an issue, to be *in* a quandary, *out* of luck, *off* your rocker—these idiomatic expressions make a kind of spatial sense as figures of speech: we can, if we stop to visualize it, imagine standing on an issue, defending our point of view, planting our feet firmly on an ideological turf we call our own. Some verbs, however, require prepositions that are arbitrary and unexplainable. The box below offers selected examples of such verb-and-preposition combinations dictated by idiom. If you are in doubt about the correct preposition to use with any other verb, a good desk dictionary will guide you.

For an extended discussion of other idiomatic aspects of English usage, see Chapter **43**.

Idiomatic Uses of Prepositions

abide *by* a decision

agree *with* a person, *to* a proposal, *on* a procedure

angry *at* or *about* something, *with* a person

argue *with* a person, *for* or *about* a measure

compatible *with*

correspond *to* or *with* a thing, *with* a person

differ *from* one another in appearance, differ *with* a person in opinion

---

Exercise 10 (page 284)

Answers will vary. One possible revision follows.

Bridges typify progress more than any other human structures. They span obstructions in people's paths and open new routes of communication. . . . Bridge engineers act as agents in this evolution of the bridge. They are directed by economic conditions over which they have no control, and they are themselves a product of these conditions. In the early days, engineers were architects unhampered by the complexity into which building operations have since fallen. They built structures that simply appeared correct to the eye. If those structures fell, they were rebuilt with sturdier proportions. . . .

interfere *with* a performance, *in* someone else's affairs
listen *to* a person, listen *at* the door
stand *by* a friend, *for* a cause, *on* an issue
wait *on* a customer, *for* a person, *at* a place, *in* the rain, *by* the
    hour

13g Using figurative language

When we express ourselves with *figurative language,* we communicate nonliterally: we compare one quite distinct thing with another on the basis of some quality we think they share, or we identify one thing by another in terms of a common quality. Figurative language is a complex and powerful means of creating, showing, or limiting relationships. Thus, when we speak of costs being *cut,* of price *gouging,* or of a state *draining* its taxpayers, we use implied comparisons to intensify and vivify our point. Of course, a merchant charged with price gouging has not, in fact, taken a chisel and scooped grooves on his or her customers any more than we have made a chest incision and inspected the right auricle and right ventricle when we speak of *getting to the heart of the subject.* These phrases are economical and precise: price *gouging* says how we feel when we think we have been defrauded (we speak of the *chiseler*); *getting to the heart of the subject* names our intent to discover the source of its life, the vital center. The right figure of speech can turn an otherwise pedestrian phrase into an arresting observation that bears the stamp of your personality and imagination.

1. Metaphor and simile

A metaphor is a direct comparison of two things on the basis of a shared quality. The word *metaphor* is itself a buried metaphor since it means *to transfer* or *carry across:* when we compare, we are carrying a trait from one thing to another as if over a bridge or road. Metaphor says that one thing is another: *All the world's a stage. Snow blanketed the ground. The road of excess leads to the palace of wisdom.*

Metaphor is one of the most powerful causes of linguistic growth, change, and vitality. To speak of large, expensive, inefficient automobiles as *gas-guzzlers,* a sharp decline in the value of currency and a sharp rise in prices as *runaway inflation,* or citizens receiving inadequate services for their money as *the public's being shortchanged* — to employ these and other metaphors that have come into general use is to be conveniently brief, exact, and vivid. In fact, whether we realize it or not, we organize whole categories of our experience through certain metaphoric structures. For example, we systematize our concepts of vitality and power through metaphors of upwardness, our concepts of debility and weakness through metaphors of downwardness: she is at the *peak* of her fame, or she *fell* from the public's favor; he is *on top* of the situation, or he is *under* the control of others. Language is always vitally metaphoric because our realities — our hopes, desires, circumstances, and fears — are constantly changing.

13g

One final, positive word about metaphors, and some advice: begin to feel their presence; make a practice of looking for them not only in nouns (the *heart* of the subject) but also in verbs. Metaphorical language gives nourishment in ways that the junk food of needlessly abstract phrasing never can — it's the difference between saying "Avoid repetitious or unnecessary phrasing" and "*Cut* out the *deadwood*." American writing is wonderfully rich in metaphors, as the following passage from Mark Twain's *The Adventures of Huckleberry Finn* may suggest.

> Once or twice of a night we would see a steamboat slipping along in the dark, and now and then she would *belch* a whole world of sparks up out of her chimbleys, and they would *rain* down in the river and look awfully pretty; then she would turn a corner and her lights would *wink* out.

Of course, Twain's carefully crafted prose in this novel takes the form of a dialect, but metaphors enrich standard English as well. In the following passage, for example, the essayist Annie Dillard uses a series of metaphorical comparisons to stress the importance of maintaining a schedule in one's life.

> A schedule defends from chaos and whim. It is a net for catching days. It is a scaffolding on which a worker can stand and labor with both hands at sections of time. A schedule is a mock-up of reason and order — willed, faked, and so brought into being; it is a peace and a haven set into the wreck of time; it is a lifeboat on which you find yourself, decades later, still living.

Like a metaphor, a *simile* asserts a comparison between two essentially unlike things, but unlike a metaphor, it uses the words *like* or *as* to do so.

> Bright *as* the sun, her eyes the gazers strike,
> And, *like* the sun, they shine on all alike.
>
> —Alexander Pope, *The Rape of the Lock*

> My heart is *like* a singing bird
> Whose nest is in a watered shoot.
>
> —Christina Rossetti, "A Birthday"

> Be thou *as* chaste *as* ice, *as* pure *as* snow, thou shalt not escape calumny.
>
> —William Shakespeare, *Hamlet*

13g

2. Analogy

A comparison can be extended into an analogy, which not only illustrates a point but also suggests an argument or point of view (Chapter **7** discusses the use of analogy in building paragraphs; Chapter **15**, its use and abuse in reasoning). Consider, for instance, Mary Ellman's startling analogy between astronauts and pregnant women.

> The astronaut's body is awkward and encumbered in the space suit as the body of a pregnant woman. It moves about with even more graceless difficulty. And being shot up into the air suggests submission too, rather than enterprise. Like a woman being carted to a delivery room, the astronaut must sit (or lie) still, and go where he is sent. Even the nerve, the genuine courage it takes simply not to run away, is much the same in both situations—to say nothing of the shared sense of having gone too far to be able to change one's mind.

3. Allusion

In an *allusion* the comparison is made between some present event, situation, or person and an event or person from history or literature. Usually, the allusion is a brief reference to something the reader is assumed to know, as when journalists allude to a recent scandal as "another possible Watergate." Sometimes the writer may employ several allusions, as when Adrienne Rich says the following of a woman who reads about women in books written by men.

She finds a terror and a dream, she finds a beautiful face, she finds La Belle Dame Sans Merci, she finds Juliet or Tess or Salome, but precisely what she does not find is that absorbed, drudging, puzzled, sometimes inspired creature, herself, who sits at a desk trying to put words together.

A sense of audience should determine what allusions, if any, are appropriate. There is no point in throwing away allusions or in alienating your readers by appearing to be more knowledgeable than they. An allusion can deepen the meaning of a statement for those who recognize the comparison, but the statement should still make perfectly clear sense without it.

4. Mixed figures of speech

Mixed figures of speech result when writers have stopped thinking about the logical and visual sense of what they're saying. Used deliberately, they make their point by comic incongruity, as in this sentence.

Whenever he saw a spark of genius, he watered it.

Most of the time, however, mixed figures of speech are confused, bizarre, or both.

Mixed   I know it sounds like sour grapes, but that's the whole kettle of fish in a nutshell.

Mixed   The southern states, being completely agricultural, hinged around the barn.

Mixed   He was saddled with a sea of grass-roots opinion that his campaigners had ferreted out for him.

13h Recognizing jargon, pretentious diction, and euphemism

Three enemies of clarity and sincerity in language remain to be discussed in this chapter—jargon, pretentious diction, and euphemism.

1. Jargon

Jargon is a label given to various types of specialized language. In its neutral sense, the word refers to the technical vocabulary that professionals in a given field rely on to communicate with one another. While perhaps obscure to outsiders, such language is nonetheless common—and necessary—in specialized fields as diverse as basketball, architecture, medicine, and chess.

But in its second—less benign—sense, the word *jargon* refers to ponderous, wordy, inflated phrasing used by writers who try to make their ideas seem more profound and their prose sound more impressive. This is the jargon that most readers object to—the language of bureaucrats and politicians who hope that by inflating their prose they can raise the commonplace to the significant.

13h

Our minds are befogged every day by phrases like *capability factor, career potential, socio-personal development, decision-making process, social interaction, holistic learning procedures, technical implementations,* and *fundamental value structures.* We cannot easily escape from this network of confused language, but if we learn to recognize the stylistic flavor of jargon, we may avoid it in our own writing. Jargon words are, by and large, abstract rather than concrete, and they typically contain more than one syllable (as if the jargon writer assumed that the addition of syllables would add weight to the word). Jargon words are often nouns masquerading as verbs: *concretize, finalize, interiorize.* Sometimes, too, nouns are turned into jargonistic adverbs or adjectives by the addition of the suffix *-wise: languagewise, subjectwise, moneywise, weatherwise.*

Jargon is best deflated by a translation into clear English.

Obscured by jargon

> The leader-follower relationship must be looked upon as a field situation and such a field will be structured and sustain its structure only when the views of the leader are acceptable to the followers. The leader-follower field will be extended to the degree that the leader is seen to have authority to assume the leader role. As the relation of the leader's apparent right to authority is moved progressively away from the problem area confronting the group, there will be an increasing tendency for the leader-follower field to disintegrate.

This specimen, while not the worst, typifies the habits of jargon— inflated prose and overuse of the passive voice. Thus *leader* and *group* become *the leader-follower relationship* in a *field situation,* and the leader's interfering becomes a movement *away from the problem area confronting the group*. Stripped of their jargon, these sentences mean no more than this.

Clarified

> A group will fall apart when its members no longer agree with the views of their leader. Whatever degree of authority a leader has is gained from the group's willingness to grant it. The more the group feels its leader is interfering, the less likely it is to follow.

In addition to being obscure and tiresome, jargon can be dangerous when it conceals or distorts the reality it describes. The phrase *antipersonnel detonating devices* obscures the chilling reality of bombs that kill men, women, and children. Similarly, the corporate chief who speaks of *anticipating the accelerated cessation of manufacturing operations* is really talking about speeding up plant closings and putting more people out of work faster.

13h

2. Pretentious diction

Pretentious diction, like the pretentious person, is stiff and phony. Our diction becomes pretentious if we always choose the polysyllabic word over the word of one syllable, a Latinate word when an Anglo-Saxon one will do, flowery phrases in place of common nouns and verbs. Writing should be as honest and forthright as plain speech, particularly when we have the opportunity to revise and edit what we write for economy and directness.

Sometimes, ordinary words seem inadequate to carry the weight we want our thoughts to have, so we decorate statements with inappropriately ornate language.

Pretentious diction

> His vigilant attention to the well-being of others profoundly influences the personal life-styles of all those fortunate enough to bear the appellation of "his friends."

This sentence says little more than, "His thoughtfulness influences the way his friends live." The fancy language is out of proportion to the statement it makes.

To guard your writing against pretentious diction, read your papers aloud, listening for phrases that you cannot imagine ever speaking to a friend or classmate. Be wary of words that dress up simple facts: *interface* for *meet, utilize* for *use, profitable enterprise* for *money-maker, decision-making process* for *leadership.* As you consult your college dictionary to develop your vocabulary, note the fine distinctions among synonyms and consider whether the words you choose will strike your reader as counterfeit or genuine. Keep in mind Samuel Johnson's advice: "Read over your compositions and, when you meet a passage which you think is particularly fine, strike it out."

13h   3.   Euphemism

Often when we want to avoid harsh facts we resort to a particular kind of circumlocution, the **euphemism.** The Greek word means "good speech," but euphemisms seldom are good for writers. Too often they are cosmetics to cover up painful realities. To avoid facing the finality of death, for example, people have always used euphemisms: *passed on* or *passed, gone west, met his Maker, gone to her reward.* The *dear departed* rests in his casket in the *slumber room,* often having been *prepared* by the *funeral director,* who today is likely to preside at a *memorial service* instead of a funeral. Ultimately, the *loved one* is not buried but *laid to rest,* not in a graveyard but in *The Valley of Memories.* Such sentimental wordiness is intended to comfort the bereaved by pretending that death is sleep, but its effect—like that of all euphemistic language—is often one of stilted insincerity.

EXERCISE 11

Analyze the following paragraphs for jargon, pretentious diction, and clichés. Translate the paragraphs into Standard English if you can, and if there are any expressions that you cannot translate, be prepared to say why.

1. A corollary of reinforcement is that the consequences of responding may be represented exhaustively along a continuum ranging from those that substantially raise response likelihood, through those that have little or no effect on response likelihood, to those that substantially reduce response likelihood. An event is a positive reinforcer if its occurrence or presentation after a response strengthens the response. Sometimes good grades, words of praise, or salary checks act as pos-

---

Exercise 11

Answers will naturally vary; two attempts at revising these paragraphs follow.

1. In terms of reinforcement, events range from those that increase the likelihood of a correct response to those that reduce it. Positive reinforcers such as good grades, words of praise, or salary checks strengthen a response. In contrast, bad grades, shame, or worthless payments are negative reinforcers, for only their elimination strengthens a response. [The word *reinforcer,* though jargon, seems unavoidable here.]
2. Each student should be required to select some courses from among those that involve practice in speaking or writing. Such a requirement would solve the problem of core requirements, since it would determine which courses will survive and which will not. But this solution is rarely tried. Professors rarely trust students to choose courses wisely;

itive reinforcers. An object or event is a negative reinforcer if its withdrawal or termination after a response strengthens the response. Often bad grades, shame, or worthless payments act as negative reinforcers. The above notion sounds complex and difficult to apply but is indeed extremely simple.

2. All courses (process or outcome) in the University system that are judged to contain written or oral communication goal statements should constitute a set of courses from which a student must select some number. This client-oriented marketplace approach to core requirements is a solution. Enrollment determines which courses will survive and which will not. However, academic tradition is rife with distrust of student judgment; and it can result in a self-fulfilling prophecy where faculty compete in playing to the "house" because they are convinced that ultimately only those who do will survive. This solution is usually condemned without trial.

13h

instead, they turn their courses into popularity contests, believing that there is no other way to survive.

For Further Reading

Altick, Richard D., and Andrea A. Lunsford. "Denotation and Connotation." "Diction." *Preface to Critical Reading.* 6th ed. New York: Holt, 1984. 1–110.

PART IV

Critical Reading and Thinking

14 *Thinking Critically*

Any expository writing that is more than just a summary of dates and events involves critical reading and thinking: interpreting evidence, making generalizations, arriving at conclusions. You may be discussing a book that you find persuasive or unpersuasive; you may be arguing for or against some new policy; you may be explaining your actions or beliefs. In each case, you are trying to convince your readers, and if you credit them with intelligence, you will want to convince them by your reasonableness. This chapter and the two that follow focus on strategies for critical reading and critical thinking that are essential to establishing such a reasonable stance.

14a The importance of knowledge

Let's begin with a principle that underlies all that follows in these chapters. It is this: *unsound reasoning is often the result of lack of knowledge rather than intentional deception or incurable bigotry; the person has not known enough, and perhaps has not cared enough, about the subject and has therefore generalized hastily.* Consider a commonplace example—the difference between uninformed drivers and skilled mechanics. A car suddenly stalls and won't start. What do drivers frequently do? They check the gas, find the tank half full, open the hood, and poke around. With luck, they happen upon the fan belt and find it intact. Now stuck, they conclude the battery must be dead because that's what happened last time. While looking for a phone and hoping that someone will stop, they again vow to take a course in auto maintenance offered at the community college and to read through the manufacturer's manual, lying unopened these past months.

Chapters **14** and **15** offer an introduction to basic principles of critical thinking and sound reasoning. Again, the inescapable format of the textbook, which conveniently collects these topics in a few separate chapters, is at odds with the reality of the writing process, which demands the writer's critical awareness from the earliest consideration of ideas to the final polishing of an essay. Part of the challenge of teaching this material, therefore, involves blending it with the rest of the term's work. Instructors should probably avoid creating a discrete logic-and-reasoning "segment" in their courses, but should instead seek ways of focusing students' attention throughout the term on the ideas introduced here.

This discussion of the reasoning that leads to sound conclusions deliberately avoids the machinery of the formal syllogism. Though it often makes for interesting classroom exercises, the syllogism is not a very useful tool for students who are new to the principles of argument. Indeed, even students who master the conventions of the syllogism often have difficulty applying it to their own reasoning processes or using it to analyze the

> ## QUICK REFERENCE: *Key Terms for Critical Thinking*
>
> A *fact* is any statement that can be proved true.
>
> **Example**   The Mississippi River forms the western border of Illinois.
>
> A *judgment* is a conclusion expressing some form of approval or disapproval.
>
> **Example**   The Mississippi River enhanced the economic development of western Illinois.
>
> An *argument* consists of two interrelated statements: a *premise* (a set of facts or a generalization presumably based on facts) that leads to an *inference,* or conclusion.
>
> **Example**   The Mississippi River floods periodically [premise]. Therefore, river towns should construct and maintain effective levees [inference].
>
> An *assumption* is a presupposed connection between a premise and an inference.
>
> **Example**   The Mississippi River floods periodically. [Assumption: Preserving river towns is worth the expense of trying to control the Mississippi River.] Therefore, river towns should construct and maintain effective levees.

14a

With skilled mechanics, it is quite otherwise. Taking their time, they proceed systematically, checking various possibilities until they find the source of trouble. Drawing on their knowledge, they reason from known effect to probable cause until they solve the problem. Because they are informed, they do not generalize rashly; because they care, they are not hasty.

The point of this rather ordinary example is, first of all, our need to recognize what we don't know and to do whatever is necessary to become knowledgeable. When our information is scanty, we cannot see complexity, nuance, or difference. We do not know how to proceed, and we risk the impulsive conclusion. (Skilled mechanics can be as

arguments of others. More valuable is a firm grasp of such concepts as premise and inference, fact and judgment.

foolish as anyone else on subjects they are ignorant about.) But most college subjects do demand that we recognize complexity, nuance, difference—as, indeed, do many of the things we study outside the academy. This chapter will present some guidelines for evaluating and shaping complex data into complex arguments and for judging among authorities in particular fields. But the starting point for any solid argument remains the same: *take the time necessary to do research and to be informed about your subject.*

14b The structure of an argument

The preliminaries of an argument are usually definitions. Having defined *capital punishment* as "execution, the death penalty for a crime," you can then argue for or against it. One argument, or reason, you might give for capital punishment is that it deters murder. An argument against it might be that it does not deter murder. Note that the words *argument* and *reason* are interchangeable and that they imply an identical process of thinking.

14b

In most discussions of logical analysis, the word *argument* signifies any two statements connected in such a way that one is based on the other. The argument has two parts: a premise (or evidence) and an inference (or immediate conclusion).

premise (evidence)	**inference (immediate conclusion)**
Capital punishment deters murder.	Therefore, it should be permitted.
Because capital punishment does not deter murder,	it should be abolished.

We use arguments constantly in writing and in speaking, and we recognize them by the actual or implied presence of connectives such as *because, so,* and *since,* and by auxiliaries such as *ought, should,* and *must.* The structure of an argument, then, is an observed fact or set of facts, or else a generalization presumably based on facts (the premise), leading to a conclusion (the inference). And usually we intend, though we may not always state explicitly, a final conclusion or point.

final conclusion ←——— **inference** ←——— **premise**

She wasn't angry. She didn't mean it, *since* she was joking about it later.

Usually, a final conclusion has several arguments, not simply one, to support it. The inference of one argument may be the premise for the next, and so on in a chainlike pattern to the final conclusion.

premise 1   **premise 2**

National prestige is fostered by   Successful countries
success in the Olympic games.   use professional athletes.
[inference from premises 1 and 2 becomes premise 3]

Since we wish to be successful in maintaining our prestige,
[inference from premise 3 becomes premise 4]

we cannot afford to field amateurs.

final conclusion

Consequently, we should begin a program of national recruiting and full-time support for our Olympic athletes.

Several distinct strands of argument may be knotted into the one final conclusion, itself often the beginning of a conversation or a paper.

14b

final conclusion

There is no good reason for our starting a program of national recruiting and full-time support for our Olympic athletes.

first argument introduced   **premise 1**

To begin with, the modern games were not founded to foster nationalism. Professionalism is contrary to the intent of the games [inference from premise 1].

second argument introduced   **premise 2**

In the second place, nationalistic rivalries have made the protection of the athletes difficult and costly. This politicizing has made the games a great burden for the host country [inference from premise 2].

third argument introduced   **premise 3**

Moreover, if one looks at the remarkable record of success that amateurs have had . . .

Just as a paragraph can develop several arguments to support one conclusion, so several paragraphs can each develop one or more arguments to support a thesis, itself a final conclusion.

If you are required to identify the premises and inferences of an argument—your own or someone else's—try constructing an outline (see **5d**). Outlining assists critical reading by isolating the major issues and evidence, and it assists critical writing by systematically pinpointing areas of disagreement.

14c Key assumptions

So far, we have considered an argument's structure, not its truthfulness. An argument's structure may be quite consistent, yet its premises and conclusions may be unsound. One of the commonest causes of unsound arguments is the writer's failure to examine the key assumptions.

A key assumption is a connection between the premise and the inference that is taken for granted *before* the argument is advanced. Consider the following example.

14c

premise 1   **premise 2**

Beth has an A– average ·   Sharon has a B– average
[inference from premises 1 and 2 becomes premise 3]

Since Beth is obviously a better student
[inference from premise 3 becomes premise 4]

she should do better work in a creative writing course.

final conclusion

Consequently, she certainly should be given preference over Sharon.

Clearly, unless you took for granted that grades and creativity are related, you couldn't very well argue that Beth's superior average was proof that she would do better work in the writing course than Sharon. Nor could you conclude that Beth ought to be given priority unless you had presupposed this relationship.

Like the premises in deductive logic, the key assumptions underlying an argument must be sound before they are built upon. If the assumptions are false or only partly true, the whole argument collapses. Writers who blithely rely on unexamined assumptions risk overlooking evidence that might undermine their conclusions. For example, if you were to assume that academic success and creativity are related (the key assumption), you would have to overlook those students with mediocre or even poor averages who are gifted painters, dancers, or poets, and you would have to ignore those intelligent honor students who seem to lack imagination, or at least seldom do more than safe, competent work.

Key assumptions occur all the time, in all kinds of arguments and contexts—letters to the editor, talk-show controversies, reviews of films and books, political campaigns. Consider the following arguments, for example. Each (in one variation or another) is popular; each rests on one or more key assumptions. We need to ask two questions about each of these arguments: (1) What are the key assumptions? (2) Do these assumptions require explaining or defending? The first argument:

14c

Argument   A great many of the movies that Hollywood makes give an unfair picture of American life because they show mainly its violence and its obsession with sex.

Assumptions   1. That movies should give a "fair" picture of whatever they are picturing.
2. That there is such a thing as a "fair picture."
3. That violence and obsession with sex are not "typical" of American life.

Question   Are these self-evident assumptions?

The second argument:

Argument   Advanced-placement courses for gifted students are a valuable addition to the high-school curriculum because such courses offer these students a chance to fulfill college requirements and to begin specializing earlier.

Assumptions   1. That college students should choose their major and specialize as soon as possible.
2. That the purpose of advanced-placement high-school courses is to satisfy college requirements, not to offer mastery of a subject for its own sake.
3. That gifted students are particularly deserving of special attention.

Question   Are these self-evident assumptions?

There are at least a couple of things you can do to help protect yourself against unsound assumptions and arguments built on them.

Exercise 1 (page 303)

Below are some of the key assumptions behind the statements in this exercise. Once students have identified these assumptions, they should consider which are valid, which need to be defended, and which are untenable.

1. (a) The only reason for a politician to run for office is to win. (b) People don't change their minds on issues during the course of a political campaign.
2. (a) Civil rights laws depend on morality. (b) Laws never change human behavior.
3. (a) Arguments over personal likes and dislikes are pointless. (b) All opinions about artistic merit or performance are equally valid because they are equally personal. (c) Artistic merit and performance cannot be evaluated according to objective criteria.
4. (a) The average person cannot know what is best for himself or herself without sophisticated information. (b) Guidelines for genetic research

First, *make it a habit* to ask what other people are taking for granted in their arguments. If their key assumptions need challenging, challenge them. Second, *make it a habit* to ask yourself what you have taken for granted in your argument. If these assumptions need explaining, explain them; if they need defending, defend them. The exercises that follow are designed to give you this kind of practice.

EXERCISE 1

Consider each of the following arguments. Each (in one form or another) is widespread; each is based on one or more key assumptions. Analyze the argument to identify its key assumptions and to determine which of these, if any, would need to be explained or defended. If you find the assumptions shaky or untenable, specify your reasons for challenging them.

1. Politicians who take an unpopular stand during an election are foolish because they simply increase their chances of losing.
2. Civil rights laws are useless because morality can't be legislated.
3. Arguments about artistic merit or performance are pointless because all such judgments are based merely on personal likes and dislikes.
4. Guidelines for genetic research should be left to the experts because the average person doesn't have enough information to know what's best.
5. It's a mistake to argue with teachers because they'll only mark you down; just give them what they want and take a good grade.

14c

EXERCISE 2

Choose one of the topics below (or one of the arguments in Exercise 1) and write one paragraph of two hundred words or so, as rapidly as you can, taking a firm stand on the issue. Then analyze your paragraph with the following questions in mind: (1) What are the key assumptions? (2) Do they need defending? (3) What kinds of arguments or evidence would support them? Then *rewrite* the paragraph in the light of your analysis and compare it with your original. Have you made significant changes in your case?

1. Colleges should (should not) have required courses for all first-year students.
2. The major television networks should (should not) be left to themselves in matters of programming and censorship.
3. Public universities should (should not) impose fixed quotas on the number of out-of-state students they will admit.

should be based primarily on sophisticated information. (c) The experts are more likely to be right.
5. (a) Teachers base grades on whether students agree with them. (b) The point of an education is to get good grades.

Exercise 2

The purpose of writing out a brief argument rapidly is to give students the chance to discover the kinds of assumptions they make almost without thinking. Several students might be asked to put their paragraphs on the board for analysis by the class, or students might discuss one another's paragraphs in small groups. Revised versions of the paragraphs should eliminate untenable assumptions and offer support for other assumptions that require it.

4. Ticket scalping at popular events should (should not) be prohibited.
5. Drunk drivers should (should not) automatically be deprived of their licenses for a fixed period of time on their first arrest.

Analyze the argument in a paper that you or your instructor found unsatisfactory, focusing on the following questions: (1) What key assumptions underlie your argument? (2) Do these assumptions require explaining or defending? (3) If so, how would you explain or defend them?

Ask the questions in Exercise 3 about an argument that you've identified in a published letter to the editor of your local newspaper.

14d The differences between fact and judgment

14d

As the preceding exercises may have suggested, what can be proved and what one approves of do not always coincide. The differences between fact and judgment, though not always easy to determine in a given case, are important.

1. Facts

A *fact* may be defined as any statement, any declarative sentence, that can be proved true. The definition says nothing about who does the proving or what method of proof is used. It merely stipulates the possibility of verifying the statement. It rules out commands, questions, and exclamations as provable assertions—no one will try to prove or disprove utterances such as these: "Shut the door!" "How old is she?" "Wow!"

Most people would agree that statements like "Water is wet" or "A yard contains three feet" are facts. But note the difference between the statement "Water is wet" and the assertion "The paint on the door is wet." The first sentence is perhaps a way of describing to a very young child the feeling of liquid on his or her fingers. In contrast with such a truth-by-definition, the second statement permits—and requires—

Exercises 3 and 4

Answers will vary.

verification. *Is* the paint actually wet? Similarly, to say "A yard contains three feet" is to state a truth-by-definition, whereas to say "The track was only ninety-nine yards long" is to present a possible fact that remains to be verified.

Sometimes we ourselves are able to verify a possible fact. We could, for instance, touch the paint on the door or—assuming we had an accurate tape measure at hand—measure the track. More often, though, we must rely on other people to collect and report data accurately. If you believe that "New York has more people than Chicago" and "Shakespeare was born in 1564" are factual statements, you are not simply accepting the authority of an almanac and an encyclopedia. You are trusting the accuracy and conscientiousness of every census taker hired in these cities by the Bureau of the Census and the reliability of scholars who have inspected the parish records of baptism in Stratford-on-Avon.

Admittedly, life is too short for anyone to verify personally more than a fraction of the facts he or she encounters, and many things have to be taken on authority. Still, you ought to cultivate the habit of skeptical analysis in reading and writing. It can help you detect those assertions that masquerade as facts but that remain ultimately unverifiable. How, for instance, can one prove (or disprove) such statements as "You can't change human nature" or "Materialism is the greatest threat to our way of life"?

14d

2. Judgments

A *judgment* is a conclusion expressing some form of approval or disapproval. The term should not be dismissed because it is taken to connote "mere opinion." There are, after all, reasonable grounds and confirming facts for "good judgment" as well as the arbitrary assumptions and disregarded facts in "poor judgment." Sometimes the judgment is a fairly simple, safe inference from the facts, as in the judgment "Helen Wills Moody was one of the finest tennis players in the game's history," which is based on her having won the Women's National Singles seven times, the Women's National Doubles three times, and the Women's Singles at Wimbledon eight times. The phrase *one of the finest* is a judgment of her record. Sometimes, a judgment is a complicated inference from many facts, none of which is immediately clear. Consider three propositions, in which the judgments are italicized.

1. In 1940, there were 131,669,275 Americans, averaging 44.2 people per square mile; by 1990, *the population was larger and denser,* 248,709,873 people, averaging 70 per square mile.
   [This first statement contains the terms *larger* and *denser,* which indicate an inference. But the overall statement is essentially factual since the inference results from a simple computation.]

2. Between 1940 and 1990, as the country *became more urbanized and heavily populated,* the American farm *became more efficient through increased mechanization and specialization.*
   [This second statement, a judgment, presupposes the first statement in the judgment *more urbanized and heavily populated.* But it assumes much more. To prove *more efficient through increased mechanization,* the writer would need figures showing the increased use of electricity and various kinds of power machinery. To prove *specialization,* the writer would need data showing the increased percentage of farms that raise only crops of livestock, or produce only dairy goods. The evidence exists, of course, to defend the judgment that the American farm has become more efficient.]

3. *Profit-seeking specialization and mechanization are destroying the small, self-sufficient family farm in America and the deep attachment to the land and tradition that are so much a part of the family farm.*
   [In this third statement, the judgment is far more conspicuous than in the first two, and the facts are less immediately evident. To prove, for example, the existence of *the small, self-sufficient family farm* with its *deep attachment to the land and tradition,* the writer would require detailed information. This information would have to include data about income, expenses, size of family, acreage worked, period of ownership without tenancy, length of political and religious affiliations, and a study of attitudes toward marriage, education, and the like. Such information might take the form of statistics or the extensive observations of qualified observers, or both. It would have to include the New York family raising some sheep and a few cows, some acres of wheat and garden tomatoes; the North Carolina family raising a hillside of tobacco and corn, supplemented by hogs and hunting; the Illinois family running a small dairy and orchard; the Colorado family

raising grain and beef near the foothills of the Rockies; and the California family raising grapefruit and oranges near the desert's edge. Then the information about all of these families would have to be analyzed to see whether there is such a type as *the small, self-sufficient family farm* with distinct values or whether there are sharply different regional variations.]

You can no more help making judgments about human actions and goals than the writer of the third statement could help feeling strongly about the changes taking place on the American farm. In fact, the writer might say that information about income and attitudes toward marriage had little to do with her judgment, that she was talking about qualities that could only be experienced personally. The grounds for this judgment might be her own life on a small Iowa farm or New Mexico ranch; novels like Willa Cather's *O Pioneers!*, Steinbeck's *The Red Pony*, or Harriette Arnow's *The Dollmaker*; short stories like those in Hamlin Garland's *Main-Travelled Roads*; movies like *Country*; or the memories of a rural doctor. But do these sources slight other qualities? Do the films, fiction, and memoirs show only loyalty, belief, the close-knit family, and hard work? What of the fatigue and boredom, the bigotry and blighted vision, the drudgery and failure they reveal? Fiction, films, and memoirs present possibilities, not facts: they can make us see, feel, and share the intensity and variety of human life in a particular time and place, but they cannot offer statistical certainty.

14d

3. Using facts and judgments

When you make judgments, then, express your facts clearly and accurately and show clearly the way in which the facts warrant your judgment; when you don't know the facts or have reason to suspect their authority, suspend judgment. And don't be reluctant to ask others to do the same. Try to distinguish between those judgments that involve personal preference and are not provable and those that may be supported by evidence and arguments. For your college writing, this advice implies your willingness to do research; to distinguish among facts, statements that may be factual, and judgments; and to tolerate uncertainty. The last is especially hard to do: often the experts in specialized fields are so much at odds that you either are tempted to give the matter up entirely or else arbitrarily decide "one side *must* be right, the other wrong, so I will choose."

If, for example, you were to look up the statistics on capital punishment, you would find no clear-cut agreement among the criminologists, psychologists, and various law-enforcement officials about what the figures prove—and no agreement among the statisticians, either. But the issue is too important to be ignored simply because you cannot prove conclusively that capital punishment is or is not a deterrent to crime. There are other factual grounds that may help you form a judgment: How many innocent men or women have been executed, or how many saved at the last minute? Do minorities, the poor, and the uneducated receive the death sentence more frequently than others convicted of murder?

4. Evaluating authorities

14d

As has been pointed out, we cannot personally verify more than a fraction of the facts we learn, and so we have to take many things on authority. Still, when experts disagree about their facts and their judgments, there are a few helpful guides.

The first guide is to be sure that a supposed expert is an authority on the subject at hand. A well-known musician may take a strong public stand on national trade policy, and a big-city mayor may be outspoken about the value of space research being conducted by NASA. But should either be considered a reliable authority on these subjects? As you formulate your position on an issue, turn to writers and scholars who have made the study of your subject their life's work.

A second guide is to consider the experts' probable motives in relation to their testimony. An executive for a major car manufacturer who testifies that "all reasonable steps have been taken to make safe, energy-efficient cars" may well not be as reliable an authority as a writer for an independent trade magazine or engineering firm.

A third guide is to see what others in the field say about the strengths or weaknesses in an expert's research. Suppose that you are doing a project on drug use among high-school students. If book reviews generally praise a research team for their studies of suburban students but criticize their failure to study inner-city students as thoroughly, you would want to confine yourself to the researchers' discus-

Exercise 5 (page 309)

1. "Last longer" and "burn cooler" are possible facts, verifiable by laboratory tests. "Cleaner" and "cheaper" may also be verifiable facts, but these terms need more precise definition: cleaner and cheaper in what sense? The same may be said about the phrase *easier on you.* Does that phrase mean less irritating to the throat, less likely to cause cancer, or what?

2. That Caesar was a Roman general and that he was killed in 44 B.C. are facts; that he was "Rome's greatest general and ruler" is a judgment requiring comparison with other generals and emperors according to specific criteria. That Caesar's assassins were "personal enemies" is a judgment that could be documented by contemporary accounts.

3. Fact (truth-by-definition).

4. Fact (truth-by-definition).

5. Judgment easily supported by reference to basketball records.

sion of suburban students only, and look elsewhere for evidence about inner-city students.

EXERCISE 5

Determine which parts of each of the following statements are facts and which parts are judgments. For each judgment, decide what kind(s) of facts or evidence, if any, could be cited to support the judgment.

1. Smoke Cigarmellos! They last longer, burn cooler, and are easier on you than cigarettes. They are cleaner and cheaper than pipes.
2. Julius Caesar, Rome's greatest general and ruler, was assassinated in 44 B.C. by Cassius, Brutus, and other personal enemies.
3. A meter equals 39.37 inches.
4. A kilometer contains 1,000 meters.
5. Michael Jordan was the finest player in the history of professional basketball.
6. If one compares the number of talented women now entering law schools with the number twenty years ago, one sees how wasteful of abilities those sexist admissions policies were.
7. The concern over computer literacy is just another educational fad, largely promoted by manufacturers rather than by genuine demand.
8. Real mastery of a foreign language means the ability to think in the language, not simply to translate headlines and signs, word by word.
9. There is no clear evidence one way or another about the effectiveness of strict gun laws in preventing crime.
10. Five daily servings of fruits and vegetables are important to good health.

14d

EXERCISE 6

Pick a controversial issue you feel strongly about and summarize your views in two or three sentences. Then analyze your sentences with the following questions in mind: What evidence can you cite to support your judgments? Do you make judgments that are difficult to support?

EXERCISE 7

Choose two of your papers—preferably a good one and a weaker one— and analyze each to determine how well the judgments are supported by evidence. Is the weaker paper characterized by unsupported judgments or unsupportable judgments? Try revising a paragraph or two to make the judgments more convincing.

6. The comparative numbers of women entering law school now and twenty years ago are facts, easily documented by admissions statistics. "Wasteful of abilities" and "sexist admissions policies" are judgments. The first could be supported by studies of talented women who were rejected by law schools twenty years ago or who wanted to apply to law school but, anticipating rejection, did not. The second could perhaps be documented by a careful study of the qualifications of male and female applicants over the last twenty years and of students actually admitted during that period.
7. A hasty judgment that ignores the heavy enrollment in computer science courses and the growing demand for and high salaries paid to employees with computer skills.
8. Judgment. Linguists, bilingual speakers, and foreign language educators might be called on to offer supporting testimony.
9. A possible fact requiring the comparative study of crime rates in states with different gun control laws. Given the many different ways of analyzing crime data and the other factors besides gun control that may

EXERCISE 8

Choose a paper to be revised (either a rough draft for a paper due or an essay that has been returned for rewriting) and go over it carefully, marking every judgment. If you find judgments that are unsupported, try revising them to make them more convincing.

EXERCISE 9

Choose a piece from your newspaper's editorial page—a signed opinion column, a letter, an editorial—and underline its judgments. Are they supported? If not, draft an answer in which you show how or why they are unreasonable or unconvincing.

14e Believability and tone

14e

The aim of most writers is believability. Novelists usually strive to make their stories realistic. Dramatists usually contrive to make their plots and characters credible. Even authors who play with the fantastic and the imaginary want to gain the reader's consent. A satirist like Jonathan Swift in *Gulliver's Travels,* a fabulist like J. R. R. Tolkien in *Lord of the Rings,* or a science fiction writer like Ursula K. Le Guin in *The Left Hand of Darkness* tries to make a fictional world that is internally consistent and that obliquely refers to our world. In applying the term *believability* specifically to argumentation, we mean the reader's belief that the writer's reasoning can be trusted.

Several factors contribute to your reader's trust in your case, including the orderliness of your argument, the plausibility of your assumptions, the persuasiveness of your evidence, and the accuracy of your logic. But these factors may not be enough to earn the reader's confidence. Even if the assumptions are defended, the conclusions supported by detail, and the arguments free of obvious errors, the tone may offend. Quite rightly, readers become skeptical when they feel the writer is trying to crowd them or compel their assent by vehement or dogmatic insistence. Consider the following passage.

Excessive vehemence distances reader

Lurking behind the walls of trailers and apartments, concealed by the privacy of homes, suppressed by the terror of its helpless victims, domestic

influence crime statistics, firm conclusions may indeed be difficult to arrive at.

10. Judgment that could perhaps be supported by data collected through medical research. For example, has the incidence of colon cancer been shown to be lower among people who eat five servings of fruits and vegetables each day? If so, such evidence would support the judgment expressed in this statement—"important to good health."

Exercises 6–9

Answers will vary. All of these exercises can be adapted for small-group work.

violence is destroying the integrity of the American family! It shatters children and marriages; it releases the most hideous emotions and feelings humans are capable of. It is the most sordid display of depravity one can imagine. No social evil is more vicious! Domestic violence threatens the very foundations of our society.

What offends here is not the writer's choice of subject (the destructiveness and prevalence of domestic violence can be documented) but his choice of tactics. He assaults his topic and reader with exclamation marks, unqualified statements, and highly charged words like *hideous, sordid,* and *vicious.* He leaves no room for honest differences of opinion and judgment; for example, readers who might feel that drug addiction or alcoholism poses as great a social problem as domestic violence does. However reasonable the rest of his case, he has risked losing the reader's trust by a lack of moderation. Now consider the same passage rewritten to earn credibility.

14e

More moderate tone engages reader

> One of the serious social problems in America is domestic violence. Because its victims, usually women and young children, are often frightened and silent, the magnitude of this problem is not always recognized. The privacy of the home—whether trailer, apartment, or house—too frequently conceals its consequences. But the bruised child, the battered wife or lover, and the angry, confused male all find themselves trapped, the law and social agencies unable to intervene until violence has already occurred, and not always easily even then.

The revision solicits concern, not unquestioning acceptance or submission.

A believable tone is a moderate one. It allows for other viewpoints and alternatives without compromising the writer's basic conviction.

Credible writer considers other positions

> For many Americans, domestic violence may seem a deplorable but less acute social disorder than alcoholism. The effects of domestic violence are not, perhaps, as visibly publicized and dramatic as certain effects of alcoholism—the televised image of the totaled car and the paramedics arriving, and the escalating rates of injury and death. But its long-term results are, far too often, the battered child who becomes the battering adult.

Although it receives less attention and less research funding than alcoholism, its consequences are not less tragic.

A moderate tone also recognizes connections where connections exist and concedes what is unknown.

Credible writer makes concessions

In reality, domestic violence and alcoholism are not wholly separate social disorders. Each frequently contributes to the other, and neither is fully understood in its causes.

In short, a moderate tone trusts its evidence and the reader's intelligence. The argument is believable because the writer invites—not compels—belief.

EXERCISE 10

Choose one of the following topics and write a paragraph in which you make the tone as dogmatic and as vehement as you can. Then rewrite the paragraph to make the tone moderate and believable.

1. A case for or against athletic scholarships.
2. A case for or against a minimum legal drinking age.
3. A case for or against prayer in public schools.
4. A case for or against police roadblocks to catch drunken drivers.
5. A case for or against the use of animals in medical research.

Exercise 10

In discussions of dogmatic and moderate tones, students might be encouraged to consider once again the issues about voice raised in Chapter **4**. How do diction and choice of detail contribute to a dogmatic stance or to a more moderate one? How does closeness to or distance from the audience?

For Further Reading

Altick, Richard D., and Andrea A. Lunsford. "Patterns of Clear Thinking." *Preface to Critical Reading*. 6th ed. New York: Holt, 1984. 268–326.

Hahn, Stephen. "Counter-Statement: Using Written Dialogue to Develop Critical Thinking and Writing." *College Composition and Communication* 38 (1987): 97–100.

Kaufer, David S., and Christine M. Neuwirth. "Integrating Formal Logic and the New Rhetoric: A Four-Stage Heuristic." *College English* 45 (1983): 380–89.

15 *Avoiding Errors in Reasoning*

The failure to examine key assumptions and the confusion of fact with judgments—discussed in the previous chapter—are not the only causes of faulty reasoning. Other reasoning errors, commonly known as *logical fallacies,* also lead to conclusions that will not stand up to scrutiny. Those faulty patterns of thinking, and the best ways of avoiding them, are the focus of this chapter.

15a Legitimate versus hasty generalizations

To generalize is to draw conclusions about a whole class or group after examining only selected members of that group. Generalizing is a type of reasoning known as *induction*—that is, reasoning that begins with a number of specific examples and uses them as the basis of broad conclusions. Young children use induction—albeit imperfectly—when, after grabbing at two or three cats, they conclude that all cats scratch. Later, when they understand what grabbing is and when they have seen more cats, they can legitimately generalize that most cats will not scratch unless they are grabbed. Pollsters use induction when they question a representative sample of voters to determine how all voters feel or will probably vote. A consumers' research organization uses induction when it purchases samples of all the different brands of washing machines, tests them carefully, and then generalizes about which brands are likely to be most efficient.

313

No presentation of critical thinking would be complete without a discussion of errors in reasoning. This chapter offers students a working knowledge of the traditional fallacies in reasoning, which they will no doubt encounter later in college and throughout life. But by deliberately preceding the discussion of these fallacies with a separate chapter on principles of argumentation, the text seeks to discourage students from regarding critical thinking as *primarily* a hunt for mistakes in reasoning. Though the ability to recognize fallacious reasoning is crucial, students should regard critical thinking as a habit of mind, not merely a keen eye for error.

15a

QUICK REFERENCE: *Errors in Reasoning*

A *hasty generalization* is a conclusion based on atypical, inadequate, irrelevant, or inaccurate evidence.

Example   Of course our student body is physically fit: just look at the success of our sports teams this year.

The *post hoc, ergo propter hoc fallacy* assumes that because B follows A, A must be the cause of B.

Example   Tourism in this city started declining right after Mayor Scott was elected. To save our tourist industry, let's replace her now!

The *reductive fallacy* occurs when simple or single causes are assumed to be responsible for complex effects.

Example   I eat turnips daily for good health. My Aunt Alice loved turnips, and she lived to be ninety-four.

A *false analogy* overlooks the fact that the differences between two things being compared are greater than their similarities.

Example   Why am I required to take certain courses before I can graduate from this university? No one requires me to buy certain groceries before I can leave the supermarket.

Begging the question occurs when a writer assumes as true the point that he or she is arguing.

Example   Improving public transportation in this city won't solve freeway congestion. Even if public transportation is clean, safe, and efficient, people will still prefer to use their cars.

An *ad hominem argument* attacks the opponent rather than his or her argument.

Example   How can anyone accept Professor Burton's plan for restructuring the curriculum? The man hasn't owned a new necktie since 1975!

A *dummy subject* is an irrelevant point that is substituted for the real issue.

Example   You want me to support increased funding for the city's museums? I guess you don't care whether or not we let the city's homeless freeze this winter!

The false *either/or argument* assumes that there are only two alternatives in a given situation.

Example   The case is clear: either we support the death penalty or we allow crime to run rampant.

A *non sequitur* occurs when there is no connection between the writer's premise and conclusion.

Example   Carolyn loved college, so I'm sure she will make an excellent teacher.

15a

1. Criteria for valid generalizations

Like most other valid arguments, legitimate generalizations rest on sound evidence. To generalize accurately, you need to consider how well your evidence will support the conclusions you wish to draw from it.

Typical evidence

Since generalizations are statements made about classes or groups, the first criterion of generalizations is that the evidence be typical of the class or group. An argument using students on the debate team as the basis for generalizing about the speaking abilities of all members of the student body would not be very convincing because the evidence being cited (a small number of articulate debaters) does not fairly represent the larger group (the whole student body).

Or suppose that you and a friend have been assigned academic advisers from the history department, and you both have found your advisers to be bright, articulate, friendly people. You might be tempted to conclude that the history department as a whole must be made up of engaging teachers. But how typical of the rest of the history faculty are your two advisers? Perhaps, indeed, they were selected for their positions because they are brighter, wittier, and more interested in students than most of their colleagues. The point is this: beware of generalizing about a group unless you can demonstrate in a reasonable way that your sample is in fact representative of the larger group.

Adequate evidence

The second criterion of generalizations is that the evidence be adequate. That is, how large is the sample you have examined in comparison with the group as a whole? Americans spending a few days in London or Europeans touring California for two weeks may acquire some accurate impressions, but such short visits will provide evidence far too superficial to support a generalization like "The English are reserved" or "Americans are friendly but ignorant."

Similarly, if your two appealing history department advisers are members of a department that consists of only three or four faculty, then you may feel much more comfortable about using them as the basis of a generalization than you could if the department were a sprawling collection of fifty or more historians. Like typicality, adequacy is sometimes difficult to judge. As a general guide, though, remember that the smaller your sample is, the more tentative you must be about the validity of your conclusions.

Relevant evidence

The third criterion of generalizations is that the evidence be relevant. When researchers at a consumers' organization test washing machines, their results will enable them to generalize only about how well different brands will wash, not about other factors such as the likelihood of costly repairs during the life of each machine. To arrive at generalizations on that subject, they would have to turn to a different body of evidence, such as reports from current owners of each brand of machine.

And what, we might ask, does the engaging manner of those history department advisers actually tell you about their teaching ability? After all, their effectiveness in a one-on-one advising situation may not translate into teaching success in a large classroom filled with students of varying levels of interest and ability. In this case, as in all generalizations, you need to be certain that your evidence is clearly germane to the point you wish to make.

Accurate evidence

The fourth criterion of generalizations is that the evidence be accurate. This standard seems self-evident, yet if you were to read through the long, careful book reviews in scholarly publications such as *Scientific American,* the *American Historical Review,* or the *Journal of American Folklore,* you would find two common criticisms: that the writer has been careless about checking facts and indiscriminate about selecting sources. In cases of extreme carelessness, the reviewer legitimately questions the author's right to be trusted, regardless of how original his or her ideas are. The most helpful guides you have are the ones for identifying expert testimony: Does the information come from a recognized source? What are the person's motives in relation to the evidence? What agreement is there among others in the field about strengths or weaknesses in the researcher's work?

2. Hasty generalizations

A generalization based on atypical, inadequate, irrelevant, or inaccurate evidence is called a *hasty generalization.* A few types of hasty generalizations are so common that they deserve special mention here.

Stereotype

A *stereotype* is a sweeping, unfounded generalization about a group of people, a profession, or a social role. The writer who suggests that all politicians are crooked, all mothers-in-law are bossy, all athletes are dumb, all accountants are dull, or all city dwellers are unfriendly is indulging in stereotyping, and any arguments founded on such false generalizations will be worthless. Stereotypes are crude caricatures that deny the variety and diversity of individuals.

Oversimplification

Oversimplification is another form of hasty generalizing. Usually, it entails making a question seem easier than it is. One source of oversimplification is the uncritical use of statistics. For example, if students in two sixth-grade classes have markedly different averages on a reading comprehension test, you could not generalize that everyone in the first class outperformed everyone in the second class. Since a few very high scores might have pulled up some mediocre ones in the averaging, you would have to compare all the individual scores to reach such a conclusion. Still less would you be entitled to simplify the results by generalizing that those in the first class were better students than those in the second. What would the vague phrase *better students* mean in this context? And how would the results of this single test support such an assertion?

Unqualified generalization

The *unqualified generalization* is a third form of hasty generalization, a claim whose exaggerated inclusiveness belies the scanty evidence that supports it. Unqualified generalizations are easy to recognize; they typically contain such blanket terms as *all, every, none,* and *no one:* "All new students think Orientation Week is a waste of time" or "Not a single woman student at this college trusts the dean." To the questions "How do you know? Have you talked with every new student or every woman?" the writer usually answers: "Of course not, but I know several people who feel . . ." A responsible writer more accurately identifies the evidence for his or her assertions: "All the new students *I have spoken with* feel that . . ." or "None of the women *on my floor* believe . . ."

15a

EXERCISE 1

Analyze each of the following generalizations by the four criteria for valid generalizations discussed in **15a**. Be prepared to explain which generalizations are defective and in what ways.

1. From a faculty committee meeting: "Students are making a farce out of the government's low-interest loan program for college financing. The percentage of students who deliberately default is steadily rising, and there's no reason to think it will drop or that students will begin to feel responsible for paying the money they owe. The whole program is just a waste of the taxpayers' money."
2. From a "Letters to the Editor" column: "How can your editorial

Exercise 1

1. Is the evidence adequate? (What *is* the percentage of students in default?) Is the evidence relevant? (Do default statistics prove that "there's no reason to think [the percentage] will drop or that students will begin to feel responsible for paying the money they owe"?)
2. Is the evidence typical? (Are there other Americans besides expressway commuters who might in fact be conserving gasoline?)
3. Is the evidence adequate? (Can we depend on the random sampling of food at other institutions by these two groups of students alone?) Is the evidence accurate? (Are the reports of these students reliable?)
4. The generalization here may be stated as follows: "Evidence other than modern medical data about the height of giants is unreliable." Is the evidence cited to prove this point typical? (Are all such early reports of giants similarly skewed?) Of the five statements in this exercise, this one seems the most legitimate.
5. Is the evidence adequate? (Does one egotistical cousin constitute sufficient evidence for a sweeping stereotype about an entire profession?)

writer deny that Americans are the most wasteful, extravagant consumers of gas in the world? Drive along any expressway or freeway at rush hours and count all the cars with only one passenger and look at the miles of bumper-to-bumper traffic."

3. From a college newspaper: "This school has the worst meals of any college in the state. Any athlete or debater can tell you the meals you get at other colleges make the ones we get look awful."

4. From the *Guinness Book of World Records:* "The only admissible evidence upon the true height of giants is that of recent date made under impartial medical supervision. Biblical claims, such as that for Og, King of Bashan, at 9 Assyrian cubits (16 feet 2½ inches) are probably due to a confusion of units. Extreme mediaeval data from bone measurements refer invariably to mastodons or other nonhuman remains. Claims of exhibitionists, normally under contract not to be measured, are usually distorted for the financial considerations of promoters. There is an example of a recent 'World's Tallest Man' of 9 feet 6 inches being in fact an acromegalic of 7 feet 3½ inches."

5. Overheard in conversation: "To be an actor, you have to be on a real ego trip. That's why people become actors. I know, because my cousin has been acting off-Broadway in New York for the last five years, and he's the most insufferably self-centered person you'd ever want to meet."

15b Mistaken causal relationships

Mistaken causal relationships are errors in reasoning about cause and effect. Perhaps the two most frequent kinds are the post hoc, ergo propter hoc fallacy and the reductive fallacy.

1.   Post hoc, ergo propter hoc

The *post hoc, ergo propter hoc fallacy* is the error of arguing that because B follows A, A is the cause of B. (In Latin, *post hoc, ergo propter hoc* means "after this, therefore because of this.") Sequence is not proof of a causal relationship. The fact that B follows A is not proof that B was caused by A. Primitive beliefs like a full moon causing pregnancy and their modern equivalent in the television commercial linking romance with a change in toothpastes are easy enough to laugh at. But clear thinking on serious social problems can be obscured by this fallacy. For example, those who complain that high-school test scores have dropped during the six months since the new mayor took office may have found a convenient scapegoat for their frustration over the state of public education, but such fallacious reasoning may cause them to over-look the real—and potentially remediable—causes of declining student performance.

2.   Reductive fallacy

The *reductive fallacy* occurs when simple or single causes are given for complex effects, creating a generalization based on insufficient evidence. Such generalizations as "Athens fell because of mob rule" and "Luther caused the Reformation" are reductive. That is, instead of specifying the mob or Luther as only one important condition, these assertions make Luther or the mob the single agent of causation. In 1964, when the U.S. surgeon general announced a high correlation between cigarette smoking and lung cancer, he indicated that one was probably a contributory cause of the other. But since not all heavy smokers die of lung cancer and since there is evidence that industrial fumes and car exhaust are also injurious in this regard, he did not say that smoking is the only cause of lung cancer or that every smoker will develop lung cancer. Insofar as they cannot directly isolate, identify, and control each factor in a sequence, scientists, like historians, usually observe the test of sufficiency: only if A alone is sufficient to produce B can it be called the cause of B.

15b

To let your readers judge the sufficiency of your argument, define its conditions and limitations as clearly as you can. With complex re-lationships, remember that there is a significant difference between saying "It is caused by" and "It has been helped by," just as there is between saying "Luther caused" and "Luther contributed to" or "The reason for the revolution" and "One reason for the revolution." The limited statement can be more exact because it is more tentative: it implies that other conditions, other contributing factors, may be as important as the one singled out for discussion.

EXERCISE 2

Analyze each of the following statements of causal relationship to deter-mine which ones are guilty of the post hoc, ergo propter hoc fallacy or the reductive fallacy.

Exercise 2

Since assigning a false cause to an effect frequently involves ignoring one or more true causes as well, the post hoc, ergo propter hoc fallacy and the reductive fallacy often go hand in hand.

1. Reductive fallacy: the writer overlooks other possible motivations among the voters (for example, concern that municipalities were fail-ing to spend tax revenues wisely).
2. Reductive fallacy: might other factors (for example, inadequate access to libraries or a dysfunctional home life) affect a child's reading ability? Post hoc, ergo propter hoc: is there any proven relationship between watching television and poor reading ability?
3. Reductive fallacy: might the stresses of the 1990s bear at least as much responsibility for the current divorce rate as the chaos of the 1960s? Post hoc, ergo propter hoc: does having grown up in the 1960s have any demonstrable connection to today's divorce rate?

1. More than two-thirds of the people in our state voted for the limitation on local property taxes and deliberately deprived their communities of all kinds of services. The only explanation is sheer selfishness; they were afraid of higher taxes.
2. All the children in the remedial reading class watch at least twenty hours of television a week. With all that passive sitting, no wonder they can't read.
3. It is not surprising that the divorce rate is climbing; all those couples splitting up now grew up during the chaos of the 1960s; they never had a chance at a stable environment.
4. Since 1940, the government has gotten bigger and bigger, and taxes have gone higher and higher. The conclusion is obvious.
5. Ever since the university instituted a foreign language requirement, the number of first-year students enrolling each year has been declining. If we intend to stabilize enrollment at this institution, we need to abolish the foreign language requirement now.

15c Reasoning by analogy

An *analogy* is a comparison between two different things or events that shows the way or ways in which they are similar. For example, to explain how the novelist works, one could draw the analogy between the writer and the potter: both begin with a rough idea or image but discover the particular shape of the plot or vase as they work with their materials, often modifying the outlines several times before they are satisfied.

1. Uses of analogies

Analogies can vividly illustrate and clarify difficult ideas. In the following student paragraph, for example, the writer has used an analogy skillfully to describe the complex techniques of satire.

> The sight of a monkey pushing through the jungle, leaping from tree to tree, seems "natural" and, perhaps, graceful. However, when a monkey is placed in a small cage or zoo, its boundings from side to floor to side to ceiling seem antic and "unnatural." Satirists employ the same techniques of limitation. They confine their subject, as it were, to a small cage, or at least one tree, for purposes of close observation. The setting in which the subject moves is limited and its barriers are precisely drawn. Satirists, in

4. Reductive fallacy: have other factors (for example, simple inflation) caused an increase in taxes?
5. Post hoc, ergo propter hoc: is there any reliable evidence that faltering enrollments are the result of students' wishing to avoid a foreign language requirement?

effect, trap their victim in the most ridiculous positions and do not allow any escape from an intensely mocking portrayal.

Analogies have been fruitful in science because they have suggested new lines of research and testing. Benjamin Franklin saw a similarity between lightning and electric sparks; the similarity between X rays and the rays emitted by uranium salts raised questions about the source and nature of this energy, and eventually led Marie Curie to discover radium; mathematicians such as John von Neumann, instrumental during the early development of computers, saw an analogy between the way the human nervous system works and the way a relay of vacuum tubes could be made to work.

2. False analogy

15c

An analogy can be illustrative or suggestive, but it cannot be conclusive. It may introduce an intriguing hypothesis or possibility, but it cannot offer proof. Consequently, you should suspect any conclusions that are supported only by an analogy, particularly when the differences between the two things being compared are equal to or greater than their similarities. To argue, for example, that the countries of Africa should have federated into a United States of Africa to solve their political and economic problems, one would have to ignore some obvious dissimilarities with the American colonies. The latter, unified by language and a common foe, had in most cases a long tradition of local self-government. African countries, in contrast, are separated from one another by deep linguistic and cultural differences and in several cases are inwardly divided by tribal rivalries. An argument based on this false analogy does not have much hope of success.

False analogies obscure and prevent clear thinking about serious and difficult questions. To detect analogies used as proof, examine the argument to see if any evidence is offered other than a comparison between two different things or events. In your own writing, if you think an analogy is essential to your argument, rethink your entire case: don't allow yourself to frame an argument solely around potentially deceptive similarities.

EXERCISE 3

Analyze each of the following analogies to determine whether it is used properly as an illustration or a hypothesis suggesting further investigation, or improperly as proof.

1. From a pamphlet: "Pornographic literature is arsenic that poisons the system. It's not enough to label it and put it on the shelf. Just as some children can't read the label on the bottle and others want to experiment, some juveniles and adults can't discriminate and others are tempted by the warning. Such books should be locked up in libraries where only scholars with reason for using them can get at them, in the same way druggists only sell arsenic from behind the counter by special permission."

2. From a medical journal: "If you place a number of mice together in fairly close quarters and then systematically introduce an increasing variety of distractions—small noises, objects, movements—you increase the probability of neurotic behavior. Cannot something like this process help explain the growth of neurotic behavior in our ever more crowded, complex society? The possibility is worth considering."

3. From a student editorial: "The administration never gets tired of telling us that the college is part of society as a whole. It harps on student responsibility for 'good taste' in plays and publications, student responsibility to obey state laws about drinking and driving, and student responsibility for property. By the same line of reasoning, then, how can the administration claim it has the final right to approve of campus organizations and their speakers? If the college is part of 'society as a whole,' it ought to recognize our rights as well as our obligations. We aren't asking for the privilege of being subversive; we are asking for the civil rights we have in 'society as a whole'—the rights to hear whom we wish and join the groups we wish."

4. From a student essay: "The college has the same obligation to satisfy the student that a store does to satisfy the customer. Students and their parents pay the bills, and they ought to have a much freer say about what courses they take. No clerk would think of telling a customer she had to buy several things she didn't want before she could buy the item she came for. And no store would keep as clerks some of the men and women the college keeps as professors. They can't even sell their product."

5. From a letter to the editor: "Think of street gangs as a kind of urban cancer. Moving through the arteries of the city, they lodge in and

15c

Exercise 3

1. Analogy used improperly as proof. Ask students to question the comparison of pornographic literature and arsenic as "poison"; who are the "experts" on pornographic literature in the same sense that druggists are experts on drugs?

2. Analogy used appropriately as hypothesis. Note the writer's tentative, rather than dogmatic, stance.

3. Analogy used improperly as proof. If the college is like the larger society, the students argue, then members of the college community should enjoy the same rights as members of the larger society. To what extent is the first analogy true?

4. Analogy used improperly as proof. Ask students to question the comparison between the clerk and the teacher, or between education and a product for sale.

5. Analogy used appropriately as illustration. The writer uses this analogy to make the point that a city, like a body, is a kind of vital organism

weaken one neighborhood after another, just as a cancer carried through the blood invades and overpowers a series of healthy organs. If we want to make our neighborhoods fully functioning organs of our urban body, then we have to find a way to eradicate the cancer of gang violence."

15d Avoiding the question

When writers fail to give relevant evidence for their arguments, they are said to be avoiding the question.

1. Begging the question

Begging the question is one such common failure. A question is begged when writers use as a proven argument the very point they are trying to prove. Consider the following argument, for example: "Permitting free parking downtown won't increase business for center-city merchants. Even if people can park for free in the city, they will still prefer to shop in suburban malls." The second statement may sound like proof of the first, but it's not; it's simply another formulation of the assertion that remains to be verified.

2. Ad hominem

The *ad hominem argument* — the argument, as the Latin phrase says, "to the man" — is a second common form of avoiding the question. Here, the tactic is to condemn the morals, motives, friends, or family of one's opponent and hence to divert attention from the substance of the opponent's argument. For instance: "How could you possibly agree with Berloff about the school bond? I hear from some people he's a real snob." The issue is the school bond, not Berloff's alleged snobbery.

The evaluation of expert testimony should not be confused with the ad hominem argument. In the former, you ask what a person's professional credentials are and the reasons for his or her position — that is, you attempt to distinguish between fact and judgment. In the latter, you insinuate by sarcasm or similar means that a case is unsound because there is something wrong with the person making it.

---

that depends for its overall health on the integrity of its various "organs." Anyone who has seen a quiet neighborhood gradually overtaken by street gangs will probably be willing to accept the comparison made here between roving gangs and cancer cells wreaking havoc throughout a healthy body.

Exercise 4 (page 326)

1. False alternatives. Recast, the sentence is equivalent to the following: Either you'll stop smoking, or you don't really care about your children's health. For some people, the addictive power of smoking might be as strong as their concern for their children.
2. Non sequitur. There may be compelling medical evidence for the link between smoking and certain types of cancer, and that evidence may be

3. Dummy subject

The *dummy subject* is another device commonly used for avoiding the question. As the label implies, the technique is to stuff, set up, and knock down a dummy issue that is substituted for the real issue. For example: "You say that drilling for oil in wilderness areas threatens the environment. But answer this: do you expect American industry and transportation to function without oil products?" The issue is not whether we are to continue to produce oil and gasoline for heating buildings and fueling cars; for the foreseeable future, at least, there cannot be any argument on this point. The dummy subject set up in this statement obscures the real issue at hand: whether the possibility of locating oil in wilderness areas outweighs the damage that may be done to the landscape and the wildlife. That's a much more complicated question than the one posed here.

15e False alternatives

The false *either/or argument* assumes that there are only two alternatives in a given situation. If parents tell a child, "You must be lazy, because the only reasons for poor schoolwork are laziness or stupidity, and we know you aren't dumb," they commit this error. They ignore other alternatives: the child may be bored with easy work, may lack adequate academic preparation, or may be unhappy for a variety of reasons. The either/or fallacy often surfaces in arguments intended to mobilize people to act: "If we don't elect Helen Fabian mayor, our public schools will continue to decline!" As careful writers know, few issues can actually be reduced to such an either/or proposition.

15f Non sequiturs

In Latin, *non sequitur* means "it does not follow." A non sequitur occurs when there is no connection between the premise and the conclusion, as in the following: "Carolyn likes algebra, so she ought to be a good treasurer." The connection between liking algebra and taking care of money is entirely unclear.

leading many smokers to quit. But the fact that people are quitting smoking does not in any way constitute proof that smoking causes cancer.
3. Begging the question. At first glance, the second assertion looks like evidence for the first, but in fact it merely restates the same idea. *Will* people still eat in restaurants if they can't smoke? That's the point to be proved, but this statement assumes the issue to be settled.
4. Ad hominem. These statements boil down to a crude personal attack based merely on hearsay.
5. Dummy subject. The issue is whether or not a ban on smoking will protect the public's health, not the alleged economic impact of such a ban on tobacco farmers and their families.

Exercise 5 (page 326)

Rare is the newspaper opinion page that doesn't provide opportunities for observing fallacious reasoning at work. Before sending your students out

EXERCISE 4

The following statements illustrate reasoning based on begging the question, ad hominem attack, the dummy subject, false alternatives, and non sequitur. Identify the fallacy in each argument.

1. If you really cared about the health of your children, then you wouldn't smoke when you're around them.
2. It's obvious that smoking causes cancer. Just look at how many people are quitting!
3. Banning smoking in restaurants won't hurt business. Whether or not people can smoke, they will still want to eat out.
4. The mayor claims to support an ordinance banning smoking in all public places in the city. But you can't believe anything she says. My brother-in-law, who's an accountant, heard that she even cheats on her taxes.
5. Banning smoking in public places to protect the populace's health is a mistake. Think of all the tobacco farmers whose livelihood will be put in jeopardy. Think of their children and the educational and personal opportunities that will be snatched away from them when their families are plunged into poverty. Is this any way for a just society to treat some of its hardest-working members?

EXERCISE 5

To sharpen your eye for others' fallacies, take a newspaper and turn to the editorial and opinion section. Go through it carefully, isolating and analyzing any errors you find. Better still, if there's a column you find particularly objectionable, write a letter to the editor pointing out how the reasoning is unsound.

EXERCISE 6

The following satire, written by a student, is deliberately based on a variety of logical fallacies, including hasty generalizations and mistaken causal relationships. How many of these logical errors can you find?

Why Have Teachers?

In the early days of America, before the establishment of compulsory schooling, moral standards were high. People were contented with the simpler virtues. Women learned to sew, cook, and keep house; men, to farm or work at some trade. Marriages were stable and happy; there was no such thing as divorce. Today this happy scene has

on their own in search of such reasoning errors, bring to class some examples that you have selected from the local newspaper so that students can observe and discuss how they function in the context of larger arguments.

Exercise 6

Among the reasoning errors in this deliberately humorous piece are the following:

1. Stereotyping, oversimplification, and unqualified generalization. The entire first paragraph is based on a naive view of early America that ignores the existence of immoral behavior and unhappy marriage and that uncritically accepts stereotypical images of women and men.
2. Post hoc, ergo propter hoc. Even if immorality in society did increase after the initiation of compulsory education (and the writer offers no facts to support this assertion), can education be identified as the cause

15f

changed—the morals of modern America have been corrupted. Every newspaper carries stories of murder, embezzlement, adultery, and divorce. What has caused this shocking situation? Is it possible to regain the happy state of early America?

The most influential institution during the formative years of each American is the school, governed and dominated by the teachers. From these teachers, obviously, children learn the human faults of blind obedience, prejudice, and the betrayal of one's kind in the form of tattling. These seeds, sown early, bear the bitter fruit of low morality. Clearly, teachers do much to undermine the morality of American children, and through them, that of society.

The obvious solution is to eliminate the teacher as much as possible. Modern children are increasingly capable of educating themselves. There are more college students today than ever before, a fact proving that youth today possess superior intelligence. By educating themselves, they would not be subjugated to the influence of teachers. They would share their knowledge willingly, each gaining from the other, with no one person dominating the others.

15f

Cynics will sneer that this system is impractical, that students need guidance and even indoctrination in fundamentals before they can think on their own. Nothing could be further from the truth! One of the most clear-thinking, intelligent leaders in this nation's history, Abraham Lincoln, was almost entirely self-educated. Think of the effect on our society of an entire generation with the training and characteristics of Lincoln. The present immorality would disappear; a high moral standard would return. The influence of the group that is undermining morality would be minimized, and the education of American youth placed where it belongs—in the hands of these same youth.

of such behavior? Similarly, in presenting Lincoln as a model for modern society, the writer makes the illogical assumption that Lincoln's morality resulted from his minimal education.

3. Reductive fallacy. The relatively large number of college students today has at least as much to do with the increased availability of postsecondary education as with the "superior intelligence" of modern youth.

Writing a deliberately flawed but at least somewhat plausible argument like this one is more difficult than it looks, but after discussing this piece, you might encourage students to try their hand at such a task. For best results, remind them to draw consciously on the specific fallacies examined in this chapter.

For Further Reading

Corbett, Edward P. J. "The Fallacies." *Classical Rhetoric for the Modern Student.* 3rd ed. New York: Oxford UP, 1990. 70–80.

16 Writing about Literature

I know noble accents
And lucid, inescapable rhythms;
But I know, too,
That the blackbird is involved
In what I know.

From "Thirteen Ways of Looking
at a Blackbird," by Wallace Stevens

Like the speaker in Stevens's poem, we as readers have known "noble accents" and "lucid, inescapable rhythms" in the poems, plays, and stories we have read. And, like the speaker reflecting on the blackbird, we have perhaps reflected on our involvement with the work. Stevens's lines suggest several major challenges in writing about literature. How to understand our relationship to the work? How to share our experience of it most effectively with other readers? How to convince others that ours is a valid way of looking at the work?

Obviously, this short chapter can offer only a few guidelines for thinking and writing about literature. These are complex subjects, certainly not to be reduced to rules such as those for the uses of the apostrophe. Nevertheless, some things can be said about the questions posed in the box on page 329 that will make your writing about literature more effective and more pleasurable. For convenience, this discussion is divided into three broad topics: Inhibiting assumptions, Productive questions, and Useful strategies.

There are both theoretical and practical reasons for the inclusion of this chapter in the text. First, the study of literature clearly offers opportunities for and practice in critical thinking and argument, the subjects of the preceding two chapters. Second, many students are required to write about literature either during a first-year composition course or in introductory literature courses taken after composition.

At the same time, of course, literary analysis involves a vocabulary and methodology beyond the scope of what can be presented here. This chapter on writing about literature is therefore necessarily only an introduction to the subject. Its goal is not to raise technical questions—questions, for example, about point of view or dramatic irony or sonnet structure—but to describe an approach to thinking about literature and literary analysis, to outline a few basic issues that anyone who wishes to read literature critically must consider. Thus, this chapter is suitable both as a brief, self-contained introduction to thinking and writing about literature, and as a preface to more detailed and extensive work in this area.

QUICK REFERENCE: *Thinking and Writing about Literature*

Ask interpretive questions.	What does the title of the work reveal? How is the work constructed? How are its parts related to one another? What patterns of images or events can you identify? Who tells the story or speaks in the poem? What is the tone of the work?
Ask evaluative questions.	How successful is the work? What are your criteria for making such a judgment? What is strange, difficult, or threatening about this text? How does it challenge your attitudes or beliefs?
Ask contextual questions.	What more do you want to know about this work or this writer? What do you want to know about the historical period or the society in which the writer worked? What do you want to know about his or her philosophical, religious, or artistic beliefs? Why do you want to know more about these things?

16a

16a Inhibiting assumptions

Inhibiting assumptions are those preconceptions and attitudes students often bring to the academic study of literature that block clear thinking and writing. Such assumptions make students distrust their abilities, or make them defensive and dogmatic, or both.

1. A special logic?

You are probably familiar with one of these inhibiting assumptions: the notion that writing about literature requires some esoteric technique or special logic, mastered only by the gifted few. You may have heard friends say (and felt yourself think) something like the following: "What does the instructor want me to say? I don't know how to write about poetry." "How am I supposed to put this essay together? I don't know what to do with the novel."

Behind these and similar remarks is the assumption that reasoning about literature is different from, say, reasoning about history, psychology, or biology. Clearly the materials being reasoned about do differ. Literary characters and events are not the same as actual persons and historical events, or the theories of perception and personality studied in psychology. But the principles of clear exposition—defining and developing a topic, observing and describing evidence accurately, supporting assertions with detail—do *not* change. Consider your own experience of discussing a film or novel with friends outside class. You agree or disagree that a character or event was or was not significant and say why (stating a thesis). You recall your impressions of the character or event as fully as you can; sometimes you are corrected by your friends, and sometimes you correct them (collecting evidence). And you connect the details you remember to the judgment you are defending (structuring an argument).

In short, the assumption that thinking and writing about literature require a special logic is questionable. But this mistaken belief that there must be some arcane technique for discussing literature can unduly inhibit us. It can make us doubt our ability to communicate effectively in the academic setting, even though we have talked intelligibly about a variety of works in more informal settings.

2. Only one correct interpretation?

Another inhibiting assumption concerns the authority of interpretations: the belief that there must be a single, unambiguous, "correct" interpretation of a given work. You recognize this view in the simple way it is often stated. In effect, it says, "Well, what *is* the right interpretation of the poem? There must be one."

Now this assumption is not entirely unwarranted. We have been taught that right answers exist. But, again, if we turn to our experience outside the classroom, we probably find that we are more discriminating. Experience has very probably taught us that right answers may be found in some areas but not in others. In matters that involve calculation or measurement—mathematics and science, for example—we reasonably expect to find the correct solution. In matters of human choice, motive, and action (the substance of literature), however, we have to master the demanding discipline of tolerating ambiguity and perplexity. The poet John Keats called this discipline "negative capability" and described it as one's ability to accept "uncertainties, mysteries, doubts, without any irritable reaching after fact and reason" (letter of December 27 [?], 1817). However strongly we may wish otherwise, we learn that adulthood involves the recognition that uncertainty has to be accepted and lived with. So, too, with plays, poems, and stories: because they so often are complex explorations of human motives and actions, they cannot be reduced to a single "correct" statement of the author's "message." If you sometimes find yourself irritably wanting to simplify the meaning of a work, resist the temptation. For the assumption that such a single, correct statement of its meaning exists can inhibit your response to the work's depth and power.

16a

3.   All interpretations equally valid?

At the other extreme is the belief that since all interpretations are wholly subjective and individual, none is better than any other. "I don't see what's wrong with my interpretation," says the person who holds this view. "After all, it's just a matter of personal opinion."

But this, too, is an assumption frequently contradicted by our behavior outside the classroom. If, for instance, we are discussing the history of science fiction or the achievements of its major writers, we are unlikely to accept all views equally. We know that some friends have read widely and deeply, while others have narrower views based on limited exposure and knowledge. The same holds true in dozens of other interests we may have—gymnastics, computers, chess, country music, whatever. We don't usually insist that others share our interests, only that they not make snap judgments and shallow assertions out of ignorance while claiming the right to do so because "it's just a matter of opinion." By contrast, we often give heed to those we know to be sensitive and informed. While not compelled to treat them as experts, we have learned that they see, feel, and grasp more; that they can make more connections; that they make us understand more fully than we can by ourselves. We don't necessarily assume that their judgments and interpretations are always right, but we recognize that their views are probably more inclusive and penetrating than other opinions—in short, better.

4.   Implications for the study of literature

16a

What does all of this imply about the study of literature? Most immediately, it implies your need to prepare and to be informed—to use dictionaries for unfamiliar words and allusions, to consult a glossary of literary terms for the meanings of terms such as *irony* and *dramatic monologue,* to reread shorter works several times and at least parts of the longer ones. Beyond such preparation, it implies an open attitude, a readiness to consider varying interpretations (including your own) as rough approximation. Consider them as hypotheses about a work's meaning. In the natural sciences, hypotheses are tested against all the facts and, other things being equal, those with the greatest explanatory power are judged better. That is, those hypotheses uniting the most features into a coherent pattern with the least complication are considered the more probably true. Admittedly, the analogy between literary interpretations and scientific hypotheses is only partial, because literature often depends on the kinds of irreducible paradoxes and ambiguities that science tries to avoid. Nevertheless, this analogy points out certain shared characteristics. Hypotheses are subject to frequent review in the light of new data, just as interpretations may be reviewed in the light of new evidence found in the text. Hypotheses are provisional and sometimes modified, just as interpretations may be tentative and sometimes revised. It's useful to think of interpretations as resembling hypotheses because such an attitude increases the likelihood of greater understanding of the work. This attitude can shift the reader's attention away from defensiveness about an entrenched view and toward what he or she shares in common with other readers—the evidence of the text. Consider the following example.

Two students in a class discussion take different viewpoints on Mark Twain's *The Adventures of Huckleberry Finn*. One interprets the novel as essentially the story of Huck's coming of age and learning he cannot trust the adult world. As evidence, the student points to Pap's abusiveness and selfishness, the unthinking violence of feuds and mobs, the barbarity of the small towns, and the duplicity of the King and the Duke. The other student interprets the novel as essentially Twain's attack on slavery. As evidence, the student points to Huck's experiences with Jim, their growing friendship, and Huck's crisis of choice when he decides he would rather go to hell by helping Jim escape than return him to slavery. If the two students regard these different interpretations as mutually exclusive alternatives, they risk becoming locked into their positions and ignoring what they might learn from each other. If, however, they construe their interpretations as tentative explanations—as hypotheses—they enhance their chances of improving their understanding. They might find, for example, that they can synthesize their separate arguments into a more comprehensive one. They might conclude that as Huck comes of age he learns he cannot trust the adult world but can trust only his personal feelings, especially in his relations with Jim. This revised interpretation is richer than the two originals because it incorporates the evidence of both. But even it is only provisional, not final. Interpretations, like hypotheses, are approximations, not absolute and unchanging truths.

16a

EXERCISE 1

1. Write a paragraph on Whitman's "The Dismantled Ship" (page 352) in which you reduce the poem to one meaning, that is, make all the images show only the loneliness of old age, *or* its feebleness, *or* its absence of activity. Then write another paragraph in which you show how much you have had to leave out of the poem in order to achieve a single meaning. Now compare the two paragraphs: How radically did you simplify the poem's imagery? What was the greatest reduction in meaning you made?

2. Write a paragraph on Whitman's "The Ship Starting" (page 354) in which you interpret the poem as, say, a reader beginning an absorbing novel, a crowd moving across a field, or a rocket accelerating off its pad. Then write a paragraph that questions the plausibility of your interpretation as a hypothesis. Now compare the two paragraphs:

Exercises 1–3

Like the chapter itself, these exercises are only suggestive. You will want to adapt them to works actually available to your students.

What is the most telling evidence you cited to question the interpretation? Why is it the most telling?

16b Productive questions

So far, we have been questioning a few assumptions that impede full responses to and clear thinking about literature. You might call these the "negative factors" and wonder about some positive ones. What are the kinds of questions and strategies that will sharpen your focus in thinking about poetry, drama, and fiction?

In one of her poems, Emily Dickinson says,

> Tell all the Truth but tell it slant—
> Success in Circuit lies
> Too bright for our infirm Delight
> The Truth's superb surprise

We may read her lines to identify three major kinds of questions to be asked. The first concerns the "slantness" and the "circuit" the writer has chosen. How is the work put together? What are the resulting effects and meanings? Why this particular direction or slant? Let's call these questions of *interpretation*. The second kind of question concerns our "Delight," infirm or otherwise. How well do we judge the work to have succeeded? By what standard? For what sort of audience? These may be labeled questions of *evaluation*. The third kind of question concerns the "Truth," all or partial, surprising or familiar. How can the individual work or writer be related to some larger background or perspective? What religious, social, or artistic ideas does the work contain? What aspects of human experience in general? These are questions of *context*.

Now clearly a given essay may address all three kinds of questions, though it will usually emphasize one kind more than the others. Normally, writers don't ask themselves whether they are interpreting, evaluating, or contextualizing, any more than they worry about which method of paragraph development they are using. Nevertheless, good criticism in the arts is primarily the act of pointing—of singling out important details or features, specifying how a particular effect is achieved, noticing resemblances among works. And effective pointing depends on asking the relevant questions to focus attention. First, then, are questions that focus attention on interpretation.

1.   Interpretive questions

To ask *what* a work means, you may find it helpful to begin with a prior question: *How* does it mean? How is it constructed? How are the parts—the stanzas, the chapters, the scenes and acts—related to one another? Through whose eyes is the story told? Why? Is there a dominant image throughout? How is it developed or modified? Any or several of these questions will help answer the fundamental question interpretation tries to answer: How are we to understand the work?

Begin with the title

If you find that your impressions are vivid but difficult to verbalize, begin with the work's title and its chapters or subtitles if it has any. Effective titles are frequently a condensed shorthand of the direction in which the writer intends to go—what Emily Dickinson means by the "slant" or "circuit." For instance, Joyce Carol Oates has written a fine novel set largely in mid-twentieth-century American cities and mainly focused on women whose lives are for the most part shaped by suffering and pain they do not understand; she has entitled the novel *them* and its first section "Children of Silence." If you were to read the novel, you would soon discover how powerfully the title unifies aspects of the work: "them" are the powerless, anonymous, marginally poor not usually written about; "them" are the losers in the pursuit of the American dream; and "them" are those other faceless figures and forces the losers blame for their suffering. Similarly, if you were to read the first section, set in the Great Depression and war years when older men were often broken by unemployment and younger men depressed and even violent, and when women endured as well as they could, you would realize that these are indeed "Children of Silence." Their lives warped by historical forces they have no words for, the men turn inward and sullen, the women to the empty clichés of romance or domesticity, and to vague hopes for a better life they cannot precisely describe.

16b

Consider who speaks

Consider the question of who tells the story or speaks in the poem, and why. What does Twain gain by having Huck tell his own story in his own words? Surely one major result is that we come to know Huck's sweetness and shrewdness, his untutored decency and wit, better than we know most people's qualities in actual life. We realize that Huck *is* his word in every sense. His arguments with and caring for Jim, the inventive lies he tells to save the two of them, his acute perceptions about the fraudulence of others, his ignorance of history and culture, and his knowledge of immediate realities—all of these elements Twain renders in Huck's words, which reveal his essential character. And, on reflection, we may raise other questions: What else has Twain made us experience through the colloquial, seemingly spontaneous language of this largely natural boy? How have we been made to feel about Pap's drunken brutality and vulgarity? About the Widow Douglas's gentility? About Tom's zeal for adventure at Jim's expense? Eventually, we may conclude that Huck's words are the ones by which we measure all else in the novel—the characters; the events; what it means to be a slave, a piece of disposable property; the possible cost of civilization itself, a loss of a vision like Huck's.

Identify a meaningful image or pattern

Another way of organizing your impressions is to identify, review, and analyze a repeated image or a recurrent pattern of action that the author has charged with meaning. In the following passage, a student is discussing Doris Lessing's novel *The Golden Notebook* and its main character, Anna Wulf, a writer whose personal and professional life is in shambles:

> During the time Anna is seeing Mother Sugar, a Jungian psychoanalyst, she has her first dream, a nightmare, about "the joy in spite." She tells Mother Sugar, "It mocked and jibed and hurt, wished murder, wished death. And yet it was always vibrant with joy." In Anna's dreams, the embodiment of this principle progresses from a jug, to a grotesque dwarf, a deformed creature, a half-human, to a person: the progression of terror of an object, to terror of the dream as myth, to terror of Saul, her actual lover. Anna must work through her fears of the principle of destruction if she is to write again. Her fear of the cruelty that destruction brings helps cause her inertia, her writer's block. She must learn to turn that force into a creative one.

Here, the student has chosen to concentrate on the importance of a progression of images. In this next example, another student has chosen a recurrent pattern of action in Ralph Ellison's novel *Invisible Man*.

> *Invisible Man* begins with a prologue that informs the reader that the black narrator is an invisible man who lives in a hole. He is invisible "simply because people refuse to see me." But he is also invisible because he has fled from seeing himself and has allowed others to manipulate him. Throughout most of the novel, the narrator is kept running by different authority/father figures or systems, submitting to each though he unconsciously rebels against them, repressing his own anger, tension, despair, and humiliation. What Ellison shows (to me, at least) is that the narrator flees not only because other people can't see beyond his blackness but also because the narrator can't accept his own humanity and his responsibility for himself.

These two examples of student writing demonstrate the value of isolating a significant image or action and asking yourself *what it adds up to*. We have used novels as illustrations so far, but you can do the same with poems, short stories, and plays. By questioning a part and teasing out its meanings and effects, you begin to see the larger pattern of the work. The resonant part may be no more than a line or two, a sentence that you marked while reading because it gave shape to your own impressions. Sometimes such lines occur near or at the end of the work as thematic summaries. The journey completed, the writer looks back to see what the direction has meant. For instance, at the end of Arthur Miller's play *Death of a Salesman,* Linda, the wife of Willy Loman, the salesman of the play's title, stands next to his grave and sobs, "I made the last payment on the house today. Today, dear. And there'll be nobody home. We're free and clear. We're free. We're free." Reading these lines, we may feel that Miller is a bit insistent, but we also certainly perceive his dramatic intent: to make us realize how *unfree* Willy was, how trapped by a certain American ideal of success, and how damaging and difficult it may be to achieve freedom from this ideal, not only for Willy's family but for us, "we," the audience.

16b

Examine the tone

Still another question you can pose concerns the tone of the work, the speaker's emotional stance toward the subject. This question is especially appropriate for (though not confined to) lyric poetry, in which there is no story, or only a suggested situation. By recognizing the tone, you can locate the cluster of feelings and attitudes that have moved you, not through the plot and events but through the curve and motion of the speaker's voice. Reading aloud, you can retrace the rises and the falls, the beckonings and the separations, the reaching outward and the drawing inward that affected you on silent reading.

In a frequently reprinted essay, the poet and critic R. P. Blackmur wrote of "Language as Gesture." This is the essence of lyric poetry—language *as* gesture. The speaker's voice gestures by greeting, by rejecting, by embracing. And as you perceive the tone, you may recall other lines or poems that echo it, that make similar gestures. One might, for instance, begin with Edward Fitzgerald's translation of *The Rubaiyat of Omar Khayyam*.

> Come fill the Cup, and in the fire of Spring
> Your Winter-garment of Repentance fling:
> The Bird of Time has but a little way
> To flutter—and the Bird is on the wing.

In turn, these lines might bring to mind Christopher Marlowe's "The Passionate Shepherd to His Love" and his invitation.

> Come live with me and be my love,
> And we will all the pleasures prove
> That valleys, groves, hills, and fields,
> Woods, or steepy mountain yields.

Catching the tone of both poems, one would discover differences as well as similarity. Both passages are a call to life, to test the joy of living in the body and through the senses; they both gesture by imploring. But Fitzgerald's lines contain a reminder, almost a warning, not found in Marlowe's—that the moment is brief, that "The Bird of Time" is "on the wing." Marlowe's tone, by contrast, is seductive in its promise of timeless youth. In fact, Sir Walter Raleigh answers Marlowe in "The Nymph's Reply to the Shepherd" with the speaker's skepticism of the young man on the make. Raleigh begins,

> If all the world and love were young,
> And truth in every shepherd's tongue,
> These pretty pleasures might me move
> To live with thee and be thy love.

and concludes,

> But could youth last and love still breed,
> Had joys no date nor age no need,
> Then these delights my mind might move
> To live with thee and be thy love.

As you may have decided by now, interpretive questions often probe by comparison and contrast. They investigate the ways titles unify diversities, parts resemble or differ, images evolve or change, voices agree or disagree. Remember that the most important thing you know about a poem or a story is what you were thinking and feeling while reading the work. Begin by asking what elements in the work account for whatever you felt and thought. Select a feature that has lingered with you; reason from effects to causes. As you move from particular to particular, you will necessarily compare and contrast. And as you find likeness and difference, you will integrate your feelings about and your understanding of the work. You will become the interpreter of meaning, the negotiator between the work and your own reader.

16b

2. Evaluative questions

In a broad sense, anyone who writes about literature evaluates continually. The scenes, characters, and lines that one discusses or omits, the themes and ideas stressed or minimized, the works themselves singled out for analysis—all of these represent choices about what is significant or insignificant in a work, what is successful or unsuccessful.

Judging a work's success

A common question you will hear is "How successful do you think the work is?" This is not the same as being asked "Did you like the work?" You can like or dislike a novel or poem for many reasons, some of which may have little to do with the work itself—for example, your sense of its relevance or irrelevance to your own life. The question "How successful do you think the work is?" should be grounded not simply in emotional responses, but in clearly formulated criteria, in a framework of discussable assumptions and terms.

One such assumption, for example, is the notion from antiquity that a literary work should have a clear beginning, middle, and end. We can productively apply this criterion for evaluation to many works, perhaps by observing how elements in the beginning of a short story foreshadow the conclusion or how the actions of a character in a play lead to inevitable consequences. But we need to recognize at the same time that any criterion's usefulness as a standard of judgment may be limited. After all, some powerful and clearly "successful" works do not end decisively; they simply stop. Ralph Ellison's *Invisible Man,* for instance, concludes with the narrator finally understanding more about himself and the world but still living in a hole. In fact, many contemporary works close with the survivors disabused of illusions or pretenses but with their futures quite uncertain—Albee's *Who's Afraid of Virginia Woolf?* and Golding's *Lord of the Flies,* to mention but two. We simply don't know what the characters are going to do after the end of the text.

16b   *Taking chances with the unfamiliar*

Be clear about the criteria by which you judge a work, but be willing to reconsider your criteria when the strangeness of a text suggests that you must. Like an unusual new acquaintance, some poems, novels, and plays may seem odd, difficult, or perhaps even threatening when you first encounter them. You may have to live with such a work for a while before you know how to assess it. Consider, for instance, what one student found after living with Tillie Olsen's fiction long enough to be moved by it:

> Raised in affluent, upper-class America, I have rarely come in contact with the poverty Tillie Olsen describes in her short stories. But her treatment of suffering powerfully conveys the despair, the broken lives, the caring, and sometimes even the hope that poverty entails. I found that Olsen develops an intensity of pain, resentment, love, and understanding that simply does not exist in more privileged communities. She made me realize the terrible destruction of human potential and personality that poverty can cause, but she also made me see how easily one can become hardened by comfort. At the end of *Tell Me a Riddle,* I had some hope that poverty can be overcome, but I found this hope tempered by the realization that as one gains affluence, one too easily loses intensity of emotion and the ability to understand.

Notice what the writer has done. Rather than hastily making up her mind about whether Olsen's stories are good or bad, she has taken the time to ask an entirely different kind of question, something like "What have I felt and understood that I had not before?" This type of question may be the most productive for works that you find unfamiliar or unsettling.

We read texts, but texts also "read" us. Certain writers and works, that is, disturb our habitual ways of thinking and feeling and our conventional notions about what literature should be. If we remain open, they make us feel our own limitations. If, as happens occasionally, you find that you are expected to write about such a work, try beginning with the following questions: Why do I find this book strange or discomforting? Is there something about myself or my beliefs that I resist coming to terms with? After thinking about these questions as honestly as you can, you may discover some things about yourself that take you on a far more interesting journey than the one defined by safer, more familiar works.

16b

3. Contextual questions

Contextual questions are those that ask about the intellectual or historical background of the work or its author. Such questions may probe the connections between the work and the writer's life or times; the work and philosophical, political, or religious ideas; the work and certain artistic movements or forms; the work and human experience in general. What, for example, does the fiction of Toni Morrison, Alice Walker, and Toni Cade Bambara say about the lives of black women in America? What did T. S. Eliot learn from Ezra Pound about poetry? What political and social ideas was Swift satirizing in *Gulliver's Travels*? How does Virginia Woolf's literary criticism illuminate her major novels? What are the relationships between Shelley's interest in philosophy and his poetry? How does Dickens's humor differ from Fielding's? Why were the Beat poets called *Beat*?

Contextual questions are often the most exciting ones you can ask. They encourage wide reading, research, and concentrated thinking. They invite you to pursue a line of inquiry in depth and to sustain it until you have found the answers that make the most sense. Courses that center on a historical period, one or two authors, a movement, a theme, or a genre naturally provoke such questions—the instructor's, your own, or both. Answering such questions may enlarge your understanding of a work by enabling you to place it in a context that illuminates some of its important features.

Defining your question

What is a good contextual question? To begin with, it should be one that is answerable. To ask "What did Salinger really have in mind when he wrote *Catcher in the Rye?*" is to ask a question that is probably unanswerable: nobody but Salinger could know, and he hasn't said. A more manageable question is "What central themes of *Catcher in the Rye* are found in Salinger's other works?" It is answerable because the texts are available. Effective contextual questions are essentially the same as those you ask in preparing to write any paper involving research and critical thinking. (See also Chapter **17** on the research process.)

Unless your instructor assigns the topic, your first question is the hardest: What more do I want to know about the work or writer? The period or society that shaped the work or writer? Some philosophical, religious, or artistic idea that permeates the work or influenced the writer? Other similar works or writers? Even if a topic is assigned, you can normally sharpen it by posing your own question and checking with the instructor to be sure it's relevant.

Clarifying your interest

A second question is closely related to the first: Why do I want to know more about this? Of course it's because you are interested, but what arouses your interest? For instance, suppose you wanted to know more about some recent feminist writers. Why? Because of their treatment of women? Of men? Of women and men? Of women's sexuality? Of mothers and daughters? Sometimes, especially at the beginning, it won't be easy to answer why, and often your interests will change as you get into the topic. But the more you can at least tentatively answer this question, the more you clarify your focus.

16b

Planning your research

A third question is also crucial: What more do I need to know to answer my question? Here your primary and secondary reading and your conversations with your instructor are essential. Occasionally, you may find that you need to know too much, that the question is too vast or complicated to be manageable. For instance, if you were to ask seriously "What are the differences between the treatment of World War I and that of World War II in American fiction?" you would be committing yourself to a very long program of reading and study. When your questions open up such expansive territories for research, you may need to define more narrowly the context in which you wish to examine a work.

Avoiding oversimplification

Like interpretive questions, contextual questions are often answered by making significant comparisons and contrasts. In doing so, you should keep two more questions in mind, both of which concern the danger of oversimplification. The first is "Have I defined a contextualizing term too loosely or applied it too glibly?" What, for example, does it mean to consider a work in terms of its relation to a "crisis of faith," a "conflict between the individual and society," or a "search for identity"? In a loose sense, a great number of novels probably do dramatize a "search for identity," but how exactly does one understand both Huckleberry Finn's flight and Hester Prynne's remaining on the scene of her disgrace in *The Scarlet Letter* as "searches"?

The second question is "Have I looked at important differences as well as important similarities?" Difference is as vital as similarity. Writers sometimes do change their themes, subject matter, or techniques and style. History does affect and modify beliefs, artistic conventions, individual lives. To echo the philosopher William James, every difference that is a difference makes a difference.

16c A sample student essay

Questions give momentum to thinking. They nudge you to move from effect to cause, impression to source, individual case to

16c

general principle. What follows is a student essay that effectively blends interpretive and contextual questions into one unified argument. The essay concerns the function of Old Hilse, a character in Gerhart Hauptmann's play *The Weavers,* a dramatization of a revolt by impoverished Silesian weavers in central Europe during the 1840s. The writer's central interpretive question is "Why is Old Hilse even in the play?" His answer is a persuasive demonstration of the way in which Old Hilse changes our understanding of the play, of the effect he has upon us.

Why Old Hilse?

What Old Hilse does *not* cause or influence

If one were to examine the contribution of Old Hilse to the plot of The Weavers, one would be hard put to find any excuse for his being in the play. He neither alters the course of the main action nor initiates any new actions. His speeches to the main characters are unheeded. He does not join the rebel weavers, nor does he come to the defense of the manufacturers. He remains neutral in the battle, in no way affecting its outcome. His only connection with the action of the play is to be an unintentional and all-but-unnoticed casualty.

Focusing question

Then why are his unheeded lines ever spoken? Why is this character brought into the play at all?

The play begins with a dispute between the younger weavers and the manufacturer's buyer, builds up the weavers' discontent with their poverty and
fatigue, and reaches a climax with
their open rebellion. It roars toward
what we hope will be its triumphant
conclusion. But it runs head—on into
Old Hilse. Here is a man whom we fully
expect to jump on the bandwagon, or at
least to act as a dramatic counterpoint
by siding with the manufacturers. <u>But
Old Hilse just states his contempt for
this particular uprising, reiterates
his belief in duty, and goes back to
his daily weaving.</u> For a moment the
<u>rapidly moving picture of a community
in revolt is frozen. The logic that has
been leading up to the great truth of
why all the weavers must kill all the
owners is stopped just short of a final
conclusion.</u> The anticipated victory of
good over evil, already foreshadowed in
the impoverished mass's sacking of a
manufacturer's estate, falters. Old

16c

Old Hilse's
action—his refusal
to join the
rebellion—and its
immediate effect
on our involvement
in the plot

Hilse, the most respected weaver, the
one most representative of simple devotion to weaving, will not join the rebellion.

In a moment the machine starts to
rumble again. The drunken and possessed
leaders of the rebellion rush out of
Hilse's house to battle the government

Further effects on the reader—the meaning(s) of Old Hilse's choice

troops. The plot starts up again. But
the reader left behind begins to question the rebels. Why won't Old Hilse
join? Why does his refusal, although
not altering the plan of the rebellion
one bit, alter the meaning of it so
greatly? Hilse is certainly not afraid.
He is a wounded veteran of a much
greater war. As he starts to talk about
the war, the rebellion raging outside
begins to shrink. It is nothing to him.
What's more, it is nothing to anyone
except those who are inside of it.

Initial statement of what Old Hilse does cause—our seeing the plot from a new perspective

Suddenly the story of the young weavers
battling for their rights and the older
ones gradually joining them becomes a
pathetic example of the pattern we see

16c

in the papers almost daily, the local
rebellion. This is Hilse's contribution. He is the only character who
stands far enough outside the battle to
see it as the futile effort it is, not
as the glorious rebellion that the
other weavers think it is. He has seen
it all before. He can even predict jail
terms for the leaders. Hilse takes us
far enough from the story to see it
clearly. Hilse, who is nothing to the
plot's outcome, is everything to its
meaning: he makes the plot change from
a story in which we are as personally
wrapped up as the characters into a
dismal pattern of the universality of
revolt born by suffering and hunger,
doomed to be led astray by its own ex-
cesses, and thus defeated.

Restatement of
Old Hilse's
function— final
answer to "Why
Old Hilse?"

16c

EXERCISE **2**

1. Pick a work—a poem, a play, or a piece of fiction—that you like and
know well and that has an effective title. Write several paragraphs in
which you show how the title acts to unify elements of the work—its
plot and characters, themes and development, images and details, and
so on. Make as many connections as you can, even if a few of them
seem a bit strained or far-fetched. When you have finished, reread the

paragraphs critically and revise them by concentrating on the most important connections that you have made. What elements of the first version became more unified in the second?

2. Choose a short story or novel and write several paragraphs in which you imagine how the work would be different if told from another point of view—for instance, *The Adventures of Huckleberry Finn* through Jim's eyes, or *Heart of Darkness* through Kurtz's eyes. What new perspectives on the work does this strategy offer?

3. Do the same with a short poem; for instance, Thomas Hardy's "Had You Wept" from the woman's point of view, Frost's "Mending Wall" through the neighbor's eyes, or Robinson Jeffers's "Hurt Hawks" through the "terrible eyes" of the bird or "the wild God."

4. Write a paragraph on Dickinson's "This quiet Dust" (page 355) in which you visualize as fully as you can *how* dust permeates the poem. For instance, how does cloth ("Frocks") look, feel, and smell as it turns to dust, or how do summer flowers ("Bloom") fade and dry?

5. Choose some type of literature you read purely for pleasure—for example, mass-market romances, science fiction, sports stories, or fantasy. What criteria would you propose for judging the success of a work of this sort? Show how your criteria might be applied to one of these texts.

6. Look through the editor's headnotes or introductions to the authors and selections in your literature anthology and find some critical judgment that you disagree with, perhaps one that points to some limitation or failure in the work or writer. Then write a thoughtful response in which you perhaps concede part of the criticism but find other grounds for valuing the writer or work.

7. Jot down three or four broad contextual questions that you might be interested in answering. For example: What connection is there between a writer's life and work? Between a historical period or event and a work? Between a religious or philosophical idea and a work? What more would you have to know to answer your questions?

8. Using the student paper "Why Old Hilse?" as a model, write an essay in which you analyze how a character is used primarily to provide some larger perspective on or understanding of a play, poem, or novel.

16d Useful strategies

Apart from the questions discussed above, you have other ways of assisting your thinking and writing about literature. The most important of these is paying close attention to the terms, themes, and techniques of analysis that your instructor stresses. There is no substitute for participating in class, asking questions, and keeping up with the reading. The more actively responsible you become for your own education, the more likely you are to get what *you* want from it. The following strategies should help you achieve this end.

1. Keeping a journal

A proven strategy for increasing one's pleasure in and understanding of literature is keeping a journal or reading log. Many students who have kept journals find they do best to set aside two or three sessions a week for writing about their class reading. Length of entry and format often vary: some students write several hundred words on each novel, play, or poem; others jot down short notes, impressions, or references to specific pages they wish to return to. The subject matter can also take varying forms: some students pursue a theme or two from work to work; some explore their personal feelings and thoughts and connect the work to their own experience; some isolate key passages, images, or characters and reflect on these; and others, depending on the work, may try a combination of these approaches. Unless assigned and collected by the instructor, such journals are entirely private. Journals allow you to write freely about any aspect of the reading in whatever way you find productive.

16d

The advantages of keeping a journal are several. To begin with, a journal allows you to explore your own reactions to a work at greater length and in greater depth than class sessions may permit. By doing so, you make the poem or story more fully your own. Moreover, the journal encourages you to sort out your impressions while they are still fresh. Sometimes, a few weeks after reading a work, you may recall having had some wonderful insights but have no idea now what they were. Journals help you remember. Finally, journals can assist your reviewing in either of two ways. Looking over your journal, you may find the same topic discussed several times; perhaps it could become a subject for a paper. Or, reviewing your journal for an in-class examination, you may rediscover evidence and ideas that you might otherwise have overlooked.

If you have not kept a journal before, you may want to review the suggestions for keeping a journal in **2a**. Don't be concerned if you find yourself a bit self-conscious and awkward when you begin. These feelings are entirely natural and usually diminish as you become more experienced. At the very least, try one for a few weeks; it's an excellent way of making the academic study of literature a more personal inquiry.

2. Summarizing

Another useful strategy is summarizing. While summarizing can take a number of forms, the technique best suited for scenes or acts of plays, sections or chapters of prose fiction, and the divisions of longer poems is to write down a few phrases or sentences that capture the primary events, themes, or images of the work. The summary thus becomes a record of your dominant impressions of the text. Here, for instance, is one student's summary of a chapter called "Pastoral," from V. S. Naipaul's moving novel *A House for Mr. Biswas,* based on the life of Naipaul's father, an Indian journalist growing up in Trinidad.

16d

```
Brief pastoral. Mr. B's birth curse, death of
calf and father: family dispersed; no home.
```

And here is the summarizing note for the next chapter, entitled "Before the Tulsis."

```
Beyond childhood: school, beatings, work with
Pundit (& disgrace), liquor store, sign painter.
This novel goes in real stages; youth—adoles-
cence, concluding with sex, hopes of love and
romance, à la Samuel Smiles.
```

The value of this kind of summarizing is most obvious for long, complex works that you are reading for the first time. Summaries help you retrace what you have read and sort out the central developments and ideas from the lesser ones; they map the major features of the territory you have just explored. Reviewing the territory later, you can inspect the details more analytically because you already have a tentative framework into which they fit. In a somewhat different fashion, summarizing can also help unravel the knotty strands of shorter but nevertheless complex pieces. Though only 204 lines, Browning's poem "Childe Roland to the Dark Tower Came" is one of his most mysterious works. Here is one reader's summary that served at least as a start toward understanding it.

```
Strange poem in several ways: dreams, snatches

of memory of picture and verse, not B's usual

control; the wasteland where all effort is fu-

tile, things mysterious and pointless—world

does not mean intensely and mean good. Note

poem filled with images of failure, betrayed

strength, weakness, aging and decay without

honor—memory no help.
```

16d

The main use of this note for the writer was that it identified several ways in which this poem differed from others by Browning and therefore highlighted key issues to be considered.

Rather like some journal entries, the summarizing note is your own record in your own words of your primary reactions. And like its journal equivalent, such a note is best used as an aid for further, more carefully detailed analysis. It is another means of engaging yourself more actively with the reading.

3.   Working with the words

Plays, poems, and fiction are made out of words, not clay or copper. When you are caught up in a short story or sonnet, you are enmeshed in the effects of words—their connotations and denotations, their plasticity and firmness, their freshness and familiarity. And when you think and write critically about the story or poem, you are partially disengaging yourself from the words in order to look at them. Themes, images, and events do not exist in the abstract; they are embedded in and realized through the words, the stuff of language. Whatever "happens" in literature happens because of the patterns that have been made out of words. Whatever "happens" in analysis and criticism happens usually because these patterns have been explicated.

Explication

To *explicate* is to unfold. To explicate a piece of literature is to unfold the ways the words have been shaped into larger units of meaning—couplets, lines, scenes, chapters, completed works. Even a short poem may include layers of suggestiveness and strands of imagery. Explication, the unfolding of these layers and strands, is essential to critical thinking about literature. And while critical thinking and writing do not end with explication, they usually begin with it. Before you can go on to larger questions—How does this writer differ from that writer? This epic compare with that epic?—you have to work with the words. Even if you do not write about the language as such, you at least have to think about it as such.

How do you think about "language as such"? To begin with, you will need to look up unfamiliar words and allusions and see how they are used in context. Beyond that, you should, at least with shorter poems and sections of plays, try reading aloud to catch the sounds, rhythms, and intonations of the language. But such a task is more easily illustrated than described. To get an idea of what's involved, first read the poem that follows, written by Walt Whitman in the last years of his life. After you have read the poem aloud a couple of times and looked up words like *hawser'd*, answer these questions: (1) How is the picture of old age embedded in particular images? (2) Why is the unifying image "The Dismantled Ship," rather than, say, "The Forgotten Ship"? (3) How can the poem be read as a picture of human loss and decay, particularly Whitman's?

16d

The Dismantled Ship

In some unused lagoon, some nameless bay,
On sluggish, lonesome waters, anchor'd near the shore,
An old, dismasted, gray and batter'd ship, disabled, done,
After free voyages to all the seas of earth, haul'd up at last and
    hawser'd tight,
Lies rusting, mouldering.

Now compare your analysis with the following, an extract from a student essay.

Whitman views a perishing human being as a model for suffering and loss: the victim loses his strength and abilities, is helpless, alone, neglected. His central image, a rotting ship, helps develop this theme because it is easily associated with a weakening body, an aging man or woman, or even, as the editors hint, the elderly Whitman himself. The image conveys not just the idea of a decaying object or thing, but a decaying person. It invites the reader to empathize, to imagine the analogy between ship and human being, both now impotent and forgotten.

Whitman's diction develops his theme. It makes the reader feel the tragedy of a person or ship perishing, of an outcast weak and abandoned. Like a ship rotting in "some unused lagoon," mired in stagnant water and cut off from the "seas of earth," so an aging man may be shut up in a nursing home or live alone, confined, separated from life. He is "anchor'd near the shore," cut off by time, space, and thought from the ships and men sailing the wide oceans. He is "dismasted . . . disabled, done"; like a "mouldering" ship that has lost its source of power, his age has cost him his Freudian source of energy—his libido. He is "dis<u>man</u>tled," unmanned. He is unable to make "voyages" of life and love from person to person and country to country, "free" to choose and "free" from cost or worry. The ship is no longer freshly painted and intact; the old man's skin is weathered, his body weakened. The "good gray poet" has become a "gray and batter'd ship."

Nor is there any returning to the days of old, for time has him "hauled up at last and hawser'd tight." The inevitable price of the years of "free voyages to all the seas of earth" is to become worn out, an empty hull to be dragged aside and secured to prevent drifting. Yet what is perhaps still worse about his decay is the lack of concern by others, for while his person cries out to be cared for—to stop the "rusting" and "mouldering"—he is alone. He is lonely but no one comes; he is feeble, but no one helps. The sluggish waters lapping against the hull are all that is heard.

Layers of meaning

Notice how the student's explication above proceeds. It finds three possible layers of meaning in the words—the image of the ship, of an aging man, and of the poet Whitman. It does not say the poem "is" one layer only or has one "message," but instead tries to find correspondences and similarities among these layers. And it argues for

16d

such correspondences by finding them embedded in the words. To put it in different terms, the explication unfolds each image to see how it may be read in relation to the ship, to an aging man, and, on occasion, to the poet. Still, the explication does not claim to be the complete or only interpretation of the poem. Explications are rarely if ever "complete." Here, indeed, the student could have done more with the sounds: Whitman's diminuendo in "*dismasted . . . disabled, done*" or his finality in "*haul*'d up *at* last and *haw*ser'd *tight*," to mention but one possibility. Nor does this explication preclude other readings with a somewhat different emphasis. Another student, having read about Whitman's last years, might unfold these meanings more fully than the writer of this essay has. And in fact, if a second student were to interpret the poem mainly as a picture of the poet's old age, that reading would supplement, not contradict, the first reading. The two readings would constitute hypotheses about the poem to be compared in relation to the evidence—the words of the text.

16d

Poems for comparison

Now, having read a poem and an explication, try working with the words of another of Whitman's poems. This one is concerned with youth, beginnings, fullness of power, and experience. Read it aloud and analyze it first for its layers of meaning—its playfulness with motion and speed, light and color, water and wind. Then juxtapose it to "The Dismantled Ship": what is the composite picture, and how is it composed by the contrasting images?

The Ship Starting

Lo, the unbounded sea,
On its breast a ship starting, spreading all sails, carrying even her
    moonsails,
The pennant is flying aloft as she speeds she speeds so stately—below
    emulous waves press forward,
They surround the ship with shining curving motions and foam.

This composite picture of youth and age, beginnings and endings, could just as easily be developed in a work quite unlike Whitman's two poems. Below is such a poem, by Emily Dickinson. In working with her words, you might begin by explicating *quiet Dust* and the connections between *Gentlemen and Ladies* and *Lads and Girls*. Then try to visualize how *Bloom and Bees / Exist an Oriental Circuit,* that is, live out a full cycle. After you have finished with Dickinson's poem, compare it with Whitman's two poems: what are the significant contrasts in the imagery and meanings?

> *This quiet Dust was Gentlemen and Ladies*
>
> This quiet Dust was Gentlemen and Ladies
> And Lads and Girls—
> Was laughter and ability and Sighing
> And Frocks and Curls.
>
> This Passive Place a Summer's nimble mansion
> Where Bloom and Bees
> Exist an Oriental Circuit
> Then cease, like these—

Recall the questions posed at the beginning of this chapter: How to understand our relationship to the work? How to share our experience of it most effectively with others? How to convince others that ours is a valid way of looking at the work? A suggestion: Begin with the words. For in and through them you have experienced "the noble accents" and "lucid, inescapable rhythms" you have known.

16d

EXERCISE 3

1. Keep a journal faithfully for at least a month, making at least two entries a week of 150 words each. Write on whatever aspects of literature you wish—how it's related to your experience, what ideas you find most interesting, why you like or dislike a particular work. At the end of the month, reread your entries with the following questions in mind: (1) Did you have any new insights or make any discoveries while writing? (2) Did writing about the literature increase your pleasure in it?

2. For an assigned work (preferably a longer one) try summarizing its parts, sections, or chapters at the end of each division. Then, after you have finished the work, reread your summaries with the following questions in mind: (1) Did the summarizing help you understand the whole section more clearly? (2) As you review your summaries, do you find you have a firmer grasp on the entire work?

3. Choose two poems that deal with the same theme—for example, love and loss, men and women misunderstanding each other, delight in a

natural setting or living creature, suffering and recovery, the passage from adolescence to adulthood. Write an analysis in which you first explicate each work and then compare the two as treatments of the theme.

4. Choose a short poem (no more than twenty-five lines) that you like. Then write as complete an explication of it as you can, unfolding every image as fully as possible and looking for the ways the images support and develop the theme. After you have finished, read your analysis with the following questions in mind: (1) Can you find images that you want to do still more with? (2) How much has your explication changed your understanding of or feelings about the poem?

5. Follow the instructions in number 4, above, but use the lyrics to a popular song (rock, country, or folk). Pose one question in addition to those listed in number 4: What happens to the lyrics when you consider the words without the music?

6. Choose a page of a short story or novel that you like and analyze it carefully with the following in mind: Do you find the kinds of images that you expect in poetry? If so, what are they and how are they used? If not, what evidence of craft or technique do you find? How, as far as you can determine, are these effects achieved? How do they affect you as a reader?

16d

For Further Reading

Comprone, Joseph J. "Literary Theory and Composition." *Teaching Composition: Twelve Bibliographical Essays*. Ed. Gary Tate. Fort Worth: Texas Christian UP, 1987. 291–330.

Deen, Rosemary. "An Interplay of Powers: Writing about Literature." *Only Connect: Uniting Reading and Writing*. Ed. Thomas Newkirk. Upper Montclair: Boynton/Cook, 1986. 174–86.

Lindberg, Gary. "Coming to Words: Writing as Process and the Reading of Literature." *Only Connect: Uniting Reading and Writing*. Ed. Thomas Newkirk. Upper Montclair: Boynton/Cook, 1986. 143–57.

PART V

The Research Paper

17

The Research Process

When we open a newspaper at the end of a busy day, we may not think that we are doing research, but we are. We are doing research as we scan the paper for reports about the mayor's latest conflict with the city council, or about the response of the stock market to the Federal Reserve Board's new monetary policy. We are doing research when we copy a recipe out of the food section, check the standings of our favorite team, read a movie review, or hunt through the classified ads for a good used lawn mower. Research is part of the texture of our lives. It answers one of our deepest needs as thinking human beings—our need for information.

Gathering information is not a mechanical task; on the contrary, it constantly calls forth our powers of judgment and evaluation. After we have seen a baseball game or a new movie, we seek out friends to discuss it with, newspaper accounts or reviews to read. Why? By considering the opinions of people around us, we come to understand our own judgments better. Which play was really the turning point in the game? Which actor's performance was central to the film's success? We question and rethink our ideas not only during a debate in a noisy cafeteria or a crowded bar, but also in our silent interaction with the printed opinions of others.

The urge to do research, then, is rooted not simply in our curiosity but in our desire to understand. Behind every fact that engages our attention lies our natural wish to comprehend its meaning, our impulse to fit it into a context or pattern. Writing papers based on research satisfies that impulse, but it does something more: through the process of gathering and evaluating information, it calls the writer into a kind of conversation with researchers who have preceded him or her. A research paper assignment is thus an invitation to become part of a

This chapter, the first of eight chapters on writing research papers, offers an overview of the research process and introduces the first issue that students and instructors alike must consider: the selection of an appropriate subject for research.

Resist the temptation to assign specific subjects for research in your classes. Such a practice not only deprives a student of the important experience of developing his or her own focus for the research paper, but also makes the entire research process artificial and unrealistic. Students who are researching subjects assigned to them by an instructor have no personal investment in the work they are doing; they are not impelled by the force that motivates all genuine researchers: the desire to answer a question, to know, to understand. Their efforts, even under the best of circumstances, cannot be more than halfhearted.

Unfortunately, some instructors feel that leaving the choice of research subjects up to individual students is an invitation to plagiarism. This need not be the case. The following approaches, used individually or together,

> QUICK REFERENCE: *Types of Research Projects*
>
> *The informative report*   Seeks to describe, explain, or analyze a specific aspect of a subject. Assimilates and focuses material in an original way in order to offer a new perspective on the topic.
>
> *The researched argument*   Attempts to persuade the reader to accept an original argument. Uses evidence from various sources to arrive at and then to support a judgment.

far-flung community of thoughtful men and women, sharing their concerns, agreeing and disagreeing with their opinions, reflecting and expanding upon their conclusions.

17a Thinking about your assignment

The starting point in planning a research project is understanding your instructor's assignment. Let's begin, therefore, by distinguishing between two different kinds of research papers, the *informative report* and the *researched argument*.

1. The informative report

The first type of research project, the informative report, attempts to describe, explain, or shed new light on a specific aspect of a subject. The writer of an informative report asks a question about this subject—a question, perhaps, that is somehow different from those that other people have asked—and answers it by collecting facts and viewpoints from various sources, by selecting whatever seems to be particularly significant or interesting, and by assimilating this information into a paper that focuses and presents it in an original way. The informative report is never a mere summary of what someone else has

make plagiarism too difficult to be worthwhile and—more important—help students appreciate the sequence of steps in the research process:

1. Establish at the outset a schedule of dates on which materials such as the following will be due: (a) a general subject area that the student is considering researching; (b) a tentatively restricted subject and a list of at least five sources of information that the student has examined; (c) a working bibliography of at least fifteen items; (d) the final restricted subject and a tentative thesis; (e) a set of sample note cards; (f) a tentative outline of the paper.
2. Indicate to students from the beginning that they will be required to submit *all* their research materials with the final paper, including all bibliography and note cards (those not actually used in writing the paper as well as those on which the paper is based), and all rough drafts of the paper.
3. Require each student to keep and submit a journal of his or her research steps, with a dated entry for each session spent working on the

said. Instead, it strongly bears the stamp of the researcher, both in the assertion that he or she makes about the subject and in the evidence that he or she chooses to support that assertion.

You will find an example of such a paper—Emmet Geary's "Recovery from the Florence Flood: A Masterpiece of Restoration"—in Chapter **21**. In this case the writer's assignment was to research any event from the 1960s and develop a paper that explored some specific aspect of that event. Like all researchers, Emmet began with a large subject—natural disasters—and only slowly zeroed in on a precise and manageable subject for investigation. The diagram on page 362 shows the stages by which he narrowed his subject.

Browsing among entries in the volumes of the *Readers' Guide to Periodical Literature* that span the 1960s (see **18c**), Emmet first moved from "disasters" to the narrower subject of "floods." One of the most destructive floods of the decade, he learned through his reading, was the flood of the Arno River that devastated the Italian city of Florence in 1966. Realizing that this subject was too broad to handle in a comprehensive or original way, Emmet posed a question about it: Was any aspect of this flood unusual? What caught his attention as he read articles about the flood were reports about the damage done to Florence's unique collection of art treasures from the Renaissance. But even this subject, he discovered with further reading, could be focused into a still narrower one for his paper: the *restoration* of the works of art damaged by the flood.

17a

Having arrived at this narrow subject, Emmet could now continue his research more efficiently, looking only for sources that dealt specifically with this topic and taking notes with a new sense of purpose and direction. The ultimate result was his tightly organized paper, which focuses on the unusual steps taken by professional restorers and concerned volunteers to save Florence's damaged treasures.

2.   The researched argument

The second type of research paper uses evidence to shape an original argument. Rather than collecting and assembling materials to describe or explain a subject, the researcher who is writing an argument uses research first to arrive at a judgment and then to defend that judgment before a reader.

paper. The journal should describe how the student went about searching for a subject, how he or she decided on a restricted subject, what sources of information were examined and why they were selected, and how he or she came to find a direction for the paper. Like any writer's journal, it should record the highs and lows of the research process, from the discovery of exactly the right piece of information needed to clinch an argument, to the frustrations of not being able to organize the final piles of notes effectively. Such a journal forces the student to reflect on and appreciate the stages of the research process, and it also helps the instructor more fully understand and more fairly evaluate each student's research efforts.

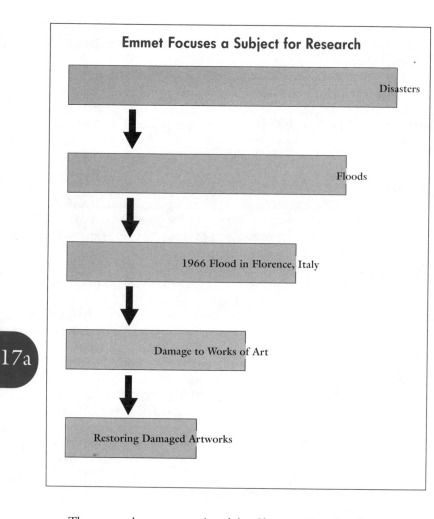

Emmet Focuses a Subject for Research

Disasters

Floods

1966 Flood in Florence, Italy

Damage to Works of Art

Restoring Damaged Artworks

17a

The research paper reprinted in Chapter **23**—Cyndi Lopardo's "Career versus Motherhood: The Debate over Education for Women at the Turn of the Century"—is an example of this second type of paper. Cyndi wanted to write about women and education, but beyond those ideas she had not defined a subject. Like Emmet, she began by reading broadly in search of a specific topic that would interest her. An article on the history of women's education in the *Encyclopedia of Edu-*

cation (see **18b**) aroused her interest in American higher education at the end of the nineteenth century, and particularly in the debate then raging over the appropriateness of rigorous academic programs for women. A bibliography at the end of the encyclopedia article sent Cyndi to two book-length histories of women's education in America, Thomas Woody's *A History of Women's Education in the United States* and Mabel Newcomer's *A Century of Higher Education for Women*.

Armed with the background information she acquired from reading the relevant portions of these two books, Cyndi next turned to the *Nineteenth Century Readers' Guide* (see **18c**) in search of a list of articles from the 1890s on the subject. Based on the articles she located there, she drew her own conclusions about the debate over higher education for women and tentatively formulated the argument she would present in her paper: that despite the increasing educational opportunities for women at the turn of the nineteenth century, much of society continued to regard higher education for women primarily as a means of enhancing roles within the home and family. The diagram on page 364 shows the stages by which Cyndi moved from her general interest in women's education to this specific argument.

3.   Shared features

This summary of Emmet's and Cyndi's research procedures has oversimplified the often slow and complicated process of identifying a workable subject, but it illustrates two features that are common to both the informative report and the researched argument.

A research paper makes an assertion

First, a good research paper is focused around a central assertion. You needn't panic if, as you start your research, you're not sure what your paper's central assertion is going to be, for the fact is that it's impossible to know what assertion you can make about a subject until you have done a considerable amount of reading. As you acquire more and more information, though, you should begin to formulate *possible* assertions for your paper. After each session of researching your subject, ask yourself the following questions:

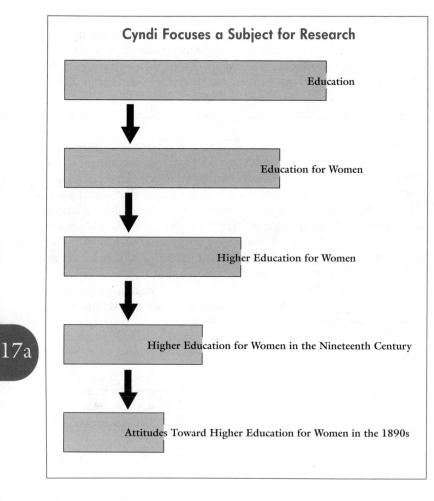

Cyndi Focuses a Subject for Research

Education

Education for Women

Higher Education for Women

Higher Education for Women in the Nineteenth Century

Attitudes Toward Higher Education for Women in the 1890s

1. What am I *now* able to assert about my subject?
2. What do I think I *might* be able to assert about my subject with further research?

Use the answers to these questions to assess your progress and to direct your next research efforts. The final assertion that you make about your subject—the assertion that unifies your paper—will take the form of a thesis statement, a sentence that states your subject and indicates the specific point you wish to make about it.

A research paper reflects its writer's originality

The second feature common to both the informative report and the researched argument is originality. You may think there is little room for your own originality as a writer in a paper that is based on what other people have written about a subject, but that isn't true. Every good research paper owes its success to the researcher's unique talents as a thinker and investigator. The more creatively you have thought about your subject, the more distinctive your paper's focus will be. The more thoroughly you have researched your subject, the more diverse the sources of information that your paper will bring together. In its final form, your research paper will gather and present information about your subject in a way not duplicated by anyone else who has written on it.

17b Thinking about a subject

If doing research is new to you, your first impulse may be to choose a topic that you already know well. Such a choice, however, is almost certain to rob your research of any interest or satisfaction, leaving you only with tedious and meaningless busywork. The purpose of research, after all, is not to document what you already know, but to discover what you do not know. As disturbing as it may sound at first, you are doing real research only if you do not know where it will lead.

17b

1. Be genuinely interested in your subject

The fundamental requirement for a topic to research is the same as that which should guide the choice of any subject for writing: your true interest in it. In a writing course, your instructor may leave the subject for your research paper entirely up to you or may allow you to choose from a list of subjects or a general subject area. Even if your instructor limits the range of subjects more narrowly, you should seek out a specific angle or focus that for some reason appeals to you.

Research is a process of discovery. You can participate in this process fully only if you select a subject that is a genuine question for you—a problem, a mystery, a tantalizing unknown quantity.

2. Be willing to search for a good subject

You may have been able to find a good subject for the other papers you have written in your composition class by turning to your personal experiences, your reading, or your entries in a journal. That will not be the case for a research paper. You will not be able to define a workable subject by sitting quietly at your desk and thinking deeply about the assignment. Instead, as the descriptions above of Emmet's and Cyndi's research procedures suggested, the process of identifying a potentially good subject for research begins with serious work in the library.

Although they were writing different kinds of papers, both Emmet and Cyndi began their hunt for a good subject in the same way: by looking for ideas and inspiration first in general sources of information. Emmet, searching for a topic from the 1960s, browsed through articles listed in the *Readers' Guide* until something in the titles he read attracted his attention. He did not complete the process of narrowing his subject—from disasters, to floods, to Florence, to the destruction of artworks, to the restoration of those works—in a single session in the library; instead, that process extended over several days of reading articles and thinking about them.

Cyndi, too, started with general reading—in her case, an encyclopedia in the field of education. When the topic of women's education in the nineteenth century caught her eye, she pursued it first by examining two general histories of women's education and then by looking at specific articles on the topic that were published at the turn of the century. Only after reading a number of these articles was Cyndi certain that there was enough material here to support an entire paper on the attitudes toward women's education in the 1890s.

The point is this: a good topic for a research paper doesn't fall ready-made into one's lap; instead, it evolves slowly, as the researcher becomes more and more familiar with the subject area. The process of finding such a topic demands patience and persistence.

17b

3. Be prepared to make changes in your subject

The process of writing usually alters a writer's conception of his or her topic. Sometimes the topic becomes narrower, as the writer becomes aware of the need to balance completeness with limitations on length. Sometimes it changes focus, as the writer thinks of related subjects and ideas. In research, many of these modifications of your topic will occur before you begin writing, during the research process itself.

As you start to explore a tentative subject, you must be ready to accept changes in your original plan. You should expect your research to lead in directions you had not anticipated, to new sources of information and new ideas that will inevitably affect your original conception of your topic. The opinions of others will modify your early ideas, leaving you with new perspectives to consider. On other occasions, unfortunately, you may find that the libraries available to you do not have enough material on your subject from which to construct a serious research paper, and you will be forced to modify your original subject radically or to abandon it altogether. Such is the life of the dedicated researcher—a combination of excitement and frustration, of discovery and disillusionment.

17c

17c Thinking about your reader

Professional researchers write with a keen awareness of their potential readers. Typically, scholars begin a research project with a specific journal in mind to which they plan eventually to submit the finished project for publication. They know what sorts of people read that journal and what those people probably already know about the subject. They also know whether they are elaborating on someone else's research or contradicting it, and as a result they have a fair sense of the extent to which their work will be regarded as innovative, controversial, or revolutionary.

It's very possible that your own professional work after college will place you in a similar situation. Whether you do research for publication in a professional journal or for in-house distribution to colleagues in a business setting, you will be writing for a community of readers whose potential reactions to your research will be constantly in your mind. For this assignment, however, your sole audience is likely to be your instructor. How can awareness of this audience affect what you write?

Two questions about audience that were presented in Chapter **3** may guide you in this situation as well: What does your reader already know about this subject? What else do you want your reader to know? If, in the case of your instructor, you're unsure about how to answer these questions, you should plan to discuss your paper with him or her as it evolves. Find out what your instructor knows about your subject and what aspects of your research he or she finds particularly intriguing. Use such discussions to direct your research efforts and to shape your paper, so that in its final form it responds to your instructor's interests and questions.

17d Planning the long paper

Perhaps the most disconcerting requirement of a research paper is its length—often five or more times longer than most of the other papers you have written in your composition class. Writing a long paper that draws on material from different sources is good practice in the kinds of writing tasks that people in many professions are called on to complete—business reports, legal briefs, case histories, and feature articles, to name just a few. But such writing makes demands that shorter, less formal essays do not.

1. Leave enough time

The finest library facilities and the best ideas for a research paper will not be of much use to you if you do not leave enough time to work on your paper. You may have been able to write a first draft of your other essays in just a few sittings—one devoted to exploring the subject, one to outlining and planning, one to composing. That approach, however, will not be sufficient for a serious research paper, which usually involves at least a few weeks of preliminary work even before you begin writing, and several composing sessions as you assimilate and structure the material you have accumulated.

You can never begin researching too early, for you must be prepared for all the setbacks that accompany research, ranging from the topic that grows increasingly complex (or that fails to develop at all) to the crucial book that you discover is missing from your library. And the task of fusing your final set of notes into a coherent whole may also be more difficult than you expect. The most important rule for research, then, is to plan ahead, leaving yourself plenty of time to gather information and several sessions for writing and revising. The research paper completed in a single coffee-soaked night is not likely to be very successful, no matter how thorough the research on which it is based.

2.   Understand the research process

The research process involves a number of steps, including identifying a subject, collecting information, selecting the material you want to use, assimilating it into a coherent, focused piece of writing, and accurately documenting your sources. To work efficiently in each of these stages, you need to understand their relation to one another and to the research process as a whole. Before you begin to work on your paper, therefore, you should at least skim through the seven chapters that follow.

17d

Locating information and taking notes

The first step in composing a research paper, of course, is gathering information. For many college writing purposes, that will mean doing substantial research in a library. You can't understand or focus your topic until you have a firm grasp of what others have written about the subject. Chapters **18** and **19** will discuss some important sources of information in the library and some strategies for taking effective notes from the material you find.

Assimilating materials and avoiding plagiarism

By definition, research draws on the work of others. One of the keys to composing a successful research paper is being able to integrate the fruits of research into your paper, smoothly incorporating the information you have collected into your own prose. A second key to successful writing that is based on research is distinguishing between the legitimate and illegitimate use of other people's ideas and words in your paper. Presenting such material as your own, whether deliberately or accidentally, is a serious offense known as plagiarism. Chapter **20** will deal with the artful—and accurate—use of these materials in your paper.

Using standard methods of documentation

Your instructor will no doubt specify which style of documentation to use to indicate your sources of information. This book presents three of the most widely used documentation methods. The first, discussed in Chapter **19**, is the method advocated by the Modern Language Association and used in literary study and many other humanities fields. The second, described in Chapter **22**, is prescribed by the American Psychological Association and is widely used in the social sciences. The third method, involving endnote citations, is less widely used today than formerly but is still the norm in some disciplines; it is presented in Chapter **24**. Chapters **21** and **23** illustrate MLA and APA documentation with the complete research papers written by Emmet Geary and Cyndi Lopardo.

17d 3. Be prepared for the recursiveness of the research process

Chapter **1** described writing as a recursive rather than a linear process, that is, a process whose stages are often cyclical rather than sequential. The same is true for the research process. You can avoid some of the frustration of doing research by preparing for the fact that composing a research paper inevitably involves backtracking: abandoning an unworkable subject and beginning anew; discarding notes that prove worthless and searching for better ones; rethinking your paper's focus again and again; returning to the library, even after you have begun writing the paper, to verify a quotation or to look for just one more source. When you feel caught in a dizzying whirl of contradictory note cards, half-completed paragraphs, citations to still unexamined sources, and maddeningly arbitrary documentation rules, you'll know that you have become a true researcher at last.

For Further Reading

Ford, James E., and Dennis R. Perry. "Research Paper Instruction in the Undergraduate Writing Program." *College English* 44 (1982): 825–31.

Grasso, Mary Ellen. "The Research Paper: Life Centered." *College English* 40 (1978): 83–86.

Larson, Richard L. "The 'Research Paper' in the Writing Course: A Non-Form of Writing." *College English* 44 (1982): 811–16.

Marshall, Colleen. "A System for Teaching College Freshmen To Write a Research Paper." *College English* 40 (1978): 87–89.

Schwegler, Robert A., and Linda K. Shamoon. "The Aims and Process of the Research Paper." *College English* 44 (1982): 817–24.

18 *The Library*

When most people think of libraries, they think of books—and with good reason, for books are the most visible of any library's holdings. When you use a library for serious research, however, you need to be familiar with the many other kinds of materials available—especially with standard reference works, magazines, journals, newspapers, and government publications. Since most American libraries use the same basic system for filing and organizing materials, you will find that the guidelines below will apply to almost any library that you have access to. But you should remember that this book offers only an introduction to library use. To get the most out of your library, you will have to discover its own particular strengths—its large microfilm holdings, for example, or its excellent collection of rare books. You will need to know where various holdings are kept and what library policies govern their use. You can learn about these and other features of your library through the official tours that many college libraries offer at the beginning of the term. Or you can give yourself a tour. Ask at the main desk for a map of the building and its features, or simply wander from floor to floor at a leisurely pace, identifying the materials available and noting their locations. Becoming familiar with the arrangement and system of your library is your first task as a serious researcher, one that will help to make your work more efficient and satisfying.

18a

18a The library catalog

The catalog of a library is the main index to its holdings. All the books, reference works, periodicals, and other materials in the library's

When many students think of a library, they think first of books, every library's most visible asset. Professional researchers, on the other hand, know that much of their material will come from other sources. This chapter, therefore, balances the traditional material about locating books in the library with extensive coverage of reference works and periodical indexes, as well as a detailed discussion of data-base searches and an introduction to the use of government documents. Of course, all of this material will need to be adapted to suit the library or libraries in which students will be working; above all, they will need to know where to locate the items described in the text and what library policies govern their use.

<table>
<tr><td colspan="2">QUICK REFERENCE: *Major Library Resources*</td></tr>
<tr><td>*Library catalog*</td><td>An on-line or card catalog that indexes a library's book and periodical holdings. Arranged alphabetically by author, title, and subject.</td></tr>
<tr><td>*Standard reference works*</td><td>Encyclopedias, dictionaries, indexes, and bibliographies providing facts on a large variety of subjects and lists of additional sources.</td></tr>
<tr><td>*Periodical indexes*</td><td>Subject and author indexes to newspapers, scholarly journals, and popular magazines.</td></tr>
<tr><td>*On-line and CD-ROM data bases*</td><td>Frequently updated data banks offering instant computerized access to millions of pieces of information in a wide range of disciplines.</td></tr>
<tr><td>*Government documents*</td><td>Information, on a variety of topics, published by the federal government in pamphlet, report, or monograph form. Indexed by subject in the *Monthly Catalog of United States Government Publications*.</td></tr>
</table>

18a

collection are listed alphabetically in either a card catalog or an on-line (that is, computerized) system.

1. Using a card catalog

In a card catalog, each book that the library holds is listed on a set of three-by-five-inch cards filed alphabetically in at least three different places: under its author's name (under each author's name if there are more than one); under its title; and under the subject or subjects it covers. In some libraries, author and title cards are collected in a single alphabetical catalog, while subject cards are filed separately, also in alphabetical order.

Reading catalog cards

Catalog cards, like those illustrated on page 374, contain a good deal of potentially important information, including the publication date of a book, the number of its pages, and notes about features such as indexes and illustrations in the book. The more you use the card catalog, the more skilled you will become in assessing this information before you actually examine the book itself. When you identify a book that you wish to look at, make a note of its *call number,* also found on the catalog card. The call number, which is based on a nationally used classification system, is your guide to the location of the book in your library. Two principal systems of classification are used by American libraries: the Dewey Decimal System (a numerical system) and the Library of Congress System (an alphabetical classification). At your library's main desk, you can get further information about the system your library follows. If your library has open stacks—that is, if library patrons are allowed to browse through the shelves and select books themselves—you will also find information there about the location of books throughout the library.

18a

Locating books

When you want to know where a specific book is located in your library, the author or title card will lead you to it fastest. When you don't know authors or titles, look through the cards under the subject

Call number

```
305.406                                    Title card
M383
S          The sound of our own voices: women's
           study clubs 1860–1910

    Martin, Theodora Penny.
        The sound of our own voices: women's study
    clubs 1860–1910 / Theodora Penny Martin. Boston:
    Beacon Press, c1987. xiv, 254 p., (16) p. of plates:
    photos. 24 cm.
```

```
305.406                                    Subject card
M383
S          Women--Education--United States--
           History

    Martin, Theodora Penny.
        The sound of our own voices: women's study
    clubs 1860–1910 / Theodora Penny Martin. Boston:
    Beacon Press, c1987. xiv, 254 p., (16) p. of plates:
    photos. 24 cm.
```

```
305.406                                    Author card
M383
S

    Martin, Theodora Penny. ————————————        Author's name
        The sound of our own voices: women's study ——  Title
    clubs 1860–1910 / Theodora Penny Martin. Boston:
    Beacon Press, c1987. xiv, 254 p., (16) p. of plates: —  Publisher and
    photos. 24 cm.                                          date of
                                                            publication
        Includes index. Bibliography: p. 227–239. ISBN  Description
    0807067105: $25.00                                      of book

    1. Women—Education—United States—History.
    2. Continuing education—United States—History. ——  Also indexed
    3. Women—United States—Societies and clubs—             under these
    History. I. Title.                                      headings
```

18a

Catalog Cards

As this illustration indicates, the author card is the primary catalog card. The other two cards differ only in the additional headings—for subject and title—that have been added to them.

you are interested in. Since both the Dewey Decimal System and the Library of Congress System are based on subject matter, you will usually find that the books your library has on a particular subject are shelved together. You can use the subject cards, therefore, not only as a listing of the library's holdings on a subject but also as a guide to the appropriate section of the book stacks. If your library has open stacks, some browsing around in this area will usually lead you to a number of useful books. Feel free to pull down from the shelves any books that look interesting, but respect your library's policies about reshelving books. To avoid the chaos created by accidental misshelving, many libraries ask that you do not put books back yourself, but instead leave them on a table or at some other designated place for library staff members to reshelve.

2. Using an on-line catalog

Increasingly, libraries are developing computer systems that enable patrons to bypass the card catalog and locate books and other materials simply by typing the author or title into a computer terminal, which then displays all of the information normally found on a card. Some computer systems also make it possible to search for books by subject. If your library has cataloged its holdings in an on-line system, you should definitely learn how to use it, for it will save you valuable time.

On-line cataloging systems vary widely, but as the illustration on page 376 indicates, the typical on-line catalog is designed above all for ease of use. Often, as shown, you begin with a computer menu (screen 1) that permits you to look up a work by entering its author or title or to request a list of works related to a subject area. If you wish to search the library's holdings for books on a specific subject, for example, you select *subject* from the menu and are prompted to indicate as precisely as possible the subject you are interested in. The computer will then display brief information about relevant titles in the library's collection (screen 2). By entering another command, you can obtain more detailed information about any one of the titles, as well as the call number of the book and its status—noncirculating, available, or already checked out (screen 3).

18a

Because on-line cataloging systems vary from library to library, students should realize that the on-line catalog that they have access to will likely operate somewhat differently from the one described here. The purpose of the illustration in this section is to demystify on-line cataloging by demonstrating how to access such a system and by emphasizing the point that on-line catalogs are designed to be easy to use.

Screen 1: Menu indicates types of searches possible

```
Welcome to ILLINET Online at DePaul University

  Select Type of Search
  - - - - - - - - - - - - - - - - - - - - - - - - - - - - - - - - -
   1. Subject
   2. Title
   3. Author
   4. Author AND Title
   5. Music
   6. Call number, ISBN, etc.
   7. Direct command mode

TO START: Enter a number from above and press <ENTER>
```

Screen 2: Brief information on relevant titles

```
Subject Search: WOMEN--EDUCATION--UNITED STATES--
                              HISTORY
No. of Items: 2

  1. TITLE:The sound of our own voices : women's
           study clubs 1860-1910/1987
     AUTHOR:Martin, Theodora Penny.

  2. TITLE:Woman's education begins : the rise of
           the women's colleges. 1971
     AUTHOR:Boas, Louise (Schutz)
- - - - - - -Press <ENTER> after making choice - - - - - - -
```

18a

Screen 3: Full information about one title

```
Subject Search: WOMEN--EDUCATION--UNITED STATES--
                              HISTORY

  CALL NO: To see the call number, enter L
    TITLE: The sound of our own voices : women's
           study clubs 1860-1910
   AUTHOR: Martin,Theodora Penny.
     PUBL: Boston : Beacon Press,
     DATE: 1987

  SUBJECT: Women--Education--United States--
           History--18th century.
           Continuing education--United States--
           History--19th century.
           Women--United States--Societies and
           clubs--History--19th century.

     ISBN: 0807067105:
    RID #: ocm15654352    (This is not a call number)
 CONTENTS: Bibliography: p. 227-239.
    NOTES: Includes index.
   FORMAT: xiv, 254 p., (16) p. of plates :
           photos. ; 24 cm.
- - - - - - -Press <ENTER> after making choice - - - - - - -

? - Help               G - Go back
M - Main idea          T - Try new subject
==> -                  L - Location/Call no.
```

Using an On-line Catalog

18b Standard reference works

You can use the library catalog to locate not only individual books by a specific author or on a particular subject but also the standard reference works owned by your library—encyclopedias, dictionaries, indexes, and bibliographies. Your personal library no doubt includes a number of reference books such as a dictionary and a desk encyclopedia; a college or public library, however, may own hundreds of specialized and useful reference works. These works fall into two general categories: books that offer facts (usually in the form of compact essays on various subjects) and books that provide bibliographies (lists of other books and articles on a given subject). As we saw in Chapter **17**, reference books in the first category are a good starting place for your research efforts because the overview of a subject that they provide will often include references to a host of interesting subtopics ideal for further exploration. Reference books in the second category will lead you to further sources of information as your research efforts begin in earnest.

Reference works, like other books, are shelved according to call number, but most libraries conveniently place their reference books together in a single section of the library, or even in a separate reference room. (The catalog listing will indicate whether that is your library's practice.) As you become familiar with the reference works in your library, you may want to keep your own list or card file of the sources that you have found especially useful, so that you can locate them quickly for future research work. Skill in using your library's reference collection, like skill in most other areas of life, will come from frequent practice.

What follows is a list of some standard reference works, grouped by type and subject. You will no doubt find many more in your library.

Guides to reference materials

> *Guide to Reference Books*
> *Guide to the Use of Books and Libraries*
> *The Reader's Adviser*

18b

General information

Collier's Encyclopedia
Dictionary of the History of Ideas
Encyclopaedia Britannica
Encyclopedia Americana
New Columbia Encyclopedia

Gazetteers and atlases

Columbia-Lippincott Gazetteer of the World
National Geographic Atlas of the World
Rand McNally Atlas of World History
The Times Atlas of the World

Reference books for special subjects

Art and architecture

Bryan's Dictionary of Painters and Engravers.
Encyclopedia of World Art.
Haggar, Reginald C. *Dictionary of Art Terms.*
Hamlin, T. F. *Architecture through the Ages.*
Myers, Bernard S., ed. *Encyclopedia of Painting.*
Zboinski, A., and L. Tyszynski. *Dictionary of Architecture and Building Trades.*

Biography

American Men and Women of Science. Includes scholars in the physical, biological, and social sciences.
Current Biography. Monthly since 1940, with brief bibliographic entries and an annual cumulative index.
Dictionary of American Biography. 20 vols. and supplements; bibliographic entries at the end of each article.
Dictionary of National Biography (British). 22 vols. and supplements; each article accompanied by a bibliography.

Directory of American Scholars.

James, Edward T., and Janet W. James, eds. *Notable American Women, 1607–1950.* Has bibliographic entries.

National Cyclopedia of American Biography. Includes supplements.

Webster's New Biographical Dictionary.

Who's Who (British), *Who's Who in America,* and *International Who's Who.* Brief accounts of living men and women; frequently revised.

Who's Who of American Women. 1958–.

Classics

Avery, C. B., ed. *New Century Classical Handbook.*

Hammond, N. G. L., and H. H. Scullard, eds. *Oxford Classical Dictionary.*

Harvey, Paul, ed. *Oxford Companion to Classical Literature.*

Current events

Americana Annual. 1923–. Annual supplement to the *Encyclopedia Americana.*

Britannica Book of the Year. 1938–. Annual supplement to the *Encyclopaedia Britannica;* some entries have a brief bibliography.

Facts on File. 1941–.

Statesman's Year Book. 1864–. A statistical and historical annual giving current information (and brief bibliographies) about countries of the world.

World Almanac. 1968–.

18b

Economics and commerce

Coman, E. T. *Sources of Business Information.* A bibliography.

Greenwald, Douglas, et al. *McGraw-Hill Dictionary of Modern Economics.* Has bibliographic references.

Historical Statistics of the United States: Colonial Times to 1970. Includes indexes and bibliographies.

International Bibliography of Economics. 1952–.

Munn, Glenn G. *Encyclopedia of Banking and Finance.* Has bibliographic entries.

Sloan, Harold S., and Arnold Zurcher. *A Dictionary of Economics.*

Statistical Abstract of the United States. 1897–.

Wyckham, Robert G. *Images and Marketing: A Selected and Annotated Bibliography.*

Education

Burke, Arvid J., and Mary A. Burke. *Documentation in Education.*

Deighton, Lee C., ed. *Encyclopedia of Education.* Has bibliographic entries.

Husen, Torsten, and T. Neville Postlethwaite, eds. *International Encyclopedia of Education.*

Knowles, Asa S. *International Encyclopedia of Higher Education.*

Mitzel, Harold E., ed. *Encyclopedia of Educational Research.*

World Survey of Education.

Film

18b

Bawden, Liz-Anne, ed. *Oxford Companion to Film.*

International Encyclopedia of Film.

History

Adams, James T., ed. *Dictionary of American History.* A bibliography accompanies each article.

American Historical Association: Guide to Historical Literature.

Cambridge Ancient History. Bibliographic footnotes.

Cambridge Medieval History. Bibliographic footnotes.

Langer, William L., ed. *Encyclopedia of World History.*

Martin, Michael R., et al. *An Encyclopedia of Latin-American History.*

Morris, Richard B., and Graham W. Irwin, eds. *Harper Encyclopedia of the Modern World.*

New Cambridge Modern History. Bibliographic footnotes.

Literature

General

Fleischmann, Wolfgang Bernard, ed. *Encyclopedia of World Literature in the Twentieth Century.* Brief bibliographies.

Grigson, Geoffrey. *The Concise Encyclopedia of Modern World Literature.* Brief bibliographic entries.

Leach, Maria, and Jerome Fried, eds. *Funk & Wagnall's Standard Dictionary of Folklore, Mythology, and Legend.*

MacCulloch, John A., et al. *Mythology of All Races.* Bibliography at end of each volume.

Preminger, Alex, F. J. Warnke, and O. B. Hardison, eds. *Princeton Encyclopedia of Poetry and Poetics.* A brief bibliography accompanies each article.

British

Baugh, A. C., et al. *A Literary History of England.* Has bibliographic entries.

Drabble, Margaret, ed. *Oxford Companion to English Literature.*

Sampson, George. *Concise Cambridge History of English Literature.*

Watson, George, ed. *New Cambridge Bibliography of English Literature.*

Wilson, F. P., and Bonamy Dobree, eds. *Oxford History of English Literature.* Excellent bibliographic essays at the end of each volume.

North American

Hart, J. D. *Oxford Companion to American Literature.*

Leary, Lewis. *Articles on American Literature.*

Spiller, Robert E., et al. *Literary History of the United States.* Entries include bibliographic essays.

Toye, William, ed. *Oxford Companion to Canadian Literature.*

Music and dance

Apel, Willi. *Harvard Dictionary of Music.* Has brief bibliographic entries.

Beaumont, Cyril W. *A Bibliography of Dancing.*

De Mille, Agnes. *The Book of the Dance.*

Ewen, David. *The World of Twentieth Century Music.* Brief bibliographic entries.

Grove, George. *Dictionary of Music and Musicians.* This work and the *Harvard Dictionary of Music* are the authorities in the field. Excellent bibliographies.

Hanna, Judith Lynne. *To Dance Is Human.*

Orrey, Leslie, ed. *Encyclopedia of Opera.*

Scholes, P. A. *Oxford Companion to Music.* Includes bibliographies.

Thompson, Oscar. *International Cyclopedia of Music and Musicians.* Brief bibliographies.

Westrup, J. A., ed. *New Oxford History of Music.* Includes bibliographies.

Philosophy

Copleston, Frederick. *A History of Western Philosophy.* Bibliography at end of each volume.

Edwards, Paul, ed. *Encyclopedia of Philosophy.* Bibliographies.

Urmson, J. O. *Concise Encyclopedia of Western Philosophy and Philosophers.* Brief bibliography at end of volume.

Political science

Levy, Leonard W., ed. *Encyclopedia of the American Constitution.*

Morgenthau, Hans. *Politics among Nations.*

Political Handbook of the World. 1927–.

Smith, Edward C., and A. J. Zurcher, eds. *Dictionary of American Politics.*

White, Carl M., et al. *Sources of Information in the Social Sciences.*

Psychology

Beigel, Hugo. *Dictionary of Psychology and Related Fields.*

Corsini, Raymond J., ed. *Encyclopedia of Psychology.*

Drever, James. *Dictionary of Psychology.*

Gregory, Richard L., ed. *Oxford Companion to the Mind.*

The Harvard List of Books in Psychology. Annotated.

Psychological Abstracts. 1927–.

Wolman, Benjamin B., ed. *International Encyclopedia of Psychiatry, Psychology, Psychoanalysis, and Neurology.*

Religion

Buttrick, G. A., et al. *Interpreter's Dictionary of the Bible: An Illustrated Encyclopedia.* Has bibliographic entries.

Cross, F. L., and Elizabeth A. Livingstone. *Oxford Dictionary of the Christian Church.* Has brief bibliographies.

Eliade, Mircea, ed. *Encyclopedia of Religion.* Brief bibliographic entries.

Encyclopedia of Islam.

Encyclopedia Judaica.

Hastings, James, ed. *Encyclopedia of Religion and Ethics.*

Jackson, S. M., et al. *New Schaff-Herzog Encyclopedia of Religious Knowledge.*

Malalasekera, G. P., ed. *Encyclopedia of Buddhism.*

New Catholic Encyclopedia.

18b

Science

General

McGraw-Hill Encyclopedia of Science and Technology.

Meyers, Robert A., ed. *Encyclopedia of Physical Science and Technology.*

Newman, James R., et al. *Harper Encyclopedia of Science.* Brief bibliographic entries.

Van Nostrand's Scientific Encyclopedia.

Life sciences

Benthall, Jonathan. *Ecology in Theory and Practice*. Includes bibliographic references.

De Bell, Garrett, ed. *The Environmental Handbook*. Bibliography at end of volume.

Gray, Peter, ed. *Encyclopedia of the Biological Sciences*. Brief bibliographic entries.

Reich, Warren T., ed. *Encyclopedia of Bioethics*.

Smith, Roger C., and W. Malcolm Reid, eds. *Guide to the Literature of the Life Sciences*.

Physical sciences

International Dictionary of Physics and Electronics.

Kemp, D. A. *Astronomy and Astrophysics: A Bibliographical Guide*.

Larousse Encyclopedia of the Earth: Geology, Paleontology, and Prehistory.

Universal Encyclopedia of Mathematics.

Van Nostrand's International Encyclopedia of Chemical Science.

18b ### Sociology and anthropology

Biennial Review of Anthropology.

International Bibliography of Sociology. 1951–.

Sills, David L., ed. *International Encyclopedia of the Social Sciences*. Each article followed by a bibliography.

Social Work Year Book. 1929–. Includes bibliographies.

Theater

Bordman, Gerald M. *Oxford Companion to American Theatre*.

Encyclopedia of World Theater.

Gassner, John, and Edward Quin, eds. *Reader's Encyclopedia of World Drama*.

Hartnoll, Phyllis, ed. *Oxford Companion to the Theatre*. Bibliography accompanies each article.

Exercise 1 (page 385)

This exercise and the following one have two objectives: to give students the experience of locating standard reference works in their library and to have them evaluate the information that specific works provide. Results in this exercise will vary, depending on which subjects students chose to look up, but the *Encyclopedia Americana* usually seems to offer the best combination of full coverage and useful bibliographies.

Consider making this exercise the subject of a one- or two-page report or adapting it for use as a small-group project. Each group might be given three or four terms from the list provided and might be asked to add two or three terms of its own; have the groups make brief oral presentations on their findings, and compare the results.

EXERCISE 1

Choose several of the subjects below and read the entries about them in *Collier's Encyclopedia,* the *Encyclopedia Americana,* and the *Encyclopaedia Britannica* (check both sections, the *Micropaedia* and the more detailed *Macropaedia*). Which encyclopedia's coverage seems generally most complete? Which one seems most up-to-date? Which supplies the best bibliographies of additional sources?

1. aging
2. crime
3. cocaine
4. Detroit
5. fencing
6. greenhouse effect
7. humor
8. Jerusalem
9. Navajo/Navaho
10. Normans
11. Frances Perkins
12. sextant
13. surfing
14. Louis Tiffany
15. trademark

EXERCISE 2

Choose one of the subject areas on pages 378–84 and locate in your library two of the listed reference works. Write a brief evaluative comparison of the two works, considering such elements as focus, arrangement, depth of coverage, and format. Identify at least one useful feature that is unique to each work.

18c

18c Indexes to periodicals

Many students new to research rely heavily—or even exclusively—on books as their sources of information. Such a strategy has its pitfalls. For one thing, books are not usually as well focused as a narrowly defined research topic, and finding the precise information you need in a towering stack of general books on a subject can become an exercise in frustration. Moreover, the time involved in producing a book means that current information—the most recent developments in Middle Eastern politics, for example, or the latest advances in AIDS research—may not be available in book form. To find such information, in addition to material on virtually any other kind of topic, you can turn to articles in periodicals.

Exercise 2

Consider adapting this exercise in one of the following ways:

1. Assign each student a different major reference work and ask him or her to produce a one-page descriptive and evaluative analysis, including the work's call number, its organization, the scope of its contents, and any special features it offers. Collect the papers and make a photocopied set for each student to keep as an introductory guide to selected reference works in your library.
2. Divide the class into groups and have each group examine and evaluate the reference works listed in one of the subject areas on pages 378–84. Which works are available in your library? Which offer the broadest coverage? Which are easiest to use? Which provide bibliographies? Have the groups report on their findings in oral presentations to the entire class, or have each group produce a one- or two-page written analysis of the works it examined that could be photocopied and distributed to everyone in the class for future reference.

Just as the library catalog provides an author, title, and subject index to your library's book holdings, periodical indexes offer a fast and easy way of locating articles in magazines, journals, and newspapers. Usually, you will find your library's periodical indexes grouped together in the reference collection. It is important to know the scope of at least the major indexes described below because they cover different kinds of periodicals. However, since many of these indexes are produced by the same publisher in similar formats, you will discover that after you have become familiar with the layout of one, you can move easily to the others. For example, note the similarities in form of the indexes illustrated on page 387. The distinguishing feature of each of these indexes is not the way it arranges its contents, but the distinctive type of periodical it covers.

Once you have used indexes to locate potentially useful articles on the subject you are researching, determine whether or not your library subscribes to the journals you need by looking them up in the library catalog. Most libraries bind back issues of periodicals like books and shelve them together in a periodical room or by call number among books in the stacks. Current issues are usually on display in a periodicals reading room. For assistance in locating the periodicals you need, ask at your library's main desk.

18c

If your library does not have a specific periodical that you need, ask at the Interlibrary Loan department about acquiring a photocopy of the article you're interested in from another library. Most libraries offer this service for a small charge. However, you should try not to depend on articles that you must order in this way. Unless your library can obtain copies of articles by fax, the ordering process can take several weeks, and the article, when it arrives, may turn out to be of less value to you than its title promised.

General periodical indexes

Readers' Guide to Periodical Literature. 1900–.
An author and subject index to more than two hundred magazines of general interest, such as *Consumer Reports, Ms., Newsweek, Sports Illustrated,* and *Popular Electronics.* Bound volumes cover a year or more; paperback supplements keep the index current usually to within a few weeks.

Readers' Guide

TELEVISION AND CHILDREN — Subject heading
    See also
      Action for Children's Television
      Cable television—Children's programs
      Television advertising and children — Cross-references
      Television broadcasting—Children's programs
Filling the news gap for children [booklet produced by Action
  for Children's Television] il *Children Today* 17:32 Mr/Ap
  '88
Like parent, like child: turn off the tube, turn on the exercise. — Title of article
  D. Groves. il *American Health* 7:44 Jl/Ag '88
My friend the television [viewing preferences of children
  with troubled home life; study by June Tangney] G. W.
  Bracey. il *Phi Delta Kappan* 70:258-9 N '88
Taming the TV monster. J. K. Rosemond. il *Better Homes
  and Gardens* 66:26-7 S '88
Today's TV toys. L. Gilman. il *American Health* 7:82 D — Author
  '88
TV: when to turn it on—and off. J. David. il *Good* — Title of periodical
  Housekeeping 207:128+ S '88 — Volume and pages
Video violence. R. K. Ross. por *Essence* 19:140 Je '88 — Date
What TV teaches children about politics. R. Coles. il *TV
  Guide* 36:2-4 F 6-12 '88
TELEVISION AND COPYRIGHT *See* Copyright—Broadcasting
  rights
TELEVISION AND HISTORY
It's The American experience—but something's missing. T.
  J. Fleming. il *TV Guide* 36:30-3 S 24-30 '88

Humanities Index

Television and children
    See also
      Television programs—Children's programs
Calming children's television fears: Mr. Rogers vs. The
  Incredible Hulk. J. Cantor and others. bibl *J Broadcast
  Electron Media* 32:271-88 Summ '88
Children's perceptions of television reality. P. Nikken
  and A. L. Peeters. *J Broadcast Electron Media* 32:441-52
  Fall '88
Children's representations of television and real-life
  stories. B. Watkins. bibl *Commun Res* 15:159-84 Ap
  '88

Social Sciences Index

Television and children
    See also
      Television advertising and children
      Television and youth
      Television programs—Children's programs
Aspects of the family and children's television viewing
  content preferences. J. P. Tangney. bibl *Child Dev*
  59:1070-9 Ag '88
Children's representations of television and real-life
  stories. B. Watkins. bibl *Commun Res* 15:159-84 Ap
  '88
Children's television-viewing frequency: individual differences and demographic correlates. J. P. Tangney
  and S. Feshbach. bibl *Pers Soc Psychol Bull* 14:145-58

18c

Periodical Indexes

Humanities Index and *Social Sciences Index.* 1974–.
Formerly a single index, published as the *Social Sciences and Humanities Index* from 1965 to 1974, and as the *International Index* from 1907 to 1965. The major general index to professional journals in the humanities (for example, *American Literature, Harvard Theological Review, Journal of Philosophy, New England Quarterly*) and the social sciences (for example, *Crime and Delinquency, Geographical Review, Journal of Economic Theory, Political Science Quarterly*). Same format as the *Readers' Guide,* though usually somewhat less current.

New York Times Index. 1913–.
An invaluable subject and author index to one of the world's great newspapers. Provides a brief summary of most articles, together with a citation to issue date, section, and page. Most libraries carry the *New York Times* on microfilm; for the location of microfilms in your library and instructions on their use, ask at the main desk or in the reference room. If you live in an area served by another major newspaper, your library may also have an index for it that will help you find information on significant current and past events in your community.

18c

Nineteenth Century Readers' Guide. 1890–99.
A two-volume supplement to the *Readers' Guide,* produced in the same format.

Poole's Index to Periodical Literature. 1802–1906.
A six-volume index of nineteenth-century periodicals by subject only. For authors, consult the *Cumulative Author Index for Poole's Index to Periodical Literature,* ed. C. Edward Wall (Ann Arbor: Pierian Press, 1971).

Biography Index. 1946–.
A subject index to articles and sections of books that are biographical in character. Note that an effective search requires consulting every volume. Same format as the *Readers' Guide.*

Many disciplines produce thorough indexes to a variety of specialized journals in the field. Whenever your research is within a specific academic discipline, you should check to see whether such an index exists. The indexes that follow, and others like them, can be located through the library catalog; you will usually find them shelved near the general periodical indexes described above. Most use the same format as the *Readers' Guide*.

Subject periodical indexes

Applied Science and Technology Index. 1957–.

Art Index. 1929–.

Biological Abstracts. 1926–.

Business Periodicals Index. 1958–.

Current Anthropology. 1960–.

Economic Abstracts. 1953–.

Education Index. 1929–.

Engineering Index. 1884–.

General Science Index. 1978–.

Historical Abstracts. 1955–.

Music Index. 1949–.

Philosopher's Index. 1940–.

Modern Language Association International Bibliography. 1956–. Formerly the *MLA American Bibliography,* 1921–55. The major bibliography of articles on English, American, and foreign language and literature.

Psychological Abstracts. 1927–.

Public Affairs Information Service. 1915–. A valuable index of articles, books, pamphlets, government documents, and other reports on public administration, international relations, and a broad range of economic and social issues.

Religious Index One: Periodicals. 1973–.

Sociological Abstracts. 1955–.

Zoological Record. 1864–.

18c

EXERCISE 3

This exercise should help you become more familiar with the format and use of periodical indexes. In a recent volume of the *Readers' Guide,* find a citation to an article by an author whose last name is the same as, or almost the same as, your own. Copy the full citation as it appears. Then locate the article in your library's holdings, skim through it, and summarize its contents in a paragraph or two. (If your library does not subscribe to the periodical in question, return to the *Readers' Guide* and begin again.)

EXERCISE 4

Use several volumes of the *Readers' Guide* to locate the earliest magazine article available in your library on one of the subjects below. Look up the article, read through it, and write a short essay explaining how our conception of the subject has changed since it was published.

1. AIDS
2. McDonald's Corporation
3. microwave cooking
4. satellites (artificial)
5. television

EXERCISE 5

Follow the directions in Exercise 3, using a recent volume of the *Humanities Index* or the *Social Sciences Index.*

18d A special index: the *Essay and General Literature Index*

This is an appropriate place to mention one other unusual index—not an index to periodicals, but an index to *sections* of books. The *Essay and General Literature Index* (1900–), whose location you can find in the library catalog, is a semiannual subject and author index to collections of essays on different subjects, often written by different authors. This index is usually the only way to locate such essays, since the title and subject classification of these books in the library catalog will ordinarily not be specific enough to help you.

Suppose, for example, that you are interested in the subject of women and art. If you look under the two headings "Women" and

---

Exercises 3, 4, and 5

These exercises are designed to give students hands-on experience in locating periodical indexes and periodical holdings in their library. Having students look up articles by authors with last names like their own is simply an arbitrary way of ensuring that everyone in the class does the exercise independently.

Exercises like these can of course be tailored to introduce students to whatever specific reference tools you wish to emphasize.

"Art" in the library catalog, you will find dozens of books on each subject, but you might spend days—or even weeks—looking through the books on women for those that also deal with art, and searching in the books on art for material on women artists. A few minutes of browsing in a recent issue of the *Essay and General Literature Index,* however, will lead you to the heading "Women in Art," and under it, entries like the following:

> Withers, J. Judy Chicago's Dinner party: a personal vision of women's history. *In* Art, the ape of nature, ed. by M. Barasch and L. F. Sandler p789–99.

What this entry means is that an essay by J. Withers entitled "Judy Chicago's Dinner Party: A Personal Vision of Women's History" is included on pages 789–99 of the book *Art, the Ape of Nature,* edited by M. Barasch and L. F. Sandler. The complete publication information for any book that you find listed is included at the back of the volume of the *Essay and General Literature Index* that you are using. With this information, you can go to the library catalog and determine whether the book is available in your library. Typically, a library would list this book in the catalog only under its title, the names of its two editors, and the broad subject heading "Art—Addresses, Essays, and Lectures." Without the *Essay and General Literature Index,* you would have no easy way of finding Withers's essay.

18e

18e Data-base searches

An increasing number of libraries offer their patrons computerized access to lists of articles, unpublished papers, and other sources of information on a wide variety of subjects. Such computerized files are known as *data bases.* Many college and university libraries provide access to such data bases in one or both of the following ways.

1.   On-line searches

Libraries may subscribe to the services of a data-base vendor, a company that makes available by computer the contents of many different data bases compiled and updated by independent companies and associations. For example, DIALOG, one of the largest such vendors, currently offers access to nearly two hundred separate data bases in business, technology, the humanities, the social sciences, and the natural sciences. In all, a DIALOG subscriber may search through more than seventy-five million records for titles relevant to a specific subject.

Conducting an on-line search

To perform a data-base search in most libraries, you will be asked by the reference librarian to complete an information form on your subject. The librarian will then enter one or more "descriptors," or relevant subject headings, into a computer terminal, and the computer will search through all of the data bases on the system and compile a list of appropriate sources. On some systems, moreover, you can order a printed copy of the full text of an article. Some libraries also subscribe to searching systems that library patrons can use directly, without the intermediary help of a librarian.

The only drawback to such on-line searching is the cost, which is usually calculated according to the length of time you are connected to the computer system. Although a ten-minute computer search may cost only a few dollars, a search that takes considerably longer can become an unrealistically expensive proposition for undergraduate research. On the other hand, data-base searches offer enormous savings of time. In just a few minutes, a computer can scan bibliographies that might take weeks to examine by hand. On-line data bases are also more current than printed reference works can be. For example, the *Wilson Journal Directory*, described in the following list of data bases, is updated twice each week, whereas the corresponding bound indexes usually lag several weeks to several months behind the current date.

18e

Check with your reference librarian to determine whether the following on-line data bases are available at your library.

Major on-line data bases

Arts and Humanities Search.
Indexes more than 1,100 journals in the arts and humanities, beginning in 1980. Updated weekly.
Dissertation Abstracts Online.
Indexes North American doctoral dissertations in all disciplines, beginning in 1861. Updated monthly.

LEXIS/NEXIS.
Provides the full text of an enormous range of documents related to law, business, and current affairs. Examples include United States legal decisions from the eighteenth century to the present; current state and federal legal codes and statutes; business and financial information from a variety of industry sources; detailed descriptive information about American corporations; articles from major American newspapers and from a wide range of journals in fields such as advertising, computer technology, criminology, economics, electronic media, energy, environmental studies, finance, foreign affairs, health care, insurance, international trade, public relations, and transportation. Continuously updated.

PsycINFO.
Indexes more than 1,000 journals in psychology, beginning in 1967.

SciSearch.
Indexes a wide range of journals in science and technology, beginning in 1974.

Social SciSearch.
Indexes more than 1,500 social science journals, beginning in 1972.

18e

Wilson Journal Directory.
An on-line version of various bound periodical indexes published by the H. W. Wilson Company, such as the *Art Index*, the *Applied Science and Technology Index*, the *Business Periodicals Index*, the *Education Index*, the *General Science Index*, the *Humanities Index*, the *Readers' Guide*, and the *Social Sciences Index*. Indexes a total of 3,700 periodicals.

2. CD-ROM searches

Many data bases are also available on laser-read compact discs, similar to the compact discs used for recording and playing back music. Libraries that receive data bases on such discs (referred to as *CD-ROM*, for "compact disc, read-only memory") often make them directly available to patrons at no charge.

Note that unlike the other on-line data bases listed in this section, which provide bibliographic citations to articles, *LEXIS/NEXIS* provides the complete text of the document in question. The necessarily brief description of *LEXIS/NEXIS* given here offers only a hint of its massive size and great usefulness.

For example, most of the Wilson periodicals, including the *Readers' Guide,* the *Humanities Index,* and the *Social Sciences Index,* are available for CD-ROM searches. All the records contained in each of these indexes since 1983 (or in some cases 1984) have been recorded on a single compact disc that is replaced with an updated version four times a year. The disc's contents are read by laser and displayed on an ordinary computer terminal. But a CD-ROM search is more than a computerized version of the browsing you might do in the printed volumes of one of these indexes. Using a command called Wilsearch, you can perform a very powerful kind of subject search that is possible only on a computer.

Using Wilsearch

The Wilsearch request menu asks you to enter up to eight descriptive words covering the topic you are interested in. The more terms you enter, the more precise—but also the more limited—your search will be. The computer then searches all of the records on the compact disc (that is, all of the articles indexed since 1983 or 1984), looking for any articles that have in common all the terms you've indicated. If it finds any matches, it displays the full citations one at a time and gives you the opportunity to print out a copy of any entries that interest you.

Suppose, for example, that you, like Cyndi, are interested in women's education in the nineteenth century. Using the Wilsondisc for the *Humanities Index,* you might begin by entering just two of your key terms, *education* and *women.* (See the illustration on page 395.) The computer then reads the disc and in this case identifies a total of eighty articles indexed since February 1984 that involve both of these subjects. To narrow the search, you could enter a third key word, *nineteenth century.* The computer would then identify and display the titles of articles that include all three key terms, like the title shown in the illustration.

Similar searching capabilities are available on a variety of other CD-ROM data bases, such as those listed below. To determine whether your library subscribes to these or other CD-ROM data bases, check with your reference librarian.

As this description of a search conducted on Wilsearch shows, CD-ROM data bases are much more than merely computerized versions of bound indexes; they dramatically increase the efficiency with which a bibliographic search can be conducted. Because the researcher using a bound index can look under only one subject at a time, many of the citations found through such a search will inevitably be irrelevant to his or her precise interest. In contrast, a CD-ROM search enables the researcher to filter out grossly irrelevant data by specifying *several* subject headings or key words. The computer produces a list of only those citations that contain all of these key words.

In the example illustration, the computer cross-matched 1,055 citations on education and 3,506 citations on women to identify eighty entries dealing with both women and education.

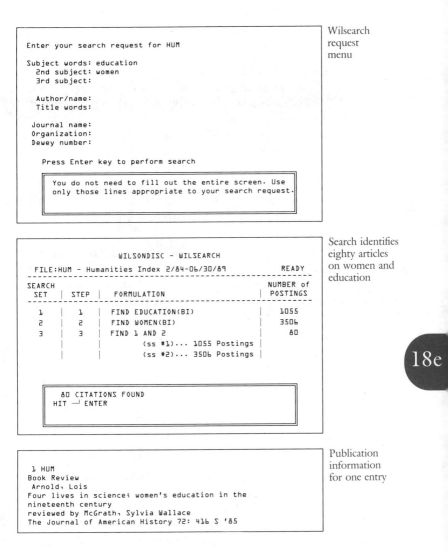

Enter your search request for HUM

Subject words: education
  2nd subject: women
  3rd subject:

  Author/name:
  Title words:

 Journal name:
 Organization:
 Dewey number:

   Press Enter key to perform search

   You do not need to fill out the entire screen. Use
   only those lines appropriate to your search request.

WILSONDISC - WILSEARCH

FILE:HUM - Humanities Index 2/84-06/30/89   READY

SEARCH SET	STEP	FORMULATION	NUMBER of POSTINGS
1	1	FIND EDUCATION(BI)	1055
2	2	FIND WOMEN(BI)	3506
3	3	FIND 1 AND 2	80
		(ss #1)... 1055 Postings	
		(ss #2)... 3506 Postings	

   80 CITATIONS FOUND
   HIT ⏎ ENTER

18e

 1 HUM
Book Review
 Arnold, Lois
Four lives in science: women's education in the
nineteenth century
reviewed by McGrath, Sylvia Wallace
The Journal of American History 72: 416 S '85

Searching a CD-ROM Data Base with Wilsearch

Major CD-ROM data bases

Academic Index.
> Indexes nearly 400 journals and magazines considered likely to be used in undergraduate research. Includes more than 500,000 citations (some as early as 1985) to periodicals in the humanities, the social sciences, and the natural sciences. Also includes citations to the *New York Times* for the most recent six-month period. Updated monthly.

ERIC on SilverPlatter.
> An index of published journal articles and unpublished research reports in the field of education, beginning in 1966. Includes more than 750,000 citations. Updated quarterly.

Magazine Index/Plus.
> Indexes more than 400 general-interest magazines, such as those indexed in the *Readers' Guide,* beginning in 1980. Also offers citations to the *New York Times* for the most recent three-month period. Includes more than 2.65 million citations. Updated monthly.

Newspaper Abstracts Ondisc.
> An index to seven major newspapers, including the *New York Times,* the *Chicago Tribune,* the *Wall Street Journal,* and the *Christian Science Monitor,* beginning in 1985. Updated monthly.

18f Government documents

One of the most often overlooked and yet one of the most valuable sources of information on a wide range of subjects is the U.S. government. Each year, the agencies of the national government publish thousands of pamphlets, booklets, magazines, and books on hundreds of subjects. Many libraries routinely receive and catalog much of this material, which is usually collected together in a single location.

The subject index in the *Monthly Catalog of United States Government Publications* is a good place to begin discovering the range and variety of government documents. The subject headings in one recent issue include everything from "Acid Rain" to "Airplane Inspection,"

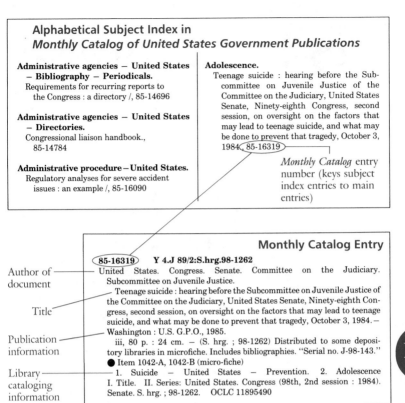

Alphabetical Subject Index in
Monthly Catalog of United States Government Publications

Administrative agencies – United States – Bibliography – Periodicals.
Requirements for recurring reports to the Congress : a directory /, 85-14696

Administrative agencies – United States – Directories.
Congressional liaison handbook., 85-14784

Administrative procedure – United States.
Regulatory analyses for severe accident issues : an example /, 85-16090

Adolescence.
Teenage suicide : hearing before the Subcommittee on Juvenile Justice of the Committee on the Judiciary, United States Senate, Ninety-eighth Congress, second session, on oversight on the factors that may lead to teenage suicide, and what may be done to prevent that tragedy, October 3, 1984, 85-16319

Monthly Catalog entry number (keys subject index entries to main entries)

Monthly Catalog Entry

85-16319   Y 4.J 89/2:S.hrg.98-1262

Author of document — United States. Congress. Senate. Committee on the Judiciary. Subcommittee on Juvenile Justice.

Title — Teenage suicide : hearing before the Subcommittee on Juvenile Justice of the Committee on the Judiciary, United States Senate, Ninety-eighth Congress, second session, on oversight on the factors that may lead to teenage suicide, and what may be done to prevent that tragedy, October 3, 1984. —

Publication information — Washington : U.S. G.P.O., 1985.
iii, 80 p. : 24 cm. – (S. hrg. ; 98-1262) Distributed to some depository libraries in microfiche. Includes bibliographies. "Serial no. J-98-143."
● Item 1042-A, 1042-B (micro-fiche)

Library cataloging information — 1. Suicide – United States – Prevention. 2. Adolescence I. Title. II. Series: United States. Congress (98th, 2nd session : 1984). Senate. S. hrg. ; 98-1262.   OCLC 11895490

18f

Locating Government Documents

from "Computer Graphics" to "Chippewa," from "Lake Trout" to "Literacy," from "Radioactive Waste Disposal" to "Retirement" to "Rhetoric" to "Rocket Engines." Once you have located some promising titles in the subject index, the government documents librarian in your library can show you how to use the index to the documents on file and how to find items in your library's collection.

For Further Reading

Schmersahl, Carmen B. "Teaching Library Research: Process, Not Product." *Journal of Teaching Writing* 6 (1987): 231–38.

19 *Working with Sources*

$\mathbb{A}$ list of books, articles, and other sources of information on a given topic is called a *bibliography*. Most research papers end with a bibliography or with a list of all the works the writer has referred to in the paper. But the research process also *begins* with the compilation of a working bibliography, that is, a list of sources that the writer intends to examine. Only after assembling such a preliminary list of sources do most researchers move to the next important stage of research, taking notes.

19a The working bibliography

The working bibliography is valuable for a number of reasons. First, it becomes your master list of sources. Over a period of several weeks of research, you will not be able to remember all of the books, articles, documents, and other sources that you consulted, some of which were useful and some of which you found irrelevant to your topic. The working bibliography offers a systematic way of keeping track of all of this information. Because it contains references to sources that you must still check, it provides an outline of the research work that remains for you to do; and since it includes the sources you have looked at, it helps to eliminate accidental backtracking. Second, the working bibliography gives you a place to make potentially useful notes about your sources as you examine them. Later, when you are putting your paper together, you will often find it helpful to be able to recall what an author's main point in an article was or what your reactions to a book were as you read it.

398

Many students (and some instructors) feel that the traditional note-card method of accumulating and organizing information for research is too cumbersome and inefficient. But while the sometimes popular alternatives—taking notes on pages of loose-leaf paper, photocopying and high-lighting magazine and journal articles, or inserting dozens of bookmarks into key pages of books—may work for brief research reports, they are unlikely to be very efficient when the research project is a major one spanning weeks of library work. Underlying this chapter's emphasis on the note-card method is the assumption that students should experience this systematic approach at least once if they are to be able to make an informed decision about its usefulness to them in future research work.

The two keys to making this system work efficiently are filling out bibliography cards correctly and taking clear notes. Keeping in mind that every system of documentation is arbitrary but inflexible, students should remember to take this book with them to the library so that they will have the MLA Works Cited forms on pages 403–16 (or the APA reference forms on pages 487–97) at hand as they compile a working bibliography.

QUICK REFERENCE: *Taking Notes*

As you collect information from your sources, remember that a researcher's notes usually fall into one of the following four categories.

Direct quotation   A brief passage copied word for word from a source and enclosed in quotation marks. Look for points stated so forcefully, cleverly, or succinctly that you cannot imagine expressing them any other way.

Paraphrase   A restatement of another writer's ideas in words that are entirely your own. An acceptable paraphrase accurately reflects the meaning of the source but is wholly original in phrasing. See **20b** for the rules governing the citation of paraphrased material.

Summary   A succinct statement of the most important point or points in a source. Look for opportunities to condense text without sacrificing essential information.

Notes to yourself   Clarifying, explanatory, or suggestive notes intended to remind you later of what you were thinking as you examined a particular source.

19a

1. Assembling a working bibliography

Use common sense in choosing items for your working bibliography. Don't waste time, for example, in collecting references to obscure publications not available in your library. Interlibrary loans are possible but may be time-consuming, unpredictable, and expensive; you will usually find it more rewarding to explore the resources of your own library. Look for information in the most likely places. If your topic is a recent event or a living person, for instance, start with newspapers and periodicals rather than with books.

Both lists provide readily accessible model citations for every type of source that an undergraduate is likely to encounter.

The most sensible way to compile your working bibliography is to enter each potentially important source that you identify on a separate three-by-five-inch card or slip of paper. On the back of each card, make your brief notes about the source. The separate cards can be sorted in any number of handy ways; for example, you might place all the sources remaining to be consulted on the top, all those you have already examined on the bottom. When you are at last ready to prepare your paper's concluding bibliography (or *Works Cited* list, as it is frequently called), you can simply remove cards for the sources not used in the paper, alphabetize the remaining cards, and type the Works Cited list directly from them.

2. Recording bibliographic information

In order to be able to use your working bibliography cards as the basis of your paper's final Works Cited list, you must be careful to include all the information needed for the bibliography entries when you fill out each card. Otherwise, you will find yourself trekking back to the library at the last minute to look up a missing year of publication or to double-check an illegibly written author's name. The best plan, as you fill out each bibliography card, is to use the precise bibliographic *form* described below, in order to expedite typing the Works Cited list from your original cards. See the illustration on page 401 for examples of working bibliography cards.

Bibliography forms vary from discipline to discipline, but most systems of citing and listing sources aim for clarity and simplicity. None is inherently superior to another. This chapter and the next two will follow the system of documentation and bibliographic (Works Cited) forms prescribed by the Modern Language Association (MLA) and used in many humanities fields. Chapters **22**, **23**, and **24** illustrate two other systems of documentation. The most important thing about using any such system is that you must follow it precisely and consistently. Though its rules are arbitrary, they cannot arbitrarily be broken.

19b MLA Works Cited forms

The box below conveniently lists the model MLA Works Cited forms found on pages 403–16. Remember to have these samples at hand when you are compiling your working bibliography so that you

Author's name in inverted order ——

First and last pages of article ——

Anonymous source begins with title ——

Indent second and subsequent lines ——

Judge, Joseph. "Florence Rises from
the Flood." *National Geographic*
July 1967 : 1-43.

"Slow Art Restoration Continues in
Florence." *New York Times*
9 Aug. 1967, late city ed.: 42.

Working Bibliography Cards

can refer to them as you fill out your bibliography cards. Note that the author's name is always given last name first for easy indexing. For the same reason, the second and subsequent lines of each entry are always indented. (For additional information about MLA Works Cited forms, see Joseph Gibaldi and Walter S. Achtert, *MLA Handbook for Writers of Research Papers*, 3rd ed. [New York: MLA, 1988].)

19b

Table of MLA Works Cited Forms

Books

1. Book by one author
2. Book by two or more authors
3. Book by a committee, commission, association, or other group
4. Anonymous book
5. Later or revised edition of a book
6. Edited book (*author's work is being cited*)
7. Edited book (*editor's work is being cited*)

8. Translated book (*author's work is being cited*)
9. Translated book (*translator's work is being cited*)
10. Book in more than one volume
11. Republished book
12. Book that is part of a series
13. Book published by a division of a press
14. Book published before 1900
15. Book with incomplete publication information

Parts of books

16. Introduction, preface, foreword, or afterword in a book
17. Essay in a collection of essays by various authors
18. Poem, short story, or other work in an anthology
19. Journal or magazine article reprinted in a collection of essays by various authors

Articles in journals and magazines

20. Article in a journal paginated by the volume (*continuous pagination*)
21. Article in a journal paginated issue by issue
22. Article in a journal with issue numbers only
23. Article in a weekly or biweekly magazine
24. Article in a monthly or bimonthly magazine

Articles in newspapers

25. Article in a newspaper
26. Editorial in a newspaper
27. Letter to the editor

Other print sources

28. Abstract in *Dissertation Abstracts International*
29. Book review
30. Dissertation, unpublished
31. Encyclopedia article (*or article in similar reference work*)
32. Government document
33. Interview, published
34. Map

35. Pamphlet
36. Proceedings of a conference

Nonprint sources

37. Computer software
38. Film
39. Interview, personal
40. Lecture
41. Microfilm or microfiche
42. Recording
43. Television program
44. Videotape

Books

1. Book by one author

```
Minatoya, Lydia.  Talking to High Monks in
     the Snow: An Asian-American Odyssey.
     New York: HarperCollins, 1993.
```

19b

- A colon separates the book's main title and subtitle.
- For nonacademic publishers, use a shortened form of the company's name: *Heath* for D. C. Heath and Company, *Knopf* for Alfred A. Knopf, Inc., and so on.

2. Book by two or more authors

```
Scholes, Robert, and Robert Kellogg.  The Na-
     ture of Narrative.  London: Oxford UP,
     1966.
```

- The abbreviation *UP* means "University Press."
- When more than one city of publication is given, use only the first in your citation (the title page of Scholes and Kellogg's book also lists Oxford and New York).

- In listing the authors' names, follow the same order used on the book's title page.
- Give the second author's name in normal rather than inverted order.
- If there are three authors, list both of the last two authors' names in normal order: `Davis, Jane, Lee O'Brien, and Sylvia Mattheson.`
- If there are more than three authors, you need give the name only of the first, following it by the Latin abbreviation *et al.* ("and others"), not underlined: `Walker, Stephen A., et al.`

3. Book by a committee, commission, association, or other group

```
American Automobile Association.  Illinois/In-
     diana/Ohio Tour Book.  Falls Church:
     American Automobile Assn., 1987.
Ground Zero.  Nuclear War: What's in It for
     You?  New York: Pocket, 1982.
```

- A parenthetical text citation for either of these books would begin with the joint author's name: (American Automobile Association 44), (Ground Zero 169). See **20d.**

4. Anonymous book

```
Kodak Guide to 35mm Photography.  Rochester:
     Eastman Kodak, 1980.
```

- A parenthetical text citation for this book would begin with a shortened form of the title: (Kodak Guide 16). See **20d.**

5. Later or revised edition of a book

```
Miller, Casey, and Kate Swift.  The Handbook
     of Nonsexist Writing.  2nd ed.  New
     York: Harper, 1988.
```

```
Townsend, John Rowe.  Written for Children:
     An Outline of English-Language Chil-
     dren's Literature.  Rev. ed.  Philadel-
     phia: Lippincott, 1975.
```

6. Edited book (*author's work is being cited*)

```
Gaskell, Elizabeth.  The Life of Charlotte
     Brontë.  Ed. Alan Shelston.  Harmonds-
     worth: Penguin, 1975.
Pope, Alexander.  The Poems of Alexander Pope.
     Ed. John Butt.  New Haven: Yale UP, 1963.
```

• When you are citing the work of the author, put the editor's name after the title.

7. Edited book (*editor's work is being cited*)

```
Garber, Frederick, ed.  The Italian.  By Ann
     Radcliffe.  London: Oxford UP, 1968.
Floyd, Samuel A., Jr., ed.  Black Music in
     the Harlem Renaissance: A Collection of
     Essays.  Knoxville: U of Tennessee P,
     1993.
```

19b

• When you are citing the work of an editor, put the author's name (if one exists) after the title.

8. Translated book (*author's work is being cited*)

```
Brumm, Ursula.  American Thought and Reli-
     gious Typology.  Trans. John Hoaglund.
     New Brunswick: Rutgers UP, 1970.
```

9. Translated book (*translator's work is being cited*)

```
Lind, L. R., trans.  The Aeneid.  By Virgil.
     Bloomington: Indiana UP, 1962.
```

10. Book in more than one volume

```
Sturzo, Luigi.  Church and State.  2 vols.
     Notre Dame: U of Notre Dame P, 1962.
Johnson, Edgar.  Sir Walter Scott: The Great
     Unknown.  Vol. 1.  New York: Macmillan,
     1970.  2 vols.
```

- If you use only one volume of a book published in multiple volumes, indicate the volume you are using after the title, and end the entry with the total number of volumes in the set.

11. Republished book

```
Shirer, William L.  Berlin Diary: The Journal
     of a Foreign Correspondent 1934-1941.
     1941.  Harmondsworth: Penguin, 1979.
```

- The copyright page of this paperbound book indicates that it was originally issued in 1941 by a different publisher. Information about the first publisher is not required in this citation, but the original publication date is given after the title.

12. Book that is part of a series

```
Radley, Virginia L.  Samuel Taylor Coleridge.
     Twayne's English Authors Ser. 36.  New
     York: Twayne, 1966.
```

- Give the name of the series and, if provided, the number of the volume in the series before you list the publication information.

19b

13. Book published by a division of a press

Ehrenreich, Barbara, and Deirdre English.

<u>For Her Own Good: 150 Years of the Ex-</u>

<u>perts' Advice to Women</u>. Garden City:

Anchor—Doubleday, 1979.

McDonnell, Thomas P., ed. <u>A Thomas Merton</u>

<u>Reader</u>. Rev. ed. Garden City: Image—

Doubleday, 1974.

- When a book is published by a division of a publishing house, give the name of the division first, followed by a hyphen and the name of the publisher.

14. Book published before 1900

Kellogg, Brainerd. <u>A Text—Book on Rhetoric</u>.

New York, 1897.

- In citations to books published before 1900, the publisher's name may be omitted. Use a comma, not a colon, between the place of publication and the date.

19b

15. Book with incomplete publication information

Marr, George S. <u>The Periodical Essayists of</u>

<u>the Eighteenth Century</u>. London: Clarke,

n.d.

- The abbreviation *n.d.* means "no date."
- If the place of publication is missing, substitute the abbreviation *N.p.* ("no place"); if the publisher's name is missing, use the abbreviation *n.p.* ("no publisher"). The citation for a book with no publication information would be as follows: N.p.: n.p., n.d.

Parts of books

16. Introduction, preface, foreword, or afterword in a book

```
Miller, J. Hillis.   Introduction.   Bleak

     House.   By Charles Dickens.   Ed. Norman

     Page.   Harmondsworth: Penguin, 1971.

     11-34.
```

17. Essay in a collection of essays by various authors

```
Young, Richard E.   "Concepts of Art and the

     Teaching of Writing."   The Rhetorical

     Tradition and Modern Writing.   Ed. James

     J. Murphy.   New York: Modern Lang.

     Assn., 1982.   130-41.
```

- Follow the title of the essay with the title of the book in which it appears and the name of the book's editor or editors.
- End the entry with the first and last pages on which the essay is found.

19b

18. Poem, short story, or other work in an anthology

```
Raleigh, Walter.   "The Advice."   The Anchor

     Anthology of Sixteenth-Century Verse.

     Ed. Richard S. Sylvester.   New York:

     Anchor-Doubleday, 1974.   330-31.
```

- End the entry with the first and last pages on which the work in question is found.

19. Journal or magazine article reprinted in a collection of essays by various authors

```
Fogle, Richard Harter.   "The Abstractness of

     Shelley."   Philological Quarterly 24
```

```
(1945): 362-79.  Rpt. in Shelley: A Col-
lection of Critical Essays.  Ed. George
M. Ridenour.  Twentieth-Century Views.
Englewood Cliffs: Prentice, 1965.
13-29.
```

- Provide information about an article's earlier publication when it is noted in the collection you are using. *Rpt. in* ("reprinted in") indicates that the reprinted version of this article is the one being cited.

Articles in journals and magazines

20. Article in a journal paginated by the volume (*continuous pagination*)

```
Miller, Jerome A.  "Horror and the Decon-
struction of the Self."  Philosophy To-
day 32 (1988): 286-98.
```

19b

- Most periodicals published quarterly or less frequently use continuous pagination for all the issues published in a single year; that is, if the year's first issue ends with page 125, the second issue begins with page 126. The citation to such a periodical includes the name of the journal, the volume number (32), the year of publication (1988), and the first and last pages of the article (286-98).

21. Article in a journal paginated issue by issue

```
Butterick, George.  "Charles Olson's 'The
Kingfishers' and the Poetics of Change."
American Poetry 6.2 (1989): 28-59.
```

- When each issue of a journal begins with page 1, the citation includes the volume (6) *and* the issue number (2) in addition to the year of publication and the first and last pages of the article.

- A title ordinarily enclosed in double quotation marks appears in single quotation marks when it is part of a larger title enclosed in quotation marks.

22. Article in a journal with issue numbers only

```
Jacobson, Paul.   "Temperature and Your Gui-
      tar's Health."   Guitar Review 75 (1988):
      17-18.
```

- When a periodical uses issue numbers but no volume numbers, give the issue number (75) as if it were a volume number. Compare with item 20 above.

23. Article in a weekly or biweekly magazine

```
Rudolph, Barbara.   "Adrift in the Doldrums."
      Time 31 July 1989: 32-34.
```

- Follow the title of the magazine by listing the date in inverted form, a colon, and the first and last pages of the article. Abbreviate months, except for May, June, and July.
- Begin the citation to an anonymous article with the title.

24. Article in a monthly or bimonthly magazine

```
Blakely, Mary Kay.   "Coma: Stories from the
      Edge of Death."   Life Aug. 1989: 80-88.
```

- For a bimonthly magazine, include both months, abbreviated if possible, connected by a hyphen: Jan.-Feb. 1995: 23-28.

Articles in newspapers

25. Article in a newspaper

```
Donoghue, Denis.   "Does America Have a Major
      Poet?"   New York Times 3 Dec. 1978, late
      city ed., sec. 7: 9+.
```

19b

```
"GM Plans Taiwan Office."  Wall Street Jour-
```
```
     nal 11 July 1989: B2.
```

- Specify the edition of the newspaper when it is indicated on the masthead.
- If the newspaper is divided into separately paginated sections, specify the section. If the sections of the newspaper are lettered, the section can be incorporated into the page citation (B2).
- Indicate an article continued on nonconsecutive pages with a plus sign after the first page of the article (9+).
- Begin the citation to an anonymous article with the headline or title.

26. Editorial in a newspaper
```
"'Restraint' Spurs Terrorists."  Editorial.
```
```
     Chicago Sun-Times 3 Aug. 1989: 42.
```

- A signed editorial begins with the author's name in inverted order.

27. Letter to the editor
```
Hayden, Lavonna.  "Broadway Blues."  Letter.
```
```
     Village Voice 28 Feb. 1989: 4.
```

19b

- The title "Broadway Blues" has been supplied by the editor. Not all published letters are given titles.

Other print sources

28. Abstract in *Dissertation Abstracts International*
```
Krantz, Susan Ellen.  "The First Fortune: The
```
```
     Plays and the Playhouse."  DAI 47 (1986):
```
```
     189A.  Tulane U.
```

29. Book review
```
Pettit, Norma.  Rev. of American Puritanism:
```
```
     Faith and Practice, by Darrett B. Rutman.
```

```
New England Quarterly 43 (1970):
504-06.
```

- If the review has a title, include it in quotation marks after the author's name.
- Publication information for the book being reviewed is not included.

30. Dissertation, unpublished

```
Rauff, James Vernon.  "Machine Translation
    with Two-Level Grammars."  Diss. North-
    western U, 1988.
```

31. Encyclopedia article (*or article in similar reference work*)

```
"Phonetics."  Encyclopaedia Britannica: Mi-
    cropaedia.  15th ed.  1986.
Dunn, Mary Maples.  "Penn, William."  Encyclope-
    dia of American Biography.  Ed. John A. Gar-
    raty.  New York: Harper, 1974.
```

- For familiar reference works such as standard encyclopedias, include the name of the author of the article (if the article is signed), the title of the entry, the name of the encyclopedia, and its edition (if given) and year of publication.
- For less familiar reference works, supply full publication information.
- Omit page and volume numbers in either type of citation when the work is organized alphabetically.

32. Government document

```
United States.  Superintendent of Documents.
    Poetry and Literature.  Washington: GPO,
    1978.
```

- Unless the name of the author of a government publication is given, begin the citation with the name of the government and the name of the agency issuing the document.
- *GPO* is an abbreviation of "Government Printing Office."

33. Interview, published

```
Drabble, Margaret.  Interview.  Interviews
     with Contemporary Novelists.  By Diana
     Cooper-Clark.  New York: St. Martin's,
     1986.  47-73.

Stern, Gerald.  "A Poet of the Mind: An In-
     terview with Gerald Stern."  By Eliza-
     beth Knight.  Poetry East 26 (1988):
     32-48.
```

- Begin citations to interviews with the name of the person interviewed.
- Identify the citation as an interview if it is untitled and provide the name of the interviewer, if known, together with standard publication information.

19b

34. Map

```
Southeastern States.  Map.  Falls Church:
     American Automobile Assn., 1988.
```

35. Pamphlet

```
Rusinow, Dennison I.  Yugoslavia's Muslim Na-
     tion.  Hanover: Universities Field Staff
     Intl., 1982.
```

- The citation form for a pamphlet is the same as that for a book.

36. Proceedings of a conference

```
Rousseas, Stephen W., ed.  Inflation: Its
    Causes, Consequences and Control.  A
    Symposium Held by the Dept. of Econom-
    ics, New York U.  31 Jan. 1968.  Wilton:
    K. Kazanjian Economics Foundation, 1968.
```

- Include the title and date of the conference before the publication information.

Nonprint sources

37. Computer software

```
Etter, Thomas, and William Chamberlain.
    Racter.  Computer software.  Mindscape,
    1984.
```

- If the software is available in different versions, indicate the version you are citing after the name of the program: `Vers. 2.2`.

38. Film

```
Casablanca.  Dir. Michael Curtiz.  With Hum-
    phrey Bogart, Ingrid Bergman, and Claude
    Rains.  Warner Bros., 1942.
```

39. Interview, personal

```
Toulouse, Teresa A.  Personal interview.
    31 Mar. 1994.
```

40. Lecture

```
Catano, James V.  "The Paradox Behind the
    Myth of Self-Making: Self-Empowerment
```

19b

```
vs. the Power of the Academy."  Confer-
     ence on College Composition and Communi-
     cation.  Seattle, 17 Mar. 1989.
```

41. Microfilm or microfiche

• When citing a publication reproduced on microfilm or microfiche, simply use the ordinary citation form appropriate for that publication.

42. Recording

```
Friendly, Fred W., and Walter Cronkite, eds.
     The Way It Was: The Sixties.  Narr. Wal-
     ter Cronkite.  CBS, F3M 38858, 1983.
Barbieri, Gato, tenor sax.  Tropico.  Audio-
     tape.  A&M, CS-4710, 1978.
```

43. Television program

19b

```
Nightline.  ABC.  WLS, Chicago.  23 Jan. 1994.
"Baka: People of the Forest."  Writ. and
     prod. Phil Agland.  National Geographic.
     PBS.  WTTW, Chicago.  7 Aug. 1989.
```

• The basic information in a citation to a television program is the title of the program, the network, the local station and city, and the date. For a specific episode of a program, begin with the episode's title.
• Information about the production of a program (writer, producer, director, narrator, etc.) may be included when appropriate.

44. Videotape

```
The Beggar's Opera.  Videocassette.  By John
     Gay.  Prod. and dir. Jonathan Miller.
```

Exercise 1 (page 416)

1. Lefkowitz, Mary R. Rev. of *Women in Roman Law and Society,* by Jane F. Gardner. *American Historical Review* 92 (1987): 1185–86. [Publication information for the book being reviewed is not included in this citation.]
2. Ailey, Alvin. Interview. "Alvin Ailey Celebrates 30 Years of Dance." By A. Peter Bailey. *Essence* Nov. 1988: 64+.
3. Egoff, Sheila A. *Thursday's Child: Trends and Patterns in Contemporary Children's Literature.* Chicago: American Library Assn., 1981.
4. Davis, Philip J. "Of Time and Mathematics." *Southern Humanities Review* 18 (1984): 193–202.
5. Gray, Frances. "The Nature of Radio Drama." *Radio Drama.* Ed. Peter Lewis. London: Longman, 1981. 48–77.
6. "Cost Estimate Jumps for Music Center Expansion." *Los Angeles Times* 12 Sept. 1984, sec. VI: 1.

```
With Roger Daltrey and Carol Hall.

BBC-TV/RM Arts, 1985.  135 min.
```

EXERCISE 1

Write a Works Cited entry in correct MLA format for each of the following sources. Note that in some cases you do not need all the information provided.

1. A review of Jane F. Gardner's book Women in Roman Law and Society, published in 1986 by the Indiana University Press in Bloomington. The review, written by Mary R. Lefkowitz, appears on pages 1185 and 1186 of volume 92 of the American Historical Review (1987), a continuously paged journal.
2. An interview with Alvin Ailey entitled Alvin Ailey Celebrates 30 Years of Dance, published in the November 1988 issue of Essence. The article begins on page 64 and continues on nonconsecutive pages later in the magazine. The interviewer is A. Peter Bailey.
3. Sheila A. Egoff's book Thursday's Child: Trends and Patterns in Contemporary Children's Literature, published in Chicago by the American Library Association. The year of publication is 1981.
4. An article entitled Of Time and Mathematics, published by Philip J. Davis in the Southern Humanities Review, volume 18, 1984. It appears on pages 193 to 202. The journal is continuously paged.
5. Frances Gray's essay The Nature of Radio Drama, in a book entitled Radio Drama and edited by Peter Lewis. The book was published in London by Longman. The year of publication is 1981. The essay appears on pages 48 to 77.
6. Cost Estimate Jumps for Music Center Expansion, an article in the September 12, 1984, issue of the Los Angeles Times. It appears on page 1 of section VI.
7. The article Sleep in the 1983 Encyclopedia Americana. Ian Oswald wrote the article, which appears on pages 31 to 33 of volume 25. No edition is given.
8. An article in the Journal of Broadcasting by Joanne Cantor, Dean Ziemke, and Glenn G. Sparks. The title is Effect of Forewarning on Emotional Responses to a Horror Film. It appears on pages 21 to 31 of volume 28, 1984. The journal is continuously paged.
9. A two-volume biography, The Life and Letters of John Gibson Lockhart, written by Andrew Lang and published in 1897 by the London publisher John C. Nimmo.

19b

---

7. Oswald, Ian. "Sleep." *Encyclopedia Americana*. 1983. [The other information provided is not included in the citation.]
8. Cantor, Joanne, Dean Ziemke, and Glenn G. Sparks. "Effect of Forewarning on Emotional Responses to a Horror Film." *Journal of Broadcasting* 28 (1984): 21–31.
9. Lang, Andrew. *The Life and Letters of John Gibson Lockhart*. 2 vols. London, 1897. [The publisher's name may be omitted from citations to books published before 1900.]
10. "Job Safety Becomes a Murder Issue." *Business Week* 6 Aug. 1984: 23.
11. Patrides, C. A. "Shakespeare and the Comedy beyond Comedy." *Kenyon Review* 10.2 (1988): 38–57.
12. Maland, Charles J. *Frank Capra*. Twayne's Theatrical Arts Ser. Boston: Twayne, 1980.
13. Shapiro, Charles. Afterword. *Hard Times*. By Charles Dickens. New York: Signet Classics-New American Library. 1961. 293–97. [MLA form also permits the abbreviation *NAL* for *New American Library*.]

10. An anonymous article on page 23 of the August 6, 1984, issue of Business Week. The title is Job Safety Becomes a Murder Issue.
11. C. A. Patrides's article Shakespeare and the Comedy beyond Comedy, published in the second number of volume 10 of the Kenyon Review, a journal that pages each issue separately. The year of publication is 1988. The article appears on pages 38 to 57.
12. A book by Charles J. Maland entitled Frank Capra. It is a volume in Twayne's Theatrical Arts Series and was published in 1980 in Boston by Twayne.
13. Charles Shapiro's afterword to Charles Dickens's novel Hard Times, published in 1961 by the Signet Classics division of New American Library in New York. The afterword is found on pages 293 to 297.
14. The article Dermatology by W. B. Shelley, found on pages 302 to 307 of The Oxford Companion to Medicine, a two-volume reference work arranged alphabetically. The editors are John Walton, Paul B. Beeson, and Ronald Bodley Scott. The book was published in Oxford by Oxford University Press in 1986.
15. A book entitled Life Insurance Companies as Financial Institutions, produced by the Life Insurance Association of America and published in 1962 by Prentice Hall in Englewood Cliffs.

19c Taking notes

After you have identified several likely sources of information on your topic, your next impulse may be to arm yourself with packages of loose-leaf paper or piles of legal tablets to be filled up with notes. But remember that you will be writing your paper directly from your notes, not from the books you've consulted (which are hard to refer to), or from the periodicals you've read (which usually cannot leave your library). The basic consideration for note taking, then, is this: how can you take notes that will be most useful and most accessible later, as you compose the paper?

1. Note cards

For most people, the answer to this question is to take notes on separate cards or slips of paper, four by six inches or larger (regular typing paper cut in half works well). The rationale for such a system is simple. Note taking is an exploratory act, not a definitive one; as you are taking notes, you can never be certain which notes you will later use and

14. Shelley, W. B. "Dermatology." *The Oxford Companion to Medicine.* Ed. John Walton, Paul B. Beeson, and Ronald Bodley Scott. 2 vols. Oxford: Oxford UP, 1986. [Page numbers are not included in the citation to a reference work whose entries are arranged alphabetically.]
15. Life Insurance Association of America. *Life Insurance Companies as Financial Institutions.* Englewood Cliffs: Prentice Hall, 1982. [MLA form also permits the abbreviation *Prentice* for *Prentice Hall.*]

Taking useful notes is a skill perfected through practice. Students often find note taking wearisome because they instinctively think that it should be a rather mechanical task, the mere copying of words from a source onto a note card. In contrast, as every researcher knows (and as sections **19c**, **19d**, and **19e** stress), good notes are the result of careful thought about the source one is reading. The time put into taking thoughtful notes is

which you will not need. If your notes are on separate cards, you will later be able to sort them out, clip them together, arrange some, and discard others. You will gain a flexibility that will enormously simplify the task of organizing and writing your paper.

For such a system of note taking to work, though, each note card must be *self-contained*. It must, in other words, contain three pieces of information:

1. *A clear, complete note*
   Be certain that the single note you put on each card is sufficiently complete to make sense to you later, when you no longer have in front of you the article or book that it came from.
2. *A reference to your source*
   To ensure that you will later be able to cite sources accurately in your paper, you must include on each note card a reference to the source from which that note was taken. Don't copy all the publication information for the source onto each note card; instead, develop a system for keying the note cards to the bibliography cards in your working bibliography. For example, you might write just the author's last name at the top of each card (but be careful to distinguish between sources if two of them share the same last name).
3. *The page number*
   You must be certain that the page number or numbers from which you took the note also appear on the note card, because you will have to cite those page numbers in your final paper.

2. Types of notes

There are four basic types of notes, and a single note card may contain just one or a combination of all four. (See the illustration of a bibliography card and a note card on page 419.)

Direct quotation

Copying direct quotations onto note cards may at first seem to be the easiest way to take notes, but often it actually creates more work for you later on. Mounds of undigested quotations lacking their original contexts are usually harder to work with as you are writing your

saved later on: a researcher who has reflected on each note during the research process approaches the writing of a research paper with some at least half-formed ideas about the paper's focus and development.

Text of Source

Once sorted and carefully taken apart at Fort Belvedere, the dried books were given a bath! The washing, pressing, and drying of the separated pages were done at the heating plant of the Florence railroad station—and a more unlikely place for the saving of a great library cannot be imagined.

In the cavernous rooms, filled with huge boilers and jungle gyms of pipes, students stood at a bank of washbasins and submerged the old handmade pages in plain tapwater mixed with fungicide. The dried pages were apt to become brittle because the old sizing had run and gathered in puddles; the washing flushed out this old glue. The crucial factor was that the old inks and handmade papers could be washed without damage. Finally, the individual pages were flattened in a press and hung out to dry (pages 26-7).

Sally Lou Smith and American binding expert now living in

Lon...

clou...

Bibliography card

Judge, Joseph. "Florence Rises from the Flood." _National Geographic_ July 1967: 1 - 43.

Note card

19c

Source —

Page —

Paraphrase —

Quotation —

Researcher's —
note to self

Judge, p. 41

Working in the crowded boiler rooms of the city's train station, students "submerged the old handmade pages [of flood-damaged books] in plain tapwater mixed with fungicide."

(example of improvised procedures in the early days of the crisis)

Source, Bibliography Card, Note Card

paper than incisive and thoughtful notes in your own words (see *Para-phrase,* below). Sometimes, however, you will find a writer who states a point so forcefully, cleverly, or succinctly that you might want to quote the author's phrasing in your paper. In such cases, when you copy an author's exact words onto your note card, be certain to enclose them in quotation marks so that later, as you compose your paper, you will be able to distinguish between your own words on your note cards and the words that belong to others.

Be certain, too, that everything within the quotation marks is exactly as it appears in the original quotation; you are not free to omit or add words randomly, or to change punctuation or spelling. If you have to add a word or phrase for clarity, you must enclose the added material in square brackets ([]), not parentheses (see **35c**). If you wish to delete part of an overly long quotation, you must show the deletion with three spaced periods (. . .) called *ellipsis marks* (see **36c**). Quotations, in short, must be handled with precision. If you fail to set them off with quotation marks, you leave yourself open to the serious charge of plagiarism, discussed in the next chapter (see **20b**). If you alter them without indicating the change, your instructor may penalize you for inexact handling of sources.

19c

Paraphrase

A paraphrase is a restatement of another writer's ideas in words that are entirely your own. Paraphrasing takes thought and care, for it must reflect the meaning of the given text but be wholly original in phrasing. You may not simply replace some of the words in another writer's sentence with your own; instead, the very structure of your sentence should be different from your source's. Good paraphrasing takes time when you are doing it, but it can save time later: if you have paraphrased well, you may be able to write your paper directly from material on your note cards (though you will still need to acknowledge the source of the ideas contained in your prose). For advice on para-phrasing properly, see **20b**.

Summary

As you get further and further along in your research, you will be better able to decide when you need to note all of the details given in a passage in one of your sources and when you can simply summarize the passage in a sentence or two. Look for opportunities to use summary effectively as a way of reducing your work without sacrificing important information.

Notes to yourself

Have you found a quotation that might make an attention-getting introduction to your paper? Are you reading a source whose ideas contradict those in other articles you've examined? Is the book in front of you the best survey of your subject that you have located so far? Because you can't expect to remember all the peripheral ideas that occur to you as you do your research, write them down on your note cards as they come to mind. Later, when you review your cards in preparation for outlining the paper, you'll be glad for the clarifying, explanatory, or suggestive notes that you made to yourself while you were deep in the research process.

3. Recognizing a potential note

As this description of notes suggests, note taking is far from being a mechanical task. It is a thoughtful, even creative, act that demands your alertness and care.

19c

You may be wondering how you will recognize a note when you encounter one in your reading. When you are just beginning to research a topic, after all, almost everything you read about it may be new. Is everything, therefore—every page, every paragraph, every sentence—a note waiting to be jotted down? If that is so, you may be thinking, note taking will mean paraphrasing or summarizing the complete contents of every article or book you pick up.

Although there are no secret tricks that will unfailingly enable you to spot potential notes hidden among the closely packed lines of an article in the *New York Times*, note taking is, fortunately, a more selective process than the description in the previous paragraph suggests. You might keep in mind the general guidelines in the box on page 422 as you decide what information to commit to your note cards.

In the early stages of your work, you should expect to take many notes that you will later discard. This is an inevitable part of research work, since, as we observed earlier, it is only through the research

---

Characteristics of Good Research Notes

Clarity Good notes make a clear point. If you can't understand what the author you're reading is saying, copying down a quotation from the article or a paraphrase of the text will not help you later. The notes you take should be clear enough for anyone looking over your note cards—even a person who had not read the original sources—to understand.

Specificity Good notes present specific information—facts, places, descriptions, examples, statistics, case histories. Like all good essays, successful research papers are grounded in specific information, information that must exist on your note cards when you begin to compose your paper.

Focus Good notes often reflect the particular attitudes or opinions of the author whom you are reading. Try to write notes that capture the essence of an author's argument, concisely restate the main point, or indicate his or her biases.

19d

---

process that you will be able to define and focus your subject clearly. Taking notes and rethinking your original topic go hand in hand. To put it more brutally: you'll have to take many notes that you will ultimately throw away before you'll know which ones to keep.

19d Assessing your sources

Above we considered the importance of approaching note taking in a thoughtful way, isolating the key ideas in a source and finding the most accurate and most concise way to record those ideas on your note cards. Effective note taking requires another kind of reflection as well: carefully considering the quality of your sources and their appropriateness to your research project.

1. How current?

How important to your paper is *recent* information about your subject? If you are writing about historical events, you may wish to examine material published over a large span of time. A paper on the San Francisco earthquake of 1906, for example, might well draw both on contemporary accounts of the disaster and on modern assessments of its influence on subsequent city planning. In contrast, if you have chosen a current subject or one that is undergoing continual change, you will need the most up-to-date sources available. In science, politics, and medicine, for example, old information is frequently useless information.

2. How authoritative?

What can you find out about your author's qualifications to write on your subject? Begin by looking at the end of an article or on the jacket of a book for a note that cites the author's professional position or other publications. In addition, be alert for citations to your author's work in other sources, either in textual references or in footnotes. Notice whether your author's name turns up frequently in bibliographies—an indication that he or she has published widely. Finally, consider the evidence that your author uses to support assertions. Is it the kind of specific and substantial information that suggests a thorough acquaintance with the subject? The better qualified the author, the more likely it is that the information you are reading is accurate and complete.

19d

3. How objective?

Whether or not you have been able to locate information about your author, you should watch for signs of the author's biases within his or her writing itself. Pure objectivity, of course, is rare, since every writer's perspective colors the handling of a subject. The question here is whether your author's biases are so strong that they may result in a distorted presentation of the subject. Is your author's work based on facts or on judgments? Does your author make questionable assumptions? (See **14b**, **14c**, and **14d**.) Does he or she satirize or ridicule those who have taken different positions? If you detect hints of bias in your author, you will want to examine a broad range of other sources as well, so that your own perspective on the subject will be as balanced as possible.

19e Assessing your subject

Use your initial note taking as a way of assessing the likelihood that the subject you've chosen will yield a successful research paper. Often, taking notes from just a few of the sources that you expect to be most promising will tell you whether your subject is going to work or not.

1. Signs of a good subject

A good subject will grow richer and more interesting as you research it. You will discover perspectives on the subject that you had not considered and will find yourself caught up in the process of discovering and synthesizing information about the topic. Your reading will suggest a number of possible directions for further research, many of which you may find intriguing.

19e

2. Signs of a poor subject

In contrast, any of the following situations should suggest to you that your subject may be unworkable.

1. All the sources you examine make the same meager points about the subject. There's less to be learned here than you expected.
2. The sources you read suggest that the topic is far more complicated than you initially realized. You begin to feel that you will never be able to comprehend, let alone focus, your subject.
3. Your reading bores you. The subject turns out to be much less interesting than you expected.

Of course, you should give any subject a fair chance of blossoming by investigating all possible types of sources—reference works, books, magazine and journal articles, newspapers, essays in collections, and nonprint sources. Be certain, moreover, to discuss your research problems with your instructor, who may be able to help you salvage a subject that appears unworkable by suggesting a new focus for your research or specific sources for you to investigate. But don't wait until just days before your paper is due to ask your instructor for help or for permission to look for another subject. Plan to talk with him or her at the first signs of trouble in your research.

EXERCISE 2

Section 19c noted that a researcher should try to summarize the major points in a source when possible rather than to copy onto a note card a host of small details. For practice in the art of summarizing, write a brief summary in your own words of each of the following passages. Try to capture both the passage's main point and its key details in no more than two sentences.

Example

Text

 Babylon—the city and its empire—flourished for almost 2000 years, from about 2225 B.C. until its capture by Alexander the Great in 331 B.C. When the Greek conqueror of the world died there, Babylon could be said to have died too. But up to that time it had been the cultural capital of the civilised world; and even after its site was lost, buried under mounds of rubble, its existence was never forgotten. The very name has always had a magical sound to it. The Hebrews placed the Garden of Eden somewhere nearby. The Greeks wrote that it contained two of the Seven Wonders of the World. The Romans described it as "the greatest city the sun ever beheld." And to the early Christians "Great Babylon" was the symbol of [human] wickedness and the wrath of God. And so it was "by the waters of Babylon" that the history of the Western world could be said to have begun.

 Although it seems unbelievable that a metropolis of such size and splendour should have vanished from the earth—its outer defences alone were ten miles in circumference, fifty feet high, and nearly fifty-five feet deep—the fact is that by the first century B.C. nothing remained but its walls. For Babylon had been devastated so often that by this time it was abandoned except for a few refugees who made their homes in the rubble. The royal palaces had been looted, the temples had fallen into ruins, and the greater part of the city inside the walls was overgrown with weeds.

—James Wellard, *Babylon*

19e

Exercise 2

Answers will vary.

1. A study by the University of Texas School of Public Health suggests that people who repeatedly gain and lose weight increase their cholesterol level and hence their risk of heart disease.
2. Medieval windmills were successful only after the problem of adjusting to changing wind directions had been solved: the windmill was balanced on a post so that it could be turned in whatever direction the wind was blowing.
3. Gayle Delaney, a San Francisco psychologist, suggests the following procedure for solving your problems through dreams: while you are falling asleep, repeat the question that you wish your dreams to answer; immediately upon awakening, write down everything that you can remember about your dreams; during the day, reflect on the possible symbolic meaning of your notes.

Summary

By the first century B.C., little except the massive walls remained of Babylon, the most magnificent city of the world from 2225 B.C. until the fourth century B.C., a city whose reputation earned it a place in Hebrew, Greek, Roman, and early Christian myth.
[The passage's central point—expressed in this summary— is the contrast between Babylon's greatness for two thousand years and its stunning obliteration by the first century B.C.]

1.   Despite the hype, losing weight doesn't always lead to better health. "Seesawers"—those who put on many pounds and then shed them—may nearly double their risk of heart disease, according to a study from the University of Texas School of Public Health. Those who gain little or no weight and those who put on weight but make no effort to lose it may run no additional risk of coronary disease.

Texas researchers, who studied 400 men ages 20 to 40, theorize that seesawers who gained 10% or more of body weight after losing pounds in weight-loss programs created a sharp rise in artery-clogging cholesterol. This apparently wasn't the case with the "no-gain" and "gain-only" groups. The risk for the gain-only group: Their large, continuous gains increased the risk of fatal cancers.

"Avoid fast-loss starvation diets," advises one of the researchers, Peggy Hamm. "If you are comfortable with your present weight, work hard at maintaining it and avoid wide fluctuations. If you're not comfortable with your weight, adjust your life-style and your eating habits so that you take the excess weight off very gradually."

—"The Downside of Dieting," *Changing Times*

19e

2.   The windmill was an inspired answer to the problem of the lack of water power, and was undoubtedly one of medieval Europe's most important inventions. Essentially an adaptation of the watermill to a new source of power, it made use of the familiar mechanism—now inverted so as to be driven by sails mounted high in the building, rather than by a waterwheel at its base. But a more fundamental alteration was also necessary. The difficulty with the windmill, and what presumably delayed its invention, was the problem of how to harness a power source that regularly changed its direction, and which would not be directed or controlled. With the watermill the water always flowed along the same channel, and at a rate the miller could vary by means of sluices; the seemingly intractable problem for the

4. Sante Fe, New Mexico, is a surprisingly tolerant, cosmopolitan community whose population includes nuclear physicists, artists, state government workers, millionaires, New Age vegetarians, Hispanics, and Sikhs.

5. The reversed positions of buttons on modern clothing for men and women can probably be traced to the fourteenth and fifteenth centuries, when the buttonhole finally replaced the earlier and less durable button loop in fashionable people's clothing. Right-handed men found it easier to fasten their clothing with the buttons on the right, but because women in this social class were dressed by maids, buttons on women's clothing were sewn on the left, where they would be more convenient for a right-handed attendant facing the wearer of the garment.

first windmill builders was to contrive a way of keeping the sails facing into the wind. The solution they came up with was to balance the windmill on a single massive upright post, so that the miller could push the whole structure around to face in whichever direction he wanted. The wind speed he could compensate for, like any sailor, by adjusting the spread of canvas on the lattice-work sails.

—Richard Holt, "The Medieval Mill—A Productivity Breakthrough?" *History Today*

3. Although dreams seem to arise unbidden, you can choose the subjects of your nighttime dramas. One technique you might try is a technique called "incubation," developed by psychologist Gayle Delaney of San Francisco. Choose a problem or question in your life, she suggests, and write down a few sentences about it. Then, just before you go to bed, compose a one-line question that sums up what you want to know, such as "Why do I fight with my spouse?" Lay the paper beside you, repeating the question over and over to yourself as you fall asleep.

When you awaken, write down everything you remember about any of your dreams. Don't reject anything as irrelevant. As Delaney says, "Dreams speak to us in symbols," so even a farfetched image may, after some wide-awake thought, be seen to bear on the incubated problem. If the technique doesn't work the first night, keep trying. Delaney reports a high success rate among her patients.

The tricky part is remembering. About the only way to capture a dream is to write it down immediately upon waking, for dreams vanish within 15 minutes. If you don't remember a dream, write down whatever is on your mind—those thoughts often come from the night's dreams and may be the first clue to retrieving them.

—"A Blueprint for Dreaming," *Newsweek*

19e

4. Santa Fe style isn't a reference to fashion or popularity. It's a blue sky, spiritual attitude towards life, and an abiding but quiet appreciation for a unique community culture that started in the early 1600s with sun-baked bricks of mud and straw.

Back then in 1610 when the city was officially founded on an empty mesa 7,000 feet above sea level, the rule of law came long distance from the king of Spain—with the tentative acquiescence of the local Pueblo Indians. Seven decades later, the natives revolted, and it was not until 1692 that the "city of holy faith" was reclaimed for Spanish colonialism by Don Diego de Vargas. The Republic of

Mexico eventually had its heyday of authority beginning in 1821, after which Anglo traders began arriving in wagons on the old Santa Fe Trail. In 1846 during the War with Mexico, General Stephen Watts Kearny claimed Sante Fe for the Stars and Stripes.

So the city's tradition of tolerance for new faces goes way back. Today that aspect of Santa Fe's culture is perhaps its most appealing. The town is made up of many subgroups that don't mesh, yet don't clash. Among them are Hispanics who trace their local lineage back hundreds of years and world-class physicists working on nuclear research at the nearby Los Alamos National Laboratory. There is a huge artistic community and an army of waitresses and desk clerks. Santa Fe being the capital city, its state-government contingent numbers in the thousands. And there's a shockingly large collection of the world's wealthiest individuals who keep very much to themselves.

This is an impossible mix. But the suspension holds—even after they stirred in the New Agers with their vegetarian dream rolfing and herbal acu-massage therapy, and the Sikhs with their turbans and beards. Santa Fe is open to almost all ways of thinking, and that makes for a far more interesting, cosmopolitan city than its size and location would ordinarily suggest.

—Paul Young, "Santa Fe Style: Impossible Cosmopolitan Mix," *American West*

19e

5.   Although the button had been known since Roman times, being inserted into a loop sewn onto the edge of a mating piece of garment, the buttonhole as we know it did not evolve until the thirteenth century, perhaps in response to the failure of a button and loop to make as tight a closure as one might like on a cold windy day, or in response to the fragility of loops and their propensity to break when one was getting dressed for some big event. Perhaps the first buttonhole was actually hastily improvised with a knife or scissors in response to a loop's breaking at the wrong time. But the unreinforced buttonhole would have torn open wider and wider with use, and thus would eventually have failed to hold its button very securely. This shortcoming might easily have led to the reinforcing provided by the now familiar specialized buttonhole stitching.

Even with the advantage that they were less likely than hooks to snag, buttons definitely still took some time to be mated with buttonholes. Nevertheless, an abundance of buttons on garments became a sign of fashion in fourteenth- and fifteenth-century Europe; and the contrasting dressing customs of privileged men and privileged women of that time are generally believed to be responsible for the fact that even today men's clothes button differently from women's. Since, presumptively, most people have always preferred the right hand, a man dressing himself would naturally have favored his right hand for manipulating a button through a buttonhole. Hence, the buttons on men's garments, even if at first attached randomly to one side or the other, would soon have migrated to the man's right-hand side. The most fashionable women, however, were commonly dressed by maids, who naturally faced their mistresses while hooking or buttoning them up. Therefore, buttons would have migrated to the side of a lady's garment that corresponded to the facing maid's right. Any other arrangement would have been inefficient.

—Henry Petroski, *The Evolution of Useful Things*

19e

For Further Reading

Gibaldi, Joseph, and Walter S. Achtert. *MLA Handbook for Writers of Research Papers.* 3rd ed. New York: Modern Lang. Assn., 1988.

20 *Composing the Research Paper*

Perhaps the most important advice to keep in mind as you organize and write your paper is that the research paper, though it may be longer than other essays you have written, is more similar to than different from a typical expository essay, and its success will depend largely on the same principles of effective writing that you have studied in other contexts. If you have learned how to formulate a thesis and introduction, how to write clearly structured paragraphs, how to use specific diction and development effectively, how to ensure coherence and maintain consistency of tone, then you should be able to write a good research paper.

There is no denying, however, that the matter of integrating other people's ideas and words with your own text complicates the task of composing a research paper. Accordingly, the first section below presents some guidelines to follow as you organize your paper, and the following three sections deal specifically with incorporating information from your sources into the paper. This chapter ends by considering some important matters of format for your final draft.

20a Organizing and writing a research paper

The more you learn about your subject from note taking, the more you may feel that you will never be able to stop examining sources without the risk of missing some potentially important new piece of information. Strictly speaking, of course, that's true. But the realities of research—whether in college or in professional life—dictate that you

430

Like all aspects of writing, the research process is inherently idiosyncratic; hence **20a** presents only guidelines for organizing materials and drafting the research paper, not rules.

To give students a perspective on the progress they make with their research projects, consider assigning them to small groups (perhaps groups defined by the writers' similar research topics) that will meet periodically during the term. The members of each group will have the opportunity to discuss the status and development of their projects, explain what steps they plan to take next, and hear how others are coping with the process of locating sources, taking notes, developing a focus, and drafting the paper.

QUICK REFERENCE: *Avoiding Plagiarism*

Plagiarism is the deliberate or accidental presentation of another's language or ideas as your own. To avoid plagiarism, use quotations and paraphrases carefully.

Quotation	Enclose every direct quotation in quotation marks and cite the source in your paper. In general, several words in succession—or even a single distinctive word—taken from another source may be said to constitute direct quotation.
Paraphrase	Cite the source of every paraphrased idea in your paper unless the idea would be considered common knowledge.
Common knowledge	An idea is common knowledge *only* if (1) you find it repeated in many sources or (2) it would be familiar to an average, educated person, even one who has not researched your subject.

For more information on quoting, paraphrasing, and citing sources, see **20b**, **20c**, and **20d**.

20a

---

must at some point call a halt to your research and begin shaping into a coherent whole the material that you have collected.

1.   Know when to stop taking notes

How will you know when you've collected enough information and can begin writing your paper? It's difficult to be certain that you've done enough research, but you might expect your work to lead to this point in stages something like the following.

Examine your major sources

First, take notes from all of your major sources, that is, all of those that you initially expected to be important sources of information on your topic, either because their titles seemed particularly promising or because you had already skimmed through them. As noted at the end of the preceding chapter, you should complete this stage of the research process with a reasonably sure sense that your subject is in some way going to provide the basis for a successful paper.

Look for connections among your notes

Once you move beyond your list of major sources and start examining others, you will probably discover a number of the same topics surfacing again and again, and you will begin to see connections among your note cards for the first time. Source Y, for example, has an opinion different from that of source X; source B confirms a point made by source A. Recognizing such connections is a good sign that you are mastering your subject. This is usually the point at which you will be able to define a more precise direction for your paper and your additional research. You will have become familiar enough with your subject to identify those aspects of it that seem most worth investigating.

Think about what your research proves

20a

At about this point, you will no doubt realize that you have developed ideas of your own about your subject, based on the reading and note taking you have done. The best researchers, after all, are less interested in mere piles of accumulated data than in ways of using the data they have collected to support their own observations and ideas.

Once you are able to see beyond your separate notes to the ways in which those notes can be used to substantiate a larger argument of your own, a sense of the completeness of your work may begin to grow upon you. You may gradually begin to develop a vague mental outline of some of the key ideas you think your paper should cover. When you reach this point, it may be time to retire from the library—for a while, at least—and have a try at writing your paper.

2. Organize your notes

The first stage in writing your paper is reviewing and sorting out all of the notes you have taken, collecting together notes from different sources that explain, comment on, or give evidence for the same specific points. If you have put your notes on separate cards or slips of paper, you will find this easy to do.

As you read each note card, decide which aspect of your subject it pertains to, and group it with others that address the same issue. Don't be surprised if you have a large miscellaneous category made up of notes whose value seems questionable; many of your early note cards may indeed be no longer important, now that you have more clearly focused your subject. Realize, however, that although sorting out your note cards will help you define the main issues to concentrate on in your paper, it may also reveal points that need further research. Some additional trips to the library in search of specific pieces of information may still be necessary before your paper is finished.

Some writers, in sorting out their note cards, attach a comment card to each note card, briefly indicating the way they expect to use the note in the paper. Later, when they have begun writing, they can easily expand the comment card into a sentence or two that establishes a clear context for the material on the note cards. This practice helps to guarantee that the finished paper will not be a mere splicing together of facts or quotations; instead, the notes will function as part of a larger argument created by the researcher.

3.   Compose a tentative outline

20a

Few writers can progress beyond this point in composing a long paper without making at least an informal outline. The piles of note cards before you will help. Each of the large piles may be one of the main points in your paper, a main heading in your outline. Within each pile you will find notes that will make up the subpoints to be covered. With your usable notes organized in groups before you, sketch out an outline of your paper on a separate sheet of paper, including all the subpoints that you have notes to support. Some writers like to mark their note cards to correspond with the points in their written outline, so that they will know just which cards to pick up as they compose the paper.

4.   Segment your writing

Even a researcher who begins writing with a firm grasp of his or her subject and a clear conception of the form for the final research paper may sometimes feel overwhelmed by the amount of material to be assimilated into the paper. For that reason, many researchers view their papers in segments, and they approach the task of writing by thinking about and working on only one segment at a time. For example, you might set as the goal of your first composing session drafting only the introduction to your paper—the opening paragraph or paragraphs that will provide the reader with necessary background on your subject and introduce the paper's thesis. If you have formulated a tentative outline, make drafting just one new section of the outline the objective of each successive composing session. Don't feel that you have to compose the paper's parts sequentially; if you get stuck while writing one segment, leave it temporarily and work on a different one instead.

As in all writing, your goal is to put down on paper a draft, not a final polished essay. Write in any way that will help you move along quickly, whether that means using a soft pencil, a ballpoint pen, a typewriter, or a word processor. Skip lines if you write by hand, so that you will have room for later additions and changes.

In **20c** below, we will consider ways of incorporating quotations into your paper. But it is appropriate here to point out that you shouldn't take the time to copy into your draft quotations that you intend to use in your text. Instead, simply clip the note card with the quotation on it to the appropriate page of the draft. The time to worry about smoothly incorporating such material into your text will come later, as you revise.

5. Leave time for rethinking and revising

When you do begin revising, you should probably be prepared to make more changes than you might have made in other papers you have written. The length of a research paper and the number of different materials on which it is based open up a variety of possibilities for its organization, and you need to be ready to reassemble your material in several ways before you find a satisfactory arrangement. Transitional words, phrases, and sentences will be more important than ever as you attempt to link together smoothly the information gathered from your various sources and your own observations and conclusions.

Be prepared, too, for the possibility that you will have to return to the library to check a source or page number, to make sense of a confusing but important note card, or even to do some additional research. For these reasons, plan to leave enough time to write your earliest draft in several sittings, to put it away for a day or two (or at least overnight), and then to return to it fresh for thorough revision. A research paper is a complex project, and you should not expect to be able to dash off a draft one evening, patch it up the next, and hand it in the following morning. Apart from matters of composition—formidable enough in a paper of this length—you will need time to double-check the accuracy of your citations, type up the paper in the correct format, and proofread carefully. Leave yourself enough time to assemble a paper worthy of the weeks of research you have completed.

20b Avoiding plagiarism

Although the research paper is similar in many respects to the other writing you have done, it presents you with at least one major new task: accurately citing the sources of your research. If you fail to distinguish between your own words and thoughts and those of your sources, you mislead your reader into assuming that everything in the paper is your own work. Passing off the language or ideas of someone else as your own is a serious violation known as *plagiarism*.

Section **20d** considers the proper format for citing sources in your paper. But first, this section looks more closely at the concept of plagiarism itself, particularly as it pertains to using quotation and paraphrase in a research paper. Those are the two basic situations in which you must cite your sources in order to avoid plagiarizing, and we will examine them separately.

20b

1.   Quoting accurately

You must enclose every direct quotation in quotation marks, and you must cite its source in the paper. This rule is easy enough to understand. If you do not enclose in quotation marks the direct quotations that you take from your sources, your reader will have no way of knowing which words are yours and which are your sources'. And once you do use quotation marks to set off these phrases or sentences, your reader's natural question will be, "Who wrote this?" Your citation of the source answers that question.

Section **20b** reduces the complicated question of plagiarism to two basic rules, one governing quotation, the other governing paraphrase. *Accurate quotation, acceptable paraphrase,* and *common knowledge* are all defined and extensively illustrated, but the complexity of these issues for beginning writers probably demands that you not only assign this section for reading but also discuss it in class. Exercise 1 on pages 458–61 provides opportunities for students to practice the careful handling of quotation and paraphrase.

A quotation must present the words of your source exactly as they appear in the original text unless you use ellipsis marks or brackets to indicate that you have made changes in the text (see **20c**, **35c**, and **36c**). Be careful not to distort the meaning of the original text by omitting key words or by using the quoted passage in a sense not intended by the original writer. Consider the following examples. (For more information about the MLA system of parenthetical citation that is illustrated here, see **20d**.)

Source

In a given area the plague accomplished its kill within four to six months and then faded, except in the larger cities, where, rooting into the close-quartered population, it abated during the winter, only to reappear in spring and rage for another six months.

—Barbara W. Tuchman, *A Distant Mirror: The Calamitous 14th Century* (New York: Knopf, 1978) 93.

Inaccurate use of quotation

20b

In fourteenth—century cities, the plague "rooted into the close population during the winter, only to reappear in spring and rage for another six months" (Tuchman 93).

[The quoted passage in this sentence resembles Tuchman's, but it is not a word-for-word reproduction of her text, and it is therefore unacceptable. This writer has changed the word *rooting* to "rooted," and has omitted the words *quartered* and *it abated.*]

Inaccurate use of quotation

According to Barbara Tuchman, the great plague of the fourteenth century lasted only "four to six months and then faded" (93).

[This writer has quoted Tuchman's words accurately but has radically distorted her meaning by ignoring the rest of her sentence, where she refers to the plague's cyclical return in the cities, year after year.]

Accurate use of quotation

```
In medieval cities, according to Barbara Tuch-
man, the plague "abated during the winter" but
typically "[reappeared] in spring and [raged]
for another six months" (93).
```

[To make Tuchman's words fit the structure of his sentence, this writer had to change the original text's *reappear* and *rage* to *reappeared* and *raged*; he indicated those changes in an acceptable way, by putting the substituted words in brackets. Otherwise, the quoted passages are faithful to the original.]

2.   Paraphrasing accurately

20b

You must cite the source of every paraphrased idea unless that idea would be considered common knowledge. To explain this documentation rule, we need to consider separately its two key terms, *paraphrase* and *common knowledge.*

Paraphrasing

To *paraphrase* an idea means to change the words in which it is expressed without materially altering its meaning. Many writers have difficulty grasping the precise point at which the wording of a quotation has been sufficiently altered to constitute an acceptable paraphrase. *In general, several words in succession taken from another source may be said to constitute direct quotation.* Thus you cannot turn a quotation into an acceptable sentence of your own simply by changing a few words in the original. Consider the following examples, based on the same excerpt from Barbara Tuchman used above.

Unacceptable paraphrase

```
In a specific area the plague killed its vic-
tims in four to six months and then receded,
except in big cities, where it declined in the
winter, only to reappear in spring and flourish
for another six months (Tuchman 93).
```

[This writer has merely substituted a few words of his own for words in the source. The structure of the sentence, however, is Tuchman's. The result is plagiarism.]

Unacceptable paraphrase

```
The plague accomplished its kill within four to
six months in most places, but in the cities it
abated during the winter and would rage again
in the spring (Tuchman 93).
```

[The structure of this writer's sentence is original, but she has used several phrases taken directly from Tuchman: *accomplished its kill within four to six months, abated during the winter.* Borrowing such phrases without enclosing them in quotation marks makes the writer guilty of plagiarism. Just the word *rage* as used here would constitute plagiarism in most readers' eyes, even though it is not part of a longer phrase taken from Tuchman, because it is such a distinctive verb in Tuchman's original sentence.]

Acceptable paraphrase

```
In the crowded cities, the plague never com-
pletely disappeared; though relatively dormant
in the winter, it returned in full force when
the weather turned warm again (Tuchman 93).
```

[This writer has captured the exact meaning of Tuchman's passage, but in a sentence that is original in structure and diction. The only major words taken from Tuchman are *cities, plague,* and *winter;* such duplication is acceptable, since it would be impossible to find synonyms for these basic terms.]

Common knowledge

As shown above, even a quotation converted into acceptable paraphrase must have its source cited in your paper unless it falls into a category often referred to as *common knowledge.* What does common knowledge mean?

In practice, writers often find it simply impossible to give sources for everything they write. Where, for instance, did these rules for avoiding plagiarism come from? It would be difficult to say, since people have talked and written about the concept of plagiarism for several centuries at least. Our sense of what the term means in the 1990s is a good example of common knowledge, part of our understanding for which we have no single identifiable source.

If you are unsure whether an idea you encounter in your research qualifies as common knowledge, you might keep in mind the following two-step test. An idea is common knowledge and its source need not be cited *only* if

1. you find it repeated in many sources, rather than stated in just one; or
2. you believe it would be familiar to an average, educated person, even one who had not researched the subject (a person, for example, like one of your classmates).

For example, the fact that the Olympic games originated in Greece would not need citation, since it fulfills both of the conditions above (it is information that would be found in many books and articles on the Olympics, *and* it is a fact familiar to most people). Nor would the fact that the modern Olympic games were begun in 1896 require citation; although that fact fails the second condition (most people you asked would probably not be able to give you this date), it passes the first (anyone doing research on the Olympics would repeatedly encounter the date in a variety of sources).

In contrast, a single author's opinion about the propaganda value of the 1936 Berlin Olympics in Nazi Germany would probably need a citation, even if the opinion were acceptably paraphrased. Such a statement would not meet either of the conditions above. As a specific writer's opinion, it would appear only in a single source (though if you found a great many writers who shared this opinion, it would then qualify as common knowledge after all). And as the statement of a presumed authority on the Olympics, it would not be information that we could expect others who had not studied the subject to know.

20c Incorporating quotations into your writing

A good research paper is more than a collection of quoted passages strung together in some vaguely logical order. As the essays by Emmet Geary and Cyndi Lopardo in Chapters **21** and **23** demonstrate, more important to a successful research project is the researcher's ability to assimilate evidence from a variety of sources, to focus effectively, to provide a clear context for major points, and to organize information coherently.

Nonetheless, quotations do play a valuable role in research writing. A particularly apt quotation can underscore or clarify a key point or provide a strong concluding statement. Notice, for example, Geary's effective use of well-chosen quotations for these purposes on the first and last pages of his paper (see pages 465 and 481). The quoted words of your sources can also add immediacy to an issue or an argument. Lopardo effectively draws on quotations throughout her essay to bring to life the debate over women's education that raged in the 1890s (see Chapter **23**).

In **20b**, we considered the guidelines for accuracy in quotation. In **20d**, we examine the mechanics of parenthetically documenting such quotations when they occur in your paper. This section focuses quite differently on the *art* of effective quotation. Its goal is to help you blend quotations into your own prose with the ease and authority of an experienced researcher.

The examples below are all based on the following brief passage.

Section **20c** offers extensive discussion of one of the thorniest problems that beginning writers encounter as they draft a research paper: smoothly incorporating quotations from sources into their own prose. It provides and illustrates a large repertoire of strategies that students can easily master.

Consider teaching this section in connection with the sample research papers in Chapters **21** and **23**. Both papers not only provide a larger context for discussing the guidelines presented here but also illustrate the virtues of balancing a few well-chosen quotations with paraphrased material and with the writer's own analysis and explanation.

Source

> Pity the Pilgrims, who stepped ashore to confront a wall of forest and a cruel joke beneath the trees. New England stands on granite. Except for the silted beaver meadows and alluvial valleys like the Connecticut, the glaciers left the colonists only a thin mantle of hilly, stony soil.
>
> —Boyd Gibbons, "Do We Treat Our Soil Like Dirt?" *National Geographic*, Sept. 1984: 376.

1. Quoting an entire sentence

When you wish to quote an entire sentence from your source, you may do so in one of two ways: by attaching an attributor to the sentence to be quoted or by casting the sentence to be quoted as a noun clause in your own sentence.

Method 1: Adding an attributor

An *attributor* may be defined as a clause or phrase added to a full-sentence quotation to identify its source. In composing an attributor, you may use either the writer's name or an appropriate identifying phrase, such as "one scholar" or "a well-known writer." (See pages 447–50 for the different citation rules that apply in these two cases.) When the attributor precedes the quoted sentence, it should be followed by a comma.

20c

Attributor precedes quoted sentence

```
Boyd Gibbons comments, "Pity the Pilgrims, who

stepped ashore to confront a wall of forest and

a cruel joke beneath the trees" (376).
```

Attributor precedes quoted sentence

```
As one writer explains, "New England stands on

granite" (Gibbons 376).
```

Attributor precedes quoted sentence

```
According to Boyd Gibbons, "Except for the

silted beaver meadows and alluvial valleys like
```

Composing an Attributor

You can choose from a wide range of verbs when you compose an attributor, provided that the verb you use fits the context of your sentence.

Boyd Gibbons

asserts,	argues,
claims,	comments,
concedes,	concludes,
explains,	notes,
observes,	points out,
proposes,	says,
states,	stresses,
suggests,	remarks,
replies,	writes,

"Pity the Pilgrims, . . ."

20c

```
the Connecticut, the glaciers left the colo-
nists only a thin mantle of hilly, stony soil"
(376).
```

An attributor also may be inserted into the middle of a quoted sentence, may stand between two sentences quoted in succession, or may be placed in a separate sentence used to introduce a quoted sentence.

Attributor inserted into quoted sentence

```
"Pity the Pilgrims," writes Boyd Gibbons, "who
stepped ashore to confront a wall of forest and
a cruel joke beneath the trees" (376).
```

Attributor inserted between quoted sentences

```
"New England stands on granite," explains Boyd
Gibbons.  "Except for the silted beaver meadows
```

```
and alluvial valleys like the Connecticut, the
glaciers left the colonists only a thin mantle
of hilly, stony soil" (376).
```

Attributor placed in introductory sentence

```
Boyd Gibbons stresses the inhospitable terrain
that settlers found in the New World.  "Except
for the silted beaver meadows and alluvial val-
leys like the Connecticut," he observes, "the
glaciers left the colonists only a thin mantle
of hilly, stony soil" (376).
```

Method 2: Using a noun clause

Often the syntax of the sentence you quote will permit you to cast it as a noun clause in some variation on the following sentence: *So-and-so states that "[full sentence to be quoted]."* Notice that this pattern always requires you to change the capital letter at the beginning of the quoted sentence to a lower-case letter, a change that must be indicated with square brackets.

20c

Quoted sentence cast as noun clause

```
Boyd Gibbons points out that "[e]xcept for the
silted beaver meadows and alluvial valleys like
the Connecticut, the glaciers left the colo-
nists only a thin mantle of hilly, stony soil"
(376).
```

2.   Quoting part of a sentence

Don't automatically quote an entire sentence when quoting a few carefully chosen words will better serve your purposes. When you quote only part of a sentence, the source may be identified in the sentence or may appear in the parenthetical citation.

Partial sentence quoted

```
Boyd Gibbons writes that the Pilgrims "stepped
ashore to confront a wall of forest and a cruel
joke beneath the trees" (376).
```

Remember that when you quote only part of a sentence, the passage you quote must perfectly fit the grammar of the new sentence in which you place it.

Incorrect: quotation used ungrammatically

```
Though they came to the New World with visions
of paradise, the Pilgrims found "the glaciers
left the colonists only a thin mantle of hilly,
stony soil" (Gibbons 376).
```

Revised: quotation fits syntax of sentence

```
Though they came to the New World with visions
of paradise, the Pilgrims found "only a thin
mantle of hilly, stony soil" (Gibbons 376).
```

In the examples above, it was not necessary to indicate the omission of other words from the source because the fragmentary nature of the quoted passage and the lower-case letter at the start of the quotation already show that the quotation begins in the middle of a sentence. However, if the quoted portion of a sentence has the grammatical appearance of a complete sentence, as in the example that follows, ellipsis marks (three *spaced* periods) are required to indicate the place where words have been omitted.

Ellipsis at end of quotation

> "Pity the Pilgrims," writes Boyd Gibbons, "who
> stepped ashore to confront a wall of forest
> . . ." (376).

In this case, the sentence's final period comes after the parenthetical citation (see **20d**).

Similarly, if you omit words from the middle of a quotation—for example, because they are irrelevant to your point—you must show the omission with ellipsis marks.

Ellipsis in middle of quotation

> Boyd Gibbons has argued that the Pilgrims
> "stepped ashore to confront . . . a cruel joke
> beneath the trees" (376).

Keep in mind that you cannot omit words from a quotation if doing so would change the intended meaning of the original sentence.

For more information about using ellipsis marks, see **36c**.

20c

3.   Altering a quotation

If you make a change in a quotation in order to clarify the meaning of the quoted passage or to fit it into the syntax of your sentence, you must indicate the change with square brackets. One such alteration, for example, might involve an addition to the text.

Clarifying meaning of original text

> Boyd Gibbons explains that "the glaciers left
> the [New England] colonists only a thin mantle
> of hilly, stony soil" (376).

Adjusting syntax of original text

```
Boyd Gibbons observes that the Pilgrims "con-
front[ed] a wall of forest and a cruel joke be-
neath the trees" (376).
```

Other alterations, including even changing a lower-case letter to upper case, or vice versa, are indicated in the same way.

Changing original text

```
As Boyd Gibbons explains, "[T]he Pilgrims . . .
stepped ashore to confront a wall of forest and
a cruel joke beneath the trees" (376).
```

For more information about using brackets, see **35c**.

20d Citing sources in MLA style

20d   In **20b**, we examined the situations in which you must indicate the sources of the material—whether quoted or paraphrased—that you have used in writing your research paper. In this section, we turn to the method of making such citations in the text of your paper.

The system of documentation adopted by the Modern Language Association of America in 1984 eliminates the elaborate footnotes used for years by both students and scholars. The simplicity of this new system and the academic prestige of its proponent, the MLA, have brought it into widespread use, particularly in the humanities. Keep in mind, however, that preferred methods of documentation vary arbitrarily from discipline to discipline. Chapters **22** and **24** present two other widely used forms of documentation, the system of parenthetical citation prescribed by the American Psychological Association and the system of endnote documentation formerly advocated by the MLA. Still other methods of documentation exist as well. The best approach for you is simply to follow closely whatever model your instructor suggests.

The basic rules of parenthetical citation in MLA style are quite straightforward; it's the variations that become confusing. Section **20d** explains and illustrates all of the major variations: long quotations, citations when the author's name already appears in the text (see **20c**), citations to works by more than one author, citations to anonymous and multivolume works, citations to more than one work by the same author, and content notes. For a parallel discussion of these cases in APA documentation style, see **22b**.

The MLA system reduces documentation to two components. First, at the end of each passage whose source must be noted, the last name of the author and the page or pages on which the material is found are inserted in parentheses with no punctuation between the name and page number.

```
(Alexander 197—98)
```

At the end of the paper, on a separate sheet with the heading "Works Cited," a complete bibliographic entry is provided for each of the sources cited in the text (see Emmet Geary's Works Cited list on page 483). These entries, which follow the forms described in **19b**, are arranged alphabetically according to the last names of the authors.

```
Alexander, Edwin P.  On the Main Line: The Penn-

     sylvania Railroad in the 19th Century.  New

     York: Potter, 1971.
```

If you properly fill out a bibliography card for each of your sources as you take notes, you will be able to alphabetize the cards for the sources you used and copy your Works Cited entries directly from them.

20d

The examples that follow illustrate how this method of documentation is used for a variety of common sources.

1. Quotations

Typically, the parenthetical citation in a text comes *after* the quotation marks that close a quotation but *before* the sentence's end punctuation.

Parenthetical citation in text

```
The definitive biography of Mahatma Gandhi re-

mains to be written.  As one Gandhi scholar has
```

explained, "Multivolume works written by Gandhi's former colleagues and published in India
are comprehensive in scope, but their objectivity suffers from the authors' reverent regard
for their subject" (Juergensmeyer 294).

Citation in works cited

Juergensmeyer, Mark.   "The Gandhi Revival--A
      Review Article."   Journal of Asian Stud-
      ies 43 (1984): 293-98.

If the quoted passage ends with a question mark or exclamation point,
however, the original end punctuation remains inside the quotation
marks and a period is added after the parenthetical citation.

Parenthetical citation in text

A noted language scholar asks, "Are all our
ideas about the world controlled by our language, so that our reality is what we say
rather than what objectively, verifiably exists?" (Daniels 77).

Citation in works cited

Daniels, Harvey A.   Famous Last Words: The
      American Language Crisis Reconsidered.
      Carbondale: Southern Illinois UP,
      1983.

Below are some variations on these basic rules for documenting quotations.

Setting off a long quotation

A quotation of more than four lines is set off from the text, indented ten spaces from the left margin, and typed without quotation marks. Such a quotation is usually introduced with a colon unless it begins in the middle of a sentence that grammatically continues the sentence that introduces it. The parenthetical citation is placed two spaces *after* the end punctuation.

Parenthetical citation in text

One editor suggests that photographers trying to publish their work should aim to surpass—not just equal—the photographs they see in print:

> Editors know where they can get pictures like the ones they've already published. If you want to get noticed, you have to take pictures better than those. This is especially true if you are looking for assignments rather than to sell existing pictures. Why take a chance on a new photographer who will come up with no better than what you already have, an editor might reason? (Scully 33)

Citation in works cited

Scully, Judith. "Seeing Pictures." <u>Modern Photography</u> May 1984: 28–33.

20d

Incorporating the author's name into the text

When you have incorporated the author's name into the sentence that presents the quoted passage (see **20c**), only the page number of the source appears in the parenthetical citation.

Parenthetical citation in text

The English, claims Richard Altick, are obsessed by love for their dogs. "Walking dogs,"
he points out, "is a ritual that proceeds independently of weather, cataclysms, and the movements of the planets; they are led or carried
everywhere, into department stores, fishmon-
gers', greengrocers', buses, trains" (286).

Citation in works cited

20d

Altick, Richard D. To Be in England. New
     York: Norton, 1969.

Parenthetical citation in text

"After watching a lot of music videos," Holly
Brubach observes, "it's hard to escape the conclusions that no one has the nerve to say no to
a rock-and-roll star and that most videos would
be better if someone did" (102).

Citation in works cited

Brubach, Holly. "Rock-and-Roll Vaudeville."
     Atlantic July 1984: 99-102.

Citing a work by more than one author

When two or three persons wrote the material that you wish to quote, include the names of all. Follow the same order in which the names are printed in the original source.

Parenthetical citation in text

```
Selvin and Wilson argue that "a concern for ef-
fective writing is not a trivial elevation of
form over content.  Good writing is a condi-
tion, slowly achieved, of . . . being what one
means to be" (207).
```

Citation in works cited

```
Selvin, Hanan C., and Everett K. Wilson.  "On
     Sharpening Sociologists' Prose."  Socio-
     logical Quarterly 25 (1984): 205-22.
```

20d

When your source is a work by more than three authors, give the name only of the first in your parenthetical text citation, followed by the abbreviation *et al.* (Latin for "and others") not underlined. For example: (Leventhal et al. 54)

Citing an anonymous work

If the author of the material you are quoting is not given, use the title, or a shortened form of the title, in your parenthetical text citation. Place the titles of articles in quotation marks; underline the titles of books.

Parenthetical citation in text

```
Environmentalists protested that a recent study
of the plan to spray herbicides on marijuana
"systematically underestimated the possibility
```

```
of damage from such spraying and exaggerated
the benefits to be achieved by a spraying pro-
gram" ("Marijuana Spraying" 14).
```

Citation in works cited

```
"Marijuana Spraying Opposed."  New York Times
     22 Aug. 1984: 14.
```

In the case of a one-page article like that above, the page number may be omitted in the parenthetical text citation.

Citing a multivolume work

The parenthetical text citation to a work in more than one volume includes the volume number and a colon before the page citation.

Parenthetical citation in text

```
The medieval manor house dominated nearby cot-
tages "not only because it was better built,
but above all because it was almost invariably
designed for defence" (Bloch 2: 300).
```

Citation in works cited

```
Bloch, Marc.  Feudal Society.  Trans. L. A.
     Manyon.  2 vols.  Chicago: U of Chicago
     P, 1961.
```

Citing two works by the same author

If your Works Cited list includes more than one work by the same author, your parenthetical text citations to this author must indicate which work you are referring to. In such cases, add a shortened version of the relevant title. In the Works Cited list, substitute three hyphens and a period for the author's name in the second citation.

Parenthetical citation in text

> "Of America's eastern rivers," writes one
> historian, "none was longer or potentially
> more important than the one the Indians accu-
> rately described as the 'Long-reach River'--
> Susquehanna" (Hanlon, Wyoming Valley 17).

Citations in works cited

> Hanlon, Edward F.   The Wyoming Valley: An
>   American Portrait.   Woodland Hills:
>   Windsor, 1983.
> ---.   "Urban-Rural Cooperation and Conflict
>   in the Congress: The Breakdown of the
>   New Deal Coalition, 1933-1938."   Diss.
>   Georgetown U, 1967.

20d

2.   Paraphrases

As noted in **20c**, a successful research paper is more than a string of quotations. Although a strategically placed quotation can help to focus a paragraph or emphasize a point, an extended series of quotations in a research paper often creates the impression of disjointedness and confusion. Look instead for opportunities to express in your own words the ideas that you have discovered during your research.

As the following examples illustrate, the rules described above for acknowledging the sources of quotations also apply to paraphrased material.

Parenthetical citation in text (author's name in parenthetical citation)

The steadily growing role of television in politics has helped to shift attention away from the politicians' stands on issues to the way they appear before the camera (Meyrowitz 51).

Citation in works cited

Meyrowitz, Joshua. "Politics in the Video Eye: Where Have All the Heroes Gone?" Psychology Today July 1984: 46–51.

Parenthetical citation in text (author's name incorporated into text)

One effect of the microscope's development in the late 1600s, Paul Fussell points out, was to change attitudes toward insects. Whereas people in the seventeenth century had considered insects innocuous creatures, eighteenth-century men and women, exposed for the first time to drawings of magnified insect bodies, regarded them as hideous and contemptible (235–36).

Citation in works cited

Fussell, Paul. The Rhetorical World of Augustan Humanism: Ethics and Imagery from Swift to Burke. London: Oxford UP, 1965.

Parenthetical citation in text (source with two authors)

Computers may be dominating the modern office, but architects are beginning to counter this technological takeover by designing comfortable and inviting office interiors (Davies and Malone 73).

Citation in works cited

Davies, Douglas, and Maggie Malone.   "Offices of the Future."   Newsweek 14 May 1984: 72+.

Parenthetical citation in text (anonymous source)

Some airport delays, it appears, can be blamed on government deregulation of the airlines.   On at least one weekday at Kennedy International Airport, for example, airlines have now scheduled over sixty arrivals between four and five o'clock, even though the airport can accommodate only forty-nine landings each hour ("Not Quite Ready" 25).

Citation in works cited

"Not Quite Ready When You Are."   Time 9 July 1984: 25.

3. Content notes

Although footnotes have been eliminated from the citing of sources in the MLA system of documentation, they may still be used to add supplementary information to the text of a research paper. Such notes, often referred to as *content notes,* are indicated in the text with consecutive superscript numerals and are placed either at the bottom of the appropriate page or together on a separate sheet, with the heading "Notes," inserted after the text of the paper and before the Works Cited page. If you collect your notes together on a separate sheet, as most instructors prefer, double-space between and within the notes. Indent the first line of each note five spaces.

Content notes offer a convenient means of including explanatory material or referring the reader to additional sources of information.

Text with superscript

The art of biographical writing in nineteenth-century England has generally been undervalued,[1] with the result that modern readers tend to regard Victorian biographies with a certain condescension and smugness.

20d

Note

[1] A few recent authors, however, have recognized the artistic merit of at least some nineteenth-century biographical writing. For useful readings of several major biographies of the period, see Gwiasda and Reed.

The full publication information for sources mentioned in notes is supplied in the Works Cited list.

Citations in works cited

Gwiasda, Karl E. "The Boswell Biographers: A
        Study of 'Life and Letters' Writing in

the Victorian Period." Diss. Northwest-

    ern U, 1969.

Reed, Joseph W., Jr. <u>English Biography in</u>

    <u>the Early Nineteenth Century, 1801–1838</u>.

    New Haven: Yale UP, 1966.

20e Formatting the research paper

    The physical appearance of a research paper makes its own contribution to the paper's effectiveness. A meticulously prepared paper naturally inclines the reader to expect content of equal quality. Haphazard typing, by contrast, can undercut the authority of even the best research and writing by giving a reader the impression of hasty and careless work. Proper format, therefore, is more than a superficial concern.

    The format guidelines below are based on those suggested by the Modern Language Association. Your instructor may give you supplementary or alternative instructions to follow.

1. Paper

    Using a typewriter with a fresh ribbon, or a computer printer, type or print out your research paper on standard 8½-by-11-inch white bond. Do not use onionskin paper, which is hard to read, or erasable typing paper, which easily smears. For convenient reading, most instructors prefer that the pages of a research paper be held together with a paper clip rather than stapled or fastened in a folder.

2. Spacing and margins

    Double-space everything in your paper—text, long quotations, notes, and Works Cited list. Double-space as well between page headings (such as "Works Cited") and the first line of text on the page.

    Leave a one-inch margin on the top, bottom, and sides of each page. Page headings such as "Notes" and "Works Cited" are centered just within this margin, one inch from the top of the page. Page

---

Following MLA style, **20e** specifies that information about the writer of the paper should appear at the top of the first page of the text, rather than on a separate title page. If you wish your students to use a title page, remember to stipulate what information you want a title page to contain.

numbers are placed outside the top margin, one-half inch from the top of the page and one inch from the right side of the page. Number all pages, including the first. You should not use punctuation or abbreviations such as *p.* with page numbers; however, to identify your paper if pages become separated and misplaced, you may precede the number on the top of each page with your last name: Smith 1, Smith 2, and so on.

3. Title page

Do not include a separate title page unless your instructor specifically requests it. Instead, on four separate double-spaced lines in the upper left corner of the first page, type your name, the name of your instructor, the course number, and the date. Double-space, center the title of your paper, and double-space to begin the text of the paper. Double-space between lines of your title if it runs onto a second line. (See the title page of Emmet Geary's paper on page 465.)

EXERCISE 1

20e

Treat each of the passages below as if it were to become part of a research paper you are writing. In each case, compose the following:

1. A few sentences of your own incorporating an acceptable paraphrase of one or more of the ideas in the passage.
2. A few sentences of your own incorporating a quotation taken from the passage. (Remember that if you quote only part of a sentence, the phrase or clause that you quote must fit into the syntax of your sentence.)
3. A citation of the source in proper form for a Works Cited list.

Remember to include appropriate parenthetical text citations in your sentences for the first two items above.

1. Los Angeles, one might reasonably guess, is the most prodigious user of water in the state of California, if not the entire world. At least 12 million people inhabit the metropolitan region, a sightless sprawl that has filled a basin twice the size of Luxembourg and is spilling into the ultramontane deserts beyond. The climate is semiarid to emphatically dry, although many people, including Anglenos, seem surprised when you point this out, because enough water comes in by aqueduct each day (about two billion gallons) to have transformed this former stub-

---

Exercise 1

This exercise, offering students realistic practice in using sources with professional facility and accuracy, is much harder than it looks. For each passage given here, have four or five students put on the chalkboard their paraphrase of the text; four or five others should put on the board their original passage incorporating a quotation from the text. The class as a whole can then discuss each student's work. Watch especially for (1) unacceptable paraphrase (whole phrases or distinctive sentence patterns from the original inadvertently incorporated into the student's own sentences); (2) inaccurate quotation (words dropped, altered, or misspelled); (3) quoted passages awkwardly or ungrammatically incorporated in the student's own sentences; (4) inaccurate form in Works Cited citations. You may wish to repeat this exercise several times.

bly grassland and alkali waste into an ersatz Miami, six times as large. Los Angeles now diverts the entire flow of the Owens River, one of the largest of the eastern Sierra Nevada streams; it appropriates a substantial share of the Colorado River, the largest by far in the American Southwest; it siphons off about a third of the flow of the Feather River, one of the biggest in the state, through an aqueduct 445 miles long. The few meager streams in and around the basin have long since been sucked dry.

In Los Angeles, even after months of habitual drought (southern California is virtually rainless from April through November), the fastidiously manicured lawns remain green. The swimming pools remain filled, eight million cars well washed. There are verdant cemeteries for humans and their pets. The Palm Springs Chamber of Commerce boasts of more than 100 golf courses, shining like green lakes in that desiccated landscape, where it rains about four inches in a typical year. Los Angeles is a palpable mirage, a vast outdoor Disneyland, the Babylon and Ur of the desert empire that is the American West.

[The opening two paragraphs of an article in the bimonthly magazine Greenpeace. The title of the article is The Emerald Desert; the author is Marc Reisner; the article appears on pages 6 to 10 of the July-August 1989 issue. This passage is on page 6.]

20e

2. What were the Romans like at that time—at the beginning of contact with the older Greeks in the middle of the third century B.C.? They were a small group of a few hundred thousand souls, one group of several that had emerged from barbarous central Europe and pushed their way into Italy in search of land, and they had long plodded on in silence at the dull task of making the soil provide food. For a while they had been subdued by the Etruscans, but taught by their conquerors to use arms in strong masses, they had applied this lesson by driving off their oppressors and re-establishing their old independent town meetings, returning again to the tilling of the soil. A prolific and puritanic folk with a strict social morality, they outgrew their boundaries and began to expand. In the contests that resulted the Romans came off the victors. In [page break] organizing the adjacent tribes into a federal union they revealed a peculiar liberalism—unmatched anywhere among the barbarians of that day—by abstaining from the exaction of tribute; they also betrayed an imagination of high quality in the invention of cooperative leagues, and unusual capacity for legal logic in the shaping of municipal and civic forms.

[A passage on pages 9 and 10 (note the page break indicated in this excerpt) in Tenney Frank's book Life and Literature in the Roman Republic, originally published in 1930 as volume seven of the Sather Classical Lectures, republished in 1965 by the University of California Press at Berkeley.]

3. In a Boston business district that lately has been overwhelmed by glass and metal office towers, oddly shaped hotels, and an abundance of trendy shops, a few vestiges of the old "Hub City" remain. Paul Revere's house still stands in a neighborhood that is fighting off condominium developers. Faneuil Hall, a revolutionary war meeting-house, is the centerpiece of a burgeoning plaza full of shops and restaurants. Baseballs still fly over the left-field wall at Fenway Park, one of the last surviving stadiums that knew Babe Ruth. And then there's South Station.

   Once South Station dominated its neighborhood in Dewey Square; now it lays in the shadow of several of those new office towers. But at age 90, South Station is nearing the end of a major facelift that will ensure its status as a Boston landmark into the next century. At the same time, South Station remains one of the busiest stations on Amtrak's busiest route, the Northeast Corridor, of which it is the northern anchor.

   [From page 38 of an article by Tom Nelligan in Trains, a monthly magazine. The article, entitled Boston South Station Revival, runs from page 38 to page 42 in the June 1989 issue.]

20e

4. In the second half of the seventeenth century, Holland, a term used to describe the seven United Provinces of the Northern Netherlands, was at the peak of its world power and prestige. With its dense, teeming population of two million hard-working Dutchmen crowded into a tiny area, Holland was by far the richest, most urbanized, most cosmopolitan state in Europe. Not surprisingly, the prosperity of this small state was a source of wonder and envy to its neighbors, and often this envy turned to greed. On such occasions, the Dutch drew on certain national characteristics to defend themselves. They were valiant, obstinate and resourceful, and when they fought—first against the Spaniards, then against the English and finally against the French—they fought in a way which was practical and, at the same time, desperately and sublimely heroic.

   [Passage is on page 178 of Peter the Great: His Life and World, by Robert K. Massie, published in 1981 in New York by

Ballantine Books. The book was first published by Alfred A. Knopf in 1980.]

5. Because girls identify positively with their mothers and then recreate the mothering role in their own lives, some psychologists believe that their capacities for nurturance and empathy are more developed than boys'. Accordingly, it is natural for a woman to define herself through her social relationships. By contrast, male exposure to the military and to competitive sports may engender such traditional male values as aggressiveness.

   Whatever the cause, where women tend to cooperate, men tend to compete. Whether in public or private communication, men are more comfortable than women in a combative "debate" style. Lecturing, arguing, pivoting on claims from reason or logic, and demanding or providing evidence are more typically male than female behaviors. Consistent with these findings, women use less hostile verbs than men. Men are more likely than women to engage in verbal dueling.

   Not only are the messages of women less verbally aggressive but they tend to be more pro-social, particularly in their stress on relationships rather than on autonomous action. In their political ads, women usually stress their strengths rather than counteract their weaknesses.
   [Passage is on page 82 of Kathleen Hall Jamieson's book Eloquence in an Electronic Age: The Transformation of Political Speechmaking, published in New York by Oxford University Press in 1988.]

20e

For Further Reading

Kohlich, Augustus M. "Plagiarism: The Worm of Reason." *College English* 45 (1983): 141–48.

van Leunen, Mary-Claire. *A Handbook for Scholars*. Rev. ed. New York: Oxford UP, 1992.

21 Student Research Paper A: MLA Documentation

The student research paper that follows, Emmet Geary's "Recovery from the Florence Flood: A Masterpiece of Restoration," is an excellent example of an informative report that is tightly focused around a precise thesis statement. As explained in Chapter **17**, Geary drew on his reading about the effects of the 1966 flood in Florence, Italy, to define a narrow subject for his paper—the efforts of professionals and volunteers to rescue and restore the city's valuable art. The thesis statement in which he introduces this focusing idea comes at the end of his first paragraph, a paragraph that compactly provides all the background needed by the reader to understand the rest of the paper.

Perhaps the best feature of this paper is Geary's skillful integration of his sources. Throughout the essay, he moves back and forth among his sources, pulling together related pieces of information and weaving them into a coherent and well-developed narrative. Excellent transitions between paragraphs help to unify the paper, and Geary's clear explanations of occasionally technical information hold the reader's interest.

From start to finish, this paper is an example of the way in which the researcher's vision of a subject can shape the diverse products of reading and note taking into a unified and original whole.

463

Among the points that might be included in a discussion of the sample research paper and its accompanying documentation in this chapter are the following:

1. Using an introduction to provide a brisk summary of background information (pages 464–65).
2. Focusing a research paper around a thesis (pages 464–67).
3. Summarizing sources effectively (pages 466–67).
4. Integrating information from several different sources (pages 470–71).
5. Using transitions effectively (pages 472–73, 476–77).
6. Echoing the paper's introduction and thesis in its conclusion (pages 480–81).

Note the effective movement of Geary's introductory paragraph. It begins with a brief but specific survey of the flood's devastating impact on Florence, then moves to the damage done to the city's art, then (with the Batini quotation) shifts to the narrower subject of art restoration, the focus of Geary's paper.

Compare the version of the Batini quotation given in the paper with the original, on Geary's note card:

21

Batini, p. 90

"Despite the various complex restoration methods briefly explained above, the havoc played by the flood among works of art in Florence presented many new problems. For example, never before had so many and diverse works of art been damaged at the same time, all of which needed to be restored at once by an army of specialists, unfortunately a rarity today."

In Geary's paper, the bracketed capital *N* at the start of the quotation and the ellipsis marks at the end indicate that only part of the original sentence is quoted here.

1/2"
1"
1

Emmet Geary

Professor P. L. Herrold

History 100

March 28, 1995

Recovery from the Florence Flood:

A Masterpiece of Restoration

On November 4, 1966, the swollen Arno River
inundated Florence, Italy. Nineteen inches of
rain had fallen in two days, causing floodwater to
reach depths of twenty feet in some parts of the
city. The damage was devastating: six thousand of
the city's ten thousand shops were destroyed, five
thousand families were left homeless, and more than
a hundred people drowned. But the primary reason
that most outsiders grieved for Florence was the
damage to its unique collection of Renaissance art
treasures and rare books. As Giorgio Batini noted,
"[N]ever before had so many and diverse works of art
been damaged at the same time, all of which needed
to be restored at once . . ." (90). The story of
this restoration is a story of commitment and
ingenuity. Though the Florence flood destroyed
some priceless masterpieces and heavily damaged

21

21 **If we compare Geary's paraphrase of Horton with the original text, we see that he has effectively and accurately summarized the source in his own words:**

A few days after the disastrous floods that occurred in Italy on November 4, 1966, a group of art lovers in the United States organized the Committee to Rescue Italian Art (CRIA). One of their first acts was to send, on November 8, two art historians to Florence and Venice, the areas where the art losses were reported to be the greatest, to assess the damage and to find out what could be done to help. Word was received from them by transatlantic telephone that restoration experts and materials were urgently needed. By November 14, there were 16 conservators on their way to Florence. Within the next week, they were joined by four more conservators. This group of 20, headed by Lawrence Majewski, acting director of the Conservation Center, Institute of Fine Arts, New York University, included: a chemist; 13 conservators of paintings, frescoes, mosaics, and furniture; two conservators of prints and drawings; one librarian; and three bookbinders, specializing in the restoration and conservation of books, manuscripts, and other library materials.

2

others, it inspired valiant efforts among professional restorers and untrained volunteers
alike, and even occasioned some discoveries in the
field of art that would otherwise never have been
made.

As the floodwater rose, the first demonstration of dedication to art was shown by
fourteen members of the staff of the Uffizi
Gallery, who risked their lives to rescue twenty-
four paintings stored in the museum's basement
(Rhode 20). When the floodwater had subsided,
generous contributions from all over the world
arrived in Florence, and hundreds of volunteers--
mainly students from throughout Europe and North
America--came to undertake the messy cleanup that
would return Florence to normal and salvage the
city's damaged treasures. The volunteers were led
by an international team of art historians and
conservators. Within only a few days of the flood,
for example, one group of American art lovers had
organized the Committee to Rescue Italian Art and
two weeks later had dispatched to Florence a team of
twenty experts, including specialists in paintings,

21

21

By inserting the citation to Ricci in the middle of his sentence, Geary makes it clear that only the information in the first half of the sentence—the specific data about the size and speed of the floodwater—comes from this source.

3

mosaics, furniture, prints, bookbindings, and
manuscripts (Horton 1035).

Two distinct types of damage to art had
resulted from the flood: that due to submersion,
and that due to water pressure, turbulence, and
friction. Submersion caused the flood's most
significant artistic loss——the great <u>Crucifix</u> by
Giovanni Cimabue, painted at the end of the
thirteenth century——as well as most of the other
damage to paintings and books. Compounding the
problem of submersion was oil, which had spilled
from ruptured fuel tanks around the city, and which
rode the top of the floodwater, coating everything
it touched. Having never before worked on
paintings stained by fuel oil, restorers were
forced to experiment with a number of solvents,
including benzene and carbon tetrachloride (Judge
39). Water pressure and turbulence created a
different kind of devastation. Sweeping through
the city at forty to fifty miles an hour, the
twelve-foot wave of water (Ricci 25) knocked
sculptures from their pedestals and damaged the
altarpieces of churches. The famous baptistry

21

Geary found his information about the damage to Ghiberti's baptistry doors in many sources; consequently, it could be considered common knowledge and did not require specific documentation.

In his paragraph describing the flood's damage to Florence's libraries, note Geary's effective integration of related material from different sources.

21

4

doors of the city's cathedral, cast by Lorenzo
Ghiberti in the fifteenth century, were violently
battered by the water, which dislodged five of the
doors' bronze panels.

The first task that restoration workers faced
was collecting the objects to be restored. Since
the last serious threat to Florence's art had come
from German artillery bombardment during World War
II, many valuable books and manuscripts had been
stored below ground for safety (Horton 1036). Now
these books had to be pulled from library basements
full of water and mud. In the Biblioteca Nazionale
alone, more than 300,000 volumes were damaged; in
the library of the Gabinetto Vieusseux, 250,000
more had been under water and needed immediate
attention ("Florentine Flood Disaster" 194). All
told, nearly two million books were damaged by the
flood (Horton 1036).

Not only the floodwater but the subsequent
growth of destructive mold spores threatened
Florence's priceless books. As Carolyn Horton
explains, mold endangered even books that had
escaped direct damage from the flood:

21

A quotation of more than four typed lines is set off by indenting ten spaces. Double-space between the last line of the text and the first line of the quotation, and double-space the quotation itself. No quotation marks are used when a quotation is set off in this way.

21

Again, the information given here about methods of restoring and drying books was available in several sources and therefore did not require documentation in Geary's paper.

Note Geary's smooth transition between the last two paragraphs, which deal with salvaging books, and this one, which moves on to consider damage done to paintings on wooden panels: "Like books . . . "

5

> Books are hygroscopic, i.e., have the
> capacity for absorbing water from the air
> around them. Therefore any books stored
> in conditions of high humidity are in
> danger of being damaged by mold. We had
> received reports that the flooded area of
> Florence had become, in effect, a huge
> humidity chamber. The wet books in rooms
> that were only partially flooded were
> humidifying the dry books on the upper
> shelves. (1035)

Salvaged books, covered with mud and oil and soaked
with water, were first washed with mild soap and
then treated with fungicides and antibiotics that
would inhibit the growth of mold and bacteria.
Then came the drying, by any means available: heating in tobacco ovens and brick kilns, interleaving
pages with absorbent paper, or spraying with powder.

   Like books, paintings on wooden panels were
particularly susceptible to damage from submersion in water. As one observer described the
problem:

21

Compare Geary's version of the quotation from the anonymous article "The Florentine Flood Disaster" with the original text:

> The situation regarding panel paintings has not changed much since the preliminary reports. The return to health will be slow and laborious. As is well known, when the water has soaked into the wood, the priming layer of glue and gesso dissolves, and the colours dissolve with it. This is not only the case with panels that were entirely submerged, as at Santa Croce (Fig. I). Even in cases where a few inches along the bottom were submerged, those parts buckle, and crack the part that seemed safe. More unexpected still, some panels which seemed quite undamaged when the flood subsided, developed blisters two or three days later, and the paint began to fall.

Note the editorial changes that Geary has made: (1) he has enclosed the initial *W* of his quotation in brackets to indicate that the first words of the original quotation have been omitted; (2) he has inserted the word *plaster* in brackets to define the unfamiliar term *gesso* for the reader; (3) he has inserted ellipsis marks to indicate an omission after his third sentence (note that the usual three periods follow a fourth period—the period of the sentence); and (4) he has inserted the word *only* in brackets to make the sense of the original quotation clearer. Geary has retained the unorthodox punctuation and the British spelling ("colours") of the original text.

21

6

[W]hen the water has soaked into the
wood, the priming layer of glue and gesso
[plaster] dissolves, and the colours
dissolve with it. . . . Even in cases
where [only] a few inches along the
bottom were submerged, those parts
buckle, and crack the part that seemed
safe. More unexpected still, some
panels which seemed quite undamaged when
the flood subsided, developed blisters
two or three days later, and the paint
began to fall. ("Florentine Flood
Disaster" 193)

21

To prevent wooden panels from drying too fast and
shrinking, thus causing the pigment to flake off,
restoration workers had to reduce the humidity
around the panels gradually. Within twelve days of
the flood, the Limonaia, a large greenhouse in one
of Florence's public parks, was converted to a
sophisticated drying facility complete with an
elaborate humidity-control system. Initially set
at ninety percent, the humidity level inside was
gradually lowered, and the panels were constantly

Another excellent transition links the two paragraphs on this page: "Even more difficult to restore . . ."

When parts of a sentence derive from different sources, insert the appropriate parenthetical citations in midsentence, as Geary does, for accurate documentation. Consider the following two note cards.

21

> "Florentine Flood Disaster," p. 193
>
> Damage to frescoes more serious than people thought at first: dampness penetrated plaster even above the level of the floodwater, causing "a breaking down of the adhesion between the plaster layers and the wall."

> "Slow Art Restoration," p. 42
>
> Salt dissolved in the floodwaters "had become lodged inside and under wood panels and frescoes, causing tiny explosions to tear the paint."

7

checked to ensure sufficiently slow drying (Batini
90-91). Only after complete drying, a process that
sometimes took many months, could the painted
panels be moved to laboratories for further restoration, which usually involved planing down the
back of the panels until only the pigment and priming layers remained, and then attaching a lami-
nated, shrink-proof panel to the back of the
painting ("Road Back" 80).

Even more difficult to restore were Florence's frescoes, paintings originally executed
directly on damp plaster, so that the pigment fused
with the surface of the wall. Besides damage from
submersion and floating fuel oil, frescoes were
affected by dampness, which caused the plaster
layers to separate from the wall ("Florentine Flood
Disaster" 193), and by salt contained in the
floodwater, which penetrated the plaster and
caused "tiny explosions" in the painted surface as
the wall dried ("Slow Art Restoration" 42). To
save frescoes, restorers used a technique called
"strapo," which involves applying a coating of glue
and a canvas sheet to the wall. After the glue

21

Geary's previous paragraphs have discussed the restoration of damaged books, paintings, and frescoes. In the final paragraph before his conclusion, Geary considers the flood's unexpectedly beneficial effects on sculptures.

21

8

has dried, the painting can be pulled from the wall intact on the canvas. Difficult as this process is, it yielded an unexpected reward: when the painted surfaces were removed, more than three hundred sinopias, or preliminary drawings for the frescoes, were uncovered on the walls ("Church Found" 35).

Surprisingly, sculpture seems to have received more benefit than harm from the flood. Some statues were actually cleaned by the swirling water, whose mud acted as a gentle abrasive, removing the grime of hundreds of years. The restorers themselves used mud to clean sections of statues that were untouched by the floodwater (Batini 103–05). Fuel oil, on the other hand, did pose a serious threat to sculpture. Since marble is a porous stone, the oil penetrated beneath the surface and had to be drawn out and absorbed by talc applied to the statues. But such thorough cleaning of these statues actually left them cleaner than they had been before the flood and led to a few surprises. For example, the restoration revealed for the first time that Donatello's statue The

21

The Ricci quotation provides the foundation for an effective concluding paragraph. It not only echoes ideas from the paper's introduction but also gives Geary the opportunity to reiterate one of his main ideas—the importance of the volunteer efforts to save Florence's art.

21

9

Magdalen had originally had gilded hair ("Florentine Flood Disaster" 194).

Only a few months after the floodwater had
devastated Florence, as the frantic restoration
work continued, Leonardo Ricci aptly described the
world's reaction to the disaster. "Many floods
indeed and natural tragedies have happened
everywhere in the world," he wrote. "But never
have we heard such a cry as for Florence. As if,
instead of a city it were a person, a loved one who
in a way belongs to everybody and without whom it is
impossible to live" (25, 32). In a real sense,
the rescued art of Florence does belong to everyone: without generous contributions of money from
around the world and the tireless efforts of an international corps of volunteers, Florence's treasures could not have survived.

21

In the Works Cited, anonymous works are arranged alphabetically by the first significant word in the title.

21

Ricci's article begins on page 25 but continues on nonconsecutive pages later in the magazine.

The March 12, 1967, issue of the *New York Times* is a Sunday edition divided into sections; the section number must therefore be included in the citation. The August 9, 1967, issue—a weekday issue—is paged continuously without section divisions; no section number is necessary, since there is only one page 42 in the issue.

1" 1/2"
10

Works Cited

Batini, Giorgio. 4 November 1966: The River Arno in the Museums of Florence. Trans. Timothy Paterson. Florence: Bonechi Editore, 1967.

"Church Found under Basilica in Florence." New York Times 4 Nov. 1967, late city ed.: 35.

"The Florentine Flood Disaster." Burlington Magazine 109 (1967): 193–94.

Horton, Carolyn. "Saving the Libraries of Florence." Wilson Library Bulletin 41 (1967): 1034–43.

Judge, Joseph. "Florence Rises from the Flood." National Geographic July 1967: 1–43.

Rhode, Eric. "Good News from Florence." New Statesman 6 Jan. 1967: 20.

Ricci, Leonard. "Exploratory Research in Urban Form and the Future of Florence." Arts and Architecture Feb. 1967: 25+.

"Road Back Is Long for Florentines." New York Times 12 Mar. 1967, late city ed., sec. 1: 80.

"Slow Art Restoration Continues in Florence." New York Times 9 Aug. 1967, late city ed.: 42.

21

22 *Using APA Documentation*

Originally formulated nearly seventy years ago to guide psychologists in the preparation of scholarly articles, the American Psychological Association's style of documentation is the norm today for professional publication not only in psychology but throughout the social sciences. This chapter will discuss and illustrate the features of APA documentation and explain the formatting of a paper prepared according to APA guidelines. It is followed by a chapter that contains a complete student research paper documented in APA style.

22a APA reference list forms

APA documentation style resembles MLA documentation in its use of brief parenthetical references in the text to a list of full citations, called a *reference list,* at the end of the paper. But subtle differences distinguish the two methods of documentation. Before considering APA guidelines for using parenthetical citations and for formatting the components of a research paper, this chapter first examines sample reference list citations in APA style for the most frequently used types of sources. The Table of APA Reference List Forms on pages 485–87 conveniently lists the model APA references found on pages 487–97. For additional information about APA citations, see the *Publication Manual of the American Psychological Association,* cited in item 3.

This chapter provides a complete guide to the forms of APA documentation as presented in the most recent (1994) edition of the APA *Publication Manual.* It presents an accessible list of model APA reference forms for virtually every source that an undergraduate might encounter (**22a**), as well as an extended discussion of the APA method of citing sources (**22b**) and a step-by-step guide to formatting a paper in APA style (**22c**).

QUICK REFERENCE: *Features of APA Documentation*

Keep in mind the following distinctive characteristics of APA reference list citations.

Author's name	In place of the author's first and middle names, use initials.
Date of publication	Always place the date of publication, enclosed in parentheses, directly after the author's name. The remaining publication information comes later in the citation.
Capitalization	When listing the title of a book or a periodical article, capitalize only the first word of the title, the first word of the subtitle, and any proper nouns in the title.
Indentation	Indent the first line of each citation five spaces.
Abbreviations	Remember that APA documentation uses fewer abbreviations than MLA style; months of the year and names of universities, for example, are spelled out.

22a

Table of APA Reference List Forms

Books

1. Book by one author
2. Book by two or more authors
3. Book by a committee, commission, association, or other group
4. Anonymous book

5. Later or revised edition of a book
6. Edited book
7. Translated book
8. Book in more than one volume
9. Republished book

Parts of books

10. Essay in a collection of essays by various authors
11. Journal or magazine article reprinted in a collection of essays by various authors

Articles in journals and magazines

12. Article in a journal paginated by the volume (*continuous pagination*)
13. Article in a journal paginated issue by issue
14. Article in a weekly magazine
15. Article in a monthly magazine

Articles in newspapers

22a

16. Article in a newspaper
17. Letter to the editor

Other print sources

18. Book review
19. Dissertation, unpublished, microfilm copy
20. Dissertation, unpublished, manuscript copy
21. Encyclopedia article
22. Government document
23. Interview, published
24. Proceedings of a conference
25. Report

Nonprint sources

26. Computer software

27. Film, videotape, audiotape, slides, chart, artwork
28. Lecture, unpublished

Books

1. Book by one author

Hayes, J. R. (1978). Cognitive psychology: Thinking and creating. Homewood, IL:
Dorsey Press.

- Leave one space between elements in the citation.
- Capitalize only the first word of the title and the first word of the subtitle (and proper nouns in the title, if any).
- Add the U.S. Postal Service abbreviation for the state if the city of publication is not well known.
- For nonacademic publishers, use a shortened form of the company's name, omitting such terms as *Co., Inc.,* and *Publishers.* However, write out in full the names of university presses.

22a

2. Book by two or more authors

Clark, H. H., & Clark, E. V. (1977).
Psychology and language: An introduction to
psycholinguistics. New York: Harcourt.

Naylor, J. C., Pritchard, R. D., & Il-
gen, D. R. (1980). A theory of behavior in
organizations. New York: Academic Press.

- Regardless of the number of authors, give the names of all in inverted order, following each name with a comma and preceding the last name with an ampersand (&).

3. Book by a committee, commission, association, or other group

```
     American Psychological Association.

(1994). Publication manual of the American

Psychological Association (4th ed.). Washing-

ton, DC: Author.
```

- When the author of the book is also its publisher, substitute the word *Author* for the name of the publisher at the end of the citation.
- The first parenthetical text citation to this work would begin with the joint author's name written out in full: (American Psychological Association [APA], 1994). Since the abbreviation of this association's name is a familiar one, subsequent parenthetical text citations may give only the abbreviation: (APA, 1994). See **22b**.

4. Anonymous book

22a

```
     Research in outdoor education: Summaries

of doctoral studies. (1973). Washington, DC:

American Association for Health, Physical Ed-

ucation, and Recreation.
```

- The parenthetical text citation for an anonymous work begins with the first two or three words of the title: (Research in Outdoor, 1973). See **22b**.

5. Later or revised edition of a book

```
     Phelps, R. R. (1986). A guide to re-

search in music education (3rd ed.). Me-

tuchen, NJ: Scarecrow.
```

Jourard, S. M. (1971). <u>The transparent
self</u> (Rev. ed.). New York: Van Nostrand.

- When information in parentheses follows the title of a book, as it does here, no punctuation appears between the title and the parentheses.

6. Edited book

Halebsky, S. (Ed.). (1973). <u>The sociology of the city.</u> New York: Scribner's.

Stam, H. J., Rogers, T. B., & Gergen, K.
J. (Eds.). (1987). <u>The analysis of psycholog-
ical theory: Metapsychological perspectives.</u>
Washington, DC: Hemisphere.

7. Translated book

Hauser, A. (1982). <u>The sociology of art</u>
(K. J. Northcott, Trans.). Chicago: University of Chicago Press. (Original work published 1974)

22a

- In parentheses after the title, supply the translator's name in normal order.
- End the citation with a parenthetical note giving the date of the book's original publication. Do not use punctuation within these parentheses.

8. Book in more than one volume

Ford, J. (1975). <u>Paradigms and fairy
tales: An introduction to the science of
meanings</u> (Vols. 1–2). London: Routledge.

- After the title, indicate which volumes of the work you refer to in your paper; that information may differ from the total number of volumes in the work.

9. Republished book

Cottrell, F. (1970). <u>Energy and society:</u>

<u>The relation between energy, social change,</u>

<u>and economic development.</u> Westport, CT:

Greenwood Press. (Original work published

1955)

- The copyright page of this book indicates that it was originally issued in 1955 by a different publisher. Although information about the first publisher is not required in this citation, the original publication date is given in a parenthetical note at the end of the citation.

Parts of books

10. Essay in a collection of essays by various authors

Boskoff, A. (1964). Recent theories of

social change. In W. J. Cahnman & A. Boskoff

(Eds.), <u>Sociology and history</u> (pp. 140–157).

New York: Free Press of Glencoe.

Tawney, J. W. (1977). Educating severely

handicapped children and their parents

through telecommunications. In N. G. Haring &

L. J. Brown (Eds.), <u>Teaching the severely</u>

<u>handicapped</u> (Vol. 2, pp. 315–340). New York:

Grune & Stratton.

- Follow the title of the essay by the name(s) of the editor(s) of the book in which it is contained, the title of the book, and the pages on which the essay is found.
- For an essay in a multivolume collection, include the appropriate volume number as shown in the second example.
- Note that when inclusive page numbers are provided in an APA citation, the complete second number is used (not 315–*40*, but 315–*340*).

11. Journal or magazine article reprinted in a collection of essays by various authors

Motokawa, K. (1965). Retinal traces and visual perception of movement. In I. M. Spigel (Ed.), Readings in the study of visually perceived movement (pp. 288–303). New York: Harper. (Reprinted from the Journal of Experimental Psychology, 1953, 45, 369–377)

- When information about an article's earlier publication is noted in the collection you are using, provide it in parentheses at the end of the citation.

22a

Articles in journals and magazines

12. Article in a journal paginated by the volume (continuous pagination)

Webster, G. R. (1989). Partisanship in American presidential, senatorial, and gubernatorial elections in ten western states. Political Geography Quarterly, 8, 161–179.

- Most periodicals published quarterly or less frequently use continuous pagination for all the issues published in a single year; that is, if the year's first issue ends with page 125, the second issue begins with page 126. The citation to such a periodical includes the name of the journal and the volume number (underlined), followed by the first and last pages of the article (without the abbreviation *pp.*).
- Do not enclose the title of the article in quotation marks.

13. Article in a journal paginated issue by issue

      Maranto, C. D. (1987). Continuing con-

cerns in music therapy ethics. Music Therapy,

6(2), 59-63.

- When each issue of a journal begins with page 1, include the issue number (2) in parentheses immediately after the underlined volume number (6).

14. Article in a weekly magazine

      Jaroff, L. (1989, July 3). Fury on the

sun. Time, 134, 46-55.

      Running up a global tab. (1989, July

10). Time, 134, 47.

- Give the date with the year first, followed by the month, unabbreviated, and the day.
- End the citation with the volume number, if it is given, and the page number or numbers of the article.
- For an anonymous article, begin the citation with the title.

15. Article in a monthly magazine

      Hill, J. V. (1989, May). The design and

procurement of training simulators. Educa-

tional Technology, 29, 26-27.

22a

Articles in newspapers

16. Article in a newspaper

Freitag, M. (1989, August 17). The battle over medical costs. New York Times, pp.
25, 28.

U.S. panel weighs birth pill warning.
(1989, March 29). Chicago Sun-Times, p. 2.

- In citations to newspaper articles, use the abbreviations *p.* or *pp.* before the page numbers.
- If an article is continued on nonconsecutive pages, give all page numbers, separated by commas: pp. 25, 28.

17. Letter to the editor

Capezza, D. (1989, July 13). Of course,
oil spills can be prevented [Letter to the
editor]. New York Times, p. A22.

- If the letter has been given a title, as here, insert the title before the bracketed notation identifying the piece as a letter.

Other print sources

18. Book review

Kimble, G. A. (1988). Psychology's brief
history [Review of the book Historical foundations of modern psychology]. Contemporary
Psychology, 33, 878-879.

Belotti, M. (1988). [Review of the book

22a

The paradox of poverty: A reappraisal of economic development policy]. Journal of Economic Literature, 26, 1233–1234.

- If the review has a title, give it before the bracketed notation identifying the piece as a review.
- Note that the name of the author of the work being reviewed does not appear in the citation.

19. Dissertation, unpublished, microfilm copy

Johnson, T. P. (1989). The social environment and health. Dissertation Abstracts
International, 49, 3514A. (University Microfilms No. 8903561)

- Use this format if your source is a university microfilm copy of a dissertation. Note that the date given refers to this volume of *Dissertation Abstracts International,* not the date of the dissertation itself.

20. Dissertation, unpublished, manuscript copy

Johnson, T. P. (1989). The social envi-
ronment and health (Doctoral dissertation,
University of Kentucky, 1988). Dissertation
Abstracts International, 49, 3514A.

- Use this format if your source is a manuscript copy of a dissertation. When the dates of the dissertation and of the publication of its abstract in *Dissertation Abstracts International* differ, as they do here, the parenthetical text citation includes both: (Johnson, 1988/1989).

21. Encyclopedia article

Dashiell, J. F. (1983). Behaviorism. In
Encyclopedia Americana (Vol. 3, pp. 469—471).
Danbury, CT: Grolier.

- Treat an encyclopedia article the same as an article in a multi-volume collection of essays by different authors (see item 10 above).

22. Government document

U.S. Women's Bureau. (1975). Handbook on
women workers. Washington, DC: U.S. Government Printing Office.

23. Interview, published

Lyman, F. (1988, January). [Interview
with Maggie Kuhn, founder of the Gray Pan-
thers]. The Progressive, 52, 29-31.

- If an interview has a title, insert the title before the bracketed notation that identifies the piece and its subject (see item 17 above).

24. Proceedings of a conference

Genaway, D. C. (Ed.). (1983). Conference
on Integrated Online Library Systems. Can-
field, OH: Genaway & Associates.

Stilson, D. W. (1957). A multidimensional psychophysical method for investigating

visual form. In J. W. Wulfeck & J. H. Taylor (Eds.), <u>Proceedings of a Symposium</u>
<u>Sponsored by the Armed Forces—NRC Committee</u>
<u>on Vision</u> (pp. 54–64). Washington, DC: Na-
tional Academy of Sciences—National Research
Council.

- Use the first form for a citation to the collected proceedings of a conference, the second for a citation to a single article in such a collection.

25. Report

Butler, E. W., Chapin, F. S., Hemmens,
G. C., Kaiser, E. J., Stegman, M. A., &
Weiss, S. F. (1969). <u>Moving behavior and res-</u>
<u>idential choice: A national survey</u> (National
Cooperative Highway Research Program Rep.
No. 81). Chapel Hill: University of North
Carolina, Center for Urban and Regional
Studies.

Price, M. E., & Botein, M. (1973). <u>Cable</u>
<u>television: Citizen participation after the</u>
<u>franchise</u> (Research Rep. No. R–1139–NSF).
Santa Monica, CA: Rand.

- If the report has been given a number, supply it in parentheses after the title.

Nonprint sources

26. Computer software

Etter T., & Chamberlain, W. (1984).
Racter [Computer software]. Northbrook, IL:
Mindscape.

27. Film, videotape, audiotape, slides, charts, artwork

Messecar, R. (Author & Producer/Editor),
& Hales, D. (Author). (1982). Theater of the
night: The science of sleep and dreams [Film].
Pleasantville, NY: Human Relations Media.

Jordan, P. (Producer & Director).
(1974). Prejudice: Causes, consequences,
cures [Videotape]. Carlsbad, CA: CRM Films.

- Identify the functions of major contributors in parentheses after their names.
- Identify the medium in brackets after the title of the work.

22a

28. Lecture, unpublished

Zappen, J. P. (1989, March). Scientific
rhetoric in the nineteenth and early twentieth centuries. Paper presented at the Conference on College Composition and Communication, Seattle, WA.

- Include the month of the meeting or conference at which the lecture was delivered.

22b Citing sources in APA style

APA text citations, like MLA citations, are inserted into the text parenthetically. But APA parenthetical citations differ from MLA citations in three ways:

1. The APA citation includes the author's name and the year of publication of the source. The page number is added only when a quotation is being cited.
2. The elements in an APA parenthetical citation are separated by commas.
3. The abbreviations *p.* and *pp.* are used with page numbers.

Compare the following examples of parenthetical citations in APA style with the corresponding MLA citations described in **20d**.

1. Quotations

As in MLA format, the parenthetical citation in the text comes *after* the quotation marks that close the quotation but *before* the sentence's end punctuation.

Parenthetical citation in text

The definitive biography of Mahatma Gandhi remains
to be written. As one Gandhi scholar has explained, "Multivolume works written by Gandhi's
former colleagues and published in India are comprehensive in scope, but their objectivity suffers
from the authors' reverent regard for their subject" (Juergensmeyer, 1984, p. 294).

Citation in reference list

Juergensmeyer, M. (1984). The Gandhi
revival--A review article. Journal of Asian
Studies, 43, 293-298.

Below are some variations on this basic method of documenting quotations.

Setting off a long quotation

A quotation of more than forty words is set off from the text and indented five spaces from the left margin. Such a quotation is commonly introduced with a colon, and the parenthetical citation is placed one space after the end punctuation.

Parenthetical citation in text

One editor suggests that photographers trying

to publish their work should aim to surpass—

not just equal—the photographs they see in

print:

    Editors know where they can get pictures

    like the ones they've already published.

    If you want to get noticed, you have to

    take pictures better than those. This

    is especially true if you are looking

    for assignments rather than to sell ex-

    isting pictures. Why take a chance on a

    new photographer who will come up with

    no better than what you already have, an

    editor might reason? (Scully, 1984,

    p. 33)

22b

Citation in reference list

Scully, J. (1984, May). Seeing pictures.

Modern Photography, 48, 28–33.

Incorporating the author's name into the text

If you introduce a quotation by mentioning the author's name in your text, use only the author's last name, unless first initials are needed to distinguish between two authors with the same surname. Follow the author's name immediately with the year of the source's publication in parentheses. The page number, also in parentheses, comes after the quotation.

Parenthetical citation in text

```
The English, claims Altick (1969), are obsessed
by love for their dogs.  "Walking dogs," he
points out, "is a ritual that proceeds indepen-
dently of weather, cataclysms, and the move-
ments of the planets; they are led or carried
everywhere, into department stores, fishmon-
gers', greengrocers', buses, trains" (p. 286).
```

22b

Citation in reference list

```
     Altick, R. D. (1969). To be in England.
New York: Norton.
```

Citing a work by more than one author

If your source was written by two authors, include the names of both in the parenthetical text citation, following the same order in which the names are printed in the original source.

Parenthetical citation in text

```
Selvin and Wilson (1984) argue that "a concern
for effective writing is not a trivial eleva-
tion of form over content.  Good writing is a
```

```
condition, slowly achieved, of . . . being what
one means to be" (p. 207).
```

or

```
Two sociologists argue that "a concern for ef-
fective writing is not a trivial elevation of
form over content.  Good writing is a condi-
tion, slowly achieved, of . . . being what one
means to be" (Selvin & Wilson, 1984, p. 207).
```

Citation in reference list

```
     Selvin, H. C., & Wilson, E. K. (1984).
On sharpening sociologists' prose. Sociologi-
cal Quarterly, 25, 205-222.
```

Note the following variations on this rule when more than two authors are involved:

22b

1. When the source was written by three to five authors, give all their names in the first parenthetical text citation, but in subsequent citations include in the parenthetical text citation the name of the first author only, followed by the abbreviation *et al.* (Latin for "and others"; the abbreviation is not underlined): (O'Malley et al., 1990, p. 101).
2. When six or more authors are involved, give the name of the first author only, followed by the abbreviation *et al.,* in all parenthetical text citations.

Note, however, that the reference list citation includes the names of all authors, regardless of the number.

Citing an anonymous work

If you quote an anonymous work, use the first few words of the title in your parenthetical text citation. Place the titles of articles in quotation marks (but note that they are not enclosed in quotation marks in the reference list citation), and underline the titles of books. Capitalize all major words of the title in the parenthetical text citation (but not in the reference list citation).

Parenthetical citation in text

```
Environmentalists protested that a recent study
of the plan to spray herbicides on marijuana
"systematically underestimated the possibility
of damage from such spraying and exaggerated
the benefits to be achieved by a spraying pro-
gram" ("Marijuana Spraying," 1984, p. 14).
```

Citation in reference list

```
     Marijuana spraying opposed. (1984, Au-
gust 22). New York Times, p. 14.
```

Citing a multivolume work

The volume number of a multivolume work appears in the parenthetical text citation only when the reference list citation indicates that more than one volume of the work has been consulted (see item 8 in **22a** above).

Parenthetical citation in text

```
The medieval manor house dominated nearby
cottages "not only because it was better
built, but above all because it was almost
invariably designed for defence" (Bloch,
1961, Vol. 2, p. 300).
```

Citation in reference list

Bloch, M. (1961). Feudal society (L. A. Manyon, Trans., Vols. 1-2). Chicago: University of Chicago Press. (Original work published 1939)

Citing two works by the same author

If the sources you use include more than one work by the same author, the date that you give in each parenthetical text citation may alone be sufficient to indicate which work is being cited. If more than one work by an author has been published in the same year, however, differentiate among works by adding lowercase letters to the dates in *both* the reference list and the parenthetical text citations.

Parenthetical citations in text

(Gilbert, 1985a, p. 112)

(Gilbert, 1985b, pp. 164-165)

Citations in reference list

Gilbert, L. A. (1985a). Dimensions of same-gender student-faculty role-model relationships. Sex Roles, 12, 111-123.

Gilbert, L. A. (1985b). Measures of psychological masculinity and femininity: A comment on Gaddy, Glass, and Arnkoff. Journal of Counseling Psychology, 32, 163-166.

2. Paraphrases

As noted above, APA documentation style departs from MLA style significantly in the case of paraphrasing. In APA style the parenthetical text citation does not include a page number when the writer is paraphrasing, rather than quoting, a source.

Parenthetical citation in text (author's name in parenthetical citation)

The steadily growing role of television in politics has helped to shift attention away from the politicians' stands on issues to the way they appear before the camera (Meyrowitz, 1984).

Citation in reference list

Meyrowitz, J. (1984, July). Politics in the video eye: Where have all the heroes gone? Psychology Today, 18, 46–51.

Parenthetical citation in text (author's name incorporated into text)

One effect of the microscope's development in the late 1600s, Fussell (1965) points out, was to change attitudes toward insects. Whereas people in the seventeenth century had considered insects innocuous creatures, eighteenth-century men and women, exposed for the first time to drawings of magnified insect bodies, regarded them as hideous and contemptible.

Citation in reference list

Fussell, P. (1965). The rhetorical world of Augustan humanism: Ethics and imagery from

22b

<u>Swift to Burke</u>. London: Oxford University
Press.

22c Formatting a paper in APA style

The manuscript style described by the American Psychological Association in its *Publication Manual* is intended primarily for authors who are submitting articles for consideration by professional journals. The writers of the manual note, therefore, that its requirements may need to be modified for use in undergraduate classes.

In the guidelines below, only the APA's title-page requirements have been modified, in order to allow for inclusion of the course number, the name of the instructor, and the date on which the paper is submitted. Check with your instructor for supplementary or alternative instructions.

1. Paper

Using a typewriter with a fresh ribbon, or a computer printer, type or print out your research paper on standard 8½-by-11-inch white bond. Avoid dot-matrix computer printers unless they print clearly and legibly. Do not use onionskin or erasable paper.

22c

2. Spacing and margins

Double-space everything in your paper—text, long quotations, footnotes, and reference list. Double-space as well between page headings (such as "References") and the first line of text on the page.

Leave a one-inch margin on the top, bottom, and sides of each page. In the upper right corner of each page (including the first), about one-half inch from the top of the page, type a manuscript page header (a shortened title consisting of the first two or three words of the paper's title) followed by five spaces and the page number, taking care to stay within the one-inch right margin. The manuscript page header identifies the paper if pages become separated. Type a maximum of twenty-seven lines of text on each page, not including the line containing the manuscript page header and the page number.

3. Title page

On four double-spaced lines centered on the title page, provide the following information:

1. The title of your paper, not enclosed in quotation marks or underlined. Capitalize only the first letters of important words in the title. Double-space between the lines of a title typed on more than one line.
2. Your name.
3. The course for which the paper is being submitted, followed by a comma and your professor's name: Psychology 100, Professor Sharon March.
4. The date of submission.

Don't forget to include your manuscript page header and first page number in the upper right corner. See the title page of Cyndi Lopardo's paper on page 510.

4. Abstract page

In APA style, a paper begins with an *abstract,* or summary, of its contents, typed on a separate page. The abstract should not exceed 960 characters and spaces (about 120 words). It should present the purpose or thesis of your paper, indicate the types of sources you investigated, and state the conclusions you arrived at.

Center the word *Abstract* one inch from the top of the page. Double-space and type your abstract in block style—that is, without the usual paragraph indentions. See Cyndi Lopardo's abstract on page 511.

5. Text pages

The text of your paper begins on page 3. Center your title one inch from the top of the page. Double-space and begin the first line of the paper.

6. References page

In APA format, the sources used in a research paper are listed alphabetically on a final page, with the heading "References" centered one inch from the top of the page. Do not underline this heading or enclose it in quotation marks. Double-space after this heading and give the citation for the first source used; double-space between lines of each citation and between citations. Alphabetize an anonymous source by the first significant word in the reference list citation. See Cyndi Lopardo's reference list on pages 533–34.

7. Footnotes page

As in MLA format, content notes, if any, are given on a separate page. In APA format, this page *follows* the reference list page or pages. One inch from the top of the page, center the heading "Footnotes" (or "Footnote," if only one note is given); again, do not underline this heading or enclose it in quotation marks. Double-space between this heading and the first footnote. Begin each footnote with a superior number indented five spaces; do not leave a space between the superior number and the first word of each footnote. Double-space between and within footnotes. See Cyndi Lopardo's footnote page on page 535.

22c

For Further Reading

American Psychological Association. *Publication Manual of the American Psychological Association*. 4th ed. Washington: APA, 1994.

23 Student Research Paper B: APA Documentation

Cyndi Lopardo's "Career versus Motherhood: The Debate over Education for Women at the Turn of the Century" is a good example of a researched argument based on what are called primary sources. Primary sources are raw data, documents, or evidence—for example, the results of experiments; original letters and diaries; historical records; and eyewitness accounts of events. Secondary sources, in contrast, are other writers' commentaries on or analyses of primary works. In this paper Cyndi's primary sources are published articles from the 1890s about the education of women.

Cyndi's task in the paper is the same one that confronts every researcher whose work is based on primary sources—to analyze the data, draw conclusions about it, and then present and defend those conclusions to her readers. Of course, the final paper does not include every article Cyndi examined. Instead, having used her reading to develop a thesis, Cyndi selects the articles that provide the best evidence for the point she wants to make: that while increasing numbers of women had access to higher education by the end of the nineteenth century, there was widespread feeling that colleges should be training women specifically for motherhood rather than for possible professional careers outside the home.

Among the points that might be included in a discussion of the sample research paper in this chapter are the following:

1. Distinguishing between primary and secondary sources (page 509).
2. Focusing a research paper around a thesis (pages 512–17).
3. Using subheadings in APA style to highlight a paper's organization (pages 516–17, 519, 527, 531).
4. Using transitions effectively (pages 520–27).
5. Citing two works by the same author in APA style (pages 526–29).
6. Using summary well (pages 530–31).
7. Echoing the paper's introduction and thesis in its conclusion (pages 530–32).

Career versus Motherhood   1

Career versus Motherhood: The Debate over Education
for Women at the Turn of the Century
Cyndi Lopardo
Education 100, Professor Karen J. Blair
March 20, 1995

23

Career versus Motherhood   2

Abstract

By 1890, the opening of colleges for women and the
advent of coeducation had settled the issue of wom-
en's access to higher education. But another question remained unresolved: the purpose of a college
education in a woman's life. Articles published
during the 1890s on the goals of higher education
for women suggest that, despite the professional
accomplishments of many educated women in the nineteenth century, social forces were at work to keep
women's education focused on the enrichment of home
and family. A woman's right to a professional career outside the home would not be recognized until
the next century.

23

The APA *Publication Manual* specifies that in papers prepared for publication, writers should leave only one space between sentences and should not hyphenate words to even out the right margin. However, the manual notes that in the interest of readability, such specifications may be relaxed when a paper is intended as a final copy. In preparing this research paper, therefore, Cyndi followed the standard practice of leaving two spaces between sentences and of using hyphenation to create a neat right margin.

Lopardo's opening paragraphs effectively provide background and focus for the paper. The first paragraph identifies educational opportunity as a key element in the women's movement of the nineteenth century; the second focuses on the status of higher education for women in the 1890s; and the third isolates a specific issue in discussions about women's education during that decade. Note the effective transitions between these paragraphs: the first sentence of each paragraph smoothly refers to the key idea in the preceding one.

The original text of the passage that Lopardo quotes from the Seneca Falls Declaration is as follows:

> He has denied her the facilities for obtaining a thorough education, all colleges being closed against her.

APA style permits changing the first letter of a quotation from uppercase to lowercase (or vice versa) without brackets. (In MLA style, such a change would have to be indicated: "[h]e has denied . . .") Cyndi clarifies the quotation by using brackets to substitute *woman* for *her*.

Career versus Motherhood: The Debate over

Education for Women at the Turn of the Century

The origins of the modern women's movement

have frequently been traced to the convention of

women organized by Elizabeth Cady Stanton and

Lucretia Mott in Seneca Falls, New York, on July 19

and 20, 1848. Besides launching the drive for

women's suffrage, the Seneca Falls Convention

produced a major document in the history of women's

rights. The Declaration of Sentiments and Resolu-

tions, modeled after the Declaration of Independen-

ce, listed both the grievances and the aspira-

tions of politically active women in the nineteenth

century. To this document the beginnings of

educational opportunities for women can also be

traced, for one of its stated grievances against

man was that "he has denied [woman] the facilities

for obtaining a thorough education, all colleges

being closed against her" ("Seneca Falls Declara-

tion," 1973, p. 316).

The participants in the Seneca Falls Conven-

tion could not have foreseen how quickly that

In APA style, paraphrased material is cited by author and date alone. Page numbers are included only after quotations.

Lopardo's third paragraph introduces the evidence she will present—published articles from the 1890s—and ends with the thesis she will argue.

23

inequity would be remedied. By 1890, many of the
women's colleges that are today associated with excellence in education had opened their doors--
among them Mt. Holyoke, Vassar, Smith, Wellesley,
Radcliffe, Bryn Mawr, and Barnard. Even more significant, by this time nearly two-thirds of all the
nation's colleges and universities were coeduca-
tional (Buckler, 1897).

On the surface, then, the story of women's education in the nineteenth century would seem to be
one of rapidly expanding opportunities. By the end
of the century, however, a new debate was raging--
not over women's access to higher education, but
over the purpose of such an education in a woman's
life. An examination of articles written during
the 1890s on the goals of higher education for women
leads one to conclude that equality of opportunity
was not yet within women's grasp. Higher education
did not open up new spheres of activity for most
women at the end of the nineteenth century; instead, these articles suggest that powerful social
forces were at work to keep education for women

APA style encourages the use of subheadings to highlight a paper's organization. Double-space before and after a subheading; do not underline or capitalize it. In a more technical paper (for example, one reporting the results of an experiment), the problem being investigated would be introduced in the opening paragraphs and the rest of the paper would be divided with the following headings: Method, Results, Discussion.

One of the strengths of this paper is Lopardo's handling of her evidence. She blends quotation, paraphrase, and summary well, providing just the right amount of detail necessary for the reader to understand each article that she cites.

focused on the enrichment and enhancement of home and family.

Supporters of Opportunities for Women

To be sure, some educators of the time did call for broader educational and professional opportunities for women. Butler (1896), for example, criticized the ways in which women's development was retarded by prevailing attitudes in society—for example, by the belief that girls' elementary and secondary education should not be as rigorous as boys'. Franklin (1898) agreed that what we today would call social conditioning was responsible for the gap between the accomplishments of men and those of women. The "youthful dreams and aspirations of a gifted boy cluster around high achievement and resounding fame," he explained, "because all that he hears and reads tends to arouse in him such ambitions" (p. 46). In contrast, the girl is taught to focus her life on "the conquest of men by beauty and charm" (pp. 46–47). No wonder, therefore, that women's professional accomplishments had not equaled those of men:

23

Quotations of more than forty words are set off by indenting five spaces from the left margin. Ellipsis marks indicate omitted material.

23

The superior number 1 refers to a content note, which is found at the end of the paper on the page following the reference list.

Men who have had the spark of genius or even of talent in them have been spurred to effort by all their surroundings, by the traditions of the race, by rivalry with their comrades, by the admiration which the opposite sex accords to brilliant achievements. . . . What of all this has there been for women? How many have been so placed as to even think of an intellectual career as a possibility? . . . The very absorption in a high intellectual interest . . . was, in the case of girls, up to the last two or three decades, universally condemned and repressed and thwarted even in the most cultivated families. (p. 43)[1]

Two Groups of Critics

Such defenses of women's intellectual rights were, however, far less typical of the 1890s than criticism of wider educational and professional opportunities for women was. The critics could hardly ignore women's recent

Note how the opening sentences of this paragraph organize the material that follows. The first sentence is transitional, contrasting the critics to be presented here with the supporters of opportunities for women discussed above. The second sentence identifies one group of critics, those who attempted to belittle women's professional accomplishments. Since Buckler is then introduced as a member of this group, the reader is prepared for a discussion that illustrates her treatment of women's accomplishments in this way.

23

Career versus Motherhood   7

achievements in such previously male fields as science, law, and medicine, but one group of these critics found ways of denigrating those accomplishments in order to assert the need for a college curriculum for women that was focused on the home and family. Buckler (1897) is representative of this group. On the one hand, she concedes that "there is no walk of life which, in some quarter of the globe at least, is not open to [women]" (p. 302). But on the other hand, even as she enumerates women's accomplishments in professional life, Buckler concludes that women have never "achieved anything absolutely first-rate, whether as creation or as discovery" (p. 303), and that there is little chance they ever will:

> If women were ever intellectually equal to men, when and why did they begin to fall behind? And if they never were equal, how can they hope to catch up now, when masculine education is advancing at as great a rate as feminine? (p. 308)

In the quotation from Buckler, Lopardo underlines the phrase *the good of the community* to emphasize the standard by which Buckler is judging women's accomplishments. Following APA style, she inserts the phrase *italics added* in brackets immediately after the underlined phrase to indicate that she has added underscoring (emphasis) not found in the original text.

23

Lopardo groups together similar pieces of evidence and clearly points out their similarities to her readers. Here, an effective transitional sentence indicates that Bolton is also included in the first group of critics, those who sought to diminish women's professional accomplishments.

Why should women pursue a professional career if they are thus doomed to second-rate accomplishments? Or, as Buckler phrases the question, "Is it for the good of the community [italics added] that she should engage in these higher branches [of literature, science, and art]?" (p. 296). In Buckler's view, women's professional accomplishments have been so meager as to be inconsequential to the community at large. Instead, she asserts, women should find satisfaction "in assisting and carrying out the creations of men. For it is in this subordinate relation that women can probably find their truest and widest sphere, that of Influence" (pp. 308–309).

Bolton (1898) approaches the issue of college education for women in a similar way. She begins by cataloging women's accomplishments from biblical times to the present, but in spite of this evidence she concludes, paradoxically, that "[women's] genius has but a limited field; while many have obtained fame through their knowledge of mathematics

Lopardo now moves to a second group of critics, those who felt that the college curriculum for women should place greater emphasis on domestic issues. Note the transitions within this paragraph that link its main examples: Brown (1896), *for example,* agrees . . . Backus (1899) *also* praises . . .

Lopardo clearly introduces each piece of evidence and indicates the specific point it is intended to make.

and its applications to astronomy, they show but
little aptitude for the natural sciences, and
rarely exhibit any inventive faculty" (pp. 510–
511). A life of learning, she claims, can therefore never offer a woman the same fulfillment as
being "a happy wife and good mother" (p. 511).
Echoing Buckler (1897), Bolton suggests that if
women's education is to be put to a worthwhile purpose, it should be to "assist some loved one to perfect his researches" (p. 511).

A second group of critics took pains to praise
the new educational opportunities open to women,
but warned of the dangers of a college curriculum
for women that neglected domestic issues. Brown
(1896), for example, agrees with Franklin and Butler that "every human being, man or woman, should
have all the education that he can take" (p. 431).
But she defends women's education only in terms of
its usefulness as preparation for motherhood, and
she concludes by warning that "whatever in the education of girls draws them away from [the home] is
an injury to civilization" (p. 432). Backus (1899)

23

23

When citing two works by the same author, include the dates of both works in parentheses, separated by a comma: (Smith, 1895, 1898) or Smith (1895, 1898). If you use a parenthetical citation to cite two or more works by different authors, arrange them in alphabetical order and separate them with a semicolon: (Jones, 1988; Smith, 1990).

The date in parentheses after the second mention of *Smith* indicates which of her articles is being discussed in this paragraph.

also praises the "new womanhood" of her decade, citing "mental ambition" as the "dominating force among intelligent modern women" (p. 461). But she leaves little room for such ambition in her concep-tion of women's higher education. Instead, her defense of the current college curriculum for women rests solely on its contribution to motherhood:

> Can we not secure better returns from col-lege training [of women] if the needs of the family, the ideals of wifehood, be kept steadily in the view of our daugh-ters—the home be made the criterion for all mental effort exercised without the home? (p. 461)

Increasing Conservatism

At least some critics of higher education for women during the 1890s became more conservative as the twentieth century approached. Two articles by Smith (1895, 1898), for example, illustrate the apparently increasing pressure for domestic educa-tion at the college level. Like Brown (1896) and Backus (1899), Smith (1895) applauds the new

As above, Lopardo uses brackets to insert words that make the quoted passage clearer. The original version begins as follows:

23

> In fact, nobody knew very well what she was there for; it seemed only fair that she should "have a chance too," but a chance for what? . . .

educational opportunities open to women whose
"distinctive intellectual bent demanded some other
outlet than housekeeping for their energies. They
wished to teach in the higher schools, or to enter
the professions of literature, law, or medicine"
(p. 27). As Smith surveys the recent history of
higher education for women, however, it becomes
clear that her own vision of women's education is a
significantly narrower one:

> In fact, nobody knew very well what [a
> woman] was [in college] for; it seemed
> only fair that she should "have a chance
> too," but a chance for what? Why, to
> marry, of course! But nobody ever said
> that aloud, and nobody thought of adapting
> her training to her probable and desirable
> business in life. (p. 28)

In the future, Smith says hopefully, the "tendency to emphasize the profession of wifehood
and motherhood in its proper relations will be
increasingly controlling in all education of
women" (p. 33).

23

Lopardo effectively summarizes Smith's entire article of 1898 in a single paragraph. Note the key passages from the last paragraph of the article that she has selected to quote (the quoted passages are italicized):

> If to all these practical and utilitarian attainments the mother can add *the graces of culture in music or art or literature,* she may give the child a background for education and a resource in life beyond the power of statistics to estimate. The elevation, enrichment, and sweetening of the family life by these contributions from the mother's own storehouse of culture are a safeguard against temptation from without not to be matched by legislation or training, or even by church influence. To *make the household sweet, wholesome, dignified,* a place of growth, is certainly a profession requiring not merely the best training, but a specific training adapted to those ends.

23

Lopardo's concluding paragraph returns smoothly to the note on which the paper began—the Seneca Falls Convention of 1848. Here she introduces a second quotation from the Seneca Falls Declaration—a passage demanding equality in career opportunities— to underscore her concluding point, that although women had access to higher education by the end of the century, they had still not gained the right to use that education in a professional career outside the home.

Career versus Motherhood   12

At the end of the decade, Smith (1898) returns
to this topic, but in an even more reactionary way.
Now she calls the idea of having women pursue the
same college curriculum as men an "experiment" (p.
522) that has failed. In its place, she proposes in
detail a curriculum that will enable a woman to
"make the household sweet, wholesome, dignified"
(p. 525)--that is, a course of study emphasizing
manual training, hygiene, "standards of honor and
honesty," and "the graces of culture in music or art
or literature" (p. 524).

Conclusions

Clearly the statistics regarding higher
education for women at the end of the nineteenth
century do not tell the whole story. It is true
that the question of women's access to higher
education had been resolved in the half-century
since the Seneca Falls Convention, for most of the
nation's colleges and universities had opened
their doors to women. But another Seneca Falls
resolution--one calling for "equal participation
with men in the various trades, professions, and

Career versus Motherhood   13

commerce" ("Seneca Falls Declaration," 1973, p. 317)--was far from fulfilled. Although the education of women had become socially acceptable, it remained focused on the enrichment of home and family life; the intellectual life available to women could be pursued only as a sort of hobby. The battle for the right to an education that was truly equivalent to men's and for the right to a career outside the home remained to be fought in the next century.

23

References

Backus, H. H. (1899, February 25). Should the college train for motherhood? Outlook, 61, 461–463.

Bolton, H. I. (1898, August). Women in science. Popular Science Monthly, 53, 505–511.

Brown, H. D. (1896, March 7). How shall we educate our girls? Outlook, 53, 431–432.

Buckler, G. G. (1897). The lesser man. North American Review, 165, 296–309.

Butler, N. M. (1896, April 4). The right training of girls under sixteen. Outlook, 53, 626–627.

Franklin, F. (1898). The intellectual powers of woman. North American Review, 166, 40–53.

The Seneca Falls declaration of sentiments and resolutions. (1973). In H. S. Commager (Ed.), Documents of American history (Vol. 1., pp. 315–317). Englewood Cliffs: Prentice.

Smith, M. R. (1895, November). Recent tendencies in the education of women. Popular Science Monthly, 48, 27–33.

23

Smith, M. R. (1898, August). Education for domestic life. Popular Science Monthly, 53, 521–525.

Woodworth, R. S. (1933). Ladd–Franklin, Christine. In D. Malone (Ed.), Dictionary of American Biography (Vol. 10, pp. 528–530). New York: Scribner's.

23

Career versus Motherhood   16

Footnote

[1]Franklin's liberal perspective on the issue of professional careers for women can perhaps be explained by a biographical detail: he was married to the well-known psychologist Christine Ladd-Franklin. Although Ladd-Franklin fulfilled the doctoral requirements at Johns Hopkins University in 1882 and went on to a distinguished career in teaching and research at Columbia University, Johns Hopkins refused to award her a degree until 1926 because it did not officially recognize women as graduate students (Woodworth, 1933).

24 *Using Endnote Documentation*

Though abandoned by the Modern Language Association in 1984 in favor of the documentation style examined in Chapters **19** and **20**, endnote documentation remains in use in other humanities fields. This method of documentation inserts superior numbers (numbers raised a half-line) into the text to refer to citations, *endnotes,* that are then collected at the end of the paper. (A more complicated alternative not considered here is to place the appropriate notes at the bottom of each page; in that case they are called *footnotes.*)

24a Using endnotes

Anyone who is familiar with the current style of MLA documentation will find the transition to using endnotes an easy one. In place of the parenthetical citation in the text prescribed in MLA documentation, the writer using endnotes inserts a slightly raised number in the text corresponding to a citation given on note pages that follow the paper. The raised numbers inserted in the text do not start over with *1* on each page but run consecutively throughout the paper. Content notes, if any, do not appear on a separate note page but are intermingled with citations to sources.

1. Features of the endnote page

In the center of the endnote page, one inch from the top, type the word *Notes,* not underlined or in quotation marks. Double-space,

Many disciplines continue to use endnotes as their standard form of documentation, and the Modern Language Association itself still provides an extended discussion of endnote documentation in the *MLA Handbook for Writers of Research Papers.* This chapter, therefore, provides sample endnote forms for all of the sources considered in Chapter **19**, together with pages from a research paper illustrating endnote documentation.

QUICK REFERENCE: *Features of Endnote Documentation*

Keep in mind the following differences between endnote forms and MLA Works Cited forms.

Author's name	Use normal rather than inverted order for the author's name.
Indentation	Indent the first line of an endnote—but not any subsequent lines—five spaces.
Parentheses	Enclose the complete publication information for books in parentheses.
Commas	Separate the elements in an endnote with commas rather than periods (but note that no punctuation ever comes before parentheses unless the word before the parentheses is an abbreviation that ends in a period).
Page citation	Always end an endnote with a page citation, unless (1) the note refers to the entire work being cited or (2) the source is one without pages (for example, computer software, a film, an interview, or a lecture).

24a

---

indent five spaces, and type a slightly raised *1*. Leave a space after the raised number before beginning the note; do not indent the second and subsequent lines of the note. Continue in the same manner with the rest of the paper's notes, double-spacing within and between notes. A bibliography page following the page or pages of endnotes is optional; if included, it is arranged like an MLA Works Cited page but given the heading "Bibliography."

2.   Multiple endnote citations

In citations to a source for which full publication information has been given in an earlier note, provide only the author's last name (or a shortened form of the title, if it is an anonymous work) and the page number:

First citation

> ¹ Alice Walker, <u>The Color Purple</u> (New York: Harcourt, 1982) 44.

Subsequent citation

> ² Walker 70–71.

If the endnotes include citations to two works by the same author, subsequent citations include a shortened form of the appropriate title to distinguish between them.

First citations

> ¹ Alice Walker, <u>The Color Purple</u> (New York: Harcourt, 1982) 23.
>
> ² Alice Walker, <u>The Temple of My Familiar</u> (San Diego: Harcourt, 1989) 101.

Subsequent citations

> ³ Walker, <u>Temple</u> 34.
>
> ⁴ Walker, <u>Color Purple</u> 70–71.

The abbreviations *ibid.* (Latin *ibidem*, "in the same place") and *op. cit.* (Latin *opere citato*, "in the work cited") are no longer used with endnotes.

24b Endnote forms

On the following pages are endnote forms corresponding to the MLA Works Cited forms given in **19b**. A hypothetical page citation has been added to the end of each note to illustrate the positioning of page numbers in endnotes.

Table of Endnote Forms

Books

1. Book by one author
2. Book by two or more authors
3. Book by a committee, commission, association, or other group
4. Anonymous book
5. Later or revised edition of a book
6. Edited book (*author's work is being cited*)
7. Edited book (*editor's work is being cited*)
8. Translated book (*author's work is being cited*)
9. Translated book (*translator's work is being cited*)
10. Book in more than one volume
11. Republished book
12. Book that is part of a series
13. Book published by a division of a press
14. Book published before 1900
15. Book with incomplete publication information

Parts of books

16. Introduction, preface, foreword, or afterword in a book
17. Essay in a collection of essays by various authors
18. Poem, short story, or other work in an anthology
19. Journal or magazine article reprinted in a collection of essays by various authors

Articles in journals and magazines

20. Article in a journal paginated by the volume (*continuous pagination*)
21. Article in a journal paginated issue by issue
22. Article in a journal with issue numbers only
23. Article in a weekly or biweekly magazine
24. Article in a monthly or bimonthly magazine

24b

Articles in newspapers

25. Article in a newspaper
26. Editorial in a newspaper
27. Letter to the editor

Other print sources

28. Abstract in *Dissertation Abstracts International*
29. Book review
30. Dissertation, unpublished
31. Encyclopedia article (*or article in similar reference work*)
32. Government document
33. Interview, published
34. Map
35. Pamphlet
36. Proceedings of a conference

Nonprint sources

37. Computer software
38. Film
39. Interview, personal
40. Lecture
41. Microfilm or microfiche
42. Recording
43. Television program
44. Videotape

Books

1. Book by one author

[1] Lydia Minatoya, Talking to High Monks in the Snow: An Asian—American Odyssey (New York: HarperCollins, 1993) 44.

2. Book by two or more authors

2 Robert Scholes and Robert Kellogg, <u>The</u> <u>Nature of Narrative</u> (London: Oxford UP, 1966) 27.

3. Book by a committee, commission, association, or other group

3 Ground Zero, <u>Nuclear War: What's in It</u> <u>for You?</u> (New York: Pocket, 1982) 66–67.

4. Anonymous book

4 <u>Kodak Guide to 35mm Photography</u> (Rochester: Eastman Kodak, 1980) 12.

5. Later or revised edition of a book

5 Casey Miller and Kate Swift, <u>The Hand-</u> <u>book of Nonsexist Writing</u>, 2nd ed. (New York: Harper, 1988) 98.

24b

6. Edited book (*author's work is being cited*)

6 Elizabeth Gaskell, <u>The Life of Charlotte</u> <u>Brontë</u>, ed. Alan Shelston (Harmondsworth: Penguin, 1975) 254–55.

7. Edited book (*editor's work is being cited*)

7 Frederick Garber, ed., <u>The Italian</u>, by Ann Radcliffe (London: Oxford UP, 1968) 201.

8. Translated book (*author's work is being cited*)

8 Ursula Brumm, <u>American Thought and Reli-</u> <u>gious Typology</u>, trans. John Hoaglund (New Brunswick: Rutgers UP, 1970) 107–08.

9. Translated book (*translator's work is being cited*)

[9] L. R. Lind, trans., The Aeneid, by Virgil (Bloomington: Indiana UP, 1962) 76.

10. Book in more than one volume

[10] Luigi Sturzo, Church and State, 2 vols. (Notre Dame: U of Notre Dame P, 1962) 1: 67.

11. Republished book

[11] William L. Shirer, Berlin Diary: The Journal of a Foreign Correspondent 1934–1941 (1941; Harmondsworth: Penguin, 1979) 198.

12. Book that is part of a series

24b

[12] Virginia L. Radley, Samuel Taylor Coleridge, Twayne's English Authors Ser. 36 (New York: Twayne, 1966) 34–36.

13. Book published by a division of a press

[13] Barbara Ehrenreich and Deirdre English, For Her Own Good: 150 Years of the Experts' Advice to Women (Garden City: Anchor–Doubleday, 1979) 333.

14. Book published before 1900

[14] Brainerd Kellogg, A Text–Book on Rhetoric (New York, 1897) 22.

15. Book with incomplete publication information

[15] George S. Marr, The Periodical Essayists of the Eighteenth Century (London: Clarke,
n.d.) 40–44.

Parts of books

16. Introduction, preface, foreword, or afterword in a book

[16] J. Hillis Miller, introduction, Bleak
House, by Charles Dickens, ed. Norman Page
(Harmondsworth: Penguin, 1971) 12.

17. Essay in a collection of essays by various authors

[17] Richard E. Young, "Concepts of Art and
the Teaching of Writing," The Rhetorical Tradition and Modern Writing, ed. James J. Murphy
(New York: Modern Lang. Assn., 1982) 133.

18. Poem, short story, or other work in an anthology

[18] Walter Raleigh, "The Advice," The An-
chor Anthology of Sixteenth-Century Verse, ed.
Richard S. Sylvester (New York: Anchor-
Doubleday, 1974) 330.

19. Journal or magazine article reprinted in a collection of essays by various authors

[19] Richard Harter Fogle, "The Abstractness
of Shelley," Philological Quarterly 24 (1945):
362–79, rpt. in Shelley: A Collection of

Critical Essays, ed. George M. Ridenour, Twentieth Century Views (Englewood Cliffs: Prentice, 1965) 28–29.

Articles in journals and magazines

20. Article in a journal paginated by the volume (*continuous pagination*)

[20] Jerome A. Miller, "Horror and the De-
construction of the Self," Philosophy Today 32
(1988): 287.

21. Article in a journal paginated issue by issue

[21] George Butterick, "Charles Olson's 'The
Kingfishers' and the Poetics of Change," American Poetry 6.2 (1989): 28–29.

22. Article in a journal with issue numbers only

[22] Paul Jacobson, "Temperature and Your
Guitar's Health," Guitar Review 75 (1988): 17.

23. Article in a weekly or biweekly magazine

[23] Barbara Rudolph, "Adrift in the Dol-
drums," Time 31 July 1989: 33.

24. Article in a monthly or bimonthly magazine

[24] Mary Kay Blakely, "Coma: Stories from
the Edge of Death," Life Aug. 1989: 82.

Articles in newspapers

25. Article in a newspaper

[25] Denis Donoghue, "Does America Have a Major Poet?" <u>New York Times</u> 3 Dec. 1978, late city ed., sec. 7: 9.

26. Editorial in a newspaper

[26] "'Restraint' Spurs Terrorists," editorial, <u>Chicago Sun-Times</u> 3 Aug. 1989: 42.

27. Letter to the editor

[27] Lavonna Hayden, "Broadway Blues," letter, <u>Village Voice</u> 28 Feb. 1989: 4.

Other print sources

28. Abstract in *Dissertation Abstracts International*

[28] Susan Ellen Krantz, "The First Fortune: The Plays and the Playhouse," <u>DAI</u> 47 (1986): 189A (Tulane U).

29. Book review

[29] Norma Pettit, rev. of <u>American Puritanism: Faith and Practice</u>, by Darrett B. Rutman, <u>New England Quarterly</u> 43 (1970): 504-05.

30. Dissertation, unpublished

[30] James Vernon Rauff, "Machine Translation with Two-Level Grammars," diss., Northwestern U, 1988, 29.

31. Encyclopedia article (*or article in similar reference work*)

[31] "Phonetics," <u>Encyclopaedia Britannica:
Micropaedia</u>, 15th ed., 1986.

32. Government document

[32] United States, Superintendent of Documents, <u>Poetry and Literature</u> (Washington: GPO, 1978) 7–8.

33. Interview, published

[33] Margaret Drabble, interview, <u>Interviews with Contemporary Novelists</u>, by Diana Cooper-Clark (New York: St. Martin's, 1986) 72–73.

34. Map

[34] <u>Southeastern States</u>, map (Falls Church: American Automobile Assn., 1988).

35. Pamphlet

[35] Dennison I. Rusinow, <u>Yugoslavia's Muslim Nation</u> (Hanover: Universities Field Staff Intl., 1982) 3.

36. Proceedings of a conference

[36] Stephen W. Rousseas, ed., <u>Inflation: Its Causes, Consequences and Control</u>, Symposium Held by the Dept. of Economics, New York U, 31 Jan. 1968 (Wilton: K. Kazanjian Economics Foundation, 1968) 77.

24b

Nonprint sources

37. Computer software

³⁷ Thomas Etter and William Chamberlain,
<u>Racter</u>, computer software, Mindscape, 1984.

38. Film

³⁸ <u>Casablanca</u>, dir. Michael Curtiz, with
Humphrey Bogart, Ingrid Bergman, and Claude
Rains, Warner Bros., 1942.

39. Interview, personal

³⁹ Teresa Toulouse, personal interview, 31
Mar. 1994.

40. Lecture

⁴⁰ James V. Catano, "The Paradox Behind
the Myth of Self-Making: Self-Empowerment vs.
the Power of the Academy," Conference on College Composition and Communication, Seattle, 17
Mar. 1989.

24b

41. Microfilm or microfiche

• When citing a publication reproduced on microfilm or microfiche, simply use the ordinary note form appropriate for that
  publication.

42. Recording

⁴² Fred W. Friendly and Walter Cronkite,
eds., <u>The Way It Was: The Sixties</u>, narr. Walter
Cronkite, CBS, F3M 38858, 1983.

43. Television program

[43] <u>Nightline</u>, ABC, WLS, Chicago, 23 Jan. 1994.

44. Videotape

[44] <u>The Beggar's Opera</u>, videocassette, by John Gay, prod. and dir. Jonathan Miller, with Roger Daltrey and Carol Hall, BBC–TV/RM Arts, 1985 (135 min.).

24c Endnotes in a student research paper

To illustrate endnotes in the context of an actual research paper, two pages from Emmet Geary's essay "Recovery from the Florence Flood: A Masterpiece of Restoration," shown in full in Chapter **21**, have been reformatted with endnotes rather than parenthetical citations and printed on the following pages, together with the complete list of endnotes that would appear after the text of the paper.

24c

1/2"

1"

1

Emmet Geary

Professor P. L. Herrold

History 100

March 28, 1995

Recovery from the Florence Flood:

A Masterpiece of Restoration

On November 4, 1966, the swollen Arno River

inundated Florence, Italy. Nineteen inches of

rain had fallen in two days, causing floodwater to

reach depths of twenty feet in some parts of the

city. The damage was devastating: six thousand of

the city's ten thousand shops were destroyed, five

thousand families were left homeless, and more than

a hundred people drowned. But the primary reason

that most outsiders grieved for Florence was the

damage to its unique collection of Renaissance art

treasures and rare books. As Giorgio Batini noted,

"[N]ever before had so many and diverse works of art

been damaged at the same time, all of which needed

to be restored at once. . . . "[1] The story of this

restoration is a story of commitment and ingenuity.

Though the Florence flood destroyed some priceless

masterpieces and heavily damaged others, it had

24c

24c

4

been stored below ground for safety.[6]   Now these
books had to be pulled from library basements full
of water and mud.   In the Biblioteca Nazionale
alone, more than 300,000 volumes were damaged; in
the library of the Gabinetto Vieusseux, 250,000
more had been under water and needed immediate attention.[7]   All told, nearly two million books were
damaged by the flood.[8]

    Not only the floodwater but the subsequent
growth of destructive mold spores threatened Florence's priceless books.   As Carolyn Horton explains, mold endangered even books that had escaped
direct damage from the flood:

> Books are hygroscopic, i.e., have the
> capacity for absorbing water from the
> air around them.   Therefore any books
> stored in conditions of high humidity
> are in danger of being damaged by
> mold.   We had received reports that
> the flooded area of Florence had be-
> come, in effect, a huge humidity
> chamber.   The wet books in rooms that

1″

Notes

[1] Batini, Giorgio. <u>4 November 1966: The River Arno in the Museums of Florence</u>, trans. Timothy Paterson (Florence: Bonechi Editore, 1967) 90.

[2] Eric Rhode, "Good News from Florence," <u>New Statesman</u> 6 Jan. 1967: 20.

[3] Carolyn Horton, "Saving the Libraries of Florence," <u>Wilson Library Bulletin</u> 41 (1967): 1035.

[4] Joseph Judge, "Florence Rises from the Flood," <u>National Geographic</u> July 1967: 39.

[5] Leonard Ricci, "Exploratory Research in Urban Form and the Future of Florence," <u>Arts and Architecture</u> Feb. 1967: 25.

[6] Horton 1036.

[7] "The Florentine Flood Disaster," <u>Burlington Magazine</u> 109 (1967): 194.

[8] Horton 1036.

[9] Horton 1035.

[10] "Florentine Flood Disaster" 193.

[11] Batini 90-91.

[12] "Road Back Is Long for Florentines,"

24c

New York Times 12 Mar. 1967, late city ed.,
sec. 1: 80.

[13] "Florentine Flood Disaster" 193.

[14] "Slow Art Restoration Continues in Florence," New York Times 9 Aug. 1967, late city
ed.: 42.

[15] "Church Found Under Basilica in Florence," New York Times 4 Nov. 1967, late city
ed.: 35.

[16] Batini 103–05

[17] "Florentine Flood Disaster" 194.

[18] Ricci 25, 32.

24c

PART VI

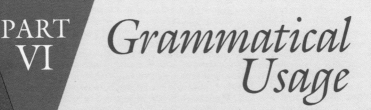

Grammatical Usage

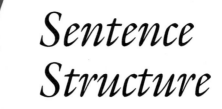

25 Sentence Structure

We all know that a sentence in grammar is a series of spoken or written words that forms the grammatically complete expression of a single thought. On the page, such a unit of discourse begins with a capital letter and ends with the appropriate end punctuation mark. Spoken aloud, the sentence is marked by voice inflection and pauses, the longest of which signals its completion. We have a well-developed, intuitive sense of the sentence because we have been hearing, speaking, writing, and reading sentences most of our lives.

If we look up the word *sentence* in the *Oxford English Dictionary*—that historian of our language—we find that it is one of those words that have contracted over the centuries: it had more meaning in Shakespeare's time than it has in ours. Some of these meanings, such as "opinion" and "way of thinking," are listed in the dictionary as obsolete and are not available to contemporary writers. Nevertheless, they point the way back to the Latin origin of the word, *sentire,* "to feel, to be of the opinion, to perceive, to judge." The word *sentence* shares the same root as *sentiment* and *sense,* and appropriately so, for the construction of a sentence, even the simplest two-word kind, requires sensing and thinking, perceiving and judging.

25a Parts of speech

To understand how sentences express the perceptions and judgments of a speaker or writer, we must first become familiar with the various classes into which words—the constituent elements of sentences—may be placed. One way to approach such a classification is to note the different forms of English words. The words *tree, audience,* and

555

The survey of traditional grammar in Chapter **25** offers students a common vocabulary for discussing sentence elements and sentence types. For more information, see Chapter **26**, "Agreement," Chapter **27**, "Case of Pronouns and Nouns," Chapter **28**, "Adjectives and Adverbs," and Chapter **29**, "Verbs."

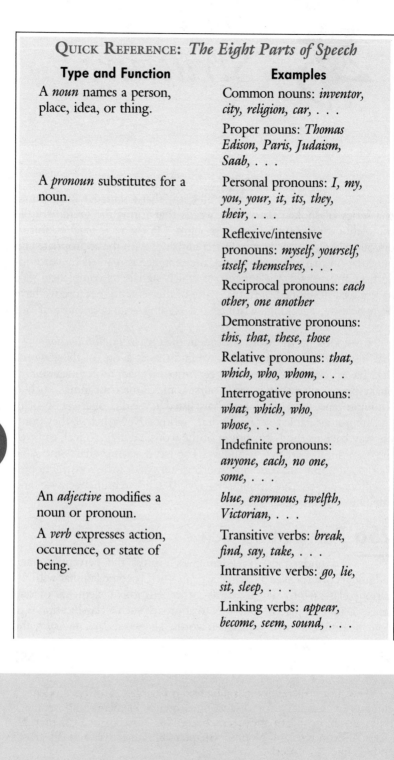

QUICK REFERENCE: *The Eight Parts of Speech*

Type and Function	Examples
A *noun* names a person, place, idea, or thing.	Common nouns: *inventor, city, religion, car, . . .*
	Proper nouns: *Thomas Edison, Paris, Judaism, Saab, . . .*
A *pronoun* substitutes for a noun.	Personal pronouns: *I, my, you, your, it, its, they, their, . . .*
	Reflexive/intensive pronouns: *myself, yourself, itself, themselves, . . .*
	Reciprocal pronouns: *each other, one another*
	Demonstrative pronouns: *this, that, these, those*
	Relative pronouns: *that, which, who, whom, . . .*
	Interrogative pronouns: *what, which, who, whose, . . .*
	Indefinite pronouns: *anyone, each, no one, some, . . .*
An *adjective* modifies a noun or pronoun.	*blue, enormous, twelfth, Victorian, . . .*
A *verb* expresses action, occurrence, or state of being.	Transitive verbs: *break, find, say, take, . . .*
	Intransitive verbs: *go, lie, sit, sleep, . . .*
	Linking verbs: *appear, become, seem, sound, . . .*

25a

	Auxiliary verbs: *could, have, may, will, . . .*
An *adverb* modifies a verb, an adjective, or another adverb.	*cleverly, quickly, soon, very, . . .*
A *preposition* precedes a noun or pronoun, indicating its relationship to another word in the sentence.	*above, between, from, in, on, through, under, with, . . .*
A *conjunction* connects words, phrases, and clauses.	Coordinating conjunctions: *and, but, for, nor, or, so, yet*
	Subordinating conjunctions: *although, because, if, unless, when, while, . . .*
	Correlative conjunctions: *both . . . and, either . . . or, neither . . . nor, not only . . . but also, whether . . . or*
	Conjunctive adverbs: *consequently, however, moreover, therefore, . . .*
An *interjection* interrupts the rhythm of a sentence to express emotion.	*ah, oh, okay, wow, . . .*

25a

belief, for example, are alike in that they may appear in a sentence after words such as *a, the,* or *this: a tree, the audience, this belief.* Words in this class also take inflectional endings to indicate the plural, usually a suffix including the letter *s: trees, audiences, beliefs.* Grammarians have traditionally called words with these formal qualities **nouns.** In a different class are words to which the inflectional suffixes *-ed* or *-d* can be added: *ask, asked; bake, baked; cry, cried.* Words in this class are identified as

verbs. Yet another class consists of words to which *-er* and *-est* can be added: *happy, happier, happiest; swift, swifter, swiftest.* These words are called **adjectives.**

By itself, however, such a formal approach to grammar cannot fully describe the elements of a sentence, for many words resist classification in a single category. In addition to a word's *form,* we need to examine its possible *functions* in a sentence.

> **noun**
> Every *dress* in the store is on sale.

> **verb**
> You may *dress* casually for the party.

> **adjective**
> Tomorrow night's *dress* rehearsal has been canceled.

Considered together, formal and functional characteristics of words yield the eight traditional categories known as the *parts of speech:* **nouns, pronouns, adjectives, verbs, adverbs, prepositions, conjunctions,** and **interjections** (see the box on pages 556–57). Recognizing the parts of speech is a first step toward understanding sentence structure.

(For additional examples and further discussion of the **boldface** terms in this chapter, see the "Glossary of Grammatical and Stylistic Terms" on pages G25–G45.)

25b Subjects and predicates

25b

A statement says something about something; to make a statement you need to *name* what you are talking about and *assert* something about it. The grammatical term for the word or words that name what you are talking about is the **subject.** The **predicate** is the assertion you make about the subject.

subject	predicate
I	like spices.
Edison	invented the light bulb.
A coyote	howled all night.
Creativity	is a gift.

The subject is usually a noun or pronoun, though it may be a **phrase** or **clause,** as we will see below. The predicate may contain a number of words with various functions, but its essential element is a verb, a word that asserts.

1.   Identifying subjects and verbs

The analysis of any sentence begins with the identification of the simple subject and the verb. Look first for the verb, often a word or group of words that states an action or occurrence.

Joe Miller *wrote* me a letter.
I *sprained* my wrist.
The fire *is burning* out of control.
She *will* never *paint* landscapes again.

Some verbs merely assert that something is—or looks like, sounds like, seems to be, or appears to be—something. Such verbs are called **linking verbs** or **copulas.**

Sara Miller *is* a gifted athlete.
You *sound* angry.
The troops *are looking* weary.
He *has* always *seemed* conceited.

Note that some forms of a verb are phrases that include one or more **auxiliary verbs**—*is* burning, *will* paint, *are* looking, *has* seemed. (For more information about verb phrases, see **29c, 29d,** and **29f.**)

Once you have found the verb in a sentence, put it in the blank in the following question: "Who or what _____ ?" The answer to the question is the subject, and if you strip away the modifiers you have the **simple subject.**

A long, dull speech *followed* the dinner.
[What followed the dinner? *A long, dull speech. Long* and *dull* are adjectives describing *speech;* the simple subject is *speech.*]
Half a mile away *rose* the spires of the cathedral.
[What rose half a mile away? The answer is the subject, *spires.*]

2.   Compound subjects and predicates

Since we can make one assertion about several persons and things, a sentence may have several nouns as its subject. Such a construction is called a **compound subject.**

compound subject	
The *trees* and *plants*	were dying.
Jane Austen, George Eliot, and *Emily Brontë*	are my favorite novelists.

Similarly, we can make several assertions about one subject. Such a construction is called a **compound predicate.**

	compound predicate
She	*wrote, revised, typed,* and *proofread* the manuscript.
Exhausted, she	*went* to bed and *slept* for twelve hours.

3.   Subjects and verbs in interrogative and imperative sentences

In an interrogative sentence—one that poses a question—the subject often follows some form of the verbs *have, do,* or *be,* or another auxiliary verb.

verb	subject	
Have	*you*	the time?
Is	*he*	qualified?

auxiliary	subject	verb	
Have	*you*	read	this novel?
Did	*she*	write	it?
May	*they*	borrow	it?

	auxiliary	subject	verb
What kind of story	did	*he*	tell?

In an imperative sentence—one that commands or requests—the subject is not expressed. Since a command is addressed directly to someone, that person need not be named.

25b

subject		verb	
(	)	Come	in.
(	)	Return	the book no later than Monday.
(	)	Take	these books to the library, please.

Pick out the simple subjects and the verbs in the following sentences. Note that either the subject or the verb may be compound.

Example

> After locking the airplane door, the flight attendants checked the passengers' seat belts.
>
> **Subject** attendants
> **Verb** checked

1. The last arrivals, searching for empty overhead bins, stowed their carry-on luggage.
2. Invisible to us, the pilot and copilot were checking the instruments.
3. Signs warning passengers not to smoke and to fasten their seat belts flashed on.
4. Directly beneath the signs was a door leading to the pilot's compartment.
5. Altogether about sixty passengers were on the plane.
6. In a few moments the plane moved, slowly at first, and then roared into life.
7. After taxiing out to the airstrip, the pilot hesitated a moment to check the runway.
8. Then with a sudden rush of speed the plane raced down the runway and gradually began to climb.
9. Below us, at the edge of the airport, were markers and signal lights.
10. The football field and the quarter-mile track enabled me to identify the high school.

25c

25c Modifiers

It is possible to make a complete sentence of only two words, a subject and a verb:

Rain fell.

Exercise 1

1. arrivals [subject] . . . stowed [verb]
2. pilot . . . copilot [subject] . . . were checking [verb]
3. Signs [subject] . . . flashed [verb]
4. was [verb] . . . door [subject]
5. passengers [subject] were [verb]
6. plane [subject] . . . moved . . . roared [verb]
7. pilot [subject] hesitated [verb]
8. plane [subject] raced . . . began [verb]
9. were [verb] markers . . . lights [subject]
10. field . . . track [subject] enabled [verb]

Few sentences, however, are as simple as this one. We usually add other words whose function is to describe the subject or the verb:

A *gentle* rain fell *steadily.*

Here *gentle* describes *rain,* and *steadily* describes how it fell. Such words are called **modifiers,** and they may be attached to almost any part of a sentence. Although modifiers usually describe, they may also indicate how many (*three* books, *few* books), which one (*this* pencil, *my* pen), or how much (*very* gently, *half* sick).

Modifiers are divided into two main classes: **adjectives** and **adverbs.** Any word that modifies a noun, pronoun, or gerund is an *adjective;* an *adverb* is any word that modifies a verb, an adjective, or another adverb.

Very hungry people *seldom* display *good* manners.

In this sentence, *hungry* and *good* are adjectives, describing or indicating what kind of people and manners. *Very* is an adverb that modifies the adjective *hungry; seldom* is an adverb modifying the verb *display.*

Adjectives and adverbs have different forms to indicate **comparison.** In addition to the regular, or positive, form (*slow, comfortable, slowly*), there are the comparative (*slower, more comfortable, more slowly*) and superlative (*slowest, most comfortable, most slowly*) degrees. The examples illustrate the rule: adjectives with more than two syllables form the comparative and superlative degrees by addition of the words *more* and *most,* instead of the suffixes -*er* and -*est.* All adverbs ending in -*ly* use *more* and *most* to indicate degrees of comparison. (For further discussion of adjectives and adverbs, see Chapter **28.**)

25d Direct and indirect objects

Verbs that make a full assertion about the subject—that require no additional words to complete the thought—are called **intransitive verbs.**

After meeting all the relatives, my cousin *left.*

In a heavy rain, cabbage may *explode.*

Transitive verbs, in contrast, are incomplete when used with a subject alone. If one says only "I bought," the listener is likely to ask, "What did you buy?" The word or words that answer such a question and complete the assertion are known as the **direct object** of the verb. The direct object is usually a noun or pronoun, though it may be a phrase or a clause, and it usually names the thing acted upon by the subject.

subject	verb	direct object
My niece	built	*a water clock.*
They	chased	*whoever came near them.*

The easiest way to identify a direct object is to say the simple subject and verb and then ask the question "What?" My niece built what? The answer, *clock,* is the direct object of the verb *built.* Note that, like subjects and predicates, direct objects may be compound.

subject	verb	compound direct object
I	borrowed	*a tent, a sleeping bag,* and *a gas stove.*

Certain verbs, such as those involving an act of giving or telling, may take not only a direct object but an **indirect object,** which designates the receiver of whatever is named by the direct object.

		indirect	
subject		object	direct object

The award gave the young *photographer* encouragement.
[What did the award give? *Encouragement* is the direct object. Who received the encouragement? *Photographer* is the indirect object—the receiver of what is named by the direct object.]

25e

The same meaning can be expressed by a phrase beginning with *to:*

The award gave encouragement *to* the young photographer.

He offered me his pen.

He offered his pen *to* me.

25e Subject and object complements

A **subject complement** follows a linking verb and completes the predicate either by further naming the subject or by describing it. A subject complement that names the subject is called a **predicate noun.**

subject   predicate noun
My mother was the *mayor* of our town.
[*Mayor*, the predicate noun, is another name for *mother*, the subject.]

When the subject complement describes the subject, it is called a **predicate adjective.**

                         predicate
        subject   adjective
My mother was exceptionally *popular*.
[The adjective *popular* describes the subject of the sentence, *mother*.]

An **object complement** follows the direct object in a sentence and performs functions similar to those of a subject complement—it either provides another name for the object or describes it.

                        object
              object complement
The townspeople elected my mother *mayor*.
[The noun *mayor* follows and completes the direct object, *mother*.]

                        object
              object complement
Everyone considered her reputation *spotless*.
[The adjective *spotless* describes the direct object, *reputation*.]

25e

EXERCISE 2

Pick out the subjects and verbs in the following sentences, and identify direct objects, indirect objects, predicate nouns, predicate adjectives, and object complements.

Example

As a housewarming present, my uncle gave us a picture.

Subject	uncle
Verb	gave
Direct object	picture
Indirect object	us

Exercise 2

1. Subject: It. Verb: was. Predicate noun: sketch.
2. Subject 1: technique. Verb 1: was. Predicate adjective: interesting. Subject 2: Dufy. Verb 2: had used. Direct object: lines.
3. Subject 1: It. Verb 1: seemed. Predicate noun: work. Subject 2: I. Verb 2: showed. Indirect object: whom. Direct object: it.
4. Subject: figures. Verb: were. Predicate noun: trio.
5. Subject: We. Verb: found. Direct object: tones. Object complement: dazzling.
6. Subject: I. Verbs: wrote, thanked. Indirect object: uncle. Direct object: him.
7. Subject 1: We. Verb 1: hung. Direct object 1: picture. Subject 2: guests. Verb 2: admired. Direct object 2: it.
8. Subject 1: We. Verb 1: enjoyed. Direct object: it. Subject 2: friend. Verb 2: told. Indirect object: us. Direct object: value.

1. It was an original sketch by Dufy.
2. The technique was interesting, since Dufy had used only a few simple lines.
3. It seemed an early work, according to a friend to whom I showed it.
4. The central figures in the picture were a trio of circus performers.
5. We found the luminous tones of the work dazzling.
6. I wrote my uncle and thanked him for the gift.
7. We hung the picture in the living room, where guests often admired it.
8. We enjoyed it for several months, until my friend told us its value.
9. Then we worried about burglars, and we wrote my uncle again asking if he would give us a less valuable picture.
10. He called us and calmed our fears about theft.

25f Phrases

A group of words that does not constitute a complete statement and that functions in a sentence like a single word is called a **phrase**.

The train *to Boston* leaves *in ten minutes*.

In this sentence, for example, the group of words *in ten minutes* modifies the verb *leaves* in exactly the same way as an adverb like *soon*. Similarly, *to Boston* functions like an adjective: it describes and identifies *train*.

1. Prepositional phrases

25f

A prepositional phrase consists of a **preposition** (a connective such as *above, by, from, on, to,* or *with*) joined to a noun or a pronoun, which is called the *object of the preposition*. Such phrases usually modify nouns or verbs, and they are described accordingly as adjective or adverb phrases.

	adjective		adverb
The leader	*of the band*	swayed	*in the sun.*
The procession	*from the church to the cemetery*	continued	*for an hour.*

9. Subject 1: we. Verb 1: worried. Subject 2: we. Verb 2: wrote. Indirect object: uncle. Subject 3: he. Verb 3: would give. Indirect object: us. Direct object: picture.
10. Subject: He. Verbs: called, calmed. Direct objects: us, fears.

2. Verbal phrases

A **verbal** is a form of a verb that functions as some other part of speech. It is important to distinguish between verb forms ending in *-ing* and *-ed* when they function as part of the verb, as in "I was turning around," and such forms when they function as adjectives to modify a noun, as in "a turning point" or "a turned ankle." A verbal that modifies a noun is called a **participle.** Note that a participle may be in the past or in the present tense—"a *used* [past] car with *splitting* [present] upholstery."

A verb form that functions as a noun is called a **gerund:** "Writing is his passion." In this sentence, *writing* is the subject of the sentence. Gerunds may also be used as the objects of verbs or of prepositions.

	object of verb		object of preposition
He loves	*writing*	and amuses himself by	*scribbling dull verses.*

A third type of verbal is the **infinitive,** the present form of the verb preceded in most cases by the word *to: to write, to scribble.* Infinitives are frequently used as nouns—as subject or object of the verb.

	subject		object
To err	is human, but remember	*to apologize.*	

Since they are verb forms, participles, gerunds, and infinitives may take objects, and they may be modified by adverbs or by prepositional phrases. A verbal with its modifier and its object, or subject, makes up a verbal phrase and functions as a single part of speech, but it does not make a full statement.

Participial phrase   *Moved by my mother's life of selfless dedication to the disadvantaged,* the townspeople voted to build a monument to her.
[Here the participle *moved,* modified by a prepositional phrase, describes the townspeople.]

Gerund phrase   *Selecting an inexpensive and appropriate site* took considerable time.
[Here the phrase—gerund, object, and the modifiers of the object—is the subject of the sentence.]

Exercise 3 (page 568)

Students may find it easier to classify prepositional phrases in this exercise if they keep in mind that phrases answering questions about verbs (Where? When? How? Why?) are adverbial phrases, whereas adjectival phrases answer questions about nouns (Of what type?).

1. *between the street and the driveway*—prepositional phrase, adverb modifying *found* [though one could also argue that this is an adjectival phrase describing the ditch]
2. *of workers*—prepositional phrase, adjective modifying *crew*
   to lay a new water main—infinitive phrase, object of *begun*
   along the curb—prepositional phrase, adverb modifying *to lay*
3. *Hoping that I would not get a ticket for overnight parking*—participial phrase modifying *I*
   for overnight parking—prepositional phrase, adjective modifying *ticket*
   in the street—prepositional phrase, adverb modifying *left*
   in front of the house—prepositional phrase, adverb modifying *left* [the entire phrase *in front of* functions as the preposition in this sentence]

Infinitive phrase The task required *us to walk for hours.*
[The infinitive phrase is the object of the verb *required.* It consists of the infinitive, *to walk,* together with its subject, *us,* and a modifying phrase, *for hours.*]

3. Absolute phrases

An **absolute phrase** is a group of words that has a subject but no verb and is not grammatically connected to the rest of the sentence. The subject of an absolute phrase is frequently followed by a participle.

The site having been selected, we met to choose a sculptor.
His hands folded on the table, one citizen questioned our decision.
A tree, *all things considered,* is a better monument than a statue.

The subject of an absolute phrase may also be followed by an adjective or a prepositional phrase.

His voice quiet, his face pale, he urged us to reconsider our decision.
We listened carefully, *our hearts in our mouths.*

Because absolute phrases are formed by the suppression of connecting elements—prepositions ("*with* our hearts in our mouths") or subordinating conjunctions and verbs ("*when* all things *are* considered")—they have a toughness and economy that can be a virtue in writing.

4. Appositive phrases

25f

An **appositive** is a noun or noun phrase added to explain another noun: "My mother, *the mayor,* was the subject of controversy all her life." Appositives with their modifiers make up phrases, since they function as a unit to give further information about a noun.

The memorial she wanted, *a grand magnolia tree,* now stands in the center of town.
The townspeople, *wise and practical citizens,* made the decision, *a radical one for that time and place.*

Appositives, like absolute constructions, compress connections by eliminating words. The last sentence could have been written, "The

4. *For three days* — prepositional phrase, adverb modifying *prevented*
   to my garage — prepositional phrase, adjective modifying *access*
5. *Finding a place to park* — gerund phrase, subject of sentence
   to park — infinitive phrase, adjective modifying *place*
   on my side — prepositional phrase, adjective modifying *neighbors*
   of the street — prepositional phrase, adjective modifying *side*
   in the same predicament — prepositional phrase, adjective modifying *neighbors*
6. *By Friday* — prepositional phrase, adverb modifying *had filled [up]*
   stained with dust and dew — participial phrase, modifying *car*
7. *The damage having been done* — absolute phrase
   to give the car a thorough cleaning — infinitive phrase used as a predicate noun
8. *Washing the car* — participial phrase modifying *I*
   with fantasies — prepositional phrase, adverb modifying *entertained*
   of suing the city or picketing the mayor's office — prepositional phrase, adjective modifying *fantasies*

townspeople, who were wise and practical citizens, made the decision, which was a radical one for that time and place," but the result would be a less economical and far less effective sentence.

EXERCISE 3

Pick out the phrases in the following sentences. Identify them as prepositional, participial, gerund, infinitive, absolute, or appositive, and be ready to describe their function in the sentence.

Example

On Tuesday, I came home expecting to drive my car, a shiny new convertible, into the garage.

On Tuesday	prepositional phrase, adverb modifying *came*
expecting to drive my car into the garage	participial phrase modifying *I*
to drive my car	infinitive phrase, object of *expecting*
a shiny new convertible	appositive, identifying *car*
into the garage	prepositional phrase, adverb modifying *to drive*

1. However, I found a ditch between the street and the driveway.
2. A crew of workers had begun to lay a new water main along the curb.
3. Hoping that I would not get a ticket for overnight parking, I left the car in the street in front of the house.
4. For three days a yawning trench prevented access to my garage.
5. Finding a place to park was difficult, since all the neighbors on my side of the street were in the same predicament.
6. By Friday the workers had filled up the ditch, but my car, stained with dust and dew, looked ten years older.
7. The damage having been done, my only option was to give the car a thorough cleaning.
8. Washing the car, I entertained myself with fantasies of suing the city or picketing the mayor's office.
9. My brother, a strong advocate of justice, suggested sending the city a bill for the job.
10. But by this time my anger had dissipated, and I decided to forget the inconvenience I had endured.

25f

9. *a strong advocate of justice* — appositive, identifying *brother*
   of justice — prepositional phrase, adjective modifying *advocate*
   sending the city a bill for the job — gerund phrase, object of *suggested*
   for the job — prepositional phrase, adjective modifying *bill*
10. *by this time* — prepositional phrase, adverb modifying *had dissipated*
    to forget the inconvenience — infinitive phrase, object of *decided*

Exercise 4 (page 571)

1. Independent clause: Griffith [subject] achieved [verb] immediate success with his first film
   Adverb clause: Shortly after he [subject] entered [verb] filmmaking in New York
   Adjective clause: which he [subject] directed [verb] in 1908

25g Clauses

A **clause** is a group of words that contains a subject and a predicate and that makes a statement. Except for elliptical questions and answers, every sentence must contain at least one clause. But not all clauses are sentences. Some clauses, instead of making an independent statement, serve only as a subordinate part of the main sentence. Such clauses, called **dependent** (or **subordinate**) **clauses,** perform a function like that of adjectives, adverbs, or nouns. **Independent clauses,** on the other hand, can stand alone as complete sentences. They provide the framework to which modifiers, phrases, and dependent clauses are attached in each sentence. Any piece of connected discourse is made up of a series of independent clauses.

"She heard the news" is a clause because it has a subject, *she,* and a verb, *heard.* It is an independent clause because it is complete in itself and can stand alone as a sentence. "When she heard the news" is also a clause because it has a subject and a predicate, but it is a dependent one. The addition of the word *when* creates a condition of incompleteness, or dependency. Any reader will expect to be told what happened when she heard the news.

dependent clause	**independent clause**
When she heard the news,	she was delighted.

Dependent clauses are usually connected to the rest of the sentence by **relative pronouns** (such as *who, which,* and *that*) or by **subordinating conjunctions** (such as *although, because, if, since, when,* and *while*). The terms *relative* and *subordinating* remind us that clauses introduced by these words are not self-sufficient; they are related or subordinated to an independent clause. Written separately, they are fragments. (For more on relative pronouns and subordinating conjunctions, see **8b**. For further discussion of sentence fragments, see Chapter **30**.)

Dependent clauses function as parts of speech. Like nouns, they can be subjects and objects, and like adverbs and adjectives, they can be modifiers.

25g

1. Noun clauses

A **noun clause** functions as a noun in a sentence. It may be the subject or the direct object in an independent clause, or the object of a preposition or of a gerund.

2. Independent clause: Between 1908 and 1913 . . . Griffith [subject] continually worked [verb] with techniques
   Adverb clause: while he [subject] was directing [verb] Westerns
   Adjective clause: that others [subject] had introduced [verb]
   Adjective clause: that he [subject] gradually refined [verb 1] and perfected [verb 2]
3. Independent clause: Griffith [subject] was delighted [verb] by the Western
   Adverb clause: because it [subject] offered [verb] opportunities for spectacle and scope
4. Independent clause: He [subject] found [verb] that the Western was an ideal genre for experimenting with close-ups and with cross-cutting
   Noun clause as direct object of *found:* that the Western [subject] was [verb] an ideal genre for experimenting with close-ups and with cross-cutting
   Adjective clause: [*that* understood; direct object of *employed;* antecedent is the appositive *techniques*] he [subject] employed [verb] to build narrative suspense

Noun clause as subject of the sentence

That Lauren was considered for the position is remarkable.

Noun clause as direct object of the verb

She said *that she would accept only under certain conditions*.

Noun clause as object of the preposition

We will give the job to *whoever is best qualified*.

Noun clause as object of a gerund

We do best for ourselves by asking *what we can do for others*.

2.   Adverb clauses

An **adverb clause** is a dependent clause used to modify a verb, an adjective, or an adverb in an independent clause.

Adverb clause that modifies a verb

We ate *whenever we felt like it*.
[The clause *whenever we felt like it* modifies the verb *ate*.]

Adverb clause that modifies an adjective

The trip was as pleasant *as we had hoped*.
[The clause *as we had hoped* modifies the adjective *pleasant*.]

Adverb clause that modifies an adverb

The train arrived sooner *than we had expected*.
[The clause *than we had expected* modifies the adverb *sooner*.]

3.   Adjective clauses

A dependent clause used to modify a noun or pronoun is called an **adjective clause**.

5. Independent clause: Some critics [subject] have pointed out [verb] that Griffith was more interested in dramatic situations
   Noun clause as direct object of *have pointed out:* that Griffith [subject] was [verb] more interested in dramatic situations
   Adjective clause: that [subject] lent [verb] themselves to lively visual treatment
   Adverb clause: than he [subject] was [verb] in the details of plot or conventional justice
6. Independent clause: He [subject] would willingly let [verb] the villains go free
   Adverb clause: whenever he [subject] felt [verb] that the dramatic situation warranted it
   Noun clause as direct object of *felt:* that the dramatic situation [subject] warranted [verb] it
7. Independent clause: The close-up [subject 1] of the outnumbered settlers grimly hanging on and the panoramic view [subject 2] of the battle seen from afar were [verb] characteristic Griffith shots. [simple sentence with compound subject]

Adjective clauses

The detective *whom we met yesterday* showed us his library, *which includes all the first editions of Dorothy Sayers.*
[The adjective clause *whom we met yesterday* modifies the noun *detective*; the adjective clause *which includes all the first editions of Dorothy Sayers* modifies the noun *library.*]

Adjective clauses are usually introduced by relative pronouns, which serve both as pronouns and as subordinating conjunctions. The following sentences illustrate how relative pronouns work.

Dorothy Sayers wrote many books; the books were widely read.
[This sentence consists of two independent clauses. It would be more idiomatic, however, if we substituted a pronoun for the second *books*.]

Dorothy Sayers wrote many books; *they* were widely read.
[If, instead of using the pronoun *they*, we now substitute the relative pronoun *that*, the second clause becomes dependent.]

Dorothy Sayers wrote many books *that* were widely read.
[*That were widely read* no longer will stand as an independent sentence. Joined to the first clause, it functions as an adjective, modifying *books*.]

The relative pronouns *who* (and *whom*), *which*, and *that* always have two simultaneous roles: (1) they serve as subordinating conjunctions, connecting dependent clauses to independent ones, and (2) they function like nouns, as subject or object in the dependent clause. Often, relative pronouns can be omitted: "She is a person I cherish." But sometimes they need to be expressed. "Hers is the kind of writing writers envy" is awkward and confusing, but "Hers is the kind of writing *that* writers envy" is not.

25g

EXERCISE 4

Find the simple subject and verb of each clause in the following sentences. Point out the independent clauses and the dependent clauses, and be prepared to state the function in each sentence of each dependent clause.

Example

The movie director who did much to perfect the one-reel Western as a distinct genre was D. W. Griffith.

---

8. Independent clause: In 1915, Griffith [subject] produced [verb] *The Birth of a Nation,* the first great spectacle movie. [simple sentence with appositive at end]
9. Independent clause: It [subject] made [verb] use of many of the techniques
   Adjective clause: [*that* understood; direct object of *had developed*] he [subject] had developed [verb]
   Adverb clause: while he [subject] was making [verb] one-reel Westerns
10. Independent clause: they [subject] have criticized [verb] its sympathetic portrayal of the Ku Klux Klan
    Adverb clause: Although film critics [subject] have praised [verb] the artistic qualities of *The Birth of a Nation*

| **Independent clause** | The movie director [subject] was [verb] D. W. Griffith |
| **Adjective clause** | who [subject] did [verb] much to perfect the one-reel Western as a distinct genre |

1. Shortly after he entered filmmaking in New York, Griffith achieved immediate success with his first film, which he directed in 1908.
2. Between 1908 and 1913, while he was directing Westerns, Griffith continually worked with techniques that others had introduced but that he gradually refined and perfected.
3. Griffith was delighted by the Western because it offered opportunities for spectacle and scope.
4. He found that the Western was an ideal genre for experimenting with close-ups and with cross-cutting, the techniques he employed to build narrative suspense.
5. Some critics have pointed out that Griffith was more interested in dramatic situations that lent themselves to lively visual treatment than he was in the details of plot or conventional justice.
6. He would willingly let the villains go free whenever he felt that the dramatic situation warranted it.
7. The close-up of the outnumbered settlers grimly hanging on and the panoramic view of the battle seen from afar were characteristic Griffith shots.
8. In 1915, Griffith produced *The Birth of a Nation,* the first great spectacle movie.
9. It made use of many of the techniques he had developed while he was making one-reel Westerns.
10. Although film critics have praised the artistic qualities of *The Birth of a Nation,* they have criticized its sympathetic portrayal of the Ku Klux Klan.

25h Types of sentences

Sentences ask questions or answer them, issue commands or requests, express strong feeling, and, most often, make statements. The **syntax** of the sentence, its arrangement of words, tells us immediately what kind of sentence it is.

| **Exclamatory** | What a ridiculous assignment! |
| **Imperative** | Write the paper. |

Exercise 5 (page 575)

1. Simple sentence with appositive phrase.
   Independent clause: Galen [subject], a physician of ancient Greece, was generally accepted [verb] as the authority on anatomy and physiology.
2. Compound sentence with appositive phrase.
   Independent clause 1: His theory [subject] of the four humors—blood, phlegm, bile, and black bile—was [verb] neat and logical
   Independent clause 2: authorities [subject] had accepted [verb] it for centuries
3. Simple sentence with participial phrase.
   Independent clause: Similarly, his account [subject] of the structure of the human body, revised by generations of scholars and appearing in many printed editions, was generally accepted [verb].

Interrogative   Are you writing the paper?
Declarative   I have written the paper.

From the standpoint of structure, sentences are traditionally classified as simple, compound, complex, and compound-complex.

1.   Simple sentences

A **simple sentence** consists of one independent clause with or without modifying words or phrases but with no dependent clauses attached.

	subject	**verb**
Simple	Harvey	despaired.

	modifying phrase	**subject**	**verb**
Simple	Nervously biting his fingernails,	Harvey	despaired

modifying phrase
of ever learning grammar.

modifying phrase
Simple   Nervously biting their fingernails,

compound subject
Harvey and his friend Zelda,

modifying phrase
puzzled once more by the red marks on their papers,

compound predicate
despaired of ever learning the fine points of grammar and
longed for the simple beauty of differential calculus.

25h

Obviously, simple sentences can be quite elaborate when the subject or the verb is modified with verbals and appositives. Still, such sentences can be reduced to a simple kernel and, as such, are limited in expressing complicated ideas or showing the relation of one idea to another. Moreover, simple sentence following simple sentence leads, at best, to tedious writing, and, at worst, to what in writing is called a *primer style*. The straightforward thrust of the simple declaration should be modulated by the careful use of other types of sentences.

4. Complex sentence.
   Adverb clause: If dissection [subject] showed [verb] a difference from Galen's account
   Independent clause: the obvious explanation [subject] was [verb] that human structure had changed since Galen's time
   Noun clause as predicate noun: that human structure [subject] had changed [verb] since Galen's time
5. Complex sentence.
   Independent clause: One person [subject] . . . was [verb] Andreas Vesalius
   Adjective clause: who [subject] refused [verb] to accept this explanation
   Adjective clause: who [subject] was studying [verb] in Italy
6. Simple sentence with participial phrase at beginning.
   Independent clause: Asked to edit the anatomical section of Galen's works, Vesalius [subject] found [verb] many errors in it.

2.   Compound sentences

The **compound sentence** consists of two or more independent clauses joined by a coordinating conjunction or by a semicolon. There are seven **coordinating conjunctions:** *and, but, for, nor, or, so,* and *yet.*

	independent clause		independent clause
Compound	He wrote for hours,	and	his hunger vanished.

	independent clause	independent clause
Compound	His style was graceful;	his sentences were lively and varied.

Compound   independent clause
His roommate left the shower running,   but

independent clause
Al did not notice.

The compound sentence offers the advantage of possible balance and antithesis. Skillfully used, it creates effective coordination and parallelism (see **8b** and **8d**).

3.   Complex sentences

A **complex sentence** contains one independent clause and one or more dependent clauses that express subordinate ideas.

25h

Complex   dependent clause
Because he was tired and hungry and discouraged,

independent clause
he did not want to rewrite the paper.

Complex   independent clause   dependent clause
Still, ideas for writing come   when we least expect them.

Complex   independent clause   dependent clause
Reluctantly, he put pen to paper,   while his roommate sang in the shower.

The complex sentence has the advantage of flexibility; it can be arranged to produce a variety of sentence patterns and to indicate subtle

7. Complex sentence.
   Independent clause: Galen's statement [subject] seemed [verb] wrong to Vesalius
   Noun clause as appositive: that the lower jaw [subject] consisted [verb] of two parts
   Adjective clause: who [subject] had never found [verb] such a structure in his own dissections
8. Complex sentence.
   Independent clause: He [subject] finally concluded [verb] that Galen was describing the anatomy of lower animals . . . and that he had never dissected a human body.
   Noun clause as first direct object of *concluded:* that Galen [subject] was describing [verb] the anatomy of lower animals—pigs, monkeys, and goats
   Noun clause as second direct object of *concluded:* that he [subject] had never dissected [verb] a human body

relationships between ideas. It also provides selective emphasis, since the subordination of dependent clauses throws the weight of the sentence onto the independent clause. Understanding when and how to subordinate is a fundamental writing skill (see **8b**).

4. Compound-complex sentences

When a compound sentence contains one or more dependent clauses, the whole is described as a **compound-complex sentence.**

	independent clause	
Compound-complex	He was surprised	

	dependent clause	
	when the water rose above his shoes	but

independent clause
he went on writing.

	dependent clause
Compound-complex	Although he was drenched to the bone,

	independent clause	
	he typed up the paper,	and

dependent clause
while his roommate bailed out the room,

independent clause
he read the finished manuscript with undampened satisfaction.

25h

EXERCISE 5

Classify the following sentences as simple, compound, complex, or compound-complex. Identify the subject and verb in each clause. Describe the function of each dependent clause.

Example

When Renaissance physicians began to study human anatomy by means of dissection, they concluded that the human body had changed since the days of antiquity.

---

9. Complex sentence.
   Adverb clause: When he [subject] realized [verb] that Galen could be wrong
   Noun clause as direct object of *realized:* that Galen [subject] could be [verb] wrong
   Independent clause: Vesalius [subject] began [verb] a study
   Adjective clause: that [subject] came [verb] to be recognized as his major work: a fully illustrated treatise on the human body based on actual observation
10. Compound sentence.
    Independent clause 1: This work [subject], the *Fabrica,* was widely criticized [verb] by Vesalius's contemporaries

Complex sentence	
Adverb clause	When Renaissance physicians [subject] began [verb] to study human anatomy by means of dissection
Independent clause	they [subject] concluded [verb] that the human body had changed since the days of antiquity
Noun clause as direct object of *concluded*	that the human body [subject] had changed [verb] since the days of antiquity

1. Galen, a physician of ancient Greece, was generally accepted as the authority on anatomy and physiology.
2. His theory of the four humors—blood, phlegm, bile, and black bile—was neat and logical, and authorities had accepted it for centuries.
3. Similarly, his account of the structure of the human body, revised by generations of scholars and appearing in many printed editions, was generally accepted.
4. If dissection showed a difference from Galen's account, the obvious explanation was that human structure had changed since Galen's time.
5. One person who refused to accept this explanation was Andreas Vesalius, a young Belgian physician who was studying in Italy.
6. Asked to edit the anatomical section of Galen's works, Vesalius found many errors in it.
7. Galen's statement that the lower jaw consisted of two parts seemed wrong to Vesalius, who had never found such a structure in his own dissections.
8. He finally concluded that Galen was describing the anatomy of lower animals—pigs, monkeys, and goats—and that he had never dissected a human body.
9. When he realized that Galen could be wrong, Vesalius began a study that came to be recognized as his major work: a fully illustrated treatise on the human body based on actual observation.
10. This work, the *Fabrica,* was widely criticized by Vesalius's contemporaries, but it played a key role in establishing the modern science of anatomy.

25h

Independent clause 2: it [subject] played [verb] a key role in establishing the modern science of anatomy

For Further Reading

Christensen, Francis. "A Generative Rhetoric of the Sentence." *College Composition and Communication* 14 (1963): 155–61.

Delahunty, Gerald P., and James J. Garvey. *Language, Grammar, and Communication: A Course for Teachers of English.* New York: McGraw-Hill, 1994.

Kolln, Martha. *Understanding English Grammar.* 3rd ed. New York: Macmillan, 1990.

Weaver, Richard M. "Some Rhetorical Aspects of Grammatical Categories." *Rhetoric and Composition: A Sourcebook for Teachers and Writers.* Rev. ed. Ed. Richard L. Graves. Upper Montclair: Boynton/Cook, 1984. 95–99.

26 *Agreement*

As in many other languages, most of the nouns, pronouns, and verbs in English have different forms that indicate their relation to one another in a sentence. Most nouns and all verbs, for example, have different singular and plural forms; for a sentence to make grammatical sense, singular verbs must be used with singular subjects, and plural verbs with plural subjects. Pronouns, too, have separate forms to indicate number (singular or plural) and person (first person: *I, we;* second person: *you;* third person: *he, she, it, they*). The matching of subjects and verbs, pronouns and nouns, according to person and number in a sentence is called **agreement.**

The rules of agreement sound simple enough in theory, but in practice they can sometimes be a bit confusing. One reason for this confusion is that most speakers of English are not very sensitive to questions of agreement, because English has relatively few inflections, or different forms, to begin with. The verb *walked,* for example, remains the same whether its subject is singular or plural, or first, second, or third person.

26

> I walked   you walked   they walked

A more unusual grammatical construction may therefore momentarily puzzle even the most meticulous user of English.

> Either Susan or Alan is?/are? going to be nominated.
> Athletics is?/are? in danger of being cut from the school budget.

To complicate matters further, dialectical variations among speakers of English often affect the rules of agreement, since various dialects may form singulars and plurals in different ways. Speakers of such dialects have two sets of rules to keep in mind: those that apply in their dialect

---

QUICK REFERENCE: *Problems with Agreement*

Subject-verb agreement

Modifying phrases after the subject do not affect the agreement of subject and verb.

> **Example**   A *load* of bricks and roofing materials *was* [not were] *delivered* to the construction site today.

Compound subjects linked by *and* are usually considered plural.

> **Example**   The *framing* and *insulating* of the new house *are* [not *is*] behind schedule.

When a linking verb connects two nouns, the first one is always the subject.

> **Example**   The main *factor* in the architect's design *was* [not were] the wishes of the homeowner.

When an expletive begins a sentence, the actual subject follows the verb.

> **Example**   There *were* [not *was*] a porch and a deck in the original design for the house.

The indefinite pronouns *each, either,* and *neither* always take singular verbs.

> **Example**   *Each* of the design problems *was* [not were] corrected before construction began.

The indefinite pronouns *all, any, more, most, none,* and *some* may be singular or plural, depending on the nouns they refer to.

> **Singular**   *Is any* mortar left?
> **Plural**   *Are any* bricks left?

Pronoun-antecedent agreement

The indefinite pronouns *anybody, anyone, each, either, everybody, everyone, neither, nobody, no one, somebody,* and *someone* are singular and should be followed by singular pronouns.

26

> **Example**   *Everyone* who builds a new house should deter-
> mine *his or her* [not *their*] design priorities.
>
> A singular noun used to refer indefinitely to a person, place, or
> thing should be followed by a singular pronoun.
>
> **Example**   An *architect* has to work closely with *his or her*
> [not *their*] client.

and those that operate in what is called Edited English, the English
commonly used in business, journalism, academics, and professional
life.

26a Agreement of subject and verb

The subject and verb of a sentence must agree in person and
number. For example, if the subject is in the first-person singular (*I*),
the verb must be also (*am*). The only highly inflected verb in English,
that is, the only verb with several different forms, is *be*.

I *am*	we *are*
you *are*	you *are*
he/she/it *is*	they *are*

In most other English verbs, the only inflection is the *s* or *-es* added to
the third-person singular in the present tense.

I know	we know
you know	you know
he/she/it knows	they know

26a

What may be confusing here is the fact that plural nouns and singular
verbs in the third-person-singular present usually end in *s,* whereas
singular nouns and plural verbs usually do not.

Singular (verb ends in *s*)

The clock tick*s* loudly.
The star shine*s* faintly.
That contestant ha*s* talent.

Plural (noun ends in *s*)

> The clock*s* tick loudly.
>
> The star*s* shine faintly.
>
> Those contestant*s* have talent.

This rule holds most of the time, but English includes some nouns whose singular *and* plural forms end in *s*, as well as a few irregular nouns whose plural forms do *not* end in *s* (for example, *man, woman, child, tooth, sheep, goose, criterion*). These unusual noun forms do not affect the correct form of the verb.

Singular (some nouns end in *s*)

> That bu*s* look*s* unreliable.
>
> Ga*s* sell*s* for less now than it did last month.

Plural (some irregular nouns do not end in *s*)

> Her feet feel tired.
>
> Those phenomena seem to be inexplicable.

These, then, are the basic rules for subject-verb agreement in English. But we must also consider several grammatical situations that are sometimes puzzling. Note that the following situations are not exceptions to the rules above; they are simply cases where it may be difficult at first to see how to apply those rules.

1.   Modifying phrases after the subject

Uncertainty about which word is the subject of the sentence can result in an agreement error. A modifying phrase placed between the subject and verb may seem to change the number of the subject, but it does not.

Incorrect   A program of two Bergman films were shown last night.

Correct   A *program* of two Bergman films *was shown* last night. [Because *films* is the noun closest to the verb, it may appear at first that the verb in this sentence should be plural. But *films* is simply the object of the preposition *of*. The subject of the sentence is *program*, and the verb must always agree with its subject no matter what words or phrases come between them.]

Phrases such as *accompanied by, as well as,* and *together with* suggest a plural idea, but they do not change the number of the subject. When you are determining whether your verb should be singular or plural, disregard these phrases and remember what your subject is.

Incorrect   The prisoner, accompanied by guards, her lawyer, and various family members, were in the courtroom.

Correct   The *prisoner,* accompanied by guards, her lawyer, and various family members, *was* in the courtroom.

Incorrect   The mansion, along with the guest house and garages, were up for sale.

Correct   The *mansion,* along with the guest house and garages, *was* up for sale.

2. Compound subject

When two subjects are joined by *and,* they are usually considered plural.

Science and *math are* my best subjects.

The *screening, hiring,* and *training* of each applicant *are* left to the Personnel Department.

Sometimes, though, two nouns are used together to indicate a single idea; in those cases the verb is singular.

Bacon and eggs *is* a typical American breakfast.

Similarly, when the two nouns of a compound subject both refer to the same person or thing, the verb is also singular.

This young novelist and social critic *is* becoming a celebrity.

Finally, when *each* or *every* is used to modify a compound subject, a singular form of the verb is also used.

Each soldier and sailor *was* given a complete examination.

Every camera and light meter *has* been reduced in price.

26a

3.   Collective nouns

Collective nouns, such as *class, committee, team, family,* and *number,* are treated as singular when they refer to the group as a unit. But if you want to emphasize the individual members of the group, you may use the plural form of the verb.

> The committee *was* unanimous in its recommendation.

> The team *were* unable to agree on a date for the party.
> [Many writers would find this sentence awkward, even though it is correct, and would rephrase it, The members of the team were unable to agree . . .]

> The number of correct answers *was* small.

> A number of papers *are* overdue.
> [*Number* is singular when preceded by *the,* plural when preceded by *a.*]

4.   Nouns ending in *s*

Some nouns that are plural in form are grammatically singular—for example, *aesthetics, economics, linguistics, mathematics, news, physics, semantics.*

> Physics *was* the hardest course I had in high school.

> The news *is* better than we had expected.

Note that certain other nouns ending in *s* have no singular form and are always plural—for example, *trousers, scissors, measles, forceps.* Finally, some nouns ending in *-ics*—such as *athletics, politics,* and *statistics*—may be either singular or plural, depending on the intended meaning.

> Athletics [the collective activity] *builds* the physique.
> Athletics [particular activities] *are* her favorite pastime.

> Statistics [the academic subject] *is* my most difficult course.
> Statistics [the collected data] *suggest* that his argument is weak.

5.   Linking verbs

When two nouns in a sentence are connected by some form of the verb *be,* remember that the first noun is the subject and that the verb always agrees with it.

Incorrect	The first thing visible on the horizon were boats loaded with tuna.
Correct	The first *thing* visible on the horizon *was* boats loaded with tuna.
Correct	*Boats* loaded with tuna *were* the first thing visible on the horizon.

6.   Inverted sentence order

Sometimes the subject of a sentence follows the verb. In these cases of inverted word order, the subject and verb still agree.

Incorrect	Beyond the old mud fort was the endless sands of the desert.
Correct	Beyond the old mud fort *were* the endless *sands* of the desert. [*Fort* is the object of the preposition *beyond* in this sentence. The subject is *sands*, and the verb must therefore be plural, *were*.]

In sentences beginning with *there is* or *there are*, *there* is an element called an *expletive* and is not the subject. The real subject of the sentence always follows the verb in these cases.

There *is* only one correct *solution* to this problem.

There *are* a million *laughs* in that movie.

There *was* a long *list* of jobs to be done before we left.

There *were* many *jobs* to be done before we left.

26a

7.   *Or/nor*

When two singular subjects are joined by *or* or *nor*, the verb is singular if both subjects are singular and plural if both are plural.

Neither the *manufacturer* nor the *consumer was* treated fairly.

Poor testing *procedures* or inadequate safety *standards were* responsible for the accident.

When one subject is singular and one is plural, the verb agrees with the subject nearer it.

Either good grades or an outstanding *recommendation is* needed for admission to the honors program.

Are good *grades* or an outstanding recommendation more important for admission?

8.   Indefinite pronouns

Some indefinite pronouns are always singular in number: *anybody, anyone, each, either, everybody, everyone, neither, nobody, no one, one, somebody, someone.* They are always correctly followed by singular verb forms.

Anyone not admitted *is* guaranteed a refund.

Each of the students *was* tested.

Somebody is quietly walking up the stairs.

Other indefinite pronouns may be singular or plural: *all, any, more, most, none, some.* To determine whether the pronoun is singular or plural, look at the noun that it refers to.

All of the food *has* been eaten.

All of the hamburgers *have* been eaten.

None of the money *was* lost.

None of the coins *were* lost.

A few indefinite pronouns are always plural: *both, few, fewer, many, others, several.*

Others are still waiting to apply, even though *fewer* than half *are* likely to be interviewed.

9.   Relative pronouns as subjects

The relative pronouns *who, which,* and *that,* when used as subjects of subordinate clauses, take a singular verb when their antecedent in the sentence is singular and a plural verb when it is plural.

Betsy is a *woman* who *loves* life in the country.

The school was destroyed by high *winds,* which *are* unusual at this time of year.

The correct number of the relative pronoun may be a bit harder to determine when the sentence contains the phrase *one of the* or *one of those*.

> This is one of those inexpensive quartz *watches* that *are* made in Japan.
> [The pronoun *that* refers to the group of watches.]
> I selected the only *one* of the watches that *is* guaranteed for ten years.
> [The pronoun *that* refers to just one of the watches, the one with the ten-year guarantee.]

EXERCISE 1

Choose the correct verb forms in the following sentences.

Example

> The McCarthy hearings, held during 1953 and 1954, (represents, represent) a dark era in American history.
>
> **Correct**   The McCarthy hearings . . . *represent* a dark era. . . .

1. Senator Joseph R. McCarthy of Wisconsin had claimed as early as 1950 that there (was, were) more than two hundred Communists in the State Department.
2. McCarthy offered no proof for this claim, but people's concern that Communists were infiltrating various government offices (was, were) strong enough to give rise to a period of national hysteria.
3. The tool that McCarthy used to support his charges (was, were) public hearings before the Senate Investigations Subcommittee, which he chaired.
4. Each of the people who (was, were) called before the committee (was, were) confronted by several equally unpleasant choices.
5. A witness could admit his or her affiliation with the Communist party, could expose a friend or an associate who (was, were) linked to the party, or could take the Fifth Amendment.
6. The last of these options (was, were) almost as good as an admission of guilt.
7. Many of the people who (was, were) branded Communists by Mc-Carthy's committee (was, were) "blacklisted"—that is, denied employment—after testifying.

26a

Exercise 1

1. there were more than two hundred Communists
2. concern . . . was
3. tool . . . was
4. people who were called
   Each . . . was confronted
5. a friend or an associate who was linked
6. last [one] . . . was
7. people who were branded
   Many . . . were "blacklisted"
8. the writer Dashiell Hammett and the musician Pete Seeger were
9. influence . . . was
10. betrayals and mistrust . . . were

8. Among the more famous of those who suffered blacklisting (was, were) the writer Dashiell Hammett and the musician Pete Seeger.
9. McCarthy's political influence, together with the waves of hysteria it spawned, (was, were) finally ended in December 1954, when the Senate voted to condemn his conduct.
10. The betrayals and mistrust of this period (was, were) the inspiration for Arthur Miller's play *The Crucible*.

EXERCISE 2

Choose the correct verb forms in the following sentences.

Example

Fads are phenomena that (touches, touch) almost every area of contemporary life.

Correct   Fads are phenomena that *touch* almost every area . . .

1. Fashion, food, recreation, music—any of these fields (is, are) likely to be affected by fads.
2. One of the many clothing fads that (seems, seem) ridiculous when we look back at them (was, were) disposable paper dresses.
3. In the 1980s, Cajun cooking, including dishes like jambalaya and blackened redfish, (was, were) suddenly popular in cities far away from the rural Cajun towns of Louisiana.
4. Among college students, the number of fads that (has, have) involved setting new records (is, are) high.
5. Sitting on flagpoles, swallowing goldfish, and packing people into phone booths (was, were) fun partly because of the publicity that such activities attracted.
6. Neither those tie-dyed T-shirts in the back of your closet nor that Hula-Hoop collection in your basement (is, are) likely to see daylight again.
7. The tattoo collector and body piercer of the 1990s (risk, risks) embarrassment if body decoration (go, goes) out of style.
8. But the skeptic or critic who (denounces, denounce) all fads will occasionally be surprised to discover that what once seemed a fad has found a permanent place in American culture.
9. (Was, Were) any of the people who scoffed at the jogging craze of the 1970s prepared to see this activity become so widespread and respectable two decades later?
10. Rock and roll (is, are) still more proof that some fads are here to stay.

26a

Exercise 2

1. any of these fields are
2. fads that seem
   One . . . was
3. cooking . . . was
4. fads that have involved
   the number . . . is
5. sitting . . . swallowing . . . and packing . . . were
6. collection . . . is
7. tattoo collector and body piercer [one person] . . . risks
   decoration goes
8. skeptic or critic who denounces
9. Were any of the people
10. Rock and roll is

26b Agreement of pronoun and antecedent

Pronouns agree in number and gender with their **antecedents,** the words in a sentence that they refer to.

> Many *people* pay a genealogist to look up *their* ancestry.
> [*People*, the antecedent, is plural, so the pronoun *their* must also be plural.]
>
> My *uncle* paid a genealogist to look up *his* ancestry.
> [*His* agrees with *uncle*.]

Like subject-verb agreement, the basic principle of agreement between pronouns and antecedents is easy enough to understand. But again, a few unusual constructions may at first seem puzzling.

1. Compound antecedents

Compound antecedents, like compound subjects, are usually considered plural when joined by *and* and singular when joined by *or* or *nor*.

> My father encouraged *Henry* and *David* to postpone *their* trip.
> Neither the *dog* nor the *cat* had touched *its* food.

2. Collective nouns as antecedents

When the antecedent is a collective noun, the singular pronoun is used to emphasize the cohesiveness of the group, the plural to emphasize the separate individuals.

26b

> The *audience* showed *its* approval by applause.
> The *audience* were on *their* feet, booing and whistling.

Note that in the second sentence the verb *were* is also plural in form. Be consistent. If the verb form indicates that the antecedent is singular, the pronoun must also be singular. If the verb is plural, the pronoun must be plural too.

Incorrect	The panel is ready to give their opinions.
Correct	The panel *is* ready to give *its* opinions.
Correct	The panel *are* ready to give *their* opinions.

The second sentence here suggests that the panel members all hold the same opinions; the last sentence suggests that the various members of the panel have different opinions to offer.

3. Indefinite antecedents

In informal usage, indefinite pronouns like *anybody, anyone, each, either, everybody, everyone, neither, nobody, no one, somebody,* and *someone* are often treated as if they were plural.

> **Informal** Almost *everyone* eats some fruit as part of *their* basic diet.

Strictly speaking, though, all of these pronouns are singular, and pronouns that follow them in Edited English must also be singular. The problem is that English lacks singular personal pronouns that can refer to both males and females. Consequently, sentences such as the following, while grammatically correct, are today considered unacceptable because they illogically exclude half the human population.

> **Illogical** *Anyone* returning merchandise must present *his* sales receipt.
>
> **Illogical** *No one* in line for the canceled tennis match got *her* money back.

Women, as well as men, may need to return merchandise, and men, as well as women, attend tennis matches. One solution to this problem is to use two pronouns, one masculine and one feminine, when the antecedent can be either male or female.

> **Correct** *Anyone* returning merchandise must present *his or her* sales receipt.
>
> **Correct** *No one* in line for the canceled tennis match got *his or her* money back.

However, some writers might consider this construction awkward, and most writers would probably reject the following similar sentence as unacceptably clumsy.

> **Correct but awkward** For once, *everyone* in the class saw *himself or herself* as *he or she* really was.

For all of these cases, a second correct—and less awkward—alternative is simply to rewrite the sentence with plural, rather than singular, nouns and pronouns.

Customers returning merchandise must present *their* sales receipts.

None of the people in line for the canceled tennis match got *their* money back.

For once, the class *members* saw *themselves* as *they* really were.

Agreement problems similar to those involving indefinite pronouns as antecedents may arise when the antecedent is a singular noun that is not intended to refer to a specific person, place, or thing.

Incorrect   When a client calls the office, do not leave them on hold for more than a minute.

Incorrect   A person who fails to keep their dog on a leash will be ticketed.

Incorrect   If a customer isn't satisfied with their purchase, we will happily refund their money.

The agreement error can be corrected by using singular forms for the pronoun.

Correct   When a *client* calls the office, do not leave *him or her* on hold for more than a minute.

Again, though, the most graceful way of solving the agreement problem in such sentences may be to change the antecedents to the plural. Remember to make other nouns in the sentence plural if logic demands that you do so.

Correct   When *clients call* the office, do not leave *them* on hold for more than a minute.

Correct   *People* who *fail* to keep *their dogs* on *leashes* will be ticketed.

Correct   If any *customers aren't* satisfied with *their purchases,* we will happily refund *their* money.

(For additional advice on avoiding sexism in writing, see **13e.**)

4. Demonstrative pronouns

When demonstrative pronouns (*this, that, these, those*) are used as adjectives, they must agree in number with the words they modify. *This* and *that* are used with singular nouns, *these* and *those* with plural nouns.

Incorrect	These kind of vegetables are grown in the valley.
Correct	*This kind* of *vegetable is* grown in the valley.
Correct	*These kinds* of *vegetables are* grown in the valley.

EXERCISE 3

Determine the causes of faulty agreement in the following sentences and correct the errors.

Example

Cramped seating, unappealing food, long airport delays, lost baggage—because of these kind of problems, many people have come to dislike traveling by plane.

Correct   . . . these *kinds* of problems . . .

1. In contrast, a person who boards a long-distance train can expect to enjoy the trip ahead of them as much as the arrival at their destination.
2. Anybody who believes that train travel is obsolete should test their belief by traveling on one of Amtrak's scenic routes.
3. No one who takes the *Pioneer* from Chicago to Seattle, for example, will be disappointed by the views from their window when the train crosses through the Rocky Mountains.
4. Because every car in the train is a double-decker, they offer passengers a spectacular view of the canyons and rivers.
5. These kind of cars are used only on Amtrak's western trains, because it could not fit through the low, nineteenth-century tunnels that are found along many eastern routes.
6. Eating your dinner as the scenery flies by outside your window is a delight, and the courteous dining-car staff is ready to do what they can to make your meal enjoyable.
7. During the evening, the lounge car offers feature films that a passenger can enjoy before their bedtime.
8. Some people are able to sleep soundly in the wide coach seats, but the compact sleeping compartments, each of which can sleep two, has its advantages.
9. Anyone interested in history will appreciate the brochure they receive highlighting some of the historical events that occurred along the train's route.
10. The typical Amtrak passenger is someone who is less interested in arriving at their destination quickly than in enjoying the experience of traveling.

26b

Exercise 3

Some answers will vary.

1. . . . people who board . . . can expect to enjoy the trip ahead of them . . .
2. Anybody . . . should test his or her belief . . .
3. No one . . . by the views from his or her window . . .
4. . . . all the cars in the train are double-deckers, they offer . . .
5. This kind of car is used . . . because it could not fit . . .
6. . . . staff are ready to do what they can . . .
7. . . . that a passenger can enjoy before his or her bedtime.
8. . . . the compact sleeping compartments . . . have their advantages.
9. Anyone . . . he or she receives . . .
10. Typical Amtrak passengers are people who are less interested in arriving at their destinations quickly . . .

27 Case of Pronouns and Nouns

Case refers to the changes in form of a noun or pronoun that show how it is used in a sentence. English nouns used to have many case forms, but today the only case endings remaining are those that indicate possession (*child's, woman's, year's*). Most pronouns, however, have three case forms: the **nominative** (or **subjective**) case when the pronoun is the subject of a verb; the **possessive** (or **genitive**) case to show possession; and the **objective** (or **accusative**) case when the pronoun functions as the object of a verb or preposition.

Nominative	I	you	he	she	it	we	they	who
Possessive	my	your	his	her	its	our	their	whose
Objective	me	you	him	her	it	us	them	whom

As with agreement, we usually get the case right without consciously thinking about it. But a few constructions can occasionally cause writers trouble.

27a

27a Compound constructions

A noun and a pronoun used together in a compound construction should be in the same case; the same principle applies to constructions like *we citizens* and to appositives. In most of these situations, you can easily check to determine that you have the pronoun in the right case by reading the sentence without the noun. It should still sound correct.

Correct   My *mother* and *I* have a good relationship.
[*Mother* and *I* are both in the nominative case because they are the compound subject of the verb *have*.]

To determine the correct pronoun case when a noun and a pronoun appear together in a compound construction, try reading the sentence without the noun.

Example   Will there be a raise *for us* [not *for we*] sales representatives this year?

Example   The director gave the highest raises *to* David and *me* [not *to I*].

To choose between *who* and *whom* in a dependent clause, try substituting a personal pronoun in the sentence.

Example   There is a bonus for *whoever* [not *whomever*] sells the most computer equipment. [*He or she,* not *him* or *her, sells . . .*]

To determine the correct case of a pronoun after *than* or *as,* mentally complete the shortened clause.

Example   Suzanne hasn't sold as much as *I* [*have*].

Use the nominative form of a pronoun when the pronoun follows a linking verb.

Example   I didn't expect the visitor to be my supervisor, but it was *she* [not *her*].

Use the possessive form of a noun or pronoun before a gerund.

Example   Sharon disapproved of *my* [not *me*] entering the sales field.

Incorrect   The doctor asked my *mother* and *I* to come in together. [Because a construction like *my mother and I* is so common, one can easily slip into it even in this sentence, where the objective pronoun is needed. The correct case of the pronoun becomes clear when we delete the noun *mother* from the compound direct object: *The doctor asked . . . I?/me? . . .*]

Correct	The doctor asked my *mother* and *me* to come in together.
Correct	*We children* always tried to please our parents by getting good grades. [The fact that the pronoun is correctly in the nominative case is clear when we read the sentence without the noun *children: We . . . always tried . . .*]
Incorrect	Our parents always rewarded *we children* for getting good grades. [The correct case of the pronoun becomes clear when we delete the noun *children* from the sentence: *Our parents always rewarded we?/us? . . .*]
Correct	Our parents always rewarded *us children* for getting good grades.
Incorrect	Most of the float was designed by only two members of the class, Howard and *I*. [Again, deleting the nouns *members* and *Howard* makes it clear that the objective case of the pronoun is needed here because the pronoun is in apposition with the object of the preposition *by: Most of the float was designed by. . .I?/me? . . .*]
Correct	Most of the float was designed by only two members of the class, Howard and *me*.
Incorrect	Between *you* and *I*, this essay hasn't got a chance of winning the contest. [Both pronouns are objects of the preposition *between*, and both must therefore be in the objective case.]
Correct	Between *you* and *me*, this essay hasn't got a chance of winning the contest.

27b *Who* and *whom* in dependent clauses

When in doubt about the case of the relative pronouns *who* and *whoever*, try a personal pronoun *(he/him, she/her, they/them)* in its place in the sentence. If *he, she,* or *they* sounds right, use the nominative, *who;* if *him, her,* or *them* fits the grammatical context, *whom* is correct.

Here is the woman *who?/whom?* can explain eclipses.

[We could say *she can explain eclipses,* but not *her can explain eclipses.* Thus, *who* is correct in this sentence; as the subject of the clause, it is in the nominative case.]

Marshall is the man *who?/whom?* I told you about.
[In this sentence, the pronoun is not the subject of the clause; instead, the clause means *I told you about he/him. Him,* rather than *he,* fits this context; the correct pronoun is thus *whom,* the object of the preposition *about.*]

Here are the extra blue books for *whoever?/whomever?* needs them.
[We could say *he needs them* or *she needs them,* but not *him needs them* or *her needs them.* The correct pronoun is thus *whoever.* It is in the nominative case because it is the subject of the verb *needs.*]

The awards will be presented to *whoever?/whomever?* the council nominates.
[We could say *the council nominates them,* but not *the council nominates they.* The correct pronoun is thus *whomever.* It is in the objective case because it is the object of the verb *nominates.*]

Note that the case of the pronoun *who* or *whom* is unaffected by the insertion of phrases like *I think* or *we know* into the dependent clause.

The artist *who?/whom?* I thought would design the awards has changed her mind.
[The sense of the dependent clause is *I thought* [that] *she/her would design the awards.* Only *she* fits into this clause, so *who* is the correct pronoun. It is in the nominative case because it is the subject of the verb *would design.*]

We trust the advice of friends *who?/whom?* we know can be objective.

[The sense of the dependent clause is *we know* [that] *they/them can be objective.* Only *they* fits this clause, so *who* is again the correct pronoun. It is in the nominative case because it is the subject of the verb *can be.*]

But compare the following different situation, where the phrase *we know* constitutes both the subject and verb of the dependent clause:

We trust the advice of the friends *who?/whom?* we know best.
[Here the dependent clause means we know they/them best.
Only *them* fits into this sentence, so the correct pronoun is
whom, the object of the verb *know.*]

27c *Who* and *whom* in interrogatives

To determine the correct case of the interrogative pronouns
who and *whom,* apply the same test described above for dependent
clauses. If the answer to the question includes the nominative form of
the personal pronoun, *who* is the correct interrogative; if the answer
includes the objective form, *whom* is correct.

Who is coming to the party? [*They* are coming.]

Whom are you expecting at the party? [I am expecting *them.*]

In speech and in much informal writing, the tendency is to use *who* as
the interrogative form, no matter what its grammatical place in the
sentence. Edited English, however, requires *whom* when the pronoun is
in the objective case.

Informal   *Who* are you expecting for dessert?
Formal   *Whom* are you expecting for dessert?

Informal   *Who* are you leaving with?
Formal   With *whom* are you leaving?

27d

27d Reflexive and intensive pronouns

A special type of objective pronoun is used to refer to a noun
or pronoun mentioned earlier in a sentence. These pronouns are called
reflexive pronouns. The reflexive form of the pronoun is used instead
of the objective form whenever the actor in a sentence and the recipient
of the action are the same.

Reflexive   *Scott* accidentally cut *himself* with the knife.
Reflexive   *We* had never seen *ourselves* on television before.

Reflexive Pronouns

Nominative form	Reflexive form
I	myself
you (singular)	yourself
he	himself
she	herself
it	itself
we	ourselves
you (plural)	yourselves
they	themselves

Note that the following forms do not exist except in nonstandard usage: *hisself, themself, theirselves.*

Since a reflexive pronoun by definition refers back to another noun or pronoun, it may appear in a sentence only if the noun or pronoun to which it refers also appears.

Incorrect	Gina and *myself* are flying to Des Moines tomorrow.
Correct	Gina and *I* are flying to Des Moines tomorrow.
Incorrect	The plane tickets arrived in an envelope addressed to my mother and *myself.*
Correct	The plane tickets arrived in an envelope addressed to my mother and *me.*

When the pronoun forms above are used to emphasize a noun or another pronoun in a sentence, rather than to designate the recipient of an action, they are known as **intensive pronouns.**

Intensive	*Scott himself* was responsible for the accident. [No one else was to blame.]
Intensive	*We* found the television studio by *ourselves.* [No one assisted us.]

27e Pronouns after *than, as,* and *but*

After *than* or *as,* the case of a pronoun is determined by its use in the shortened clause of which it is a part.

My cousin is taller than *I* [am].
They take more photographs than *we* [do].
I can type as well as *he* [can].

Sometimes a comparison involving *than* or *as* can be completed in two possible ways. In such situations, the case of the pronoun will determine how the reader understands the sentence.

They like Kelley more than *I* [do].
They like Kelley more than [they like] *me.*
Kelley cares about them as much as *I* [do].
Kelley cares about them as much as [she cares about] *me.*

The word *but* is sometimes used as a preposition meaning "except." A pronoun that follows *but* in such constructions is the object of the preposition and should therefore be in the objective case.

Incorrect	All the guests at the party had a good time but Judy and *I.*
Correct	All the guests at the party had a good time but Judy and *me.*

27f Pronouns with linking verbs

27f

The subject complement of a linking verb, such as a form of the verb *be,* is in the nominative case (see **25e**). Despite the widespread tolerance in spoken English of forms like "It is me" and "I thought it was her," the correct, nominative form of a pronoun should be used when the pronoun follows a linking verb in writing.

Incorrect	When the voice on the telephone asked for Dr. Kim, I said, "This *is her.*"
Correct	When the voice on the telephone asked for Dr. Kim, I said, "This *is she.*"

Incorrect	I expected the caller to be Richard Markson, but it *was* not *him*.
Correct	I expected the caller to be Richard Markson, but it *was* not *he*.
Incorrect	It appears that the members of the delegation *will be* Mr. Rosen, Ms. Kowalski, and *me*.
Correct	It appears that the members of the delegation *will be* Mr. Rosen, Ms. Kowalski, and *I*.

27g Pronouns with infinitives

Both the subject and the object of an infinitive (usually a verb form preceded by *to*) are in the objective case (see **25f**). The objective form of a pronoun must be used when the pronoun is in either of these positions in the sentence.

Subject of infinitive	The company president wanted *me to lie* when I testified before the committee.
Object of infinitive	I would not like *to be him* when the company's wrongdoing is revealed.

27h Pronouns and nouns with gerunds

In grammatical terms, gerunds function in a sentence like nouns (see **25f**). Therefore, a noun or pronoun modifying a gerund, like a noun or pronoun modifying any noun, must be in the possessive case.

Incorrect	Alan's parents disapproved of *him traveling* alone in Greece.
Correct	Alan's parents disapproved of *his traveling* alone in Greece. [The first sentence erroneously suggests that Alan's parents disapproved of *him*. In the second sentence, the possessive pronoun *his* identifies the gerund *traveling* as the actual object of the preposition *of*.]
Incorrect	They also objected to his *sister bicycling* through Canada.
Correct	They also objected to his *sister's bicycling* through Canada. [The first sentence suggests that they found his *sister*

objectionable. In the second sentence, the possessive noun *sister's* identifies the gerund *bicycling* as the actual object of the preposition *to*.]

EXERCISE 1

Choose the correct case for the pronoun in each of the following sentences.

Example

John Fitzgerald Kennedy, the man (who, whom) we remember as America's thirty-fifth President, was born in Massachusetts in 1917.

Correct   . . . the man *whom* we remember . . .

1. For decades, his family and (he, him) figured prominently in the news.
2. Political observers were consequently not surprised by (him, his) deciding to run for President in 1960.
3. Whatever people thought of Kennedy's politics, they agreed that few presidential candidates had been as charismatic as (he, him).
4. The presidential debates between the two candidates, Richard Nixon and (he, him), were the first ever to be televised.
5. It was Kennedy (who, whom) the analysts declared to be victor.
6. After the debates Kennedy's support grew, and although the election was one of the closest ever in terms of the popular vote, the winner was finally determined to be (he, him).
7. Kennedy's administration was marked by noble goals from the beginning; after all, it was (he, him) who said, "And so, my fellow Americans, ask not what your country can do for you; ask what you can do for your country."
8. Kennedy was the leader (who, whom) a new generation of Americans looked to for inspiration.
9. Few American presidents have been so often idealized as (he, him).
10. In his short lifetime, Kennedy left his mark on American politics—indeed, on all of (we, us) Americans.

27h

EXERCISE 2

Choose the correct case for the pronoun in each of the following sentences.

Example

Gertrude Stein, (who, whom) critics continue to regard as one of the great creative figures in modern literature, was born in Pennsylvania in 1874 but spent most of her life abroad.

Exercise 1

1. he
2. his
3. he
4. him
5. whom
6. him
7. he
8. whom
9. he
10. us

Exercise 2

1. Who
2. she
3. she

Correct   . . . *whom* critics continue to regard . . .

1. (Who, Whom) would have guessed that this Radcliffe undergraduate would go on to influence art and literature in the early decades of the twentieth century?
2. After moving to Paris in 1903, Stein used her personal wealth to support young artists; indeed, no one of the time was a more dedicated patron of art than (she, her).
3. Pablo Picasso and (she, her) became friends soon after he moved to Paris in 1904.
4. Stein's experiments in literary form propelled her into the world of literature and made her a writer (who, whom) dazzled and inspired her contemporaries in the 1920s.
5. Ernest Hemingway, F. Scott Fitzgerald, and Ezra Pound were among the authors (who, whom) she encouraged and influenced.
6. It was (she, her) who coined the now-famous phrase *a lost generation* to describe such writers after World War I.
7. Stein's witty autobiography, *The Autobiography of Alice B. Toklas* (1933), has remained popular among readers (who, whom) want to understand (she, her) and her times.
8. Stylistic innovations established Stein as a major literary figure, and it is largely because of (they, them) that her reputation has endured.
9. With the rise of feminist criticism, Stein has inspired new attention from scholars (who, whom) regard her as a pioneer in women's modes of writing.
10. Admittedly, though, Stein's often difficult style can sometimes be as puzzling to (we, us) readers today as it was to her contemporaries.

27h

4. who
5. whom
6. she
7. who, her
8. them
9. who
10. us

28 *Adjectives and Adverbs*

Adjectives and adverbs are similar types of modifiers with slightly different functions. **Adjectives** modify nouns and pronouns; they provide such information as the color, size, type, or manner of the words they describe.

The car came to a *sudden* stop.

The performers began an *elegant* dance.
[In these sentences, *sudden* describes the kind of stop that the car made, and *elegant* describes the dance done by the performers.]

Adverbs, on the other hand, modify verbs, adjectives, and other adverbs. They answer questions like *when? where? why? in what way? to what degree?*

The car *suddenly* stopped.

The performers began an *unusually* elegant dance.
[In the first sentence here, the adverb *suddenly* modifies the verb *stopped.* In the second, the adverb *unusually* modifies the adjective *elegant* (not the dance, but its elegance, was unusual).]

Most adverbs are formed by adding *-ly* to the adjective: *clear, clearly; immediate, immediately.* But like other rules of English, this one has its exceptions. Some adjectives and adverbs have the same form: the *far* corner, *much* pleased, I *little* thought, do it *right*, run *fast*. And a few adjectives and adverbs have completely different forms: a *good* job, a job done *well*. Finally, some adjectives already end in *-ly*: a *friendly* gesture, a *manly* appearance, a *leisurely* vacation. In some of these cases, the

> QUICK REFERENCE: *Problems with Adjectives and Adverbs*
>
> Remember that adjectives and adverbs like *unique/uniquely, perfect/perfectly, fatal/fatally,* and *unanimous/unanimously* do not logically have comparative and superlative forms.
>
> **Example** This is the *most unusual* [not most unique] automobile I have ever seen.
>
> Use the comparative form, not the superlative, in comparisons involving only two persons or things.
>
> **Example** Both of these antique cars are rare, but the 1934 Chevrolet is the *more* [not most] valuable.
>
> Use adjectives, not adverbs, after linking verbs.
>
> **Example** I feel *bad* [not badly] about having sold my 1965 Mustang.
>
> Hyphenate compound adjectives when they precede a noun.
>
> **Example** The *antique-car* auction will continue until Saturday.

adverb form is the same; in others, there is no corresponding adverb in English. A dictionary is your best guide.

28a Comparative and superlative forms

For establishing **comparisons**, most adjectives and adverbs have three different forms: the *positive* (or dictionary) form, the *comparative* form, and the *superlative* form.

1. Comparative and superlative forms of adjectives

Adjectives usually form the comparative by adding *-er* and the superlative by adding *-est*.

tall	taller	tallest
lively	livelier	liveliest

Many adjectives of two syllables and all longer adjectives form the comparative and superlative by adding *more* and *most*.

alert	more alert	most alert
ambitious	more ambitious	most ambitious

All adjectives indicate lesser degree by adding *less* for the comparative and *least* for the superlative.

lively	less lively	least lively
ambitious	less ambitious	least ambitious

2. Comparative and superlative forms of adverbs

Adverbs nearly always form the comparative and superlative with *more* and *most*.

slowly	more slowly	most slowly
beautifully	more beautifully	most beautifully

A few adverbs that do not end in -*ly* form the comparative and superlative by adding -*er* and -*est*.

fast	faster	fastest
near	nearer	nearest

28a

All adverbs indicate lesser degree by adding *less* for the comparative and *least* for the superlative.

slowly	less slowly	least slowly
beautifully	less beautifully	least beautifully

3. Irregular comparative and superlative forms

A few adjectives and adverbs form the comparative and superlative irregularly.

Irregular adjectives

bad	worse	worst
good	better	best
little	less	least
many	more	most
much	more	most
some	more	most

Irregular adverbs

badly	worse	worst
well	better	best

4. Adjectives and adverbs without comparative and superlative forms

Some adjectives and adverbs, like *unique/uniquely, perfect/perfectly, infinite/infinitely, fatal/fatally, unanimous/unanimously,* and *chief/chiefly,* cannot logically take comparative or superlative forms. Since unique means "one of a kind," no object can be more unique than another. Similarly, a thing is either perfect or not perfect; strictly speaking, no degree of perfection is possible.

Edited English, therefore, tends to avoid expressions like *more perfect* or *most unique,* although you may use modifiers like *nearly* and *almost* that indicate an approach to the absolute.

Correct   Records have disappeared from the shelves of music stores now that compact discs offer *more nearly perfect* sound reproduction.

Correct   The brilliance of this diamond makes it an *almost unique* gem.

In informal writing, the comparative and superlative forms *more perfect* and *most perfect* are occasionally accepted.

Acceptable informally   This is the *most perfect* pumpkin in the field.

The forms *more unique* and *most unique*, however, remain unacceptable in any context to the vast majority of users of English.

> **Unacceptable** That abstract painting is the *most unique* representation of the New York City skyline that I have seen.

5. Correct use of comparative and superlative forms

In Edited English, the comparative is used for comparisons involving two persons or things, and the superlative for comparisons involving three or more persons or things.

> Of my two brothers, Jack was the *taller*.
>
> She was the *quickest* person on the team.

In speech and informal writing, this distinction is not always observed, and the superlative is often used even when only two things are being compared: "Of the two styles offered, the first was the *most popular*."

Be careful to avoid double comparisons—that is, constructions that combine *more* or *most, less* or *least* with an adjective or adverb that already ends in *-er* or *-est*.

> **Incorrect** I prefer this *more darker* shade of green paint.
>
> **Correct** I prefer this *darker* shade of green paint.
>
> **Incorrect** The salesperson says that of all the paints on the market, this one dries *most fastest*.
>
> **Correct** The salesperson says that of all the paints on the market, this one dries *fastest*.

For advice on avoiding incomplete comparisons, see **12g**.

28b

28b Adjectives with linking verbs

Linking verbs such as *be, become, seem,* and *appear,* as well as verbs associated with the five senses (*look, feel, taste, sound, smell*) and certain other verbs suggesting development (*become, grow, prove*), are often used to link a subject and a modifying adjective, the subject complement (see **25e**).

$$\text{The swimmer} \left\{ \begin{array}{l} \text{was} \\ \text{seemed} \\ \text{looked} \\ \text{felt} \\ \text{sounded} \\ \text{became} \end{array} \right\} \; cold.$$

Note that a subject complement can never be an adverb, because adverbs modify only verbs, adjectives, and other adverbs, not nouns or pronouns.

Incorrect	I felt *badly* about Carolyn's accident. [Since the only word in this sentence that the adverb *badly* can modify is the verb *felt*, the sentence seems to suggest that the writer's ability to feel was deficient.]
Correct	I felt *bad* about Carolyn's accident. [The adjective *bad* correctly modifies the subject, *I*.]
Incorrect	George looks *well* in a tuxedo. [Since the only word in this sentence that the adverb *well* can modify is the verb *looks*, the sentence seems to suggest that wearing a tuxedo enhances George's vision.]
Correct	George looks *good* in a tuxedo. [The adjective *good* correctly modifies the subject, George.]

Of course, a verb in the list above may be followed by an adverb, but in such a case it ceases to function as a linking verb. Consider the following examples:

Adjective and linking verb	The *gong* sounded *hollow*. [It seemed to be hollow.]
Adverb	The gong *sounded hollowly*. [It made a hollow sound when it was rung.]
Adjective and linking verb	*Gail* looked *weary* to me. [I thought she appeared weary.]
Adverb	Gail *looked wearily* to me. [She turned to me in a weary manner.]

Adjective and linking verb	My opponent's *argument* proved *convincing*. [It turned out to be a convincing argument.]
Adverb	My opponent's argument *proved convincingly* that she had not adequately prepared for the debate. [It offered convincing proof that she was unprepared.]

28c Nouns used as adjectives

Nouns in English frequently function as adjectives modifying other nouns.

Contract negotiations are stalled over the issue of *salary increases* for the *night shift*.

Our lives are full of concrete things and abstract concepts identified by such noun-plus-noun combinations: *light bulb, sofa bed, turkey sandwich, gas station, movie review, smog alert, computer literacy, investment opportunity*. The main point to remember in using nouns as adjectives is that more than three nouns in a row can make for a dense, confusing sentence.

Confusing	The spring office softball tournament preparations are proceeding smoothly.

Such a sentence can be clarified by breaking up the cluster of nouns and by using possessive nouns where possible.

Clearer	Preparations for the office's spring softball tournament are proceeding smoothly.

28d

28d Compound adjectives

When a compound adjective is formed from two nouns, from an adjective and a noun, or from two adjectives, the compound is hyphenated when it precedes the noun that it modifies.

The *locker-room* brawl left six players injured.

My favorite *high-school* teacher was Ms. Resnick.

Marcia looked out over the *blue-green* waters of the gulf.

All the elements of a phrase used as an adjective are also hyphenated.

> I wish I had her *never-say-die* attitude.
> Peter knew the invitation was a *once-in-a-lifetime* opportunity.

Remember, though, that *-ly* adverbs used with adjectives are a different grammatical situation. Such adverbs are modifiers, not parts of a compound, and they are not hyphenated.

> Their first apartment was in an *exceptionally decrepit* building.

However, similar constructions with the term *well* usually *are* hyphenated when they precede the modified noun: *a well-managed business, a well-done steak* (but *a steak well done*). See also **36a**.

28e Colloquial forms

In some spoken contexts, the following pairs of modifiers may be used interchangeably: *real/really, sure/surely, almost/most*. Edited English demands more careful distinctions between them.

Real is an adjective; in writing, it should not be used in place of the adverb *really* ("truly") to modify verbs, adverbs, or other adjectives.

Acceptable in speech	Ever since our house was burglarized, we haven't been sleeping *real* well at night.
Preferred in writing	Ever since our house was burglarized, we haven't been sleeping *really* well at night.

Sure, another adjective, should not take the place of the adverb *surely* ("certainly") in writing.

Acceptable in speech	Steve *sure* feels bad about having left the back door unlocked.
Preferred in writing	Steve *surely* feels bad about having left the back door unlocked.

When *most* functions as an adverb, it means "very" or "to the greatest extent": "Last quarter's sales report is *most* encouraging." It should not be used in writing to mean "nearly," a sense reserved for the adverb *almost*.

28e

| **Acceptable in speech** | *Most* every night since the burglary he's gone downstairs to recheck the locks. |
| **Preferred in writing** | *Almost* every night since the burglary he's gone downstairs to recheck the locks. |

EXERCISE 1

Correct the use of adjectives and adverbs in the following sentences so that it conforms to the standards of Edited English.

Example

Learning to write is a bit like learning to play a musical instrument such as the piano. You can spend hours listening to CDs or tapes and still play bad, for only practice will bring real results.

Correct . . . and still play *badly* . . .

1. In the same way, you may study a composition textbook and grasp all of its abstractest principles, but they will remain abstract until you actually write.
2. If you pick up a little piano playing on your own and then study the instrument more formal, you will experience the difficulty of overcoming bad habits.
3. By the same token, in a college writing class you are not really a beginner, since you have had years of high school practice, but you may have been writing without consciously paying attention to details.
4. As a sophisticated writer, you will need to discover a more unique voice, a self projected onto the page, just as a musician finds a style that seems real natural.
5. In addition, you will need to develop a more subtler understanding of the audiences you write for.
6. There's room for developing your technical expertise as well. Just as the novice pianist masters the keyboard by practicing drills and scales, you will find that the college composition textbook grammar exercises that your instructor assigns will contribute to your mastery of the language.
7. In this comparison of the pianist and the writer, does the latter's task seem to be the most difficult?
8. In one way, at least, it is: unlike the pianist, the writer most always has to find his or her own subject. That challenge is a great one, for

28e

Exercise 1

1. . . . all of its most abstract principles, . . .
2. . . . study the instrument more formally, . . .
3. . . . years of high-school practice, . . .
4. . . . to discover a unique voice, . . . a style that seems really natural.
5. . . . to develop a subtler understanding . . .
6. . . . the grammar exercises that your instructor assigns in your college composition textbook . . .
7. . . . the more difficult?
8. . . . the writer almost always . . . to avoid run-of-the-mill topics . . .
9. . . . the most difficult part . . .
10. . . . see the world freshly.
11. . . . one-time performance.
12. . . . really creative risks . . .
13. . . . as slowly as you wish.
14. . . . fixed firmly on the page . . .
15. . . . their imperfect ones.

readers expect a writer to avoid run of the mill topics and to strive for originality.

9. For many writers, finding an original perspective is the most infinitely difficult part of the writing process.

10. Some writers read widely, some keep journals, some use a variety of brainstorming strategies—all in the hope that they will see the world fresh.

11. Writers do enjoy one advantage denied to musicians, though: they are free from the terror of a live, one time performance.

12. Unlike a musician performing before a live audience, a writer can take real creative risks without fearing instant judgment.

13. As a writer you can work in private as slow as you wish.

14. You can revise your essay over and over, and your audience will not see it until it is fixed firm on the page exactly as you want it.

15. In contrast, pianists never know how their performances will turn out, and they do not have the opportunity to take back their less perfect ones.

28e

29 *Verbs*

At the center of every sentence stands a verb, a word describing an action or a condition. Chapter **25** examined the syntactic relationship between the verb and other elements in a sentence. This chapter focuses on verb forms — in particular, the forms that indicate tense, voice, and mood.

29a Verb forms

Verbs not only present an action or a condition, but also indicate a time frame within which that action or condition occurs — at present, in the past, in the future. This indication of time depends on verb forms known as **tenses,** which in English are constructed from the five verb forms illustrated in the tables below. The first three of these forms — base, past, and past participle — are known as the **principal parts** of a verb. Depending on how they form their principal parts, verbs are classified either as **regular** or as **irregular.**

Regular verbs

Base	Past	Past participle	Present participle	-s form
trust	trusted	trusted	trusting	trusts
agree	agreed	agreed	agreeing	agrees
deny	denied	denied	denying	denies

As these examples illustrate, the past and past participle of regular verbs are both formed by adding *-ed* or (when the verb already ends in *e*) *-d.*

QUICK REFERENCE: *Verbs*

Tense

By *tense* we mean variations in the form of a verb that indicate differences in time. English verbs have six principal tenses.

Present	I *promise* to be on time.
Past	I *promised* to be on time.
Future	I *will promise* to be on time.
Present perfect	I *have promised* to be on time.
Past perfect	I *had promised* to be on time.
Future perfect	I *will have promised* to be on time.

Voice

The word *voice* denotes a verb form that indicates whether the subject of a sentence acts or is acted upon. Transitive verbs in English have two voices.

Active voice	The hurricane *obliterated* three coastal villages. [The subject— hurricane — acts.]
Passive voice	Three coastal villages *were obliterated* by the hurricane. [The subject— villages —is acted upon.]

Mood

English verbs express the speaker's or writer's attitude by what is called *mood*. English verbs have three possible moods.

Indicative mood	I *was sitting* in the front row. [The indicative mood is used to state a fact or ask a question.]
Imperative mood	*Sit* in the front row, please. [The imperative mood is used in a command or request.]
Subjunctive mood	I feel as if I *were sitting* in the back row. I wish I *were sitting* in the front row! May I ask that I *be seated* in the front row? [The subjunctive mood is used to state a

> condition contrary to fact, to express a
> wish, or to state a request or demand in a
> clause beginning with *that.*]

Irregular verbs

Base	Past	Past participle	Present participle	-s form
sing	sang	sung	singing	sings
have	had	had	having	has
cut	cut	cut	cutting	cuts

By definition, irregular verbs form their principal parts in unpredictable ways. As these examples indicate, some change an internal vowel, others change an ending, and still others retain the same spelling in all three principal parts. For examples of some of the additional variations among irregular verb forms, see **29b** below.

One irregular English verb, *be,* is exceptional in that it has eight different forms rather than five.

Forms of *be*

Base	Past	Past participle	Present participle	-s form	Additional forms
be	was	been	being	is	am
	were				are

29a

Be in the present and past tenses

	Present	Past
I	am	was
you (singular)	are	were
he/she/it	is	was
we	are	were
you (plural)	are	were
they	are	were

29b Irregular verbs

As noted above, a number of frequently used English verbs form their principal parts in irregular ways. Below are some of the most common and most commonly confused of these irregular verbs. Remember that your dictionary is a more complete guide. You can find the principal parts of any irregular verb in a desk dictionary by looking under its base form.

29b

Common Irregular Verbs

Base	Past	Past participle
arise	arose	arisen
awake	awoke, awaked	awaked, awoken
become	became	become
begin	began	begun
bid (offer)	bid	bid
bid (command)	bade	bidden
bite	bit	bitten
blow	blew	blown
break	broke	broken
bring	brought	brought
build	built	built
burn	burned, burnt	burned, burnt
burst	burst	burst
buy	bought	bought
catch	caught	caught
choose	chose	chosen
cling	clung	clung
come	came	come
cost	cost	cost
creep	crept	crept
deal	dealt	dealt
do	did	done

Base	Past	Past participle
draw	drew	drawn
drink	drank	drunk
drive	drove	driven
eat	ate	eaten
fall	fell	fallen
fight	fought	fought
find	found	found
fling	flung	flung
fly	flew	flown
forget	forgot	forgotten, forgot
freeze	froze	frozen
get	got	got, gotten
give	gave	given
go	went	gone
grow	grew	grown
hang (suspend)	hung	hung
hear	heard	heard
hide	hid	hidden, hid
hit	hit	hit
know	knew	known
lay (put)	laid	laid
lead	led	led
leap	leaped, leapt	leaped, leapt
lend	lent	lent
lie (recline)	lay	lain
plead	pleaded, pled	pleaded, pled
rid	rid, ridded	rid, ridded
ride	rode	ridden
ring	rang	rung
rise	rose	risen
run	ran	run

29b

Base	Past	Past participle
see	saw	seen
shake	shook	shaken
show	showed	shown, showed
shrink	shrank, shrunk	shrunk, shrunken
sing	sang	sung
sink	sank	sunk
sit	sat	sat
slay	slew	slain
speak	spoke	spoken
spin	spun	spun
spring	sprang, sprung	sprung
steal	stole	stolen
strike	struck	struck, stricken
strive	strove, strived	striven, strived
swear	swore	sworn
swim	swam	swum
swing	swung	swung
take	took	taken
teach	taught	taught
tear	tore	torn
think	thought	thought
throw	threw	thrown
wake	woke, waked	waked, woken
wear	wore	worn
weave	wove	woven
wed	wedded	wed, wedded
wind	wound	wound
wring	wrung	wrung
write	wrote	written

29b

The following *regular* verbs are sometimes confused with similar irregular verbs:

1. dive/dived/dived

   The past form *dove* is widespread in speech, but it remains unacceptable in writing to many users of English. *Dived* is the safer choice.

2. hang/hanged/hanged

   In the sense "to execute," *hang* is a regular verb: "Despite protests from opponents of the death penalty, the convicted murderer was *hanged* at dawn." Compare with *hang* ("to suspend") above.

3. lie/lied/lied

   In the sense "to tell an untruth," *lie* is a regular verb. Compare with *lie* ("to recline") above.

4. weave/weaved/weaved

   In the sense "to move in and out," *weave* is a regular verb: "The car ahead of me *weaved* recklessly through the heavy traffic." Compare with *weave* ("to make cloth") above.

29c Verb tenses

As explained above, by *tense* we mean variations in the form of a verb that indicate differences in time. English verbs have six principal tenses.

1. Present tense

The present tense designates a current act or condition, or an act that is regularly repeated. It is expressed with the base form of the verb or, in the third person singular, with the *-s* form.

> Some scientists *believe* that the so-called greenhouse effect *is* already apparent.
>
> The earth's average temperature *rises* slightly each year because of increased amounts of carbon dioxide in the atmosphere.

The present tense is also used in discussions of literary and artistic works.

When Hamlet *is* alone, he *contemplates* suicide.

Combined with modifiers that indicate time, the present tense can assert that an act or condition will occur in the future.

Are you available for tomorrow's staff meeting?

No, my flight *leaves* tonight at eight o'clock.

2. Past tense

The past tense designates an act or condition that occurred at a specific time in the past. It is expressed with the past form of the verb.

On September 7, 1940, the German Luftwaffe *began* its night bombing of London.

The British people *were* ready for the attacks.

The past tense also indicates recurrent actions in the past that have not continued into the present.

Every night for two months, Londoners *took* refuge from the bombs in the city's vast network of subway stations.

3. Future tense

The future tense designates an act or condition that will occur at some time in the future. It is formed by preceding the base form of the verb with *will* or *shall*. Note that earlier differences in meaning between *will* and *shall* have largely disappeared, and *shall* is rarely used today in American English except in questions: "Shall we eat out tonight?"

The doctor *will see* you first thing tomorrow morning.

She *will be* pleased to hear that your condition has improved.

4. Present perfect tense

The present perfect tense designates an act or condition that occurred at an indefinite time in the past, or one that began in the past and continues in the present. It is formed by preceding the past participle form of the verb with *have* or *has*.

Professor Maguire *has finished* his most recent novel.

Several publishers *have been* interested in the manuscript since he began it.

5. Past perfect tense

The past perfect tense designates an act completed or a condition existing in the past before some other specific time in the past. It is formed by preceding the past participle form of the verb with *had*.

I *had* already *composed* my letter of resignation when the telephone rang.

My supervisor wanted to know why I *had seemed* so unhappy during the previous weeks.

6. Future perfect tense

The future perfect tense designates an act that will be completed or a condition that will exist before some other specific time in the future. It is formed by preceding the past participle form of the verb with *will have*.

By March 1, the state transportation department *will have submitted* its plans for the new highway to the airport.

Unfortunately, projected increases in airport traffic suggest that the highway *will* already *have become* obsolete by the time it is completed next year.

29d Progressive forms of verbs

29d

Each of the verb tenses in English also has a so-called *progressive form* to indicate that an act extends continuously over a period of time. The progressive form is created by substituting the present participle for the form of the verb used in each tense and adding a form of the verb *be*. Compare the following sentences in the progressive tense with their counterparts in **29c**.

Present progressive   The earth's average temperature *is rising* slightly each year because of increased amounts of carbon dioxide in the atmosphere.

Past progressive   The British people *were preparing* for the attacks.

Future progressive	The doctor *will be seeing* more patients this afternoon than she expected.
Present perfect progressive	Professor Maguire *has been finishing* his most recent novel for several months.
Past perfect progressive	I *had been composing* my letter of resignation for two hours when the telephone rang.
Future perfect progressive	By March 1, the state transportation department *will have been planning* the new highway to the airport for two years.

For a discussion of English verbs that do not have progressive forms, see **43d**.

29e Sequence of tenses

Almost any extended passage of English prose contains verbs in different tenses.

> I suddenly *remembered* [past] that Chris *is* [present] often late for business meetings and *wished* [past] that I *had called* [past perfect] to make sure he *was* [past] on his way. If he *fails* [present] to show up, I *thought* [past], the client *will* probably *drop* [future] us from the project and we *will have wasted* [future perfect] a month of work.

The trick is determining which tenses can logically follow one another, particularly in a sentence containing one or more dependent clauses. As the following sentences indicate, the relationships among tenses can sometimes be more complicated than they first appear.

Incorrect	When the mayor died, her fellow citizens realized how much she contributed to the community, and since then they collected money for a memorial.
Correct	When the mayor died, her fellow citizens realized how much she *had contributed* [before her death] to the community, and since then they *have collected* [from that time to the present] money for a memorial.

1. Sequence of tenses in dependent clauses

There are no absolute rules governing the correct sequence of tenses in sentences that contain dependent clauses. Instead, you have to let the sense of the sentence be your guide. The examples below illustrate some, but not all, of the possibilities.

Main verb in present tense

The motor *starts* when I *press* this button.
[Present + present. The verbs in both the independent clause and the dependent clause are properly in the present tense because the sense of the sentence is to describe two recurring actions: "The motor starts *every time* I press this button."]

Main verb in past tense

The motor *started* when I *pressed* this button.
[Past + past. When the verb in an independent clause is in the past tense, the verb in a dependent clause is often in the past tense as well. In this sentence the two verbs designate actions that occurred approximately simultaneously in the past and that have not continued into the present.]

The motor *started* after I *had pressed* this button.
[Past + past perfect. When the verb in an independent clause is in the past tense, the verb in the dependent clause may be in the past perfect tense. In this sentence the verb in the dependent clause designates an action in the past that occurred before the action designated by the verb in the independent clause.]

The motor *started* even though it *is* old.
[Past + present. When the verb in an independent clause is in the past tense, the verb in the dependent clause may be in the present tense. In this sentence the verb in the dependent clause designates a condition that is true without respect to time: the motor was old yesterday, it is old today, and it will be old tomorrow. This use of the present tense is sometimes called the *timeless present*.]

29e

Main verb in future tense

The motor *will start* when I *press* this button.
[Future + present. When the verb in an independent clause is

in the future tense, the verb in the dependent clause may be in the present tense, because the present tense, as we have seen, may in some contexts refer to the future. The sense of this sentence is: "The motor will start *if* I *will* press this button."]

The motor *will start* once I *have pressed* this button.
[Future + present perfect. When the verb in an independent clause is in the future tense, the verb in the dependent clause may be in the present perfect tense. In this sentence, the verb in the dependent clause designates an action that will occur before the action designated by the verb in the independent clause.]

Main verb in present perfect tense

The motor *has started* because I *pressed* this button.
[Present perfect + past. When the verb in an independent clause is in the present perfect tense, the verb in a dependent clause is usually in the past tense. In this sentence the verb in the dependent clause designates a past action that has not continued into the present, whereas the verb in the independent clause designates a past action that has continued into the present.]

Main verb in past perfect tense

The motor *had started* before I *pressed* this button.
[Past perfect + past. When the verb in an independent clause is in the past perfect tense, the verb in a dependent clause is usually in the past tense. In this sentence the verb in the independent clause designates an action in the past that occurred before the action designated by the verb in the dependent clause.]

29e

Main verb in future perfect tense

The motor *will have started* by the time I *press* [or *have pressed*] this button.
[Future perfect + present or present perfect. When the verb in an independent clause is in the future perfect tense, the verb in a dependent clause is usually in the present or present perfect tense. In this sentence the verb in the independent clause

designates an action in the future that will occur before the action designated by the verb in the dependent clause.]

2. Sequence of tenses with infinitives

Use an infinitive in its present-tense form (*to* + base form of verb) unless it represents an action earlier than that of the sentence's main verb. In that case, the correct infinitive form is the perfect infinitive (*to* + *have* + past participle of verb).

Incorrect July 14, 1789, was a thrilling day to have been alive in Paris.

Correct July 14, 1789, was a thrilling day *to be* alive in Paris. [The sentence discusses the thrill of being alive on July 14, 1789, not before that date. The present infinitive is correct.]

Incorrect Many modern historians would like to witness the events of that day.

Correct Many modern historians would like *to have witnessed* the events of that day. [Witnessing events in the eighteenth century would necessarily precede desiring to do so in the twentieth. The perfect infinitive is correct.]

3. Sequence of tenses with participles

When the action designated by a participle occurs at the same time as the action designated by the main verb in the sentence, the present participle is correct.

29e

Believing the defendant to have been a victim of circumstances, the jury found her not guilty. [The jury's belief and their decision occurred at the same time, so the present participle is correct. The perfect infinitive *to have been* appears in the sentence because the defendant's status as a victim preceded the jury's belief about her (see "Sequence of tenses with infinitives" above).]

When the action designated by a participle occurs before the action designated by the main verb, the present perfect participle (*having* + past participle) is correct.

Having announced their verdict, the jury members felt relieved. [First they announced their verdict; then they felt relief. The present perfect participle is correct.]

EXERCISE 1

Choose the correct tenses of verbs, infinitives, and participles in the following sentences.

Example

> Thomas Edison (1847–1931), America's most prolific inventor, (had, had had) only three months of formal education as a child.
>
> **Correct**   Thomas Edison . . . *had* only three months of formal education. . . .

1. Before he (became, had become) a telegraph operator at the age of sixteen, Edison (sold, had sold) newspapers and candy on trains in Michigan.
2. By the time he was twenty-two, Edison (patented, had patented) his first two inventions, an electric vote recorder and an improved stock ticker.
3. Consumed by energy and ideas, Edison seldom (slept, had slept) through the night.
4. In 1870, (selling, having sold) his interest in an electrical engineering firm that he (helped, had helped) to found, Edison (went, had gone) into business manufacturing his new stock ticker.
5. The research laboratory that he (established, had established) in Menlo Park, New Jersey, a few years later was the first such lab (to bring, to have brought) together a creative team of full-time researchers.
6. (Working, Having worked) in his New Jersey lab, Edison invented the phonograph, a device that (will always be, had always been) associated with the man known as the Wizard of Menlo Park.
7. The apex of Edison's accomplishments in the field of electric lighting was his design for the Pearl Street power plant in New York City, which was the first electric-light power plant in the world when it (opened, had opened) in 1892.
8. Edison's lightbulb manufacturing company (evolved, has evolved) into the corporation that we (know, have known) today as General Electric.

29e

Exercise 1

1. became, had sold
2. had patented
3. slept
4. having sold, had helped, went
5. established, to bring
6. Working, will always be
7. opened
8. has evolved, know
9. held, had established
10. had planned, to do

9. When Edison died in 1931, he (held, had held) more than a thousand patents and (established, had established) himself as the leading technological genius of his era.
10. To honor Edison, President Hoover (planned, had planned) to turn off the country's electrical power for a few minutes during the inventor's funeral, until his advisers warned that (to do, to have done) so would throw the nation into chaos.

29f Auxiliary verbs

We have already seen how forms of the verbs *have* and *be* are combined with the principal parts of verbs to create the tenses of verbs, infinitives, and participles. When used in this way, *have* and *be* are called **auxiliary verbs.** A few other auxiliary verbs remain to be considered.

1. *Do*

Like the verbs *have* and *be, do* may function both as a main verb ("I *did* the laundry this morning") and as an auxiliary verb. In the latter role, it has three functions: to form negative constructions, to form interrogatives, and to add emphasis to a verb. The auxiliary *do* is always combined with the base form of a verb.

Negative construction	Kate's religion *does not permit* her to receive blood transfusions.
Interrogative	*Did* she *share* her belief with the doctor?
Emphasis	I *do try* to see both sides of an issue like this, even when I find it perplexing.

29f

2. Modal auxiliaries

Nine verbs in English are known as *modal auxiliaries*. Each adds a specific shade of meaning to the main verb that it is used with.

1. *Can* expresses ability: "Since my car is fixed, I can leave for California tomorrow."
2. *Could* expresses condition: "If my suitcases were packed, I could leave for California tomorrow."

3. *May* expresses possibility ("I may leave tomorrow, but I may not") or permission: "May I leave for California tomorrow, or would you prefer that I stay?"
4. *Might* expresses weaker possibility than *may:* "Depending on the weather, I might leave for California tomorrow."
5. *Must* expresses necessity: "I must leave for California tomorrow if I expect to get there by Friday."
6. *Ought to* expresses obligation: "Jon called from Los Angeles to say that he needs my help. I ought to leave for California tomorrow."
7. *Should* expresses obligation: "I should stop procrastinating and leave for California tomorrow."
8. *Will* expresses intention: "I've put this trip off long enough. Tomorrow I will leave for California."
9. *Would* expresses condition: "If I were to leave for California tomorrow, would you come with me?"

Note that unlike the other auxiliary verbs *have, be,* and *do,* each modal auxiliary has only one form. It is therefore unaffected by the person or number of the subject:

> I *should* leave tomorrow.
>
> She *should* have left yesterday.
>
> They *should* be leaving soon.

EXERCISE 2

29f

Insert a modal auxiliary into each of the following sentences to create the meaning indicated.

Example

> Anyone who has gratefully reached for a candy bar during a long afternoon of work or an evening of tedious study (   ) thank the ancient Aztecs. [Obligation]
>
> **Correct**   . . . *should* (or *ought to*) thank the ancient Aztecs.

1. If it seems strange that we owe chocolate to the Aztecs, we (   ) remember that the cacao tree, on which the cocoa bean grows, is native to South America. [Necessity]
2. Even the word *chocolate* (   ) be traced to the Aztec word *xocolalt,* meaning "bitter water." [Ability]

Exercise 2

1. must
2. can
3. would
4. must
5. may/might
6. would
7. ought to/should
8. may
9. can
10. may/might, will

3. You (   ) understand that origin of the word *chocolate* if you tasted an unprocessed cocoa bean. [Condition]
4. Credit for introducing chocolate to Europe (   ) be given to the sixteenth-century Spanish explorers who first tasted it in the New World and returned with it to their native land. [Necessity]
5. It (   ) be hard for us to believe, but as recently as the seventeenth century, chocolate was a luxury in England, commanding prices that put it out of reach of all but a few. [Possibility]
6. If you were asked about the origins of the chocolate industry in North America, (   ) you know that chocolate was not produced here until 1765? [Condition]
7. Milk chocolate came still later; for that we (   ) be grateful to the Swiss, who perfected its formula at the end of the nineteenth century. [Obligation]
8. A century later, the Food and Drug Administration continues to stipulate that only chocolate containing milk or cream (   ) be sold in the United States under the label "milk chocolate." [Permission]
9. Today, chocolate flavoring (   ) be found in products ranging from breakfast cereal to pharmaceuticals. [Ability]
10. Chocolate (   ) not be addictive, but chocolate lovers know how difficult it is to decide that they (   ) reduce their consumption of the sweet. [Possibility/Intention]

29g Voice

Transitive verbs in English have two forms, called **voices,** to indicate whether the subject of the sentence is the actor in the sentence or is acted upon. In a sentence whose verb is in the **active voice,** the subject does the action that the verb describes.

Active verbs

actor———→action →recipient
New Orleans *has inspired* writers for more than two centuries.

actor———→action ————————→recipient
A writer *cannot escape* the city's influence.

By contrast, in a sentence whose verb is in the **passive voice,** the subject is acted upon by an actor that may or may not be named in the sentence.

Passive verbs

recipient⟵ action⟵ actor
Writers *have been inspired* by New Orleans for more than two centuries.

recipient⟵ action
The city's influence *cannot be escaped*.

1. Forming passive verbs

The passive voice is created by combining appropriate forms of *be* and the past participle. Notice how the passive verb in each of the following tenses reverses the meaning of the corresponding active sentence.

	Active	**Passive**
Present	I trust you.	I *am trusted* by you.
Past	I trusted you.	I *was trusted* by you.
Future	I will trust you.	I *will be trusted* by you.
Present perfect	I have trusted you.	I *have been trusted* by you.
Past perfect	I had trusted you.	I *had been trusted* by you.
Future perfect	I will have trusted you.	I *will have been trusted* by you.

Passive verbs form the progressive by adding the appropriate progressive form of *be* to the past participle. Among the progressive forms in the passive voice, the present and past progressive are the most common.

Present progressive passive   I *am being trusted* by you.
Past progressive passive   I *was being trusted* by you.

2. Using active and passive verbs

We need passive verbs to express actions when the actor is unimportant or cannot be identified. In the following sentence, for example, the passive verb effectively focuses attention on the action and the recipient of that action and de-emphasizes the unknown actors.

recipient ⟵ action
Our apartment *was burglarized* yesterday.

The corresponding active sentence would in this case be ludicrously redundant: "Burglars burglarized our apartment yesterday."

But when the actor in a sentence is known and may be significant, the active voice is usually preferable for two reasons. First, a passive verb always requires more words than an active verb to express the same idea; when overused, passive verbs thus result in wordy writing. Second, a passive verb may de-emphasize or obscure an actor that should in fact be identified in a sentence, as in the following case.

Passive verb obscures actor   It *has* long *been asserted* that cigarette smoking is not necessarily harmful to your health.

Active verb indicates actor   Tobacco companies *have* long *asserted* that cigarette smoking is not necessarily harmful to your health.

Who does the asserting here makes all the difference. Without an active verb and an expressed actor, we can't adequately evaluate the claim. For more on the stylistic advantages of the active voice, see **8c**.

EXERCISE 3

Identify passive verbs in the following sentences. If a sentence would be improved by using the active voice instead, revise it, making up likely actors if necessary.

Example

   Carmen was working for the state government when she discovered that important tax records were apparently being removed from the office at night.

Passive verb   were being removed

Analysis   The passive verb in this sentence is acceptable, since the actor is unknown. However, an active verb used with an indefinite pronoun would perhaps heighten the sense of mystery: ". . . when she discovered that *someone was* apparently *removing* important tax records from the office at night."

1. Sometimes records would be missing for days; then suddenly, mysteriously, they would be returned to their file cabinets.
2. When the situation was analyzed by Carmen, the possibility of malfeasance could not be dismissed.
3. The decision was finally made by Carmen to determine who was responsible.

Exercise 3

1. The passive verb is *would be returned;* as in the example, it's acceptable, since the actor is unknown.
2. The passive verbs are *was analyzed* and *could be dismissed*. Revise for directness: "When Carmen analyzed the situation, she could not dismiss the possibility of malfeasance."
3. The passive verb is *was made*. Revise for directness: "Carmen finally made the decision to determine who was responsible."
4. The passive verb is *would be caught*. Revise for parallelism: "She would conceal herself in the office at night and would catch the culprit in the act."
5. The passive verb is *was selected*. Revise for directness: "As her hiding place, she selected an empty cabinet large enough to sit in."
6. The passive verb is *had been vacated*. Revise for directness: ". . . until her co-workers had vacated the office."

4. She would conceal herself in the office at night, and the culprit would be caught in the act.
5. An empty cabinet large enough to sit in was selected as her hiding place.
6. One Monday afternoon at five o'clock, Carmen slowly straightened her desk until the office had been vacated by her co-workers.
7. Into the cabinet she crawled, making sure that a crack was left through which the thief could be seen.
8. After an hour, Carmen realized that her left leg had been positioned in a way that cut off circulation to her foot.
9. As her legs were untangled, she bumped the cabinet door, which clicked shut, trapping her inside.
10. As the long night wore on, Carmen consoled herself by reflecting that she had been hired for her expertise as an accountant, not as a sleuth.

29h Mood

Verbs express a speaker's or writer's attitude by what is called their **mood**. English verbs have three possible moods: **indicative, imperative,** and **subjunctive.**

1. Indicative mood

The indicative mood is by far the most frequently encountered in English. It is used to state a fact or ask a question.

I *was sitting* next to Nancy.
Were you *sitting* nearby?

2. Imperative mood

The verb in a command is said to be in the imperative mood.

Sit next to Nancy, please.

3. Subjunctive mood

The subjunctive mood is used to express conditions contrary to fact and to state certain demands and requests. In modern English, subjunctive verb forms differ from indicative forms in only two cases:

7. The passive verbs are *was left* and *could be seen.* Revise for directness: "Into the cabinet she crawled, making sure that she left a crack through which she could see the thief."
8. The passive verb is *had been positioned.* Revise for directness: "After an hour, Carmen realized that she had positioned her left leg . . ."
9. The passive verb is *were untangled.* Revise for directness: "As she untangled her legs, . . ."
10. The passive verb is *had been hired;* it's acceptable in this sentence, since the actor is unimportant and irrelevant.

1. The present subjunctive uses the base form of the verb for all persons and numbers, *including the third-person singular,* where indicative verbs use the *-s* form.
2. The past subjunctive form of the verb *be* is *were* for all persons and numbers.

Though used much less today than formerly, the subjunctive mood still surfaces in a number of idiomatic expressions ("*Be* that as it may," "Far *be* it from me") and in the three specific situations described below.

Clauses beginning with *if, as if,* or *as though* and stating a condition contrary to fact

If I *were* [not *was*] you, I would pay no attention to Steve's investment advice.
[In reality, I am not you.]

Steve confidently offers advice *as if* he *were* [not *was*] an experienced investor.
[In reality, he is not experienced.]

He talks *as though* the stock market's future *were* [not *was*] predictable.
[In reality, it is not predictable.]

Clauses expressing a wish or desire

I wish that your Hungarian cooking class *weren't* [not *wasn't*] already full.

If only I *were* [not *was*] able to enroll!

29h

Clauses beginning with *that* and stating a demand, a request, a recommendation, or a requirement

I demand *that* I *be* [not *am*] allowed to address the council!

May I ask *that* my friends *be* [not *are*] recognized as well?

We suggest *that* the council *take* [not *takes*] immediate action to preserve the historic Pelham Building on Market Square.

The legislation we are proposing stipulates *that* developers *be* [not *are*] prohibited from demolishing the building under any circumstances.

EXERCISE 4

Correct the following sentences by changing verbs in the indicative mood to the subjunctive mood where necessary.

Example

> If the winter in Alaska was less harsh, the state's population would probably increase dramatically.
>
> **Correct** If the winter in Alaska *were* less harsh, . . .

1. My friends Tom and Lori, who live outside Anchorage, talk about the state as if it was the only place on earth to live.
2. If I moved to Alaska, they tell me, I would feel as if I was beginning my life again.
3. They wish my home was closer to Alaska so that I could visit them more often than I do now.
4. Like many other Alaskans, they feel they have a right to demand that every tourist respects the pristine condition of the state's wilderness lands.
5. Together with a group of their neighbors, they are collecting signatures on a petition requiring that all future plans to drill for oil in Alaska's wilderness areas are reviewed by environmental experts.

29h

Exercise 4

1. My friends Tom and Lori, who live outside Anchorage, talk about the state as if it *were* the only place on earth to live. [condition contrary to fact]
2. If I moved to Alaska, they tell me, I would feel as if I *were* beginning my life again. [condition contrary to fact]
3. They wish my home *were* closer to Alaska so that I could visit them more often than I do now. [wish]
4. Like many other Alaskans, they feel they have a right to demand that every tourist *respect* the pristine condition of the state's wilderness lands. [demand]
5. Together with a group of their neighbors, they are collecting signatures on a petition requiring that all future plans to drill for oil in Alaska's wilderness areas *be* reviewed by environmental experts. [requirement]

30 Sentence Fragments, Comma Splices, Fused Sentences

Sentences broken into fragments or incorrectly joined together should be avoided in most writing not simply because they violate rules of grammatical usage, but because they may distract and confuse a reader. An eye trained to spot subjects and verbs and an ear tuned to the intonations of speech are usually sufficient to catch fragmented and run-together sentences. To strengthen your feel for complete sentences, read your writing aloud. Listen to the accents, pitch, and rhythms of the words on the page. Notice the different breath pauses for different marks of punctuation, the rising and falling pitch at different points in the sentence. Read aloud the sentences of other writers for cadence and intonation. Remember that grammar and the human voice often coincide in remarkable ways.

30a Types of sentence fragments

When part of a sentence is punctuated as if it were a complete sentence, it is called a **sentence fragment.** A sentence fragment is typically either a dependent clause or a phrase lacking a full verb.

Fragment   The network newscasts on television each night provide only twenty-three minutes of news coverage. Thereby making superficial reporting almost inevitable.

Quick Reference: *Sentence Errors*

Sentence fragments

A sentence fragment is part of a sentence punctuated as if it were a complete sentence.

> **Fragment**   The tax increase was approved. *Although many key senators opposed it.*

Correct a sentence fragment by joining it to a complete sentence.

> **Correct**   The tax increase was approved, although many key senators opposed it.

Comma splices

A comma splice occurs when two independent clauses are connected only with a comma.

> **Comma splice**   Taxes on the wealthy will increase, however, most other citizens will be unaffected.

Correct a comma splice by connecting the clauses with a semicolon, a coordinating conjunction, or a subordinating conjunction.

> **Correct**   Taxes on the wealthy will increase; however, most other citizens will be unaffected.

> **Correct**   Taxes on the wealthy will increase, *but* most other citizens will be unaffected.

> **Correct**   *Although* taxes on the wealthy will increase, most other citizens will be unaffected.

Fused sentences

A fused sentence occurs when two independent clauses are joined with no punctuation or conjunction between them.

> **Fused**   The debate over the tax increase was rancorous many senators felt personally attacked by their colleagues.

> Correct a fused sentence by using any of the strategies above.
>
> **Correct**   The debate over the tax increase was ran-
> corous, *and* many senators felt personally
> attacked by their colleagues.

Though its opening capital letter and concluding period at first make it look like a sentence, the second group of words here is a fragment—in this case, a participial phrase without a subject or a full verb. It should be joined to the sentence that precedes it.

Correct   The network newscasts on television each night provide only twenty-three minutes of news coverage, thereby making superficial reporting almost inevitable.

Most fragments result from inadvertently punctuating one of the following constructions as a sentence.

1.   Dependent clause as fragment

A dependent clause must either be joined to the sentence of which it is logically a part or be rewritten as an independent clause.

Fragment   Often I stay up late in my room, studying, writing, or thinking about the future. While all the other people in the dorm are asleep.

Correct   Often I stay up late in my room, studying, writing, or thinking about the future while all the other people in the dorm are asleep.

Fragment   I was grateful to learn of the college's loan funds. Because I didn't know where I could turn for help or see how I could take a part-time job.

Correct   I was grateful to learn of the college's loan funds because I didn't know where I could turn for help or see how I could take a part-time job.

30a

The fragments above might have been eliminated by omitting the conjunctions *while* and *because* to change the dependent clauses into independent clauses. Note, however, that without the conjunction the precise connection between the two clauses in each case is lost.

Correct but weak	Often I stay up late in my room, studying, writing, or thinking about the future. All the other people in the dorm are asleep.
Correct but weak	I was grateful to learn of the college's loan funds. I didn't know where I could turn for help or see how I could take a part-time job.

2.   Participial or absolute phrase as fragment

A **participial phrase** functions as an adjective and must be joined to the sentence containing the noun or pronoun that it modifies.

Fragment	I was surprised at the commotion in the magazine's office. Reporters and secretaries were rushing all over the place. Running up and down the aisles, conferring with the editors, and talking in little groups. [*Who are running, conferring,* and *talking?* Those three participles describe the reporters and secretaries, so they cannot be separated from the second sentence in this passage.]
Correct	I was surprised at the commotion in the magazine's office. Reporters and secretaries were rushing all over the place, running up and down the aisles, conferring with the editors, and talking in little groups.
Fragment	I stepped into the chaotic room in search of a desk with my name on it. Having already decided that working here would be an adventure. [A phrase constructed around the participle *having decided* cannot stand by itself. It must be joined to the sentence that names the decision maker. In this case it is *I.*]
Correct	Having already decided that working here would be an adventure, I stepped into the chaotic room in search of a desk with my name on it.

30a

A participial phrase may also be rewritten as an independent clause, though the result is often a somewhat less economical style.

Correct   I was surprised at the commotion in the magazine's office. Reporters and secretaries were rushing all over the place. *They were* running up and down the aisles, conferring with the editors, and talking in little groups.

Remember that joining a noun or pronoun with a participle produces an **absolute phrase** (see **25f**), not a complete sentence. Such a fragment can be revised in several ways.

Fragment   The confusion in the office mounting. I despaired of finding anyone who could help me.
[The participle *mounting* modifies the noun *confusion*, but this construction cannot stand alone because it has no verb.]

Correct   The confusion in the office was mounting. I despaired of finding anyone who could help me.
[An absolute phrase can always be revised as a complete sentence by substituting a verb—in this case, *was mounting* or *mounted*—for the participle.]

Correct   The confusion in the office mounting, I despaired of finding anyone who could help me.
[When an absolute phrase expresses an idea that is related to a complete sentence, the phrase can simply be attached to the sentence with a comma.]

Correct   Because the confusion in the office was mounting, I despaired of finding anyone who could help me.
[In some cases, an absolute phrase can be revised as a dependent clause. The subordinating conjunction *because* and the verb *was mounting* create a dependent clause that modifies the verb *despaired* in the independent clause.]

30a

3. Infinitive phrase as fragment

An **infinitive phrase,** a group of words constructed around *to* plus a verb form, does not convey a complete thought and cannot stand alone.

Fragment   After a long discussion, I finally received permission from my parents. To spend the summer and fall with El Centro de Paz, a work project in Mexico.

Correct   After a long discussion, I finally received permission from my parents to spend the summer and fall with El Centro de Paz, a work project in Mexico.

4. Prepositional phrase as fragment

A **preposition** (such as *at, for, in, over, through, with*), its object, and any modifiers constitute a prepositional phrase. A prepositional phrase modifies another word in a sentence and must always be joined to the sentence containing that word.

Fragment   Many people, seeking a perfect carpet of green grass, pour chemicals on their lawns each summer. Without a thought about the possible hazards of these concoctions.
[*Without a thought about the possible hazards of these concoctions* is a prepositional phrase modifying the verb *pour* and must be joined to the sentence in which that word appears.]

Correct   Many people, seeking a perfect carpet of green grass, pour chemicals on their lawns each summer without a thought about the possible hazards of these concoctions.

In some cases, it may be possible to expand a prepositional phrase into a full sentence.

Correct   Many people, seeking a perfect carpet of green grass, pour chemicals on their lawns each summer. *They don't think* about the possible hazards of these concoctions.

30a

5. Appositive phrase as fragment

An **appositive phrase** is typically a noun phrase that describes or explains another noun or a pronoun. Such a phrase cannot stand alone, but must be linked to the word it describes, usually with a comma or dash.

Fragment   The emergency-room physician recognized the signs of shock in the accident victim. Elevated pulse rate, low blood pressure, and clammy skin.

Correct   The emergency-room physician recognized the signs of shock in the accident victim—elevated pulse rate, low blood pressure, and clammy skin.
[The appositive phrase *elevated pulse rate, low blood pressure, and clammy skin* explains the word *signs*.]

An appositive phrase may contain within it a dependent clause, but the phrase remains incomplete and must be connected to the sentence containing the word that it describes.

Fragment   No one could identify the victim. A woman in her late twenties who had staggered into the hospital before collapsing.

Correct   No one could identify the victim, a woman in her late twenties who had staggered into the hospital before collapsing.

Sometimes an appositive can be rewritten as an independent clause without any loss of conciseness.

Correct   No one could identify the victim. A woman in her late twenties, *she* had staggered into the hospital before collapsing.
[*A woman in her late twenties* is now in apposition with the pronoun *she*.]

30b Acceptable incomplete sentences

30b

Professional writers sometimes use sentence fragments deliberately to create specific effects. In the following description of a London railway station, for example, the series of fragments re-creates the way in which impressions bombard the arriving traveler.

Acceptable fragments for effect

Waterloo Station: big, bustling, not sepulchral like today's American termini. Numerous stalls for magazines, flowers, tea, and every other railway-station vendible; direction signs everywhere, plain, explicit, always helpful—no traveler who can read is in danger of being misled in Britain. To the taxi stand, and another gratifyingly authentic touch of London, the high-slung, dignified taxi with its pipe-smoking, tweed-jacketed, cloth-capped driver.

—Richard D. Altick, *To Be in England*

Fragments are acceptable, even desirable, when they are used in such a self-conscious and effective way.

Fragments are also acceptable in speech and in some informal writing when the speaker's or writer's full meaning is clear. Permissible fragments include those in the categories below.

Elliptical expressions

Just wanted to thank you for dinner last night.

Hope to see you soon.

Questions and answers

Why not? Because it's late.

How much? Two dollars.

Exclamations

No way!

At last!

Requests

This way, please.

If I could have your attention for a moment.

30b

Informal transitions

So much for the first point.

Now to consider the next question.

EXERCISE 1

Some of the passages below contain sentence fragments; others do not. Locate each sentence fragment, identify its type, and revise the passage in order to eliminate it.

Exercise 1

1. In ancient Greece and Rome, surgery was a highly developed art. Greek and Roman surgeons operated with great skill and with surprising concern for cleanliness, thanks to the teachings of Hippocrates, the influential Greek physician who lived about 400 B.C. [appositive phrase as fragment]
2. [no sentence fragment]
3. Lacking the understanding of surgery that the Romans had possessed, most medieval physicians wanted nothing to do with it. Surgery thus became part of the practice of barbers. [participial phrase as fragment]
4. Surgery remained distinct from, and subordinate to, the practice of medicine until well into the nineteenth century. And for patients, surgical procedures remained experiences in terror. In the absence of any effective anesthetic, the surgeon's assistants would position themselves around the operating table to hold the patient down. [prepositional phrase as fragment]

Example

Surgery has its roots in prehistoric times. Archaeological evidence suggests that the prehistoric surgeon's tool for making incisions was a sharpened piece of flint. Amputations apparently performed with crude saws made out of bone.

Fragment Amputations apparently performed with crude saws made out of bone. [absolute phrase]

Revised Amputations *were* apparently *performed* with crude saws made out of bone.

1. In ancient Greece and Rome, surgery was a highly developed art. Greek and Roman surgeons operated with great skill and with surprising concern for cleanliness, thanks to the teachings of Hippocrates. The influential Greek physician who lived about 400 B.C.
2. But the ancient tradition of excellence in surgery was short-lived. The advances made by the Romans were lost when the Roman Empire collapsed and the world entered the Dark Ages.
3. Lacking the understanding of surgery that the Romans had possessed. Most medieval physicians wanted nothing to do with it. Surgery thus became part of the practice of barbers.
4. Surgery remained distinct from, and subordinate to, the practice of medicine until well into the nineteenth century. And for patients, surgical procedures remained experiences in terror. In the absence of any effective anesthetic. The surgeon's assistants would position themselves around the operating table to hold the patient down.
5. Perhaps the most important attribute that a nineteenth-century surgeon could possess was speed. The best surgeons performed an amputation in little more than a minute and a half. To minimize the patient's agony.
6. One of the most dramatic advances in surgery came in the 1840s with the development of ether. An anesthetic that allowed the surgeon to work more slowly and carefully. Without the distraction of the patient's screaming and thrashing.
7. But infection remained a serious — and baffling — problem. Until Joseph Lister discovered in the 1860s that operating in a room full of carbolic acid mist greatly reduced the occurrence of postoperative gangrene.
8. The first surgical gloves were not intended to protect the patient from germs on the surgeon's hands. But to protect the hands of the surgeon and the nurses from irritation caused by the carbolic acid spray.

30b

5. Perhaps the most important attribute that a nineteenth-century surgeon could possess was speed. The best surgeons performed an amputation in little more than a minute and a half, to minimize the patient's agony. [infinitive phrase as fragment]
6. One of the most dramatic advances in surgery came in the 1840s with the development of ether, an anesthetic that allowed the surgeon to work more slowly and carefully, without the distraction of the patient's screaming and thrashing. [appositive phrase as fragment, prepositional phrase as fragment]
7. But infection remained a serious — and baffling — problem, until Joseph Lister discovered in the 1860s that operating in a room full of carbolic acid mist greatly reduced the occurrence of postoperative gangrene. [dependent clause as fragment]
8. The first surgical gloves were not intended to protect the patient from germs on the surgeon's hands, but to protect the hands of the surgeon and the nurses from irritation caused by the carbolic acid spray. [infinitive phrase as fragment]

9. At about the same time, some operating teams adopted surgical suits. A replacement for the blood-stained mackintoshes that surgeons previously wore.
10. Blood transfusions were another mystery to nineteenth-century physicians. Some transfusions were successful. Whereas others had disastrous results. It was not until the turn of the century, when blood typing was finally understood, that transfusions could be performed safely.

30c Comma splices

A **comma splice**—sometimes called a *comma fault*—occurs when two independent clauses are joined only with a comma. Comma splices are distracting to a reader, and they can often lead to misreading.

Comma splice   My nephew stood in the doorway, soaked from the rain, the stray dog lay at his feet.

Is it the nephew who is soaked from the rain, or the stray dog? The confusion results because the comma by itself is not a strong enough punctuation mark to indicate the end of an independent clause. Two stronger punctuation marks are the period and the semicolon; note how they can be used to interpret the incorrectly joined clauses above.

Correct   My nephew stood in the doorway, soaked from the rain. The stray dog lay at his feet.
[The nephew is soaked.]

Correct   My nephew stood in the doorway; soaked from the rain, the stray dog lay at his feet.
[The dog is soaked.]

30c

You can sometimes catch comma splices in revision by reading your paper aloud. If you naturally drop your voice or pause substantially at a comma, check to see whether you have mistakenly used the comma to connect independent clauses. To correct a comma splice, try one of the strategies below.

1. Use a period to divide the clauses into separate sentences

Correct the comma splice by making each main clause a sentence punctuated with a period. This strategy works well when a tran-

---

9. At about the same time, some operating teams adopted surgical suits, a replacement for the blood-stained mackintoshes that surgeons previously wore. [appositive phrase as fragment]
10. Blood transfusions were another mystery to nineteenth-century physicians. Some transfusions were successful, whereas others had disastrous results. It was not until the turn of the century, when blood typing was finally understood, that transfusions could be performed safely. [dependent clause as fragment]

sitional word, phrase, or clause is present to express the relationship between the two sentences that you create.

Comma splice	There was an extremely heavy rain on Monday night, after the storm had passed, the streams were overflowing.
Correct	There was an extremely heavy rain on Monday night. After the storm had passed, the streams were overflowing.
	[The adverbial clause *after the storm had passed* links the two new sentences chronologically.]

2. Use a semicolon to connect the clauses

Correct the comma splice by replacing the comma with a semicolon. A semicolon may be used by itself or together with a conjunctive adverb or a transitional phrase.

Semicolon by itself between independent clauses

A semicolon alone can connect two independent clauses when the two clauses are so closely related that their relationship does not need to be stated explicitly with a conjunction or transitional phrase.

| Comma splice | Gambling is like a drug, after a while the gambler finds it impossible to stop. |
| Correct | Gambling is like a drug; after a while the gambler finds it impossible to stop. |

Note that a semicolon must be preceded *and* followed by an independent clause. If it is not, a sentence fragment results.

| Fragment | Gambling is like a drug; *after a while, impossible to stop.* |

Semicolon with conjunctive adverb or transitional phrase

When two independent clauses are linked by a **conjunctive adverb** such as *consequently, however, moreover, nonetheless, then,* or *therefore,* or by a transitional phrase like *as a result, for example,* or *on the other* *hand,* a semicolon is required. A comma used with a conjunctive adverb or transitional phrase creates a comma splice.

Comma splice	To most of the economists at the conference, a rise in inflation seemed inevitable, however, three of the experts predicted the opposite.
Correct	To most of the economists at the conference, a rise in inflation seemed inevitable; however, three of the experts predicted the opposite.
Comma splice	The three optimists came with evidence to support their prediction, for example, they cited a slight decline in the gross national product during recent months.
Correct	The three optimists came with evidence to support their prediction; for example, they cited a slight decline in the gross national product during recent months.

As an alternative, of course, two independent clauses linked by a conjunctive adverb or by a transitional phrase may be divided into separate sentences.

Correct	To most of the economists at the conference, a rise in inflation seemed inevitable. However, three of the experts predicted the opposite.
Correct	The three optimists came with evidence to support their prediction. For example, they cited a slight decline in the gross national product during recent months.

Note that a conjunctive adverb, unlike a coordinating conjunction or subordinating conjunction, need not come first in a clause but may be inserted in a number of places. It is preceded by a semicolon *only* when it comes at the beginning of a clause and serves as the connective between two independent clauses.

Incorrect	The paint remover was difficult to apply. Its fumes; moreover, irritated our eyes and throats.
Correct	The paint remover was difficult to apply. Its fumes, moreover, irritated our eyes and throats. [The conjunctive adverb *moreover* is not preceded

by a semicolon because it is not used as a
connective between two clauses.]

Correct   The paint remover was difficult to apply; moreover,
its fumes irritated our eyes and throats.
[Here *moreover* is preceded by a semicolon
because it begins the second clause and serves
as a connective between the two clauses.]

3. Use a coordinating conjunction to connect the two clauses

Use a coordinating conjunction—*and, but, for, nor, or, so, yet*—to connect two independent clauses when you wish to give them equal emphasis. A coordinating conjunction is usually preceded by a comma.

Comma splice   The parks in this city are very poorly maintained, the
two public swimming pools are in bad condition as
well.

Correct   The parks in this city are very poorly maintained, *and*
the two public swimming pools are in bad condition
as well.

Comma splice   We would be willing to pay higher taxes, we just
want some assurance that the city will use our money
wisely.

Correct   We would be willing to pay higher taxes, *but* we just
want some assurance that the city will use our money
wisely.

30c

When a coordinating conjunction joins two independent clauses that are punctuated internally with commas, a semicolon rather than a comma may be used with the coordinating conjunction to show the main division of the sentence more clearly.

Comma splice   As the development of the atomic bomb, of computer
systems, and of guided missiles shows, technology,
indeed basic scientific research itself, is often determined by political and military considerations, many
people do not recognize this interdependence and instead regard changes in technology as changes that
simply "happen."

Correct   As the development of the atomic bomb, of computer systems, and of guided missiles shows, technology, indeed basic scientific research itself, is often determined by political and military considerations; *but* many people do not recognize this interdependence and instead regard changes in technology as changes that simply "happen."

For more on using coordination effectively, see **8b**.

4. Use a subordinating conjunction or a relative pronoun to subordinate one clause

If a comma joins two independent clauses that are unequal in importance, you may be able to correct the comma splice by subordinating one clause with a subordinating conjunction (such as *after, although, because, since, while, whereas,* and *when*), or with a relative pronoun (such as *that, which,* and *who*).

Comma splice   Marjorie has stopped lending her nephew money, she doesn't trust him any longer.

Correct   Marjorie has stopped lending her nephew money, *because* she doesn't trust him any longer.

Comma splice   Last week he asked her for a loan of $200, he said he needed it for car repairs.

Correct   Last week he asked her for a loan of $200, *which* he said he needed for car repairs.

For more on using subordination effectively, see **8b**.

30d

30d Acceptable comma splices

A few minor exceptions to the rules governing comma splices should be mentioned here. Short parallel independent clauses are sometimes joined only with commas, particularly in narratives.

Acceptable   The sky darkened, the wind blew, the cold rain began to fall.

Also, an elliptical question is attached to the end of a related independent clause with only a comma.

Exercise 2 (page 647)

Answers will vary.

1. On May 2, 1970, President Richard Nixon expanded the war in Vietnam by ordering American troops into Cambodia, which was a neutral country in the conflict. [comma splice corrected with relative pronoun]
2. [no comma splice]
3. A million and a half college students nationwide responded by walking out of classes and joining massive protests. President Nixon publicly referred to the protesters as "bums." [comma splice corrected with period]
4. On May 4, 1970, edgy National Guard troops protecting the campus of Kent State University in Ohio fired into a crowd of unarmed students and killed four persons. Two were protesters; two were bystanders. [comma splices corrected with period, semicolon]

Acceptable   You told Sam to meet us at three o'clock, didn't you?

Acceptable   Sam's not very reliable, is he?

EXERCISE 2

Some of the passages below contain comma splices; others do not. Locate each comma splice and revise the passage in order to correct it.

Example

The 1960s are remembered as a time of idealism, protest, and change in America, however, the first year of the next decade was no less turbulent.

> **Revised**   The 1960s are remembered as a time of idealism, protest, and change in America. However, the first year of the next decade was no less turbulent.

1. On May 2, 1970, President Richard Nixon expanded the war in Vietnam by ordering American troops into Cambodia, it was a neutral country in the conflict.
2. A storm of protest broke out around the nation, for even many people who had not opposed the role of the United States in Vietnam felt that this step was wrong.
3. A million and a half college students nationwide responded by walking out of classes and joining massive protests, President Nixon publicly referred to the protesters as "bums."
4. On May 4, 1970, edgy National Guard troops protecting the campus of Kent State University in Ohio fired into a crowd of unarmed students and killed four persons, two were protesters, two were bystanders.
5. Many of the year's movies reflected the nation's social and political concerns, *Woodstock* and *M*A*S*H,* for example, were popular films.
6. The former was a documentary account of the massive three-day rock concert that had been held a year earlier in upstate New York, and the latter was the satirical antiwar film that gave rise to the popular television series of the same name.
7. The year also brought the drug-related deaths of two talented musicians, Jimi Hendrix and Janis Joplin, both of them were twenty-seven years old.
8. Perhaps to escape from such serious concerns, people were buying books with other themes, the two best-sellers in 1970 were *Love Story* and *Everything You Always Wanted to Know about Sex but Were Afraid to Ask.*

30d

5. Many of the year's movies reflected the nation's social and political concerns; *Woodstock* and *M*A*S*H,* for example, were popular films. [comma splice corrected with semicolon]
6. [no comma splice]
7. The year also brought the drug-related deaths of two talented musicians, Jimi Hendrix and Janis Joplin, both of whom were twenty-seven years old. [comma splice corrected with relative pronoun]
8. Perhaps to escape from such serious concerns, people were buying books with other themes. The two best-sellers in 1970 were *Love Story* and *Everything You Always Wanted to Know about Sex but Were Afraid to Ask.* [comma splice corrected with period]
9. [no comma splice]
10. The major early issues of the women's movement were child care and job discrimination, which are among the issues that remain important to many women and men today. [comma splice corrected with relative pronoun]

9. Although an August 26 celebration of the fiftieth anniversary of women's suffrage focused attention on equal rights, the campaign for an Equal Rights Amendment that began in 1970 ended in failure more than a decade later.

10. The major early issues of the women's movement were child care and job discrimination, they are among the issues that remain important to many women and men today.

11. Jobs in particular were on the minds of all Americans, in 1970 almost two million more people were out of work than in 1969.

12. The nation's unemployed reached four million, it was the highest number since the Great Depression of the 1930s.

13. Many people forget, however, that it was during the Nixon administration that concern for the environment was institutionalized, in July of 1970 the Environmental Protection Agency, commonly known today by its initials EPA, was formed.

14. And the Voting Rights Act of 1970 lowered the voting age to eighteen, although it applied only to federal elections.

15. The twelve months of 1970 brought changes that would be felt for years, their wounds, too, would take longer to heal than most people realized.

30e Fused sentences

A **fused sentence** is one in which two independent clauses are joined with no punctuation or conjunction between them.

> **Fused** The Senate passed the bill only after long hours of debate both sides had strong feelings about the measure.

The fused sentence is an even more serious error than the comma splice because it makes the reader's task of deciphering the sentence's meaning extremely difficult. To correct a fused sentence, use any of the strategies discussed above for correcting comma splices.

Use a period

> The Senate passed the bill only after long hours of debate. Both sides had strong feelings about the measure.

Use a semicolon

> The Senate passed the bill only after long hours of debate; both sides had strong feelings about the measure.

11. Jobs in particular were on the minds of all Americans, because in 1970 almost two million more people were out of work than in 1969. [comma splice corrected with subordinating conjunction]

12. The nation's unemployed reached four million, which was the highest number since the Great Depression of the 1930s. [comma splice corrected with relative pronoun]

13. Many people forget, however, that it was during the Nixon administration that concern for the environment was institutionalized. In July of 1970 the Environmental Protection Agency, commonly known today by its initials EPA, was formed. [comma splice corrected with period]

14. [no comma splice]

15. The twelve months of 1970 brought changes that would be felt for years. Their wounds, too, would take longer to heal than most people realized. [comma splice corrected with period]

Use a semicolon and a conjunctive adverb

Both sides had strong feelings about the bill; *consequently,* the Senate passed it only after long hours of debate.

Use a semicolon and a transitional phrase

Both sides had strong feelings about the bill; *as a result,* the Senate passed it only after long hours of debate.

Use a comma and a coordinating conjunction

The Senate passed the bill only after long hours of debate, *for* both sides had strong feelings about the measure.

Use a comma and a subordinating conjunction

The Senate passed the bill only after long hours of debate, *because* both sides had strong feelings about the measure.

EXERCISE 3

Some of the passages below consist of fused sentences; others do not. Locate the fused sentences and revise them appropriately.

Example

Amber is the fossil resin of extinct evergreens the creation of amber began sixty to seventy million years ago.

> **Revised**   Amber is the fossil resin of extinct evergreens. The creation of amber began sixty to seventy million years ago.

30e

1. The color of amber ranges from pale cream to deep reddish-brown the most valuable amber is clear to translucent.
2. Amber feels warm to the touch and very lightweight some people initially mistake real amber for plastic.
3. Like some plastics, amber becomes charged with static electricity when it is rubbed with a soft cloth.
4. Most true amber comes from the Baltic coast similar but softer resins of inferior value occur elsewhere in the world.
5. Baltic amber was highly prized in the ancient world archaeologists have found it in Bronze-Age excavations throughout the Mediterranean.

Exercise 3

Answers will vary.

1. The color of amber ranges from pale cream to deep reddish-brown; however, the most valuable amber is clear to translucent. [fused sentences corrected with semicolon and conjunctive adverb]
2. Amber feels warm to the touch and very lightweight. Some people initially mistake real amber for plastic. [fused sentences corrected with period]
3. [no fused sentences]
4. Most true amber comes from the Baltic coast; similar but softer resins of inferior value occur elsewhere in the world. [fused sentences corrected with semicolon]
5. Baltic amber was highly prized in the ancient world; archaeologists have found it in Bronze-Age excavations throughout the Mediterranean. [fused sentences corrected with semicolon]

6. Amber has been made into ornamental objects for centuries because it can be polished to a lustrous sheen.
7. Roman matrons wore amber amulets for protection from witchcraft even today, superstition continues to surround amber.
8. Many people believe it offers protection from bad luck modern Lithuanian brides still wear amber for this purpose.
9. Because amber is petrified tree sap, it sometimes contains fossilized insects experts find these preserved specimens fascinating.
10. Amber featured prominently in Steven Spielberg's film *Jurassic Park* the dinosaurs in the movie were brought to life through the preservative qualities of this fascinating fossil.

30e

6. [no fused sentences]
7. Roman matrons wore amber amulets for protection from witchcraft, and even today, superstition continues to surround amber. [fused sentences corrected with comma and coordinating conjunction]
8. Many people believe it offers protection from bad luck; modern Lithuanian brides, for example, still wear amber for this purpose. [fused sentences corrected with semicolon and transitional phrase]
9. Because amber is petrified tree sap, it sometimes contains fossilized insects. Experts find these preserved specimens fascinating. [fused sentences corrected with period]
10. Amber featured prominently in Steven Spielberg's film *Jurassic Park*; the dinosaurs in the movie were brought to life through the preservative qualities of this fascinating fossil. [fused sentences corrected with semicolon]

PART VII

Punctuation, Spelling, Mechanics

31

End Punctuation: Period, Question Mark, Exclamation Point

Punctuation is to writing what notation is to music: it allows the eye to re-create from the page the sounds that the author of the composition had in mind. Both are necessary and exacting systems. Just as musicians know the crucial difference between a quarter note and a half note, so writers know the crucial difference between a comma and a semicolon, between brackets and parentheses. The brief, moderate, or extended pauses noted by punctuation give cadence and rhythm to prose, but more important, they signal meaning. Only a person who understands punctuation knows how the drop in the voice signaled by the commas gives the following two sentences very different meanings.

> The students who have worked diligently and completed all the assignments on time will not have to take the final.
>
> The students, who have worked diligently and completed all the assignments on time, will not have to take the final.

If you have come to believe that correctly punctuating sentences is a mysterious art, this chapter and the five chapters that follow it may help to demystify punctuation for you. These chapters present, explain,

653

QUICK REFERENCE: *End Punctuation*

Period

Use only one period at the end of a declarative sentence, even if the sentence ends with an abbreviation or a quotation.

Incorrect	Rehearsal will begin promptly at 6:30 p.m..
Correct	Rehearsal will begin promptly at 6:30 p.m.
Incorrect	No one should say, "I didn't know what time to be here.".
Correct	No one should say, "I didn't know what time to be here."

Question mark

If an abbreviation ends a question, do not omit the last period before the question mark.

Incorrect	Is Dr. Marcus an M.D. or a Ph.D?
Correct	Is Dr. Marcus an M.D. or a Ph.D.?

But omit the period after a quoted sentence that ends a question.

Incorrect	Did you say, "I don't know."?
Correct	Did you say, "I don't know"?

Exclamation point

If an abbreviation ends an emphatic statement, do not omit the last period before the exclamation point.

Incorrect	You didn't tell me that the invitation said R.S.V.P!
Correct	You didn't tell me that the invitation said R.S.V.P.!

But omit the period after a quoted sentence that ends an emphatic statement.

Incorrect	Don't say, "Yes, I did."!
Correct	Don't say, "Yes, I did"!

For additional information about punctuating quotations, see **34b**.

31

and illustrate the rules that specify the main places where punctuation marks are needed, as well as some places where punctuation should be avoided.

First to be considered, then, are the three punctuation marks used at the ends of English sentences.

31a The period

Periods are used as end punctuation primarily in sentences that make a statement, but they may also end other kinds of sentences. In addition, periods are part of many abbreviations, and they have some special functions in quotation and dialogue.

1. Period after a declarative or mildly imperative sentence

Use a period after a sentence that makes a statement or issues a mild command.

A declarative sentence, like this one, ends with a period.

Don't forget to end a mild command with a period, too.

A period at the end of the sentence is never combined with another punctuation mark. For example, if a statement ends with an abbreviation that includes a period, a second period to end the sentence is not necessary.

Incorrect   Amtrak's *Crescent* leaves New Orleans every day at 7:25 A.M..

Correct   Amtrak's *Crescent* leaves New Orleans every day at 7:25 A.M.

Similarly, if a declarative sentence ends with a quotation, the final punctuation within the quotation marks suffices for the entire sentence.

31a

Incorrect   Michael looked at me oddly and said, "I never received your letter.".

Correct   Michael looked at me oddly and said, "I never received your letter."

Incorrect   I gasped, "What!".

Correct   I gasped, "What!"

For additional information about punctuating quotations, see **34b**.

2. Period after an indirect question or a polite request

Use a period, not a question mark, to end an indirect question, that is, a question that has been rephrased as a statement.

> I wonder how many people would know that this is an indirect question.

Similarly, use a period, not a question mark, to end a request that has been phrased as a question for the sake of politeness.

> Will you please remember to use a question mark only after a direct question, not after an indirect one.

3. Periods with abbreviations

Many abbreviations include or are followed by periods.

Mr.	D.V.M.	B.C.
Ms.	M.B.A.	etc.
Rev.	Ph.D.	Inc.

However, note that some abbreviations, like the U.S. Postal Service abbreviations for states, are not followed by periods: *IL, LA, NY, WA*. Many organizations and agencies, also, are represented by their initials without periods: *CBS, FAA, NAACP*. Finally, periods are not used with acronyms, abbreviations spoken as words: *DOS* (disk operating system), *ERIC* (Educational Resources Information Center), *SADD* (Students against Drunk Driving).

For additional information about abbreviations, see **38d**.

31a

4. Periods with ellipsis marks

Three periods—with spaces before, after, and between them—are called ellipsis marks; they are used to indicate the omission of a word or words from a quoted passage. If the omitted words come at the end of a sentence, the ellipsis marks follow the period that closes the sentence.

"I pledge allegiance to the flag . . . and to the Republic for which it stands. . . ."

For additional information about ellipsis marks, see **20c** and **36c**.

5. Periods in dialogue

Three (or at the end of a sentence, four) periods are sometimes used in writing dialogue to indicate hesitation and pauses.

"I've been around. Went to that Tom Petty concert at the . . . Forum. He sang that song, oh, you know, that song we always used to listen to. . . ." Julian closes his eyes and tries to remember the song.

—Bret Easton Ellis, *Less Than Zero*

31b The question mark

Question marks close questions and indicate doubtful information.

1. Question marks after direct questions or questions in a series

A direct question ends with a question mark.

Isn't this the kind of question that must end with a question mark?

Short questions in a series also end with question marks, whether or not they are complete sentences.

Shouldn't you use a question mark at the end of this question? And this one? And what about this one?

If a question ends with an abbreviation that includes a period, the question mark does not replace the period, but follows it.

Incorrect   Did the invitation say R.S.V.P?
Correct   Did the invitation say R.S.V.P.?

In other situations, though, a question mark is not combined with other punctuation marks. For example, if a question ends with a quoted declarative sentence, the period that would ordinarily end the sentence is omitted.

31b

Incorrect   Did you say, "I'm not going to the party."?

Correct   Did you say, "I'm not going to the party"?

For additional information about punctuating quotations, see **34b**.

2.   Question mark indicating doubtful information

You may use a question mark in parentheses to indicate that the information you provide in a sentence is of doubtful accuracy.

> Hippocrates, the renowned Greek physician for whom the Hippocratic oath is named, was born on the island of Cos in 460 (?) B.C.

However, don't use a question mark in parentheses to be sarcastic; find words to convey your feelings instead.

Avoid   The prize I won in the drawing was a lovely (?) landscape painted on black velvet.

Better   The prize I won in the drawing was a tacky landscape painted on black velvet.

31c The exclamation point

An exclamation point is appropriate only after statements, commands, or interjections that would be given unusual emphasis if spoken.

I will *not* go to this party with your cousin!

Don't try to make me!

No!

If an emphatic statement ends with an abbreviation that contains a period, the exclamation point does not replace the period, but follows it.

Incorrect   I refuse to leave for the party before nine P.M!

Correct   I refuse to leave for the party before nine P.M.!

In other situations, though, an exclamation point is not combined with a period. For example, if an emphatic statement ends with a quoted

31c

declarative sentence, the period that would ordinarily end the sentence is omitted.

> **Incorrect**   All right! I said, "I'll go."!
> **Correct**   All right! I said, "I'll go"!

For additional information about punctuating quotations, see **34b**.

Use exclamation points sparingly, and never use them in parentheses for an attempt at irony.

> **Avoid**   Your cousin's personality is just a little (!) bland.
> **Better**   Your cousin has the personality of a potato.

EXERCISE 1

Provide appropriate end punctuation where needed in the sentences below.

Example

Have you ever wondered about the man behind the legend of Pancho Villa

> **Punctuated**   Have you ever wondered about the man behind the legend of Pancho Villa?

1. A hero of the Mexican Revolution, Francisco Villa (1878–1923) has sometimes been referred to by American historians as "the Border Bandit"
2. Self-educated, Villa represented himself as a champion of Mexican peasants, but he was a sophisticated media manager
3. Did you know that his battles were recorded by early newsreel films that are now stored in the Smithsonian Institution in Washington, D.C.
4. Villa's campaign against the government of the corrupt Mexican president Porfirio Diaz in 1910–11 was covered by the journalist John Reed, most famous for his book *Ten Days That Shook the World,* an account of the birth of the U.S.S.R.
5. When Villa rode into Chihuahua City to receive a medal for personal heroism, the people filled the air with cries of "Villa, the friend of the poor"
6. Why, then, has Villa had an ambiguous reputation in the United States

31c

Exercise 1

1. A hero of the Mexican Revolution, Francisco Villa (1878–1923) has sometimes been referred to by American historians as "the Border Bandit."
2. Self-educated, Villa represented himself as a champion of Mexican peasants, but he was a sophisticated media manager.
3. Did you know that his battles were recorded by early newsreel films that are now stored in the Smithsonian Institution in Washington, D.C.?
4. [no additional end punctuation needed]
5. When Villa rode into Chihuahua City to receive a medal for personal heroism, the people filled the air with cries of "Villa, the friend of the poor!"
6. Why, then, has Villa had an ambiguous reputation in the United States?

7. The answer lies at least partly in lingering memories of his 1916 raid on Columbus, New Mexico

8. Villa's troops were retaliating for the earlier shooting of bandits in Chihuahua by a group of Americans

9. A prominent attorney living today in El Paso, Texas, recalls, "He killed a lot of people, including my great uncle, but then, my uncle had sold him wooden bullets"

10. Villa was assassinated in 1923, but Mexican art, legend, and literature preserve his memory

31c

7. The answer lies at least partly in lingering memories of his 1916 raid on Columbus, New Mexico.

8. Villa's troops were retaliating for the earlier shooting of bandits in Chihuahua by a group of Americans.

9. A prominent attorney living today in El Paso, Texas, recalls, "He killed a lot of people, including my great uncle, but then, my uncle had sold him wooden bullets."

10. Villa was assassinated in 1923, but Mexican art, legend, and literature preserve his memory.

32 Comma

The comma is perhaps the most used and, consequently, the most abused punctuation mark. It separates coordinate elements within a sentence and sets off certain subordinate constructions from the rest of the sentence. But because it represents the shortest breath pause and the least emphatic break, it cannot separate two complete sentences.

A primary function of the comma is to make a sentence clear. Use commas whenever necessary to prevent misreading—to separate words that might be erroneously grouped together by the reader.

32a Comma with coordinating conjunction between independent clauses

Two independent clauses linked by a coordinating conjunction (*and, but, for, nor, or, so, yet*) should be separated by a comma. Note that the comma is always placed *before* the conjunction.

32a

Incorrect	I failed German in my senior year of high school and, it took me a long time to regain any interest in foreign languages.
Incorrect	I went through the motions of studying but, my mind was elsewhere.
Correct	I failed German in my senior year of high school, *and* it took me a long time to regain any interest in foreign languages.
Correct	I went through the motions of studying, *but* my mind was elsewhere.

QUICK REFERENCE: *Major Uses of the Comma*

Use a comma between independent clauses linked by a coordinating conjunction.

> **Example**   I saw this antique oak desk at a garage sale, *and* I knew I had to own it.

Use a comma to set off an introductory element.

> **Example**   *When I learned the price of this desk,* I realized that I could afford it.

Use commas to separate elements in a series.

> **Example**   The *sides, drawers,* and *feet* of the desk feature hand-carved details.

Use a comma to separate coordinate modifiers.

> **Example**   The *clear, smooth* finish of the desk's top is particularly attractive.

Use commas to set off a nonrestrictive modifier.

> **Example**   Desks like this one, *which is constructed of solid oak,* have not been made for decades.

Use commas to set off a parenthetic element.

> **Example**   This desk, *in my opinion,* is worth far more than I paid for it.

Very short independent clauses need not be separated by a comma if they are closely connected in meaning.

32a   **Comma omitted between short independent clauses**

> The bell rang and everyone left.

When the independent clauses of a compound sentence are long and are also subdivided by commas, a semicolon rather than a comma may be used with the coordinating conjunction to show the main division of the sentence more clearly.

Semicolon in place of comma for clarity

For purposes of discussion, we will recognize two main varieties of English, Standard and Nonstandard; and we will divide the first type into Formal, Informal, and Colloquial English.

32b Comma to set off an introductory element

An introductory element is a clause or phrase that precedes the subject of the sentence. An introductory dependent clause is almost always set off from the sentence with a comma.

Dependent clause

Whenever I read about the nineteenth century, I am struck by the sufferings of the poor.

An introductory verbal phrase (participial, gerund, or infinitive) is also usually followed by a comma.

Participial phrase

Suffering from disease, overcrowding, and poverty, the people of Manchester were prime victims of the early Industrial Revolution in England.

Gerund phrase

After seeing the poverty and unfair treatment of the working-class people, Elizabeth Gaskell wrote several protest novels.

Infinitive phrase

To appreciate Gaskell's sympathy for the urban poor, one should read her novel *Mary Barton*.

32b

A short prepositional phrase at the beginning of a sentence is usually not set off by a comma, but a long introductory prepositional phrase or a series of prepositional phrases is often followed by a comma for clarity.

Short prepositional phrase (no comma)

On Tuesday I started reading Gaskell's novel.

Long prepositional phrase

Despite many interruptions during the following days, I reached the book's dramatic courtroom scene by Friday.

A conjunctive adverb or transitional phrase (see **11b**) at the beginning of a sentence is also set off with a comma.

Conjunctive adverb

Still, Dickens's novels about the condition of the Victorian working class remain my favorites.

Transitional phrase

For example, his short novel *Hard Times* brilliantly attacks the hypocrisy of wealthy factory owners.

32c Commas to separate elements in a series

Separate words, phrases, or clauses in a series by commas. However, if *all* the elements of a series are joined by coordinating conjunctions (*a and b and c*), no commas are necessary to separate them.

Series of nouns

Books, papers, and *photographs* were strewn about the room.

Series of adjectives

The shy devilfish blushes in *blue, red, green,* or *brown*.

Series of prepositional phrases

Water flooded *over the riverbanks, across the asphalt road,* and *into the basements* of nearby homes.

Series of verbal phrases

Running a mile or two, swimming laps, and *playing tennis* are all excellent ways to improve one's aerobic conditioning.

Series of predicates

The bear *jumped away from the garbage can, snarled at the camper,* and *raced up the tree.*

Series of dependent clauses

If you feel faint, if your vision becomes blurred, or *if you have difficulty breathing,* then discontinue this medication.

Series of independent clauses

Greek revival architecture swept through this country from 1820 until about 1860, the Italianate style was popular well into the 1870s, and *the Romanesque revival dominated the last decades of the century.*

The comma before the last item in a series is omitted by some writers, but its use is generally preferred because it can prevent misreading.

Misleading	Congress is about to consider legislation dealing with international trade, changes in taxation rates, funding for health care and gun control. [Without a final comma, the sentence seems to say that Congress will consider funding for gun control. No such misreading occurs if the comma is included.]
Clearer	Congress is about to consider legislation dealing with international trade, changes in taxation rates, funding for health care, *and* gun control.

32d Commas with coordinate modifiers

Adjectives modifying the same noun should be separated by commas if they are coordinate in meaning. Coordinate adjectives are those that could be joined by *and* without distorting the meaning of a sentence.

Bus lines provide *inexpensive, efficient* transportation.
[The adjectives are coordinate because one could speak of transportation that is inexpensive *and* efficient.]

When one adjective is so closely linked with a noun that it is thought of as part of the noun, it is not coordinate with a preceding adjective. No comma is used between such adjectives.

The Paynes bought a *spacious summer* cabin.
[One could not speak of a spacious *and* summer cabin. The adjectives are not coordinate.]

Note that numbers are not coordinate with other adjectives and are not separated by commas.

They screened in *two large, airy* outdoor porches.
[*Two* and *large* should not be separated by a comma. But because one could describe the porches as large *and* airy, a comma is used to separate these two coordinate adjectives.]

32e Commas to set off a nonrestrictive modifier

A dependent clause, participial phrase, or appositive is **nonrestrictive** when it can be omitted without changing the main idea of the sentence. Providing additional but not essential information about the noun to which it refers, a nonrestrictive modifier is always set off by commas. In contrast, a **restrictive** modifier provides essential information about the word it modifies. It cannot be omitted without changing the main idea of the sentence, and it is never set off by commas.

1.   Nonrestrictive clauses

Two commas are required to set off a nonrestrictive clause in the middle of a sentence, one comma if the clause occurs at the end of the sentence.

nonrestrictive clause
My faculty adviser, *who had to sign the program card*, was hard to find.
[The clause is not required to identify the adviser in question. It

could be omitted without changing the point of the sentence—
that the writer's adviser was hard to find.]

restrictive clause

Faculty advisers *who are never in their offices* make registration
difficult.
[In contrast, omitting the clause in this case would entirely
change the sense of the sentence, for the clause specifies that
only certain advisers—those who are never in their offices—
are being discussed.]

Notice how the meaning of a sentence may be altered by the addition
or the omission of commas.

nonrestrictive clause

The board sent questionnaires to all members, *who are on Social
Security.*
[The sentence implies that all members are on Social Security.]

restrictive clause

The board sent questionnaires to all members *who are on Social
Security.*
[Only some members are on Social Security, and only they
received the questionnaire.]

In relative clauses beginning with *which* or *that, which* is used in nonrestrictive clauses (with commas), *that* in restrictive clauses (without
commas).

nonrestrictive clause

I found the letter under the door, *which had been locked.*

restrictive clause

The letter *that I found under the door* was a mystery.

Punctuating Nonrestrictive and Restrictive Clauses

.32e

Type of clause	Essential information?	Use commas?	Use *that* or *which*?
Nonrestrictive	No	Yes	*which*
Restrictive	Yes	No	*that*

2. Nonrestrictive participial phrases

Like clauses, participial phrases may be nonrestrictive or restrictive. The former are set off by commas; the latter are not.

nonrestrictive phrase

Uncle Sid's letter, *lying unclaimed in the dead-letter office,* contained the missing document.
[The participial phrase is not needed to identify the letter in question.]

restrictive phrase

We have had many complaints about letters *undelivered because of careless addressing.*
[The participial phrase is needed to specify which letters have generated complaints.]

3. Nonrestrictive appositives

An appositive—a word or phrase placed next to a noun to further identify it—may also be nonrestrictive or restrictive. Use commas with nonrestrictive appositives only.

nonrestrictive appositive

Reaching absolute zero, *273.15 degrees below zero Celsius,* is one goal of scientists working in cryogenics.
[The appositive explains the noun that precedes it—absolute zero—but is not essential to the meaning of the sentence.]

restrictive appositive

The noun *cryogenics* comes from a Greek word meaning "icy cold."
[Which noun is the writer discussing? The sentence would be meaningless without the appositive.]

Note that including or omitting commas with an appositive significantly changes the meaning of a sentence.

nonrestrictive appositive

My roommate's pet snake, *Slither,* has been missing from its cage for a week.
[Since the appositive is nonrestrictive and hence not essential

to the meaning of the sentence, the sentence implies that the
roommate has only one pet snake—the missing one.]

restrictive appositive

My roommate's pet snake *Slither* has been missing from its cage for
a week.
[A restrictive appositive indicates the need to specify which
snake is missing and hence implies that there is more than one
snake in the roommate's collection.]

An appositive used to define a word is often introduced by the conjunction *or*. Such appositives are always set off by commas to distinguish them from the common construction in which *or* joins two coordinate nouns.

appositive

The class found a speciment of pyrite, or *fool's gold*.

coordinate nouns

Was the specimen *pyrite* or *genuine gold*?

An abbreviated title or degree (for example, *K.C.B., USMC, M.D.,
Ph.D.*) is punctuated as a nonrestrictive appositive when it follows a
proper name.

He was introduced as Robert Harrison, *LL.D.*, and he added that
he also held a Ph.D. from Cornell.

32f Commas to set off a parenthetic element

Parenthetic is a general term describing explanatory words and
phrases that interrupt the normal sentence pattern to supply additional,
but not essential, information. Parenthetic elements are usually set off
by commas, though they may also be set off by dashes or parentheses
(see **35a** and **35b**). In the widest sense of the term, parenthetic elements
include the nonrestrictive modifiers discussed above. Any other sentence element may also become parenthetic if it is removed from its
regular place in the sentence and inserted so that it interrupts the sentence's normal order—for instance, by falling in between the subject
and verb.

32f

Notice in the following case how adjectives are moved from their normal position before the noun they modify to become parenthetic elements that must be set off by commas.

Adjectives in normal position

Two *tired and hungry* boys wandered into camp.

Adjectives as parenthetic element

Two boys, *tired and hungry*, wandered into camp.

In the same way, the parenthetic elements in the following sentences must be set off by commas.

Prepositional phrase as parenthetic element

Placing a powerful telescope in orbit may, *in the opinion of some astronomers*, radically change our conception of the galaxy.

Clause as parenthetic element

Space research, *I am convinced*, should remain one of this nation's highest priorities.

Conjunctive adverbs (such as *consequently, furthermore, however, moreover, nonetheless,* and *therefore*) and transitional phrases like *as a result, for example,* and *on the other hand* frequently function as parenthetic elements and are set off with two commas when they occur in the middle of a sentence and with a single comma when they appear at the end.

Conjunctive adverb as parenthetic element

Beef should be bright red and marbled with pure white fat. Packaged meat may appear fresher than it is because of tinted lighting in a supermarket, *however*.

Transitional phrase as parenthetic element

Shoppers should, *as a result*, take care to examine meat packages carefully.

32g Commas to set off an absolute phrase

An absolute phrase typically consists of a noun and a participle or adjective (see **25f**). It is not grammatically part of the sentence in which it appears and is set off with commas.

The hurricane having passed, workers began to clear trees and debris from the roads.

Residents of the town, *their faces sorrowful*, slowly returned to their damaged homes.

32h Commas in comparative and contrastive constructions

Commas are used to separate some idiomatic coordinate constructions involving a comparison of adjectives or adverbs. Such constructions include the formulas *the more . . . , the more . . .* and *the more . . . , the less. . . .*

The older the tree, *the weaker* its resistance to disease.

The more I study forestry, *the less* I understand what role human beings should play in forest management.

Coordinate words or phrases that are contrasted are also separated by a comma.

We are *a contentious group*, not *a belligerent one.*

Our aim is to encourage *question and debate*, not *criticism and personal attacks.*

32i Commas with interjections, direct address, and tag questions

32i

Interjections and nouns used as terms of direct address are set off by commas.

Oh, is it my turn to talk?

Yes, I am prepared to address the assembly.

Exercise 1 (page 675)

1. My friend Theodore, who lives in Brooklyn, knows better. [Nonrestrictive relative clause. The clause could be restrictive only if the writer had two friends named Theodore, one of whom did not live in Brooklyn.]
2. Theodore, who is in his late twenties, never finished high school. [Nonrestrictive relative clause.]
3. He was one of those students who find school frustrating because of undiagnosed learning disabilities. [Restrictive relative clause identifying the specific students in question.]
4. His friends who graduated got jobs or went on to college. [Restrictive relative clause, distinguishing the friends in question from those who did not graduate. The clause would be nonrestrictive only if all of Theodore's friends graduated from high school.]
5. But Theodore's reading ability, which is at the third-grade level, makes it difficult for him to find a job that is worthwhile. [The first relative

Ms. Kuhn, may I speak frankly?

This absurd budget proposal, *ladies and gentlemen,* raises questions about the school board's competence.

An elliptical question, or tag question, attached to the end of a related statement is set off by a comma.

You can't defend this proposal, *can you?*

32j Commas with dates, addresses, place names, and numbers

If only one element in a date (month and day, or month and year), place name, or address (number and street) appears in a sentence, no comma is required.

April 4 is Sandy's birthday.

She has lived in Bloomington since June 1989.

She recently bought the house at 15 Center Street.

But multiple elements in dates, place names, and addresses are set off by commas. (Exception: no comma appears between the state and the ZIP code in an address.)

Sandy was born on *Monday, April 4, 1960,* in *Scranton, Pennsylvania.*

She has lived in *Bloomington, Indiana,* for several years.

Her new address is *15 Center Street, Bloomington, Indiana 47401.*

A comma is not included when a date is written in inverted style: *7 December 1941.*

Commas are used to divide numbers of more than four digits into groups of three in order to designate thousands, millions, billions, and so on.

About *110,000* people live in Tempe, Arizona.

It's part of the Phoenix metropolitan area, whose population exceeds *1,500,000.*

Four-digit numbers may include commas as well.

There are *5,280* feet in a mile.

clause is nonrestrictive, supplying incidental rather than essential information about Theodore's reading ability. The second relative clause is restrictive; it specifies a particular kind of job.]

6. Theodore lives at home with his mother and sister, who work in Manhattan. [The relative clause in this sentence could be restrictive only if Theodore had more than one mother and sister.]

7. He rarely sees his old high-school friends who are working during the day. [The relative clause in this sentence could be restrictive or nonrestrictive, depending on the writer's intended meaning. If restrictive, as here, it indicates that there are other high-school friends whom Theodore does see regularly—specifically, those who are not working during the day. If the clause is punctuated as nonrestrictive, then the sentence would say that all of Theodore's old high-school friends work during the day.]

8. But Theodore has now enrolled in a literacy education program, which operates out of his local public library. [The context suggests that the

But do not use commas in numbers referring to pages, years, or addresses.

> On page 2522 of my almanac is a calendar for all the years from
> 1801 to the present.

32k Commas with direct quotations

The words used to identify the speaker of a quotation—such as *he said, she asked, they exclaimed*—are set off by commas when used with a direct quotation.

> "When I was in Africa," *Brad said*, "I learned a great deal about the plight of elephants."
> "The poaching of elephants for their tusks is decimating herds," *he explained.*

But do not use a comma at the end of a quotation that is already punctuated with a question mark or exclamation point.

> "Does anyone really need ivory jewelry?" Brad asked.

When the quotation contains two independent clauses, use a semicolon after the words identifying the speaker when they occur between the clauses, in order to avoid a comma splice or a fused sentence.

> "The future of African elephants depends on the world outside Africa," *Brad pointed out*; "we have to insure that the market for ivory trinkets disappears."

Do not use a comma in an indirect quotation.

> Brad said that most countries have now banned the importation of ivory.

For additional rules regarding the punctuation of direct quotations, see **34b**.

321

32l Commas to prevent misreading

Use a comma whenever necessary to prevent accidental misreading. For the sake of clarity, even an introductory element consisting of only a single word or two may need to be set off from the sentence by a comma.

relative clause is describing rather than specifying the literacy program; hence, it is nonrestrictive.]
9. Already the progress that he has made is remarkable. [This sentence makes no sense without the restrictive relative clause. What progress are we talking about?]
10. Theodore's first goal, which is to obtain a driver's license, now seems within reach. [A person can have only one "first" goal; the nonrestrictive relative clause does not distinguish among goals but simply describes the goal in question.]

Confusing	Ever since he has devoted himself to athletics.
Clear	*Ever since*, he has devoted himself to athletics.
Confusing	Inside the house was brightly lighted.
Clear	*Inside*, the house was brightly lighted.
Confusing	Soon after the minister entered the chapel.
Clear	*Soon after*, the minister entered the chapel.
Confusing	To elaborate the art of flower arranging begins with simplicity.
Clear	*To elaborate*, the art of flower arranging begins with simplicity.

32m Misuse of the comma

Since modern practice is to use less rather than more punctuation in expository and narrative prose, a good working rule for beginning writers is to use no commas except for those required by the preceding conventions. Be especially careful to avoid the incorrect use of commas illustrated below.

Comma erroneously separates subject and verb

Ted's ability to solve the most complicated problems on the spur of the moment, never failed to impress his co-workers.

Comma erroneously precedes first element of a series

For lunch I usually have, a sandwich, some fruit, and milk.

Comma erroneously follows last element in a series

New Jersey, Rhode Island, and Massachusetts, were the most densely populated states as of the last census.

Comma erroneously divides indirect quotation

During chapel the minister announced, that the choir would sing Handel's *Messiah* for Easter.

Exercise 2 (page 675)

1. Though I wasn't much of a musician, I could at least march in step, and that put me ahead of most of the others. [32b, comma to set off introductory element; 32a, comma with coordinating conjunction between independent clauses]
2. My high-school marching band was, to tell the truth, among the worst in the state of Pennsylvania. [32f, commas to set off parenthetic element]
3. Our football team sometimes reached the regional semifinals, but our band never enjoyed such success. [32a, comma with coordinating conjunction between independent clauses]
4. I still remember our morning practice sessions, which were held in a playground near a doughnut factory. [32e, comma to set off nonrestrictive relative clause]
5. We had to report at seven o'clock each morning, a full ninety minutes before the school day began. [32e, comma to set off nonrestrictive appositive]

Comma erroneously splits idiomatic construction

Joy is so tall, that she may well break the school's record for rebounds.

EXERCISE 1

In the following sentences, insert commas where they are needed to set off nonrestrictive modifiers, or change *which* to *that*. In doubtful cases, explain the two possible meanings of the sentence.

Example

> Many people who have never been to the United States think of it as a country of luxury and ease for all.

> **Analysis**   No commas needed. The clause *who have never been to the United States* is a restrictive modifier, required to indicate which people are being discussed.

1. My friend Theodore who lives in Brooklyn knows better.
2. Theodore who is in his late twenties never finished high school.
3. He was one of those students who find school frustrating because of undiagnosed learning disabilities.
4. His friends who graduated got jobs or went on to college.
5. But Theodore's reading ability which is at the third-grade level makes it difficult for him to find a job which is worthwhile.
6. Theodore lives at home with his mother and sister who work in Manhattan.
7. He rarely sees his old high-school friends who are working during the day.
8. But Theodore has now enrolled in a literacy education program which operates out of his local public library.
9. Already the progress which he has made is remarkable.
10. Theodore's first goal which is to obtain a driver's license now seems within reach.

32m

EXERCISE 2

Add commas where they are needed in the following sentences, and be prepared to justify your punctuation according to the rules discussed in this chapter.

6. The weather was bitter, the field was frozen, and the instruments were icy, but somehow the smell of doughnuts baking across the street made the long, tedious practice sessions bearable. [32c, two commas to separate clauses in a series; 32a, comma with coordinating conjunction between independent clauses; 32d, comma with coordinate modifiers]
7. Everyone having arrived, Mr. Bell, our band director, would sketch out the marching routine we were to learn. [32g, comma to set off absolute phrase; 32e, commas to set off nonrestrictive appositive]
8. His explanations, of course, could just as well have been delivered to us in Greek. [32f, commas to set off parenthetic element]
9. Marching in step was difficult enough for most members of the band, but simultaneously marching, playing music, and avoiding holes in the uneven field usually proved impossible. [32a, comma with coordinating conjunction between independent clauses; 32c, commas to separate gerunds in a series]
10. We were terrible, not just bad, and everybody knew it. [32h, comma with contrastive construction; 32a, comma with coordinating conjunction between independent clauses]

Example

> I have some fond memories of high school but playing the cornet in my high-school marching band is not one of them.

> **Punctuated**   I have some fond memories of high school, but playing the cornet in my high-school marching band is not one of them. [32a, comma with coordinating conjunction between independent clauses]

1. Though I wasn't much of a musician I could at least march in step and that put me ahead of most of the others.
2. My high-school marching band was to tell the truth among the worst in the state of Pennsylvania.
3. Our football team sometimes reached the regional semifinals but our band never enjoyed such success.
4. I still remember our morning practice sessions which were held in a playground near a doughnut factory.
5. We had to report at seven o'clock each morning a full ninety minutes before the school day began.
6. The weather was bitter the field was frozen and the instruments were icy but somehow the smell of doughnuts baking across the street made the long tedious practice sessions bearable.
7. Everyone having arrived Mr. Bell our band director would sketch out the marching routine we were to learn.
8. His explanations of course could just as well have been delivered to us in Greek.
9. Marching in step was difficult enough for most members of the band but simultaneously marching playing music and avoiding holes in the uneven field usually proved impossible.
10. We were terrible not just bad and everyone knew it.
11. Mr. Bell's philosophy however was "the more you practice the better you become."
12. Well that wasn't quite true in our case.
13. On one particularly memorable occasion we were practicing a routine that required the sousaphone players to bow to the audience at the end of the song.
14. Having done the routine over and over for nearly an hour the sousaphonists were becoming tired and dizzy for the instrument is heavy.
15. Mr. Bell frustrated and tired himself asked us to try the routine one final time.
16. Across the field we marched a sousaphone leading each column.

32m

11. Mr. Bell's philosophy, however, was "the more you practice, the better you become." [32f, commas to set off parenthetic element; 32h, comma with comparative construction]
12. Well, that wasn't quite true in our case. [32i, comma with interjection]
13. On one particularly memorable occasion, we were practicing a routine that required the sousaphone players to bow to the audience at the end of the song. [32b, comma to set off introductory element]
14. Having done the routine over and over for nearly an hour, the sousaphonists were becoming tired and dizzy, for the instrument is heavy. [32b, comma to set off introductory element; 32a, comma with coordinating conjunction between independent clauses]
15. Mr. Bell, frustrated and tired himself, asked us to try the routine one final time. [32f, commas to set off parenthetic element]
16. Across the field we marched, a sousaphone leading each column. [32g, comma to set off absolute phrase]
17. The music ended, and the time came for the sousaphonists to bow. [32a, comma with coordinating conjunction between independent clauses]

17. The music ended and the time came for the sousaphonists to bow.
18. Exhausted they all toppled over in different directions.
19. One tipped sideways and landed on Mr. Bell another went face first into the ground and a third fell backward into the startled woodwind section.
20. After a long cold morning on the drill field the marching routine was no better than it had been when we started and now six people were injured.

32m

18. Exhausted, they all toppled over in different directions. [32b, comma to set off introductory element]
19. One tipped sideways and landed on Mr. Bell, another went face first into the ground, and a third fell backward into the startled woodwind section. [32c, commas to separate independent clauses in a series]
20. After a long, cold morning on the drill field, the marching routine was no better than it had been when we started, and now six people were injured. [32d, comma with coordinate modifiers; 32b, comma to set off introductory element; 32a, comma with coordinating conjunction between independent clauses]

Semicolon and Colon

Although they sound and look similar, semicolons and colons function differently. A stronger mark of punctuation than the comma, a semicolon can be used without a conjunction to link independent clauses. A colon also creates a substantial break in a sentence, but, unlike the semicolon, it always indicates a specific relationship between the parts of a sentence that precede and follow it.

33a The semicolon

The semicolon indicates a greater break in a sentence than the comma does, but it does not have the finality of a period.

1. Semicolon to connect independent clauses not linked by a coordinating conjunction

When the independent clauses of a compound sentence are not joined by a coordinating conjunction, a semicolon is required. Use a semicolon in place of a comma and coordinating conjunction when the relationship between two clauses is so clear that it does not need to be stated explicitly.

> I'm not saying that these stories are untrue; I'm just a bit doubtful about your source.
>
> You trust Terry; I don't.

A semicolon used in this way must be preceded *and* followed by an independent clause. If it is not, a sentence fragment results (see **30a**).

Fragment   I'm not saying these stories are untrue; *just doubtful, perhaps.*

33a

QUICK REFERENCE: *Semicolon and Colon*

Semicolon

Use a semicolon to connect independent clauses that are not linked by a coordinating conjunction (*and, but, for, nor, or, so, yet*).

Example	Your argument is convincing; however, your statistics are inaccurate.

Make sure that you have a complete sentence on both sides of a semicolon; otherwise, a sentence fragment results.

Fragment	I'm not disputing your argument; *just your statistics.*
Correct	I'm not disputing your argument; I'm only questioning your statistics.

Colon

Use a colon to introduce a list, quotation, or explanatory statement.

List	There's an old saying that a wise real estate investment depends on three factors: location, location, and location.
Quotation	My father used to say one thing about real estate: "Consider the location of the property first."
Explanatory statement	This house meets my primary criterion for a sound real estate investment: its location is outstanding.

A semicolon is also necessary when two independent clauses are linked by a conjunctive adverb such as *consequently, however, moreover, nonetheless, then,* or *therefore.* A comma used with a conjunctive adverb creates a comma splice (see **30c**).

> Our plan was to sail from Naples to New York; *however,* an emergency at home forced us to fly back instead.

We were understandably tense on the flight back; *moreover,* when we landed, we learned that our bags were lost.

Note that in these cases, the conjunctive adverb functions as an introductory element in the second clause and is therefore appropriately followed by a comma (see **32b**).

2. Semicolon to separate independent clauses with internal punctuation

When two independent clauses with internal punctuation are joined by a coordinating conjunction and a comma, the dividing point between the clauses may at first be difficult to perceive. In such a case, a semicolon instead of a comma may be used with the coordinating conjunction to show the main division of the sentence more clearly.

Confusing In recognition of her years of service, the principal received a farewell dinner, a framed picture of the student body and the faculty, and a compact edition of the *Oxford English Dictionary,* and later the library in the elementary school, after considerable discussion by the school board, was named for her.
[The list of gifts for the principal at first seems to include the elementary-school library.]

Clearer In recognition of her years of service, the principal received a farewell dinner, a framed picture of the student body and the faculty, and a compact edition of the *Oxford English Dictionary*; and later the library in the elementary school, after considerable discussion by the school board, was named for her.

3. Semicolon to separate elements in a series

When elements in a series contain internal commas, a comma is not a strong enough mark of punctuation to separate those elements clearly. In this case, use semicolons instead.

Confusing The parents' day discussion was led by Mr. Joseph, the chaplain, Ms. Smith, a French instructor, the dean, and his assistant.
[How many people in all participated?]

Clearer   The parents' day discussion was led by Mr. Joseph, the chaplain; Ms. Smith, a French instructor; the dean; and his assistant.

Do not use a semicolon to *introduce* a list or series; the proper punctuation for that purpose is a colon or dash.

Incorrect   The guest list included the following distinguished citizens; the mayor and her husband, the members of the city council, and the president of the school board.

Correct   The guest list included the following distinguished citizens: the mayor and her husband, the members of the city council, and the president of the school board.

EXERCISE 1

Some of the following sentences are correct. In the others, insert semicolons where they should appear.

Example

In 1871, Chicago was the nation's railroad, livestock, and grain center, then the great fire erupted.

Punctuated   In 1871, Chicago was the nation's railroad, livestock, and grain center; then the great fire erupted. [semicolon connects independent clauses not linked by a coordinating conjunction]

1. Only forty years earlier, Chicago's population had been barely 100, now it was more than 300,000.
2. After the fire had finally burned itself out, four square miles of the city lay devastated, moreover, 100,000 people were homeless.
3. The city's stone water tower survived unscathed, rising above the devastation, it became a symbol of the people's will to rebuild.
4. The rubble from the fire was plowed into Lake Michigan, on top of it today sits beautiful Grant Park.
5. Rebuilding the city was complicated by the fact that the fire had destroyed deeds and other key documents, therefore, it was difficult at first to determine who rightfully owned the burned-out but still-valuable land.

33a

Exercise 1

1. Only forty years earlier, Chicago's population had been barely 100; now it was more than 300,000.
2. After the fire had finally burned itself out, four square miles of the city lay devastated; moreover, 100,000 people were homeless.
3. The city's stone water tower survived unscathed; rising above the devastation, it became a symbol of the people's will to rebuild.
4. The rubble from the fire was plowed into Lake Michigan; on top of it today sits beautiful Grant Park.
5. Rebuilding the city was complicated by the fact that the fire had destroyed deeds and other key documents; therefore, it was difficult at first to determine who rightfully owned the burned-out but still-valuable land.
6. [correct as it stands]
7. Among the technological innovations that affected the new buildings erected in Chicago after the fire were elevators, which had been introduced in the 1860s; new, stronger foundations, which could support

6. The city council acted swiftly, if belatedly, to ban frame buildings in the downtown area, and as a result architects streamed into Chicago to help design the new city.
7. Among the technological innovations that affected the new buildings erected in Chicago after the fire were elevators, which had been introduced in the 1860s, new, stronger foundations, which could support taller, heavier buildings, and the skeletal frame, which made the modern skyscraper possible.
8. By the 1890s, Chicago was home to the tallest office buildings in the world, rising sixteen, even seventeen, stories above street level.
9. During this decade the word *skyscraper* was applied to buildings for the first time, previously it had referred only to ships' sails, big horses, and tall tales.
10. Many of Chicago's famous early skyscrapers remain in use as desirable office buildings, others have been converted into chic apartments and condominiums.

33b The colon

Unlike the semicolon, which makes a reader pause in the middle of a sentence, a colon urges a reader to continue by suggesting a relationship between the information that precedes and follows it.

1. Colon to introduce a list, quotation, or explanation

The colon is used primarily to introduce a formal enumeration or list, a quotation, or an explanatory statement.

> Consider these three viewpoints: political, economic, and social.
>
> Tocqueville expresses one view: "In the United States we easily perceive how the legal profession is qualified by its attributes . . . to neutralize the vices inherent in popular government. . . ."
>
> I remember which way to move the clock when changing from Daylight Savings Time to Standard Time by applying a simple rule: spring ahead, fall backward.

Note that a list introduced by a colon should be in apposition to a preceding word; that is, the sentence preceding the colon should be grammatically complete without the list.

taller, heavier buildings; and the skeletal frame, which made the modern skyscraper possible.
8. [correct as it stands]
9. During this decade the word *skyscraper* was applied to buildings for the first time; previously it had referred only to ships' sails, big horses, and tall tales.
10. Many of Chicago's famous early skyscrapers remain in use as desirable office buildings; others have been converted into chic apartments and condominiums.

Incorrect	We provide: fishing permit, rod, hooks, bait, lunch, boat, and oars.
Correct	We provide the following items: fishing permit, rod, hooks, bait, lunch, boat, and oars.
Correct	We provide the following: fishing permit, rod, hooks, bait, lunch, boat, and oars.
Correct	The following items are provided: fishing permit, rod, hooks, bait, lunch, boat, and oars.

2. Colon between independent clauses

The colon may be used between two independent clauses when the second clause explains or develops the first.

Intercollegiate athletics continues to be big business, but Robert Hutchins long ago pointed out a simple remedy: colleges should stop charging admission to football games.

3. Other uses of the colon

A colon is used after a formal salutation in a business letter.

Dear Sir or Madam: Dear Mr. Harris: Ladies and Gentlemen:

A colon is used to separate hour and minutes in numerals indicating time.

The train leaves at 9:27 A.M. and arrives at Joplin at 8:15 P.M.

It also separates the title and subtitle of a book.

Winifred Gérin's *Charlotte Brontë: The Evolution of Genius*

The Kings and Queens of England: A Tourist Guide, by Jane Murray

In bibliographical references, a colon is used between the place of publication and the name of the publisher.

New York: Oxford UP

Finally, a colon is often used to separate chapter and verse in a biblical citation.

Proverbs 28:20

33b

EXERCISE **2**

Insert colons where they are needed in the following sentences.

Example

Performance is essential to dance education the stage teaches lessons that the classroom can't duplicate.

> **Punctuated**   Performance is essential to dance education: the stage teaches lessons that the classroom can't duplicate. [second clause explains the first]

1. Please pay special attention to two points in the following memo required costumes and rehearsal time.
2. Technical rehearsal week demands total cooperation the cast and crew must work together for the first time as a coordinated unit.
3. If you are new to recitals, you will find it helpful to read *Best Foot Forward A Dancer's Guide to Audition and Performance.*
4. All dancers must appear in identical apparel black unitards, red tunics, and black jazz boots.
5. The orchestra rehearsal will run precisely from 630 P.M. to 945 P.M.

Exercise 2

1. Please pay special attention to two points in the following memo: required costumes and rehearsal time. [colon introduces list]
2. Technical rehearsal week demands total cooperation: the cast and crew must work together for the first time as a coordinated unit. [second clause explains first]
3. If you are new to recitals, you will find it helpful to read *Best Foot Forward: A Dancer's Guide to Audition and Performance.* [colon between title and subtitle]
4. All dancers must appear in identical apparel: black unitards, red tunics, and black jazz boots. [colon introduces explanatory statement]
5. The orchestra rehearsal will run precisely from 6:30 P.M. to 9:45 P.M. [colon with numerals indicating time]

34 Apostrophe and Quotation Marks

Like semicolons and colons, apostrophes and quotation marks bear some resemblance in appearance, but they serve very different functions.

34a The apostrophe

The chief uses of the apostrophe are to indicate the possessive case of nouns and indefinite pronouns, to mark the omission of letters in a contracted word or date, and to indicate the plurals of letters and numerals.

1. Apostrophe to indicate the possessive case

All singular nouns and indefinite pronouns, including those that already end in -*s*, form the possessive by adding -'*s*.

a child's toy	the bus's exhaust
someone's wallet	Agnes's clarinet
day's end	Charles Dickens's novels
a week's delay	Camus's humanism

An exception to this rule exists only when the addition of -'*s* would create an awkward-sounding proper name. In those few cases, the singular possessive may be formed by adding the apostrophe alone.

Moses' life
Xerxes' conquests
Euripides' plays

QUICK REFERENCE: *Apostrophe and Quotation Marks*

Apostrophe

Form the possessive of all singular nouns and indefinite pronouns, including words that end in -*s*, by adding -*'s*: *a dog's life, anyone's guess, James's idea.*

Form the possessive of all plural nouns that do not end in -*s* by adding -*'s*: *the children's welfare, those moose's antlers.*

Form the possessive of all plural nouns that end in -*s* by adding an apostrophe alone: *these animals' cages, the Joneses' party.*

Use an apostrophe to indicate contractions and to form the plurals of letters and numerals: *it's, o'clock, p's, 7's.*

Quotation marks

Periods and commas are always placed *inside* quotation marks.

Example   "And now," said the lecturer, "I will answer your questions."

Colons and semicolons are always placed *outside* quotation marks.

Example   A woman in the rear rose and said, "I have a question"; immediately, everyone in the front rows turned to look at her.

Question marks and exclamation points are placed inside quotation marks if the quotation is a question or exclamation, outside the quotation marks if the whole sentence is a question or exclamation.

Example   The lecturer asked, "Can you speak a bit louder?"

Example   Did anyone expect her to respond, "No, I can't"?

34a

All plural nouns that do not end in -*s* also form the possessive by adding -'*s*.

children's games   two deer's tracks

men's and women's clothes   two moose's antlers

All plural nouns that end in -*s* form the possessive by adding the apostrophe alone.

boys' and girls' games   the two buses' engines

in two hours' time   the Kennedys' estate

both babies' cries   the Douglases' party

Compound nouns and pronouns form the possessive by adding -'*s* to the final word.

the team captain's decision

someone else's book

my sister-in-law's visit

In a phrase that indicates joint possession, the last noun takes the possessive form; in a phrase that indicates individual possession, each noun takes the possessive form.

Marshall and Ward's Minneapolis branch

John's, Pamela's, and Harold's separate claims

Note that personal pronouns *never* take an apostrophe, even though their possessive forms end in -*s*.

his   ours

hers   yours

its   theirs

2.   Apostrophe to form contractions

Use an apostrophe to indicate omissions in contracted words and dates.

it's = it is   o'clock = of the clock

I'm = I am   class of '98 = class of 1998

let's = let us   doesn't = does not

we're = we are   haven't = have not

3. Apostrophe to form the plurals of letters, numerals, and words considered as words

The plurals of letters and numerals are formed by adding -'s.

> Her *w*'s were like *m*'s, and her *6*'s resembled *G*'s.

Form the plural of a word considered as a word in the same way.

> His conversation is too full of *you know*'s punctuated by *well*'s.

34b Quotation marks

Quotation marks are used primarily to indicate dialogue, the word-for-word citation of printed material, and certain types of titles.

1. Quotation marks to enclose direct quotations

Use quotation marks to enclose a direct quotation, but not an indirect quotation. A direct quotation gives the exact words of a speaker; an indirect quotation is the writer's paraphrase of what someone said.

> **Direct quotation**   He said, "I will call."
> **Indirect quotation**   He said that he would call.

Expressions like *he said* and *she explained* are never included within the quotation marks. If the actual quotation is divided by such an expression, both halves must be enclosed by quotation marks.

> "I am interested," he said, "so let's talk it over."
> "It all began accidentally," Jackson explained. "My remark was misunderstood."

If a quotation consists of several sentences uninterrupted by a *he said* or *she said* expression, use one set of marks to enclose the entire quotation. Do not enclose each separate sentence.

> Barbara replied, "Right now? But I haven't finished my paper for economics. Call me in a couple of hours."

If a quotation consists of several paragraphs, put quotation marks at the beginning of each paragraph and at the end of only the last paragraph.

Poor Richard's Almanack has a number of things to say about diet: "They that study much ought not to eat so much as those that work hard, their digestion being not so good.

"If thou art dull and heavy after meat, it's a sign thou hast exceeded the due measure; for meat and drink ought to refresh the body and make it chearful, and not to dull and oppress it.

"A sober diet makes a man die without pain; it maintains the senses in vigour; it mitigates the violence of the passions and affections."

Quotations within quotations

A quotation within a quotation is enclosed with single quotation marks. Be sure to conclude the original quotation with double marks.

The lecture began, "As Proust said, 'Any mental activity is easy if it need not take reality into account.' "

In the rare instance when a third set of marks must be included within a quoted passage, they become double:

In her edition of Flannery O'Connor's letters, Sally Fitzgerald comments: "Anything but dour, she never ceased to be amused, even in extremis. In a letter after her return from the hospital and surgery, in 1964, she wrote: 'One of my nurses was a dead ringer for Mrs. Turpin. . . . Her favorite grammatical construction was "it were." . . . I reckon she increased my pain about 100%.' "

Long quotations

When a quoted passage runs more than four typed lines, it should be set off by indenting ten spaces and double-spacing. Quotation marks are not used to set off such material, though they may be required within the quotation.

34b

```
T. S. Eliot begins the essay "Tradition and the

Individual Talent" as follows:

      In English writing we seldom speak of

      tradition, though we occasionally apply
```

```
its name in deploring its absence.
We cannot refer to "the tradition" or
to "a tradition"; at most, we employ
the adjective in saying that the po-
etry of So-and-so is "traditional" or
even "too traditional." Seldom, per-
haps, does the word appear except in
a phrase of censure.  If otherwise,
it is vaguely approbative, with the
implication, as to the work approved,
of some pleasing archaeological re-
construction.
```

For information on documenting such a quotation, see **20d**.

Verse quotations

A quotation of one line of verse, or part of a line, should be enclosed in quotation marks and incorporated into the text.

> Lytton disliked the false heroics of Henley's "My head is bloody but unbowed."

If two or three lines of verse are run into the text, indicate the line breaks by a slash (see **36b**).

> Stark Young and Rex Stout both found book titles in Fitzgerald's "never grows so red / The rose as where some buried Caesar bled."

A quotation of more than three lines of poetry should be set off by indenting ten spaces and double-spacing, without quotation marks. Be sure to keep the line lengths exactly as they are in the original, and indicate the line numbers being quoted with a parenthetical citation placed two spaces after the end of the final line.

```
Blake characterizes this freshness of perception
at the beginning of "Auguries of Innocence":
                To see a World in a Grain of Sand
                And a Heaven in a Wild Flower,
                Hold Infinity in the palm of your hand
                And Eternity in a hour.  (1-4)
```

2.   Quotation marks to indicate titles

Use quotation marks for titles of articles, short stories, short poems, songs, chapters of books, lectures and speeches, and individual episodes of radio and television shows.

"Sharp Drop in Unemployment" (newspaper article)

"Doris Lessing's Heroes" (journal article)

"Young Goodman Brown" (short story)

"Mending Wall" (poem)

"Jane Austen and the Dance" (lecture)

"Summertime" (song)

"Fictions" (chapter)

"Prelude to Tragedy" (episode of the television show *The Spanish Civil War*)

When one of the titles above (for example, the title of a short story) appears in a title that would itself be enclosed in quotation marks (for example, the title of an article), the shorter title is enclosed in single quotation marks:

"Understanding the Misfit in Flannery O'Connor's 'A Good Man Is Hard to Find' "

The titles of books, plays, long poems, pamphlets, periodicals, films, radio and television programs, and major works of opera, dance, and music are represented by italics or, on a typewriter, by underlining (see **38e**). Note that the titles of books of sacred scripture and the names of books of the Bible are neither underlined nor enclosed in quotation marks.

34b

Exodus	Vedas	Qur'an
Old Testament	Talmud	Upanishads

3. Quotation marks with words used in a special sense

Use quotation marks to enclose a word used in a special way—for example, in a specific technical context, or with an intended ironic meaning. But when defining a technical term, use italics or underlining rather than quotation marks (see **38e**).

Technical context

> When people speak of "modernist" architecture, they are usually thinking of the style popularized in this country by Ludwig Mies van der Rohe.

Ironic context

> The "complexity" of modernist architecture lies in its apparent simplicity.

However, avoid using quotation marks as an implicit apology for slang or other inappropriate language.

Inappropriate use of quotation marks

> That comedian's monologue really "slayed" me.

If you feel the need to apologize for a word, look for an alternative way of expressing your idea.

4. Quotation marks with other punctuation

At the end of a quotation, a period or comma is placed inside the quotation mark; a semicolon or colon is placed outside the quotation mark.

> "Quick," said my cousin, "hand me the flashlight."
>
> The bride and groom in the film said, "I do"; the audience in the theater cheered.
>
> I have only one comment when you say, "All people are equal": I wish it were true.

A question mark or exclamation point goes inside the quotation mark if it applies to the quotation only, and outside the quotation mark if it applies to the whole sentence.

"Did you arrive on time?" asked my mother.

Did the invitation say "R.S.V.P."?

He called irritably, "Move over!"

Above all, don't let anyone hear you say, "I give up"!

EXERCISE 1

Insert apostrophes and quotation marks where they are needed in the following sentences.

Example

Has anyone downstairs seen my calculus book? called Louis from the second floor, where he was searching his room unsuccessfully.

Punctuated　　"Has anyone downstairs seen my calculus book?" called Louis from the second floor, where he was searching his room unsuccessfully.　[quotation marks with direct quotation]

1. Whats it called? responded his sister Toni, looking up from a tabloid article whose headline was Martians Told Me to Live the Rest of My Life in Belgium.
2. I cant remember, said Louis. All I know is that its cover is green and that its not where I left it.
3. Louiss cry hadnt attracted anyone elses attention.
4. In the kitchen, his father was engrossed in a cookbook chapter entitled Chocolate and You; somewhere in it he hoped to find a dessert to make for that evenings dinner.
5. In the garden, his mother wasnt noticing anything except the curious disease that was rapidly withering both of her prize rosebushes leaves.
6. On the sunporch, his brother Nicholas was cleaning his snakes cage while its wriggling resident looked on from a temporary container.
7. In two days time, said Louis as he walked down the stairs, Ive got to know a lot more about solving integrals with algebraic substitutions than I do now.
8. Yesterday, he explained to Toni, my math professor unexpectedly said, Im sorry, but were going to have to have our midterm exam a

34b

Exercise 1

1. "What's it called?" responded his sister Toni, looking up from a tabloid article whose headline was "Martians Told Me to Live the Rest of My Life in Belgium."
2. "I can't remember," said Louis. "All I know is that its cover is green and that it's not where I left it."
3. Louis's cry hadn't attracted anyone else's attention.
4. In the kitchen, his father was engrossed in a cookbook chapter entitled "Chocolate and You"; somewhere in it he hoped to find a dessert to make for that evening's dinner.
5. In the garden, his mother wasn't noticing anything except the curious disease that was rapidly withering both of her prize rosebushes' leaves.
6. On the sunporch, his brother Nicholas was cleaning his snake's cage while its wriggling resident looked on from a temporary container.

week earlier than Id planned, since the examination day on my original syllabus is a holiday.

9. Louis had barely finished speaking when Bruno, the family collie, came into the room, dropped the moist shreds of a green book at his feet, raised its eyes proudly, and said, Woof!

10. It looks as if my calculus grade has literally gone to the dogs, said Louis weakly.

34b

7. "In two days' time," said Louis as he walked down the stairs, "I've got to know a lot more about solving integrals with algebraic substitutions than I do now."

8. "Yesterday," he explained to Toni, "my math professor unexpectedly said, 'I'm sorry, but we're going to have to have our midterm exam a week earlier than I'd planned, since the examination day on my original syllabus is a holiday.'"

9. Louis had barely finished speaking when Bruno, the family collie, came into the room, dropped the moist shreds of a green book at his feet, raised its eyes proudly, and said "Woof!"

10. "It looks as if my calculus grade has literally gone to the dogs," said Louis weakly.

35 Parenthetic Punctuation: Dash, Parentheses, Brackets

T he term *parenthetic,* which comes to us from the Greek word meaning "to insert," is used to denote an explanatory or amplifying comment that is inserted into a sentence but that may lack a grammatical connection with the rest of the sentence. Some parenthetic elements may be set off by commas (see **32f**), but others require stronger punctuation—dashes, parentheses, or brackets.

35a The dash

The dash, as its name suggests, is a dramatic mark. Like the comma and parentheses, it separates elements within the sentence, but what parentheses say quietly the dash stresses. Note that on a typewriter, a dash consists of two hyphens with no spaces before, after, or between them.

1. Dash with parenthetic element

Dashes are frequently used to insert an amplifying, qualifying, explanatory, or descriptive comment into the middle of a sentence or to attach such a comment to the end of an otherwise grammatically complete sentence.

QUICK REFERENCE: *Parenthetic Punctuation*

Dash

Use a dash to emphasize a comment inserted into a sentence.

Example   The town of my childhood—it now exists only in my imagination—was ravaged by a flood.

Use a dash to sum up an introductory list in a sentence.

Example   Streets, cars, houses, trees—all were covered with gray mud when the floodwater retreated.

Parentheses

Use parentheses to insert a comment of secondary importance into a sentence.

Example   Despite efforts to replicate Dr. Petroski's experiment (and they have been considerable), no one has produced his results.

Brackets

Use brackets to insert a clarifying or explanatory comment into a quotation.

Example   According to Thomas Jefferson, George Washington "was determined the experiment [of the United States Constitution] should have a fair trial and would lose the last drop of his blood in support of it."

35a

Every woman is a human being—one cannot repeat that too often—and a human being *must* have an occupation, if he or she is not to become a nuisance to the world.

—Dorothy Sayers, "Are Women Human?" *Unpopular Opinions*

One of the main reasons for the continuation of the Cold War—indeed, for some of its bloodiest episodes—was the unexpected appearance of Communist regimes in unexpected places around the globe.

—John Lukacs, "The End of the Twentieth Century," *Harper's Magazine*

The assistant warden believed that female inmates should wear no cosmetics other than what she herself used—a bit of mascara and a light shade of lipstick.

—Kimberly Wozencraft, "Notes from the Country Club," *Witness*

We examined the hole. It looked as though it had been dug with a tablespoon—shapely and neat, a little wider at the bottom than at the top.

—Franklin Burroughs, "A Snapping Turtle in June," *Georgia Review*

The dash is an essential punctuation mark in two situations. First, when a parenthetic element consists of an independent clause, the clause must be set off with dashes (or else with parentheses). Punctuated with commas, such a sentence would be ungrammatical and hopelessly confusing.

Incorrect	By the time the speech was over, it lasted two hours, most of the audience members were in a stupor.
Correct	By the time the speech was over—it lasted two hours—most of the audience members were in a stupor.

Second, to avoid confusion when an appositive or other parenthetic element contains commas, the element should be set off with dashes rather than commas.

Confusing	Three works of art, a watercolor, an oil, and a silk-screen print, hung on the west wall. [Are there three—or six—pieces in all?]
Clearer	Three works of art—a watercolor, an oil, and a silk-screen print—hung on the west wall.

2.   Dash following an introductory list

When a sentence begins with a series or list, a dash is commonly used to link the list with the statement of summary or comment that follows it.

35a

The soldier in combat who sees his friend killed twenty yards away while he himself is unhurt, the pupil who sees another child get into trouble for copying on a test—they don't wish their friends ill, but they can't help feeling an embarrassing spasm of gratitude that it happened to someone else and not to them.

—Harold S. Kushner, *When Bad Things Happen to Good People*

3.   Dash for emphasis

Any sentence element set off with dashes acquires special emphasis. In the following sentences, for example, commas would be acceptable, but dashes add a dramatic effect.

> Shame plagued me—and shame is the older brother to disease.
>
> —Leonard Kriegel, "Falling into Life," *The American Scholar*

> An intellectual weakness—and saving grace—of American students has always been that they are unable to sit still for ideology and its tight flemish-bonded logics and dialectics.
>
> —Tom Wolfe, *From Bauhaus to Our House*

Frequently a dash is used to indicate a sharp and perhaps unexpected turn of thought in a sentence.

> He suffered from claustrophobia. He wanted to run away—either to run away or to smash the place up.
>
> —Doris Lessing, *The Grass Is Singing*

> She had a strong impulse to get up, walk across the rug, and slap his face. That'll make him wink, she thought, rising, dizzy, half out of her seat—and then subsiding in horror at the idea of the spectacle she had nearly created.
>
> —Alison Lurie, *The Nowhere City*

Finally, to introduce a list, the dash is at once more informal and more dramatic than the colon.

> They hugged the memories of illnesses to their bosoms. They licked their lips and clucked their tongues in fond remembrance of the pains they had endured—childbirth, rheumatism, croup, sprains, backaches, piles.
>
> —Toni Morrison, *The Bluest Eye*

35b   Use the dash cautiously. Its flashy interruption can create energy and drama in a sentence, but its overuse weakens rather than intensifies that effect.

35b Parentheses

Like commas and dashes, parentheses are used to enclose or set off parenthetic, explanatory, or supplementary material. But unlike commas, parentheses usually enclose material that is less closely related in thought or structure to the rest of the sentence. And unlike dashes, parentheses reduce rather than increase dramatic effect.

1. Parentheses with parenthetic element

Parentheses are often used to include material of the sort we might expect to find in a footnote—useful information that is not essential to the sentence.

> He commonly had more important things to think about than his shortness (and average height then was less than it is now) but the chief references in his letters . . . suggest that it was often in his mind.
>
> —Douglas Bush, *John Keats*

They also provide opportunities for the writer's comments and asides.

> Acting out of volition and necessity he had "chosen" (to the extent that it was a matter of choice) his distinctive mode, muckraking.
>
> —Justin Kaplan, *Lincoln Steffens: A Biography*

2. Parentheses with numbered items and with documented sources

Parentheses are used to enclose numbers that mark an enumeration within a sentence.

> The types of noncreative thinking listed by Robinson are (1) reverie, or daydreaming; (2) making minor decisions; and (3) rationalizing, or justifying our prejudices.

Finally, parentheses are used in the formal documentation of research. For more information about that function, see Chapters **19** through **24**.

35b

3. Parentheses with other punctuation

When a passage in parentheses is part of a sentence element that is set off by a comma, the comma is placed outside the parentheses. If the material within parentheses is an exclamation or question, appropriate punctuation goes inside the parentheses.

> If we are willing to commit ourselves to a true war on drugs (and shouldn't we be willing to do so?), then we need to begin not with drugs, but with poverty and lack of opportunity in our inner cities.

When parentheses are used to enclose a separate sentence, the sentence's end punctuation is placed inside the parentheses.

> All of the settlements appear to be made up of two parts. First is the group of prefab houses that are finished and inhabited. Usually behind them, standing row upon row, is the second part—houses that are unfinished, empty, and awaiting money for completion. (Sometimes the "houses" are simply trailer homes.)
>
> —Edward W. Said, "Palestine, Then and Now," *Harper's Magazine*

35c Brackets

Square brackets are used to enclose a word or words inserted into a quotation by the person quoting. Such insertions typically comment on the quotation or provide an explanation of a word or phrase in the quotation that would otherwise be unclear.

> "Everyone in the metropolitan area [the company's report claimed] will welcome the opening of City Waste Disposal's newest incineration facility."
>
> "In a typical Chicago building of the turn of the century, the spandrels [horizontal panels under the windows] are recessed and discontinuous so that the building's uninterrupted vertical piers dominate the viewer's perception."

Sometimes in a quotation a noun in brackets replaces a pronoun whose antecedent does not otherwise appear in the quoted passage. In the following passage, for example, the bracketed material has been substituted for the pronoun *its*.

> "We know more about [the English language's] state in the later Middle Ages than earlier, and from the time of Shakespeare on, our information is quite complete."

The word *sic* (Latin for "thus"), enclosed in brackets, is inserted into a quotation after a misspelling or other error to indicate that the error occurs in the original text.

He sent the following written confession: "She followed us into the kitchen, snatched a craving [sic] knife from the table, and came toward me with it."

Finally, if one parenthetical expression falls within another, brackets replace the inner parentheses. (Avoid this situation when possible. Usually [as here] it is distracting to the reader.)

EXERCISE 1

Insert dashes, parentheses, and brackets where they are needed in the following sentences.

Example

The cities of Florida's central Gulf Coast Clearwater, St. Petersburg, and Tampa offer tourists a varied but low-key vacation.

Punctuated The cities of Florida's central Gulf Coast—Clearwater, St. Petersburg, and Tampa—offer tourists a varied but low-key vacation.

1. St. Petersburg it was named for the Russian birthplace of its founder offers resorts that flourished in the Roaring Twenties.
2. Clearwater's main attraction is simple and irresistible four miles of white-sand beach.
3. Warmly tinted stucco buildings, red tiled roofs, cool colonnades all of these architectural details point to Tampa's Spanish heritage, which reaches back to 1528.
4. According to one guidebook, "Museums in the area include the Salvador Dali Museum in St. Petersburg and the Spongeorama not a misprint! in nearby Tarpon Springs."
5. Excursion boats take visitors to historic sites on the keys a local term for small offshore islands, as well as to the habitat of the most lovable of endangered species the manatee.

35c

Exercise 1

1. St. Petersburg (it was named for the Russian birthplace of its founder) offers resorts that flourished in the Roaring Twenties. [dashes also acceptable]
2. Clearwater's main attraction is simple and irresistible—four miles of white-sand beach.
3. Warmly tinted stucco buildings, red tiled roofs, cool colonnades—all of these architectural details point to Tampa's Spanish heritage, which reaches back to 1528.
4. According to one guidebook, "Museums in the area include the Salvador Dali Museum in St. Petersburg and the Spongeorama [not a misprint!] in nearby Tarpon Springs."
5. Excursion boats take visitors to historic sites on the keys (a local term for small offshore islands), as well as to the habitat of the most lovable of endangered species—the manatee.

36 Other Punctuation: Hyphen, Slash, Ellipsis Marks

Three punctuation marks with very different functions remain to be discussed—the hyphen, the slash, and ellipsis marks.

36a The hyphen

Although the general tendency of modern English usage seems to be away from hyphenation, hyphens are still used in a number of compound constructions.

1. Hyphen with some compound nouns

Compound nouns—nouns formed by combining two or more individual words—fall into three categories: *open compounds* are written as separate words; *closed compounds* are written as single words; and *hyphenated compounds* connect their constituent elements with hyphens.

In general, hyphenated compounds are recently coined terms or terms that are still in the process of coming into general use. As the following examples suggest, however, usage varies considerably. Your

---

QUICK REFERENCE: *Hyphen, Slash, Ellipsis Marks*

Hyphen

Use a hyphen with a compound adjective when it precedes a noun.

> **Example**   Pamela's junior-college internship offered on-the-job training in accounting.

Use a hyphen between a prefix and a proper noun, but do not use a hyphen between most prefixes and common nouns: *sub-Saharan, subheading*.

Slash

Use a slash to separate quoted lines of poetry.

> **Example**   In Edwin Arlington Robinson's poem, Richard Cory is initially described as "a gentleman from sole to crown, / Clean favored, and imperially slim" (3–4).

Ellipsis marks

Use ellipsis marks (three spaced periods) to indicate an omission from a quoted passage.

> **Example**   Virginia Woolf has written that the reader of a novel "must be capable . . . of great boldness of imagination."

For further information about quoting and citing sources, see **20b**, **20c**, and **20d**.

---

best guide is the latest edition of a good desk dictionary such as those described in Chapter **9**.

Open compound	Closed compound	Hyphenated compound
court order	courthouse	court-martial
eye opener	eyedropper	eye-catcher

half note	halftime	half-moon
horse sense	horsepower	horse-trading
time zone	timepiece	time-share

2.   Hyphen with compound adjectives

Compound adjectives—two or more words used as a single adjective *before* a noun—are usually hyphenated.

air-conditioned office	second-floor bedroom
ground-breaking research	three-year-old child
high-school prom	twenty-first-century technology
no-win situation	upper-middle-class background
grilled-cheese sandwich	well-informed leader

But most compound adjectives are not hyphenated when they *follow* a noun.

The *snow-covered* mountains lay ahead.

The mountains ahead were *snow covered*.

Some compound adjectives are always hyphenated; for guidance, consult a good desk dictionary.

Their *old-fashioned* ideas were surprising.

I found their ideas *old-fashioned*.

See also **28d**.

3.   Hyphens with prefixes

Most prefixes are attached to words without hyphens, but a compound formed by a prefix and a proper noun usually is hyphenated.

36a

antismoking	anti-Semitic
midcentury	mid-January
postcolonial	post-Vietnam
preconception	pre-Christian
unaddressed	un-American

Note that in some cases a hyphen may be required after a prefix to distinguish between words with different meanings.

She *recovered* her strength.

She *re-covered* her sofa.

Hyphens are used after the prefix *ex-* in the sense of "former" (*ex-president*) and in other cases when the absence of a hyphen after a prefix might be awkward or confusing (*anti-intellectual, co-owner, pro-choice, pro-life*).

4. Hyphens with numbers

A hyphen is used when the numbers 21 through 99 are written out.

twenty-six

one hundred sixty-three

A hyphen is used when a fraction is written out.

two-thirds

ten and one-half

5. Suspensive hyphen

When two compound words are connected by *and* or *or* and the second word in both compounds is the same, you may indicate the first compound by writing just its first word followed by a hyphen and a space.

four- and six-cylinder engines

full- or part-time employment

The same principle applies when two prefixes are joined to the same word.

pre- and postgame activities

(For discussion of hyphens used to mark syllabication, see **38f**.)

36a

EXERCISE 1

Should the compounds in the following sentences be written as one word, with a hyphen, or as two words? Consult a recent edition of a good dictionary, if necessary.

1. We need an eight foot rod.
2. All the creeks are bone dry.

Exercise 1

Words written as single words below follow the *American Heritage College Dictionary.*

1. eight-foot
2. bone dry
3. one-fourth
4. world power
5. go-between
6. good-looking
7. ne'er-do-well
8. all together
9. T-shaped
10. badly needed
11. all ready
12. subbasement
13. anti-British
14. halfhearted
15. chip-on-the-shoulder
16. self-reliant
17. high-school
18. secondhand
19. pigheaded
20. second-rate

3. She gave away one fourth of her income.
4. The United States is a world power.
5. Who was your go between?
6. He is extremely good looking.
7. The younger son was a ne'er do well.
8. Let us sing the chorus all together.
9. They are building a T shaped addition.
10. She is getting a badly needed rest.
11. Are you all ready?
12. The leak was in the sub basement.
13. He was anti British.
14. She does her work in a half hearted manner.
15. I don't like your chip on the shoulder attitude.
16. They always were self reliant.
17. A high school course is required for admission.
18. I do not trust second hand information.
19. He is as pig headed a man as I ever knew.
20. She will not accept anything second rate.

36b The slash

The most common use of the slash, also known as the *virgule* or *solidus,* is to separate quoted lines of poetry.

1. Slash with quoted lines of poetry

When up to three lines of poetry are quoted, they should be incorporated into the text. Use a slash with a space on either side to mark the line breaks, retaining the poem's capitalization and punctuation between lines. Indicate the line numbers of the quotation with a parenthetical citation.

36b

> In "Dover Beach," Matthew Arnold pessimistically depicts humanity "on a darkling plain / Swept with confused alarms of struggle and flight, / Where ignorant armies clash by night" (35–37).

If you quote more than three lines of verse, the quoted lines should be set off from the text and indented ten spaces (see **34b** and **38a**).

2. Slash to express alternative wording

A slash is sometimes used in statements that include alternative wording. Do not leave a space on either side of the slash in these cases.

[Unlike the safety belt,] the air bag is a popular safety device. The reason is its invisibility, which enables the driver to forget/repress the danger of accident.

—Wolfgang Schivelbusch, *The Railway Journey*

3. Slash with dates, fractions, and other numbers

In informal, technical, or scientific writing, a slash may be used between the month, day, and year when a date is expressed entirely in numbers; in fractions that would otherwise be written out; and as a substitute for the word *per* in expressions of measurement. Do not leave a space on either side of the slash in these cases.

January 10, 1995	1/10/95
three-fifths	3/5
thirty-two feet per second	32 ft/sec

EXERCISE 2

Compose a sentence that includes a quotation of two or three lines from the following poem by Robert Burns (1759–96).

A Red, Red Rose

O, my luve is like a red, red rose
    That's newly sprung in June:
O, my luve is like the melodie
    That's sweetly play'd in tune.

So fair art thou, my bonnie lass,
    So deep in luve am I:
And I will luve thee still, my dear,
    Till a' the seas gang dry.

Till a' the seas gang dry, my dear,
    And the rocks melt wi' the sun:
And I will luve thee still, my dear,
    While the sands o' life shall run.

And fair thee weel, my only luve,
    And fair thee weel awhile!
And I will come again, my luve,
    Tho' it were ten thousand mile.

36b

Exercise 2

Answers will, of course, vary. The following are some possibilities.

Burns's poem opens with a comparison between his love and "a red, red rose / That's newly sprung in June" (1–2).

The poet promises to be faithful "Till a' the seas gang dry, my dear, / And the rocks melt wi' the sun" (9–10).

The poem concludes with the following pledge: "And I will come again, my luve, / Tho' it were ten thousand mile" (15–16).

36c Ellipsis marks

The deliberate omission of words from a quoted text is called an *ellipsis*. To indicate such an omission from the middle of a quoted passage, use three spaced periods known as *ellipsis marks*.

Source

On the evidence of her work and what she has said about it, Georgia O'Keeffe is neither "crusty" nor eccentric. She is simply hard, a straight shooter, a woman clean of received wisdom and open to what she sees.

> —Joan Didion, "Georgia O'Keeffe," *The White Album* (1979; New York: Pocket, 1980) 127.

Ellipsis marks indicate omitted words

"On the evidence of her work and what she has said about it," writes Joan Didion, "Georgia O'Keeffe is . . . simply hard, . . . a woman clean of received wisdom and open to what she sees" (127).

Ellipsis marks are not used to indicate an omission at the beginning or end of a quotation unless the quoted portion of a sentence has the grammatical appearance of a complete sentence. Consider the following cases.

Incorrect In Didion's view, Georgia O'Keeffe is ". . . a straight shooter . . ." (127).

Correct In Didion's view, Georgia O'Keeffe is "a straight shooter" (127).
[Because the quoted phrase—*a straight shooter*—is clearly part of a larger sentence, no ellipsis marks should be used before or after it.]

Correct According to Didion, ". . . Georgia O'Keeffe is neither " 'crusty' nor eccentric" (127).

Correct "On the evidence of her work and what she has said about it," notes Didion, "Georgia O'Keeffe is neither 'crusty' nor eccentric. She is simply hard . . ." (127).
[In both cases, the quoted passage appears to be a complete sentence. Ellipsis marks are therefore required to indicate that words in the original sentence have been omitted.]

Note that when an ellipsis occurs at the end of a sentence, a fourth period follows the parenthetical page citation to close the sentence. If such a sentence ends without a page citation, the order is reversed: the ellipsis marks follow the end punctuation of the sentence.

> "I pledge allegiance to the flag . . . and to the Republic for which it stands. . . ."

Ellipsis marks may also indicate the omission of one or more entire sentences from the middle of a quotation. In this case, they follow the end punctuation of the last sentence before the omission.

Source

> The fact is that plastic will soon be to modern Americans what the walrus was to the Aleut or the buffalo was to the Sioux: nothing less than the basis of an entire material culture. In some form or other, we wear it, eat with it, write with it, cover our floors with it, insulate our houses with it—the list is practically endless. Being less spiritually evolved than the Aleut or the Sioux, though, we loathe plastic instead of respect it; we're addicted to it, but make fun of it.
>
> —JoAnn Gutin, "Plastics-A-Go-Go," *Mother Jones* March/April 1992: 56.

Ellipsis marks indicate omitted sentence

> "The fact is," JoAnn Gutin wryly observes, "that plastic will soon be to modern Americans what the walrus was to the Aleut or the buffalo was to the Sioux: nothing less than the basis of an entire material culture. . . . Being less spiritually evolved than the Aleut or the Sioux, though, we loathe plastic instead of respect it; we're addicted to it, but make fun of it" (56).

For further information about quoting and citing sources, see **20b**, **20c**, and **20d**.

36c

EXERCISE 3

Compose a passage that quotes a portion of the following text and that uses ellipsis marks to indicate the omission of several words or of one or more entire sentences.

> Two major forces in our culture cooperate to produce linguistic insecurity: the ranking of social and geographical dialects as superior

Exercise 3

Answers will vary.

and inferior, and an educational system based on a doctrine of correctness and purity in language that invariably conflicts with the observable facts of English usage. Linguistic insecurity may very well be a sociolinguistic given for many Americans. It is induced by formal language study in the schools—the ascertaining of standards, the writing of grammars, the instruction in English for speakers of English—and by the self-appointed language elite that has emerged in every age to defend standards and to regulate the language behavior of others. These are the gatekeepers of language, and their attitudes are sometimes liberal, sometimes conservative, often contradictory, and invariably prescriptive. These experts variously appeal to and reject reason, custom, authority, taste, morality, and their own personal vision. They defend the language by mounting attacks on its speakers. And they do not concern themselves so much with keeping the enemy out—particularly at the present time—for they are firmly convinced that the barbarians are those already inside. So we find them, sitting at their gates, constantly watching our grammar.

—Dennis E. Baron, *Grammar and Good Taste: Reforming the American Language* (New Haven: Yale UP, 1982) 228.

36c

37 *Spelling*

The word *orthography*, meaning the art of correct spelling, is derived from two Greek roots: *orthos* (straight) and *graphein* (write). Spelling right, then, is writing straight. Since the time of Aristotle, correct spelling has distinguished the scholar from the dolt. Indeed, Lord Chesterton could write in the eighteenth century that one false spelling would fix shame on a writer for life: "I know many of quality," he claimed, "who never recovered from the ridicule of having spelled *wholesome* without the *w*."

Chesterton's comment may seem to reflect the exaggerated propriety of a bygone age, but even today, many readers expect accurate spelling, and fairly or not, they regard a writer's spelling mistakes as indications of a general sloppiness of mind. Like so many other aspects of writing, then, good spelling has a *rhetorical* function: it helps a writer to establish a persona characterized by precision and carefulness.

37a Trouble spots

Learn to look for and concentrate on trouble spots in words. If you can remember the correct spelling of the trouble spot, the rest of the word will often take care of itself. *Receive*, like *deceive, perceive,* and *conceive,* is troublesome only because of the *ei* combination; if you recall that it is *ei* after *c*, you will have mastered these words. Similarly, to spell *beginning* or *planning* correctly, all you need to remember is the double *n*.

Careful pronunciation may help you to avoid errors at trouble spots. In the following words, the letters in boldface are often omitted.

QUICK REFERENCE: *Spelling Rules*

Drop final e? Drop a final *e* before suffixes beginning with a vowel, but retain a final *e* before suffixes beginning with a consonant: *hope, hoping, hopeful.* (Some exceptions: *awful, judgment, ninth, truly.*)

Double final consonant? Double a final consonant that is preceded by a vowel when you add a suffix beginning with a vowel and the accent falls on the final syllable of the original word: *occurring,* but *profiting.* (Some exceptions: *excellent, transferable.*)

Change final y *to* i? Change a final *y* that is preceded by a consonant to *i* when you add any suffix except *-ing: accompaniment,* but *accompanying.* (Some exceptions: *laid, paid, said.*)

Use ie *or* ei? Put *i* before *e* except after *c: achieve, ceiling.* (Some exceptions: *either, leisure, neither, seize, weird.*)

Pronounce the words aloud, exaggerating the sound of the boldface letters.

accidenta**ll**y	liable	recognize
candi**d**ate	library	sophomore
everybody	lite**r**ature	strictly
February	occasiona**ll**y	surprise
genera**ll**y	probably	temperament
lab**o**ratory	quantity	usually

37a

Many people add letters incorrectly to the following words. Pronounce the words, making sure that no extra syllable creeps in at spots indicated by boldface type.

ath**l**etics	ent**r**ance	mischie**v**ous
disast**r**ous	height	remem**br**ance
drown**ed**	hind**r**ance	simila**r**
e**lm**	light**n**ing	umbrella

Trouble spots in the following words are caused by a tendency to transpose the boldface letters. Careful pronunciation may help you to remember the proper order.

child**re**n	**per**form	pre**ju**dice
hund**re**d	**per**spiration	**pre**scription
irrelevant	**pre**fer	trag**e**dy

37b Similar words frequently confused

Learn the meaning and spelling of similar words. Many errors are caused by confusion of such words as *effect* and *affect*. It is useless to spell *principal* correctly if the word that belongs in your sentence is *principle*. The following list distinguishes briefly between words that are frequently confused.

accept	receive		berth	bed
except	aside from		birth	being born
access	admittance		boarder	one who boards
excess	greater amount		border	edge
advice	noun		breath	noun
advise	verb		breathe	verb
affect	to influence (verb)		capital	city
effect	result (noun)		capitol	building
effect	to bring about (verb)		choose	present
aisle	in church		chose	past
isle	island		clothes	garments
all ready	prepared		cloths	kinds of cloth
already	previously		coarse	not fine
allusion	reference		course	path
illusion	misconception		complement	to complete
altar	shrine		compliment	to praise
alter	change		conscience	sense of right and wrong
angel	celestial being		conscious	aware
angle	corner		corps	group
ascent	climbing		corpse	dead body
assent	agreement			

costume	dress	personal	private
custom	social convention	personnel	work force
council	governmental group	precede	come before
counsel	advice	proceed	continue
dairy	milk supplier	principal	most important
diary	daily record	principle	basic doctrine
decent	proper	quiet	still
descent	slope	quite	entirely
desert	wasteland	respectfully	with respect
dessert	food	respectively	in the order named
device	noun	shone	from *shine*
devise	verb	shown	from *show*
dual	twofold	stationary	not moving
duel	fight	stationery	writing supplies
formally	in a formal manner	than	comparison
formerly	previously	then	at that time
forth	forward	their	possessive
fourth	4th	there	in that place
ingenious	clever	they're	they are
ingenuous	frank	to	as in *go to bed*
its	of it	too	as in *too bad, me too*
it's	it is	two	the number 2
later	subsequently	weather	rain or shine
latter	second of two	whether	which of two
lead	metal	who's	who is
led	past tense of the verb *lead*	whose	possessive
loose	not tight	you're	you are
lose	misplace	your	possessive
peace	not war		
piece	a portion		

37c Spelling rules

The available spelling rules in English apply to a relatively small number of words, and unfortunately almost all rules have exceptions. Nevertheless, some of the rules may help you to spell common words that cause you trouble, especially those words formed with suffixes.

It is as important to learn when a rule may be used as it is to understand the rule itself. Applied in the wrong places, rules will make your spelling worse, not better.

1. Final silent *e*

Drop a final silent *e* before suffixes beginning with a vowel (*-ing, -age, -able*). Keep a final silent *e* before suffixes beginning with a consonant (*-ful, -ly, -ness*).

arrange + ment = arrangement	nine + teen = nineteen
bale + ful = baleful	pale + ness = paleness
dote + age = dotage	plume + age = plumage
guide + ance = guidance	sincere + ly = sincerely
hope + ful = hopeful	stone + y = stony
hope + ing = hoping	white + wash = whitewash
late + ly = lately	white + ish = whitish
love + able = lovable	write + ing = writing

Note the following exceptions:

awful	dyeing	judgment	truly
duly	hoeing	ninth	wholly

The *e* is retained in such words as the following in order to keep the soft sound of *c* and *g:*

courageous	outrageous
noticeable	peaceable

EXERCISE 1

Following the rule above, write the correct spelling of each word indicated below.

37c

use + ing	pale + ing
use + ful	manage + ment
argue + ment	write + ing
nine + ty	refuse + al
white + ness	waste + ful

Exercise 1

using	paling
useful	management
argument	writing
ninety	refusal
whiteness	wasteful
immediately	hopeless
pleasure	absolutely
manageable	surely

immediate + ly   hope + less
please + ure   absolute + ly
manage + able   sure + ly

EXERCISE 2

Write the following words together with the adjectives ending in *-able* derived from them (e.g., *love, lovable*).

dispose   prove   console   imagine   measure
move   compare   blame   cure

EXERCISE 3

Write the following words together with the adjectives ending in *-able* derived from them (e.g., *notice, noticeable*).

trace   change   charge   damage   manage
service   marriage   place   peace

2. Double the final consonant

When adding a suffix beginning with a vowel to words ending in one consonant preceded by one vowel (*red, redder*), notice where the word is accented. If it is accented on the last syllable or if it is a monosyllable, *double* the final consonant.

*bé*nefit + ed = benefited   pre*fér* + ed = preferred
*díf*fer + ence = difference   *pró*fit + ing = profiting
oc*cúr* + ence = occurrence   *réd* + er = redder
o*mít* + ing = omitting   *trá*vel + er = traveler

Note that in some words the accent shifts when the suffix is added.

re*fér*red   *ré*ference
pre*fér*ring   *pré*ference

There are a few exceptions to this rule, such as *transferable* and *excellent;* and a good many words that should follow the rule have alternative spellings—for example, *worshiped* or *worshipped; traveling, traveler,* or *travelling, traveller.*

Exercise 2

disposable   blamable (or blameable)
movable (or moveable)   imaginable
provable   curable
comparable   measurable
consolable

Exercise 3

traceable   placeable
serviceable   damageable
changeable   peaceable
marriageable   manageable
chargeable

EXERCISE 4

Make as many combinations as you can of the following words and suffixes. Give your reason for doubling or not doubling the final consonant. Suffixes: *-able, -ible, -ary, -ery, -er, -est, -ance, -ence, -ess, -ed, -ish, -ing, -ly, -ful, -ment, -ness, -hood.*

occur	equip	man	expel
happen	commit	defer	rival
begin	equal	sum	glad
shrub	ravel	stop	profit
scrap	kidnap	clan	level
red	rid	libel	jewel

EXERCISE 5

Write the present participle and the past participle of each of the following verbs (e.g., *stop, stopping, stopped*).

prefer	begin	acquit	equip
profit	hop	commit	recur
slam	differ	drag	confer

3. Words ending in *y*

If the *y* is preceded by a consonant, change the *y* to *i* before any suffix except *-ing.*

accompany + es = accompanies   lonely + ness = loneliness
ally + es = allies   study + ing = studying
lady + es = ladies   try + ed = tried

The *y* is usually retained if it is preceded by a vowel:

displayed   monkeys   valleys

Note the following exceptions: laid, paid, said.

37c

EXERCISE 6

Add suffixes to the following words. State your reason for spelling the word as you do.

mercy	relay	hardy	bounty	medley
duty	study	wordy	jockey	galley
pulley	essay	fancy	modify	body

Exercise 4

occurrence, occurred, occurring (accented on final syllable)
happened, happening (accented on first syllable)
beginning (accented on final syllable)
shrubbery (monosyllable)
scrapped, scrapping (monosyllable)
redder, reddest, redly (monosyllable)
equipped, equipping, equipment (accented on final syllable)
committed, committing, commitment (accented on final syllable)
equaled (or equalled), equaling (or equalling), equally (accented on first syllable, but either spelling acceptable)
raveled (or ravelled), raveling (or ravelling) (accented on first syllable, but either spelling acceptable)
kidnaped (or kidnapped), kidnaping (or kidnapping) (accented on first syllable, but either spelling acceptable)
ridded, ridding (monosyllable)

37d

EXERCISE 7

Write the plural of the following nouns (e.g., *lady, ladies*).

baby	remedy	treaty	turkey
hobby	enemy	delay	decoy
democracy	poppy	alley	alloy
policy	diary	attorney	corduroy
tragedy	laundry	journey	convoy

EXERCISE 8

Write the third-person present and the first-person past of the following verbs (e.g., *he/she cries, I cried*).

fancy	spy	vary	worry
qualify	reply	dry	pity
accompany	occupy	ferry	envy

4. *ie* or *ei*

When *ie* or *ei* is used to spell the sound *ee*, put *i* before *e*, except after *c*.

achieve	grieve	retrieve	ceiling
belief	niece	shield	conceit
believe	piece	shriek	conceive
brief	pierce	siege	deceit
chief	relief	thief	deceive
field	relieve	wield	perceive
grief	reprieve	yield	receive

Note the following exceptions: *either, leisure, neither, seize, weird.*

37d Words commonly misspelled

Below is a list of some ordinary words that are often misspelled. Have a friend test you on these words—fifty at a time. Then concentrate on the ones you miss. To help you remember correct spellings, trouble spots are indicated by boldface type in most of the words.

absence	absurd	academic
absorption	abundant	accidentally

manly, manful, manhood (monosyllable)
deferred, deferring, deferment, (accented on final syllable), deference (accented on first syllable)
summary, summed, summing (monosyllable)
stopped, stopping (monosyllable)
clannish (monosyllable)
libeled (or libelled), libeling (or libelling) (accented on first syllable, but either spelling acceptable)
expelled, expelling (accented on final syllable)
rivaled (or rivalled), rivaling (or rivalling) (accented on first syllable, but either spelling acceptable)
gladder, gladdest, gladly (monosyllable)
profitable, profited, profiting (accented on first syllable)
leveled (or levelled), leveling (or levelling) (accented on first syllable, but either spelling acceptable)
jeweler (or jeweller), jeweled (or jewelled) (accented on first syllable, but either spelling acceptable)

accommodate
accumulate
accurate
achievement
acquainted
acquire
across
additionally
address
adequately
aggravate
airplane
allotment
allotted
all right
already
altogether
always
amateur
among
analysis
annually
apology
apparatus
apparent
appearance
appetite
appreciate
appropriate
arctic
argument
arithmetic
arrangement
article
ascend
association
athletic

attacked
attendance
audience
available
awkward
bargain
basically
becoming
beginning
believe
benefited
boundary
brilliant
Britain
business
calendar
candidate
career
category
cemetery
certain
challenge
changeable
changing
Christian
column
coming
commission
committee
comparatively
competent
competition
conceit
concentrate
condemn
confidence
conqueror

conscientious
conscious
consider
consistent
contemporary
continuous
controlled
convenience
coolly
copies
courteous
criticism
dealt
deceive
decision
definitely
descendant
describe
description
desirable
despair
desperate
dictionary
different
difficult
dining room
disappear
disappoint
disastrous
discipline
disease
dissatisfied
dissipate
divide
doctor
dying
effect

37d

Exercise 5 (page 717)

prefer, preferring, preferred
profit, profiting, profited
slam, slamming, slammed
begin, beginning, began
hop, hopping, hopped
differ, differing, differed
acquit, acquitting, acquitted
commit, committing, committed
drag, dragging, dragged
equip, equipping, equipped
recur, recurring, recurred
confer, conferring, conferred

eighth	humorous	meant
eliminate	hurriedly	medieval
embarrass	hypocrisy	merely
emphasize	illiterate	miniature
entirely	imagination	municipal
entrance	imitation	murmur
environment	immediately	mysterious
equipped	incidentally	necessary
especially	incredibly	neither
etc. (et cetera)	independent	nineteen
exaggerate	indispensable	noticeable
exceed	infinite	nowadays
excellent	initiative	nuclear
exceptionally	intelligence	obstacle
exercise	interest	occasionally
existence	involve	occurred
exorbitant	irrelevant	occurrence
expense	irresistible	omission
experience	itself	omitted
explanation	jealousy	opinion
familiar	knowledge	opportunity
fascinate	laboratory	optimism
feasible	laid	origin
February	led	paid
fictitious	leisure	pamphlet
finally	library	parallel
foreign	license	paralyzed
forty	literature	parliament
friend	loneliness	particularly
gauge	lose	partner
government	luxury	pastime
grammar	magazine	perform
guard	maintenance	perhaps
harass	manufacturer	permanent
hardening	marriage	permissible
height	mathematics	persistent
hindrance	mattress	personnel

37d

Exercise 6 (page 717)

mercies, merciful (*y* preceded by consonant)
duties, dutiful (*y* preceded by consonant)
pulleys (*y* preceded by vowel)
relays, relaying (*y* preceded by vowel)
studies, studying (*y* preceded by consonant)
essays, essayed (*y* preceded by vowel)
hardiest (*y* preceded by consonant)
wordiest (*y* preceded by consonant)
fanciest (*y* preceded by consonant)
bountiful (*y* preceded by consonant)
jockeyed, jockeying (*y* preceded by vowel)
modified, modifying (*y* preceded by consonant)
medleys (*y* preceded by vowel)
galleys (*y* preceded by vowel)
bodies (*y* preceded by consonant)

persuade	recognize	strenuous
physical	recommend	stretch
pleasant	reference	studying
politician	referred	succeed
possess	religious	suppress
possible	reminisce	surprise
practically	repetition	susceptible
preceding	representative	syllable
predominant	rhythm	sympathize
prejudice	ridiculous	temperament
preparation	sacrifice	tendency
prevalent	safety	thorough
primitive	schedule	together
privilege	secretary	tragedy
probably	seize	transferred
procedure	sense	truly
proceed	separate	typical
profession	sergeant	tyranny
professor	severely	undoubtedly
prominent	shining	unnecessary
pronunciation	siege	until
prove	similar	using
psychology	sincerely	usually
pursue	soliloquy	vengeance
questionnaire	sophomore	village
quizzes	specimen	villain
really	speech	weird
receive	stopping	writing

EXERCISE 9

37d

Study the following words, observing that in all of them the prefix is not *diss-* but *dis-*.

dis + advantage	dis + obedient
dis + agree	dis + orderly
dis + approve	dis + organize
dis + interested	dis + own

Exercise 7 (page 718)

babies	treaties
hobbies	delays
democracies	alleys
policies	attorneys
tragedies	journeys
remedies	turkeys
enemies	decoys
poppies	alloys
diaries	corduroys
laundries	convoys

Exercise 8 (page 718)

he fancies, I fancied
she qualifies, I qualified

EXERCISE 10

Study the following words, observing that in all of them the prefix is not *u-* but *un-*.

un + natural   un + numbered
un + necessary   un + named
un + noticed   un + neighborly

EXERCISE 11

Study the following words, distinguishing between the prefixes *per-* and *pre-*. Keep in mind that *per-* means "through," "throughout," "by," or "for," and that *pre-* means "before."

perform	perhaps	precept
perception	perspective	precipitate
peremptory	perspiration	precise
perforce	precarious	precocious
perfunctory	precaution	prescription

EXERCISE 12

Study the following adjectives, observing that in all of them the suffix is not *-full*, but *-ful*.

peaceful	graceful	grateful	pitiful
dreadful	forceful	faithful	thankful
handful	shameful	healthful	plentiful

EXERCISE 13

Study the following words, observing that in all of them the ending is not *-us*, but *-ous*.

advantageous	specious	fastidious
gorgeous	precious	studious
courteous	vicious	religious
dubious	conscious	perilous

EXERCISE 14

Study the following words, observing that in all of them the suffix *-al* precedes *-ly*.

accidentally   terrifically   exceptionally

he accompanies, I accompanied
she spies, I spied
he replies, I replied
she occupies, I occupied
he varies, I varied
she dries, I dried
he ferries, I ferried
she worries, I worried
he pities, I pitied
she envies, I envied

apologetically	specifically	elementally
pathetically	emphatically	professionally
typically	finally	critically

EXERCISE 15

Study the following words, observing that the suffix is not -*ess*, but -*ness*.

clean + ness	plain + ness	stern + ness
drunken + ness	stubborn + ness	keen + ness
mean + ness	sudden + ness	green + ness

EXERCISE 16

Study the following words, observing that the suffix is not -*able*, but -*ible*.

accessible	horrible	legible
admissible	imperceptible	perceptible
audible	impossible	permissible
compatible	incompatible	plausible
contemptible	incredible	possible
convertible	indefensible	reprehensible
discernible	indelible	responsible
eligible	intelligible	sensible
feasible	invincible	susceptible
flexible	invisible	tangible
forcible	irresistible	terrible

EXERCISE 17

Study the following groups of words.

-*ain*	-*ain*	-*ian*	-*ian*
Britain	curtain	barbarian	guardian
captain	fountain	Christian	musician
certain	mountain	civilian	physician
chieftain	villain	collegian	politician

37d

EXERCISE 18

Study the following groups of words.

-*ede*	-*ede*	-*eed*
accede	precede	exceed
antecede	recede	proceed
concede	secede	succeed

Exercise 19 (page 724)

1. principle   4. principle
2. principle   5. principal
3. principal

EXERCISE 19

Fill the blanks with *principal* or *principle*. *Principle* is always a noun; *principal* is usually an adjective. *Principal* is also occasionally a noun: the *principal* of the school, both *principal* and *interest*.

1. Her refusal was based on _____.
2. This is my _____ for going.
3. The _____ has asked that we hold our meeting tomorrow.
4. He did not even know the first _____ of the game.
5. Can you give the _____ parts of the verb?

EXERCISE 20

Fill the blanks with *affect* or *effect*.

1. An entrance was _____ed by force.
2. The _____ upon her is noticeable.
3. The law will take _____ in July.
4. The hot weather will _____ the crops.
5. There was no serious after_____.

EXERCISE 21

Fill the blanks with *passed* or *past*. *Passed* is the past tense or past participle of the verb *pass*; *past* can be an adjective, noun, adverb, or preposition.

1. We _____ your house.
2. She went _____ me.
3. My cousin is a _____ master at the art of lying.
4. That vocalist is _____ her prime.
5. Many years _____ before he returned.

EXERCISE 22

37d

Fill the blanks with one of the words in each set.

1. *Its* (pronoun in the possessive case) or *it's* (contraction of *it is*).
   a. _____ raining.
   b. The cat has had _____ supper.
   c. The clock is in _____ old place again.
   d. _____ now six years since the accident.
   e. I think that _____ too late to go.

Exercise 20

1. effected   4. affect
2. effect   5. aftereffect
3. effect

Exercise 21

1. passed   4. past
2. past   5. passed
3. past

Exercise 22

1. (a) It's   (d) It's
   (b) its   (e) it's
   (c) its

2. *Your* (pronoun in the possessive case) or *you're* (contraction of *you are*).
   a. _____ mistaken; it is _____ fault.
   b. _____ position is assured.
   c. _____ to go tomorrow.
   d. I hope that _____ taking _____ vacation in July.
   e. I appreciate _____ arriving on time.

3. *There* (adverb or interjection), or *their* (pronoun in the possessive case), or *they're* (contraction of *they are*).
   a. It is _____ turn.
   b. _____ ready to go.
   c. _____ , that is over with.
   d. _____ car was stolen.
   e. _____ back from _____ trip.

4. *Whose* (pronoun in the possessive case) or *who's* (contraction of *who is*).
   a. _____ turn is it?
   b. _____ responsible for this?
   c. He is one _____ word can be trusted.
   d. Bring me a copy of _____ *Who*.
   e. _____ ready to go?

EXERCISE 23

Choose the correct italicized word in each of the following sentences. Consult section **37b** if necessary.

1. Everyone is going *accept, except* me.
2. People came to her every day for *advice, advise,* and she was always ready to *advice, advise* them.
3. At so high an altitude it was hard to *breath, breathe*.
4. Albany is the *capital, capitol* of New York.
5. The tickets were sent with the *complements, compliments* of the manager.
6. The country was as dry and dreary as a *desert, dessert*.
7. The shack in which we *formally, formerly* lived is still standing.
8. It's *later, latter* than you think.
9. The winners were *lead, led* up onto the stage.
10. Button the money in your pocket so you won't *lose, loose* it.

37d

2. (a) You're/your   (d) you're/your
   (b) Your   (e) your
   (c) You're
3. (a) their   (d) Their
   (b) They're   (e) They're/their
   (c) There
4. (a) Whose   (d) *Who's*
   (b) Who's   (e) Who's
   (c) whose

Exercise 23

1. except   6. desert
2. advice/advise   7. formerly
3. breathe   8. later
4. capital   9. led
5. compliments   10. lose

Mechanics

The appearance of a paper, like the appearance of a person, indicates regard for self and for the world at large. Accurate typing, a clean page, observance of editing conventions—all of these suggest a writer's confidence and authority. Wise writers use any available means—including care with mechanics—to win the favor and attention of their readers.

38a Manuscript preparation

Unless your instructor specifies otherwise, you should prepare your essays on standard 8½-by-11-inch white paper. Typed papers—which are preferable—should be double-spaced on unruled white bond. If your instructor permits handwritten papers, use wide-ruled paper, write legibly in black or dark blue ink, and skip lines. An instructor or an editor grows weary with a manuscript that has to be puzzled out one word at a time. Give your thoughts and sentences a fair chance by presenting them neatly on the page.

1. Format

Below are some widely accepted conventions for arranging the text on your page. Your instructor may have additional, or different, requirements.

1. Type or write on one side of the sheet only.
2. Leave a margin of one inch on the top, bottom, and sides of typed papers, slightly more for handwritten essays.
3. On four double-spaced lines in the upper left corner of the first page, give your name, your instructor's name, the course number,

38a

QUICK REFERENCE: *Mechanics*

Capital letters

Capitalize proper nouns, the names of particular people, places, or things: *Monday, General Mills, Democrats, Middle Ages, Lake Erie, African-American, The Book of Mormon, Motorola, Aunt Alice, Mars.*

Capitalize the first word and all important words in the titles and subtitles of books, plays, articles, musical compositions, pictures, and other literary or artistic works. Unimportant words in a title are the articles *a, an,* and *the;* the coordinating conjunctions (*and, but, for, nor, or, so, yet*), and all prepositions (as well as the word *to* when used in an infinitive).

Numbers

Write out numbers from one through ninety-nine: *six, sixth, twenty-one, twenty-first.*

Write out round numbers above ninety-nine that can be expressed in one or two words, and round numbers in the hundreds of thousands: *two thousand, sixteen hundred, five hundred thousand.*

Abbreviations

Do not use periods with postal abbreviations for states, with the abbreviations for certain organizations and agencies, or with acronyms (abbreviations spoken as words): *CA, TX, DAR, FAA, OPEC, UNICEF.*

Do not abbreviate civil, religious, military, or academic titles unless they are followed by a person's full name: *Senator Kennedy, Sen. Edward Kennedy; Father O'Malley, Fr. John J. O'Malley.*

38a

Italics

Italicize all words in the titles of books and monographs; plays, motion pictures, and television and radio series; magazines, journals, and newspapers; paintings and sculpture; and long poems and musical compositions.

> Do not use italics with titles of parts of published works, articles in magazines, or episodes of television shows. Enclose these titles in quotation marks.
>
> Italicize the names of ships, planes, trains, and spacecraft.
>
> Italicize foreign words that have not yet become accepted in English, as well as words referred to as words.

and the date. Double-space again (or skip another line) and center your title. Do not use quotation marks or underline your title unless it includes words that require such punctuation (see **38e**). Capitalize all words in the title except articles, coordinating conjunctions, and prepositions. Double-space after your title and begin the first line of your essay.

4. Indent paragraphs five spaces when you type. In handwritten manuscripts, indent about an inch.

5. Number all pages with arabic numbers in the upper right corner, one-half inch from the top of the page.

2. Quotations

When you reproduce quotations in your text, observe the following conventions. (For an extended discussion of the correct use of quotations, see **20c** and **20d**. For detailed instructions on the use of quotation marks, see **34b**.)

1. A quotation of only a few words should be incorporated into your sentences.

```
In Childhood and Society, Erik Erikson notes

that the young adult, "emerging from the

search for and insistence on identity," has

become "ready for intimacy."
```

2. A quotation of more than four typed lines of prose, or more than three lines of verse, should be set off from the main text without

quotation marks by indenting. Introduce the quotation with a co-lon unless the quotation begins in the middle of a sentence that grammatically continues your own sentence of introduction; in that case, use no punctuation. Indent the quotation ten spaces from the left margin, double-spacing between the last line of your text and the first line of the quotation, and between the lines of the quotation itself.

3. A quotation of poetry should be divided into lines exactly as the original is divided. If an entire line of verse does not fit on one line of the page, the words left over should be indented on the next line.

```
Allons! the inducements shall be greater,

We will sail pathless and wild seas,

We will go where winds blow, waves dash,

     and the Yankee clipper speeds by

     under full sail.
```

4. When quoting dialogue from a story, novel, or play, be sure to reproduce the paragraphing and punctuation of the quotation ex-actly as in the original.

```
     "Are you better, Minet-Chéri?"

     "Yes. I can't think what came over me."

     The grey eyes, gradually reassured, dwelt

on mine.

     "I think I know what it was.  A smart

little rap on the knuckles from Above."

     I remained pale and troubled and my

mother misunderstood:

     "There, there now.  There's nothing so

terrible as all that in the birth of a
```

38a

```
child, nothing terrible at all.  It's much

more beautiful in real life.  The suffering

is so quickly forgotten, you'll see!  The

proof that all women forget is that it is

only men--and what business was it of Zo-

la's, anyway?--who write stories about it."
```

Note, incidentally, that British writers and publishers commonly use a single quotation mark (') where American convention requires double quotation marks(").

3. Manuscript corrections

If a reading of your final draft shows the need for minor corrections, make them unmistakably clear. It is not necessary to recopy an entire page for the sake of one or two small insertions or alterations, but recopying is called for if the number of corrections would make the page difficult to read or messy in appearance. Words to be inserted should be typed or written above the line, and their proper position should be indicated by a caret (^) placed below the line.

```
                  other
On the^hand, Nightingale's books on the nursing

profession remained influential for years after

her death.
```

Inserted words should not be enclosed in parentheses or brackets unless these marks are required by the sentence. Cancel words by drawing a neat line through them, not by enclosing them in parentheses or brackets.

38b Capital letters

The general principle governing capitalization is that proper nouns are capitalized and common nouns are not. A proper noun is the name of a particular person, place, or thing.

Richard Wright	Alaska	the Capitol
Virginia Woolf	New Orleans	the Golden Gate Bridge

A common noun is a more general term that can be used as a name for a number of persons, places, or things.

author	state	building
woman	city	bridge

Note that the same word may be used as both a proper and a common noun.

Of all the *peaks* in the Rocky Mountains, *Pike's Peak* is the mountain I would most like to climb.

Our beginning *history* class studied *legislative* procedure and the part our *representatives* play in it. When I took *History 27,* our class visited the *Legislative* Committee hearing in which *Representative* Cella expressed his views on the Alliance for Progress.

Abbreviations are capitalized when the words they stand for would be capitalized: USN, ROTC, NBC.

1. Proper nouns

Capitalize proper nouns and adjectives derived from them. Proper nouns include the following examples.

1. Days of the week, months, and holidays.

Sunday	Thanksgiving
October	New Year's Eve

2. Organizations such as political parties, governmental bodies and departments, societies, institutions, clubs, churches, and corporations.

Socialist Party	Boston Public Library
U.S. Senate	Optimist's Club
Department of the Interior	Greek Orthodox Church
American Cancer Society	Raytheon Company

38b

3. Members of organizations.

Republicans	Buddhists
Lions	Girl Scouts

4. Historical events, periods, and documents.

Battle of Hastings	Declaration of Independence
Middle Ages	Stamp Act
Baroque Era	Magna Carta

5. Specific places and geographical areas.

Latin America	Colorado River
Ellis Island	the Far East
Sahara Desert	the Midwest

6. Names of races, ethnic groups, and languages (but not the words *white* and *black* when used to refer to races).

Caucasian	Japanese
African-American	Italian

7. Names of religions, religious figures and holidays, and sacred books.

the Lord	the Bible
the Son of God	the Book of Mormon
Allah	Day of Atonement
Lutheran	All Saints' Day

8. Registered trademarks.

Coca-Cola	Volvo
Tide	Sony

38b

9. Terms identifying family members only when such words are used in place of proper names.

My sister and brother both received letters from Grandma and Grandpa.

10. Titles of persons only when they precede proper names.

Senator Marsh	the senator's voting record
Professor Helen Stein	a professor of chemistry
Aunt Elsa	my favorite aunt

11. In biological nomenclature, the names of genera but not of species.

     Homo sapiens   *Equus caballus*
     Salmo irideus   *Aquila heliaca*

12. Stars, constellations, and planets, but not the words *earth, sun,* or *moon* unless they are used as astronomical names.

     Sirius   the Milky Way
     Arcturus   Jupiter

2. Titles of works

Capitalize the first word and the important words of the titles and subtitles of books, plays, articles, musical compositions, paintings, and other literary or artistic works. Unimportant words in a title are the articles *a, an,* and *the;* the coordinating conjunctions (*and, but, for, nor, or, so, yet*); and all prepositions (as well as the word *to* when used in an infinitive).

Matthew Arnold's *Culture and Anarchy*
Brahms's *Variations on a Theme by Handel*
Browning's "Love among the Ruins"
Joan Didion's *Slouching towards Bethlehem*
Shakespeare's *Measure for Measure*
Bruce Springsteen's "Born in the U.S.A."
Telling Lives: The Biographer's Art
"Who and What Is American?"

3. Sentences and quotations

Capitalize the first word of every sentence and of every direct quotation in dialogue. Note that a capital letter is not used for the part of a quotation that follows an interpolated expression like *he said,* unless that expression begins a new sentence.

"Mow the lawn diagonally," said Mr. Grant, "and go over it twice."

"Mow the lawn twice diagonally," said Mr. Grant. "It will be even smoother if the second mowing crosses over the first one."

Mr. Grant said, "Mow the lawn twice."

Following a colon, the first words in a series of short questions or sentences may be capitalized.

The first-aid questions were dull but important: What are the first signs of shock in accident victims? Should they be kept warm? Should they eat? Should they drink?

Capitalize the first word of every line of poetry except when the poem itself does not use a capital letter.

I'll walk where my own nature would be leading:
    It vexes me to choose another guide:
Where the grey flocks in ferny glens are feeding;
    Where the wild wind blows on the mountain-side.

—Emily Brontë

last night i heard
a pseudobird;
or possibly
the usual bird
heard pseudome.

—Ebenezer Peabody

38c Numbers

In general, treat all numbers in a particular context similarly; in the interest of consistency, do not use words for some and figures for others. The following additional guidelines for writing numbers are widely accepted.

1. Numbers from one through ninety-nine and round numbers that can be expressed in one or two words are usually written out.

three people in line

twenty-five flavors

seven hundred reserved seats

325 hotel rooms

Round numbers in the hundreds of thousands are also written out.

three hundred thousand citizens

126,000 votes

Adjectival forms of numbers are also written out when they can be expressed in one or two words.

second chance

thirty-fifth floor

the *ten-thousandth* customer

All numbers that begin a sentence are written out, even though they would ordinarily be represented by figures.

Four hundred sixty dollars was too much.

2. To indicate a range of numbers, use the complete second number for numbers through 99.

33–34   90–99

For larger numbers, use the last two digits of the second number unless more are required.

123–25   100–09

399–401   12,500–13,000

3. Use figures to express the day of the month and the year in a date.

December 7, 1941   14 July 1789

References to centuries and decades are usually written out in lowercase letters but may be expressed in figures. In the latter case, the figures are followed by an *s* without an apostrophe.

the *nineteenth* century   the 1800s

the *sixties*   the 1960s, the ’60s

Write out the names of centuries when they are used as adjectives.

a *twentieth*-century invention

38c

4. Use figures for numbers in street addresses; long numbers; chapter and page numbers; time citations followed directly by A.M. or P.M.; and decimals.

525 Spring Street   page 33

11337 Palm Boulevard   9:00 P.M. [but *nine o'clock*]

1,275 gallons   7:25 A.M.
Chapter 12   8.5 percent

Use figures with abbreviations and symbols.

80 lbs.   66%
55 mph   6′1″

5. Use figures after a dollar sign.

$12.50 $1,000

If the amount of money in question can be expressed in one or two words, it may be written out.

fifty-five cents   *sixteen* dollars

Amounts of money in the millions, billions, or trillions of dollars may be expressed with a combination of figures and words when a dollar sign is used.

$12 million (but *twelve million dollars*)

38d Abbreviations

Minimize the use of abbreviations in expository prose. As a general rule, spell out the first names of people, the words in addresses (*North, Street, New Jersey*), the days of the week and the months of the year, and units of measurement (*ounces, pounds, kilometers, hours, quarts*).

Elliott Brodie of 327 *West* 27th *Avenue*, Kenosha, *Wisconsin*, died on *December* 16, 1989.

38d

Abbreviations cannot be avoided entirely, however, and it is important to be familiar with the most important conventions governing their use.

1. Some abbreviations are always written with periods.

Mr.   Ph.D.
etc.   i.e.
A.D.   P.M.

Others, such as the U.S. Postal Service abbreviations for states and the abbreviations for many organizations and agencies, are written without periods.

CA   DAR
TX   FAA

Acronyms (abbreviations spoken as words) are also written without periods.

NATO   UNICEF
MADD   OPEC

Still other abbreviations may be written with or without periods.

mph or m.p.h.   USA or U.S.A.
rpm or r.p.m.   PTA or P.T.A.

Your best guide to the proper punctuation of an abbreviation is a good desk dictionary. Many such dictionaries conveniently collect all abbreviations in a separate appendix.

2. Civil, religious, military, and academic titles are usually written out.

Senator Kennedy   Governor Cuomo
Secretary Baker   Colonel Mason
Father O'Malley   Professor Meyer

Such titles may be abbreviated only when they are followed by a person's full name: *Sen. Edward Kennedy,* but not *Sen. Kennedy.* The titles *Reverend* and *Honorable* must be followed by a full name *and* preceded by the word *the.*

the Reverend Thomas Jones (not *the Reverend Jones*)
the Honorable Alice Simpson (not *the Honorable Simpson*)

38d

The word *the* is dropped if these titles are abbreviated, but the abbreviated forms must also be followed by a full name.

Rev. Thomas Jones (not *Rev. Jones*)
Hon. Alice Simpson (not *Hon. Simpson*)

3. The titles below are abbreviated when they precede names.

   Mr.   Mrs.
   Messrs.   Dr.
   Ms.   St. [Saint]

   Titles and degrees such as the following are also abbreviated after names.

   Sr.   Ph.D.
   Jr.   M.A.
   M.D.   LL.D.
   D.D.S.   Esq.

   Do not duplicate a title before *and* after a name.

   Incorrect   Dr. Rinard Z. Hart, *M.D.*
   Correct   Rinard Z. Hart, *M.D.*, or *Dr.* Rinard Z. Hart

4. The words *volume, chapter, edition,* and *page* should be written out in references within a text, but abbreviated in parenthetical citations and bibliographies.

   I found this quotation on *page* 267 of the third *edition.*

   For further information on proper terms for addressing dignitaries, consult the Appendix of your style manual (*pp.* 664–80).

5. In technical writing, directions, recipes, and the like, terms of measurement are often abbreviated when used with figures.

   32° F   ½ tsp.
   5 cc   32 mpg
   12 ft.   4 hrs

6. When referring to corporations, use the ampersand (&) and abbreviations such as *Co., Inc.,* and *Bros.* only when a company uses such an abbreviation in its official title.

   Incorrect   D. C. Heath & Co.
   Correct   D. C. Heath and Company

7. Abbreviations that end in a period form their plurals by adding *-'s.*

   two *Ph.D.'s*   M.A.'s in several disciplines

   Abbreviations that do not end in a period usually form their plurals by adding *-s* without an apostrophe.

   the *PTAs* of both schools

   a fraternity house full of *BMOCs*

38e Italics

Italics are used for certain titles, unnaturalized foreign words, scientific names, names of ships and aircraft, and words used as words. To italicize a word in a manuscript, draw one straight line below it, or use the underlining key on the keyboard: King Lear.

1. Italicize all words in the titles of books and monographs; plays, motion pictures, and television and radio series; magazines, journals, and newspapers; paintings and sculpture; and long poems and long musical compositions. The article *the* preceding the title of a newspaper is not italicized or capitalized.

   Stephen Crane's *The Red Badge of Courage*

   Arthur Miller's *Death of a Salesman*

   The Wizard of Oz

   Sesame Street

   Newsweek

   the *Southern Review*

   the *Chicago Tribune*

   Michelangelo's *David*

   Alexander Pope's *The Rape of the Lock*

   Ravel's *Bolero*

38e

Titles of parts of published works, articles in magazines, and episodes of television shows are enclosed in quotation marks.

The assignment is "Despondency" from William Wordsworth's long narrative poem *The Excursion*.

In the *New Yorker,* I always read filler material entitled "Letters We Never Finished Reading."

She hoped to publish her story entitled "Nobody Lives Here" in a magazine like *Harper's.*

2. Italicize the names of ships, planes, trains, and spacecraft.

The S.S. *Constitution* sails for Africa tomorrow.

We saw Lindbergh's *Spirit of St. Louis* when we visited Washington last month.

I'm going to Baltimore on Amtrak's *Yankee Clipper.*

Voyager 2 is still sending back information from deep space.

3. Italicize foreign words that have not yet become accepted in the English language. If you are not certain whether a foreign word has become naturalized, consult a dictionary. Be sure to consult the dictionary's explanatory notes to see how foreign words are indicated. Italicize the Latin scientific names for plants and animals.

A feeling of *gemütlichkeit* pervaded the hotel we stayed at in Munich.

The technical name of Steller's jay is *Cyanocitta stelleri.*

4. Italicize a word referred to as such, as well as a technical term (particularly one accompanied by its definition) when it appears for the first time in your text.

The word *November* had been omitted from the invitations.

An *isotope* is an atom with the same atomic number as another atom but with a different atomic weight.

38f Syllabication

In published writing, dividing a word at the end of a line is mainly a printer's problem. In manuscripts it is not necessary to keep the right-hand margin absolutely even, so it is seldom necessary to divide a word at the end of a line. If such a division is essential, observe the following principles, and mark the division with a hyphen (-).

1. Divide words only *between* syllables—that is, between the normal sound divisions of a word. When in doubt as to where the division between syllables comes, consult a dictionary. One-syllable words,

Exercise 1 (page 741)

1. The Romans built incredible bridges out of rocks and concrete; some still stand two thousand years later.
2. Many bridges were built by twelfth-century Christians who wanted to carry their message all over Europe.
3. According to the book *Great Bridges of the World,* bridge building, already sophisticated in many ways, became a science in the 1700s.
4. Iron was introduced in bridges in 1779, and in the last half of the nineteenth century bridge builders began using steel.
5. There are four main kinds of bridges—beam, arch, suspension, and cantilever—and two types of moveable bridges, pivot and vertical lift, which are a far cry from the drawbridges of medieval times.
6. The longest cantilever bridge, 3,239 feet overall, is the Quebec Bridge over the Saint Lawrence River in Canada.
7. The Lake Pontchartrain Causeway in Louisiana, called the longest bridge in the world, is 23.87 miles long.

such as *though* or *strength,* cannot be divided. Syllables of one letter should not be divided from the rest of the word. Nor should a division be made between two letters that indicate a single sound. For example, never divide *th* as in *brother, sh* as in *fashion, ck* as in *Kentucky, oa* as in *reproaching,* or *ai* as in *maintain.* Such combinations of letters may be divided only if they indicate two distinct sounds: *post-haste, dis-hon-or, co-au-thor.*

Incorrect   a-dult, burg-lar-ize, co-ord-in-a-tion, li-mit, ver-y

Correct   adult, bur-glar-ize, co-or-di-na-tion, lim-it, very

2. A division usually comes at the point where a prefix or suffix joins the root word.

    anti-dote, be-half, con-vene, de-tract, sub-way

    fall-en, Flem-ish, lik-able (or like-able), like-ly, place-ment, tall-er, tall-est

    This rule does not hold when it contradicts the normal pronunciation of the word.

    bus-tling, jog-gled, prej-u-dice, prel-ate, res-ti-tu-tion, twin-kling

3. When two consonants come between vowels (me*mb*er), the division is between the consonants if pronunciation permits (*mem-ber*). If the consonant is doubled before a suffix, the second consonant goes with the suffix (*plan-ning*).

    at-tend, bur-lesque, clas-sic, dif-fer, fas-ten, fit-ting, hin-der, im-por-tant, laun-der, nar-rate, pas-sage, rab-bit, rum-mage, ser-geant, ten-don
    BUT NOTE: knowl-edge

4. The division comes after a vowel if pronunciation permits.

    devi-ate, modi-fier, ora-torical, oscilla-tor

38f

EXERCISE **1**

Correct any errors in capitalization, numbers, abbreviations, and italics.

Example

> The 1st bridges on the Earth were natural ones, formed by rocks and fallen trees.

8. Bridges are technically fascinating, but a person doesn't have to be a professor of engineering to appreciate their beauty.
9. The Brooklyn Bridge in New York City has inspired artists and writers, including John Marin and Hart Crane.
10. Many bridges—such as the Golden Gate Bridge in San Francisco, California, and the famous London Bridge, which was dismantled and moved to Arizona—are tourist attractions.

Exercise 2 (page 742)

1. Early images of Native Americans were of savages, hundreds of godless warmongers who attacked small groups of innocent settlers, and an occasional Native American who recognized the value of the white man's ways.
2. In some movies, at least a few of the whites were equally bad, stealing land and carrying off Native American women, but the larger evils of government exploitation and genocide were never suggested.

> **Corrected** The first bridges on the earth were natural ones, formed by rocks and fallen trees.

1. The romans built incredible bridges out of rocks and concrete; some still stand 2,000 yrs. later.
2. Many bridges were built by 12th-century christians who wanted to carry their message all over europe.
3. According to the book Great Bridges of the World, bridge building, already sophisticated in many ways, became a Science in the seventeen hundreds.
4. Iron was introduced in bridges in seventeen seventy-nine, and in the last ½ of the 19 cent. bridge builders began using steel.
5. There are 4 main kinds of bridges—beam, arch, suspension, and cantilever—and 2 types of moveable bridges, pivot and vertical lift, which are a far cry from the drawbridges of Medieval Times.
6. The longest cantilever bridge, 3,239 ft. overall, is the quebec bridge over the saint lawrence river in Canada.
7. The lake pontchartrain causeway in La., called the longest bridge in the world, is 23.87 mi. long.
8. Bridges are technically fascinating, but a person doesn't have to be a Professor of Engineering to appreciate their beauty.
9. The brooklyn bridge in NYC has inspired Artists and Writers, including John Marin & Hart Crane.
10. Many bridges—such as the golden gate bridge in San Francisco, CA, and the famous london bridge, which was dismantled and moved to Ariz.—are Tourist attractions.

EXERCISE 2

Correct any errors in capitalization, numbers, abbreviations, and italics.

Example

Because movies are a reliable gauge of the Country's social attitudes, analyzing images of native americans in films can reveal a great deal.

> **Corrected** Because movies are a reliable gauge of the country's social attitudes, analyzing images of Native Americans in films can reveal a great deal.

1. Early images of native americans were of Savages, 100s of Godless warmongers who attacked small groups of innocent Settlers, and an occasional native american who recognized the value of the White Man's ways.

3. One of the first movies to break this trend was *Broken Arrow,* which appeared in 1950.
4. In the 1957 movie *Run of the Arrow,* Rod Steiger played an outcast who considered becoming a Sioux but became an American citizen instead.
5. Over the next fifteen years, movies began to recognize the existence of Native American cultures beyond the stereotypical tepees and peace pipes.
6. For example, eighty percent of the dialogue in *A Man Called Horse* is in Sioux.
7. It was not until *Little Big Man* in 1970 that a Native American, Chief Dan George, was cast in a lead role in a major motion picture.
8. The 1980 film *Windwalker* also stands out; even though a British actor played the lead, the entire movie was done in the Cheyenne and Crow languages, with subtitles in English.
9. In the nineties [or '90s], films like *Dances with Wolves* and *Thunderheart* reversed stereotypes by portraying government agencies as villains.

38f

2. In some movies, at least a few of the Whites were equally bad, stealing land and carrying off native american women, but the larger evils of Government exploitation and genocide were never suggested.
3. One of the 1st movies to break this trend was Broken Arrow, which appeared in nineteen fifty.
4. In the 1957 movie Run of the Arrow, Rod Steiger played an outcast who considered becoming a sioux but became an american citizen instead.
5. Over the next 15 yrs., movies began to recognize the existence of nat. am. cultures beyond the stereotypical tepees and peace pipes.
6. For ex., eighty % of the dialogue in A Man called Horse is in sioux.
7. It was not until Little big man in 1970 that a native american, chief Dan George, was cast in a lead role in a major motion picture.
8. The nineteen-eighty film Windwalker also stands out; even though a Brit. actor played the lead, the entire movie was done in the cheyenne and crow languages, with subtitles in english.
9. In the nineties, films like Dances with Wolves and Thunderheart reversed stereotypes by portraying government agencies as villains.
10. Perhaps these changes indicate a recognition in Mainstream American Culture that the role of native americans in this country transcends cowboy-and-indian games.

38f

10. Perhaps these changes indicate a recognition in mainstream American culture that the role of Native Americans in the country transcends cowboy-and-Indian games.

PART VIII

Special Writing Situations

39 *Writing Business Letters*

The process of composing a business letter involves many of the same issues that are important in other writing tasks. What is your main point, and what do you wish to accomplish? How much do you know about your readers and their probable response? What tone should you adopt? How much specific detail must you include? But beyond these matters of content, the appearance of a business letter is also critical. An effective business letter *looks* like a business letter; it wins its reader's attention partly by following the conventions that characterize business correspondence. This chapter, therefore, deals not only with questions of content but also with important matters of form.

39a The rhetoric of business correspondence

We write business letters for many reasons—to request information, to place orders, to voice complaints, to offer thanks. Each business letter takes shape in a unique rhetorical situation, a specific relationship to be developed between writer and reader. The best letters build on that relationship to accomplish their writers' purposes.

1. Consider your reader

Whenever possible, address your letter by name to a specific person rather than to a mere job title such as "Personnel Director" or "Customer Relations Manager." Particularly for application letters or letters of complaint, it may well be worth the small cost to telephone a company and ask the name of the person to whom you should write.

Good writing in a business letter has the same qualities as good writing anywhere, including clear organization, adequate specific development, and sensitivity to audience. But as anyone who regularly receives business correspondence knows, the conventions of form make almost as large a contribution to the effect of a business letter as its content does. This chapter and the next, therefore, deal with both content and form in letter writing and include models of letters written in the three most common styles—indented, block, and modified block.

For a suggestion about creating writing assignments that provide experience in letter writing, see page 40.

QUICK REFERENCE: *Parts of a Business Letter*

A business letter contains five essential elements. Except as noted below, single-space throughout the letter, centering the text neatly on the page.

Heading	Three lines at the top of the letter containing your street address; your city, state, and ZIP code; and today's date. Double-space or quadruple-space after the heading.
Inside address	Identical to the address you type on the envelope. Double-space after the inside address.
Salutation	Repeats the name given on the first line of the inside address, omitting the addressee's first name: *Dear Mr. Agee, Dear Professor Wilcox.* Follow the salutation with a colon, and double-space before the first paragraph of the body.
Body	Begins by clearly stating your purpose for writing. Continues with concise, specific, and clear development. Double-space or quadruple-space after the last line of the body.
Close	An appropriate concluding phrase (*Sincerely, Yours truly, Best wishes,*), followed by a comma. Quadruple-space and type your name. Sign your letter in the space between the two lines.

Letters addressed impersonally to a mere title will eventually land on the correct desk, but they lack the impressive sense of direct contact conveyed by letters written to a specific individual.

Think carefully about your reader, and try to strike an appropriate tone. A snarling letter of complaint may offer a temporary outlet for your frustrations, but it is less likely to resolve your problem than a letter that suggests your patience and reasonableness. As you organize the contents of your letter, keep in mind the suggestions for effective

39a

writing discussed elsewhere in this book. Provide your reader with specific information, and arrange it in paragraphs that are coherent and complete; no reader making his or her way through a stack of incoming correspondence will be willing to puzzle over your intended meaning. Give your letter the attention to style that suggests a sophisticated writer, and proofread the final copy with professional accuracy.

2. Consider your form

Business letters, even short ones, are usually typed, single-spaced, on one side of 8½-by-11-inch paper. Neat centering on the page is more important than adherence to standard margins. In what is called *block style,* all the parts of a letter are typed flush against the left margin, and the first lines of paragraphs are not indented (see sample on page 759). In the less formal *indented style,* by contrast, the inside address and the close are typed on the right side of the page and the first line of each paragraph is indented five spaces (see sample on page 753). The *modified block style* follows the general arrangement of the indented style, but without indentation of the first lines of paragraphs (see sample on page 752).

39b Parts of a business letter

A typical business letter has five parts.

1. The heading

The heading consists of your address and the date, usually typed on three lines, and placed either flush against the upper left margin (block style) or in the upper right corner (indented style). It is included so that the person who receives your letter will be able to respond to you even if your envelope is lost or discarded.

The first line of the heading contains your street address; the second, your city, state, and ZIP code; the third, today's date. If you abbreviate your state, use the standard two-letter abbreviation (without periods) prescribed by the U.S. Postal Service. Double-space or quadruple-space after the last line of the heading.

39b

2.   The inside address

The inside address is identical to the address that you type on the envelope. Including it inside the letter ensures that your letter will reach its addressee even if it is opened by someone else in an office and becomes separated from its envelope.

On the first line of the inside address, use the appropriate abbreviated title with the full name of the person you are writing to: Mr. David Hunt, Dr. Elizabeth Aikers, Ms. Harriet Sweeney, Rev. Stephen Jules. If the person has an official position within a company, the title of the position and the name of the company are given on the second line, separated by a comma, or on the second and third lines.

```
Mr. Robert O'Malley
Editor in Chief, The Indianapolis Courier

Ms. Margaret Wilson
Vice President
Blindex Corporation
```

The next line of the inside address contains the street address, followed on the concluding line with the city, state, and ZIP code. Again, if you abbreviate the state, use the U.S. Postal Service abbreviation. Double-space after the inside address.

3.   The salutation

The salutation repeats the name given on the first line of your inside address, omitting the person's first name. In business letters the salutation is followed by a colon.

```
Dear Mr. O'Malley:

Dear Ms. Wilson:
```

If you are unable to obtain the name of the person to whom your letter should be addressed, use one of the following salutations:

```
Dear Sir or Madam:
```
[Use this salutation when you are writing to a specific person whose name you do not know—for example, the editor of a newspaper or the chief of surgery in a hospital.]

39b

Ladies and Gentlemen:
[Use this salutation when you must address your letter to a company or organization rather than to a specific person.]

If you know the sex but not the name of the person to whom you are writing, you may use the salutation *Dear Sir* or *Dear Madam.*

Avoid the salutations *Dear Sirs* and *Gentlemen,* both of which illogically exclude women. And never open a standard business letter with the phrase *To Whom It May Concern;* this salutation is used only in letters such as personal recommendations that are intended for distribution to various people unknown to the writer.

Double-space after your salutation.

4. The body

Clearly state your purpose for writing — to apply for a job, to order a replacement part, or to express a complaint — as early as possible in your letter. Major corporations and large government offices receive hundreds — if not thousands — of letters every day, and your correspondence will get the fastest possible treatment if the person who opens your letter can immediately determine what you want. For the same reason, be concise, specific, and clear.

5. The close

Double-space or quadruple-space after the last line of the body of your letter, and type an appropriate close: very formal (*Very truly yours,*), formal (*Yours truly, Sincerely yours, Sincerely,*), or relatively informal (*Best wishes,*). The close is positioned under the inside address, either flush left (block style) or at the right side of the page (indented style). Capitalize only the first word, and follow the close with a comma. Leave room for your signature by quadruple-spacing, and type your name exactly as you will sign it.

Sincerely yours,

William A. Quinn

William A. Quinn

39b

Business letters are usually mailed in long (9½-inch) envelopes. Type your name and address in the upper left corner, and center the name and address of your correspondent, just as they appear in your letter's inside address.

```
Maureen Brown
218 East 10th Street
Columbus, OH 43202



                Mr. Stephen Hernandez
                Circulation Manager
                Book Collectors' Digest
                2121 Peachtree Plaza
                Atlanta, GA 30309
```

Sample business letter (modified block style)

```
                        218 East 10th Street
                        Columbus, OH 43202
                        February 8, 1994

Mr. Stephen Hernandez
Circulation Manager
Book Collectors' Digest
2121 Peachtree Plaza
Atlanta, GA 30309

Dear Mr. Hernandez:

For the second consecutive month, I have
not received my issue of Book Collectors' Di-
gest.  Since my address has not changed, I am
inclined to think that a mailing problem exists
```

39b

somewhere in your office, and I would appreciate your looking into the matter. My subscription number is B2184-886.

Because I have missed two issues of my subscription through this delivery problem, may I
ask that you extend my subscription by two
months, until October of this year? I enjoy
your magazine and look forward to remaining one
of your subscribers.

                    Sincerely,

                    Maureen Brown

                    Maureen Brown

Sample business letter (indented style)

                    90 North Thomas Avenue
                    Kingston, New York 12401
                    May 16, 1994

Catalog Department
Gillespie Furniture Creations
3101 Fontaine Road
Denver, CO 80203

Ladies and Gentlemen:

     On April 26 I ordered a chrome-and-glass
coffee table (model C261/LY) from your spring
1994 catalog. When it arrived yesterday, I discovered that several pieces of hardware needed
for assembly were missing. Would you please
send me the following missing parts:

               6-#17 metal screws
               1-connecting rod "B"
               2-chrome finishing caps

39b

For your information, I have enclosed a copy of the shipping invoice. I appreciate your assistance and look forward to hearing from you.

Yours truly,

Mark Wallace

Mark Wallace

Enclosure

40 *Composing Résumés and Job Applications*

Job applications are among the most important letters that anyone writes. When you compose a résumé and write an accompanying letter of application, you must rely on your writing to persuade a potential employer that your qualifications, personality, and interests make you the best candidate for the job.

40a Designing a résumé

A *résumé*, sometimes called a *vita* (the Latin word for "life"), lists chronologically the activities of your life that qualify you for a job. It is an essential part of every job application.

1. Format

There is no fixed format for a résumé, but you should keep in mind a few general guidelines. Above all, make the content of your résumé clear and easy to follow, and arrange it attractively. Make headings and subheadings stand out by underlining or using boldface type. Leave wide margins and sufficient white space between the major sections of your résumé. Don't feel that you have to crowd everything onto a single page, but don't pad your résumé with needless detail or trivial facts simply to extend its length.

40a

QUICK REFERENCE: *Designing a Résumé*

Make the contents of your résumé clear and easy to follow, arrange information neatly on the page, help headings and sub-headings to stand out by using underlining or boldface type, and leave wide margins and sufficient white space on the page. Include the following essential elements:

Personal information	Provide your full name, your current address, and your telephone number or numbers.
Education	In reverse chronological order, list institutions attended (with accurate dates), fields of study, and degrees earned.
Experience	In reverse chronological order, list positions held (with accurate dates) and briefly describe responsibilities or accomplishments.
References	Indicate that references are available upon request, or list the names, addresses, and telephone numbers of persons whom the reader can contact directly.

---

2. Content

Every résumé should begin with your full name (avoid nicknames), your current address, and your telephone number (include both a home and an office number if you are willing to receive calls from potential employers at your present place of work). Typically, the major categories under which the remaining material on a résumé is placed are "Education" and "Experience." List items in reverse chronological order, and provide accurate dates, so that a reader can see what you have done in each recent year of your life. It is acceptable for a résumé to continue on additional pages; more important than length are the substance of the information you present and a neat, uncrowded appearance. A résumé usually ends either with a notation such as "Ref-

40a

erences available on request" or with the names, addresses, and tele-phone numbers of persons whom the reader can contact directly for more information about you.

Some employers also like to find something about a candidate's outside interests on a résumé; others consider such information irrele-vant padding. Use your best judgment, based on what you can learn and surmise about your reader. In any case, you should not include such personal information as height, weight, or marital status unless it has direct bearing on the job you are applying for. (See the sample résumé on pages 760–61.)

40b Letters of application

A résumé is usually accompanied by a cover letter, called a *letter of application,* that is personally addressed to a potential employer. Such a letter should be complete but normally should not exceed one page. Its contents are usually divided into three sections.

1. Introduction

Use your introductory paragraph (which may be no longer than a sentence or two) to accomplish three things. First, make it clear that you are writing a letter of application. Businesses receive many kinds of letters every day, and you want to be sure that yours is imme-diately grouped with those of other job applicants. Second, state the specific job that you are applying for. Often a company will advertise several positions at once; it is to your advantage, obviously, to be sure that your letter correctly places you in competition for the job you want. Finally, indicate how you learned of the opening you are apply-ing for—whether you read a newspaper advertisement, for example, or were referred by a friend who knew of the company's hiring plans.

2. Body

The body of your letter should summarize your qualifications clearly and specifically. Don't simply repeat all the facts on your résumé; instead, use your letter to *comment* on the résumé, emphasizing your most important qualifications and providing additional information about your background where appropriate.

40b

At the same time, let the style of your writing reveal something about your personality. Ideally, the tone of an application letter should be businesslike but not stuffy, natural but not chatty. Be positive, but without being pushy or insistent; most employers, like most general readers, are impressed by confidence but not by raw aggressiveness. Don't make insupportable assertions about your suitability for the job in question ("I am unquestionably the candidate you are looking for"). Similarly, don't offer glowing evaluations of your accomplishments ("My course work in economics has given me outstanding mastery of the field"). Take a more objective stance instead, and let the facts in your background speak for themselves ("At my graduation I was named Outstanding Student in Economics on the basis of the 4.00 grade-point average that I earned in my economics course work."). Finally, avoid a highly idiosyncratic style or an unorthodox approach in your letter unless you are certain that it is appropriate for your potential employer.

3. Conclusion

Use the brief conclusion of your letter to direct the reader's attention to the résumé that you have enclosed, to state your willingness to be interviewed for the position, and to provide information about when and where you would be available for a possible interview. Some employment counselors recommend that a letter of application end with the applicant's offer to call the reader in the near future in order to arrange an interview; others argue that such calls are presumptuous and will only alienate a potential employer. You must decide which approach is suitable for the employers you address.

Sample cover letter (block style)

2094 Neil Avenue, Apt. 45
Des Moines, Iowa 50312
June 17, 1993

Mr. William Prewett
Personnel Director, A&G Associates
1212 Milliken Drive
Cedar Rapids, Iowa 52401

Dear Mr. Prewett:

I wish to apply for the position of Public Relations Assistant that you advertised in the
Des Moines Register last week.

I received my B.A. in May from the University
of Iowa with a major in history and a minor in
communications. My major field has given me
not only the broad intellectual background of a
liberal arts curriculum, but also substantial
experience in research and report writing.
Through my minor in communications, moreover, I
have gained experience in the areas of inter-
personal communication, group dynamics, and organizational and small-group communication.

From my extracurricular work, I have gained
practical experience in publications and editing. As managing editor of the University of
Iowa student literary magazine for the past two
years, I shared responsibility for all editorial decisions with the magazine's editor in
chief. In addition, I had primary responsibility for overseeing the actual production of
each semester's issue. During my junior year,
I was one of two student assistants employed by
the Office of the Dean of Students to prepare
office memoranda for distribution throughout
the campus.

40b

My résumé is enclosed. Although I am currently
living in Des Moines, I would be happy to come

to Cedar Rapids at any time for an interview. I appreciate your consideration and look forward to hearing from you.

Sincerely,

Phyllis Wainwright

Phyllis Wainwright

Enclosure

Sample résumé

RÉSUMÉ

Phyllis Wainwright
2094 Neil Avenue, Apt. 45
Des Moines, Iowa 50312
(515) 555-6682

Education   B.A., cum laude, University of Iowa, 1993.
     Major: History
     Minor: Communications

Experience Managing Editor, Iowa Literary Journal, 1991-93.
     Solicited student submissions of fiction and poetry; shared responsibility for all editorial decisions; supervised proofreading, design, and layout of magazine.

Student Assistant, Office of the Dean of Students, University of Iowa, 1991-92.
     Responsible for preparing and distributing office memoranda, distributing incoming mail, and helping to maintain office files.

Host, Macmillan's Restaurant, Des Moines, Iowa, Summer, 1991.

40b

```
              Peer Tutor, Department of History,
              University of Iowa, 1990-92.
                  Tutored students in History 121,
                  122 (European History I, II).
```

```
References    Dr. Rosemary Eddins
              Faculty Adviser, Iowa Literary
              Journal
              Department of English
              University of Iowa
              Iowa City, Iowa 52240
              (515) 555-4283

              Mr. Nathaniel Robinson
              Dean of Students
              University of Iowa
              Iowa City, Iowa 52240
              (515) 555-9032

              Dr. Alice Voros
              Chair, Department of History
              University of Iowa
              Iowa City, Iowa 52240
              (515) 555-6930
```

40b

For Further Reading

Beatty, Richard H. *The Perfect Cover Letter*. New York: Wiley, 1989.

Hansen, Katharine. *Dynamite Cover Letters*. Berkeley: Ten Speed Press, 1990.

Lathrop, Richard. *Who's Hiring Who*. Rev. ed. Berkeley: Ten Speed Press, 1989.

41 *Writing under Pressure*

Earlier chapters of this book stressed the extended and recursive nature of the writing process—isolating a subject, analyzing your audience, exploring your ideas, considering possible methods of development, planning the organization of a paper, drafting, revising, reconsidering, redrafting. But some kinds of academic writing (not to mention much writing done in professional life) don't permit us to plan, write, and revise with the leisure we would prefer. Short-answer tests, midterm examinations, two-hour final examinations with three or more questions to be answered—such examples of academic writing are reminders of the limits that the classroom situation may impose on your writing process. The focus of this chapter is techniques for effective economizing, that is, for composing efficiently and confidently despite such restrictions.

41a Preparing for the essay examination

Of course, none of the strategies described in this chapter are substitutes for mastering the content of a course; no strategy will conceal the fact that a writer has little to say about the subject at hand. The starting point for effective writing under pressure, therefore, is acquiring thorough familiarity with the material assigned for an examination.

Plan your time so that you can review systematically and fully. Begin by going over your class notes and your underlinings in your text or texts. In doing so, pay special attention to the concepts and ideas that your instructor has stressed and the information or key examples that flesh out these primary ideas. For instance, in an introductory film

41a

Students sometimes think of in-class writing as an activity completely separate from the writing they do in out-of-class essays. Chapter **41** attempts to break down this distinction, and at the same time to suggest some special strategies for writing effectively under examination conditions.

> QUICK REFERENCE: *Tips for Writing an Essay Examination*
>
> *Understand the directions.*   Know the difference between explaining, analyzing, comparing, summarizing, and evaluating, and follow your instructor's directions carefully.
>
> *Plan your answer.*   Take a few moments to outline your response or to list key terms, names, or details.
>
> *Be brisk.*   Begin answering the question immediately, with minimal background or introduction.
>
> *Be responsive.*   Make sure that your essay actually answers the question that your instructor has posed.
>
> *Be analytical.*   Don't substitute mere summary for analysis, explanation, and evaluation.
>
> *Be specific.*   Provide specific evidence and explain how it substantiates your assertions.
>
> *Review your answer.*   Take time to review the form and content of your essay before handing in the examination booklet.

course you would need to know the concept of "shooting angle" and to be able to illustrate it by a specific reference to Hitchcock or some other master. Take the time to acquire a firm grasp of concepts that you may understand only in a general way. For instance, in a course on educational tests and measurements, you would want to be able to explain in detail how to determine the validity and reliability of a test. Start, then, by reviewing the major course topics, techniques of analysis, and key illustrations.

You can also prepare by trying to anticipate the kind of question you are likely to be asked. One way of doing this is to pose such questions for yourself and to think through how you would answer them. For example, if you had just finished a long unit on the Civil War in an American history course, you could easily frame questions on the Civil War's early roots, its more immediate causes, and its major phases. Posing such questions is excellent preparation in two ways: it facilitates

41a

your reviewing, and it enables you to synthesize the materials into your own understanding of them. Many students have found it helpful to work together in framing and answering possible essay examination questions.

41b Reading the examination

Once the examination has been handed out, *read it through carefully*. As you read, keep in mind the number of questions you are expected to answer and the suggested time limits, if any, for each question. If the instructor has not indicated the weight of each question by suggesting time limits, you will have to make these choices yourself. Usually, you will have a pretty good idea of which questions are harder and therefore require more time, and which are easier and require less.

1. Understand the directions

After having read the examination and tentatively allocated your time, go back and reread the questions you plan to answer, paying special attention to the directions for each one. Note in particular the verb that indicates what you are required to do in your answer.

Explain = Spell out the reasons, causes, connections.

("Explain why Britain adopted the VAT" = spell out the reasons Britain adopted the value-added tax.)

Analyze = Break up, separate, segment into parts, steps, phases, sections, causes.

("Analyze the effects of the Cold War on French foreign policy" = separate into phases the effects of the Cold War on French foreign policy.)

Compare = Place side by side and **point out** significant similarities, differences, or both.

("Compare the role of the government in Keynesian and monetary economic theory" = place the roles of government in Keynesian and monetary economic theory side by side.)

41b

Summarize = Reduce, abbreviate to the major aspects, features, events, arguments, without distortion.

("Summarize Hume's views on causation" = abbreviate Hume's major arguments on causation.)

Evaluate = Judge, take a position on the merits of, adequacy of, reasons for or against, consequences of.

("Evaluate Piaget's views on how children learn" = judge the merits or adequacy of Piaget's views on how children learn.)

But what about *discuss,* that open-ended verb so often used for exam questions? Broadly, *discuss* means to open up, reflect on, show that you know about and have thought about the subject. Sometimes, the context makes clear what is called for. "Discuss the pros and cons of federal intervention in abortion," for instance, means "Summarize, compare, and evaluate the case for and against federal intervention in abortion." If you are in doubt, try turning the command into a question in order to discover which analytic skills are called for. To take a few examples:

1. Discuss the plausibility of Jung's doctrine of the collective unconscious = How convincing is Jung's doctrine? = **Evaluate.**
2. Discuss the major therapies in the treatment of autistic children = What are the major therapies? = **Summarize** and **compare.**
3. Discuss the significant changes in Hester Prynne's attitude toward her sin in *The Scarlet Letter* = What are the major changes? = **Analyze.**

If, even with these guidelines in mind, you are not certain what your instructor is looking for, ask for clarification. Your bewilderment or doubts are likely shared by other students.

2.   Plan your answer

Once you are clear on what is called for, *plan your answer.* This is the most important step you can take before you begin writing. Except for brief quizzes, you always have at least a few minutes to think before answering; take them. Strategies for planning answers vary:

41b

some students jot down an informal outline, with major headings and subheadings; others simply list key terms, phrases, names, or details and then look for a logical pattern or sequence; still others frame a precise thesis and work out an organizational plan before diving in. All of these techniques are valuable. The point is simply to understand the topic thoroughly before you begin writing, so that you don't use up half your time in desperate false starts. By planning, you not only gain focus; you also make yourself an active searcher in pursuit of an answer, instead of remaining a passive spectator waiting for something to happen.

41c Writing the essay

In writing your answer, you should strive for the same qualities of effective exposition that are expected in papers written out of class. Obviously, though, time won't always allow you to polish and review your answer as fully as you and your teacher would like. Sometimes, you will be pushed just to finish and to have a few minutes for proofreading. Nevertheless, while writing you should try to keep the following principles in mind.

1. Start briskly

Don't begin with long, prefatory remarks, but *go quickly and directly to the question.* Answers that begin with sentences like "This is a very controversial issue on which people hold many different viewpoints" or "This is a very complicated subject and solutions are hard to find" and that run on this way for a whole paragraph are mere throat-clearing. If the issue is controversial, your analysis should make that fact clear in its treatment of the viewpoints; if the issue is complex, your analysis should reflect that complexity. Similarly, don't begin with a long digression on something you haven't been asked about. If, for instance, you were asked to discuss the effects of the Vietnam War on America in the 1960s, you would simply be avoiding the question if you started with a long paragraph on French colonial policy or the history of the Monroe Doctrine. Such false starts are rather like the complaint of one of Saul Bellow's characters in *Seize the Day:* "If you wanted to talk about a glass of water, you had to start back with God creating the heavens and earth."

41c

2.   Respond to the question

Your beginning is a promise to yourself and the instructor about your intended direction. Often, your opening will be framed by the terms of the topic.

> Discuss three causes of . . .
>
> Compare X's and Y's theories of . . .
>
> Summarize the features of . . .

Go directly to the causes, theories, or features that you are asked to write about, approaching them in an orderly way. In cases where the wording of the topic is more open-ended, try turning the directions into a question. Thus, for example, if you were directed to "Write an essay on some significant aspect of Cézanne's achievement as a painter," you could easily ask yourself "What *is* a significant aspect of his achievement as a painter?" If, as sometimes happens, you do find yourself off to a false start, stop immediately. Return to the question and redirect your thinking to it.

3.   Be analytical

One of the more common but easily avoidable failures in essay answers is the substitution of summary for analysis. If, for instance, you are asked to compare two major historical figures, a mere description, which only outlines each, will not do: you are asked to bring prominent similarities and differences together—to highlight these features. Similarly, if you are asked to analyze or evaluate a case, a plot, or an event, don't give a summary. A sure sign that thought is absent is the writer's stating what happened without shaping an argument, making connections, or offering an interpretation—the summary that all too often runs as follows: "This was said and that happened and this was the result, so thus and such also was said and led to another result, and . . ."

4.   Provide specific evidence

The crucial choices you face in the body of the answer concern examples: what kind? how many? how thoroughly discussed? First, unless asked to give all examples, be selective, not exhaustive. Pick the

41c

most telling or typical ones. For instance, if you were discussing Huck Finn's essential decency, his humaneness, you couldn't list all cases—the novel is full of them—but you could focus on his growing awareness of his concern for Jim and on his resolve to help Jim escape, and you could point to the risks Huck takes to help the Wilks girls. Perhaps other examples interest you more—Huck's shock at the feud or pity for the tarred-and-feathered Duke and King, despite their treachery. Whatever the case, *limit* your choices to a few pointed ones.

Second, *do* something with your evidence. Merely mentioning an example or two in a sentence is not enough. Until you show by concrete development how the example applies, how it makes your point, you haven't fully answered the question. For instance, if you were discussing why Japanese car manufacturers have taken over a significant part of the American market, you couldn't merely drop the names Nissan and Toyota. What about them—better engineering and design? quicker anticipation of the demand for small cars and flexibility in planning and retooling? lower cost to the consumer because of gas economy and cheaper production costs? better marketing and servicing? Any or several of these may be relevant. However, until you specifically discuss, say, what is better in the engineering of a major Japanese model, you haven't done anything with your evidence or answered the question "Why?"

5. Review what you have written

As you come to the end of your essay, look over what you have written to determine whether you need a conclusion or not. Usually, a short summary paragraph that restates your argument or recapitulates your main points will serve well enough. Finally, when finished take a few minutes to proofread, not just skimming for obvious errors but considering changes in wording, insertions, even the renumbering of paragraphs. You haven't really finished until you turn in the exam booklet.

41d Two sample essays

41d

The two esssays that follow, both written in response to the same question, illustrate some of the differences between an ineffective and an effective answer.

Question

What did William James mean by "the moral equivalent of war" and how does his idea illustrate pragmatism as a philosophy?

Ineffective essay

William James was the brother of the novelist Henry James and was Gertrude Stein's teacher. James taught at Harvard for many years, along with such other notables as Santayana and Royce. James was one of the founders of pragmatism, a philosophy that judges ideas by their practicality. By "the moral equivalent of war," James meant something to replace war with. James speaks of war as "a school of strenuous life and heroism." He believed war was destructive and hardened soldiers. He also believed war promoted discipline and was a universal model of heroism. He wanted to discover a peaceful equivalent of war. That was what he meant by "the moral equivalent of war."

You can easily see why this answer is ineffective. The opening two sentences are a false start; they have nothing to do with the question. The third sentence—on pragmatism— is brief, unclear, and left dangling, unrelated to the question or the answer. The rest of the paragraph consists of choppy, disconnected sentences that lack focus. And except for the quotation from James, there isn't much concreteness.

Effective essay

By "the moral equivalent of war," James means a spiritual or social equivalent that would appeal as universally to our capacity for discipline and bravery as war does, but without its terrible destructiveness. Defining war as "a school of strenuous life and heroism," James recognizes how it hardens soldiers but also how it is the only model of selflessness available to the mass of humanity. He observes that voluntary poverty might be one example of a disciplined life that does not rely on hurting others. Pragmatism, a philosophy that tests concepts by looking at their actual consequences in life, is clearly expressed in James's suggestion. In effect, he looks at the facts—the consequences—and says that if something as vicious as the idea of war can still draw out heroic qualities, then we ought to be able to find a noble idea—"a moral equivalent of war"—that brings out the best in us.

In contrast with the first example, this effective answer begins by defining James's idea and develops it clearly and coherently. This second

41d

answer is much more tightly organized and precisely worded than the first. And it *connects* James's idea to pragmatism, as directed by the question, while also defining pragmatism more adequately than the first answer defines it. Finally, the second answer closes strongly with a firm restatement of James's idea. The second paragraph isn't much longer than the first, but it contains far more information and is much easier to follow. It answers the question.

41d

42 *Writing with a Word Processor*

The writing process has been transformed during the past decade or so by the widespread availability of personal computers and computer programs known as word processors. If you have never used a word processor, or if you have tried word processing but did not feel comfortable with it, this chapter is for you. The pages that follow discuss some of the capabilities common to all word processors and suggest ways of making the best use of them as you compose and revise your manuscript.

42a Understanding word processing

A word processor is a computer program that allows a writer to create and manipulate a text on an electronic screen, called a *monitor,* and then send it to a printer to be reproduced on paper. Word processing offers two key advantages over other methods of composing and revising. First, the electronic text is infinitely flexible; a writer can add, delete, and move words in the document at the touch of a keyboard key. Second, since the text is stored on a computer disk after each working session, the writer needs to type it only once; after making whatever changes are necessary, he or she prints the paper electronically without further retyping.

If you find it difficult to get started on a writing assignment, or if you have trouble finding ways to revise your writing once you've put a draft down on paper, then word processing could make your writing sessions easier and more productive. Don't put off learning word processing because you are intimidated by computers; you don't need to know anything about how a computer works to use a word processor. And don't be concerned about damaging the computer you're working

42a

771

QUICK REFERENCE: *Word-Processing Terminology*

File	The text of the document you create, held in the computer's memory while you are working on it or permanently stored on disk.
Backup	An extra copy of the document you are working on, saved on disk in case the current copy should be lost.
Save	The computer function that enables you to make backup copies of a document or to store the final copy on disk.
Word wrap	The automatic advancing of the text to a new line when one line is full, eliminating the need for a typewriter-style carriage return.
Insert	The computer function that permits the addition of a letter, a word, or a page or more of text into the middle of a document.
Delete	The computer function that eliminates from a document text that you no longer want.
Move	The computer function that moves a portion of text—a word, a phrase, a paragraph, or more—from one position to another in a document, or from one document to another.
Copy	The computer function that copies a portion of text—a word, a phrase, a paragraph, or more—from one position to another in a document, or from one document to another.
Spelling checker	A computer program that compares the words in your document against a large number of correctly spelled words in the computer program's memory and highlights any words that it is unable to match.

42a

Style checker	A computer program that analyzes certain grammatical and stylistic features of your document—for example, agreement errors, sentence length, and diction—and prints out comments and suggestions for revision.

on by inadvertently striking the wrong keys on the keyboard; it's impossible to harm a computer that way (though it's true that you can damage or even lose the document you are working on).

On most campuses, comuter labs are staffed by assistants who will be happy to get you started on the equipment available there—usually microcomputers like IBM PCs or Apple Macintoshes. If that's not the case where you are, ask a friend to show you how to turn the computer on, how to use a computer disk, and how to begin working with whatever word-processing program is available. All of us who now use word processing effortlessly started out feeling stupid and clumsy; it's a feeling that quickly passes.

1. Basic word-processing functions

Word-processing programs differ in their capabilities and complexity, but all such programs share the features described below, and the basic functions of many are so easy to use that even a novice can begin to compose and edit a text during his or her first working session.

Word wrap

Unlike a typewriter, a word processor does not force you to hit a carriage-return key at the end of each line. Instead, by a function known as *word wrap,* the program automatically advances you to a new line. As a result, you are free to type continuously, without ever thinking about how close you are to the right margin.

Backup and save

When you create a text (usually referred to as a *document* or a *file*) on a word processor, it is held electronically in the computer's

42a

memory as you work on it. However, should the power go off while you are writing on a computer, or should a surge of electricity cause the computer to malfunction, the document you are working on may be lost. All word-processing programs, consequently, enable you to make electronic *backup copies* of your document while you are working on it—copies that will be preserved on a disk even in the event of a power outage. When you finish a word-processing session, you *save* the final version of your work on a disk; with most word processors, this last version replaces all the interim backup copies that you made as you were composing.

Insert and delete text

All word processors allow you to make additions to a text by a command called *insert*. The additions can be as small as a letter or a word, or as large as a paragraph or a page or more of text. When you activate the insert command, the existing text moves aside to make space for whatever you wish to add. Conversely, the *delete* command is used to eliminate part of a text that you no longer want. The rest of your text then automatically moves up to fill in its place.

Move text

A word processor lets you electronically mark a portion of your text—a word, a phrase, a paragraph, or more—and move it to a different position in the text. When you use the *move* command, the first sentence in a paragraph can become the last, or your concluding paragraph can become your introduction, all with just the touch of a key.

Copy text

A word processor allows you to *copy* a passage in your text and insert it at another point in the text as well, or to copy it into an entirely separate document.

2.   Basic formatting functions

Besides enabling you to manipulate the words of your text on the screen, every word-processing program allows you to format your final printed document in a number of ways.

Spacing and margins

You can print out your text single-spaced or double-spaced, with margins of any size that you wish (many word processors allow other line spacing as well). Moreover, you can change the margins or spacing within a document as often as you want. Word processors also permit automatic centering of part of a text (for example, a title) and automatic indenting of blocks of text (such as long quotations in a research paper).

Automatic headers and page numbers

With a word processor, you can create a *header*—that is, a repeated heading—that will automatically print out at the top of each page of your final text (an example of such a header is the manuscript page header required on the pages of a research paper prepared according to APA style [see Chapter **23**]). If you wish your header to include the page number, the word processor will also consecutively number your pages when it prints them—and it will automatically renumber them if you make additions to or deletions from the original text.

Hyphenation and right justification

To even up the text's appearance on the page, some word-processing programs automatically break and hyphenate words at the end of the line; most others allow you to insert hyphens manually. Most word processors also allow you to print your text with what is called a *right-justified* margin; that is, they will automatically space out the words in each line so that all the lines of print extend evenly to the right margin. Check with your instructor to see whether he or she prefers a right-justified text or the usual uneven right margin, known as a *ragged right* margin.

Special fonts

In addition to underlining words, some word processors allow you to print words in boldface, or even in a variety of *fonts,* or type styles. The range of possibilities will depend not only on your word-processing program but on the kind of printer you are using.

42a

42b Getting the most out of word processing

When you sit down at the computer for your first session of word processing, you should bring with you a real project that you are about to begin—for example, an essay assignment due in a few weeks in one of your classes. Without such a task to focus your efforts, you may find that your first few sessions of word processing amount only to aimless experimentation. In contrast, if you begin by working on a genuine assignment, you will more quickly learn the word processor's most important commands, and your working sessions will give you a greater feeling of accomplishment.

1. Planning your paper on a word processor

All of the planning strategies discussed in Chapter **2** work effectively with a word processor. Indeed, you may discover that a word processor makes you more efficient and more creative as you plan and organize a paper.

Brainstorming

Instead of brainstorming with paper and pen, try filling your computer screen with the ideas that occur to you as you think about your subject. Because a word processor lets you shift words and phrases around on the screen, you can finish a brainstorming session by re-arranging the ideas you've generated, moving the best ones to the top of your list. In subsequent brainstorming sessions, you can go back and add new ideas to this list or delete those that no longer seem important. And when you are ready to begin serious work on a paper, you can print out a copy of all the ideas that you accumulated in several sessions of brainstorming, organized in any way that you wish.

Free writing

Some people who freeze up when they confront a blank sheet of paper have just the opposite reaction when they sit down before a blank computer screen. The blinking cursor on the screen seems to

42b

invite them to compose, and the ease with which the text goes up on the screen somehow dissolves their writer's block. If you want to try free writing without the distraction of the computer screen, simply turn the monitor off as you write; you may discover that writing without seeing what you write helps you focus on what you really want to say.

Keeping a journal

If you have access to a word processor on a regular basis, you might consider keeping a journal on a floppy disk. If you decide that parts of your journal might be the core of a good paper, you don't need to copy them out by hand; instead, you can electronically copy them out of the journal and into a separate document that will become the genesis of your paper.

Using structured methods of discovery

To use the structured approach to discovery discussed in **2b**, simply type onto the screen each of the questions to be answered, and add underneath each one as many responses as you can produce. You can save the results of one working session on disk, and then come back the next day and add to it. When you've completely answered all the questions, print out your responses and circle those you might use in your paper. If you go back to the original document and copy out all the responses you've circled into a separate file, you'll have the beginnings of your paper.

Outlining

If you like to write from an outline, the flexibility that word processing offers can be particularly useful. As your ideas change, you can easily modify the outline that you create on a word processor by adding new ideas, deleting those you've discarded, and moving ideas around to different places. You can also print the outline at the beginning of each draft of your paper to guide you as you revise. When you're ready to print the final version of the paper, simply delete the outline before sending the text to the printer. (For a review of outlining, see **5d**.)

42b

2. Writing with a word processor

Don't feel that you have to give up your preferred method of composing when you write on a computer; instead, use the computer in a way that is compatible with the composing process that's most natural to you. Here, for example, are three alternative ways of getting your text onto a computer disk.

Composing on the screen

Some people like to compose directly on the screen. Fast writers like this approach because it's easier than writing out a paper longhand; they can produce a rough draft in a fraction of the time that it would take to compose with pen and paper. Slower, more methodical writers often like composing on the screen as well; it enables them to pause and play with the wording of each sentence before going on to the next one.

Transferring a longhand draft to the computer

Many writers find that they simply cannot get a firm grasp on their ideas unless they begin with paper and pen. That's fine too. After you've composed a longhand draft, type it into the computer to begin your revising. Remember that you will never have to retype the entire paper again.

Alternating between computer composing and longhand composing

Some writers start with a partial handwritten draft and develop enough momentum while typing it into the computer to continue writing directly on the word processor. Others compose parts of a paper on the computer screen, print out their work, fill in the other sections by hand, and then return to the computer to type in the new handwritten portions.

3. Revising with a word processor

42b

As useful as word processing can be in the planning and drafting stages of the writing process, many writers find that it is even more valuable when they begin to revise. No longer do you have to stumble through a draft attempting to decipher the changes that you penciled in between the lines last night, or last week. Now, after each revising session, you can print out a new copy of your text that incorporates all the changes you have made. Reading such a clean copy of each version of your paper will make your revising more efficient by helping you to evaluate the revisions you have made and to spot opportunities for other changes.

To revise effectively with a word processor, though, you have to take advantage of the features that set word processing apart from mere typing—especially the insert, move, and copy commands.

Insert

The ease with which you can add new material to your draft should make you more willing to consider substantial changes in your original version. Have you thought of a new example to use in one of your paragraphs? Have you realized that your introduction needs to be expanded? With a typed or handwritten page, you may feel that the additions you can make to your draft are restricted by the amount of white space available between lines or in the margins. But the situation is vastly different when you add new material to the text that appears on a computer screen. At the touch of the insert key, the text moves aside, creating as much room as you need for your new ideas.

Move

In a handwritten or typed draft, the parts of the paper are fixed in a rigid order. That's not so with the electronic version of a paper created on a word processor. By touching the key that activates your program's move function, you can effortlessly switch sentences around within paragraphs or move whole paragraphs to different positions in the paper. Print out a copy of the changes you've made and decide whether the new arrangement of ideas is an improvement. If not, it's an easy matter to move elements back to their original places.

Copy

Some writers are hesitant to make major changes when they revise because they are afraid that the new version of a draft will be

42b

worse than the original and that they will never be able to reconstruct the text they started with. But you needn't have that fear with word processing, which invites experimentation. If you think you'd like to try a drastic revision of your draft, simply copy the entire draft into a new file and try out the changes you have in mind. If you decide that they don't work, you can delete this new file and go back to the original version of the paper.

4.   Editing with a word processor

Revising involves rethinking the contents, organization, and phrasing of a paper; editing, in contrast, is a matter of correcting small errors that slipped into a paper while it was being drafted. Two supplementary computer programs that are available with many word processors can help you spot and correct at least some of the errors that should be edited out of your final text.

Spelling checkers

Many word processors include a special program called a *spelling checker,* which compares the words in your text against a large number of correctly spelled words held in the program's memory and then highlights any of your words that it is unable to match. A spelling checker is a handy device; it not only alerts you to incorrectly spelled words but also picks out typographical errors that you may have overlooked. One caution is in order, however. A spelling checker will not identify a correctly spelled word that you have accidentally used incorrectly—*it's* in place of *its,* for example. Thus you can't rely on a spelling checker alone to make your spelling free of errors, though it will help you take a major step in that direction.

Style checkers

Another kind of auxiliary computer program analyzes certain stylistic features of a text and prints out comments and suggestions for revision. Typically, *style checkers* flag such matters as errors in agreement (for example, plural pronouns used with singular antecedents), unusual sentence length (for example, very long sentences), weak verbs (for example, linking verbs and passives), and inappropriate diction (for

42b

example, clichés and slang). Some style checkers can also produce a statistical analysis of your prose (average sentence length, average paragraph length, and so on). A style checker is an intriguing aid, but because its analysis is often inexact, you have to be ready to overrule its advice when you have a good reason for doing so. The style checker can't tell, for example, when a long sentence or a passive verb is appropriate, but by marking those features in your text it at least gives you one last opportunity to reflect on what you have written and to make a deliberate choice.

42b

For Further Reading

Burns, Hugh. "Computers and Composition." *Teaching Composition: Twelve Bibliographical Essays*. Ed. Gary Tate. Fort Worth: Texas Christian UP, 1987. 378–400.

Crew, Louie. "The Style-Checker as Tonic, not Tranquilizer." *Journal of Advanced Composition* 8 (1988): 66–69.

McDaniel, Ellen, "Bibliography of Text-Analysis and Writing-Instruction Software." *Journal of Advanced Composition* 7 (1987): 139–70.

Schwartz, Helen, and Lillian S. Bridwell. "A Selected Bibliography on Computers in Composition." *College Composition and Communication* 35 (1984): 71–77.

Schwartz, Helen J., and Lillian S. Bridwell-Bowles. "A Selected Bibliography on Computers in Composition: An Update." *College Composition and Communication* 38 (1987): 453–57.

43 *Writing English as a Second Language*

If English is your second language, then you have no doubt confronted the double challenge of mastering the rules of English syntax while at the same time keeping them distinct from the rules that govern the grammar of your first language. All of us who have learned a second language and have lived in the culture where that language is spoken have had the fascinating, if often exasperating, experience of seeing firsthand how grammatical systems vary from language to language.

Of course, even native speakers of English find some of their language's rules confusing. The rules governing subject-verb agreement and pronoun-antecedent agreement, for example, are simple enough in theory, but in certain grammatical situations they can be difficult to understand and remember, even for people who have been speaking English all of their lives. The same is true for the conventions of English punctuation, mechanics, and spelling. The frustrations that you may have experienced in learning these rules were probably shared by some of your peers who have been speaking English since infancy.

But other aspects of English syntax are so much a part of the habitual usage of any native speaker that such a person rarely, if ever, gets them wrong. This chapter surveys several such features that may cause confusion for the speaker and writer of English as a second language. However, because exceptions are so common in English, you should treat the following points as guidelines rather than absolute rules.

43

782

QUICK REFERENCE: *Special Notes for ESL Writers*

Indefinite and definite articles

Use an indefinite article only before a count noun, not before a noncount noun.

Incorrect	I received a good news today.
Correct	I received *good news* today.
Correct	I received *a piece of* good news today.

Use the definite article before a specifically identified count noun or noncount noun.

Incorrect	I need help of a good math tutor.
Correct	I need *the* help of a good math tutor.

Subjects and verbs in sentences

Do not omit the subject or verb in a sentence, even if the meaning of the remaining words is clear.

Incorrect	Took a trip to New Orleans last month.
Correct	*I* took a trip to New Orleans last month.
Incorrect	The weather in New Orleans very humid.
Correct	The weather in New Orleans *is* very humid.

Phrasal verbs

Phrasal (two-word) verbs in English have meanings that usually cannot be inferred from the words that constitute them.

look over = examine   look after = care for
look up = visit   look into = investigate

Some phrasal verbs may be separated in a sentence with no change in meaning.

Correct	We *looked over* the used car.
Correct	We *looked* the used car *over*.

43

Other phrasal verbs may never be separated.

Incorrect   Susan looked my plants after while I was away.
Correct   Susan *looked after* my plants while I was away.

Progressive verb forms

Some verbs in English do not have progressive forms.

Example   I *dislike* [not *am disliking*] the food served in our cafeteria.

Gerunds and infinitives after verbs

Some verbs cannot be followed by a gerund; others cannot be followed by an infinitive.

Example   I want *to buy* [not *buying*] a new bicycle.
Example   I enjoy *bicycling* [not *to bicycle*].

Adjectives

Multiple adjectives before a noun are usually arranged in the following order: number, quality, size, shape, color.

Example   *Two large, white* swans swam in the *clear, round* pond.

Adverbs

An adverb is never placed between a verb and its direct object.

Incorrect   I have today a math exam.
Correct   I have a math exam *today*.

43a Indefinite and definite articles (*a, an, the*)

43a

The words *a* and *an* are the *indefinite articles;* the word *the* is the *definite article*. One of the most confusing areas of English syntax for nonnative speakers is knowing when to use the definite article, when to use an indefinite article, and when to use no article at all before a noun. Generally, the article depends on the kind of noun used.

1. An indefinite article does not precede a noncount noun

A *count noun* names things that can be counted: one *dog*, two *ideas*, three *books*. A *noncount noun*, in contrast, names things that cannot be counted. In ordinary usage, noncount nouns do not have plural forms. Consider the following pairs:

Count nouns	Noncount nouns
message	news
beverage	juice
car	transportation
grain	flour
virtue	honesty

In English, the indefinite articles are never used before noncount nouns.

Incorrect	I received a good news this morning.
Correct	I received good news this morning.

Incorrect	Would you like a juice with your breakfast?
Correct	Would you like juice with your breakfast?

Incorrect	Susan needs a transportation to the party.
Correct	Susan needs transportation to the party.

An indefinite article may, however, appear before a noncount noun in a construction such as the following: *a* [count noun] *of* [noncount noun].

I received *a piece of* good news.
Would you like *a glass of* juice?

Used with numbers or with some indefinite pronouns, such a construction enables speakers of English to "count" many noncount nouns.

a stick of butter   *two sticks of* butter

43a

an item of furniture   *several items of* furniture
a gallon of gasoline   *ten gallons of* gasoline

2. The definite article precedes a specifically identified noncount noun

As we have seen, noncount nouns may be used without any articles before them. However, when the context of your sentence specifically identifies a noncount noun, the noun should be preceded by the definite article *the*.

Correct   I need help.

Correct   Patience is admirable.
              [*Help* and *patience* are noncount nouns. Because the
              sentences do not specify what kind of help or patience
              is being discussed, no definite article is used.]

Incorrect I need help of a good math tutor.

Incorrect Patience of Marie's English tutor is admirable.
              [In these sentences, the types of help and patience are
              specifically identified. The noncount nouns must be
              preceded by the definite article.]

Correct   I need *the* help of a good math tutor.

Correct   *The* patience of Marie's English tutor is admirable.

3. The definite article precedes a specifically identified count noun

Unlike noncount nouns, singular count nouns may be preceded either by an indefinite article or by the definite article. Use an indefinite article before singular count nouns that are not specifically indentified by the context of your sentence, but use the definite article before singular count nouns that are specifically identified.

Incorrect My sister is youngest student in a sophomore class.
              [There can be only one youngest student in the class,
              and there is only one sophomore class under dis-
              cussion. Because both the student and the class are
              specifically identified, both nouns must be preceded by
              the definite article.]

43a

Correct	My sister is *the* youngest student in *the* sophomore class.
Incorrect	My roommate borrowed a book from me last week. Where is a book that he borrowed? [The indefinite article *a* is correct in the first sentence because the book has not yet been identified. The definite article is required in the second sentence because the context now identifies the book as the one borrowed by the roommate.]
Correct	My roommate borrowed a book from me last week. Where is *the* book that he borrowed?

4.   The definite article precedes certain proper nouns

Most proper nouns are not preceded by an article, but the definite article is used before certain types of proper nouns.

Oceans, seas, rivers, canals, and geographical regions

the Atlantic Ocean, the Baltic Sea, the Mississippi River, the Panama Canal, the West

Plural place names

the Alps, the Carolinas, the Golan Heights, the Hawaiian Islands, the Netherlands, the United States, the West Indies

Museums, theaters, libraries, hotels, and restaurants

the Smithsonian Institution, the Chicago Theater, the New York Public Library, the Hilton Hotel, the Hard Rock Café

Names of places and institutions containing the word *of*

the Avenue of the Americas, the Bay of Bengal, the Cape of Good Hope, the People's Republic of China, the University of Nebraska

Unless they also fall into one of the categories above, proper nouns in the following categories are usually not preceded by definite or indefinite articles: names of individuals (Harrison Ford, Queen Elizabeth); names of streets (Fifth Avenue, Main Street); names of parks

43a

(Central Park, Golden Gate Park); names of cities, states, and countries (Los Angeles, Florida, Egypt); names of lakes and continents (Lake Erie, Africa); names of days, holidays, and months (Tuesday, Memorial Day, December).

43b Subjects and verbs in sentences

Unlike sentences in some other languages, English sentences consist of one or more clauses, each of which must contain both a subject and a verb.

1. Always state the subject, except in requests and commands

The subject of a declarative English sentence must always be expressed.

Incorrect	Went to high school in California.
Correct	*I* went to high school in California.
Incorrect	When visit Santa Cruz this summer, will see my old friends.
Correct	When *I* visit Santa Cruz this summer, *I* will see my old friends.

In requests and commands, however, the subject *you* is understood and is omitted.

Incorrect	You come to California with me in June!
Correct	Come to California with me in June!

2. State the subject only once

The subject of an English sentence is not repeated, even for emphasis.

Incorrect	Santa Cruz it is very beautiful.
Correct	Santa Cruz is very beautiful.
Incorrect	The experiences that I had there they were interesting.
Correct	The experiences that I had there were interesting.

43b

3. Do not omit the expletives *there* or *it*

A common pattern in English is to begin a sentence with the expletive *there* or *it*.

There are twenty students in my composition class.

It is difficult to learn the exceptions in English grammar.

In these constructions, the subject of the sentence follows the verb, as we see if we reverse the word order in each case.

Twenty students are in my composition class.

To learn the exceptions in English grammar is difficult.

Nonetheless, in sentences that employ expletives, the words *there* and *it* cannot be omitted.

Incorrect Are dark clouds on the horizon.
Correct *There* are dark clouds on the horizon.

Incorrect Is likely that the weather will change.
Correct *It* is likely that the weather will change.

4. Always include the verb

Even when the connection between a subject and a predicate noun or predicate adjective (see **25e**) is obvious, the linking verb in an English sentence cannot be omitted.

Incorrect Marcia a good friend of mine.
Correct Marcia *is* a good friend of mine.

Incorrect My math test very hard.
Correct My math test *was* very hard.

43c Phrasal (two-word) verbs

From its Germanic origins, English has acquired many verbs that consist of a verb followed by a preposition or adverb called a *particle*. Known as *phrasal verbs* or *two-word verbs*, these constructions are understandably troublesome for nonnative speakers of English. In the first place, the meaning of a phrasal verb often cannot be inferred

43c

from the words that compose it. There is nothing in the words *bring up*, for example, that would enable a nonnative speaker to understand that one meaning of this verb is "mention in conversation," nor do the words *figure out* suggest that the meaning of this verb is "solve."

A second complication arises from the fact that some constructions look like phrasal verbs but are actually ordinary verbs followed by prepositional phrases. Compare the following sentences:

> We *looked over* the contract carefully.
> [The verb *looked over* is a phrasal verb that means "examined."]
>
> We *looked* over the wall into the garden.
> [There is no phrasal verb in this sentence. *Over the wall* is a prepositional phrase that answers the question "Where did we look?"]

Phrasal verbs fall into three main categories: transitive phrasal verbs with separable particles, transitive phrasal verbs with inseparable particles, and intransitive phrasal verbs.

1. Transitive phrasal verbs with separable particles

A transitive verb is a verb that must be followed by a direct object (see **25d**). With some transitive phrasal verbs, the direct object may come after the particle or between the verb and the particle.

> David *tried on* the new sweater.
> David *tried* the new sweater *on*.

But notice that when the direct object is a pronoun rather than a noun, it always appears between the verb and the particle.

> **Incorrect**   David tried on it.
> **Correct**   David *tried* it *on*.

Transitive phrasal verbs with separable particles include the following:

back up	break up	call off
blow up	bring up	call up
break off	burn down	cheer up

clean up	hold up	take in
cross off	leave out	take off
cross out	let down	take over
cut down	look over	think over
cut up	look up	think through
draw out	make up	throw away
drop off	pick out	try on
figure out	pick up	try out
fill in	point out	turn down
fill out	put away	turn off
find out	put off	turn on
give away	put on	turn up
give back	put together	use up
hand in	show off	wake up
hand out	shut off	wear out
hang up	take back	work out

2. Transitive phrasal verbs with inseparable particles

Some transitive phrasal verbs have inseparable particles; that is, the direct object can never occur between the verb and the particle but must always directly follow the particle.

Incorrect   We get the bus off at the next stop.
Correct   We *get off* the bus at the next stop.

Transitive phrasal verbs with inseparable particles include the following:

call on	get over	pick on
come across	get through	run across
get in	go over	run into
get off	look after	see through
get on	look into	wait on

43c

3.   Intransitive phrasal verbs

Intransitive phrasal verbs do not take a direct or indirect object. The particle in an intransitive phrasal verb is always inseparable.

Incorrect   The airplane took at noon off.
Correct   The airplane *took off* at noon.

Intransitive phrasal verbs include the following.

back down	get on	sit up
break down	get up	speak out
burn down	give in	speak up
catch on	go away	stand out
catch up	go out	stand up
come about	grow up	stay up
drop in	hold out	talk back
drop out	play around	turn out
get along	run away	turn up
get back	set out	wake up
get in	sit down	wear out

43d Progressive verb forms

Section **29d** describes the progressive forms of English verbs—forms that enable a speaker or writer to indicate that an action is or was continuing over a period of time. Compare the following examples:

I *studied* for my math exam after dinner.
[Past tense. The action occurred at a specific time in the past.]

I *was studying* for my math exam when you telephoned.
[Past progressive tense. The action was in progress when you telephoned.]

43d

However, not all verbs in English follow this pattern. Many verbs that express emotion, perception, states of mind, and possession or containment cannot take progressive forms, even though a speaker or writer may wish to convey the idea of an action or a mental state that continues over a period of time.

| **Incorrect** | I am disliking my new roommate. |
| **Correct** | I *dislike* my new roommate. |

| **Incorrect** | That piano was sounding out of tune all night. |
| **Correct** | That piano *sounded* out of tune all night. |

| **Incorrect** | I have been knowing Mark since I came to this country. |
| **Correct** | I *have known* Mark since I came to this country. |

| **Incorrect** | My mother has been owning a collection of antique dolls since she was a young girl. |
| **Correct** | My mother *has owned* a collection of antique dolls since she was a young girl. |

The following list includes some of the English verbs that normally do not have progressive forms.

appear	have	possess	sound
believe	hear	prefer	suppose
belong	know	realize	suit
contain	like	recognize	surprise
deserve	love	remember	taste
disagree	mean	resemble	think
dislike	need	see	understand
feel	own	seem	want
hate	please	smell	wish

43e Gerunds and infinitives after verbs

Gerunds and infinitives are verb forms that function like nouns (see **25f**). Gerunds are formed by adding *-ing* to a verb, infinitives by preceding the verb with the word *to*.

43e

Verb	Gerund	Infinitive
walk	walking	to walk
study	studying	to study
believe	believing	to believe

Because they are nouns, gerunds and infinitives can be used as the subject of a sentence, as a predicate noun, or as a direct object.

Some English verbs can be followed by either a gerund or an infinitive in the direct-object position.

> I like *reading* Victorian novels.
> I like *to read* Victorian novels.

The problem for nonnative speakers is that there are other verbs that can be followed by a gerund but not by an infinitive, and still others that can be followed by an infinitive but not by a gerund.

Incorrect	I enjoy to read Victorian novels.
Correct	I enjoy *reading* Victorian novels.
	[An infinitive cannot follow the verb *enjoy*.]
Incorrect	I want reading Victorian novels.
Correct	I want *to read* Victorian novels.
	[A gerund cannot follow the verb *want*.]

1. Verbs followed by either a gerund or an infinitive

The verbs in the list below may be followed by a gerund or by an infinitive.

attempt	hate	neglect
begin	hesitate	prefer
continue	intend	propose
dread	like	start
fear	love	try

43e In the case of a few other verbs, including *forget, remember,* and *stop,* the choice of a gerund or an infinitive produces a significant change in meaning.

I almost forgot *calling* my mother last week.
[I nearly forgot that I had called her.]
I almost forgot *to call* my mother last week.
[I nearly failed to call her.]

I remember *locking* the doors when I parked the car.
[I recall a past action.]
I remember *to lock* the doors when I park the car.
[I never forget to do so.]

My brother has stopped *buying* chewing gum.
[He no longer buys it.]
My brother has stopped *to buy* chewing gum.
[He has paused to buy it.]

2. Verbs followed by a gerund

The verbs in the list below may be followed by a gerund but not by an infinitive.

admit	escape	put off
appreciate	finish	quit
avoid	imagine	recall
consider	keep	resent
deny	keep on	resist
detest	miss	risk
discuss	postpone	suggest
enjoy	practice	talk over

3. Verbs followed by an infinitive

The verbs in the list below may be followed by an infinitive but not by a gerund.

agree	expect	pretend
ask	have	promise
beg	hope	refuse
care	learn	wait
decide	offer	want
endeavor	plan	wish

43e

4. Verbs followed by an object and an infinitive

One other pattern involving infinitives that should be noted is a verb followed by a noun or pronoun that is then followed by an infinitive.

I advise *you to study* infinitives.

In this sentence, *you* is the direct object of *advise*, but it is also referred to as the subject of the infinitive *to study*. The verbs in the list below, some of which also fit into the categories above, may be used with infinitives in this type of construction.

advise	encourage	persuade
allow	expect	remind
ask	force	require
beg	instruct	teach
cause	invite	tell
command	oblige	urge
convince	order	warn

43f Adjectives

You already know that in English an adjective usually precedes the noun that it modifies.

a *marble* statue

a *large* statue

a *gray* statue

But when two or more adjectives are used together before a noun, a fixed hierarchy governs the sequence in which the adjectives may occur. Among the following combinations, for example, only one would sound correct to native speakers of English.

Incorrect	a marble, large, gray statue
Incorrect	a gray, marble, large statue
Correct	a large, gray, marble statue

In situations like this one, the sequence of adjective types described in the following list dictates the way native speakers of English arrange their modifiers. Note that there are always exceptions and, of course, that one would be unlikely to write a sentence that used adjectives in all of these categories before a single noun.

Adjective type	Examples
1. article	a, an, the
2. number	two, several, few
3. quality	calm, loud, valuable
4. size	small, tiny, microscopic
5. shape	square, round, oval
6. color	blue, green, yellowish
7. adjective formed from a proper noun	Canadian, Hawaiian, Jewish
8. noun used as an adjective	cotton, plastic, steel
9. the noun modified	painter, village, door

The following phrases illustrate this sequence.

two elegant, blue, silk shirts [2-3-6-8-9]

the four massive, square, steel columns [1-2-4-5-8-9]

an enormous Swiss-cheese sandwich [1-4-7-8-9]

ominous, dark storm clouds [3-6-8-9]

For an explanation of the rules that determine when commas and hyphens are used between modifiers, see **32d** and **36a**.

43g Adverbs

An adverb that modifies an adjective or another adverb is always positioned directly before the word it modifies.

I have an *extremely* high fever.

The doctor has agreed to see me *very* soon.

43g

But adverbs or adverb phrases that modify verbs may occur in various places within a sentence. Adverbs of manner, for example, may often be placed at the beginning of a sentence, before the verb, or after the verb without materially altering the meaning of the sentence.

> *Gradually*, my writing improved.
>
> My writing *gradually* improved.
>
> My writing improved *gradually*.

Not all adverbs, however, can be moved about so freely. Below are several guidelines for positioning other types of adverbs in a sentence.

1. An adverb does not separate a verb and its direct object

One rule of English syntax that applies in almost all cases is that an adverb or adverb phrase cannot occur between the verb and the direct object in a sentence.

Incorrect	I conducted carefully the experiment.
Correct	I conducted the experiment *carefully*.

Incorrect	I will submit on Tuesday my lab report.
Correct	*On Tuesday* I will submit my lab report.

2. Adverbs of degree or probability precede the main verb

Adverbs that indicate degree (for example, *almost, hardly, nearly, quite*) and adverbs that indicate probability (for example, *certainly, possibly, probably, surely*) are usually placed before the main verb but after any auxiliary verbs that may be present.

Incorrect	I have finished my lab report almost.
Correct	I have *almost* finished my lab report.

Incorrect	It will be ready certainly tomorrow.
Correct	It will *certainly* be ready tomorrow.

3. Adverbs of indefinite time precede the main verb

Like adverbs of degree and probability, adverbs that denote indefinite time (for example, *always, never, sometimes, usually*) are usually placed before the main verb but after any auxiliary verbs that may be present.

Incorrect	I study in the library usually.
Correct	I *usually* study in the library.

Incorrect	You can find me sometimes on the fifth floor.
Correct	You can *sometimes* find me on the fifth floor.

4. Adverbs of definite time are placed at the beginning or the end of a sentence

Unlike adverbs of indefinite time, adverbs and adverb phrases that indicate a specific time (for example, *at nine o'clock, next week, on Monday, tomorrow*) are usually placed at the beginning or the end of a sentence.

Incorrect	I left my chemistry book last night in the library.
Correct	*Last night* I left my chemistry book in the library.
Correct	I left my chemistry book in the library *last night*.

Incorrect	I will today try to find my book.
Correct	*Today* I will try to find my book.
Correct	I will try to find my book *today*.

43g

For Further Reading

Reid, Joy M. *Teaching ESL Writing*. Englewood Cliffs: Regents/Prentice Hall, 1993.

Glossary of Usage

This Glossary discusses a number of commonly misused words; for more complete advice on questions of usage, you should rely on a good college dictionary (see Chapter **9**).

a, an Indefinite articles. *A* is used before words beginning with a consonant sound, *an* before words beginning with a vowel sound. Before words beginning with *h,* use *an* when the *h* is silent, as in *hour,* but *a* when the *h* is pronounced, as in *history.*

accept, except Different verbs that sound alike. *Accept* means "to receive," *except* "to leave out."

> I **accepted** the diploma.
>
> When assigning jobs, the dean **excepted** students who had already worked on a project.

A.D. An abbreviation of the Latin *anno Domini,* "in the year of the lord." It is properly placed *before* the date in question. See **B.C.** An alternative abbreviation for designating years in the Christian era is C.E. ("Common Era").

adapt, adopt To *adapt* is to change or modify to suit a new need, purpose, or condition.

> Human beings can **adapt** to many environments.
>
> The movie was **adapted** from a novel.

To *adopt* something is to make it one's own, to choose it.

> The couple **adopted** a child.
>
> Our club **adopted** "Opportunity knocks" as its motto.

G1

us

adverse, averse   *Adverse* means "antagonistic" or "unfavorable."

> **Adverse** weather forced postponement of the regatta.

Averse means "opposed to"; only sentient beings can be *averse*.

> She was **averse** to sailing under such conditions.

advice, advise   *Advice* is a noun, *advise* a verb.

> He gave me some good **advice.**
> I **advise** you to listen carefully.

affect, effect   Words close in sound and therefore often confused. *Affect* as a verb means "to influence." *Effect* as a verb means "to bring about."

> Smoking **affects** the heart.
> How can we **effect** a change in the law?

As a noun, *effect* means "result."

> One **effect** of her treatment was a bad case of hives.

aggravate   Means "to intensify" or "to make worse."

> The shock **aggravated** his misery.

In colloquial usage, *aggravate* also means "to annoy," "irritate," "arouse the anger of."

ain't   A nonstandard contraction of *am not, is not,* or *are not.* Not to be used in most writing.

all ready, already   Not synonyms. *All ready* refers to a state of readiness.

> The twirlers were **all ready** for the halftime show.

Already means "by or before the present time."

> Has the game **already** started?

all together, altogether   *All together* refers to a group with no missing elements.

> If we can get our members **all together,** we can begin the meeting.

Altogether means "completely."

> You are **altogether** mistaken about that.

allude, refer   To *allude* is to make an indirect reference.

> Did her letter **allude** to Sam's difficulties?

To *refer* is to call attention specifically to something.

> The instructor **referred** us to Baudelaire's translations of Poe.

allusion, illusion   An *allusion* is a brief, indirect reference.

> Anyone who speaks of "cabbages and kings" is making an **allusion** to *Alice in Wonderland.*

An *illusion* is a deceptive impression.

> He enjoyed the **illusion** of luxury created by his imitation Oriental rugs.

alot, a lot   The only correct spelling is *a lot.*

alright, all right   The only correct spelling is *all right.*

among, between   *Among* always refers to more than two people or objects.

> He lived **among** a tribe of cannibals.

Between is used to refer to two people or objects or to more than two when they are considered separately rather than as a collective group.

> The scenery is spectacular **between** Portland and Seattle.
>
> The governors signed the agreement **between** all three states.

amoral, immoral   Anything *amoral* is outside morality, not to be judged by moral standards.

> The behavior of animals and the orbits of the planets are equally **amoral.**

Anything *immoral* is in direct violation of some moral standard.

> Plagiarism is generally considered to be an **immoral** act.

amount, number *Amount* is used as a general indicator of quantity; *number* refers only to what can be counted.

> An immense **amount** of food was prepared for the picnic, but only a small **number** of people came.

an See **a.**

and Despite widespread belief to the contrary, *and* is perfectly acceptable as a sentence opener.

> I don't like your attitude. **And** I also don't like your haircut.

ante, anti As a prefix, *ante* means "before": *ante*date, *ante*cedent. *Anti* means "against": *anti*war, *anti*knock.

anxious, eager *Anxious* refers to worry about the future.

> He was **anxious** about the outcome of his exam.

Eager indicates hopeful excitement.

> She was **eager** to meet her relatives from Ohio.

anybody, any body *Anybody* is an indefinite pronoun that means "any person." *Any body* is a phrase that refers to a "body."

> Stranded in the desert, the travelers longed to see **anybody** on the horizon.
>
> Stranded in the desert, the travelers longed to see **any body** of water on the horizon.

anymore, any more *Anymore* is an adverb that means "any longer" or "now." In Standard English, the word is used in interrogative and negative (but not positive) constructions. *Any more* is a phrase that refers to an additional amount of something.

> I don't eat eggs **anymore,** but do you have **any more** bacon?

anyone, any one *Anyone* is an indefinite pronoun that means "any person." *Any one* is a phrase that refers to one particular person or thing in a group.

> **Anyone** may enter the contest.
>
> **Any one** of the entrants will win the new car.

apt   See **liable.**

as   Dialectal when used in place of *that* or *who*.

> I don't know **that** [not **as**] we can go.
>
> There are some **who** [not **as**] trust him.

Because and *since* are clearer than **as** for introducing clauses showing causal relationship.

> **Because** [not **as**] I was late, I missed the opening curtain.

at about   Prefer *about* in writing; *at about* is redundant.

> It happened **about** [not **at about**] three o'clock.

awhile, a while   *Awhile* is an adverb.

> I'm tired, so I'll sit **awhile.**

A while consists of an article and a noun, often used as the object of a preposition.

> I'm tired, so I'll sit for **a while.**

bad, badly   As an adjective, *bad,* not *badly,* is properly used after linking verbs like *feel* and *look.*

> I feel **bad** [not **badly**] about my impolite behavior.

Badly is an adverb used with other verbs.

> I served **badly** during the tennis match because of my headache.

barely   See **hardly.**

B.C.   Abbreviation of "before Christ," placed after the date in question. See **A.D.** An alternative abbreviation for designating years before the Christian era is B.C.E. ("before the Common Era").

between   See **among.**

but   Often used colloquially in such idioms as *I can't help but think.* In writing, *I can't help thinking* is preferred. Despite widespread belief to the contrary, *but* is perfectly acceptable as a sentence opener.

> I don't like most country music. **But** I love Patsy Cline.

can, may   In Standard English, *can* is used to indicate ability, *may* to indicate permission.

> If you **can** open that box, you **may** have whatever is in it.

In informal situations, *can* is often used even though permission is meant.

> **Can** I try it next? Why **can't** I?

censor, censure   To *censor* something (such as a book, letter, or film) is to evaluate it on the basis of certain arbitrary standards to determine whether it may be made public.

> All announcements for the bulletin board are **censored** by the department secretary.

Censure means "to find fault with," "to criticize officially."

> Several officers were **censured** for their participation in the affair.

compare to, compare with, contrast with   *Compare to* is used to show similarities between different kinds of things.

> Sir James Jeans **compared** the universe **to** a corrugated soap bubble.

Compare with means "to examine in order to note either similarities or differences."

> **Compare** this example **with** the preceding one.

Contrast with is used to show differences only.

> **Contrast** the life of a student today **with** that of a student in the Middle Ages.

complementary, complimentary   *Complementary* means "serving to fill out" or "to complete."

> His tenor and her soprano are **complementary.**

Complimentary means "freely given" or "giving praise."

> Members of the audience were quite **complimentary** about the couple's recital.

compose, comprise *Compose* means "to make up or constitute." In contrast, *comprise* means "to be composed of." Remember that *compose* can be followed by *of*, but *comprise* can't be.

> The orchestra was **composed** [not **comprised**] entirely **of** grade-school students.

concur in, concur with *Concur in* refers to agreement with a principle or policy.

> She **concurred in** their judgment that the manager should be given a raise.

Concur with refers to agreement with a person.

> She **concurred with** him in his decision to give the manager a raise.

conscious, conscience *Conscious* is an adjective meaning "aware of."

> She was **conscious** of the others in the room.

Conscience is a noun meaning "the sense of moral goodness or badness."

> Her **conscience** told her to leave.

continual, continuous The first is widely used to indicate an action that is repeated frequently, the second to indicate uninterrupted action.

> We heard the **continual** whimpering of the dog.
> The dog kept a **continuous** vigil beside the body of its dead master.

contrast with See **compare to.**

data, criteria, phenomena Latin plural, not singular, forms, and hence used as English plurals in writing.

> These **data** have been taken from the last Census Report.

The use of *data* (rather than *datum*) as a singular noun is widespread, particularly in speech, but *criteria* and *phenomena* are always plural. The singular forms are *criterion* and *phenomenon*.

us

Scientists encountered a **phenomenon** that could not be evaluated under existing **criteria.**

different from, different than   Despite widespread use of the construction *different than, different from* remains the preferred form, particularly in writing.

College is **different from** [not **different than**] what I had expected.

dilemma, problem   A *dilemma* is a choice between two equally distasteful alternatives.

We faced the **dilemma** of paying the fine or spending three days in jail.

A *problem* is wider in meaning, referring to a difficulty or a question that must be solved.

The United States must soon resolve the **problem** of guaranteeing an energy supply for the twenty-first century.

disinterested, uninterested   *Disinterested* means "unbiased," "impartial." *Uninterested* means "without any interest in," or "lacking interest."

Although we were **uninterested** in her general topic, we had to admire her **disinterested** treatment of its controversial aspects.

don't   A contraction of *do not*. Not to be used with a subject in the third-person singular.

Nonstandard   He **don't** know.
Standard   He **doesn't** know.

due to   In writing, *due to* should not be used adverbially to mean *because of*. Because *due* is an adjective, it properly follows some form of the verb *be*.

The carpenter made many mistakes **because of** [not **due to**] carelessness.

The carpenter's many mistakes **were due** to carelessness.

each other, one another   When two individuals are involved in a reciprocal relationship, *each other* is used.

My sister and I respect **each other.**

When more than two individuals are mutually related, *one another* is appropriate.

The sheep rubbed against **one another** in the chill.

eager   See **anxious.**

effect   See **affect.**

either, neither   As subjects, both words are singular. When referring to more than two, use *none* rather than *neither.*

> **Either** red or pink is appropriate.
>
> I asked Leahy, Mahoney, and another colleague, but **none** of them **were** willing.

eminent, imminent   *Eminent* means "prominent," "well known."

> She was an **eminent** judge.

Imminent means "impending," "menacing," "about to occur."

> The jury's verdict is **imminent.**

enthused   Either as a verb (he *enthused*) or adjective (he was *enthused*), the word is strictly colloquial. In writing, use *showed enthusiasm* or *was enthusiastic.*

equally as good   A confusion of two phrases: *equally good* and *just as good.* Use either of the two phrases in place of *equally as good.*

> Their VCR cost much more than ours, but ours is **equally good.**
>
> Our VCR is **just as good** as theirs.

-ess   A feminine ending that is now considered unacceptable because it implies that women are functioning in roles defined by men and must be distinguished from their male counterparts: *poetess, authoress, sculptress, stewardess, hostess. Actress,* one of the last such terms still in use, is rapidly giving way to *actor,* and *waiter* and *waitress* have been widely replaced by the sex-neutral *server.*

etc.   Abbreviation of the Latin *et cetera* ("and others"). Avoid the vague use of *etc.;* use it only to prevent useless repetition or informally to represent terms that are entirely obvious from the context.

us

Vague	The judge was honorable, upright, dependable, etc.
Preferred	The judge was honorable, upright, **and** dependable.
Acceptable	Use even numbers—four, eight, ten, **etc.**

Avoid *and etc.,* which is redundant.

everybody, every body   *Everybody* is an indefinite pronoun that means "every person." *Every body* is a phrase that refers to a "body."

> From the balcony, I could see **everybody** on the street below.
>
> From the plane, I could see **every body** of water below.

everyday, every day   *Everyday* is an adjective meaning "ordinary, commonplace." *Every day* is a noun phrase that functions like an adverb; it modifies a verb by answering the question *When?*

> Heart disease has become an **everyday** topic of conversation.
>
> To avoid heart disease, I exercise **every day.**

everyone, every one   *Everyone* is an indefinite pronoun that means "every person." *Every one* is a phrase that refers to each particular person or thing in a group.

> **Everyone** on the team was late for practice.
>
> **Every one** of the players was late for practice.

except   See **accept.**

expect   Colloquial when used to mean "suppose" or "presume."

Colloquial	I **expect** it's time for us to go.
Preferred	I **suppose** it's time for us to go.

farther, further   In careful usage *farther* indicates distance; *further* indicates degree and may also mean "additional." Both are used as adjectives and as adverbs: *a mile farther, further disintegration, further details.*

faze, phase   *Faze* is a colloquial verb meaning "to perturb," "to disconcert." *Phase* as a noun means "stage of development" (a passing *phase*); as a verb it means "to carry out in stages."

fewer, less   *Fewer* refers to number, *less* to amount. Use *fewer* when referring to things that can be counted and *less* when referring to things that can be measured but not counted.

> **Fewer** persons enrolled in medical schools this year than last.
>
> **Less** studying was required to pass chemistry than we had anticipated.

flaunt, flout   Commonly misspelled, mispronounced, and, therefore, confused. *Flaunt* means "to exhibit arrogantly," "show off."

> He **flaunted** his photographic memory in class.

Flout means "to reject with contempt."

> They **flouted** the tradition of wearing gowns at graduation by showing up in blue jeans.

former, latter   Preferably used to designate one of two persons or things. For designating one of three or more, write *first* or *last*.

further   See **farther.**

get, got, gotten   *Get to (go), get away with, get back at, get with* (something), and *got to* (for *must*) are acceptable in colloquial usage but should be avoided in writing. Either *got* or *gotten* is acceptable as the past participle of *get*.

good   An adjective. Should not be used as an adverb meaning "well."

> She plays a **good** game of tennis.
> She knows the game **well** [not **good**].

had of   Nonstandard when used for *had*.

> If he **had** [not **had of**] tried harder, he would have succeeded.

hanged, hung   When *hang* means "to suspend," *hung* is its past tense.

> The guard **hung** a black flag from the prison to signal the execution.

When *hang* means "to execute," *hanged* is the correct past tense.

> After the flag was **hung,** the prisoner was **hanged.**

us

hardly, barely, scarcely   Since these words convey the idea of negation, they should not be used with another negative.

Nonstandard	We **couldn't hardly** see in the darkness.
	We **hadn't barely** finished.
Standard	We **could hardly** see.
	We **had barely** finished.

hopefully   Although widely used in speech to mean "it is to be hoped," or "I hope" ("*Hopefully,* a check will arrive tomorrow"), the adverb *hopefully* is used in writing to mean "in a hopeful manner."

They spoke **hopefully** of world peace.

illusion   See **allusion.**

imminent   See **eminent.**

immoral   See **amoral.**

impact   Used colloquially (and in bureaucratic writing) as a verb meaning "to have an effect on": "Will this power plant *impact* the environment negatively?" Not yet well-enough established for use in most writing.

imply, infer   *Imply* means "to suggest" or "hint"; *infer* means "to reach a conclusion from facts or premises."

His tone **implied** contempt; I **inferred** from his voice that he did not like me.

incident, incidence   An *incident* is a specific occurrence. *Incidence* refers to the rate or frequency of occurrence.

There was another **incident** of burglary on our block last night.

The **incidence** of burglary on our block is steadily increasing.

incredible, incredulous   Both are adjectives, or, more rarely, nouns, but *incredible* means "unbelievable," "unlikely," while *incredulous* means "skeptical," "unbelieving."

The ad made **incredible** claims for the product. I remained **incredulous.**

inside of   Omit the superfluous *of* when *inside* is used as a preposition.

I'll meet you **inside** the station.

See **outside of.**

inter, intra   As a prefix *inter* means "between" or "among": *international, intermarry; intra* means "within" or "inside of": *intramuscular, intramural.*

irony   See **sarcasm.**

irregardless   A nonstandard combination of *irrespective* and *regardless.*

> **Regardless** [or **irrespective**] of the minority opinion, we included the platform in the campaign.

is when, is where   Avoid using these phrases as parts of a definition. See **12f.**

> Smog is polluted air [rather than "Smog **is when** the air is polluted"].
>
> Literacy is the ability to read and write [rather than "Literacy **is where** a person can read and write"].

its, it's   *Its* is the possessive form of *it.*

> My suitcase has lost one of **its** handles.

It's is the contracted form of *it is* or *it has.*

> **It's** a good day for sailing.
>
> **It's** been a month since I mailed the check.

There is no such form as *its'.*

kind, sort, type   Singular nouns that must be used with singular pronouns and verbs.

> **Incorrect**   These **kind** of books **are** trash.
>
> **Correct**   This **kind** of book **is** trash.
> These **kinds** of books **are** classics.

In questions, the number of the verb depends on the noun that follows *kind* (or *sort* or *type*).

> What kind of **book is** this?
>
> What kind of **books are** these?

us

kind of, sort of   Colloquial when used to mean "rather," these forms should be avoided in writing.

> **Colloquial**   I thought the lecture was **kind of** dull.
> **Standard**   I thought the lecture was **rather** dull.

later, latter   *Later* designates time; *latter* designates the second of two items, choices, or objects.

> I'll see you **later** in the day.
> The pound had a young poodle and a young terrier. I chose the **latter.**

See also **former.**

latest, last   *Latest* means "most recent"; *last* means "final."

> I doubt that their **latest** contract proposal represents their **last** offer.

lay, lie   *Lay* is a transitive verb meaning "to put" or "place" something. It always takes an object. Its principal parts are *lay, laid, laid. Lie* is intransitive; that is, it does not take an object. It means "to recline" or "to remain." Its principal parts are *lie, lay, lain.* When in doubt, try substituting the verb *place.* If it fits the context, use some form of *lay.*

> **Present tense**   Every morning I **lay** the paper by his plate.
> I **lie** down every afternoon.
>
> **Past tense**   I **laid** the paper by his plate two hours ago.
> I **lay** down yesterday after dinner.
>
> **Present**   I **have laid** the paper by his plate many times.
> **perfect tense**   I **have lain** here for several hours.

lend   See **loan.**

less   See **fewer.**

let's   Contraction of *let us.* In writing, it should be used only where *let us* can be used.

> **Colloquial**   **Let's don't** leave yet. **Let's us** go.
> **Standard**   **Let's not** leave yet. **Let's go.**

liable, likely, apt In careful writing, the words are not interchangeable. *Likely* is used to indicate a mere probability.

> They are **likely** to be chosen.

Liable is used when the probability is unpleasant.

> We are **liable** to get a parking ticket.

Apt implies a natural tendency.

> She is **apt** to be annoyed by your behavior.

lie See **lay.**

like The use of the preposition *like* to introduce a clause may be widespread in speech, but it should be avoided in writing. Use *as, as if,* or *as though* instead.

> You should treat other people **as** [not **like**] you want to be treated.

literally Means "precisely," "without any figurative sense," "strictly." It is often inaccurately used as an intensive, to emphasize a figure of speech: "I was *literally* floating on air." (This construction makes sense only if one is capable of levitation.) Use the word *literally* with caution in writing.

loan, lend Traditionally, *lend* is a verb, *loan* a noun.

> Can you **lend** [not **loan**] me a hand with this task?

But *loan* is firmly established as a verb in American English when the context involves the literal lending of money or other physical items.

> Can you **lend** [or **loan**] me twenty dollars until Friday?

loose, lose *Loose* is usually an adjective meaning "unfixed," "unattached." *Lose* is a verb meaning "to misplace," "forget."

> The screws are **loose** and the door wobbles.
> Don't **lose** patience and don't **lose** your temper.

may See **can.**

us

media   Though widely misused as a singular noun, particularly in the context of news or broadcasting organizations, *media* is the plural form of *medium* and should be used with plural verbs and pronouns.

> Many people think that the media **are** [not **is**] covering the governor's campaign inadequately.

moral, morale   As an adjective or noun, *moral* refers to ethical conduct or values. *Morale,* a noun, refers to a prevailing mood or level of confidence.

> She is a **moral** person.
> He always looks for the **moral** of the novel.
> His last three failures have hurt his **morale**.

most   As a noun or adjective, *most* means "more than half."

> **Most** of us plan to go to the dance.
> **Most** people admire her paintings.

As an adverb, *most* means "very."

> His playing was **most** impressive.

much   See **very.**

myself   One of the reflexive pronouns (*myself, yourself, himself, herself, itself, ourselves, yourselves, themselves*). Since a reflexive pronoun by definition refers back to another noun or pronoun, it may appear in a sentence only if the noun or pronoun to which it refers also appears. See also **27d**.

> | **Incorrect** | Uncle Ed sent plane tickets for my brother and **myself.** |
> | **Correct** | Uncle Ed sent plane tickets for my brother and **me.** |

neither   See **either.**

notorious   Means "of bad repute": a *notorious* gambler. Not to be used for "famous," "celebrated," or "noted."

number   See **amount.**

of *Could of, may of, might of, must of, should of,* and *would of* are slurred pronunciations for *could have, may have, might have, must have, should have,* and *would have;* they are nonstandard forms to be avoided in writing.

us

off of A colloquial usage in which *of* is superfluous.

one another See **each other.**

outside of Correct as noun: "He painted the *outside of* the house." Colloquial as a preposition: "He was waiting *outside of* the house." Omit the *of* in writing. Colloquial as a substitute for *except for, aside from.*

over with *With* is superfluous.

>   The regatta is **over** [not **over with**].

part, portion A *part* is any piece of a whole; a *portion* is that part specifically allotted to some person, cause, or use.

>   We planted beans in one **part** of our garden.
>
>   She left a **portion** of her estate to charity.

party Colloquial when used to mean "person," as in "The *party* who telephoned left no message." Write *person.*

percent In formal writing use *percent,* or *per cent,* only after an exact figure, whether spelled out (*fifty*) or written as a numeral (*50*). The word *percentage,* meaning "a part or proportion of a whole," is used when an exact amount is not indicated.

>   Thirty-one **percent** of the city's residents were government employees.
>
>   A large **percentage** of the city's residents were government employees.

The percent symbol (%) is used only in strictly commercial writing and should be avoided in other contexts.

phase See **faze.**

phenomena See **data.**

portion See **part.**

principal, principle As a noun, a *principal* is the head or leading figure in an institution, an event, or a play.

> The **principals** in the contract negotiations met with the press to discuss their progress.

Used as an adjective, *principal* refers to a leading feature or element in a group.

> The **principal** types of telescopes are the refracting and the reflecting, or Newtonian, telescope.

A *principle* is a rule.

> The main **principle** in skiing is to keep on one's feet.

problem See **dilemma.**

quotation, quote *Quote* is a verb; *quotation* is a noun signifying the words quoted. Avoid using *quote* as a noun except in extremely informal contexts.

> Only one **quotation** [not **quote**] from the mayor's press conference was reported in the newspaper.

raise, rise Remember that *raise* means to "cause something to rise." Therefore *raise* must always have an object. Remember the principal parts of each verb:

Standard	I rise	I rose	I have risen
	I raise	I raised	I have raised
	(something)	(something)	(something)
Standard	I **rise** at six o'clock every morning.		
	I **raise** flowers for sale.		
	I **rose** at six o'clock.		
	I **raised** flowers for sale.		
	I **have risen** at six o'clock for years.		
	I **have raised** flowers for years.		

real Colloquial when used for *very.* Write *very* hot (not *real* hot).

reason is because Revise this mixed construction by eliminating either *because* or *reason is.* See also **12f.**

Mixed	The **reason** we came **is because** we knew you needed help.
Revised	The **reason** we came **is that** we knew you needed help.
Revised	We came **because** we knew you needed help.

refer   See **allude.**

regarding, in regard to, with regard to, in relation to, in terms of These windy phrases are usually dispensable. Replace them with concrete terms.

Wordy	**With regard to** grades, she was very good.
Concise	She earned very good grades.

respectfully, respectively   *Respectfully* means "showing respect." *Respectively* means "in the order specified."

sarcasm, irony   *Sarcasm* is not interchangeable with *irony*. *Sarcastic* remarks, like *ironic* remarks, convey a message obliquely, but sarcasm contains the notion of ridicule, of an intention on the part of the writer to wound. Events are *ironic* when they are different from what had been expected.

> The sergeant inquired **sarcastically** whether any of us could tell time; it was **ironic** that his watch turned out to be ten minutes fast.

scarcely   See **hardly.**

sensual, sensuous   Both words refer to impressions made upon the senses. Their connotations, however, are widely different. *Sensual* often carries unfavorable connotations. It is frequently applied to the gratification of appetite and lust.

> **Sensual** delights are often considered inferior to spiritual pleasures.

Sensuous, on the other hand, is used literally or approvingly of appeals to the senses (the *sensuous* delight of a swim on a hot day), even such abstract appeals as those found in poetry.

> Milton's **sensuous** imagery calls upon sight, touch, and smell to form the reader's impression of Eden.

us

set, sit   *Set* is a transitive verb meaning "to put" or "place" something. It should be distinguished from *sit,* an intransitive verb.

Present tense	I **sit** in the chair.
	I **set** the book on the chair.
Past tense	I **sat** on the chair.
	I **set** the book on the table.
Present perfect tense	I **have sat** in the chair.
	I **have set** the book on the table.

shall, will   In American usage, the distinction between these words is rapidly fading, and *will* is used almost exclusively. *Shall* may still be found in certain interrogatives ("*Shall* we eat out tonight?") and in sentences where a special emphasis is desired ("I *shall* be heard!").

should, would   *Should* substitutes for "ought to" ("He *should* go on a diet"), *would* for "wanted to" ("He could do it if he *would*"). *Should* indicates probability ("I *should* be finished in an hour"); *would* indicates custom ("He *would* always call when he got home").

so, such   Avoid using *so* and *such* as vague intensifiers: "I am *so* glad." "I had *such* a good time." *So . . . that,* however, is an acceptable idiomatic construction.

> I was **so** glad to find this print **that** I bought copies for all my friends.

somebody, some body   *Somebody* is an indefinite pronoun that means "some person." *Some body* is a phrase that refers to a "body."

> Adrift in the ocean, the survivors longed to see **somebody** on the horizon.

> Adrift in the ocean, the survivors longed to see **some body** of land on the horizon.

someone, some one   *Someone* is an indefinite pronoun that means "some person." *Some one* is a phrase that refers to a single specified person or thing.

> I need **someone** to shovel the snow in my driveway this winter.

> Can you help me find **some one** reliable person to hire?

sometime, some time, sometimes *Sometime* and *sometimes* are adverbs. The former means "at some unspecified time"; the latter means "occasionally."

us

> Can we have lunch together **sometime** next week?
>
> I usually eat lunch in my office, but **sometimes** I go out to a restaurant.

Some time is a phrase that refers to an amount of time.

> I have **some time** free on Tuesday, if that would be convenient for you.

sort See **kind, sort, type.**

sort of See **kind of.**

stationary, stationery *Stationary* is an adjective that means "not moving."

> A **stationary** but menacing dog barred my way.

Stationery is a noun referring to writing paper and similar office supplies.

> When you write that letter, use the **stationery** with our new corporate logo.

such See **so.**

sure Colloquial when used for "certainly" or "surely," as in "He *sure* can play poker."

that, which *That* is used to introduce restrictive clauses, which limit or define the antecedent's meaning and are not set off by commas.

> The law **that** gave women the right to vote was passed in 1920.

Which is used to introduce nonrestrictive clauses, which do not limit or define the meaning of the antecedent. Nonrestrictive clauses are always set off by commas. See also **32e.**

> The Nineteenth Amendment, **which** gave women the right to vote, was passed in 1920.

that, who Use *that* in restrictive relative clauses that refer to things, but *who* in clauses that refer to people.

Incorrect	I can't tolerate being around people **that** smoke.
Correct	I can't tolerate being around people **who** smoke.
Incorrect	There's the clerk **that** overcharged me.
Correct	There's the clerk **who** overcharged me.

their, there, they're   *Their* is the possessive form of *they*.

> **Their** time will come.

There refers to place.

> Put the book **there.**

They're is a contraction of *they are*.

> I like Ken and Alicia; **they're** honest, caring people.

this here, these here, that there, those there   Nonstandard. Use *this, these, that,* or *those*.

to, too, two   *To* is a preposition.

> We went **to** the late movie.

Too is an adverb meaning "more than enough" or "also."

> He has made the same mistake **too** many times.
> She **too** shares this feeling.

Two is an adjective or a noun designating number.

> **Two** people arrived early.

toward, towards   Interchangeable. *Toward* is more common in America, *towards* in Great Britain.

transpire   In formal writing, where the word properly belongs, *transpire* means "to become known." It is colloquial in the sense of "happen," or "come to pass."

try and   Often used for "try to," but should be avoided in writing.

> I must **try to** [not **try and**] find a job.

type   See **kind, sort, type.**

uninterested   See **disinterested.**

unique   Since *unique* means "one of a kind," the colloquial—but il-logical—forms *very unique* and *most unique* remain unacceptable to most writers.

up   Do not add a superfluous *up* to verbs: "We opened *up* the box and divided *up* the money." Write: "We opened the box and divided the money."

very, very much   Unless it is commonly used as an adjective, a past participle should not be immediately preceded by the adverb *very*. Use *very much* or *very greatly* instead.

> **Incorrect**   Our guest this evening is a **very admired** philanthropist.
>
> **Correct**   Our guest this evening is a **very much admired** philanthropist.

wait on   Colloquial for *wait for*.

> **Colloquial**   I can't leave yet; I have to **wait on** my cousin.
>
> **Preferred in writing**   I can't leave yet; I have to **wait for** my cousin.

ways   Colloquial in such expressions as *a little ways*. In writing, the singular is preferred: *a little way*.

where . . . to, where . . . at   Colloquialisms whose prepositions are redundant or dialectal.

> **Colloquial**   **Where** are you going **to**? **Where** is he **at**?
>
> **Preferred in writing**   **Where** are you going? **Where** is he?

who, whom   For extended discussion of the difference between these forms, see **27b**.

whose, who's   *Whose* is a possessive pronoun.

> **Whose** book is this?

Who's is a contraction of *who is* or *who has*.

> **Who's** at the door?

us

will See **shall.**

-wise Commercial jargon when attached to nouns in such combinations as *taxwise, languagewise, timewise,* and *moneywise.* To be avoided in serious writing.

would See **should.**

would have Colloquial when used in *if* clauses instead of *had.*

Colloquial	If he **would have stood** by us, we might have won.
Preferred in writing	If he **had stood** by us, we might have won.

you was Nonstandard. Use *you were.*

your, you're *Your* is the possessive of *you.*

> **Your** train is late.

You're is a contraction of *you are.*

> If **you're** ready, we can leave.

Glossary of Grammatical and Stylistic Terms

absolute phrase   A phrase consisting of a noun followed by a participle, an adjective, or a prepositional phrase. Not grammatically connected to any word in a sentence, an absolute phrase modifies the entire sentence and usually tells when, why, or how something happened. See also **25f, 30a**.

> **The floodwater having receded,** people began returning to their homes.
>
> David stormed into the room, **fire in his eyes, a gun in his hand.**

abstract noun   A noun that names a general and intangible quality, concept, or condition: *generosity, motivation, fear*. See **concrete noun.** See also **13b**.

active voice   See **voice.**

adjective   A part of speech that modifies a noun or pronoun. An adjective may describe (*good* food, *true* friends) or limit (*a* dog, *two* cities) the word that it modifies. See also Chapter **28**, **43f**. Note that the kinds of pronouns listed below regularly perform the function of an adjective. See **pronoun.**

> **Possessive**   **my** book, **his** sister, **your** house
> **Demonstrative** **this** chair, **these** papers

gr

Interrogative	whose hat? **which** one?
Indefinite	**any** card, **each** boy, **some** candy

adjective clause   See **clause.**

adverb   A part of speech that modifies a verb, an adjective, or another adverb. Adverbs typically answer the questions *Where? When? How? Why?* or *To what degree?* See also Chapter **28**, **43g**.

> Our host bowed **politely.**
> [*Politely* modifies the verb *bowed.*]
>
> A **very** valuable painting hung behind him.
> [*Very* modifies the adjective *valuable.*]
>
> I was **too** much impressed with his hospitality to notice.
> [*Too* modifies the adverb *much.*]

Note that nouns may occasionally be used adverbially.

> He walked **miles** without seeing another person.
> [*Miles* modifies the verb *walked.*]

adverb clause   See **clause.**

agreement   The correspondence in number and person between the subject and verb in a sentence and the correspondence in number, person, and gender between a pronoun and its antecedent. See also Chapter **26.**

antecedent   The noun or pronoun to which a pronoun refers. See also **12a, 26b.**

> I saw the **house** long before I reached **it.**
> [*House* is the antecedent of *it.*]

appositive   A noun or noun phrase that follows another noun and that denotes the same person or thing. The second noun renames or defines the first, and the two are said to be *in apposition*. See also **25f.**

> My cousin **Alice** was enjoying her favorite sport, **sailing.**
> [*Alice* is in apposition with *cousin; sailing* is in apposition with *sport.*]

article   The words *a, an,* and *the,* which in function are classed with adjectives. *The* is called the **definite article;** *a* and *an* are the **indefinite articles.** See also **43a.**

auxiliary verb   A verb used with another verb to express its tense, mood, or voice or to form an interrogative. Three auxiliary verbs in English—*be, have,* and *do*—may also function as main verbs.

> I **have** several rare coins in my collection.
> [*Have is the main verb in the sentence.*]
>
> I **have collected** coins for more than a decade.
> [*Have is an auxiliary verb, used to form the present perfect tense of the verb collect.*]

Nine other auxiliary verbs—*can, could, may, might, must, ought to, should, will,* and *would*—have only one form and cannot function as main verbs. Known as **modal auxiliaries,** they are used with other verbs to express ability, condition, possibility, necessity, obligation, and intention. See also **29f.**

gr

case   The inflection, or change in form, of a noun or pronoun to show its relationship to other words. See also Chapter **27.** The **nominative** (or **subjective**) case indicates a word used as the subject or predicate noun in a sentence.

> When the caller asked for Karen Goldman, **I** said, "This is **she.**"
> [*I is the subject of the sentence; she is a predicate noun.*]

The **possessive** (or **genitive**) case indicates possession or ownership.

> The **caller's** voice aroused **my** curiosity.
> [*Caller's and my indicate possession.*]

The **objective** (or **accusative**) case indicates a word used as a direct or indirect object or as the object of a preposition.

> Without speaking further to **me,** the caller hung up.
> [*Me is the object of the preposition to.*]

In modern English, nouns are inflected only in the possessive case: *Bill's* car, the *workers'* pension plan. Pronouns, however, have different forms in all three cases. See **pronoun.**

Nominative pronouns	I, you, he, she, it, we, they, who
Possessive pronouns	my, your, his, her, its, our, their, whose

Objective pronouns	me, you, him, her, it, us, them, whom

clause   A group of words containing a subject and a predicate. Clauses that can stand alone as complete sentences are called **independent** (or **main**) clauses. Clauses that are not by themselves complete in meaning are called **dependent** (or **subordinate**) clauses. Dependent clauses are used as nouns, adjectives, or adverbs. They are usually introduced by subordinating conjunctions or relative pronouns. See also **8b, 25g**.

> **That Sean will be late** is almost certain.
> [The dependent clause is used as a noun, the subject of the sentence.]
>
> Anyone **who thinks otherwise** is mistaken.
> [The dependent clause is used an an adjective modifying the pronoun *anyone*.]
>
> Sean will arrive **when he is ready.**
> [The dependent clause is used as an adverb modifying the verb *will arrive*.]

collective noun   A noun that is singular in form (*crowd, orchestra, team*) but that denotes a group of members. Depending on the intended meaning, collective nouns may be used with singular or plural verbs and pronouns. See also **26a, 26b**.

comma splice   A sentence error in which two independent clauses are joined only with a comma. Also known as a **comma fault.** A comma splice can often be corrected by inserting an appropriate coordinating conjunction (*and, but, for, nor, or, so, yet*) between the clauses.

> **Comma splice**   The car was an ancient model, it broke down twice during the trip.
>
> **Revised**   The car was an ancient model, **and** it broke down twice during the trip.

For additional ways of correcting a comma splice, see **30c**.

comparison   The inflection, or change in form, of an adjective or adverb to indicate an increasing degree of quality, quantity, or manner. Adjectives usually form the comparative degree by adding

-er and the superlative by adding *-est: cold, colder, coldest.* Many adjectives of two syllables and all longer adjectives form the comparative and superlative by adding *more* and *most: serious, more serious, most serious.* Adverbs nearly always form the comparative and superlative with *more* and *most: softly, more softly, most softly.* Some adjectives and adverbs form the comparative and superlative irregularly. See also **28a**.

gr

complement   A word or phrase that completes the predicate of a sentence. See also **25e**. **Subject complements** follow linking verbs and are of two types: a **predicate noun** renames the subject, and a **predicate adjective** describes the subject.

> **Predicate noun**   Our destination was **Tucson.**
>
> **Predicate adjective**   The Arizona desert is **beautiful.**

An **object complement** follows the direct object in a sentence; it either renames or describes the direct object.

> **Object complements**   We consider Tucson an ideal **community,** although we found its weather **hotter** than we had expected.

complete predicate   See **predicate.**

complete subject   See **subject.**

complex sentence   A sentence containing one independent clause and one or more dependent clauses. See also **25h**.

compound-complex sentence   A compound sentence that also contains one or more dependent clauses. See **compound sentence.** See also **25h**.

compound predicate   See **predicate.**

compound sentence   A sentence consisting of two or more independent clauses joined by a coordinating conjunction or a semicolon. See also **25h**.

compound subject   See **subject.**

concrete noun   A noun that names a specific person, place, or thing perceptible to the senses: *grandmother, mathematician, synagogue, Minneapolis, butter, ice.* See **abstract noun.** See also **13b**.

conjugation   The inflections, or changes in form, of verbs that show person, number, tense, voice, and mood. See **inflection.** Below is a conjugation of the indicative mood of the verb *see.* See also **29a, 29b, 29c, 29g,** and **29h.**

gr

		Active voice	Passive voice
		Present tense	
singular	1.	I see	I am seen
	2.	you see	you are seen
	3.	he/she/it sees	he/she/it is seen
plural	1.	we see	we are seen
	2.	you see	you are seen
	3.	they see	they are seen
		Past tense	
singular	1.	I saw	I was seen
	2.	you saw	you were seen
	3.	he/she/it saw	he/she/it was seen
plural	1.	we saw	we were seen
	2.	you saw	you were seen
	3.	they saw	they were seen
		Future tense	
singular	1.	I will see	I will be seen
	2.	you will see	you will be seen
	3.	he/she/it will see	he/she/it will be seen
plural	1.	we will see	we will be seen
	2.	you will see	you will be seen
	3.	they will see	they will be seen
		Present perfect tense	
singular	1.	I have seen	I have been seen
	2.	you have seen	you have been seen
	3.	he/she/it has seen	he/she/it has been seen
plural	1.	we have seen	we have been seen
	2.	you have seen	you have been seen
	3.	they have seen	they have been seen

	Active voice	**Passive voice**
	Past perfect tense	
singular	1. I had seen	I had been seen
	2. you had seen	you had been seen
	3. he/she/it had seen	he/she/it had been seen
plural	1. we had seen	we had been seen
	2. you had seen	you had been seen
	3. they had seen	they had been seen
	Future perfect tense	
singular	1. I will have seen	I will have been seen
	2. you will have seen	you will have been seen
	3. he/she/it will have seen	he/she/it will have been seen
plural	1. we will have seen	we will have been seen
	2. you will have seen	you will have been seen
	3. they will have seen	they will have been seen

gr

conjunction A part of speech that connects words, phrases, or clauses. **Coordinating conjunctions** connect sentence elements that are logically and grammatically equal. See also **8b**.

> **Coordinating**   and, but, for, nor, or, so, yet
> **conjunctions**

Correlative conjunctions also connect grammatically equivalent elements; because they always occur in pairs, they may be used to create additional emphasis. See also **8d**.

> **Correlative**   both . . . and, either . . . or, neither . . .
> **conjunctions**   nor, not only . . . but also

Subordinating conjunctions connect dependent clauses to independent clauses. See also **8b**.

> **Subordinating**   after, although, as, as if, as though, because,
> **conjunctions**   before, even though, how, if, since, so that,
> than, though, unless, until, when, whenever,
> where, whereas, wherever, whether, while

Conjunctive adverbs connect independent clauses. A semicolon, rather than a comma, is required between two clauses linked by a conjunctive adverb. See also **30c**.

Conjunctive adverbs	accordingly, also, besides, consequently, finally, furthermore, hence, however, indeed, instead, likewise, meanwhile, moreover, nevertheless, next, nonetheless, otherwise, similarly, still, subsequently, then, therefore, thus

conjunctive adverb   See **conjunction.**

connotation The associations, suggestions, and feelings that a word brings to mind, as opposed to its literal, or dictionary, meaning. See **denotation.** See also **13a.**

coordinate clauses Two or more independent clauses connected by a coordinating conjunction.

coordinating conjunction   See **conjunction.**

coordination A relationship of grammatical equality between sentence elements. See **subordination.** See also **8b.**

copula   See **linking verb.**

correlative conjunction   See **conjunction.**

dangling modifier A word or phrase that cannot logically modify the word to which it has been linked by the syntax of the sentence. See also **12b.**

Dangling	Completed in 1974, the world has not yet seen a building taller than the Sears Tower.
Revised	Completed in 1974, the Sears Tower remains the world's tallest building.

declension The change in form of nouns to indicate number and the possessive case. See **inflection.**

demonstrative adjective   See **adjective.** See also **26b.**

demonstrative pronoun   See **pronoun.** See also **26b.**

denotation The literal, or dictionary, definition of a word. See **connotation.** See also **13a.**

diction Choice of words, especially as those words affect the tone of a piece of writing. See also Chapters **4, 9,** and **13.**

direct address   A grammatical construction in which the speaker or writer names the person being addressed. Words of direct address are set off by commas. See also **32i**.

> **Direct address**   Mary, please meet me at two o'clock.

direct object   See **object**.

double negative   A nonstandard grammatical construction that uses two negative forms to express one negative idea within a sentence.

> **Double negative**   He **doesn't** have **no** place to go.
>
> **Revised**   He **doesn't** have **any** place to go.

elliptical construction   A phrase or clause that is grammatically incomplete but whose meaning is clear because the omitted words can easily be inferred. See also **12b**.

> **Elliptical clause**   If [it is] possible, please arrive by ten o'clock.

euphemism   The substitution of an often trite or sentimental expression for one considered to be unpleasant or indelicate: *in an interesting condition* or *in the family way* are old-fashioned euphemisms for *pregnant*. See also **13h**.

expletive   A construction usually consisting of the word *there* or *it* followed by a form of the verb *be* and used to begin a sentence. Employed effectively, an expletive creates emphasis by postponing the true subject of the sentence; careless use of expletives, however, often results in wordiness. See also **8c**, **43b**.

> **Expletive**   There is one reason to re-elect our mayor—his commitment to the region's economic development.

finite verb   A verb that makes an assertion and that can serve as a predicate, as distinguished from a verbal (an infinitive, a participle, or a gerund). Sometimes called a **full verb.**

> **Finite verbs**   The alarm **rang** and I **awoke.**
>
> **Verbals**   The **ringing** alarm forced me **to awake.**

full verb   See **finite verb**.

gr

gr

fused sentence   A sentence error in which two independent clauses are joined without any punctuation or conjunction. See **30e**.

> **Fused**   The car stalled at the corner it was out of gas.
>
> **Revised**   The car stalled at the corner. It was out of gas.

gender   In grammar, the classification of some nouns and personal pronouns according to sex—masculine (*man, he*), feminine (*woman, she*), and neuter (*book, it*).

gerund   A verb form that ends in *-ing* and that functions as a noun. The gerund should be distinguished from the present participle, which also ends in *-ing* but functions as an adjective. See **participle.** See also **12b, 25f, 27h, 43e**.

> **Subject of verb**   **Fishing** is tiresome.
> **Object of verb**   I hate **fishing**.
> **Object of preposition**   I have a dislike of **fishing**.
> **Predicate noun**   The sport I like least is **fishing**.

Like a noun, the gerund may be modified by an adjective. In the sentence *They were tired of his long-winded preaching, his* and *long-winded* modify the gerund *preaching*. A noun or pronoun preceding a gerund is normally in the possessive—in this case, *his* preaching. Since a gerund is a verb form, it may take an object and be modified by an adverb.

> He disapproved of our **taking luggage** with us.
> [*Luggage* is the object of the gerund *taking*.]
>
> Our success depends upon his **acting promptly**.
> [*Promptly* is an adverb modifying the gerund *acting*.]

idiom   An expression that is understood and used by speakers of a particular language or region, but whose meaning cannot be determined from the literal meaning of the individual words. See also **13f**.

> She was **taken in** by the practical jokes.
>
> **Every now and then,** I **have a mind** to **tell her off.**
>
> He is, **after all,** my brother, and I have to **stick up for him.**
>
> He was **out of his head** for a while, but he finally **pulled himself together.**

imperative   See **mood**.

indefinite pronoun   See **pronoun**. See also **26a, 26b**.

indicative   See **mood**.

indirect object   See **object**.

infinitive   The base form of a verb, usually preceded by *to*. The infinitive may function as a noun, an adjective, or an adverb. See also **12b, 12d, 25f, 27g, 29e, 30a, 43e**.

> **Noun**   **To err** is human.
>
> **Adjective**   I found a magazine **to read**.
>
> **Adverb**   We are happy **to help**.

Since an infinitive is a verb form, it can have a subject, can take an object or complement, and can be modified by an adverb.

> They wanted **me to go.**
> [*Me* is the subject of *to go*.]
>
> They asked **to meet him.**
> [*Him* is the object of *to meet*.]
>
> We hope **to hear soon.**
> [*Soon* is the adverbial modifier of *to hear*.]

infinitive phrase   An infinitive with its complements and modifiers. See **infinitive**. See also **25f**.

inflection   A change in the form of a word to indicate a change in meaning or use. Nouns may be inflected to show number (*child, children*) and the possessive case (*dog, dog's*). Pronouns may be inflected to show case (*he, him*), person (*I, you*), number (*it, they*), and gender (*his, hers*). Verbs are inflected to show person (I *go*, he *goes*), number (she *is*, they *are*), tense (he *is*, he *was*), voice (I *received* your letter, your letter *was received*), and mood (if this *be* treason). Adjectives and adverbs are inflected to show relative degree (*strong, stronger, strongest*). The inflection of nouns is called **declension;** that of verbs, **conjugation;** that of adjectives and adverbs, **comparison.**

intensive pronoun   See **pronoun**. See also **27d**.

interjection   A part of speech that expresses emotion but that is grammatically independent of the rest of the sentence: *ah, oh, alas.*

interrogative pronoun See **pronoun.** See also **27c.**

intransitive verb See **verb.**

irregular verb A verb that does not form its past tense and past participle by adding *-ed* or *-d: sing, sang, sung; drive, drove, driven.* See also **29a, 29b.**

gr

jargon The specialized language that is used by members of a particular profession or group but that is likely to be unintelligible to the general public. See also **13h.**

linking verb A verb such as *be, appear, become, feel, look,* or *seem* that connects a subject and a predicate adjective or predicate noun. See **verb.** See also **13c, 25b, 27f, 28b, 43b.**

misplaced modifier A modifier that is awkwardly placed—usually too far from the term it modifies—so that its relation to the rest of the sentence is confusing. See also **12c.**

> **Misplaced**   Jeremy darted into the street full of traffic **on skates.**
>
> **Revised**   Jeremy darted **on skates** into the street full of traffic.

mixed construction A sentence that begins with one grammatical construction and then shifts to another. See also **12f.**

> **Mixed**   By exercising regularly is one way for busy people to reduce stress.
>
> **Revised**   Exercising regularly is one way for busy people to reduce stress.

modifier A word or group of words that functions as an adjective or an adverb to limit, define, or qualify another word or group of words. In the sentence *I dislike these sour oranges, sour* describes the noun *oranges,* and *these* limits the noun to a particular group of oranges at hand. Both modifiers function adjectivally. In the sentence *She sang for half an hour,* the phrase *for half an hour,* which tells how long she sang, is an adverbial modifier. See also **adjective, adverb,** and **misplaced modifier.**

mood Inflection, or change in form, of a verb to indicate whether it is intended to make a statement, express a command, or express a wish or a condition contrary to fact. See also **29h**. The **indicative** mood is used to state a fact or to ask a question.

> The rain **is falling** hard.
>
> **Did** you **expect** such severe weather?

The **imperative** mood is used to express a command or a request.

> Please **answer** the telephone.

The **subjunctive** mood is used to express a wish or desire, a doubt, a concession, or a condition contrary to fact.

> I wish that I **were** [not **was**] able to help.
>
> If she **were** [not **was**] older, she would understand.

nominalization   The noun form of a verb. Used in place of verbs, nominalizations often create wordiness. See also **8c**.

Nominalizations	Jane **reached the conclusion** that her brother **was in need of** professional help.
Revised	Jane **concluded** that her brother **needed** professional help.

nominative   See **case**.

nonrestrictive modifier   A word, phrase, or clause that adds information to a sentence but that is not necessary to define or limit the word it modifies. A nonrestrictive modifier is typically set off with commas. See also **32e**.

noun   A part of speech that names a person, place, thing, or abstract concept or quality. A **common noun** refers to any member of a group or class of things (*novelist, city, book, war*) or to an abstract concept (*assistance, courage, devotion*). Common nouns are not capitalized. A **proper noun** is the name of a particular person, place, thing, or event (*Jane Austen, Toronto, Domesday Book, War of Independence*). Proper nouns are capitalized. A noun may also act as a modifier: *town* meeting, *cheese* sandwich. See **abstract noun, collective noun,** and **concrete noun**. See also **26b, 28c, 38b, 43a**.

noun clause   See **clause**.

number   The inflection, or change in form, of a noun, pronoun, or verb to indicate whether it is singular or plural.

object   The noun or pronoun that completes the assertion made by a transitive verb (**direct object**), that names the person or thing to whom something is given or told or for whom something is done (**indirect object**), or that follows a preposition in a prepositional phrase (**object of the preposition**). See also **25d, 25f**.

Direct object	I trusted **Denise** and followed her **suggestions**.
Indirect object	Denise always gave **me** sound advice.
Object of the preposition	I have always listened to **her**.

object complement   See **complement**.

objective   See **case**.

parallelism   The stylistic device of placing equal ideas in equivalent grammatical constructions. See also **8d**.

Parallel words	Margot wants **fame, prestige,** and **power** in the legal community.
Parallel phrases	She **trusts in her knowledge of the law** and **believes in her ability to succeed.**
Parallel clauses	She is undeterred by the fact **that she must work long hours, that many obstacles stand in her way,** and **that few colleagues encourage her efforts.**

participial phrase   A participle with its complements and modifiers. See **participle**. See also **25f**.

participle   A verb form used as an adjective. The present participle ends in *-ing: eating, running*. The past participle ends in *-ed, -d, -t, -en,* or *-n* or is formed by vowel change: *stopped, told, slept, fallen, known, sung*. The present perfect participle consists of *having* followed by the past participle form. See also **12b, 25f, 29e, 30a**.

Present participle	An **inquiring** reporter stopped me as I left my office.
Present perfect participle	**Having** just **returned** from vacation, I had no information to offer her.
Past participle	**Undaunted,** she continued to press me for facts about the case.

Since a participle is a verb, it may take a direct or indirect object and may be modified by an adverb.

> **Wishing her success,** I walked away.
> [*Her* is the indirect object and *success* is the direct object of the participle *wishing*.]

> **Walking briskly,** she followed me to my car.
> [*Briskly* is an adverb modifying the participle *walking*.]

gr

parts of speech The traditional classification of words into eight categories according to their functions in a sentence: nouns, pronouns, adjectives, verbs, adverbs, prepositions, conjunctions, and interjections. See also **25a**.

passive voice See **voice**.

person The inflection, or change in form, of verbs and personal pronouns to indicate the speaker (*first person*), the person spoken to (*second person*), and the person spoken of (*third person*).

> **First person** I am, we are; I go, we go.
> **Second person** you are; you go.
> **Third person** she is, they are; he goes, they go.

personal pronoun See **pronoun**.

phrase A group of words without a subject and/or a predicate, used as a single part of speech—as a noun, a verb, an adjective, or an adverb. See also **25f**.

possessive See **case**.

possessive pronoun See **pronoun**.

predicate A word or group of words that makes a statement about or asks a question about the subject of a sentence. The essential element in a predicate is a finite verb. See also **25b**. The **simple predicate** is the verb or verb phrase alone, without its objects, complements, or modifiers.

> Jim **backed** his car through the garage door.

The **complete predicate** is the verb or verb phrase together with its objects, complements, and modifiers.

> Jim **backed his car through the garage door.**

A sentence with more than one simple predicate is said to include a **compound predicate.**

> Jim **backed** his car through the garage door and narrowly **escaped** serious injury.

predicate adjective   See **complement.**

gr

predicate noun   See **complement.**

prefix   Letters added before a root word to form a new word: *non*violent, *pre*suppose, *re*design, *un*desirable. See **suffix.** See also **36a.**

preposition   A part of speech that indicates a relationship between a noun or pronoun and another word in the sentence. The word that completes the meaning of the preposition is called the **object of the preposition.** See **object.** See also **25f, 30a.**

> **Prepositions**   about, above, according to, across, after, against, ahead of, along, among, around, as well as, at, because of, before, behind, below, beneath, beside, besides, between, beyond, but, by, concerning, despite, down, during, except, for, from, in, in addition to, in back of, in front of, inside, in spite of, instead of, into, like, near, of, off, onto, out, outside, over, past, regarding, since, through, throughout, till, to, toward, under, underneath, unlike, until, up, upon, with, within, without

Many of the words above may be used either as prepositions or as adverbs. If the word is followed by a noun or pronoun that completes a phrase, it is a preposition. If it stands alone and modifies a verb, it is an adverb.

> **Prepositions**   I would like to invest **in** real estate **during** the coming year.
>
> **Adverbs**   Please come **in** and sit **down.**

principal parts   In English, the three forms of a verb from which all other forms are derived. They are (1) the base form, (2) the past form, and (3) the past participle: *send, sent, sent; choose, chose, chosen; swim, swam, swum.* All present- and future-tense forms, including the present participle, are derived from the first principal part: I *send,* he *sends,* we *will send.* The second principal part is used for the simple past tense: he *sent,* I *chose,* you *swam.* Compound past tenses and the forms of the passive voice employ the third principal part: he *has chosen,* they *had swum,* the package *was sent,* or *may be sent, is being sent, will be sent.* The verb *be* is too irregular to be reduced to three principal parts. See also **29a, 29b, 29c.**

gr

pronoun   A part of speech that substitutes for a noun already used or implied. See also **26b,** Chapter **27.** Pronouns fall into nine categories. A **personal pronoun** refers to a person or thing: *I* have explained the problem to Robert, but *he* doesn't seem to understand *it.*

Personal pronouns	[singular] I, me, you, he, him, she, her, it; [plural] we, us, you, they, them

A **possessive pronoun** is used to indicate possession: *Our* farm is larger than *theirs.*

Possessive pronouns	[singular] my, mine, you, yours, his, her, hers, its; [plural] our, ours, your, yours, their, theirs

A **demonstrative pronoun** identifies a particular noun on the basis of proximity or distance: *These* are ripe bananas; *those* are rotten. See also **26b.**

Demonstrative pronouns	[singular] this, that; [plural] these, those

An **interrogative pronoun** is used to construct a question: *Who* left this book behind? See also **27c.**

Interrogative pronouns	who, whom, whose, which, what

A **relative pronoun** introduces an adjective clause: I know a restaurant *that* you will enjoy. A relative pronoun simultaneously serves as a subordinating conjunction and as a substitute for a noun in the dependent clause. See also **25g, 26a, 27b.**

Relative pronouns	who, whom, whose, which, that

An **intensive pronoun** is used in apposition with a noun or personal pronoun for emphasis: I *myself* painted the house. See also **27d**.

> **Intensive** [singular] myself, yourself, himself, herself, itself;
> **pronouns** [plural] ourselves, yourselves, themselves

gr

A **reflexive pronoun** is used in place of the objective form of a personal pronoun when the actor and recipient of the action in a sentence are the same: Marla and Toni found *themselves* in more trouble than they had expected. See also **27d**.

> **Reflexive** [singular] myself, yourself, himself, herself, itself;
> **pronouns** [plural] ourselves, yourselves, themselves

A **reciprocal pronoun** refers individually to the persons or things named by a plural antecedent: The eastbound and westbound trains pass *each other* at two o'clock.

> **Reciprocal** each other, one another
> **pronouns**

An **indefinite pronoun** is a pronoun that does not refer to a specific person or thing: *Everyone* should learn to play a musical instrument. See also **26a, 26b**.

> **Indefinite** all, another, any, anybody, anyone, anything,
> **pronouns** both, each, either, everybody, everyone,
> everything, few, many, more, most, neither,
> nobody, none, no one, nothing, one, several,
> some, somebody, someone, something

reciprocal pronoun See **pronoun**.

reflexive pronoun See **pronoun**. See also **27d**.

regular verb A verb that forms its past tense and past participle form by adding *-ed* or *-t: start, started; dream, dreamed/dreamt*. See also **29a, 29b**.

relative pronoun See **pronoun**. See also **25g, 26a, 27b**.

restrictive modifier A word, phrase, or clause that is required in a sentence to define or limit the word it modifies. A restrictive modifier is not set off with commas. See also **32e**.

gr

sentence   An independent utterance that includes a subject and predicate and that expresses a complete idea. A sentence is set off by an initial capital letter and a final period, question mark, or exclamation point. Classified according to meaning or function, sentences fall into four categories. A **declarative sentence** asserts something about a subject.

> The man felt ill and called the doctor.

An **interrogative sentence** asks a question.

> When is she coming?

An **imperative sentence** expresses a command.

> Call her again.

An **exclamatory sentence** expresses strong feeling.

> How sick he was!

See also **complex sentence, compound sentence, compound-complex sentence, simple sentence.** See also Chapters **8, 12, 25,** and **30.**

sentence fragment   A phrase or dependent clause that is punctuated as a sentence. Unless deliberately written for a specific effect, a sentence fragment should be joined to an independent clause or revised as one. See also **30a, 30b.**

simple predicate   See **predicate.**

simple sentence   A sentence that consists of one independent clause. See also **25h.**

simple subject   See **subject.**

split infinitive   An infinitive that includes a modifier between *to* and the verb. Unless the alternatives would be unacceptably awkward, split infinitives should be avoided. See also **12d.**

> **Split**   Be sure **to carefully measure** the ingredients.
> **Revised**   Be sure **to measure** the ingredients carefully.

subject   The part of a sentence or clause that names the person or thing about which something is said. The subject of a sentence is usually a noun or pronoun, but it may be a verbal, a phrase, or a noun clause. See also **25b**, **43b**.

Noun	Beyond the ridge lay a high **plateau.**
Verbal	Nowadays **flying** is both safe and cheap.
Phrase	**To fear the worst** oft cures the worse.
Clause	**That she will be promoted** is certain.

The **simple subject** is usually a noun or pronoun. The **complete subject** is the simple subject and its modifiers.

> The young trees that we planted last year have grown tall.
> [*Trees* is the simple subject. *The young trees that we planted last year* is the complete subject.]

subject complement   See **complement.**

subjective   See **case.**

subjunctive   See **mood.**

subordination   A relationship of grammatical inequality or dependence between one element of a sentence and another. See **coordination.** See also **8b**, Chapter **25**.

suffix   Letters added after a root word to form a new word: differ*ence*, steward*ship*, travel*er*, window*less*. See **prefix.** See also **37c**.

syntax   The combination or arrangement of words that indicates their relationship to one another in a sentence.

tense   The change in form of verbs that indicates time. There are six tenses in English: present, past, future, present perfect, past perfect, future perfect. See also **29c**, **29e**.

transitive verb   See **verb.**

verb   A part of speech whose function is to assert that the subject acts, is acted upon, or exists in a certain state. A verb may be a single word or a group of words, but in either case its form changes to indicate time, number, voice, and mood. See **auxiliary verb.** See also Chapter **29**, **43c**.

A **transitive verb** is a verb that requires a direct object to complete its meaning.

He **closed** the **door.**

They **greeted her** warmly.

An **intransitive verb** is a verb that does not require a direct object.

After a heated argument, he **walked** out.

The family **huddled** around the fire.

A **linking verb** acts as a connecting link between the subject and a predicate noun or a predicate adjective.

Richard **is** a brilliant pianist.

Your answer **seems** correct.

verbal   A form of a verb that is used as a noun (*Stealing* is wrong), an adjective (*Stolen* fruit is sweeter), or an adverb (Criminals are willing *to steal*). See **gerund, participle, infinitive.**

voice   The inflection, or change in form, of a verb to indicate the relation of the subject to the action expressed by the verb. A verb is in the **active voice** when its subject is the doer of the action. A verb is in the **passive voice** when its subject is acted upon. See also **29g**.

Active voice   I **rang** the bell.
[The subject *I* did the act of ringing.]

Passive voice   The bell **was rung** by me.
[The subject *bell* was acted upon by me.]

Index

Section numbers are in **boldface;** page numbers are in regular type. Thus **39b:**749 refers to Section 39b, page 749.

in

in

in

in

in

in

in

in

in

in

in

in

in

in

in

in

in

in

Index of Quick-Reference and In-Chapter Boxes